The Women of Pliny's

Pliny's letters offer a significant source of information about the lives of Roman women, predominately, though not exclusively, upper-class, during the late first and early second centuries CE. In the 368 letters included in his ten published books of epistles, Pliny mentions over 30 women by name, addresses letters to seven, and refers to well over 40 anonymous women. Many of the references are brief comments in letters whose topics are the activities of Pliny's male acquaintances. Nonetheless his letters inform us about the roles of women in Roman families, marriages, and households, and also record the involvement of women in such matters as court cases, property ownership, religious orders, social networks, and political activities.

This book has two aims. The first is to bring these women to the foreground, to explore their kinships, relationships, and activities, and to illuminate their lives by viewing them in the social, cultural, and political environments of the period in which they lived. This book utilizes historical, literary, legal, and epigraphical sources to examine the events, circumstances, and attitudes that were the contexts for the lives of these women. The first aim, then, is to gain insight into the reality of their lives.

The second aim of this book is to investigate how Pliny defines the ideal behavior for women. In his accounts of the actions of both women and men, Pliny frequently shapes his narratives to promote moral lessons. In several of his letters about women, he elevates his subject to the status of a role model. *The Women of Pliny's Letters* offers an important view, through the medium of Pliny's letters, of women within the Roman world.

Jo-Ann Shelton is Research Professor of Classics at the University of California, Santa Barbara.

The Women of Pliny's Letters

Jo-Ann Shelton

Routledge
Taylor & Francis Group

LONDON AND NEW YORK

First published 2013
by Routledge

2 Park Square, Milton Park, Abingdon, Oxon OX14 4RN
711 Third Avenue, New York, NY 10017, USA

Routledge is an imprint of the Taylor & Francis Group, an informa business

First issued in paperback 2017

British Library Cataloguing in Publication Data
A catalogue record for this book is available from the British Library

Library of Congress Cataloging-in-Publication Data
Shelton, Jo-Ann.
The women of Pliny's letters / Jo-Ann Shelton.
p. cm.
Includes bibliographical references and index.
1. Pliny, the Younger--Correspondence--Criticism, Textual.
2. Women--Rome--History. I. Title.
PA6638.A4 2012
876'.01--dc23
2012009075

ISBN: 978-0-415-37428-6 (hbk)
ISBN: 978-1-138-08578-7 (pbk)

Typeset in Sabon
by Taylor & Francis Books

Coniugi optissimo et carissimo

Contents

List of figures

Acknowledgements

I am grateful to the series editors, Ronnie Ancona and Sarah Pomeroy, for suggesting that I undertake to write this book. And I am indebted to the editorial staff at Routledge, particularly Ruth Berry, Amy Davis-Poynter, and Sandra Stafford for their guidance and patience. Many colleagues, students, and friends, both in and outside academe, advised, assisted, and supported me in many different ways, and they all deserve my thanks. Progress on this book was interrupted several times by ill health. Many skillful and compassionate medical professionals enabled me to finish the book, and they, too, deserve my gratitude. Most of all, I could never have completed this project without the unflagging support, unfailing encouragement, and unwavering love of my husband, Daniel Higgins, to whom the book is dedicated.

Abbreviations

ADA = *Acta Divi Augusti*
AE = *L'Année épigraphique*
CIL = *Corpus Inscriptionum Latinarum*
FIRA = *Fontes Iuris Romani Antejustiniani*
ILS = *Inscriptiones Latinae Selectae*
PIR = *Prosopographia Imperii Romani*
PFOS = *Prosopographie des femmes de l'ordre sénatorial*

Genealogy Chart 1: The family of Arria

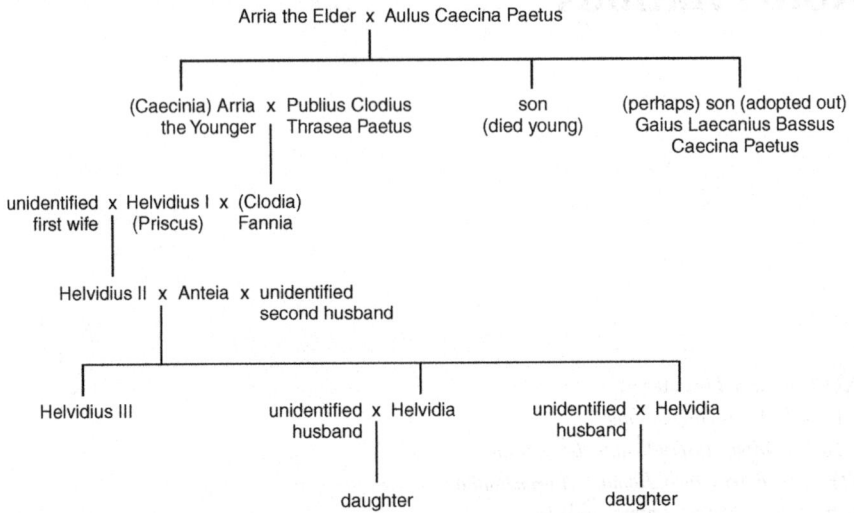

Arria the Elder x Aulus Caecina Paetus

(Caecinia) Arria x Publius Clodius
the Younger | Thrasea Paetus

son
(died young)

(perhaps) son (adopted out)
Gaius Laecanius Bassus
Caecina Paetus

unidentified x Helvidius I x (Clodia)
first wife | (Priscus) | Fannia

Helvidius II x Anteia x unidentified
second husband

Helvidius III

unidentified x Helvidia
husband

daughter

unidentified x Helvidia
husband

daughter

Genealogy Chart 2: The family of Junius

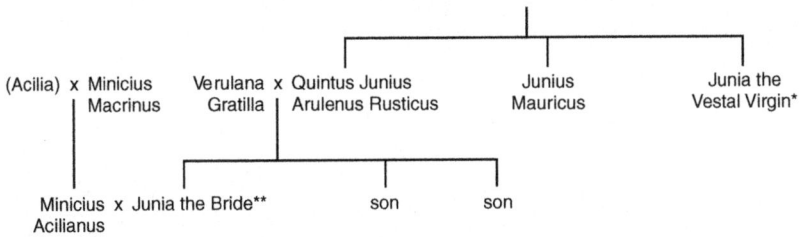

(Acilia) x Minicius
| Macrinus

Verulana x Quintus Junius
Gratilla | Arulenus Rusticus

Junius
Mauricus

Junia the
Vestal Virgin*

Minicius x Junia the Bride**
Acilianus

son

son

* Junia the Vestal Virgin may have been (1) the sister of the Junius brothers, (2) the daughter of one of the Junius
brothers, or (3) a member of a different Junius family.
In *Letter* 7.19, Pliny notes that Junia and Fannia (see Genealogy Chart 1) were kinswomen (*adfinis*), but he does
not specify the nature of their kinship.

** The name of this daughter does not appear in Pliny's published letters, but traditionally she would have been
known by the feminine form of her family's *nomen*, Junius.

Genealogy Chart 3: The family of Pliny

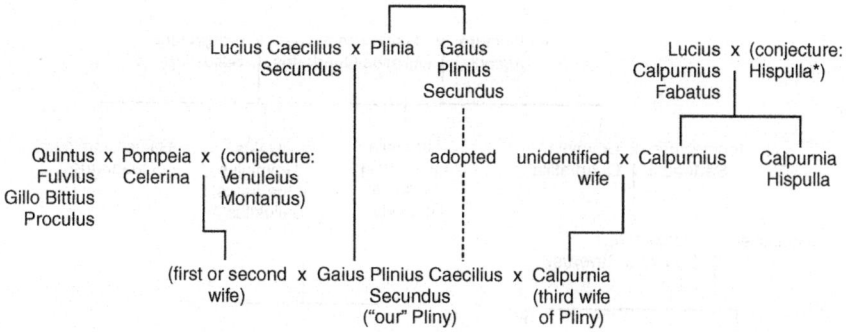

Lucius Caecilius x Plinia   Gaius
          Secundus   Plinius
                           Secundus

Lucius x (conjecture:
Calpurnius   Hispulla*)
Fabatus

Quintus x Pompeia x (conjecture:
Fulvius   Celerina   Venuleius
Gillo Bittius   Montanus)
Proculus

adopted   unidentified x Calpurnius   Calpurnia
                wife   Hispulla

(first or second x Gaius Plinius Caecilius x Calpurnia
      wife)   Secundus   (third wife
                     ("our" Pliny)   of Pliny)

* If the name of this wife was indeed Hispulla, she may have been related to, perhaps even a sister of, the wife of
  Pliny's mentor, Corellius Rufus; see Genealogy Chart 4.

Genealogy Chart 4: The family of Corellius

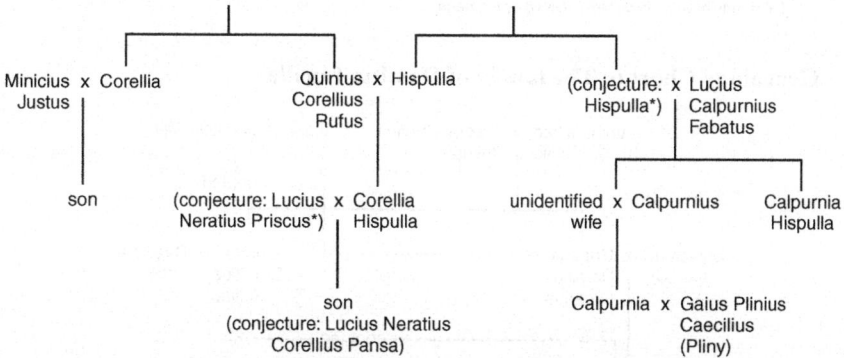

Minicius x Corellia   Quintus x Hispulla   (conjecture: x Lucius
Justus   Corellius   Hispulla*) Calpurnius
                           Rufus   Fabatus

son   (conjecture: Lucius x Corellia   unidentified x Calpurnius   Calpurnia
           Neratius Priscus*)   Hispulla   wife   Hispulla

                    son   Calpurnia x Gaius Plinius
           (conjecture: Lucius Neratius   Caecilius
                Corellius Pansa)   (Pliny)

* Raepsaet-Charlier (1987), Stemma XLVIII, conjectures that the mother of Lucius Neratius Priscus (husband of
  Corellia Hispulla) was a sister of Anteia, wife of Helvidius II (see Genealogy Chart 1). If this conjecture is correct, and
  also the conjecture that Calpurnius Fabatus was married to the sister of Corellius Rufus' wife, then Pliny was
  very distantly related by marriage to the Helvidius family.

Genealogy Chart 5: The family of Ummidia Quadratilla

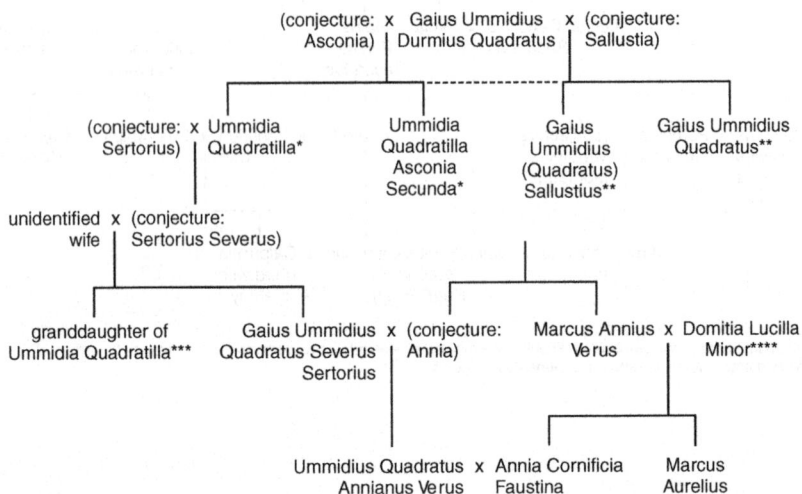

(conjecture: x Gaius Ummidius x (conjecture:
Asconia) | Durmius Quadratus | Sallustia)

(conjecture: x Ummidia
Sertorius) | Quadratilla*

Ummidia
Quadratilla
Asconia
Secunda*

Gaius
Ummidius
(Quadratus)
Sallustius**

Gaius Ummidius
Quadratus**

unidentified x (conjecture:
wife | Sertorius Severus)

granddaughter of
Ummidia Quadratilla***

Gaius Ummidius x (conjecture:
Quadratus Severus | Annia)
Sertorius

Marcus Annius x Domitia Lucilla
Verus | Minor****

Ummidius Quadratus x Annia Cornificia
Annianus Verus | Faustina

Marcus
Aurelius

* These may be the same person.
** These may be the same person.
*** The parents of this woman may not have been the same as those of Ummidia Quadratilla's grandson. i.e.
Ummidia Quadratilla may have had two children who each had at least one child.
**** Domitia Lucilla Minor (the Younger) appears also in Genealogy Chart 6. Ummidia Quadratilla and Domitius
Tullus may have been distantly related by marriage.

Genealogy Chart 6: The family of Domitia Lucilla

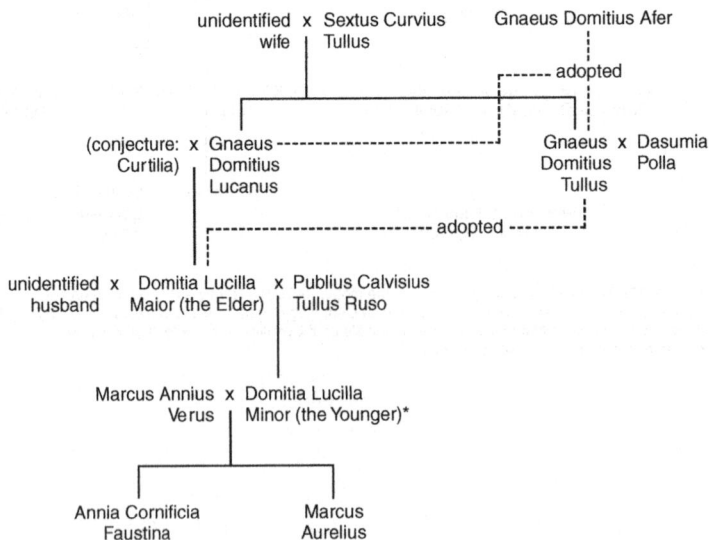

unidentified x Sextus Curvius
wife | Tullus

Gnaeus Domitius Afer

------ adopted

(conjecture: x Gnaeus ------------------------
Curtilia) | Domitius
Lucanus

Gnaeus x Dasumia
Domitius Polla
Tullus

-------------------------- adopted ---------

unidentified x Domitia Lucilla x Publius Calvisius
husband | Maior (the Elder) | Tullus Ruso

Marcus Annius x Domitia Lucilla
Verus | Minor (the Younger)*

Annia Cornificia
Faustina

Marcus
Aurelius

* Domitia Lucilla Minor (the Younger) appears also in Genealogy Chart 5. Ummidia Quadratilla and Domitius Tullus
may have been distantly related by marriage.

Introduction: writing about lives

The enduring popularity of biographies, as well as celebrity gossip magazines and "reality" television programs, is a testament to the human interest in the lives of other people. Pliny's letters offer a significant source of information about the lives of Roman women, mainly, though not exclusively, upper-class, during the late first and early second centuries CE. In the 368 letters included in his ten books of epistles, Pliny mentions over 30 women by name, addresses letters to seven women, and refers to well over 40 other women, though not by name. Many of the references are brief comments in letters whose topics are the activities of Pliny's male acquaintances, but the references nonetheless provide valuable evidence about women's activities. The letters inform us, for example, about the structure and dynamics of Roman households and family life. In addition, they record the involvement of women in such matters as court cases, property ownership, religious orders, social networks, and political activities, and thus allow us to learn about their participation in a wider and often public context. The letters also, and not inconsequentially, give a beneficial counterpoint to the negative portrayals of women found in the writings of Pliny's contemporaries, Juvenal, Martial, Suetonius, and Tacitus. Pliny's letters have therefore been extensively "mined" for data about women's roles in Roman society. Little attention has been paid, however, to capturing images of the lives of the individual women he mentions. The primary aim of this book therefore is to bring these women to the foreground, to examine their activities and relationships, and to illuminate their lives by viewing them in the context of the period in which they lived.

Admittedly, the task is not an easy one. Two major challenges are the paucity of source material and the biases of our sources. In broadest terms, an account of someone's life is a biography. However, the biographies that I am constructing can unfortunately be only very incomplete accounts, and, because we are so far removed from the time of the subjects, accuracy will always be an issue. Even in our modern age, where the lives of all of us can be tracked by a significant trail of personal and professional records preserved on paper and film or stored digitally, and where live interviews and inspection of diaries are possible, a biographer does not have access to every piece of information and is rarely privy to the subject's intimate thoughts. The construction of a coherent account of the life of a person long dead is substantially more difficult, and particularly when the subject is a woman living in a period when women were considered of much less importance than men. The paucity of sources for the biographies of ancient persons makes impossible the type of comprehensive cradle-to-grave accounts that can be produced for contemporary persons. Even for Pliny himself, the author of several hundred personal letters and the subject of several inscriptions, we can produce only a sketchy outline of his life events, and we lack even the basic information about when he was born and or when he died. From the women he mentions, we have no first-hand accounts in which they express their thoughts, describe their lives, or communicate their aspirations. And yet, for some of them, we have something that we lack for Pliny himself – observations about their behavior, and comments about how they were perceived by people around them. Unfortunately, in most cases Pliny provides little more than a snapshot, a portrait of behavior in a particular situation. And, of course, we need to be concerned about the biases of his own observations and of his reports about the perceptions of others. Additionally, we face the problem of ascertaining Pliny's reasons for writing his letters and of determining how these reasons influenced his choices and treatment of subjects.

For some of the women, we can find in the letters information about their families and friends to add more detail to the portraits. In several cases, moreover, supplemental data can be gathered from other ancient authors and from epigraphic material. Prosopography, particularly the important work of Syme (to whom frequent reference is made in this book), enables us to trace the familial and regional networks of many of these women. Nonetheless, we are undeniably dealing with what can be called either scraps of information, or pieces of a jigsaw puzzle. Although a completed puzzle will always elude us, the image of the jigsaw puzzle is fitting because it corresponds to the goal of the biographer, which is to collect, evaluate, interpret, and arrange random pieces of information in a way which enables the reader to gain at least a partial picture of the life and personality of the subject and the reasons for her/his actions. In accordance with this goal, one component of my project has been to collect and collate the available "vital statistics" about these women – the scraps of information about, for example, when and where they lived and who their nearest kin were. I have also, however, examined the data within a framework of contemporary situations and tried to construct the background from which the women can emerge or be evoked. Sources other than Pliny – historical, literary, legal, epigraphical, and artistic – provide us with information about the events, circumstances, and attitudes that were the contexts for the lives of the women in Pliny's letters, and they can thus enhance our understanding of these women. Laws, conventions, and beliefs play a significant role in defining the lives of all of us. Another component of the project therefore is to investigate the social and cultural environment of the early imperial period in which these women lived so that we can gain a better perspective on their lives.

A scarcity of source material is not the only challenge that must be addressed by someone investigating the lives of ancient Romans. A second challenge is our dependence on ancient sources that have filtered, shaped, and assembled the data about a subject's personal life to conform to their own biases. It is perhaps impossible for any author – however much professing impartiality – not to color her/his subject matter. Every selection and placement of information is a process of personal decision-making. In our use of ancient sources, we face an additional difficulty in that ancient authors had objectives quite different from those of modern biographers. The emphasis of the ancient biographers was to extract moral lessons from the lives of others, to hold up their subjects as models of behavior, and to produce stories that would illustrate general truths. The conviction among ancient biographers that biography should teach moral lessons makes the utilization of their texts a challenge for modern scholars, who are faced with the problem of trying to extract the true person from the general truth. The work of Plutarch, who lived about the same time as Pliny and was the author of *The Lives of Famous Greek and Roman Men*, and that of Tacitus, a contemporary of Pliny, who wrote a monograph about the life of his father-in-law, Agricola, certainly offer evidence of biographies whose purpose is didactic. Indeed, Plutarch stated that he used the narratives of the lives of famous men "as a mirror, trying to shape and adjust my own life to conform with their virtues."[1] And in the opening of his monograph about Agricola, Tacitus wrote that "it is an ancient custom to hand down to posterity accounts of the deeds and characters of famous men."[2]

Although there is not extant among the writings of Pliny a monograph about the life of an ancient person, many of his letters do contain biographical anecdotes. And, in most cases, one purpose of these anecdotes is to supply the reader with models of behavior. Pliny records the actions and events particular to the subject's life, but his interest in these actions and events often lies in how they demonstrate that the subject has met or exceeded a standard of moral excellence (or, in a few instances, moral frailty) and can therefore be used by readers to evaluate and inspire their own behavior. Several of his letters about women follow this pattern.

The use of real people as models for behavior was pervasive in Roman society. Referring behavior – one's own and others' – to an exemplary standard had a long tradition. Mayer describes this practice as the "cornerstone of Roman moral training."[3] From childhood, Romans were enjoined to pattern their behavior after that of people, living or historical, who embodied the virtues endorsed by their society. The Romans believed that moral instruction was done better by example from real life than by appeal to the abstract theories of Greek ethical philosophy. Pliny's rhetoric teacher, Quintilian drew an explicit contrast between the two systems of moral instruction: "However much the Greeks excel in moral precepts, so much do the Romans excel in real examples, which is a far greater thing."[4] In similar vein, Seneca the Younger asserted: "The road of moral progress is long if one follows precepts, but short and effective if one follows real models."[5] The Roman system of instruction was considered preferable because it offered people a readily comprehended image of virtue in action, and it asked them to emulate the characters of those who were like them, in terms of being members of the community. The models were capable of extraordinary achievements, but they were nonetheless familiar and therefore possible to imitate. Mayer comments that the use of *exempla* in Roman writing of all genres is a presentation of "the sort of actions which lead us to conceptualize *virtus*."[6]

In accordance with this Roman propensity to fabricate a pattern for imitation from the deeds of real people, Pliny seems, in many of his portraits of women, to represent them as individuals whose outstanding character elevates them to the level of ideal role models. Indeed, in several of his descriptions Pliny comments unequivocally that the women serve as examples for others. These letters are thus prescriptive, as well as descriptive – extolling, but also advocating certain patterns of behavior. Our interpretation of his portraits must therefore take into account his desire to advocate behavioral standards and his tendency to shape his narrative to accommodate a moral purpose. And, even when Pliny is not explicitly promoting women as models, his accounts of their actions often seem motivated by a wish to portray them as fulfilling the expectations of their families and society. In particular, they seem to aspire to roles designed by men to meet men's ideal of the perfect wife. They are individualized in the sense that they may be shown responding in a specific way to a specific situation – a threat to their family, for example – but Pliny construes their identities in terms of general virtues.

A related difficulty in any attempt to retrieve a true person from our sources is the tendency among ancient authors to reduce individuals to stereotypes. All our sources of information are male, and, in Roman literature, descriptions of women and observations about them may represent men's opinions, expectations, attitudes, and ideology about women more than the reality about the women. Dixon has expressed skepticism about the possibility of finding any traces of "real" Roman women or of reconstructing the lives of Roman women, given that we have only scraps of information.[7] In addition, because we do not have any words written by the women themselves, it seems impossible to recover a female voice from the ancient texts. Dixon maintains that our male-centered texts give neither an accurate representation of individual women, nor an accurate reflection of women in general. She asserts that the texts employ rhetorical constructions of women and cultural stereotypes from which we learn only about norms, ideologies, and male fantasies. She contends that, "Perhaps the most we can hope for from most sources, whatever they purport to record, is an idea of Roman social norms and ideals rather than actual behaviour and events."[8] In his biography of Agrippina, Barrett acknowledges the tendency of ancient sources "to think in stereotypes and to tailor the evidence to fit some imaginary preconceived type-model."[9] However, Barrett is less pessimistic than Dixon about the possibility of finding meaningful representations of women in ancient sources. He believes that "even behind reports that are contradictory or, when consistent, patently absurd, there lurks a reality capable of being at least partially unearthed."[10] His advice about how to gain insight into the life and experiences of Agrippina is applicable to the women of Pliny's letters: we can understand them by understanding the system that shaped and defined them.

Like Barrett, I believe that it is possible to discover a reality in our sources, even where the appeal to stereotypes and ideals is pervasive. Nonetheless, because Pliny has often embedded biographical details in a portrait whose elements are conventional, one component of this book is an investigation into what Pliny's employment of stereotypes can tell us about the behavior that was expected and admired in Roman women of this period. It is unlikely that Pliny's concept of appropriate behavior would have startled his contemporaries. He undoubtedly believed that his letters explored topics that were of interest and pleasure to his readers and that his letters would gain for him the approval and respect of his social peers. Therefore, it seems reasonable to assume that Pliny's reports of female behavior drew on constructs that were familiar and acceptable to his readers, that the values he endorses reflect the values of his peers, and that the letters thus provide insight into contemporary conventions and practices. His immediate "peers" may have been the landed gentry from his home region of northern Italy, men of wealth and ambition who, like him, were new to political life of Rome. Perhaps they were more morally conservative than native Romans. The portraits drawn by Pliny certainly contrast remarkably with the portraits of female depravity in the satires of his contemporary, Juvenal. Yet the writings of both men seem to presume the existence of a standard or model of ideal female behavior to which they both refer, Pliny praising women who conform to it, and Juvenal castigating women who do not. This book therefore not only brings into the light the distinctive features of the individual women whom Pliny mentions, but also investigates how the concept of the model Roman woman is constructed in Pliny and elsewhere in our ancient sources. The two topics are, of course, intertwined. We cannot effectively evaluate the information that Pliny provides about women without analyzing his reasons for choosing to include them in his letters and without taking into account the importance he placed on models.

Determining why Pliny chose to write about certain women is an essential element to interpreting his portraits of them. And the issue is complicated further by our interest in determining why he made public the letters he wrote. In the first letter of the first book, a letter addressed to a man named Septicius Clarus, Pliny states that, at the urging of Septicius, he has collected and published those of his letters that were composed with some care. He confesses that his published collection does not follow the chronological order in which the letters were written. Rather, the arrangement reflects the order in which he located each of the letters. (Presumably he retrieved the original letters from the addressees or found copies his scribe had made.) Pliny also asserts that he will, in the future, publish other letters as he locates them, as well as letters that he has yet to write. As Ash notes, Pliny "allowed himself scope to include letters which he had not yet written, about events which had not yet happened."[11] This brief programmatic letter informs us that it was Pliny himself who selected and published the letters that appear in Books 1 to 9 (Book 10 seems to have been published after his death), and that all nine books were not published at the same time, but rather in intervals. Because Pliny chose not to include the dates of composition of each letter (unlike Cicero's published letters, which do contain the dates of composition), and because he says that he chose not to publish them in the chronological order in which they were written, we cannot determine what their chronological relationship is to one another.[12]

The knowledge that the correspondence was self-published raises several questions about the nature of the letters. The first question is whether the letters as we have them are "genuine", "real," and "authentic" correspondence, "genuine," "real," and "authentic" here being defined as correspondence that was truly intended as communication with the specified addressee. Since Pliny was the editor of his letters, he was able to arrange them in the order of his choice, and not only to select, but also to reject letters for publication. He had the opportunity, moreover, to revise and alter the letters, deleting portions and perhaps even adding new sections. The letters therefore provide only the information that he, upon careful reflection, wished to release to the public. In addition, because Pliny knew, even as he was composing his letters, that he would publish some of them, there is the possibility that he created letters specifically for public consumption. He had the opportunity to produce letters that may well have been sent to the addressee, but been generated primarily to be included in the published collection. In this way, Pliny could be sure that topics of interest to him would be available to a wider audience. Moreover, he controlled who the recipients of the letters would be. Henderson observes, for example, that eleven of the 247 letters published in Books 1 to 9 are addressed to the historian Tacitus.[13] No other addressee appears so often in Books 1 to 9. The relatively large number of letters to the well-known historian gives the reader the impression that Pliny and Tacitus were close friends, but we have no way of knowing whether this was true, or whether Pliny simply insinuated a close friendship by publishing letters addressed to Tacitus, hoping to impress readers with the celebrity of his addressees.

We do not know whether or how often Tacitus responded to Pliny. Pliny did not include in his published collection any letters that he received from family members and friends. It would, of course, be useful to our assessment of Pliny, and of the women about and to whom he wrote, to learn what others wrote to him. Nonetheless we should keep in mind that each person to whom Pliny addressed a letter had an effect on that letter. As De Pretis explains, there is a circular motion to a letter: the writer is influenced by and responds to the image which s/he creates of the addressee, which, in turn, influences the self-image which the writer constructs in the letter.[14] Although a letter provides us with only one side, as it were, of a conversation, the writer, during the process of composition, tailors the letter to correspond to how s/he believes the recipient will react upon reading it. We may thus retrieve from a letter from Pliny a small perception of the addressee as s/he appeared to Pliny.

However, his publication of the letters indicates that Pliny was aiming also for a larger audience. If the letters in the published collection were edited or even specifically written for readers far beyond Pliny's circle of friends and for readers in succeeding generations, we are arguably justified in reading them as documents that differ from a letter never intended for anyone but the person to whom it was addressed. We cannot ascertain the degree of editing that Pliny did, but it is important to keep in mind that, by choosing to self-publish, he wanted his letters to serve a purpose beyond simply communicating with a friend.

Of course, even letters intended only for the recipient served an important purpose in ancient Roman society. A letter is a medium for communicating information and thoughts to people who are absent from us. Today, with the proliferation of electronic gadgets, we have many ways of communicating. In the ancient world, the letter was, aside from a messenger, the only method of keeping in touch with those from whom you were physically separated. And people were frequently separated, since a distance of even ten miles was considerable before the age of motorized vehicles. The dependence on letters as a method of sharing experiences is attested to by Pliny in *Letter* 6.17.1, where he is eager to tell a friend about the rude behavior of several guests at a social event he attended: "I must divulge my little pique of indignation to you in a letter since it is not possible to do so in person." Men of senatorial rank, like Pliny, often traveled considerable distances, inspecting their estates and serving in military and administrative positions in Italy and the far-flung provinces. They devoted much time to composing both business and personal correspondence, and therefore effective letter-writing was a highly desirable skill among the elite class. As Hutchinson has noted, letter-writing was a vital medium for the maintenance of social friendships and political alliances.[15] And letters not only sustained friendships; they might also be used to generate them, even over long distances. Regarding the correspondence addressed to Tacitus, perhaps Pliny was not a close friend, but rather was using the letters to introduce himself to the historian and to try to foster a friendship with him. Several scholars have discussed the exchange of correspondence among the Roman elite in terms of symbolic capital and the currency of friendship.[16] Letter-writing was an essential element in the development of a network of allies and thus also in the advancement of one's career. Moreover, addressees frequently circulated letters among friends, and a writer might well expect his letter to reach an audience of more than one person. It was therefore crucial that letters display a rhetorical proficiency that would impress and engage readers. Hutchinson's comments on letter-writing in the republican period are equally true of Pliny's early imperial period. "The character of that society and the place of letter-writing within it were such as to encourage the appearance of letters written with art and ability."[17]

A beautifully polished and thoughtfully composed letter can, of course, be just as "genuine," "real," and "authentic" as one hastily and crudely composed. However, De Pretis asks: "Can a learned person (especially an ancient Roman man, imbued with rhetoric) write something 'immediate'?" She answers herself that "the ideal of the completely sincere text, the verbal embodiment of its writer's heart, is ultimately a Romantic chimera."[18] Letters do more than just convey information and thoughts. By their nature, they are expressions of the writer and therefore they are – however brief or informal or seemingly spontaneously generated – a form of self-representation. All letters are compositions that are produced upon reflection, and thus they do not provide a completely unmediated or unguarded account of an event. Even if a writer thinks s/he is producing a message or a description that is untainted by personal response to the situation, s/he will intrude into the composition. Often, however, the writer intentionally uses the letter to create an image of her/himself. As Carlon comments, "The most casual of written communication is fashioned to some extent by its author for the eye of the reader; even a simple note of thanks may express both real gratitude and the writer's desire to be seen as a polite and genuinely grateful recipient."[19] Letters may reveal a writer's innermost thoughts, but only the thoughts that s/he chooses to reveal. The writer has control over what information appears in the letter and how that information is presented. Thus, particularly in the hands of a skillful writer, a letter becomes a medium for creating and manipulating a persona to present to the world. This was especially true in ancient Rome, where the intense rhetorical training that elite men received made them very proficient at self-fashioning and self-promotion. Indeed, letters were an ideal medium for presenting a self-portrait. Letters belonged to the world of social interaction, and a recipient would consider the writer's words to be less formal and perhaps more immediate and sincere than was possible in public oratory. On the other hand, the letter-writer could monitor his words more carefully than was possible in a casual conversation. For example, although the opening of *Letter* 6.17 (quoted earlier) gives the impression of immediacy and implies that Pliny is breathlessly communicating with his friend just as he would in a face-to-face conversation, he has in fact skillfully composed a letter in which he portrays himself as someone concerned about both good manners and literature – all the while seeming to be simply documenting an event. Thus letters provided the perfect medium for drawing the attention of others to your virtues and controlling the image that they developed of you, while appearing to be transmitting information.

Because Pliny published his correspondence, he had further opportunities to manipulate the image that he wished the public and posterity to have of him. Morello and Gibson have aptly described the published letters as having been "cut and polished to precisely calibrated dimensions and assembled by the epistolary craftsman into a masterly design."[20] Because the letters were so carefully crafted and edited, a study of the literary strategies that Pliny employed is an important aspect of understanding his authorial intentions. But what was the self-image he wanted to present? Pliny had two primary goals for the publication of his letters: he wanted to be recognized as a highly regarded writer and to be remembered as a virtuous man. He never states directly his reasons for publishing a selection of his letters. On several occasions, however, he comments on the ability of written records to bestow a kind of immortality. He mentions in *Letter* 5.8.1, for example, that he is considering writing a history because it is a noble deed to keep alive the memory of those to whom *aeternitas* (immortality) is owed, and also because historical writings allow the author to acquire fame by memorializing others. Clearly he had in mind that his ability to write well about the deeds of others might gain him immortality.

If Pliny did, in fact, compose books of history, no trace of them remains.[21] However, several letters – such as *Letter* 6.16, which recounts the heroism of Pliny's uncle during the eruption of Vesuvius – appear designed to serve as carefully crafted historical records that will guarantee fame for both the subject and the author. *Letter* 6.16 was specifically composed, Pliny tells us, at the request of Tacitus for inclusion in the history he was writing. However, several other letters, not prompted by or addressed to Tacitus, are similarly dedicated to historical anecdotes and accounts of heroic behavior. In these letters, Pliny devotes basically the entire letter to a narrative about someone else's deeds. *Letter* 7.19, for example, which is addressed to Priscus, makes no personal reference at all to the recipient, but instead reports to him the illness of a woman named Fannia and then describes her admirable support of her husband's interests. Rather than a chatty transmission of news, the addressee receives what might be categorized as a hagiography. Ash comments that Pliny is disingenuous both in his insistence in *Letter* 1.1 that he is not compiling history, and in his statement in *Letter* 6.16.22 that "a letter is one thing, history is another." In fact, he deliberately blurs the seemingly clear boundary between history and letter writing.[22] Indeed, Pliny was acutely aware that historical narratives and anecdotes were categories of literary composition that earned approval for a writer. He therefore embedded in his letters the types of anecdotes about people's lives, and also their deaths ("death scenes"), that were popular features of historical works.[23] As Ash observes, Pliny "found a way to inscribe the most valuable elements of 'history' within the *Epistles* without being hampered by the constraints of the genre" (i.e. the constraints of grand scale).[24] The embedded anecdotes produced lasting renown for the subjects and offered role models to readers, but also, and just as importantly, brought distinction to Pliny as someone who had written something worth reading. Although he did not produce a continuous, chronological narrative, his effectiveness as a composer of historical set pieces would earn him praise for proficiency in historiography.

Pliny was not content, however, to be remembered only as a writer and orator. It was also his goal to make sure that posterity was mindful that the conduct of his life had been honorable and admirable. In *Letter* 9.3.1, he declared: "I deem as very blessed the man who enjoys the anticipation of a good and enduring fame and lives confident of his continued impact and future glory." In essence, Pliny used the publication of his letters to create an autobiography, or, as Henderson describes it, a "self-dramatization, a literary stab at self-immortalization."[25] In *Letter* 6.16.3, the letter to Tacitus about Vesuvius, Pliny comments that the most fortunate man is one who, like his uncle, has both done deeds worth recording and has also written something worth reading. Pliny was anxious to be remembered as someone who, like his uncle, had also "done deeds worth recording." And he was not reluctant to announce in his published letters that he desired to be immortalized. For example, in *Letter* 7.33.1, where he uses the letter format to send to Tacitus an unsolicited, self-laudatory narrative about his behavior during a court proceeding, he unabashedly confesses that he wants to be mentioned in Tacitus' historical writings, which will themselves, he predicts, become immortal. He even expresses the hope that Tacitus, who did not invite the letter, will refine and embellish the material Pliny provides. And in *Letter* 9.31.1, sent to another author of a history book, he gleefully reports that he has read again and again the passages about himself which were included in the book. However, although Pliny was eager to be commemorated in the works of Tacitus and other historians, he knew there were advantages to leaving behind for posterity his own reports, the most obvious being that he could control the material and fashion a flattering self-image. Thus, in several of his narratives, Pliny himself appears as an actor, allowing him to manipulate the public memory of his role in the events by releasing his own description of his actions. Not surprisingly, the author/actor appears modest, but wise and brave. And the reader is thus led to making a positive assessment of him. In *Letter* 3.11, for example, a letter which purports to be an encomium of the philosopher Artemidorus, Pliny's clever rhetorical manipulation allows him to make his own courage and generosity a central theme in the letter while nonetheless appearing unassuming and reluctant to reveal his own virtues.[26] The publication of his letters thus enabled Pliny to produce a most flattering autobiography and to ensure that his life would be remembered even if historians ignored him. Certainly the publication of *Letter* 7.33, addressed to (but not solicited by) Tacitus, served to make Pliny's version of events widely known even if Tacitus declined to write about him. A comment attributed to Winston Churchill might be applicable to Pliny: "History will be kind to me because I intend to write it."

Pliny's ambition to leave for posterity favorable evidence of his literary talent and his public and personal life was not an unusual ambition, particularly for a Roman senator. Leach, comparing the idealized portrait of Pliny produced by his letters with the imperial sculpture of his time, maintains that self-fashioning was pervasive in late first century Rome.[27] The self-portrait that Pliny chose to create in his letters was that of a hard-working and admired statesman, a respected literary figure, a wise counselor, a valuable patron, a prudent landowner, a considerate slave owner, a loving husband, and a generous and loyal friend. Moreover, he presents himself as a man disinterested in financial matters although his wealth suggests that he was an astute manager of money. Carlon, in her study of the letters which Pliny wrote to and about women, and Radicke, in his examination of all the letters in Book 3, both indicate how each of Pliny's letters contributes to the development of a comprehensive self-portrait of a person with many different facets of character and activity.[28] Quite significantly, he seems eager to publicize his support of people who opposed Domitian, who was emperor 81 to 96 CE. McNeill, discussing another Roman author, has observed that "Horace as he appears is a carefully developed characterization, representing solely those aspects of a projected personality that he wanted us to see and believe in, in a variety of contexts."[29] The same might be said of Pliny, although he sometimes unintentionally reveals aspects of his character that he did not intend to.

Pliny's letters were published after the assassination of Domitian, and thus Pliny ran no risk of angering the emperor. His insistence on developing a portrait of himself as an anti-Domitian sympathizer is curious, particularly when we consider that his career flourished under Domitian. He held the quaestorship, tribuneship, and praetorship, and then the prefecture of the military treasury. Although Pliny claims in the *Panegyricus* (his only extant speech) to have suspended his career plans when Domitian proclaimed his hatred of good men, his tenure of the prefecture suggests, on the contrary, that he remained in Domitian's favor until the emperor's assassination in September 96.[30] However, Pliny never mentions the prefecture in his published letters. The information is found only in inscriptions.[31]

If the inscriptional evidence were not available, we would have no reason to doubt Pliny's claim that he preferred to suspend his career plans rather than to serve Domitian. He may have deliberately omitted, or removed during revision, references to the prefecture in the published letters because he did not wish to remind readers that he had remained in Domitian's favor. Whatever the reasons for the omission, his claim in the *Panegyricus* to have withdrawn from public life betrays a desire to modify the history of his conduct under Domitian.

Pliny was undoubtedly not the only man to feel uncomfortable about his conduct during the final years of the first century CE. These years were a period of anxiety for members of the senatorial class who resented their own loss of influence in public affairs and were offended by Domitian's arrogance. Few men, however, were openly hostile toward the emperor. The majority remained politically ambitious and chose to ensure their public and personal survival by adopting a prudent policy of acquiescence. They vied for and held public office and, if they resented Domitian, they did not reveal it. Of course, once Domitian had been assassinated, everyone was keen to divorce himself from any association with the emperor and to justify his own actions during the reign of terror. In the *Agricola*, Tacitus took up the defense of his late father-in-law and pointed out, that although Agricola appeared to be in Domitian's favor because he received prominent appointments, he was in reality hated by Domitian, and that, in any case, it is not impossible for a good man to serve a bad emperor.[32] The return to Rome of those people who had been exiled by Domitian, and whose loved ones had been killed by Domitian, probably produced uneasiness and shame among those who had survived his reign unharmed, and undoubtedly prompted many loud declarations of friendship and sympathy for those who had suffered. Sometimes vindication of one's own conduct meant pointing a finger at someone else, and there was a flurry of accusations and prosecutions during the reign of the next emperor, Nerva, as Pliny reports in *Letter* 9.13.4.

In the aftermath of Domitian's assassination, biographies of the few people who had challenged his authority – and the authority of earlier emperors – became very popular. Tacitus, moreover, was composing his chronicles of events during the reigns of the Julio-Claudians and their successors. His *Annals* and *Histories* are replete with stories of the prosecutions, persecutions, and deaths of the Roman elite, giving the impression, as Edwards has remarked, that the emperors had been waging war against the senatorial class.[33] Now that a more collegial emperor had taken control, apparently the Roman reading public could not get enough of biographies of men (and a few women) who had suffered under earlier imperial rulers. Pliny was eager to show how supportive he was of such literary projects. In *Letter* 8.12, for example, he writes to a friend that it is both his pious duty and his desire to attend a reading which Titinius Capito is giving because Capito is composing a volume on the deaths of illustrious men, some of whom, Pliny is keen to note, were very dear to him.[34] In celebrating the victims of earlier emperors, particularly Domitian, people who had survived unscathed and whose careers had flourished were eager to make it clear where their loyalties had rested during the difficult periods.

Pliny may well have been concerned about how posterity would view his behavior under Domitian. Leach has commented that Pliny feared that his actions would be misinterpreted, and that the publication of his letters, with their highly selective representation of his experiences, allowed him to apply hindsight in shaping the record of past events.[35] In essence, he used the letters to recast his activities during Domitian's reign. Although he had not been overtly willing to jeopardize his career or his life to support the opposition to Domitian, he did not want posterity to conclude that he had been inactive while brave men and women suffered. In *Letter* 3.11, for example, which will be examined later in this book, Pliny's rhetoric leads us to conclude that, in 93 CE, when several opponents to Domitian were killed or exiled, Pliny risked his own life to help them. And yet, at this very time, as we know from inscriptional evidence, he enjoyed the favor of Domitian. His behavior may therefore not have been as brave as he insinuates, but he was eager to have his account of events made public – after Domitian's assassination, of course. He was also careful to include, in his published collection, letters in which he mentions his friendships with the opponents and his kind favors to them and their families. He thus constructs an image of a man who was closely connected and sympathetic to Domitian's critics. Moreover, by alluding to how instrumental these critics were in the overthrow of Domitian, Pliny magnifies the significance of his support of them. His desire to construct this image of someone involved at least peripherally with Domitian's downfall and of someone on warm terms with Domitian's opponents is an important issue for this book because several of the opponents were women. In order to develop portraits of these women, we need to understand why and how Pliny chose to use their stories in order to paint a favorable picture of his own behavior.

Pliny's descriptions of the courageous actions of these women also serve to provide models of behavior for his readers. He depicts Roman society of the early second century CE, under the benevolent rule of the emperor Trajan, as a society that was intent on regaining the stability and civility that had been lost under Domitian. Hoffer suggests that "the *Panegyric* makes explicit what is implicit throughout the letters," that a good emperor enables his subjects to devote themselves to honorable political activities, to engage in worthy literary projects, to be secure in their enjoyment of their wealth, and to be loyal friends.[36] It is noteworthy that Pliny's letters give the impression that he cultivated friendships that were honest and supportive and eschewed the treachery of previous regimes. Representing himself as an advocate for the change which the reign of Trajan seemed to promise, Pliny offers prescriptions and paradigms for appropriate behavior, the paradigms being the virtuous men (himself included) and women whose actions he records in the letters. Trajan promoted an ideology of values in which women adhered to traditional roles and expectations. Pliny's portraits of women showcase and affirm this ideology and also give moral guidance to the reader. In addition, they reward the "models" for their integrity by immortalizing them (or, in a few cases, punish those who behaved badly), as well as granting distinction to the men who trained their wives and daughters to act virtuously. Pliny's portraits demonstrate, moreover, that he, through his skills as an historical reporter and a champion of moral conduct, played an important role in the restoration process. And therefore his glorification of others is a crucial element of his strategy to promote himself. A further purpose of the letters extolling virtuous behavior may be to prompt readers to remark on Pliny's good judgment in associating himself with such admirable people. Pliny thus persuades his readers that he is a counselor worth heeding and a writer worth reading because he himself has behaved appropriately and because admirable people value his friendship.[37]

Thus, in reading Pliny's reports about women and trying to retrieve some of the truth about them, we must keep in mind his reasons for choosing to write and publish. We cannot expect a simple statement of facts by an impartial reporter (if such a person has ever existed). On the other hand, the information that he furnishes sometimes tells us something more, or something different, than he perhaps intended, both about his subjects and about him, especially when we compare and augment it with historical, legal, epigraphical, literary, and artistic sources. Women were constrained by custom and law to accept roles as subordinates to men. Pliny's letters provide a context and a human face, by supplying evidence of how specific women were affected by the customs and laws, and how these women negotiated their roles. The letters thus deepen our understanding of the lives of women in the late first and early second century CE. They reveal that women adapted their behavior to the roles that they were expected to play, but that they also adapted the roles to suit their needs. We learn from the letters that women formed and maintained friendships with men, were instrumental in arranging marriages, participated in family decision-making, and were important components in the complex social networks which men established. In addition, Pliny's references to the distribution of property by women suggests that, despite legal restrictions, women did possess and exercise considerable control over property. His letters also inform us that women took legal action to protect their families. They instruct us, moreover, that women could take part in political controversies and (unlike Sallust's Sempronia) be praised for doing so. Finally, Pliny's letters furnish some of our best evidence for the value assigned to affective relationships between men and women. In particular, his letters about his love for his wife, and about conjugal devotion in other marriages, indicate that such devotion was valued. We need not believe that Pliny was always, or even ever, as loyal a friend and as loving a husband as the character he created for himself in the letters. It is significant, however, that he wanted his contemporaries to see him as such. Pliny's composition of his letters was shaped by a desire for reader approval. He must have believed therefore that his readers were interested in stories about the establishment and maintenance of affective bonds and that they would applaud his efforts to produce such stories and to appear to pattern his own life to conform to these values. Pliny's letters about his wife admittedly teach us more about him and about the expectations of Roman society than about her. Nonetheless, they allow us to recover information about her activities from which we can develop an image of how she responded to those expectations. The same is true of the other women about whom Pliny reports. In the following pages, we will bring the activities and relationships of these women to the foreground and focus on what we can learn about their lives.

Figure 1 Agrippina the Elder (c. 14 BCE – 33 CE), wife of Germanicus, granddaughter of the emperor Augustus, mother of the emperor Caligula, and grandmother of the emperor Nero. Museo Capitolini, Rome. © 2012. Photo: Scala, Florence.

1 Arria the Elder and the heroism of women

Our investigation into the lives of the women who appear in Pliny's letters starts with a group of women connected to one another through blood or marriage. Their stories begin in the last years of the principate of Augustus and extend well into the reign of Trajan, a period of about 100 years. They were the wives and daughters of men who were critical of the form of government established by Augustus and consolidated by his successors. They were, however, more than passive witnesses to events of this period; some played a vital role in perpetuating discontent with imperial rule. For their loyalty to the men in their family, and for their hostility to the emperors, these women paid heavy prices. Tacitus and Suetonius, historians who were contemporaries of Pliny, record the activities of the men who fostered dissent, but offer very little information about the women. Pliny, however, pays considerable attention to the women of this family. For most, he is our sole source of information about their lives. His letters thus grant us the invaluable opportunity to become acquainted with women who would otherwise be unknown. From the letters, we receive the impression that it was the women who linked the family together from generation to generation, preserved its history, and instilled in each new generation a respect for and a desire to emulate the family tradition of dissent. In addition, these women undertook to encourage the creation of a written narrative about the deeds of family members and to secure it for an audience far larger than just the family. They thus ensured that the fame of these family members would endure. Although Pliny's accounts provide information about this family of dissidents that is additional, rather than alternative, to Tacitus and Suetonius, his highlighting of the activities of the women offers us a different perspective and enables us to learn how the events of the first century CE affected these women, and how they, in turn, influenced events.

It is possible that Pliny's interest in recording the activities of these women was kindled by the zeal and persistence of the women themselves in telling their tales and promulgating their family history. However, his desire to bring their lives to public attention may have been motivated, in large part, by his anxiety about his own reputation, an anxiety discussed earlier in the Introduction. Several of these women had been prosecuted in 93 CE, toward the end of Domitian's reign, at a time when Pliny himself had remained unscathed and had even enjoyed career advancement. In the period after Domitian's death in 96, many men in the senatorial class, which had acquiesced in the emperor's atrocious deeds, were eager to explain their behavior. Pliny asserted in his letters that he had, in fact, been a good friend to these women (*Letters* 3.11.3 and 9.13.3) and had provided them with substantial assistance, both during the darkest hours of their punishment and afterward, when they sought to clear the family name by censuring their persecutors. By claiming that he had not deserted these women, even when his concern for their welfare put his own career and life in peril, Pliny created in his letters – and left for posterity – a portrait of himself as a courageous and effective friend whose contributions to the opposition to Domitian had simply gone unnoticed.[1] In addition, to impress upon readers that the family's reputation for courage extended back several generations, Pliny included a letter about the brave deeds of the grandmother of one of the women prosecuted in 93 CE – deeds which had occurred five decades earlier, and two decades before Pliny's birth. Although Pliny's knowledge of this woman was second-hand, by recording her deeds in a letter, he gives the impression that his concern for and connections to the family were long-standing. We might justifiably wonder to what extent Pliny manipulated his accounts not only of his own activities, but also of the activities of these women in order to embellish his self-portrait. It is certainly important to remember that we are viewing the actions of these women through Pliny's filter. We can nonetheless still gather from his letters information not available elsewhere about their responses to the challenges in their lives. We can also illuminate their lives by understanding the contexts in which they grew up, married, and raised children. Therefore, in my attempts to reconstruct the life stories of these women, I have included discussions about events, laws, customs, and conventions that framed their lives and shaped the decisions that they made. My intent has been to construct the setting for their lives and decisions. The "background information" provided in this first chapter will also be pertinent to gaining an understanding of the lives of women discussed in later chapters.

Arria the Elder (Arria Maior)

Arria the Elder ended her life by plunging a dagger into her chest. The year of her death was 42 CE. She was perhaps about 40 years old. We know nothing about Arria's childhood or her natal family.[2] By tradition, girls were usually assigned the feminine form of their father's *nomen* – that is, his gentile (family) name – and we might therefore suppose that Arria's father (and his father before him) had been an Arrius. We cannot be certain, however, because, by the early imperial period, it was not unusual for children to be assigned names that would instead preserve the name of the family of their mother, or of the family of their father's mother.[3] Although Pliny addresses three letters (*Letters* 4.3, 4.18, and 5.15; see also *Letter* 4.27) to a man named Arrius Antoninus, who would have been a child at the time of Arria's death, he does not indicate that they were related.[4] The Latin word *maior*, which means "elder," has been attached to Arria's name to distinguish her from her daughter, who was also named Arria (a good example of a daughter receiving her name from her mother, not her father). Arria the Elder will henceforth be designated as "Arria E."

Arria E was married to Aulus Caecina Paetus, a man of senatorial rank from a family in Etruria.[5] He served as a suffect consul in 37 CE.[6] From Pliny's letters, we know that Arria E gave birth to at least two children, a son who died in childhood, and a daughter who survived to adulthood. (See Genealogy Chart 1.) Quite possibly there was also a second son, if the Caecina Paetus recorded in inscriptions is indeed her son.[7] Although his name at birth would have been derived from his birth father's family, hence Caecina Paetus, he was apparently adopted by Gaius Laecanius Bassus and thus also took the name of his adoptive family.[8] It was not unusual for male Roman citizens to be adopted when they were already adults and when their natal parents were still alive. A family with more than one son might give one up for adoption to a family with no son. The motivation of the natal parents would be to concentrate family funds on one son's career, and to gain for the son they had adopted out the financial resources and social connections necessary for a successful political career.[9] However, since one son of Arria E and Paetus had died in childhood, it is unlikely that they would have adopted out their one remaining son while they were alive. The adoption may have occurred after their deaths.

Arria E's husband, Aulus Caecina Paetus, incurred the wrath of the emperor Claudius. However, the man presumed to be their biological son had a successful career in Roman public life. Emperors were sometimes kind to the children of men they had sentenced to death, perhaps in order to persuade people that they were benevolent by nature and inclined to punish only those undeniably guilty of treason.[10] He was suffect consul in 70 or 71 CE, served as curator of the Tiber River in 74 CE, and was proconsul of the province of Asia after that.[11] If this man was indeed the biological son of Arria E and Aulus Caecina Paetus, it is odd that he is not mentioned by Pliny, who claimed a close association with the family. Perhaps he, unlike his sister, had renounced the political sympathies of his birth parents and chosen to distance himself from his natal family.

Arria E's daughter was already married at the time of Arria E's suicide in 42 CE. I speculate that there was an age gap of approximately – very approximately – 20 years between mother and daughter. Roman "women" married at a young age; it was not unusual to be a bride at the age of 15 and to be wed to a much older man. Working back from the year of the suicide, we know that the daughter was already married then and was therefore perhaps about 18 years old – that is, born about 24 CE. If Arria E had married Paetus when she was 15 years old, and given birth to her daughter when she was about 18, then she was born about 4 CE, and was approximately 38 years old at the time of her death. (Of course, if the daughter were the youngest of her children, Arria E might have given birth to her at the age of 30 or beyond, and thus been about 50 at the time of her suicide.) It is possible that Arria's marriage to Paetus was not her first marriage. A girl of 15 who had been married to a much older man might well be widowed while still young and then remarried, but we have no evidence that this was a second marriage for Arria. Indeed, the circumstances of her suicide (which will be discussed later) suggest that she was determined to be remembered as a woman who had had only one husband.

Arria E's other son died in childhood. Her behavior, at the time of his death, is recounted by Pliny in *Letter* 3.16 as evidence of the strength of her character and of her willingness to sacrifice her own welfare for the interests of her husband. Pliny had learned from a conversation with Arria E's granddaughter that, on one occasion, Arria E's son and husband were both gravely ill. The son died. Though grief-stricken, Arria E concealed his death from her sick husband in order to protect him from the distress of bad news. When he inquired about the boy's health, Arria deceived him by replying: "He has rested well and willingly taken food" (*Letter* 3.16.4). She arranged and attended the funeral without her husband's knowledge. Repressing her anguish, she assumed a happy and comforting countenance when she entered his bedroom, and pretended that their son was still alive and even recovering. Only when she left the bedroom did she allow herself to dissolve into tears. As Pliny comments, she continued to play the role of mother although she had lost her son. And she chose to endure the strain of feigning good cheer in order not to jeopardize the recovery of her husband.

Pliny depicts her son's death as a traumatic experience for Arria E. Nonetheless, the loss of a child was not a rare event for Roman women. Arria E lived in an era when the incidences of miscarriage and stillbirth and of mortality among infants and children were high. Although conclusive statistical evidence is not available, scholars have estimated that the infant mortality rate may have been as high as 30%.[12] And, in an era when medical care was primitive, many young children who survived their first year nonetheless died young as a result of diseases, accidents, or poor nutrition. It is estimated that 25% or more of children between the ages of one and ten did not survive. One funerary inscription records the deaths of two brothers at the ages of five and eight. Another records the death of a six-year-old girl. A third informs us of a woman who bore two sons, only one of whom survived her.[13] Cornelia, the mother of Tiberius and Gaius Gracchus, bore 12 children, of whom only three survived to adulthood.[14] Veturia, the wife of a soldier, bore six children, of whom only one survived her when she herself died at the age of 27.[15] Agrippina the Elder (see Figure 1) bore nine children, two of whom died in infancy and a third in early childhood.[16] Quintilian, the scholar of oratory and Pliny's teacher, lost both his sons, one at age five, the other at age nine. (And his wife had died when she was only 18 years old.)[17]

The Julian laws

It is quite possible that Arria E experienced more than three pregnancies and more than one loss of an infant or child. In any case, her bearing of one or two children who survived beyond childhood would have been proof that, as a wife, she had fulfilled her most important social duty: the production of the next generation of Roman citizens. About the time that Arria E herself had been born, the emperor Augustus (who himself had only one child, a daughter, Julia) was expressing concern about the declining population of Roman citizens, which he blamed in part on the reluctance of people to marry and to become parents. The entrance into Italy of immigrants and slaves, and the birth of slaves within Italy kept the population at a stable level, but Augustus wanted more citizen families, and perhaps particularly more upper-class families. He therefore sponsored legislation to encourage marriage and child-bearing. This legislation was remarkable because it authorized the intrusion of the state into matters which had traditionally been family concerns. Citizens were now urged to consider that they had not just a family responsibility, but even a civic duty to produce children. As Severy comments, Augustus' legislation "officially made proper family behavior part of a citizens' duty. The laws heavily encouraged citizens to marry and procreate in a chaste and respectable manner for the good of the *res publica*. One's family responsibilities thus became primary duties to the community, in addition to the monitoring of other families' failures in this regard. … (A)lthough official concern for marriage and childbearing was not unprecedented, the ways in which Augustus legislated these areas of private life changed in some critical ways the conceptual relationship of the family to the state."[18]

The first set of these laws was passed in 18 BCE and became known as the Lex Julia. (Julius was Augustus' family or gentile name after his adoption by his great-uncle, Julius Caesar.) Augustus' subjects did not, however, embrace the legislation with enthusiasm, and, in 9 CE, he reiterated his concerns in a revised version of the laws, known as the Lex Papia Poppaea, named after the two consuls of the year who, ironically, were both childless bachelors. Unfortunately, a complete record of the original laws has not been preserved. Moreover, the distinctions between the two sets has been obscured because later jurists generally referred to them as if one body of legislation. Hence the term "the Julian laws" is often used to designate both sets of laws.[19] The legislation was directed at men between the ages of 25 and 60, and women between the ages of 20 and 50. The establishment of an upper limit of 50 years of age for women – the end of a woman's childbearing years – indicates that Augustus' intent in encouraging marriage was to increase the population of Roman citizens. The legislation penalized celibacy and childlessness by preventing unmarried persons from receiving certain types of inheritances and legacies, and by limiting the amount of inheritance and legacy which a married childless person could receive. In order to avoid penalization, a person was required to remarry after the death of a spouse or a divorce. By the Lex Julia, remarriage was required within one year of a spouse's death, or within six months after a divorce. The Lex Papia Poppaea extended the grace periods to two years after death, and 18 months after divorce. The rewards for producing legitimate children (that is, within a legal marriage) were, for men, preference and acceleration in appointments to public office and exemption from the burdensome task of *tutela* – that is, service as a guardian (which will be discussed later). As an incentive for marriage, preference in appointments was a substantial reward, but only among the elite class, since only they had the wealth to support such careers. By the same token, restrictions on inheritances would have held scant interest for the majority of Roman citizens, who were poor and whose family and friends had little property to bequeath. Adopted children counted equally with natural children.

There was thus incentive for elite childless couples to adopt, and, given the high mortality rate among the young, many adoptive parents chose to adopt not an infant, or even a child, but an adult (and usually a male).[20] Perhaps Arria E's putative son was adopted by a couple who wanted to enjoy the privileges of having a child.

Augustus took seriously his title of *Pater Patriae*, "Father of the Fatherland." He portrayed the state as a family and himself as the strict, but benevolent father of its citizens. He continued to promote his ideology of family values, for example praising in a public speech of 9 CE a group of men who had produced a new generation of citizens by fathering legitimate children. At the same time, he chided men who did not have children with the reproach that they were surely annihilating the Roman race and destroying the Roman state by disobeying its laws and remaining childless.[21]. To offer a model for emulation, he was fond of appearing at public events accompanied by his grandchildren and great-grandchildren.[22] He also had his family depicted conspicuously on public monuments such as the Ara Pacis, to underscore his theme of family harmony, stability, and fertility.[23]

Despite his efforts to change the moral culture of his time, Augustus was not very successful at encouraging Roman citizens to have large families. Writing about 100 years later, Pliny (who did not himself have children) praised a friend who had several children, and commented that he "had thus fulfilled the obligation of the best of citizens because he was very willing to make use of the fertility of his wife, in an era in which the rewards of childlessness make even one child seem to many to be burdensome" (*Letter* 4.15.3).[24] Tacitus reports that the enactment of Augustus' legislation encouraged the rise of informers who spied on households and reported violations. According to Tacitus, the nefarious actions of these informers ruined many families and caused panic for all. He also comments, however, that the Augustan laws failed to be effective because childlessness offered too many advantages.[25]

Arria E grew to maturity at a time when people were talking about Augustus' remarkable legislation and its ramifications. She was raised, moreover, in a period when the ideology of family stability became a prominent feature of imperial propaganda.[26] In the speech referred to earlier, in which Augustus praised men who were fathers, he also posed this rhetorical question: "What can be better than a wife who exercises personal self-control, stays at home, can manage the house for you and bring up your children, gladden you in health and tend you in sickness, share your successes and console you in your failures?" Augustus' image of the ideal wife was not novel. Roman society had traditionally instructed women to place their husbands' interests above their own. Augustus' propaganda, however, firmly linked the behavior of women to the health of the state. Arria's own thoughts about marriage and the role of a wife must surely have been influenced by the discussions of her day.

Guardians

If Arria bore three children, she would have been eligible for a privilege granted to women by the Julian laws: release from the oversight of a "guardian" or "protector." This privilege was known in Latin as *ius trium liberorum*, "the three-children privilege." It is not known whether the children had to survive to a certain age in order for the woman to qualify for the exemption, or whether even those children who died shortly after birth were counted. Gardner maintains that three was the requisite number of live births and that the children need not have survived to any specified age.[27] Freedwomen (slaves who had been freed) qualified for the exemption if they had four children, born after they had been emancipated. (Any children born while they were still slaves became the property of the slave-owner.)

The Latin word for guardian or protector is *tutor*; "guardianship" is *tutela*. When a girl or woman's *paterfamilias* died, she was released from the *patria potestas*, or "paternal control," and became *sui iuris* – that is, "under her own regulation." Nonetheless, Roman girls and women of all ages, whether single or married, were required to have a male guardian, usually a relative, appointed to them, for the rest of their lives, when their *paterfamilias* died. The *paterfamilias* was a person's oldest direct male ascendant, either the grandfather or, if he was deceased, the father.[28] The *paterfamilias* was the head of the agnate family. A legitimate child was formally a member of her/his father's family, and relatives on the father's side, such as paternal aunts and uncles, were "agnates." Relatives on the mother's side, such as maternal uncles and aunts, were "cognates."[29] Although a child undoubtedly had social interactions with cognates (the mother's family), her/his legal family was the agnates (the father's family).

Until the Julian laws, the only women who were granted exemptions from *tutela mulierum* ("guardianship of women") were Vestal Virgins.[30] The function of the guardian was not to oversee the moral instruction or physical welfare of the girl/woman, but rather to supervise the management of her finances. Usually the guardian or *tutor* was her closest male agnate, a paternal uncle or brother, for instance, and had been nominated in her father's will. For example, Junius Mauricus, who will be discussed in Chapter 2, apparently served as *tutor* for the daughter of his deceased brother (*Letter* 1.14).[31] However, a non-agnate or even a non-relative might be appointed if there was no surviving male agnate to fill the role. For example, when the younger Helvidius, who will also be discussed in Chapter 2, died in 93 CE, with no surviving adult male agnates, the consuls appointed Gaius Julius Cornutus Tertullus, who was not an agnate family member, to be guardian for one of his two daughters (*Letter* 9.13.16). The fact that they did not appoint him *tutor* also for the other daughter suggests that *tutela* was considered burdensome.[32]

While the *paterfamilias* was alive, he had legal ownership of and power of management over all the property of the agnate *familia*. Even adult men did not legally own property if their *paterfamilias* was alive. However, upon the death of the *paterfamilias*, both his son(s) and his daughter(s) were eligible to inherit the property. Roman women were legally empowered to own property (real and moveable) and to hold it separate from their husbands. This right is quite remarkable. After the fall of the Roman empire, it was removed from most European women and not reinstated again until the late 19th and early 20th centuries. However, "legal capacity" – that is, the capacity to be a holder of rights – is not the same as the capacity to exercise those rights. Although Roman women could own property, they did not have free rein on the management of it. Their wealth was acquired mainly through inheritance from a natal family member. The role of the guardian or *tutor* of a married woman was to preserve – that is, to "guard" the value of what was essentially the property of her (not her husband's) agnate family and to ensure that, at the woman's death, it was passed on to other members of her agnate family. The very concept of guardianship for adult women implies that male lawmakers believed that women were not capable of making intelligent decisions about finances.[33]

Of course, the appointment of a guardian would have been of considerably more importance to families of wealth – such as Arria E's – than to poor families, with no property to pass on. The guardian's consent was required, for example, if the woman wished to sell real estate, slaves, or draught animals, manumit (set free) slaves, arrange a dowry, or make a will. The guardian made sure that his ward did not squander the property she owned or fall prey to unscrupulous schemers who would misuse, reduce, or steal the property. Even a woman's husband might be regarded by her natal family with some suspicion. When a guardian was an agnate, he had a vested interest in safeguarding property that he himself or his children might inherit. He might be reluctant to approve a will in which a woman left property to her own children, because a woman's children, though biologically related, were not her agnates. They belonged legally to her husband's natal family, not hers. However, there was a social expectation that a mother would make provisions for her children in her will, a procedure which essentially meant passing some property of her own natal family to her husband's natal family.[34] Thus there was a potential for conflict between a woman and her guardian in the drawing up of her will. By the time of the emperor Claudius (41 to 54 CE), however, male agnates who found the responsibilities of being a guardian too burdensome were allowed to transfer them to a non-agnate person, perhaps opening the position to someone with no vested interest in guarding the property, and no reason to advise a woman against leaving her property to her children or friends.[35]

There has been considerable scholarly debate about whether the necessity of a *tutor*, without whose approval a woman could not conclude business and legal transactions, restricted and irritated women. It was certainly enough of a nuisance that Augustus, when he was designing incentives to encourage women to bear children, included a clause that free women who had borne three children were granted an exemption from guardianship. His legislation offered women an interesting trade off: freedom from the traditional oversight of their financial affairs in return for accepting the traditional burden of bearing several children. The decision to bear several children might not, however, arise (only) from a woman's desire to avoid the constraints of tutelage. A man who wanted to advance rapidly through the ranks of public service might want his wife to bear several children so that he would be eligible for the privileges accorded to the fathers of children. The birth of even one child qualified a politically ambitious man for acceleration in appointment to public office.[36]

Although we do not know the amount of wealth that Arria E possessed in her own right, or whether she chafed under the financial control of a guardian, she had probably, by the time of her death, achieved an exemption by the bearing of at least three children and was therefore legally free to manage her own finances, and leave her estate to her children (or to anyone else) if she so wished.

Roman women in the provinces

About 40 CE, Arria E traveled with her husband to Dalmatia, a Roman territory on the eastern Adriatic coast. Although few Roman women – or men, for that matter – would have had the opportunity that Arria E did to travel far from home, it was not unusual during the imperial period for women of the senatorial class to accompany husbands who were sent overseas on administrative and military assignments. However, accompanying one's husband had been frowned upon only a few decades before Arria E's journey, and it is instructive to view her travels in the context of the controversy which surrounded the issue of women in the provinces. The next few paragraphs will look at stories about the activities of women who traveled with their husbands on administrative or military duties. Several were charged, along with their husbands, with misconduct. An examination of the behavior of these women when their husbands were tried and sentenced is quite relevant both to the final chapter of Arria E's life and to our understanding of the lives of several women discussed in later chapters, especially Chapter 3.

In the republican period, it had been the custom for a woman to remain in Italy while her husband was overseas, to raise the children, protect family interests, and keep him informed about local events (and, of course, be sexually abstinent). Attitudes began to change during the late first century BCE.[37] Octavia, the sister of Augustus, was married to Mark Antony, and traveled with him to Greece and bore two children there.[38] Augustus was accompanied on his tours of the provinces by his third wife Livia, who not only kept him company, but also cultivated friends and allies in those regions.[39] The imperial family advertised the values of family stability and fertility by establishing a pattern of keeping family members together. When Augustus' stepson Drusus (Livia's son) was on military command in northern Gaul, his wife Antonia was with him and gave birth at Lugdunum (now Lyons) in 10 BCE to a son who later became the emperor Claudius.[40] Augustus' granddaughter, Agrippina the Elder (see Figure 1), traveled extensively with her husband Germanicus (Claudius' brother). Of the nine children she bore (two of whom died in infancy and a third in early childhood; see earlier), one, Gaius Caligula (emperor 37–41), was born in 12 CE and raised in an army camp in the Rhine area where his father was on campaign. Another child, a girl, was born a couple of years later while Agrippina was still on the Rhine frontier. In 17 CE, Germanicus was given oversight of the eastern provinces and the couple's youngest child was born on the eastern Mediterranean island of Lesbos in 18 CE.[41]

Germanicus and Agrippina projected the image of the family values that their grandfather Augustus promoted. Their devotion to one another was proved by their desire to remain together, even when Germanicus was posted in territories where war was being waged. They had, moreover, satisfied the most important function of marriage: they had produced many children, even when camped at the very frontiers of the empire. In addition, their success in producing and raising children in unsettled territories was a demonstration of the success of Augustus' military efforts to bring *pax* – law and order – to the far-flung Roman world.

With the establishment of the imperial form of government, men of senatorial rank who accepted overseas assignments could expect their periods of service to be longer than those of republican senators had generally been, and many wanted their wives and children near them. Army officers were also sometimes accompanied to their postings by their wives (Germanicus and Agrippina being one example). In contrast, however, rank and file soldiers were not allowed to marry, in accordance with a ban on such marriages instituted by, ironically, Augustus.[42] An army camp was therefore a distinctly masculine world, and the few Roman wives in one must have felt lonely and isolated.[43] Wives who accompanied their husbands to settled provinces, where the Roman administrative staff was based in a city, may have had the company of the wives of Roman merchants or of local dignitaries. Nonetheless, they would still experience the isolation of being surrounded by people speaking a different language and having different customs.

We have no information about what Arria E's experiences were in Dalmatia or why her husband, Caecina Paetus, was there. By the time that she traveled to Dalmatia, about 40 CE, her presence there, at the side of her husband, would have been unremarkable. About 20 years earlier, however, some senators had voiced discomfort with the practice of wives accompanying husbands to the provinces. In 21 CE, Aulus Caecina Severus proposed legislation in the Senate to forbid a man appointed as governor of a province from taking his wife with him.[44] He maintained that he and his wife had a harmonious relationship and had produced six children, but, during his 40 years of service in several different provinces, he had left her at home in Italy. His reasons for proposing the legislation were that women were frail, both physically and morally, and were thus impediments to the effective functioning of a governor's staff and army. He claimed, moreover, that they meddled in military and business matters, and sometimes fell prey to scam artists. Caecina Severus alleged, in addition, that when officials were charged with extortion in the provinces, it was often their wives who had instigated the corruption.[45]

Few senators, however, supported Caecina Severus' proposal. One argued that the provinces were no longer such militarily dangerous places for women. Moreover, the failure of a few husbands to control the avaricious and scheming behavior of their wives was not a good reason to deprive the majority of them of their wives' company and support. In addition, having wives travel with their husbands reduced the women's temptation to be sexually unfaithful at home, and thus kept marriages stronger. The final word in the debate was spoken by Drusus, son of then emperor Tiberius, who reminded the Senate of the precedents set by women of the imperial family and noted that he himself was not willing to be separated from his beloved wife and his children.

Caecina Severus' concern about the behavior of senatorial women in the provinces may have been prompted by an incident that had occurred a short time before the Senate debate of 21 CE. In 17, the emperor Tiberius appointed Gnaeus Calpurnius Piso to be governor of Syria. His wife, Munatia Plancina, accompanied him to his province. About the same time, Tiberius' nephew, Germanicus, was given over-sight of the eastern provinces, with an authority that transcended that of Piso. His wife Agrippina traveled with him and, as noted earlier, gave birth there to their youngest child. In Tacitus's account, a power struggle developed almost immedi-ately between Germanicus and Piso, and their suspicion and hatred of one another was mirrored by the tension between their wives, Agrippina and Plancina.[46] In 19 CE, Germanicus fell ill and died, although not before accusing Piso and Plancina of having poisoned him. When Piso and Plancina returned to Rome in 20 CE, Piso was charged with treason (*maiestas*), and he and Plancina together were charged with killing Germanicus by the use of poison and magic. Plancina at first promised that she would share her husband's fate, and even be his companion in death. However, when conviction looked likely, and she learned that Livia (Tiberius' mother and Augustus' wife) could obtain a pardon for her, Plancina decided to separate her case from that of her husband. In despair at his wife's decision, Piso went home and slit his throat. He was convicted posthumously on the treason charge. Ultimately the Senate, in deference to Livia, decided to drop the charges against Plancina.[47] Although she was never convicted, public response to the scandalous stories of Plancina's villainous behavior in Syria undoubtedly prompted many senators to weigh the advantages and disadvantages of allowing wives to travel with husbands on official business.

Despite public anger at Piso and Plancina, Severus' proposal of 21 CE to prohibit wives from accompanying governors failed to win support. A few years later, however, in 24 CE, the Senate did enact a measure that Roman officials were to be held accountable for harm that their wives did in the provinces.[48] Again, the measure may have been prompted by a situation which occurred that same year and involved a senatorial wife. When Gaius Silius, who had commanded an army in Upper Germany, on the Rhine frontier, was tried for treason and extortion, his wife, Sosia Galla, was tried as his co-defendant.[49] Anticipating a conviction, Silius, like Piso, chose to commit suicide rather than face execution.[50] Sosia, unlike Plancina, did not abandon her husband. She was convicted and sent into exile. In the aftermath of this case, the Senate enacted the legislation that government officials should be punished for their wives' wrongdoing in the provinces.[51]

The legislation of 24 CE did not, however, prevent further acts of misconduct and impropriety in the provinces. In 35 CE, for example, Pomponius Labeo was charged with misgovernment of the province of Moesia. He committed suicide. His wife, Paxaea, whom Tacitus declares was also guilty, but not in danger of being condemned to execution, nonetheless followed him in suicide.[52] Of course, stories of scandalous women (and men) always attract more attention than stories of virtue. It would be wrong to conclude, on the basis of several reprehensible incidents, that every wife who traveled to the provinces was an avaricious meddler who corrupted her husband. Consider the maternal aunt of

Seneca, the statesman and philosopher, who accompanied her husband when he was governor of Egypt for 16 years (16–31 CE). Seneca relates that, during her time in Egypt, she was never seen in public, never admitted a provincial into her house, never asked a favor from her husband, and never allowed a favor to be asked of her. The Egyptians regarded her as a *unicum sanctitatis exemplum*, a unique example of moral integrity.[53]

It is unlikely that Arria E, while in Dalmatia, kept as low a profile as did Seneca's aunt. As the anecdote about her son's death indicates, she was fiercely protective of her husband, Caecina Paetus, and undoubtedly maintained a lively interest in his affairs. In Dalmatia, Paetus became involved in activities that put them both in jeopardy. When Caligula was assassinated in 41 CE, some senators, who had hoped either to restore the republican constitution or to be themselves selected as the next emperor, were bitterly disappointed by the Praetorian Guards' installation of Claudius as emperor. In 42 CE, they formed a plan to depose Claudius. Pliny records, in *Letter* 3.16.7, that Paetus joined a plot hatched by Furius Camillus Scribonianus, who was governor of Dalmatia. Scribonianus tried to incite his soldiers to revolt against the emperor, promising them that he would bring back the republican constitution. When they balked, the conspiracy collapsed. Scribonianus fled, but soon either committed suicide or was executed.[54] Paetus was apprehended and taken back to Rome by ship for trial. Arria E begged the soldiers to allow her to accompany her husband on the ship, saying that she would act only as his slave. "Surely you were going to give to a man of consular rank a few little slaves, from whose hand he might take food, by whom he might be dressed, and by whom his shoes might be put on. I, by myself, will perform all these tasks" (*Letter* 3.16.8). The soldiers refused permission. Undaunted, Arria E then acquired a small fishing boat and followed the military ship back to Rome.

It is noteworthy that Arria E volunteered to take on the role of a slave – that is, to abase herself completely in order to comfort her husband. As a legal institution, slavery (*servitium* or *servitus*) was the condition of someone without rights and subject to the domination of others. The opposite of *servitium* was *libertas* (liberty), which ensured rights and the absence of subjection.[55] All Roman citizens, both male and female, legally possessed *libertas* in the sense of basic civic rights. However, men – especially elite men – were much freer of domination than any women. As the earlier section on guardians has indicated, women were subject to more legal restrictions. Moreover, by custom, if not by law, women were expected to serve their husbands. (Our English word "serve" is derived from the Latin word *servus*, meaning a slave or a servant.) Therefore, although *libertas* and *servitium* were antithetical in legal terms, Arria E's willingness to take on the role of a slave was not a complete reversal of her role as a wife.[56] On the other hand, it would have been very startling to learn that a husband had offered to assume the role of a slave in order to help his wife.

Suicide

The conspirators in Dalmatia were tried and convicted of treason in the Senate in the presence of the emperor Claudius.[57] Knowing that the death penalty was certain, Paetus faced the choice that Piso, Silius, and Pomponius (see earlier) had faced: await execution or pre-empt it by committing suicide. Suicide had long been a behavior that was socially sanctioned in ancient Rome, if it were invoked to provide escape from an impossible situation, such as intolerable physical pain, or a humiliating loss of fortune or political power.[58] In the imperial period, however, the number of reported self-inflicted deaths among aristocrats increased substantially, even as trials for treason became more common. At the same time, self-inflicted deaths were not voluntary in the same sense that they had been earlier. In 46 BCE, for example, at the end of the republican period, Cato chose to kill himself rather than acknowledge as legitimate the ascendancy of his political opponent Julius Caesar, who had offered him clemency. His death was a voluntary suicide. He could have saved his life by surrendering and renouncing his political philosophy, but he chose not to. He thus became the archetype of an ethical suicide. As already noted, *libertas* meant the possession of basic civic rights. However, in reference to their own activities, men of the senatorial class, like Cato, used the term *libertas* to denote freedom of expression and action in the pursuit of one's political ambitions. In the same context, preventing someone from voicing his opinion was considered tantamount to imposing slavery, although, in reality, the loss of free expression of speech was certainly not the equivalent of *servitium*. Nonetheless, Cato's self-inflicted death conveyed the message that he valued *libertas*, in this senatorial sense, over life, and that he preferred death to the slavery of imposed silence. As will be discussed later, in the imperial period, *libertas* became the rallying cry for people who thought that the emperor restricted their ability to contribute to the political process. To return, for a moment, to Arria E's plea to become her husband's slave, her gesture of preferring slavery to allowing her husband to suffer discomfort was laudable because she was fulfilling a woman's duty. Cato's gesture of preferring a self-inflicted death to the slavery of accepting Caesar's ascendancy was laudable because it demonstrated masculine courage. For a woman, subservience was honorable; for a man of the senatorial class, it was dishonorable.

Cato could have chosen to live, albeit in retirement from the political process. He chose instead to kill himself. In the imperial period, in contrast, people convicted of capital offences, such as treason, were not given a choice of life or death, but rather a choice of death by execution or of death by one's own hand. Tacitus uses the seemingly paradoxical or ironic phrase *liberum mortis arbitrium*, "free choice of death."[59] The self-inflicted death was, by strict definition, a voluntary suicide, but the condemned chose not honorable death over humiliating life, but rather honorable death over dishonorable death. Nonetheless, in recording the self-inflicted deaths of the early imperial period, aristocratic authors like Tacitus do not make a value distinction between voluntary suicide and what we may call coerced suicide or pre-emptive suicide. Both types of action were admired. The Romans recognized that even coerced suicide required the courage to accept death with equanimity. And Roman aristocrats of the early imperial period, who might feel that the repressive new political system deprived them of opportunities to emulate the bold self-assertiveness of their republican ancestors, could attain glory through a self-inflicted death. As Edwards comments, the process of dying became a new arena for the exercise of virtue.[60] Plass – who defines these deaths as a "passive activism" – comments that suicide became not solely a gesture of personal despair, but "something imposed by the political system and – as virtue made of necessity – a way to assert political freedom."[61]

Suicide thus became the honorable option for aristocrats who had been convicted (or were likely to be convicted). Pliny writes, for example, that Caecilius Classicus, who had been charged with mismanagement of his province, "forestalled the accusations against him by a death which was either fortuitous (that is, natural) or voluntary (that is, suicide)" (*Letter* 3.9.5).[62] And of Silius, who was mentioned earlier, Tacitus writes that "he forestalled his imminent condemnation by a voluntary end.".[63] However, suicide was an honorable option not just because it averted the humiliation of a public execution. There were material incentives as well. The property of people who were executed was confiscated by the state, and they were forbidden funerary rites. Suicides, however, were allowed funerary rites, and most of their property remained in the possession of their families, although the emperor might still confiscate part of it.[64] Execution might leave one's family destitute and in disgrace. Suicide therefore preserved the family's fortune and honor. These concessions were made to people of high rank in order to induce them to choose suicide. (And, no doubt, their families, worried about destitution and disgrace, often encouraged this choice.) It was also hoped that the emperor might be more lenient to the wife and children of a suicide.[65] The putative son of Arria E and Caecina Paetus, who was adopted into another family, seems not to have suffered the wrath of the emperor Claudius, despite the treasonous activity of his father. And Claudius pointed to his decision not to persecute the son of Scribonianus, the instigator of the failed coup in Dalmatia, as an illustration of his merciful nature.[66]

In high profile cases, moreover, where the defendant was of a noble family, the decision to kill oneself relieved senatorial prosecutors of the responsibility of, in effect, sanctioning the murder of one of their own class. Suicide also freed the emperor of culpability. As Plass has demonstrated, political suicide, or voluntary enforced suicide, evolved in the early imperial period into an intricate play for power between the emperor and those who challenged his authority. Ultimately, of course, power rested with the emperor, and he was able to eliminate those who opposed him. However, by allowing an enemy charged with subversive activity to carry out his own death and thus protect his family, the emperor not only avoided the appearance of being a vengeful executioner, but also even created the appearance of being a benevolent ruler.[67] By conceding a right to die with dignity, he could display a sensitivity to considerations of aristocratic honor, even while at the same time eliminating a perceived political rival.[68] On the other hand, from the perspective of the condemned person, the choice of suicide over execution could be construed as the final act of resistance against the emperor and the final assertion of one's freedom, even under imperial rule, to demonstrate moral autonomy.

In the end, death was inescapable for the condemned, and suicide was the only aggressive countermove possible in the power game. The emperor won the game, but the person who chose to end his own life left a legacy of a noble death. For those who believed that the corrupt and repressive tactics of the imperial system curtailed the ability of the individual to make manifest his virtues, suicide offered a glorious opportunity to demonstrate courage, fortitude, and moral integrity. As Edwards observes, choosing to be the agent of one's own death conveyed a political message. "To celebrate death as a means of escape is to undermine the power of a regime that seeks to control its subjects through the threat of lethal punishment".[69] Furthermore, if the condemned could prove, by the nobility of his death, that he was a valuable asset now lost to the state, he could diminish the respect of the public for the emperor who demanded his death. Writing about 150 years after Pliny and Tacitus, Dio noted that the emperors had imposed a passivity upon the senatorial class, and he commented that, as early as the rule of Claudius, "things had progressed to the point that excellence was no longer considered anything other than dying nobly".[70] In other words, the opportunities to display virtue were limited to dying well.

Although coerced suicide enabled a condemned individual to avoid becoming a public spectacle at an execution, it was important nonetheless that the self-inflicted death receive wide publicity if the individual's desire for lasting memorialization was to be achieved. Family members and friends therefore often attended the death, lending it a theatrical atmosphere, and then issued reports which focused on celebrating the fortitude of the deceased. Roman suicide was "very much a social act, performed in front of an audience."[71] Subsequent commemoration of the suicide of an imperial opponent then became itself a form of political protest. Accounts of these exemplary deaths were, in addition, intended to inspire others to emulate them. There were, in effect, two audiences for a suicide: the people present at the death, and the people who would (like us!) read or hear about it later. Death scene literature, moreover, brought distinction to the writers who fashioned the eyewitness reports into compelling reading. Both Pliny and Tacitus chose courageous deaths as topics for their literary creations, in part, because they knew that Roman readers were fascinated by these stories and cherished them as evidence that the imperial system had not completely eradicated honorable behavior. Tacitus assured his readers that the period was not so barren of virtues that it did not produce some good examples, such as distinguished men bravely enduring supreme hardships and making their final moments equal to the lauded deaths of their ancestors.[72]

Nonetheless, by the end of the first century CE, self-inflicted deaths, staged as political protests, were apparently so frequent that Tacitus, in his defense of his father-in-law Agricola's (and perhaps his own) unwillingness to challenge the authority of the emperor Domitian, implied that some men actually courted imperial persecution by their defiant posturings, and welcomed suicide as a martyrdom. Their actions, Tacitus maintains, were perilous, but ultimately of no utility to the state, although the men became famous for an ostentatious death.[73] The poet Martial, who lived at the same time as Pliny and Tacitus, also criticized the penchant for seeking renown by emulating the suicides of Cato (mentioned earlier) and Thrasea Paetus (mentioned later). "I don't want a man who buys his fame with easy blood. I want a man who can be praised without death."[74]

Arria's valor

Despite Martial's criticism of people who sought fame through a celebrated suicide, he himself glorified the self-inflicted death of Arria E.[75] We don't know if Arria E was charged along with her husband as a conspirator. The fact that she was not transported to Rome in the ship carrying her husband suggests that she was not. However, Dio reports that women, as well as men, were executed for participation in the conspiracy.[76] He tells us, moreover, that Messalina, who was the third wife of the emperor Claudius, was energetic in wreaking vengeance on those who had plotted against Claudius, but was also instrumental in saving the lives of guilty people who offered her favors or bribes.[77] In addition, Dio informs us that Arria E was a good friend of Messalina.[78] Some modern historians are skeptical of this statement, assuming it improbable that a friendship would develop between the virtuous Arria and a woman whom Dio describes as shameless and lustful. However, the one-dimensional portraits which appear in ancient authors – the former woman depicted as a saint, the latter as a sexual deviant – may reflect literary designs more than reality. We cannot, therefore, deny the possibility that a friendship existed between Arria E and Messalina. If Arria E had been a defendant in the trial of the conspirators, and had indeed been a friend of Messalina, she might have obtained a pardon, just as Plancina had obtained a pardon through Livia's influence. However, Arria E did not forsake her husband, as Plancina did so ignobly in order to save her own life. In fact, Pliny tells us that, at the trial of the conspirators, Arria E was outraged to see Vibia, the wife of Scribonianus, the man who had instigated the failed rebellion. She chided her with the words, "Am I supposed to listen to you? Scribonianus died in your arms – and yet you are still alive?" (*Letter* 3.16.9). Clearly she was expressing outrage that Vibia had chosen to survive her husband.[79]

As Caecina Paetus pondered his options – execution or suicide –, Arria E was in no doubt about her course of action. Indeed, looking back at the events that surrounded Paetus' trial, her family realized that Arria E had been determined to die with her husband, and that her self-inflicted death was not a sudden impulse. The narrative which her granddaughter passed on to Pliny stresses that Arria E's suicide was consistent with her earlier behavior. In his account, however, Pliny implies that Arria E seized upon her husband's fate as an opportunity to choreograph for herself a death that would ensure perpetual fame. According to her granddaughter, when Arria E's intention to die with her husband became evident, her daughter and son-in-law tried to persuade her not to kill herself. Her son-in-law asked: "Would you want your daughter to die with me if I had to die?" Arria E's reported response was: "Yes, I would, if she had lived with you for as long and in such harmony as I have lived with Paetus" (*Letter* 3.16.10). (It is interesting that, in this situation where she is expressing affection, she calls him by his *cognomen*, Paetus, rather than, as we might expect, his *praenomen*, Aulus.) When the family then established a suicide watch on her, she is reported to have said: "You are wasting your time. You can bring it about that I die a bad death, but you cannot keep me from dying" (*Letter* 3.16.11). She then leapt up from her chair, ran toward a wall, and, smashing her head on it with great force, fell to the ground. When she recovered, she said: "See! I told you that I would find some harsh method of death if you denied me an easy one" (*Letter* 3.16.12).

Paetus chose suicide over execution, but when the moment came for him to kill himself, he apparently hesitated. The resolute Arria E took control of the situation. As Pliny describes the scene, she served as both a solace and a model of death for her husband, *marito et solacium mortis et exemplum fuit* (*Letter* 3.16.2). She pulled out a dagger, stabbed herself with it, extracted it from her mortally wounded body, and handed it to Paetus with the words – which Pliny characterizes as immortal and almost divine – "Paetus, it does not hurt," *Paete, non dolet* (*Letter* 3.16.6). Pliny remarks that, at the moment of her self-sacrifice, she was inspired by the prospect of the fame and immortality she would gain by her noble deed. He then suggests that her earlier self-sacrifice, when she concealed her son's death from her husband, may, in fact, have been more heroic because it was done without the expectation of eternal glory.

Dio reports that Paetus displayed cowardice in the face of death, and therefore Arria E, in order to strengthen his resolve, took the dagger, stabbed herself, and then handed it to him with the words, "Paetus, I am not in pain."[80] Dio notes that she won praise for her courageous deed, but he also comments immediately thereafter, in a sentence that was quoted earlier, that during this period "things had progressed to the point that excellence was no longer considered anything other than dying nobly."[81]

The account of Arria E's suicide by the poet Martial offers a few intriguing details. In Martial's account, as Arria E handed to her husband the dagger which she had pulled out of her own body, she said: "Trust me. The wound which I have made does not hurt, but what you are about to do, Paetus – this hurts me."[82] There is an ambiguity about the phrase "what you are about to do." Did Arria E, in Martial's portrait, mean: "your hesitation is an attempt to avoid doing the necessary and honorable thing – and this hurts me"? This interpretation is supported by Dio's statement, already noted, that Paetus displayed cowardice, and by Pliny's comment that Arria E served as a model of death for her husband. Therefore, Arria E's insistence that the self-inflicted fatal wound did not hurt implies that she was trying to convince a wavering Paetus that he would not suffer. If so, was she concerned that the family would lose face, or that her children would lose their estate if Paetus was executed? Was she admonishing Paetus to "do the right thing"? Or, perhaps the phrase means: "what you are about to do – that is, end your life – causes me pain. I don't want to live without you." Dio's account supports this interpretation as well, because he relates that Arria E refused to live on if Paetus was dead.[83] Most scholars think that Martial intended to portray Arria E as expressing despair at the thought of living without Paetus. Certainly her scathing remark to Vibia, the wife who survived Scribonianus, implies that she thought that a wife should die with her husband. Pliny's comment, moreover, that Arria E was a solace, as well as a model (*Letter* 3.16.2), for her husband suggests that, in his final moments, she provided him with the comfort of being assured of the eternal loyalty of his wife.

If Arria E sought enduring renown, as Pliny's account implies, she achieved her goal. Two thousand years after her death, we are still reading the accounts of Pliny, Martial, and Dio, and are still impressed by her unflinching valor. Although most of her contemporaries were familiar only with the tale of her self-inflicted death, Arria E's suicide, as described by Pliny, was the final act of an adult life devoted to the interests of her husband. Soon after her death, she became celebrated as a paragon of wifely virtue. A funerary inscription from the early second century CE, for example, cites her as the foremost Roman example of a wife so loyal to her husband that she killed herself at the time of his death.[84] And yet Pliny's account also discloses that her courageous self-sacrifice had a strong element of self-interest; Arria E was motivated, in part, by a desire to be celebrated eternally. However, she lived in a society which did not sanction public careers for women and she was therefore restricted in her quest for distinction to performing selfless and noble deeds that enhanced her husband's reputation. A Roman woman could win approbation as an outstanding wife, and for responding courageously to situations involving her family, but not for pursuing any independent initiatives. For modern readers, it seems perhaps ironic that Arria E was braver than her husband, Paetus, who faltered when courage was needed, but she could be celebrated only for inspiring him, by her own death, to perform an honorable action. For ancient readers, however, the limitations on her opportunities to demonstrate her strength of character would have seemed appropriate. Certainly Pliny raises the issue in *Letter* 3.16 of whether our judgment of Arria should be based on some of her other deeds, but even the deeds he reports are one's intended to benefit her husband. Consider the episode discussed earlier, where Arria E volunteered to assume the role of a slave in order to ease her husband's hardships. A courageous man chose death over slavery; a courageous woman chose slavery over the discomfort of her husband. And when, at the end, Arria E had the opportunity to win renown by making the ultimate gesture of courage – giving up her life – her action was still one of sacrifice to her husband's interests.

As already mentioned, the presence of witnesses was an essential element at the self-inflicted death of anyone aspiring to leave a record of valorous behavior. We know the details of Arria E's suicide because there were witnesses, most likely family and household members. They, in turn, recorded the event for posterity. It is not unlikely, of course, that the accounts were filtered and embroidered for public consumption. (One wonders why Caecina Paetus' family allowed so unflattering an account of his final moments to circulate.) It was Arria E's granddaughter, who had likely learned the stories from her mother, who informed Pliny not only about the suicide, but also about some of Arria E's less known deeds. His report therefore gives the impression that the information in it was derived from people who were close to Arria E and were observers of her actions and auditors of her words. As Carlon has pointed out, Pliny's letter about Arria E contains a remarkable number of direct quotations, one from her son-in-law, and eight from Arria E herself.[85] (The phrase "Paetus, it does not hurt" is cited twice). Only two other letters (*Letters* 1.5 and 9.13) include more quotations, and these are both letters regarding Pliny's activities in defense of people persecuted by Domitian, including members of Arria E's family. In addition, nowhere else does Pliny employ as many as eight quotations from one person. Carlon remarks that "Pliny chooses to let Arria speak for herself."[86] But is this really Arria E's voice? We cannot be certain that the words which Pliny records are exactly those spoken by Arria E. Pliny is, after all, providing his reader not with a transcript of an interview he had with Arria E, but rather with a report on a conversation he had with her granddaughter, who may not yet have been born in 42 CE or may have been too young then to have a personal memory of the event. We do not know to what extent family members may have modified Arria E's original words, or how they may have decided on which expressions to include in (or exclude from) the story. We must also keep in mind that ultimately Pliny controlled the narrative he crafted; he determined what material to use (or not use) to create his portrait. The quotations which Pliny attributes to Arria E cannot be disregarded. We must, however, be aware that what they may reveal is evidence of how Arria E's character was judged by others and of how they wanted her to be remembered.

There are several reasons why Pliny included so many quotations. They certainly make his account more dramatic and therefore more compelling. In addition, because Pliny leads readers to believe that he learned of the quotations just a day previous to his composition of the letter, during a conversation with Arria E's granddaughter, whom we assume has "insider information," the quotations establish the credibility of his account. Furthermore, by publicizing his close friendship with the granddaughter, whose own heroic deeds will be discussed later, Pliny persuades readers that he was an intimate of the people who were critical of imperial rule. Carlon suggests that the style of composition provides clues to another motive Pliny may have had for publicizing this conversation with the granddaughter. She observes that Pliny's account of Arria E's unheralded strength – that is, her concealment of her son's death to protect her ill husband – occupies a significant portion of the letter. The letter opens and concludes, moreover, with the statement that some words and deeds are more famous, but others are greater. Of Arria E's handling of her son's death, Pliny suggests that this was a "greater" deed than her suicide because she did it without the expectation of enduring fame. He thus instructs the reader that the character of an individual cannot be judged solely on the basis of celebrated actions. Carlon argues convincingly that Pliny may be encouraging the reader to consider that he himself engaged in admirable behavior which has simply not been become widely known (although he does his best to make it so in the letters!).[87]

Suicides of women

Arria E's willingness to sacrifice herself for her husband was memorable, but not unique in Roman culture. Indeed, in *Letter* 6.24, Pliny recounts the story of a woman living in the same area of northern Italy where he was raised (Lake Como) who committed suicide with her terminally ill husband. Like Arria E, she initiated their self-inflicted deaths. As Pliny describes the situation, she was not just a companion (*comes*) to her husband in his death, but even the leader (*dux*), the model (*exemplum*) and, in fact, the very cause (*necessitas*) of his death, because she tied herself to her husband and then jumped out of a window of their villa, into Lake Como, taking him with her. Pliny expresses surprise that he had learned only recently about this woman's self-sacrifice, despite the fact that he lived in the same area. He comments that her brave action remained uncelebrated not because it was less distinguished than Arria E's illustrious action, but because the woman herself was less distinguished (*Letter* 6.24.5). (And, although Pliny gives the woman a modicum of fame by reporting her death, he does not record her name and therefore does not rescue her from anonymity.) He muses that deeds of the same nature are either praised to the skies or relegated to deepest oblivion depending on the eminence or obscurity of the persons who did them (*Letter* 6.24.1). Pliny's statement is, however, misleading. Arria E's deed was not celebrated because Arria E was illustrious before her death. In any case, as Pliny himself commented in *Letter* 3.16, a person's best-known deeds are not always his or her greatest deeds. He cited several of Arria E's earlier displays of fortitude which were unknown except to her family, and would have remained unknown except for the efforts of her granddaughter to publicize them. Arria E's suicide was remembered not because she was previously famous, but because it occurred in the context of an event which received much notoriety. The news of the conspiracy which her husband, Caecina Paetus, had joined was widely broadcast not only because of its audacity, but also because the emperor Claudius and his wife Messalina wreaked so terrible a vengeance on the unsuccessful conspirators and their allies.[88] The unnamed woman of Lake Como had assisted a husband who was terminally ill. Although her decision to sacrifice her own life required great fortitude, their self-inflicted deaths were private matters, not the "voluntary enforced suicides" that could be publicized as the ultimate gesture of opposition to the emperor. In contrast, Arria E's suicide could be interpreted as a tragic consequence of a cruel imperial regime. In nobly sacrificing herself to assist Paetus in his final moment of defiance, Arria E could also be perceived as committing a political act.

The suicides of women had long played a significant role in Roman discourse on political opposition and change. Indeed, the impetus for the expulsion of the monarchy from Rome in the late sixth century BCE and the subsequent establishment of the republican constitution was attributed to the suicide of Lucretia.[89] She stabbed herself with a dagger after having been raped by the son of the king. Because her decision to kill herself incited her husband, Brutus, to lead a revolt against the monarchy, she was thus indirectly responsible for the birth of the Roman republic. Lucretia's glory derived from her willingness to sacrifice herself both in the interests of her husband, who may have felt embarrassment because his wife was now a "defiled" woman, and also in the interests of her community. She used her suicide to make a statement about moral behavior. Although she judged herself to be innocent of adultery because she had not willingly submitted to her assaulter, she was determined to end her life, concerned that, if she remained alive, other women might use her story as an excuse for adultery.[90]

There was no expectation that Lucretia's husband would chose to take his own life rather than live without her. Indeed, the purpose of her suicide was to enable him to live a life free of criticism. On the other hand, stories like Arria E's, about women who chose to die at the same time as their husbands, were not uncommon. Seneca the Elder, for example, cites the case of a woman who loyally followed her husband into exile and took poison along with him when he declared that he wished to die. She died of the fatal dose. Her husband, however, survived.[91] One story with elements similar to Arria E's is that of Porcia.[92] She was related by blood and marriage to two men whose names became synonymous with efforts to preserve the republican constitution and senatorial freedom. She was the daughter of the famous Stoic statesman, Marcus Porcius Cato, who had fought against Julius Caesar and who committed suicide in 46 BCE as the army of Caesar closed in on his (see earlier). Porcia was also the wife (and cousin) of Marcus Junius Brutus, who organized the assassination of Julius Caesar in 44 BCE. She was angry that Brutus had not confided in her about the plot because he thought that a woman could not be trusted with a secret, especially if tortured for information. She therefore stabbed herself in the leg to prove her ability to withstand pain. The plot to assassinate Julius Caesar was successful, but Brutus' effort to restore the republic was not. In 42 BCE, after the defeat of his army at Philippi by the forces of Octavianus (who later became known as Augustus) and Mark Antony, Brutus realized that his cause was hopeless, and committed suicide. His self-inflicted death made the statement that he, like his father-in-law Cato (who was also his uncle), cherished *libertas* more than life. When the news reached Porcia, she was determined to kill herself. Her family and friends hid all possible weapons, trying to prevent her suicide, but she outwitted them. She killed herself by swallowing burning coals.[93]

Martial, whose epigram on the suicide of Arria E has already been discussed, also composed an epigram about Porcia's suicide.[94] "When Porcia learned of the fate of her husband, Brutus, she demanded in her grief the weapons which had been removed from her. She asked, 'Have you not yet learned that death cannot be forbidden? I would have thought that the death of my father had taught you this.' She spoke and swallowed the burning ashes." Porcia's suicide was also memorialized by Valerius Maximus who wrote: "Porcia, daughter of Cato, henceforth all generations will honor with deserved admiration your very virtuous fires. Since a blade was denied you, you did not hesitate to swallow burning coals. Though of feminine spirit you imitated the manly suicide of your father. But perhaps your accomplishment was greater, because he ended his life in a traditional fashion (with a sword), while you ended yours in a novel manner."[95]

Porcia's suicide followed that of her husband, while Arria E killed herself in the presence of a husband whose own resolve was wavering. Nonetheless, there are several similarities in the stories of the behavior of the two women. Both were devoted to the welfare of husbands who sought to restore the republican constitution. Both had a history of enduring distress in order to comfort their husbands. Arria E concealed the death of their son; Porcia stabbed herself in order to convince her husband that he could trust her. Both made it clear to their families that they did not intend to survive their husbands. Both, despite the vigilance of their families, found methods to join their husbands in death and not incidentally gained posthumous recognition. And both demonstrated that they possessed a virtue expected of the best men: the ability to tolerate pain and scorn death. Despite Arria E's insistence that her stabbing did not hurt, Roman readers would have considered her death to have been a painful one. And Porcia, as Valerius Maximus describes her, was of feminine spirit, but imitated the manly suicide of her father. The behavior of both women was therefore, in a sense, virile. The Latin word for "man" is *vir*, for "manly," *virilis*. Cicero noted that the Latin word *virtus* – from which we derive our English word "virtue" – was derived from *vir*. He also commented that fortitude was an appropriate virtue for a man, and that fortitude entailed a contempt for both pain and death.[96] In his account of the courageous suicide of Lucretia, Valerius Maximus comments that a masculine spirit (*virilis animus*) had taken over her female body *by error*.[97] Nonetheless, although Arria and Porcia had taken on masculine characteristics, they were not criticized for overstepping gender boundaries because their behavior was directed toward enhancing the reputations of their husbands. Plutarch is careful to point out, moreover, that Porcia was possessed of the appropriate feminine virtues: she had an affectionate nature, and was chaste and loyal to her husband.[98] Arria's manner of death – stabbing herself (as Lucretia also did) – was considered the honorable choice of suicide for men. However, Arria did not have the option of choosing a suicide more appropriate for women; she needed to stab herself in order to inspire her husband to do the same.[99]

A few years after Porcia's suicide, her unusual method of death was imitated by Servilia, the wife of Marcus Aemilius Lepidus.[100] In 30 BCE, Lepidus plotted to assassinate Octavianus (later known as Augustus), perhaps in emulation of Caesar's assassin, Brutus (who was his uncle). The plot was discovered, and Lepidus was executed. His wife, Servilia, then killed herself by swallowing live coals. Velleius comments that she compensated for her untimely loss of life by gaining the immortality of a celebrated name. Velleius also records the death of Calpurnia, who stabbed herself in 83 BCE after her husband, Antistius, was assassinated by his enemies in the Senate.[101] Velleius expresses the hope that the glory of Calpurnia's noble deed will not be forgotten. He then remarks that the reputation of her husband was enhanced by her courage. Velleius' comment suggests that the prestige of a husband might be augmented posthumously by his having been married to a self-sacrificing wife. We might speculate on whether wives might be prevailed upon by others to commit suicide specifically in order to increase the renown of their husbands.

Arria E was probably familiar with the stories of these republican era women and well aware that their selfless actions had earned them lasting celebrity. Among her contemporaries, too, she could find examples of wives who chose to die with their husbands. As treason trials became more numerous in the imperial period, so did the recorded occurrences of self-inflicted deaths of wives. The tale of Paxaea has already been mentioned. In 35 CE, just seven years before the deaths of Arria E and Paetus, she followed the example of her husband who cut his veins and bled to death.[102] In the same year, Mamercus Aemilius Scaurus, who had offended Tiberius by writing verses allegedly critical of him, was charged not with treason, but with magic and with adultery with Livilla (the niece of Tiberius). Anticipating a verdict of "guilty" and a sentence of execution, he committed suicide, at the urging of his wife, Sextia. Like Arria E, she both inspired her husband and joined him in death.[103] In 30 CE, when Gaius Fufius Geminus was charged with treason, he took his will to the Senate to show that he had left his inheritance in equal portions to his children and the emperor. Undoubtedly, Fufius hoped thereby to demonstrate to Tiberius that he was not hostile to him and also to remind him that the property of a suicide should not be confiscated. However, fearing a capital sentence, Fufius went home and stabbed himself, exhorting the witnesses to his death (again, note the importance of witnesses) with these words: "Report to the Senate that it is thus that he who is a man dies." His wife, Mutilia Prisca, then also died "like a man." She went to a Senate meeting and stabbed herself with a dagger that she had smuggled in, making all the senators present her witnesses.[104]

In all these stories, and also in Arria E's case, the wife's suicide was voluntary, as was that of the republican Cato, mentioned earlier. However, unlike Cato, who gave up his life because he could not submit to the new political structure, the women are portrayed as taking their own lives because they believed, or were persuaded, that death was preferable to life without their husbands. Furthermore, Arria E's reproach of Vibia, who did not die with her husband, Scribonianus, suggests that some women believed that it was shameful for a wife to survive a husband. As we learn from Velleius's comment, the self-sacrificing actions of the wives shed a positive light on their husbands. The harsher or even reprehensible aspects of a husband's character were mitigated by public knowledge that he was apparently worthy of inspiring such impressive devotion. There is, however, a strangely contradictory element to the depictions of these women, including Arria E. Their apparent reluctance to carry on without their husbands makes them seem, on the one hand, weak and passive. On the other hand, they demonstrate a remarkable strength, determination, and resourcefulness in their ability to take their own lives and in ways that were painful. Arria E, moreover, is portrayed by Pliny, though perhaps not intentionally, as having calculated that her death would bring her undying acclaim and was therefore a desirable goal. Thus, although it was her husband's arrest that provided the occasion for her suicide, she seems to have seized the opportunity to fulfill her own aspirations. Ultimately, women like Arria E acquired reputations for fortitude in the only area in which women were rewarded for fortitude: support of family members. The intent of their self-sacrificing deed can thus be viewed on one level as personal and private. Nonetheless, their suicides can also be construed as having political significance. As Plass remarks, when a wife elected to die freely with her husband, their deaths "would inevitably become a powerful political symbol of loyalty beyond the emperor's reach."[105]

The expectation that a self-inflicted death could make an individual a revered model of behavior is illustrated by Tacitus' narrative of the suicide of the Stoic philosopher and statesman, Lucius Annaeus Seneca (Seneca the Younger).[106] In 65 CE, 23 years after the suicides of Arria E and Paetus, Seneca was accused of complicity in a plot (the Pisonian conspiracy) to assassinate the emperor Nero, whose teacher and close advisor he had once been. A soldier arrived at his villa and notified him that he had been sentenced to death. In so much of his writing, Seneca had meditated about the good death. Now the moment had arrived when he could put his teachings into practice. Seneca turned to his friends (the requisite witnesses to the death scene) and, according to Tacitus, said: "I leave you my one remaining possession, but it is my finest: the pattern of my life *(imago vitae)*."[107] He then embraced his wife, Paulina, and implored her to find solace in contemplating that he had spent his life in the pursuit of virtue *(vitae per virtutem actae)*. However, she insisted on dying with him. Seneca replied: "I recommended to you the soothing pleasures of life, but you prefer the glory of death. I will not begrudge you the opportunity to set an example. We will share equally in the valor of this courageous death, but your death will be more illustrious."

In Tacitus' account, both Seneca and Paulina appear well aware that a self-inflicted death could bring glory, and that a woman's decision to die with her husband was especially laudatory. Nonetheless, the behavior of Paulina offers important insights into the pressure placed on women to appear loyal to their husbands. Both Paulina and Seneca cut their veins in order to bleed to death. Because Seneca bled sluggishly, he also drank hemlock (as Socrates had) to speed up the process of death. When the poison seemed to have little effect, he was placed first in a bath of warm water, and then in hot steam where he finally suffocated, but not before making a libation to Jupiter the Liberator. Paulina remained alive during the long and agonizing death of her husband. Tacitus reports that Nero, anxious to contain his reputation for cruelty, ordered soldiers to bandage her arms and stop the bleeding. Paulina's failure to die, as she had announced she would, later prompted criticism. Tacitus scoffs that some people believed (though he does not) that she had sought the glory of dying with her husband only as long as she feared that Nero was implacable. However, when she realized that the emperor would be lenient, she preferred the allurements of life. She lived a few more years, cherishing the memory of her husband. However, Tacitus relates, she remained very pale, revealing that the blood lost during her suicide attempt had drained away her energy.[108] Although Tacitus believes that Paulina was forcibly prevented from completing the suicide, his description of her life after Seneca's death suggests that she atoned, as it were, for her survival by neglecting her own health and continuing to devote herself to his interests. In some respects, her survival might therefore have appeared to require even more fortitude than a suicide. And, despite the Julian legislation to promote remarriage, Paulina remained a grieving widow. Antistia Pollitta offers an example of a grieving widow determined to keep her husband's death and her suffering before the public eye. After her husband was assassinated in 62 CE, three years before the suicide of Seneca, she mourned unceasingly.[109] She kept his blood-soaked clothes (she had been present at his assassination), maintained a disheveled appearance, and ate only enough food to stay alive.[110] The stories of the behavior of Paulina and Antistia after their husbands' deaths imply that women who did not share the violent fates of their husbands and did not remarry were expected to give proof that their concern for their husbands was abiding.

In Tacitus' account, Paulina is depicted as a strong and decisive individual. Dio's description of her behavior, however, presents a portrait of a woman who was manipulated by her husband.[111] He reports that Seneca wanted Paulina (who was probably considerably younger than he) to die with him and had even schooled her to believe that she wanted to accompany him in death. When the moment for suicide arrived, he cut her veins. There is no mention in Dio of Nero's ordering soldiers to stem her bleeding, or about her life after Seneca's death. Dio tells us only that she was still alive when her husband died, and that she survived him. Since there are discrepancies in the accounts of Tacitus and Dio, we cannot know with certainty how Paulina behaved when faced with the prospect of death. Nonetheless, Dio's depiction of the situation, as one in which the husband demanded that his wife die with him, raises the question of how many of the suicides of wives in this period were truly willing and self-inflicted. The depiction also, however, indicates that it was important to men that their wives exhibit the fortitude to die with them. Tacitus's representation of the situation, moreover, makes it clear that a woman who chose suicide with her husband could anticipate that she would be rewarded with enduring fame, and that a woman who survived her husband's suicide could expect to be criticized for not being loyal.

In Arria E's case, not only was her suicide voluntary, but also she used it to inspire a faltering husband to fulfill his duty. For her unselfish action, she achieved iconic status as a prominent model of behavior. In Roman culture, this reward was of considerable significance because it was an assurance of a fame that death could not destroy. As discussed in the Introduction, behavioral models drawn from the lives of real people played a central role in Roman society. The Romans believed that such examples provided more effective tools for moral instruction than abstract philosophical arguments. When Seneca announced to the witnesses to his death that he was leaving them his finest possession, the pattern of his life (*imago vitae*), he was emphasizing the importance he placed, as a moral philosopher, on the use of models. Throughout his philosophical writings, he urged readers to chose a virtuous person whose behavior they could strive to emulate, and to keep the pattern of that person's life in mind.[112] He referred to Cato as a living pattern of virtue (*virtutum viva imago*).[113] Cato was, of course, physically dead at the time that Seneca was writing, but he lived on as a model of behavior. And when Seneca's own death was imminent, he exhorted his friends to use him as a "living" model of virtue. So, too, Arria E was elevated to the enduring existence of a role model, as the inscription cited earlier and the stories passed on by Pliny, Martial, and Dio indicate. She continued to be honored as a woman whose loyalty to her husband led her to sacrifice her own life.

Martial's poem about Arria E opens with the word *casta*, "chaste." In reference to a married woman, *casta* denotes sexual fidelity to one's husband. The use of this word, in so emphatic a position in Martial's poem, perhaps denotes that Arria E had been married only once, to Paetus. In Roman society, a *univira*, a woman who had had, during her lifetime, only one husband was lauded as a model of wifely loyalty.[114] Valerius Maximus wrote that "those women who had been content with one marriage were honored with a crown of virtue (*pudicitia*)."[115] He adds that "people believed that the experience of several marriages was an indication of intemperance, even if it was lawful." The frequency of epitaphs which draw attention to the deceased woman's status as a *univira* offers testimony to the respect accorded in Roman culture to this status.[116] A woman named Cornelia, who died in 16 BCE, was memorialized by the elegiac poet, Propertius. In an elegy in which the poet imagines that Cornelia is speaking from her tomb, she expresses pride in having borne three children who lived to adulthood. Under the Julian Laws, instituted just two years before her death, this accomplishment would have earned her honor and privileges. She also implores her survivors: "Let me be known on my tombstone as having been married to just one man." And to her daughter, she offers this advice: "Take care that you have only one husband."[117]

In 42 CE, Arria E considered what the circumstances of her life might be if she lived on after her husband had either nobly taken his own life or been ignobly executed. The situation of widows is discussed in the next chapter. Arria E's daughter and son-in-law tried to persuade her to choose survival (*Letter* 3.16.10). However, as a widow, Arria E would feel pressure to relinquish her *univira* status and remarry. In some families, though perhaps not Arria E's, widows were considered a financial burden. Even if Arria E's family did not insist that she acquire a new husband, the Julian Laws encouraged remarriage. A new husband would require a whole new set of adjustments. And if she remained a widow, would she be expected to spend the remainder of her life demonstrating inconsolable grief, as Paulina and Antistia did? Arria E's reproach of Vibia, for not dying with her husband Scribonianus, as well as her statement to her daughter and son-in-law, indicate that she held a conviction that wives should not survive their husbands. Moreover, according to Pliny she realized that her suicide provided an opportunity to gain glory. Pliny's letter also stresses, however, the depth of Arria E's devotion to her husband. Perhaps she simply could not face the prospect of life without him. We cannot know if Arria E "loved" Paetus. In Pliny's account, she is reported to have asserted that she and Paetus had lived together in great harmony, *concordia*. This situation was apparently very satisfactory for her. It is notable that, when she recommended that her daughter follow her example, she included the condition "if she had lived with her husband for as long and in such harmony as I have lived with Paetus" (*Letter* 3.16.10). The condition suggests that, for Arria E, self-sacrifice was not simply an act of duty which any wife was obligated to perform, but the action of a wife who had found satisfaction in her marriage. We might wonder perhaps whether the harmony of which she boasts had been achieved mainly by Arria E's sacrificing her own interests to those of her husband. This aspect of Roman marriages will be discussed in following chapters. However, in the final moments of their life together the interests of Arria E and Caecina Paetus coincided, and she was able to fulfill her desire for perpetual glory precisely because his best interest required that he be convinced to kill himself.

Figure 2 Ulpia Marciana (c. 48 – c. 112 CE), sister of the emperor Trajan. Museo Capitolini, Rome. © 2012. Photo: Scala, Florence.

2 Arria's family and the tradition of dissent

Arria the Younger (Arria Minor)

Arria E was survived by a daughter who may have received at birth the name Caecinia – that is, the feminine form of the family (or gentile) name of her father, Caecina. However, for reasons unknown to us, she is referred to by Roman writers by the same name as her mother: Arria.[1] Modern scholars have attached to her name the Latin word *minor*, which means "younger," to distinguish her from her mother. Henceforth she will be identified as Arria Y, or Arria the Younger. A speculative and very approximate date for the birth of Arria Y is about 24 CE.[2] We do not know if she was older or younger than the brother whose death as a child is recorded by Pliny in *Letter* 3.16.3. She may have had a second brother who was adopted by Gaius Laecanius Bassus and, as an adult, enjoyed a successful career in public service (see Chapter 1). It was not unusual for adoptees, who were often adults at the time of their adoption, to maintain affective bonds with their birth families. However, we do not know whether Arria Y and this putative brother remained in contact. The fact that Pliny, who professes to have been a friend to several generations of the family, never mentions him suggests perhaps that, if he were the brother of Arria Y, he chose to sever his ties to his birth family.

Among the extended relatives of Arria the Younger was the poet Aulus Persius Flaccus (34–62 CE) who was about ten years her junior. She is described as his *cognata* ("relative"), a term which is too general for us to establish the precise nature of their kin relationship.[3] Persius, like Arria Y's father, Caecina Paetus, had family origins in Etruria. From his biography we learn that he was so well-liked by Arria Y's husband that the two sometimes traveled together. (The difference in the ages of the two men would have been at least a couple of decades.) Persius wrote a few verses about Arria the Elder, "who had killed herself in front of (or, before in time) her husband."[4] We don't know the content of these verses, but they may have extolled Arria E as an innocent victim of a repressive regime and thus been offensive to the emperor because, after Persius' death, his teacher, Lucius Annaeus Cornutus, recommended to Persius' mother that the verses be destroyed. Cornutus was a Stoic philosopher, and Persius became a dedicated student of that philosophy. Through his teacher, Persius became acquainted with the epic poet Marcus Annaeus Lucanus (Lucan) and the statesman and Stoic philosopher, Lucius Annaeus Seneca (who was Lucan's uncle and whose suicide is discussed in Chapter 1).

We do not know whether Arria Y was, like her kinsman, Persius, acquainted with Seneca, Lucan, and Cornutus, and whether she, too, was a disciple of Stoic philosophy. Nor do we know to what extent Arria Y's parents were influenced by Stoic teachings, particularly those about the importance of personal freedom. However, theirs was a household where opposition to imperial rule was not just discussed and endorsed, but was, in fact, with the planned mutiny of Scribonianus, acted on. Arria Y's convictions and behavior were undoubtedly shaped by her experiences growing up in this family. She must have been aware of the potential dangers in which her father's political views placed the family, and was perhaps anxious about her own safety and that of family members. However, she was raised by a mother whom Pliny characterizes as unflinching in stressful situations and who therefore probably did not tolerate any display of cowardice in her daughter. Nonetheless, from her mother's example, Arria Y also learned that it was a wife's duty to subordinate her own needs and desires to those of her husband, and to share his fate.

The capture and trial of her father, and the suicides of her parents in 42 CE must have been traumatic for Arria Y. Although she was probably still in her teens at this time, she was already married. We know that, perhaps after the deaths of her parents, she had one daughter. (See Genealogy Chart 1.) We hear of no other children and do not know whether Arria Y gave birth only to one daughter or whether she bore other children who subsequently died (as her brother had). Her husband was Publius Clodius Thrasea Paetus[5] who originated from the northern Italian town of Patavium (modern Padua). His family name was Clodius, but he is usually referred by ancient authors as Thrasea Paetus (or sometimes as Paetus Thrasea). Modern scholars conjecture that he had appended the name Paetus out of respect or affection for his father-in-law, Caecina Paetus, although we do not know whether he assumed the name "Paetus" before or after the suicide.[6] Of Aulus Caecina Paetus' three names, Paetus was apparently the one employed affectionately by family members. It is what Arria E called him in their final moments: "Paetus, it does not hurt." In any case, Thrasea's assumption of the name suggests that he and his father-in-law had a warm relationship.

Arria Y's husband and the opposition to emperors

In ancient Roman society, marriages, especially among the elite, were usually arranged by family members. We do not know why or how Thrasea Paetus, who may have been about ten years older than Arria Y, was chosen as a husband for her. A friendship between him and her father may have been the basis for this arrangement. Thrasea's acquaintance with Arria Y's kinsman, Persius, who was only about eight years old when her parents killed themselves, probably developed after the marriage and was therefore not a factor in arranging it. Nonetheless, Thrasea's affection for the poet who ardently embraced Stoicism is a component in our understanding of the milieu in which Arria Y lived. Her husband and some of her family members were sympathetic to the teachings of that philosophy, and Arria Y may well have been an auditor to or even participant in family discussions about how to exercise personal responsibility and maintain personal freedom in the autocratic imperial system.

Stoics were not categorically opposed to the notion of rule by one man.[7] Indeed, they believed that a wise and benevolent monarch might be the ideal form of government. They were, however, critical of a ruler whose tyrannical practices obstructed an individual's quest for integrity and autonomy. The focus of the Stoics' disapprobation was thus not the constitutional form of a government, but rather the nature of the ruler's exercise of his power. The autocratic form of government which had evolved under the emperors was a source of considerable discontent among Stoics of the first century CE. And their declarations of this discontent provoked the suspicion and anger of the emperors, who perceived criticism as treachery.

At the same time, it was not just Stoics who found the imperial system vexatious. Many men of the senatorial class discovered that the new political system deprived them of the opportunities that their republican ancestors had had to wield power and compete for honor. Most senators of the first century CE understood that it was not realistic to demand the complete abolition of the imperial system created by Augustus. It was Augustus, after all, who had brought peace after a long period of brutal civil war. Any attempt to reconstitute a government without an emperor risked returning Rome to the chaos of civil war. Perhaps Scribonianus's soldiers in Dalmatia had feared this outcome in 42 CE when they balked at his call to rebel against Claudius (see Chapter 1). Nevertheless the senators of the first century CE resented the loss of prestige and authority which they had suffered when power became concentrated in the hands of an emperor. They were expected to attend Senate meetings and assume a burden of administrative duties, but decisions of the greatest import were now made by the emperor. A façade of shared governance remained, but, in reality, the influence of the Senate was severely restricted. Moreover, discussions in the Senate were tempered by fear of offending the emperor. A political career could be fraught with anxiety, because those who fell afoul of the emperor sometimes paid with their lives.[8] In order not to risk the wrath of the emperor, many senators adopted a sycophantic behavior, believing that it was essential not just to their political careers, but even to their very survival. They practiced *dissimulatio*, the concealment of their true feelings.[9] They feared the *delatores*, the informers, who might report to the emperor a conversation or even a gesture that could be construed as evidence of disloyalty, which in turn might lead to a charge of treason, *maiestas*.[10] Publicly, many senators tried to collaborate with the emperor and feign contentment with his policies. Privately, they lamented the loss of *libertas*, the freedom which had allowed their republican ancestors to express their opinions openly, to pursue independent political initiatives, and thereby to gain *dignitas* (personal glory) and *auctoritas* (influence).[11]

When Arria Y married and moved from the home of her father to that of her husband, she continued to live in an environment where concern was expressed about the demise of republican traditions. In fact, her husband became an outspoken defender of these traditions. Arria Y's father had joined an unsuccessful conspiracy to topple Claudius shortly after his accession as emperor. Upon the death of Claudius in 54 CE, his 16-year-old stepson Nero, was appointed emperor. During the first few years of his reign, the young emperor indicated an interest in developing a good working relationship with the Senate. He was influenced, no doubt, by the views of Seneca, the Stoic philosopher who had been Nero's tutor and was now his chief advisor. Perhaps the philosopher had cherished the notion that he might train Nero to be the ideal Stoic monarch. Seneca was also the uncle of the poet Lucan, who, as noted earlier, was a good friend of Arria Y's kinsman, the poet Persius. In 56 CE, Arria Y's husband, Thrasea Paetus, was selected to the position of suffect consul, perhaps upon the recommendation of Seneca, with whom he shared family friendships and an interest in Stoicism. Thrasea's selection indicates that, at this time, his relationship with Nero was amicable. Within a few years, however, Nero became a more autocratic ruler, and his personal behavior became increasingly bizarre and dissolute. Thus, in addition to their disgruntlement about being deprived of the power enjoyed by their republican ancestors, senators were dismayed by Nero's conduct. Of course, as Wirszubski has pointed out, it is impossible to separate a tyrant's exercise of power from his character. "(A) despot's power is what the despot makes it."[12] Many senators were offended by Nero's actions and uncomfortable about serving an emperor of whom they disapproved, but most acquiesced in order to preserve their positions and lives. Pliny described the last years of Nero's reign as a period when it was dangerous to engage in any kind of relatively independent and honorable research and writing (*Letter* 3.5.5).[13]

Despite the dangers, Arria Y's husband, Thrasea Paetus, was not hesitant to make manifest his disapproval both of the Nero's actions and of the servility of the Senate toward the emperor. Most of our information about Thrasea Paetus derives from Tacitus, whose narrative is shaped by his intent to represent the collapse of Rome's republican institutions in terms of sharply conflicting personalities. Thus Thrasea is constructed as an uncompromising champion of republican values, and one of the few men courageous enough to challenge the emperor and chastise his fellow senators.[14] Determined to recapture the strength, dignity, and *libertas* of the Senate, he attempted on several occasions to persuade his colleagues to act autonomously.[15] At other times, he chose to indicate his disapproval by remaining silent. In 59 CE, for example, when Nero's letter about the murder of his mother, Agrippina, was read out in the Senate, justifying the murder as necessary to prevent a treasonous conspiracy, and when sycophantic senators were expressing gratitude to the emperor, Thrasea left the meeting without a word.[16] He was absent, moreover, from events where Nero was singing or playing his lyre, presumably not wanting to signal endorsement of behavior he considered indecorous for an emperor.[17] Although Tacitus depicts Thrasea as being confrontational, Pliny records that Thrasea was *vir mitissimus*, a very gentle man, who often said: "He who hates faults, hates mankind" (*Letter* 8.22.3).[18] His statement suggests a tolerance for human frailty. The difference in the portraits may be explained by a difference in authorial intent. Pliny, whose mention of Thrasea is admittedly brief, may have omitted any reference to Thrasea's provocative actions in order to make him appear even more of an innocent victim of a tyrannical ruler.

Arria Y's husband, Thrasea, was committed to acting according to his conscience. He believed that Rome's republican ancestors had achieved greatness because they had embodied personal virtues, such as moderation and courage, which his contemporaries, and especially the emperor, lacked. He undertook to develop these virtues in himself and to lead a life of austerity. In addition, he wrote a biography of Cato the Younger, who had become to later generations, and to Stoics in particular, an icon of self-restraint and fortitude.[19] Thrasea and his son-in-law also celebrated the birthdays of Brutus and Cassius, the assassins of Julius Caesar, the man whose ambitions had ushered in the imperial period.[20] To his critics, Thrasea's veneration of Cato and of Caesar's assassins was construed as a promotion of anti-imperialism and therefore as a threat to the emperor. His abstemious lifestyle, moreover, was seen as a deliberate affront to the self-indulgent and decadent Nero.[21]

Thrasea's admiration of Cato and his adoption of an austere lifestyle might signify that he was a devotee of Stoicism. Equally, however, they might reflect his political philosophy and his dedication to the ideal of republican *libertas* and to the virtues of independence and integrity that Cato had come to symbolize. Some modern historians have maintained that Arria Y's husband was the leader of a Stoic opposition movement.[22] The claim is debatable, however, in terms both of the composition of such a movement and of Thrasea's role. Neither Pliny nor Tacitus identifies Thrasea directly as a Stoic. Their contemporary Martial implies that Thrasea and Cato held the same *dogmata* (doctrines or opinions). However, he does not label them as Stoics.[23] Tacitus records that one of Nero's henchmen accused the Stoics of having a reputation for being arrogant, seditious and eager to cause trouble, but Thrasea's name does not appear in this context.[24] It is credible that in the first century CE, some people who professed to be Stoics (but not all Stoics) were loudly and persistently critical of the imperial government. But did their criticism emanate from their Stoic principles? As already noted, Stoicism was not in theory opposed to monarchy. However, some Stoics may have found it difficult to separate their distaste for the moral character of an emperor like Nero from his exercise of power. Many non-Stoic members of the Roman elite also had reason to deplore the emperor's conduct. For some it might be disagreement with Nero's political or ethical ideas. For others, it might be a personal animosity based on perceived mistreatment. Thus, although a group of Stoics may have been prominent in expressions of dissent and activities of resistance, they were not the only opponents of Nero's tyranny.

With respect to the characterization of Arria Y's husband Thrasea as a Stoic, Rudich has commented that Thrasea was "a Stoic by temperament and inclination," in the sense that he admired the values of integrity and self-discipline which Stoicism promoted.[25] He probably also, like many of his fellow Romans, felt more comfortable with moral instruction by example, than by appeal to abstract theories. The Roman Stoic Seneca's advocacy of learning virtue through the study of role models has been discussed in the Introduction. Thrasea's focus, however, seems to have been on fostering not Stoicism, but rather the recovery of the authority that the Senate had once enjoyed. It is not possible to determine whether he actively sought the role of leader and, as his critics charged, encouraged the subversion of the imperial system. Nevertheless, whatever the reality may have been about his philosophic convictions and his designs for recovering the republican constitution, his outspokenness and rigorous self-discipline both inspired admirers and generated detractors. To his admirers, he became a model of uncompromising moral and political integrity. His enemies, however, chided him for arrogantly thinking that he could govern better than Nero.[26]

Thrasea was well aware that his behavior infuriated Nero, but he did not temper his criticism. In fact, he embraced a Stoic scorn of death. Dio reports that Thrasea often said, "Nero can kill me, but he cannot harm me."[27] Suetonius informs us that Nero disliked Thrasea because he was too cheerless and had the countenance of a schoolmaster.[28] Clearly Nero interpreted Thrasea's austere demeanor as a condemnation of his own flamboyant behavior. In 63 CE, Nero forbade Thrasea to attend a celebration for the birth of the emperor's daughter. Thrasea bore this imperial affront calmly, even though, according to Tacitus, it foreshadowed his death.[29] However, although he had previously been indefatigable in the performance of his senatorial duties, he did not again attend a Senate meeting.[30] Nonetheless, his abstention from public life did not guarantee his safety. Now his enemies began to accuse him of dereliction of duty and to construe his abstention as an attempt to dissociate himself from the regime, an action tantamount to treason. And when he did not participate in the annual senatorial oath to support the acts of emperor, and was absent from the annual vows for the emperor's safety, he was accused of contemptuous disregard for the welfare of the state and the emperor.[31] Rudich has explained well that it is the nature of any repressive regime "to turn its subjects into accomplices by imposing on them, as a test of loyalty, various mandatory rituals. In the eyes of the authorities, a refusal to comply with these demands automatically signals subversion, so that one's mere absence in a designated place at a designated time can be taken as proof of *animus nocendi*. Innocence thus ceases to guarantee one's security. Furthermore, it is not even one's motives or intent that matter, but their official interpretation, however perverse."[32] (*Animus nocendi* means "intent to harm.")

In 66 CE, Thrasea's enemies persuaded Nero to instigate in the Senate a charge of treason against Thrasea. According to Tacitus, the emperor did not require much persuading. Of course, Nero's anxiety about sedition is understandable. In the previous year, a plot to overthrow him – the Pisonian conspiracy – had been discovered. Among the alleged participants were Seneca and his nephew Lucan, both acquaintances of the family of Arria Y, and both dedicated Stoics. Both men chose to commit suicide.[33] Thrasea's connection to these two men and his overt condemnation of the emperor's behavior may have been factors in the emperor's distrust of him. Tacitus represents the antagonism between the two men as a conflict between good and evil and reports that Nero longed to destroy

Virtue itself by killing Thrasea.[34] In a private meeting with Nero, Thrasea's enemies painted a picture of a situation where a revolution was imminent, reporting that a citizenry eager for civil dissension was comparing Thrasea to Cato and Nero to Caesar.[35] They also warned that Thrasea had attracted a group of followers, who might not yet be openly expressing their opposition to the emperor, but who, by imitating the dour appearance and conduct of Thrasea, revealed their disapproval of Nero's amusements. And, as if to convince Nero that Thrasea's treasonous ideas were gaining wide-spread influence, they mentioned that, throughout the empire, people were reading official reports with particular care in order to find out what Thrasea had *refused* to do. Now his inaction seemed to his enemies a form of subversion. We cannot determine whether Thrasea intended to do more than point out the excesses of Nero's regime – that is, whether he ever talked about rebellion. Nonetheless, his enemies convinced Nero that Arria Y's husband was dangerous. It is striking, however, that there are no extant reports in the ancient historians that Thrasea's enemies specifically made a charge that he was involved with Stoic dissidents.

Thrasea consulted friends about whether to appear before the Senate and attempt to defend himself, or whether to stay away from the trial.[36] Some urged him to attend and offer a spirited and memorable defense. Others recommended that he stay home rather than subject himself to insults. They also pointed out that, in attempting to defend himself, he might provoke Nero to harm his wife, Arria Y, and daughter. An eager young tribune named Junius Arulenus Rusticus, offered to veto the Senate's decree.[37] However, Thrasea declined his offer stating that he did not want Arulenus to risk his life on his behalf. He told Arulenus that he himself would not abandon his own unwavering pattern of life, but that the young tribune, who was just beginning his political career, needed to consider carefully the course of action most appropriate for him. Thrasea was not recommending political expediency, but rather a cautious behavior that would enable Arulenus to live to fight other battles. (And more about Arulenus will be said later).

On the day of the trial, Praetorian Guards were posted in the area of the Forum to intimidate the senators. At the trial, charges were presented against Thrasea and four other men, including Thrasea's son-in-law. First, a message from Nero was read out, in which, without naming Thrasea specifically, the emperor rebuked senators who neglected their official duties. Thrasea's senatorial opponents then argued that his absences from the Senate and oath-taking ceremonies constituted treasonous behavior.[38] They also challenged him to appear before them, claiming that his expressed criticisms would be more tolerable than the implied condemnation of his silence. What Thrasea's accusers do not seem to have stated publicly were the sentiments that they had shared with Nero: they feared Thrasea's growing prominence as a moral *exemplum* and they hated his obvious contempt for them. Dio reports that Thrasea received a death sentence not because he was accused of conspiring, but simply because of who he was.[39]

Thrasea was convicted, but allowed to arrange his own death – that is, he was given a "free choice of death."[40] The quaestor[41] sent to deliver the verdict found him at his home, attended by a large group of men and women and discussing the nature of the soul with a philosopher. He urged his weeping friends to leave, lest they suffer by their association with a condemned man, and advised his wife, Arria Y, not to attempt suicide. He then retired to a bedroom with the philosopher and with his son-in-law, Helvidius Priscus, and stretched out his arms to expose the veins to be cut. When the blood began to flow, he sprinkled some of it on the ground as a libation to Jupiter the Liberator. In offering a libation to the same deity as Seneca had (see Chapter 1), Thrasea may have intended to prompt his audience (both those present and the many people who would later hear and read about his self-inflicted death) to compare his death favorably with that of Seneca just a year previously. Like Seneca, he probably hoped to leave to posterity a model of a life lived with moral integrity and of a death faced with serenity. To the quaestor who had delivered the message he said "Look! You have been born into times in which it is useful to strengthen the soul with examples of fortitude." The imperative "Look!" (Latin: *Specta!*) is emphatic. Thrasea wanted an audience to witness his death and record its meaning.[42] He hoped that his willingness to take his own life exposed the weakness of a regime that tried to control its critics by threats of execution. In terms of Plass' theory of the "game" of voluntary enforced suicide, Nero won, in the sense that he eliminated someone who challenged his authority. However, Thrasea, by his suicide, was able to assert his freedom, even under imperial rule, to act with moral autonomy. Unfortunately, Tacitus' account breaks off at this point, but we do not doubt that he described Thrasea as dying with nobility.[43]

Arria Y after her husband's death

Arria Y did not die with her husband. Tacitus relates that she wanted to share Thrasea's fate and to follow the example of her mother, but he admonished her to save her life and not deprive their daughter of her only support.[44] Despite her mother's assertion, 24 years earlier, that suicide with one's husband was the appropriate course of action, Arria Y chose to follow her husband's advice. Her decision provides an insight into how suicides affected family members. As noted in Chapter I, a suicide which pre-empted execution saved the family property from confiscation. A suicide's children were thus not victimized by destitution. However, the loss of one and especially of both parents would be a devastating blow, especially if the reasons for the death seemed unjust. An only child, such as the daughter of Arria Y and Thrasea seems to have been, had no siblings with whom to share her grief. Their daughter (perhaps still in her teens) was now married, as Arria Y had been when her parents took their lives, and was therefore not a young orphan without any emotional support. Nonetheless, both Arria Y and Thrasea may have remembered how desolate Arria felt at the time of her parents' deaths and hoped to spare their daughter similar pain. From Tacitus' account, we cannot ascertain whether Thrasea insisted or whether he only strongly recommended that Arria Y stay alive. (Tacitus uses the verb *monere*, "to admonish.") As noted in Chapter 1, it seems that husbands could exert considerable psychological pressure on their wives, who perhaps did not want to die, to join them in suicide. In this case, we have a reverse situation: the wife wanted to die, but the husband either forbade or dissuaded her. If Arria Y had cherished any hope of achieving the same distinction as her mother had, she let the opportunity slip away with her decision to remain alive. But perhaps her concern for her daughter outweighed the lure of eternal fame, and perhaps she believed that she could contribute more to her family by "selfishly" living on, rather than by providing another *exemplum* of, a "selflessly" courageous death.

We have no way of knowing the nature of the marriage relationship between Arria Y and Thrasea. As noted, Nero's reign was an anxious time for all senatorial families. For Arria Y's family, it was especially stressful because her husband acted in ways that alienated some of his fellow senators and provoked the anger of the emperor. Perhaps she was unhappy and fearful about Thrasea's putting ideology above family security. Or perhaps she was as passionate as he about reforming the state. Was it a strain living with a man of uncompromising principles who advocated austerity and cultivated a cheerless demeanor? Or did Arria Y willingly embrace this lifestyle? The persistence of their marriage over 25 years or more implies that Arria Y learned to cope with the challenges that her marriage produced, but we do not know how she coped. Perhaps she played the role of the submissive wife, not voicing objections to her husband's behavior, but silently resenting it for putting the family in peril. Or, had her mother trained her so well to devote herself to her husband's interests that she did not question his decisions? Or perhaps, inspired by her father's involvement in opposition to Claudius' imperial regime, she was enthusiastically supportive of her husband Thrasea's political endeavors. Her continued engagement in the causes he championed (a topic that is addressed later in this chapter), even long after his death, is a clue perhaps to the reality of her interest and involvement during their marriage.

No ancient source provides information about how Arria Y responded to the death of her husband – that is, whether she kept her grief private, or whether, like Antistia Pollitta, she signaled her loss publicly by an unkempt appearance and incessant laments. Her fate was not similar to that of Paulina, who died just a few years after the suicide of her husband, Seneca, never having regained her health after his death. (On Antistia and Paulina, see Chapter I.) Arria Y, in contrast, survived Thrasea by more than 30 years. Like Paulina, however, she cherished the memory of her husband. She seems not to have remarried, despite the Julian legislation encouraging remarriage for women between the ages of 20 and 50. If, as is likely, she was wed only once, she was entitled to designation as a *univira*. Her mother, Arria E, was a *univira* when she died at the same time as her husband. The Cornelia about whom Propertius wrote was a *univira* when she died before her husband (see Chapter I). The status of *univira* might also, however, belong to a widow like Arria Y. Because there was considerable social and financial pressure on widows to remarry, resistance to another matrimony required strength of character. One of the best-known examples of a *univira* widow is another Cornelia, who was the daughter of Cornelius Scipio Africanus (the hero of the Second Punic War), the wife of Tiberius Sempronius Gracchus, and the mother of the two Gracchi who were assassinated in 133 and 121 BCE. Cornelia lived in the second century BCE and was revered by later generations of Romans as an ideal of feminine virtue.[45] She bore 12 children, only three of whom lived to adulthood. Unlike the Cornelia eulogized by Propertius, this Cornelia achieved the status of *univira* by rejecting remarriage after the death of her husband in 154 BCE. She even refused a marriage proposal from the very wealthy King Ptolemy of Egypt.[46]

Another well-known *univira* widow was Antonia, the wife of Drusus.[47] When her husband died in 9 BCE, although she was, as Valerius Maximus tells us, in the flower of beauty and age, she refused to remarry. She was just 27 years old. Her resistance must have been quite an embarrassment to her father-in-law (and uncle), the emperor Augustus, who had sponsored legislation to promote marriage. In violation of the Julian laws, Antonia lived as a widow for the next 46 years, until her death in 37 CE. Perhaps she was allowed to remain unmarried because she had borne three children to Drusus. Valerius Maximus comments that she was a virtuous woman who repaid her husband's love with her exceptional loyalty.[48]

The Romans maintained two quite contradictory attitudes towards widows. On the one hand, a woman was praised as a *univira* for demonstrating such fidelity to her husband that she married only once, but on the other hand, society expected (and the Julian laws legislated) that an adult woman of child-bearing age would have a husband and would therefore remarry if her husband died. The designation of *univira* may have generated respect, but it could not compensate for the loss of social status which many widows experienced. A widow was problematic in Roman society because she no longer fulfilled the role expected of women: to be a helpmeet to a husband. McGinn contends that, because a marriage in which the wife is dependent on her husband has traditionally been considered the most appropriate situation for adult women, widows in many societies have been a source of male anxiety. He maintains that two contrasting – though both negative – stereotypes of widows have developed. The first is the stereotype of the vulnerable widow, in need of protection and resources, who becomes a financial burden to her family and community because she consumes material resources, but contributes nothing.[49] The second stereotype is that of the lusty widow, the sexually experienced woman, now free of the control of a husband, who rouses suspicion about inappropriate sexual activity. One of the most memorable portraits of a "merry widow" is Cicero's description, in the *Pro Caelio*, of Clodia and her pursuit of young men. Even widows who may have been more restrained than the Clodia described by Cicero sometimes fell prey to unscrupulous men. In *Letter* 4.11.6, Pliny reports a rumor that the emperor Domitian seduced his own brother's daughter, Julia, when she became a widow.[50] Antonia, who was widowed at the age of 27, refused to remarry (as was noted earlier), but kept her life free from reproach. She maintained an unsullied reputation by sleeping in the same bed as her mother-in-law, Livia.[51]

A widow might, in addition, if she were wealthy, be suspected not only of engaging in sexual activity, but also of indulging in such inappropriate behavior as the squandering of her resources to satisfy her own pleasures. As McGinn admits, these broad stereotypes were constructed by men, and we are not able to recover what thoughts women had about how widows did or should behave. These unsympathetic stereotypes present the situation in terms of male fears, and gloss over the actual difficulties that widows faced. In the ancient world, the reality of widows' lived experience was often bleak, especially for women from poor families, for whom widowhood usually meant a dwindling of financial resources. And for all widows, the loss of a husband meant a loss of social identity and restrictions on social interactions. For some women, remarriage might have appeared to be the only practical means of escaping destitution, avoiding aspersions on one's moral character, or averting social isolation. On the other hand, the search for a new husband presented its own set of difficulties, especially for a wealthy widow who might worry about falling victim to a man who was attracted only by her fortune. A widow whose *paterfamilias* was deceased, as was Arria Y's, was able to negotiate her own dowry. This capacity might give her considerable control over the arrangement of a new marriage. On the other hand, a woman who had not previously been allowed to manage her own finances might be very vulnerable to the schemes of an unscrupulous suitor. And, although widowhood often meant a reduction in one's opportunities for social interactions, wealthy widows, particularly if they were aging and childless, might find themselves beset by men who offered assiduous attention and feigned affection, with the goal of being included in their wills.[52] In *Letter* 2.20, Pliny describes the odious behavior of Marcus Aquilius Regulus who cajoled and hounded at least two women into putting him in their wills.

The survival of lower-class widows, whose husbands would have had no property to bequeath to them, was always precarious. Because both Arria Y's parents and Thrasea were members of the senatorial elite, she was undoubtedly provided for through inheritances and bequests, and not in danger of being destitute.[53] However, we have no specific knowledge of what financial resources she had during her decades of widowhood, or how these resources were managed. As the mother of just one child, she would not be eligible for exemption from the oversight of a guardian, who would have been appointed for her at the death of her father. Lower-class widows generally became dependent on their children for material support. The upper-class Arria Y would have been more self-sufficient financially, but it is possible that she lived with her daughter and son-in-law. The two women seem to have remained close. The execution of the son-in-law in the 70s CE may have brought them even closer. Pliny, who was about five years old when Thrasea committed suicide, claims to have been a good friend of both women (although he was significantly younger than them, and his relationship with them may not have begun until the early 90s CE) (*Letters* 7.19.10 and 9.13.3). His accounts suggest that the two women shared a devotion to preserving the memory of the courage of their family members.

We have no information about Arria Y's activities from the time of Thrasea's death in 66 CE until 93 CE. In the intervening years, Nero was overthrown by a military coup (68 CE). Abandoned by his guards and his friends, he fled from

Rome. In a villa outside the city, accompanied by only a few servants, he committed suicide.[54] Arria Y undoubtedly felt some satisfaction when she learned of the humiliating end of her husband's persecutor. News of Nero's death was met with elation among the senators, who believed that they would regain their former power and dignity.[55] However, his death was followed by more than a year of brutal civil war, from which Vespasian emerged as emperor. He ruled from 69 to 79 CE and was succeeded first by his son Titus (until 81 CE) and then by his son Domitian, who was assassinated in 96 CE. The hope of the senatorial class for a restoration of *libertas* was not realized. Domitian was an autocratic ruler who was not disposed to cultivate the good will of the Senate or to entertain the concept of shared power.[56] After an unsuccessful revolt in 89 failed to dislodge him, Domitian became even more suspicious of Senate members and was quick to punish his critics, often by death. We learn from Pliny's letters that, in 93 CE, Arria Y and her daughter were punished for criticism of the emperor (*Letters* 3.11.3 and 7.19.5). Although her daughter attempted at the trial to establish that her mother was innocent of alleged treasonous activities, both women were convicted and sentenced to exile. Arria Y's step-grandson, who was prosecuted at the same time, was executed. We do not know where the two women spent their exile or whether they spent it together. Arria Y would have been about 70 years old at this time. The stress of a judicial hearing, the upheaval of exile, and the execution of her step-grandson must have been difficult for her. But she was resilient. She and her daughter returned to Rome, probably in early 97 CE, after the assassination of Domitian in September of 96 (*Letter* 9.13.5). Shortly after their return, they were approached by Pliny about a plan to prosecute one of the men who had initiated the charges against Arria Y's step-grandson. More will be said later about the events of 93 and 97.

We hear nothing about Arria Y's activities after 97. In *Letter* 7.19, which was probably written about 107 CE, Pliny discloses that she is deceased, but we cannot ascertain if her death was recent. We know only that it occurred within the period between her return to Rome in 97 and the writing of that letter. Pliny declares that he had been a good friend and was deeply grieved by Arria Y's death. However, he has nothing specific or personal to say about her character or actions, leaving us with the impression that he did not perhaps know her as well as he implies. His tribute to her is brief and vague: "[S]he was the mother of so great a woman; I can say nothing more ennobling" (*Letter* 7.19.9). The focus of this letter is the exemplary character of Arria Y's daughter (discussed later), and we should not expect Pliny to devote much space to Arria Y. Having shown that the daughter developed into a brave and sympathetic woman, Pliny has also indirectly revealed the admirable character of the mother who educated her. Despite the brevity of his comment, Pliny nevertheless prompts the reader to consider the contributions which Arria Y made to her family. In the course of her relatively long life, she herself survived the hostility of brutal emperors, but suffered the loss of several close family members to the animosity of these emperors. Arria Y did not acquire the celebrity that her mother had, but her role in the history of her family was just as important, for it was she who seems to have been responsible for preserving and promulgating the accounts of the family's stalwart opposition to the emperors through several generations. It was she who apparently inspired younger generations of the family to continue the tradition of challenging autocratic rulers. And it was she who raised a daughter who carried on the task of promoting the family reputation.

Fannia

The daughter of Arria Y and Thrasea presumably received the name Clodia at birth – that is, the feminine form of the family name of her father, Publius Clodius Thrasea. However, Pliny, who is the only ancient author to refer to the daughter by name, uses, for reasons unknown to us, the name Fannia. Fannius may have been a family name on Thrasea's mother's side of the family, or in the family of his paternal grandmother.[57] In *Letter* 5.5, Pliny reports the death of a man named Gaius Fannius and expresses regret that Fannius died before completing the volumes he was writing about the fates of people put to death or banished by Nero. Presumably his subjects would have included Thrasea and also Fannia's husband, who was exiled in 66 CE at the time that Thrasea was given a "free choice of death." Fannius' choice of topics suggests that he had interests that coincided with those of Fannia's family, and it is tempting to postulate that he and Fannia were kin, but we cannot go beyond speculation. Pliny, who was so eager to advertise his intimacy with Thrasea's family, writes that he was very fond of Fannius and had solicited advice from him, but does not indicate that Fannius was related to Thrasea's family.

When Fannia's grandparents ended their lives in 42 CE, her parents were already married. Fannia may have been born about 44 CE. (Again, these dates of birth are speculations.) She seems to have been their only child or perhaps their only child who survived to adulthood. The household in which she grew up has already been discussed. Her mother kept alive the story of the courageous self-sacrifice of Arria the Elder, Fannia's grandmother. She probably also instilled in Fannia, as had been instilled in her, a belief that it was her duty to support her husband. Her father led an austere life and perhaps he insisted that his wife and daughter also do so. By the time that Fannia had reached her teens, her father had gained a reputation as an outspoken critic of Nero's excesses and the Senate's complacency. His behavior put his own life and the fate of his family in peril.

Fannia's marriage

Fannia was married to a man named Gaius Helvidius Priscus, who will be designated henceforth as Helvidius I, to distinguish him from his son and grandson.[58] His father was an army officer but of a rank lower than that generally assigned to men of the elite class.[59] Helvidius I may not have been born into the senatorial class. However, he was a very bright and ambitious individual who, in his youth, devoted himself to his studies so that he might embark upon a political career. He followed teachers of philosophy who considered only virtues to be "good things" and only vices to be "bad things," and who counted power, noble birth, and other things external to one's soul to be neither "good things" nor "bad things." Tacitus' description of Helvidius I's choice of teachers indicates that he was particularly interested in Stoicism, and indeed Dio tells us that Helvidus I was brought up in the doctrines of Stoics.[60] However, the aspect of Stoicism which seems to have interested him most was the practical advice it offered on how to fortify oneself against adversity through self-discipline and restraint. Stoicism encouraged participation in public affairs, and Helvidius I did indeed embark upon a political career. He was elected to the office of quaestor for 56 CE.[61] The term of office for quaestors was only one year, but the position provided entry into and a life-long membership in the Senate. The quaestorship was generally considered the stepping stone to higher offices, but we have no record of Helvidius holding another public office during the reign of Nero. Perhaps our record is simply incomplete. Or, perhaps his outspokenness had made him unpopular with the emperor and some of his fellow senators.

Helvidius I's willingness, even as a junior magistrate, to speak his mind may have offended some senators, but it apparently attracted the favorable attention of Thrasea Paetus, who chose Helvidius I to be his son-in-law.[62] In the imperial period, holders of the quaestorship were required to be at least 25 years old. Thus we know that Helvidius was at least 25 in 56 CE. We don't know when the wedding of Fannia and Helvidius took place. It may have been around 59 or 60 CE, when Fannia would have been in her mid-teens. The age difference between this husband and wife may have been about 15 years, which was not an unusual difference. This was probably Fannia's first (and only) marriage, but Helvidius I had been previously married. (We do not know the identity of his first wife.) The Julian laws encouraged marriage for men between the ages of 25 and 60 and granted accelerated political advancement to married men with legitimate children. Young men aspiring to hold public office therefore generally married in their early 20s in order to take advantage of these perquisites.[63] Helvidius I had done so, and had at least one child from this marriage, a son (henceforth, Helvidius II). The teen-aged Fannia thus became a stepmother upon marriage. Becoming a stepmother at a young age was far from rare in the ancient Roman world because death from natural causes claimed many people in their 20s and 30s, leaving children without one parent. If the surviving parent was the father, who then married a girl much younger than himself, the children acquired a young stepmother. There is no record that Fannia and Helvidius I had any children, or any who survived to adulthood.

Since Helvidius I's family seems not to have been of the elite class, Thrasea did not arrange this match for his daughter because he hoped that it would enhance the social distinction of his own family. Instead he chose Helvidius as his son-in-law because he recognized in him qualities that he admired and cultivated in himself. Tacitus reports that Helvidius I was, as a citizen, senator, husband, son-in-law, and friend consistent, scornful of wealth, resolutely supportive of righteousness, and undaunted in the face of fear.[64] From his father-in-law, he acquired a devotion to *libertas*. Dio, who is more critical of Helvidius I than is

Tacitus, reveals that Helvidius I imitated Thrasea's frankness of speech, though not always at the appropriate time.[65] The creation of ties through marriage had always been an important or sometimes even the main consideration in arranging a match. The relationship which developed between Thrasea and Helvidius I may have been similar to the apparently warm relationship between Thrasea and his father-in-law, Caecina Paetus. We can imagine the moments the two men enjoyed together, drinking toasts, for example, to celebrate the birthdays of those republican defenders of *libertas*, Brutus and Cassius.[66] In fact, the compatibility of the two men may well have been a more important consideration in the arrangement of the marriage than the possible compatibility of the bride and groom. Of course, it is perhaps the nature of fathers to assume that their daughters would be delighted with a husband similar to them. One wonders, however, what the young Fannia thought when she was presented with a groom who seemed to mirror her father.

The banishment of Fannia's husband

Certainly Fannia's life in her husband's home was no less fraught with anxiety and danger than her childhood had been. When her father was sentenced to death in 66 CE, her husband was banished from Italy.[67] Their accusers chided Senate members for allowing Thrasea and his son-in-law, who had been caught up "in the same madness," to ridicule them with impunity.[68] However, we do not know what the "same madness" was or what specific charges were brought against Helvidius I. Apparently some of the senators pitied Helvidius I, believing that he was an innocent man being prosecuted because of his marriage relationship.[69]

As already recounted, Helvidius I remained at Thrasea's side during his suicide. He then departed from Rome. Pliny reports that Fannia accompanied her husband into exile (*Letter* 7.19.4). Her mother, Arria Y, had been persuaded by Thrasea to remain alive in order to support their daughter. We do not know whether Fannia left her mother, who would have been grieving the loss of her husband, or whether perhaps Arria Y joined the daughter and son-in-law in banishment. It is also possible that Fannia did not remain the full time with her husband in the place of banishment, but traveled back to Rome to succor her mother.

Sentences of banishment varied in severity, and we are not certain of the terms of Helvidius I's banishment. When writing of the banishment of 66 CE, and of a second banishment which is discussed later, Pliny uses the Latin word *exsilium* (*Letter* 7.19.4). Tacitus uses the same word in *Histories* 4.6. In the *Annals*, however, Tacitus comments of the banishment in 66 CE that Helvidius I was expelled from Italy (*Italia depelluntur*), and banned from Italy (*Italia arceri*)[70] Of the second banishment, Suetonius states that Helvidius I was relegated (*relegatum*).[71] *Relegatio*, in legal terms, was the imposition, on a person condemned of a capital offence, of "an interdiction from water and fire" (*aquae et ignis interdictio*). Thus the person was prohibited from using water and fire – that is, the necessities of life – within Italy.[72] To remain alive, s/he had to leave the country. *Exsilium* (also: *deportatio*) was a much more severe punishment. In addition to the interdiction from water and fire, the condemned suffered the confiscation of citizenship and property. Despite Pliny's use of the word *exsilium* in *Letter* 7.19, Helvidius I may, on the two occasions of his banishment, have been only relegated, as Suetonius' account states, and thus allowed to retain his rights as a Roman citizen and his property. His retention of his property would have eased the hardships his family endured during his banishment.

In some situations, particularly if a person threatened with prosecution voluntarily withdrew from Rome prior to sentencing, s/he was allowed to choose a place of exile. In other situations, the place was specified in the sentencing. In 8 CE, for example, the poet Ovid was relegated to the remote town of Tomis, on the west shore of the Black Sea, a location which this sophisticated urbanite would never have chosen for himself. He missed the cultural milieu of Rome, considered residents of Tomis to be barbarians, and constantly lamented the torture of having to live among them. In a poem which he wrote in Tomis, he was careful to make clear that his sentence was one of *relegatio*, not *exsilium* or *deportatio*.[73] Until his death in Tomis in 18 CE, he continued to hope that he would be granted a pardon and recalled from banishment.

We do not know where Helvidius I spent either of his two exiles, or whether Fannia stayed with him during the entire period of banishment.[74] Most wives stayed in Italy. Tacitus, however, praises women who followed their husband into exile as virtuous.[75] It was so unusual for wives to accompany their husbands that the few who did were given special mention by ancient authors. For example, Appian and Valerius Maximus both give brief reports of the actions of a woman named Sulpicia.[76] When her husband Lentulus was forced to flee from Rome during the proscriptions of 43 BCE, she wanted to join him in flight. He refused to allow her to do so and even kept his destination a secret from her. Her mother, moreover, kept a close watch over her to prevent her from leaving. However, when Sulpicia learned that Lentulus had taken up residence in Sicily, she disguised herself as a slave and traveled there to be with him. (Like Arria E, Sulpicia was willing to play the role of a slave in order to assist her husband.) Our authors do not report what Lentulus' response was – that is, whether he was pleased or displeased to have her join him.

Wives of exiles

Despite Tacitus' comment about the virtue of following one's husband into banishment, there were very practical reasons why a man would prefer that his wife remain in Italy. The wife of a man in exile was expected to play a critical role in tending to her husband's interests. She kept an eye on the management of his finances, petitioned officials for his pardon, and cultivated the alliances and friendships that were so crucial to his hopes of recall. Ovid's poems from Tomis and Cicero's letters from his exile in Greece provide us with insights into what behavior a banished husband expected of his wife, and what difficulties she might encounter as she fulfilled her duties to him.[77] We also have an account of the activities of a wife, referred to by scholars as "Turia," whose husband was forced to flee from Rome (as a fugitive, rather than an exile), initially when Julius Caesar crossed the Rubicon River in 49 BCE and sent Pompey's supporters into flight, and then, after Caesar's assassination, to escape the proscriptions implemented by the Second Triumvirate in 43 BCE.[78] Unfortunately, we have only the husbands' perspectives on the situations. Nonetheless, their accounts may instruct us about the types of experiences with which Fannia may have had to deal.

Cicero went into exile in 58 BCE when he faced prosecution for executing Roman citizens during the Catilinarian conspiracy of 63 BCE. Because he feared that a formal prosecution would result in his own execution, or that he would be shamed into committing suicide, he withdrew voluntarily from Rome. The interdiction from water and fire was put in place after his departure. He was allowed to choose his place of banishment, and he chose to reside in Thessalonica, Greece, until his recall in 57 BCE. Neither Cicero's wife nor Ovid's wife joined her husband in exile, although both had apparently offered to do so.[79] Ovid states that he persuaded his wife to stay in Italy so that she could provide him with practical assistance; Cicero encouraged his wife, Terentia, to work toward his recall.[80]

The wife of an exile would be called upon to offer her husband emotional support, to keep herself and him informed about affairs in Rome, and perhaps to counsel him about courses of action. In addition, it was essential that she take on the management of the household and its resources. Many of the matters with which Cicero's wife, Terentia, had to cope were financial. He vehemently advised her not to sell a row of houses that she owned in Rome, lest their son (now six years old) be left without an inheritance.[81] Cicero also tried to relieve Terentia's anxiety about the considerable financial loss the family would incur if the household slaves whom he owned were confiscated by the state along with his other property.[82] If confiscation was imminent, he planned to manumit the slaves, thereby depriving the state of the income from their sale. If confiscation was not demanded, they would continue to be the slaves of his family. Cicero also, however, commented that Terentia had made arrangements for *her* slaves (in the text, *your* slaves). His remark implies that she owned slaves separately from him (even as she owned real estate separately from him). She may have been given slaves as part of the dowry which she brought to the marriage, or she may have inherited them or purchased them with money she inherited.[83]

The concerns which Cicero expressed about property – both slaves and real estate – bring into view several important issues about women and property ownership in ancient Rome which are relevant also to the women of Pliny's letters. Some of these issues, such as the appointment of guardians, are mentioned in Chapter 1. Although women were required to have guardians – that is, men who supervised the management of their property – women were nonetheless allowed to own property in their own names. In a Roman marriage, there was little "joint property." Each spouse (at least those from families well enough off to have property) entered the marriage with property, and the financial records of these properties were kept separately.[84] The woman's property would have come primarily from inheritances from her father and other family members. Hence the interest of her family in having a guardian appointed to her. Even the dowry which Roman women brought to their marriages was essentially a loan rather than a gift. The husband could utilize the property and benefit from the profit it brought, but was required to return to his wife's family the principal in the case of divorce.[85] It is difficult for us to understand how this system of separate book-keeping worked. However, it provided for Roman women a financial independence that most European women did not again enjoy from the fall of the Roman empire until quite modern times.

Consider Cicero's remark about Terentia's slaves. We don't know how the duties of the separately owned slaves were divided up or whether, on a day to day basis, any account was taken of whose slaves did what or how much each slave ate. And when Cicero spoke of the row of houses that Terentia was thinking about selling, these were houses that Terentia owned. Decisions about their disposition would be made by Terentia and her guardian. It was not unusual for a wife to involve her husband in the decision-making, but she was not legally bound to. The husband of "Turia," in his eulogy for his wife, notes that she had handed over to him the estate that she inherited from her parents. He adds, however, that they shared responsibilities and that he acted as custodian of her fortune and she served as protector of his. She used her estate, in part, to provide dowries for her female relatives.[86] Cicero's concern about the sale of the houses which Terentia owned was precipitated by his hope that she would bequeath them to their son. As noted earlier, children belonged to the family of the father, in this case, to Cicero's family (the Tullius family). They could therefore expect to be named as heirs in the will of their father or to inherit his estate if he died intestate. Their mother, however, held the property of her father's family (in this case, the Terentius family), and her children had no legal claim on it. Indeed, her siblings might well want her to bequeath the property to them. Nonetheless, there was a social expectation that a mother would provide some financial support to her children in her will, and it is this expectation to which Cicero is referring.[87]

In his letters from exile, Cicero consoles Terentia on the news that his house in Rome had been looted and burned down by his enemies on the very day he went into exile.[88] Ovid, too, mentions that his wife must guard against his enemies, who are eager to strip away his property, like a wolf prowling for sheep or a hungry vulture searching for a corpse.[89] And "Turia," during her husband's absence as a fugitive from Rome, was forced to defend the family house when her husband's enemies tried to break in and plunder it.[90] In addition, wives of exiles were apparently vulnerable to physical and emotional abuse. Cicero expresses concern for the ordeal which Terentia endured when she was forcibly removed from the compound of the Vestal Virgins (where her half-sister was a Vestal and where she had perhaps sought refuge) and taken before a tribunal, perhaps to be questioned about a family financial matter.[91] Cicero and Ovid needed to maintain the good will of their wives and to appear remorseful for the aggravations that their banishments were causing. They may therefore, in order to seem very sympathetic, have exaggerated the brutality of the abuse that their wives experienced. However, being a victim of violence and humiliation was also the fate of

"Turia." She gave all her gold and gemstone jewelry (that is, her own property) to her fugitive husband, as well as part of their household income, so that he could purchase slaves and provisions and live in a dignified manner.[92] She worked tirelessly to secure a pardon for her husband. On one occasion, when she approached the triumvir, Marcus Aemilius Lepidus, and lay prostrate at his feet, he had her brutally dragged away "like a slave." She endured bruises and insulting words but, nonetheless, her husband remarks in his eulogy, her spirit remained unbroken. Ovid, too, was aware that just the designation as "wife of an exile" – a phrase he uses several times – could be a source of humiliation.[93]

Perhaps the most important of the duties of the "wife of an exile" was to lobby for her husband's recall. To do so, it was essential that she assiduously cultivate his friends and family members and exhort and persuade them to act on his behalf. She thus assumed a prominent role in the creation and maintenance of social and political alliances. It was also critical that she be willing to negotiate on her husband's behalf, and advocate for him, as "Turia" had done, before powerful men, and that she be able to do so effectively. In some cases, the "woman" who was asked to undertake these duties was quite young. Because it was common for girls to be married at the age of 14 or 15, to much older men, it is possible that the wife of an exile or fugitive might be still in her teens or in her early 20s and that she had led a quite sheltered life. Fulfilling the demands made on an exile's wife would be trying for any woman, but particularly for a young woman. "Turia," for example, was probably in her early 20s and had been married only a few years when she was called upon to perform so heroically on behalf of her husband. (At an even younger age, this remarkable woman had prosecuted the murderers of her parents and fought off the attempts of relatives to gain control of her parents' estates.)[94] Ovid begged his wife to conquer her fear of approaching officials.[95]

Moreover, the banishment of a husband produced an inversion of conventional gender roles and marriage relationships.[96] Having a husband in exile forced a woman to emerge from the private and sheltered sphere of home and family, considered the appropriate sphere for women, and to make herself conspicuous in the sphere of public places, such as the forum and judicial assemblies, and to become involved in activities traditionally considered the domain of men. She was, moreover – though she had been trained to cultivate the feminine virtues of obedience, modesty, and loyalty – now required to develop and display virtues considered masculine such as courage, self-control, and fortitude. The exile's wife was now expected to assume an active and public role, while her husband was forced to accept a passive and dependent position. His communication with family, friends, and public officials could be done only through letters and messengers, which would take many weeks for delivery. The shift in the balance of power in the family must have produced a stressful situation for elite men. Nonetheless, the basic premise remained: a good wife supported her husband. The wife of an exile was praised if she put all her efforts into her husband's interests, not if she used his absence to promote her own interests. Ovid urged his wife to be "the model of the good wife."[97] Her reward for supporting him, he wrote, was that he would sing her praises in his poetry, and she would thus win immortal fame.[98] As was noted with Arria E, wives achieved immortal fame primarily through activities that assisted their husbands.

In the words they address to their wives, both Cicero and Ovid express love for them and sorrow at being separated. The emotions may be real, but, of course, these husbands needed to stay in their wives' good graces if they expected them to continue to be supportive. Because the distances were so great and communications so slow and unreliable, there were moments when the husbands doubted the loyalty of their wives and must have despaired at the thought that the persons on whom they were most dependent might have ceased to support them. As is perhaps not unexpected, there were inevitably recriminations. Both Cicero and Ovid occasionally express frustration and irritation, and reproach their wives for seeming not, after all, to be exerting every effort possible on their behalves.[99] We wish that the wives' side of the story had been preserved.

Fannia and Helvidius may have struggled with similar frustrations. If she stayed with him during the entire time of his banishment, she was available to provide immediate comfort, but was not able to perform a role as his advocate in Rome. If, however, she remained in the city for part of the time, her time and attention were occupied with maintaining a network of support for his recall and ensuring that the family finances remained sound. She may, moreover, have endured hardships and humiliations similar to those suffered by the wives of Cicero and Ovid and by "Turia." At this time, she was probably in her early 20s, a young age to be saddled with so much responsibility.

Fannia's husband and the opposition to the emperors

The overthrow and death of Nero in 68 CE brought to an end the family dynasty of Julio-Claudian emperors that had begun when Augustus seized power.[100] Members of the senatorial class hoped that the elimination of the debauched and cruel Nero would usher in a new era of co-operation between the emperor and the Senate. Instead, Rome was beset by more than a year of civil war and anarchy, during which three men (Galba, Otho, Vitellius) in quick succession were proclaimed emperor. The end of 69 CE then saw the installation of a new dynasty established by Vespasian.

Helvidius I returned to Rome shortly after Nero's death. If Fannia expected to enjoy a life of tranquility, she was disappointed. Exile had not dulled her husband's determination to restore *libertas* to the Senate. During the brief reign of Galba (emperor June 68 to January 69), Helvidius I attempted to avenge the death of his father-in-law, Thrasea Paetus, by bringing charges against Eprius Marcellus, one of the informers (*delatores*) who had been instrumental in securing the conviction of Thrasea.[101] In the end, however, he dropped the charges. This was a surprising reversal perhaps for a man so intent on exposing the crimes of the previous regime, but he was persuaded by his fellow senators that this prosecution would cause damaging divisions in the Senate, because so many members had collaborated with Nero or, at any rate, acquiesced in his brutality. Helvidius

I was, however, rarely conciliatory. At a Senate meeting in 69 CE, he provoked the anger of Vitellius (emperor April to December 69) by speaking against one of his proposals.[102] And, almost as soon as Vespasian assumed the position of emperor in December of 69, Helvidius I offended him. When proposals favored by Vespasian were presented to the Senate, most senators approved them, continuing the pattern of dissimulation and sycophancy that had kept them safe under the Julio-Claudian emperors.[103] Helvidius I, however, refused to curry favor with insincere praise. His behavior on the day on which the Senate installed Vespasian was, Tacitus reports, the beginning both of great harm and of great renown for Helvidius I. Nevertheless, he was elected to and, in 70 CE, served in the office of praetor. His year in this office was apparently turbulent because he was not hesitant to disagree with his senatorial colleagues or criticize the emperor. Although Helvidius I had dropped his original case against Thrasea's informer, Eprius Marcellus, he did not cease to harass him by raising objections to his proposals and continuing to remind the Senate that Marcellus had induced Nero to take the lives of so many innocent men, including Thrasea.[104] In response Marcellus pointed out that, under Nero, most anxious senators had been forced to condone the emperor's actions in order to survive.[105] He himself, he said, (in an egregious statement of political expediency) prayed for good emperors, but tolerated any sort. Let Helvidius be considered the equal of Cato and Brutus in firmness and fortitude, said Marcellus. He and the rest of the Senate would continue to serve the regime.

Under Vespasian, several senators again made attempts to bring to justice those colleagues who had abetted Nero. Junius Mauricus (brother of Junius Arulenus who, as tribune, had offered to veto the conviction of Thrasea) submitted an official request that the emperor make available to the Senate the imperial records of who the informers were under Nero.[106] About this time, Helvidius I saw another chance to prosecute Marcellus for the treatment of Thrasea.[107] As the senators listened to Helvidius I's accusatory speech, Marcellus rose as if to leave the Senate house. Immediately all the senators took sides (a concern that had kept Helvidius I from pursuing his prosecution under Galba), and the day was consumed by this discord. The emperor's son, Domitian, attended the next Senate meeting and urged the members to cast aside the anger and resentment of the past.[108] At this moment, Tacitus writes, the senators let slip away the *libertas* that they had almost grasped.

Tacitus depicts Marcellus as a cynical and craven political opportunist, whose only concern was the retention of his own status and life. Helvidius I, by contrast, is portrayed as a brave individual who was willing to risk his life in order to regain the dignity that the Senate had allowed to slip away. Although Marcellus might have considered his comparison of Helvidius I to those republican champions of *libertas*, Cato and Brutus, as a warning that such republican resistance was self-destructive, Tacitus utilizes the comment to emphasize the nobility of Helvidius I's goals. The historian's sympathies are definitely with Helvidius I. It is therefore worth observing that Tacitus nonetheless records several situations in which the majority of senators sided with Marcellus or ignored Helvidius I's proposals.[109] Tacitus might have attributed the senators' lack of support for Helvidius I to their fear of the emperor. It is quite possible, however, that his colleagues did not so much fear Vespasian as dislike Helvidius I's uncompromising refusal to make any concessions toward establishing peace after so disastrous a civil war. To them, he may have appeared as a provocateur whose goal was self-promotion rather than the good of the state. Indeed, even Tacitus reports that some people believed that Helvidius I seemed too eager for fame, and that the desire for glory is the last thing that is cast off, even by philosophers.[110]

Dio's description of Helvidius I's behavior is decidedly less favorable than Tacitus'.[111] He reports that Helvidius would not desist from railing at the emperor, and may even have proposed that Vespasian not appoint his son as his heir – that is, not start a new family dynasty. Dio adds that it was very clear that Vespasian hated Helvidius I because he was an agitator who cultivated the mob and was always denouncing monarchy and praising democracy. In addition, Dio reports that Helvidius I gathered men to his side, as if it were the function of philosophy to abuse those in power, stir up the masses, throw into confusion the established order, and cause a revolution. Helvidius I was Thrasea's son-in-law and tried to imitate him, but, Dio asserts, failed. Thrasea had not attempted to ingratiate himself with the emperor Nero, but neither had he, according to Dio, said or done anything insulting to him. Helvidius I, on the other hand, was very hostile toward Vespasian and would not leave him alone either in private or in public. Therefore, Dio maintains, Helvidius I invited a deadly response and was destined to pay the penalty for his trouble-making. Suetonius, too, relates that Helvidius I was rude toward the emperor, who nonetheless checked his anger until the excessiveness of Helvidius I's very insolent wrangling had all but humiliated him.[112]

The Stoic philosopher Epictetus is said to have provided this account of an exchange between Helvidius I and Vespasian, an exchange which illustrates Helvidius I's confrontational behavior and perhaps a determination to force the emperor to punish him.[113] When Vespasian ordered Helvidius Priscus not to attend the Senate meeting, he replied, "It is up to you not to allow me to be a Senate member, but until then, I must go in." The emperor said, "Well, go in then, but be silent." Helvidius replied, "Do not ask my opinion, and I will be silent." The emperor said, "But I must ask your opinion." Helvidius replied, "And I must say what appears to me to be right." The emperor said, "But if you speak, I shall kill you." Helvidius replied, "When did I say that I am immortal? You will play your part, and I will play mine: yours is to kill; mine is to die without trembling; yours is to banish; mine is to depart without sorrow."

In the early 70s CE, Vespasian was persuaded by an advisor to expel from Rome men who were drawing on Stoic principles and, under the guise of philosophy, teaching doctrines deemed by him unsuitable to the times. An additional charge was that the Stoics arrogantly boasted of being wise, brave, and righteous, even while insulting everyone else.[114] We do not know how closely Helvidius I may have been connected to the philosophers who were expelled. Suetonius tells us that Vespasian relegated Helvidius I because he was no longer able to tolerate his insulting behavior.[115] He does not mention Helvidius I's philosophic beliefs as a cause of the relegation. It was presumably at this time that Fannia accompanied him to the second exile (Pliny, *Letter* 7.19.4). Again we do not know the location of the exile. While Helvidius I was in banishment, Vespasian (who Suetonius asserts never punished an innocent man and who sighed even over the punishment of those deserving it) ordered his execution.[116] Soon afterward, he changed his mind and sent messengers to recall the executioners. However, a false report that Helvidius I had already been slain unfortunately meant that the reprieve was not delivered. We cannot date his execution any more precisely than the early to mid-70s CE. Fate denied Helvidius I the opportunity to leave behind an example of a noble self-inflicted death.

Fannia's life after her husband's death

Thus perished Fannia's husband. We do not know how Fannia felt about her marriage. Although she had grown up with a father who was a critic of the imperial system, it cannot have been easy to be married to a man so persistent in his castigations of the emperors and of his fellow senators, so tenacious in his desire to avenge Nero's victims, and so determined, it seemed, to court the death penalty. We have no words from Fannia or her friends that would reveal whether she resented Helvidius I's uncompromising and perilous behavior and the sacrifices it demanded of her, or whether she enthusiastically supported his behavior and embraced the challenges it produced. Her actions, both before and after his death, indicate that she was devoted to his interests. Whether this devotion resulted from affection and fondness or from a strong sense of duty is something we cannot ascertain. The facts that Fannia did not remarry, maintained a close relationship with Helvidius I's son (her stepson), and continued to be involved in the causes he had fought for suggest that her devotion to her husband was more than a role she played while he was alive.

We know that Fannia had accompanied Helvidius I into his second exile (*Letter* 7.19.4). However, we don't know if she was at his side when he was killed, like Antistia Pollitta, mentioned in Chapter I, who was present at the assassination of her husband and kept his bloody clothing. Nor do we know if she contemplated suicide. If she did, perhaps she rejected that idea and decided to stay alive for the sake of her widowed mother. Arria the Elder had chosen the fame of a self-inflicted death; her daughter and granddaughter, however, while honoring her courage and preserving the memory of her deed, chose to live on. Their choices represent not timidity, but a different kind of fortitude. Life without a husband posed challenges for any woman. The challenges for Arria Y and Fannia may have been more numerous because their husbands had been among the foremost critics of the imperial system, and they may therefore have been regarded with suspicion by Vespasian and the sons who succeeded him. However, despite the possible dangers to themselves, they did not allow the reputations of their family members to be tarnished or buried in obscurity. Indeed, their decisions to survive may have been based, in part, on a determination to keep alive their husbands' stories.

With Helvidius I's death, Fannia became a widow. She was relatively young, probably around 30 years old, and she survived her husband by more than 30 years. Although the Julian legislation encouraged remarriage, we have no evidence that Fannia had a second husband. Like her mother, she was apparently a *univira*. Nor do we have information about her financial situation or who her guardian was. A guardian would have been required because she could not claim a three-children exemption. If Helvidius I's sentence had been, as our sources other than Pliny suggest, relegation (*relegatio*), rather than exile (*exsilium*), his property may not have been confiscated.[117] His son, Helvidius II, was undoubtedly his primary heir. However, he likely left some financial support to Fannia. And, as the only child of Thrasea Paetus, she had probably also inherited from him. Her mother, Arria Y, had likely received inheritances from both her parents upon their suicides in 42 CE. Perhaps Fannia and Arria Y lived together. Such an arrangement would have been advantageous for financial, social, and emotional reasons. As noted earlier, widows found themselves in an awkward social position, having lost the role – providing support to a husband – for which they had been groomed and, with it, their status in the community. In addition, as a widow without children, Fannia would not have the role of caring for a younger generation (as did her own mother, Arria Y), although she seems to have remained close to her stepson, Helvidius II. Childless widows, especially those without financial resources, were among the most vulnerable members of society because they did not have the security of knowing that younger family members were available to help them. Fannia, however, was not destitute and, by maintaining ties with her stepson, she presumably had family on whom she could depend.

McGinn's observations about the stereotypes of widows have already been discussed. A widow who wished to remain unmarried, but to continue the social contacts that she had had while her husband was still alive, had to be careful to preserve a reputation for propriety. As already noted, Antonia, who survived her husband by over 40 years, never remarried, but kept her reputation unsullied by sleeping in the same bed as her mother-in-law. It is possible that Fannia and her mother, Arria Y, shared a household (not necessarily a bed) after the deaths of their husbands.[118] However, in contrast to McGinn's comments about the social isolation of widows, Fannia and Arria Y seem to have been able to maintain the network of friends they enjoyed when their husbands were alive. We don't know whether these two widows were preyed upon by *captatores*, "legacy hunters."

We do not have information about the activities of Fannia and Arria Y in the period of about 20 years from Helvidius' execution until 93 CE. As noted earlier, Vespasian died in 79 CE and was succeeded first by his son, Titus (79–81), and then by his son Domitian, who was assassinated in 96 CE. The senatorial class did not recover the *libertas* for which Thrasea and Helvidius had fought. The autocratic Domitian was not interested in developing a good rapport with the Senate or sharing power with it. When an unsuccessful revolt in 89 threatened his life, Domitian became even more suspicious and brutal. He ruthlessly suppressed any perceived criticism of his manner of governing the empire or any perceived insult to himself personally. Punishment on the capital charge of treason was not restricted to people actually plotting sedition.[119] Informers (*delatores*) were quick to report to Domitian any disparaging words about the current regime or any admiration for people who in the past had advocated the restoration of republican *libertas*. Many senators safeguarded their survival by remaining silent. Tacitus provides a chilling description of the terror imposed by Domitian, when not just speaking candid words, but simply listening to them could be construed as a treasonous activity. "We gave a grand display of our submissiveness. Just as a previous age had experienced the ultimate in *libertas*, so we experienced the ultimate in *servitus* (slavery), when the inquisitions deprived us of the intercourse of speaking and even of listening."[120]

Despite the tactics of terror employed by Domitian, a few people dared to express concern for the loss of *libertas*. In consequence, they were punished for posing a threat to Domitian's regime. Around 89 CE and perhaps again in 93, philosophers were expelled from Rome.[121] In 93 CE, Fannia and Arria Y were prosecuted, along with five other people (henceforth designated as "the Seven") from the network of friends that had developed at least as early as Nero's regime.[122] Apparently, the family and friends of Thrasea Paetus had sustained over several decades an interest in restoring the dignity of the senatorial class. Along with Fannia and Arria Y, these were the people who Pliny tells us were prosecuted in 93.

Junius Arulenus Rusticus was the tribune who, in 66 CE, had offered to veto the Senate's death sentence against Thrasea Paetus. He had been selected to the office of praetor for 69, apparently having taken to heart Thrasea's advice to continue his political career. After a long period without public office, he was selected to the office of consul for 92 CE.[123]

Junius Mauricus was the brother of Arulenus Rusticus (see Genealogy Chart 2) and the man who in 70 CE had asked to have the imperial diaries put at the disposal of the senate so that it could discover who Nero's informers were.[124]

Herennius Senecio was a native of Baetica (southern Spain). He had, at an unknown date, served in the office of quaestor and thus gained a seat in the Senate, but did not again serve in public office. His reluctance to do so had offended Domitian.[125]

Helvidius Priscus II was the son of Fannia's husband, Helvidius I (Helvidius Priscus). He was a suffect consul in the 80s CE.[126]

Gratilla was probably the wife of Junius Arulenus Rusticus.[127]

The accusations against "the Seven" seem to have involved charges of participation in treasonous activities (*maiestas*).[128] However, none of our sources record that they were charged specifically with plotting to overthrow or assassinate Domitian. One of the charges seems to have been the promulgation of literature that might seem hostile to the imperial regime because it eulogized earlier critics. Junius Rusticus Arulenus was charged with writing a laudatory biography of Arria Y's husband, Thrasea Paetus, in which he called him a very morally upright man. Herennius Senecio was similarly charged with writing a biography of Fannia's husband, Helvidius I.[129] Tacitus reports that these activities were in themselves capital offences, and that destruction was mandated not just for the authors of the biographies, but even for their books, which were ordered to be burned in the

Forum.[130] We are also informed by Dio that Herennius was cited for not campaigning for a public office beyond the quaestorship.[131] As was the case with
Thrasea almost three decades earlier, refusal to participate in the government
could be construed as an affront to the emperor and to the Senate, and thus a
form of treason.[132] Herennius may also have angered Domitian because of his
feud with Marcus Aquilius Regulus, who had been an informer under Nero and
was apparently a supporter of Domitian[133], and because he had sought to defend
a man at whom Domitian was angry.[134] Non-participation in public office
could not have been the charge against Helvidius II because he had held
the consulship in the 80s. However, he was accused of using the characters in a
farce he had composed for the stage to criticize Domitian's divorce from his
wife.[135] We have no information about the charges against Junius Mauricus.

Fannia was charged with abetting Herennius in his writing of the biography of
her husband, Helvidius I. In fact, at the trial, he admitted that he had written it
at her request (Pliny, *Letter* 7.19.5). (Did this admission indicate a lack of gallantry
on his part?) Fannia confirmed that his statement was true and, moreover, that
she had lent him her husband's diaries (*commentarii*). However, when the prosecutor asked whether her mother knew of this activity, she replied with a curt
"No." Despite Fannia's attempt to establish her mother's innocence, both women,
and Gratilla as well, were convicted and sentenced to banishment.[136] Of the
men, Arulenus, Herennius, and Helvidius II received death sentences. Junius
Mauricus, like the women, received a sentence of banishment. We are not told
whether the men who received the death sentence preempted execution by committing suicide and, if so, whether they had an audience for a final and courageous
demonstration of defiance.

Although it is tempting to surmise that Domitian had long harbored a dislike of
this group of people who had connections to Thrasea Paetus and to Helvidius I,
the man who had harassed his father, Vespasian, several of them seem to have
done well under his regime. Helvidius II, as already noted, reached the consulship
in the 80s. Arulenus Rusticus was consul in 92, just a year before his prosecution.
Domitian had apparently been willing to endure their criticisms during the first
decade of his reign without retaliation. Or, perhaps "the Seven" and their friends
had at first been circumspect in their comments. However, the sedition in 89 had
made Domitian intolerant of any criticism, and, in turn, his harsh responses may
have generated even more hostility toward him. Pliny relates that, at about the
same time as the prosecutions of 93, there was an expulsion of philosophers from
Rome (*Letter* 3.11.2).[137] However, we don't know what the charges were or who
was defined as a "philosopher." There are reasons to speculate that "the Seven"
prosecuted in 93 may have been targeted, at least in part, because of their philosophic beliefs. Dio relates that Arulenus Rusticus was sentenced to death
because he studied philosophy and that other philosophers were banished at the
same time.[138] Marcus Aquilius Regulus, who participated in the prosecution of
Arulenus Rusticus, called him "an ape of the Stoics" (and spoke abusively of
Herennius Senecio).[139] A friendship between Arulenus Rusticus and the Stoic
philosopher, Musonius Rufus, had developed years earlier, in 69 CE.[140] It seems

very likely that Arulenus and the others in his circle had a strong interest in Stoicism and may have aimed, as did Thrasea, to incorporate Stoic teachings into their personal lives. It is less certain, however, that they were victims of a campaign to suppress philosophy per se. Their dislike of Domitian and their anger at his repressive practices were not by any means exclusive to adherents of Stoicism, although the Stoics may have been more overt and vociferous than most other complainants. Their criticisms of the imperial system, moreover, and desire for *libertas* were grounded in a political ideology that again was not exclusively Stoic, even if the Stoics at the time may have been among its most persistent and annoying advocates. The Seven prosecuted in 93 had angered Domitian not because they were Stoics, but because their refusal to endorse his notion of the proper relationship between an emperor and his subjects seemed to him to threaten the stability of his regime.

The trial of the Seven had taken place in the Senate, whose members served as jurymen and judges. Tacitus later blamed all the senators, including himself, for complicity in the conviction and punishment of the Seven. "Our own hands dragged Helvidius into prison, the wretched spectacle of Mauricus and Rusticus defiled us, and Senecio stained us with his innocent blood."[141] Although each senator did not literally lay hands on Helvidius II, nor become stained with the blood of Herennius Senecio, Tacitus imputes to them all the responsibility for the death sentences and banishments.[142]

Pliny's relationships with the Seven

Pliny, who, like Tacitus, was a young senator at this time and undoubtedly participated in the senate meetings at which the Seven were condemned, did not, like Tacitus, admit blame. Instead, he wrote and published a letter (*Letter* 3.11) in which he implies that he made valiant efforts to aid the people prosecuted in 93 CE. He omits, however, any specifics about his efforts, and also about his conduct at the Senate trial at which the Seven were convicted. He asserts that he was a friend of all seven of the defendants (*Letter* 3.11.3), but he never states explicitly how or when the friendships began. In the years immediately following Domitian's death, when the next emperors – Nerva (96 to 98) and Trajan (98 to 117) – allowed more freedom of expression, Pliny and his fellow senators were eager to advertise that they had not collaborated with Domitian and to insist that those who had collaborated should be punished. Pliny informs us that he brought charges against Publicius Certus (*Letter* 9.13) and also considered indicting Aquilius Regulus (*Letter* 1.5) for their roles in the prosecution of the Seven.[143] In addition, he announced that he had published the speeches in vindication of Helvidius II that he had composed for the trial of Publicius Certus (*Letters* 4.21.3 and 9.13.1). As his justification for bringing Publicius to trial, Pliny writes: "Once Domitian was dead, I deliberated with myself and decided that this was an important and glorious opportunity to attack the guilty, avenge the injured, and advance myself" (*Letter* 9.13.2). Pliny is not the least bit embarrassed to announce that one of his motivations was self-promotion.

Another method of convincing his contemporaries and posterity that his sympathies had always lain with the opponents of Domitian was to publish letters (though after the death of that emperor) in which he recorded the assistance he had offered Domitian's victims. In *Letter* 3.11, moreover, he draws attention to the fact that he, though at great peril to himself (he is careful to note), provided help to Artemidorus, one of the philosophers expelled from the city by Domitian in 93 CE. Artemidorus was the son-in-law of the notable Stoic philosopher, Gaius Musonius Rufus (who had himself been expelled by both Nero and Vespasian).[144] Pliny asserts that he loved Musonius Rufus, and that his friendship with Artemidorus stretched back over ten years (*Letter* 3.11.5). By mentioning his friendships with these two men, Pliny is, in effect, advertising his credentials as a long-standing associate of people who were prominent members of the Stoic community.[145] With regard to his claims that he had been a friend of the Seven who were prosecuted in 93 CE, we may wonder whether, in the post-Domitianic period, Pliny exaggerated the closeness of his relationships with the Seven, or perhaps cultivated them more assiduously in order to shine a favorable light upon himself.

It is instructive to assess how Pliny characterizes his associations with the Seven. About Fannia and Arria Y, Pliny writes: "I cherished and loved them both" (*Letter* 7.19.10; cf. *Letter* 9.13.3). About Helvidius II, Fannia's stepson, he remarks, after Helvidius II's death, that he loved him most steadfastly and enjoyed a friendship with him, at least as much as friendship was possible with someone who, through fear of the times, concealed his famous name and equally famous virtues by withdrawing from the public eye (*Letter* 9.13.3). Helvidius II's "withdrawing" must have occurred in the late 80s or perhaps the early 90s because, until the mid-80s, he was selected for several public offices, including the prestigious consulship. The comments which Pliny makes about his relationship with Fannia and Arria Y lead the reader to believe that he had known them well over a long period of time. He may have become acquainted with Helvidius II in the Senate in the late 80s, which was when Pliny began his political career, but was also the period when Helvidius II was "withdrawing." However, if their friendship did not blossom until after Helvidius II had decided to seclude himself from the public arena, it is possible that Pliny's association with the entire family was still quite recent at the time of the prosecutions in 93. I have suggested previously that Pliny may have acted generously toward the families of the Seven in the post-Domitianic period, and then published letters about his generosity in order to construct a positive image of himself. It is also possible that Fannia was happy to engage Pliny in a friendship because she found him useful to her goals. It was, after all, she who passed on to Pliny the tales about the courage of her grandmother, Arria the Elder. She may well have anticipated that he would publish a letter reporting these tales. Pliny had written to Tacitus, "I predict that your histories will be immortal, and therefore I am all the more eager (I freely admit) to be included in them" (*Letter* 7.33.1). Perhaps Fannia saw in Pliny (as Pliny saw in Tacitus) an opportunity to ensure that the stories of her family would receive wide publicity.

We know more about the nature and length of the relationship between Pliny and the Junius brothers. Shortly after his return in 97 CE from the exile imposed by Domitian, Junius Mauricus had asked Pliny to help him arrange a marriage for his niece, the daughter of Junius Arulenus Rusticus, who had been sentenced to death in 93 CE. In *Letter* 1.14.1, Pliny replies that he is happy to accept this task because he had looked up to and loved Arulenus, who had supported him with advice when he was a young man and, by his praise, made Pliny become worthy of praise. In *Letter* 1.14.4, he adds that he was influenced and educated as a young man by both the Junius brothers. The relationship between Pliny and the Junius brothers, who were several decades older than Pliny and seem to have served as mentors when he was beginning his political career, was apparently one of long-standing. In *Letter* 2.18, where Pliny replies to Mauricus' request to recommend a teacher for Arulenus' children, who had been orphaned by his death, he again expresses his eagerness to repay the early kindness of the brothers toward him: "I owe to you and to the memory of your brother this loyalty (*fides*) and devotion (*studium*) (*Letter* 2.18.4).[146] At an unknown date, but obviously before his death in 93 CE, Arulenus had asked Pliny to serve as counsel for a woman named Arrionilla in a court case where Aquilius Regulus was a prosecutor (*Letter* 1.5.5). Arrionilla is otherwise unknown to us, but her name tantalizingly suggests that she was related to Arria.[147] Of course, the connection between Thrasea's (and Fannia's) family and the Junii had existed for several decades, at least back to the day in 66 CE when Arulenus Rusticus offered to interpose his tribunicial veto to prevent the condemnation of Thrasea Paetus. Members of the families were also connected by a shared interest in Stoicism and a distaste for tyrannical emperors. In addition, there appears to have been a kin relationship between the two families, which is discussed later. Pliny may have been introduced to Thrasea's family by the Junii when he was still a young man, or at a later date, when he had become a successful counsel and was asked to defend Arrionilla.

We don't know how Herennius Senecio, who was a native of Spain, had become connected with Fannia's family and the Junii, or when his friendship with Pliny began. By 90 CE, the two men were both senators and would therefore have been acquainted with one another. Their social interactions with mutual friends may have brought them closer together. Or, the friendship may not have developed until 93 CE, when the Senate appointed Pliny and Senecio to be advocates for the province of Baetica (southern Spain) in its suit against Baebius Massa on charges of extortion (*Letter* 7.33). In this case, however, the friendship would have been of brief duration, since Senecio was condemned to death just a few months later.

Fannia and the burning of books

Herennius Senecio received the death sentence for having written about the life of Fannia's husband, Helvidius I. Fannia received a sentence of relegation for having, as Senecio revealed, asked him to write the book and having given him her husband's diaries. Clearly the idea for this project to immortalize Helvidius I was generated and guided by Fannia. Despite Fannia's assertion at the trial that her mother had not been involved in the project, Arria Y also received a sentence of relegation. We do not know if Arria Y was punished for abetting the biography project (that is, the senatorial judges did not believe Fannia), or whether there were additional charges. At the time of the prosecutions and punishments of 93 CE, the Senate ordered Arulenus Rusticus' biography of Thrasea Paetus, and Herennius Senecio's biography of Helvidius I to be destroyed.[148] It is possible that they also ordered Helvidius I's diaries to be destroyed. Pliny remarks that this senatorial order for book-burning was motivated by exigency and the fear prevalent at the time (*Letter* 7.19.6). Fannia, however, did not destroy the biographies of her father and husband. She saved them (and presumably also the diaries) and, as Pliny elegantly describes the situation, she took into exile the cause of her exile (*Letter* 7.19.6). Her courage in disobeying the Senate order, at a time when she was most vulnerable, reveals her determination to preserve the history of her family.

Fannia's rescue of books documenting events of the first century CE was not a unique occurrence. In 25 CE, during the reign of Tiberius, Aulus Cremutius Cordus was put on trial on charges relating to a book he had written many years earlier about the reign of Augustus, a book which had been read by Augustus himself.[149] One charge, which Tacitus calls "new and previously unheard of," was that Cremutius had praised Brutus and described Cassius as the "last of the Romans."[150] Other charges were that Cremutius had criticized the Senate and, although not maligning Caesar and Augustus, had not shown them sufficient respect. Since Augustus had apparently not disapproved of the book, Tiberius' perception that it was treasonous may be attributed to a personal hostility toward Cremutius and/or a desire to suppress any material which depicted Caesar's assassins favorably. After speaking in his own defense in the Senate, Cremutius went home and committed suicide by starvation. The Stoic Seneca tells us that Cremutius considered death to be an escape from slavery – that is, from an intolerable subservience to Tiberius.[151] After his death, the Senate ordered his books to be burned. However, his daughter, Marcia, preserved copies and had them published after the death of Tiberius.[152]

Writing about 85 years after the event, Tacitus created for Cremutius a very eloquent speech in his own defense at his trial in the Senate.[153] In the speech, Cremutius points out that authors before him had written positively about Brutus and Cassius, and even insulted Caesar and Augustus, yet not incurred accusations of treason. The words which Tacitus assigns to Cremutius reveal the historian's interest in portraying events of the imperial period as a struggle to regain *libertas*. In addition, Tacitus calls attention to the value of the work of historians, like himself and Cremutius.[154] He scoffs at the foolishness of believing that someone in power can destroy memories and deprive future generations of information. On the contrary, remarks Tacitus, the authority of great writers increases if they are punished, with the result that tyrants produce only shame for themselves and glory for those they persecute.[155] Tacitus did not, however, comment on the significance of the efforts of the people who rescued Cremutius' work from the flames. Writing about 40 CE, much closer to the time of the Cremutius trial, Seneca wrote an essay to Cremutius' daughter, Marcia, who had saved his work from oblivion: *Consolatio ad Marciam*. The purpose of the essay was to persuade Marcia to desist from her excessive mourning for her dead son. One of the first arguments that Seneca presents is that grief destroys, rather than preserves, the memory of a person. Seneca reminds Marcia that, when her father died, rather than burying herself in grief, she took an active and courageous role in making sure that his books survived. She therefore, Seneca assures her, did an illustrious service to her father, for whom she secured a form of immortality, and to future generations, who would have a record of the achievements of Rome's outstanding ancestors and, just as importantly, would find in her father an *exemplum* of a true Roman and of a free man.[156] By his suicide, Cremutius had traded his mortal life for the enduring glory of a man who refused to accept the constraints imposed by a tyrant. In turn, historians would grant his self-sacrifice an abiding place in the annals of Rome. Moreover, because Marcia had ensured that his books would be available to future generations, she ensured that future generations would become acquainted not just with a record of his suicide, but also with the genius of his mind, as it was displayed in his writing. Seneca asserts that Cremutius would live forever in two senses: the memory of his deed and the genius of his writing. Pliny, writing to Tacitus about his (Pliny's) uncle, expressed a similar sentiment: "I consider those men blessed to whom the gods have granted the gift either to do something worth writing about or to write something worth reading. But most blessed are those to whom both have been granted" (*Letter* 6.16.3).

Like Marcia, Fannia recognized the value of historical records, both those diaries that her husband had kept, and those biographies written by men like Herennius Senecio and Arulenus Rusticus. Unlike the men in their families, the women could not aspire to perform public deeds that were "worth writing about" or "to write something worth reading." Although they might, if given a chance, have proved to be talented writers, their society considered literary pursuits, as well as public affairs, to be activities suitable only for men. Women could, however, undertake projects that enhanced the accomplishments of the men in their families. Both Fannia and Marcia were clever enough and educated enough to realize that writing endowed men with both the immortality of having one's own words live on in published work and the immortality of having a story about oneself written by others. Women, though denied the opportunity to gain lasting renown as writers, might strive to be remembered for engaging in dangerous activities that supported male ambitions. Both Fannia and Marcia had the courage to preserve written works when it was perilous to do so. When the frightened senators voted to burn books that offended the emperor, Fannia refused to obey. It is likely that Fannia (whose father was an acquaintance, perhaps even a friend of Seneca) was familiar with Seneca's essay to Marcia and its praise of Marcia's services to her father and to her fellow Romans. The essay may have inspired Fannia's understanding of the role which she could play in exalting her family. Fannia, however, extended her activities well beyond the range of Marcia's. She actively solicited a biography from Herennius Senecio (and may also have encouraged Pliny to write about her family). When put on trial, she expressed no fear as she defiantly acknowledged that she had requested the biography and aided in its composition (*Letter* 7.19.5).

For her activities in promoting literature by and about her family members, literature apparently considered treasonous by the imperial court, Fannia (and her mother, Arria Y) received a sentence of banishment.[157] We do not know where the two widows spent their exile or whether they spent it together. For Fannia, this was her third banishment, though probably the first time that it was her own activity, rather than her husband's, that had led to exile. (We cannot be certain that Fannia was not also charged and punished, along with her husband, during his prosecution in the early 70s. However, there are no reports that accusations were made against her at that time.) The strain which exile placed on families has already been discussed. In *Letters* 3.11.3 and 7.19.4, Pliny states that the women were relegated, which usually meant that the condemned person's property was not confiscated. In *Letter* 7.19.6, however, Pliny states that Fannia's possessions had in fact been confiscated (*publicatis bonis*). If this were true, we do not know what funds were available to Fannia during her period of banishment. (Presumably her property was restored to her after the death of Domitian, when she was allowed to return to Rome.) Nor do we know who in Rome managed the affairs of the mother and daughter during their absence, and who undertook the important task of lobbying for their return. Fannia did not have siblings or children of her own. Her stepson, Helvidius II, had been executed at the time of her relegation. He left behind a wife, Anteia, and three children, two daughters and a son. However, these children were very young in 93 CE and cannot have been of much assistance to Fannia. Although Pliny was eager for the world to know that he was a friend of Fannia and Arria Y, he left no record of any specific assistance he gave them during their time in exile.

We will return to Fannia shortly, but will look now at the other women in the families of the Seven.

Anteia

Following the assassination of Domitian in September of 96, Fannia and Arria Y returned to Rome, probably in early 97 CE. At this time, Anteia, the widow of Fannia's stepson, Helvidius II, was building a new life for herself (*Letter* 9.13.5). We know little about Anteia. She may have been a daughter or granddaughter of Publius Anteius Rufus, a senator who had served as governor of Dalmatia and Syria, and who was forced to suicide in 66 CE, which was also the year of Thrasea's suicide and Helvidius I's first banishment.[158] Like Thrasea, Anteius had incurred the anger of Nero, but we have no information about whether the two men were friends. It is possible, however, that the marriage of Anteia and Helvidius II was arranged on the basis of family ties, and that her family was sympathetic to the criticisms of the imperial system voiced by Thrasea and Helvidius I. Rogers suggests that Anteia was also related to two other Anteii – one executed by Caligula, and the other by bodyguards of Caligula.[159] Raepsaet-Charlier advances a hypothesis that Anteia may also have been distantly related by marriage to Corellia Hispulla, a friend of Pliny's who will be discussed in Chapter 4.[160] We cannot be certain that Anteia was the mother of Helvidius' three children (that is, that he did not have a previous wife). However, his two daughters were described by Pliny as being in the flower of youth in about 105 CE (*Letter* 4.21.2), which would mean that they were born about 90 CE – that is, just a few years before their father's death. If this supposition is correct, it is likely that Anteia was their mother. We do not know if Anteia shared her husband's political views. The fact that she was not prosecuted along with Fannia, Arria Y, and Gratilla in 93 CE suggests that, even if she did, she may have been cautious about expressing her opinions. Perhaps she felt that the mother of young children needed to be circumspect.

Anteia did not commit suicide when her husband was condemned to death in 93 CE, nor did she aspire to the role of *univira*. In compliance with the Julian laws, Anteia apparently remarried after the death of Helvidius II. I use the word "apparently" because our only clue about her remarriage is Pliny's comment that the mother and stepfather of Helvidius II's daughter had chosen Gaius Julius Cornutus Tertullus to be the guardian for her (*Letter* 9.13.16). The identity of Anteia's second husband, however, is unknown. Nor do we know whether the three children of Helvidius II joined Anteia in her new household. Traditionally children belonged to the family of the father, and it was therefore the duty of the paternal family to care for them when their father died. However, Helvidius II seems not to have had any close agnates. (Fannia and Arria Y were step-relatives.) His children may thus have continued to be cared for by their mother, in the home of a stepfather. Both the daughters, and the son also if he were still underage, were required to have guardians.

We do not know the basis of the choice of Cornutus Tertullus as guardian (*tutor*) for one of the daughters (or who the *tutor* for the other daughter was). The fact that he was appointed only to one daughter may indicate that the responsibilities of a *tutor* could be a burden. Or, perhaps families did not want the same person to oversee more than one share of what was essentially the family property. Although guardians were often agnates of the child, this type of kinship was not required in the imperial period.[161] In any case, it is not clear that there were any adult male agnates of Helvidius II to be asked. Tertullus may therefore have been not a relative, but a family friend. He was also a friend of Pliny who declares in *Letters* 5.14.3 and 4, written about 105 CE, that he has come to know Tertullus well through long personal experience and that they enjoy a close bond built on the friendships they share with both men and women who are exemplary in their behavior.[162] Pliny may be referring to the families of the Seven (and, once again, advertising, in the post-Domitianic period, his friendship with them). We do not know how far back his personal relationship with Tertullus, who was about 15 years older than Pliny, may have extended.

Tertullus proved to be a loyal family friend not only to Anteia, but also to Arria Y and Fannia, on whose behalf he spoke at a Senate hearing in 97 CE, which is discussed later. The pattern of his public career implies that he may have had reason to be as unhappy with Domitian as was Helvidius II's family. Tertullus had been selected for a praetorship under Vespasian, but served in no public office under Domitian. Perhaps his political career had been arrested by the emperor, or perhaps he had voluntarily withdrawn from public life because of a dislike of Domitian's actions. In any case, after Domitian's death, he was again selected to several prestigious posts, including the prefecture of the treasury of Saturn for 98 to 100 CE and the suffect consulship of 100 CE, in both of which positions he served alongside Pliny. In the post-Domitianic period, Pliny was pleased to be able to claim a friendship with a foe of Domitian.

Vengeance for Anteia, Arria Y, and Fannia

Although Anteia was apparently settled in a new household when Fannia and Arria Y returned to Rome in 97 CE, she did not sever her ties to Helvidius II's stepfamily or lose interest in honoring his memory. Thus, when Pliny decided to demand justice for the men condemned to death in 93 CE, he approached Anteia. Before requesting a hearing in the Senate, which was, after all, the same group that had condemned the Seven, and whose members might therefore be reluctant to admit a miscarriage of justice, Pliny considered it prudent to consult with the families of the victims.[163] He needed to ascertain the commitment of the family and the level of support it could muster among the senators. The fact that he mentions speaking only with the women of Helvidius II's family suggests that there were no adult male relatives of Helvidius II to be consulted. Pliny also knew that his case would be stronger if he could present himself to the Senate as the representative of grieving family members, especially a widow, orphans, and an aging stepmother.

Roman law barred women from bringing forward suits in criminal cases.[164] Thus the women of Helvidius II's family would have required the services of a senatorial rank man to request a hearing before the Senate, which, in the imperial period, served as a criminal court. Pliny had contemplated prosecuting Aquilius Regulus, who had assisted in the conviction of Junius Arulenus Rusticus and rejoiced in his death (*Letter* 1.5.2).[165] He waited, however, to consult with Arulenus' brother, Junius Mauricus, when he, like Fannia and Arria Y, returned from exile (*Letters* 1.5.10 and 15). Since Pliny never records that such a prosecution subsequently took place, perhaps we can surmise that Mauricus advised Pliny against it, arguing that Regulus was a wealthy man and a faction leader supported by many and feared by more (*Letter* 1.5.15). Pliny's target, in his efforts to avenge Helvidius II, was Publicius Certus, one of the men who had encouraged the accusations in the Senate against Helvidius II. Pliny leaves obscure, however, what charges he brought against Certus.[166] He describes Certus' conduct as having been particularly egregious, even during a period of atrocious deeds (*Letter* 9.13.2). For example, Certus, a senator, had the audacity to attack Helvidius II, another senator, right in the Senate itself.[167] Bauman suggests that Pliny may have accused Certus of treason on the grounds that, by his violent behavior, he had breached his duty as a senator toward another senator.[168] Pliny maintains that he was incited to demand a hearing not so much because of his personal obligations to his friends, but rather because of public justice, the outrageousness of the conduct, and a concern about precedent (*Letter* 9.13.3). Nonetheless, although he discounted the motivating factor of personal obligations, he was careful to consult with family members.

Although Pliny identifies himself in his letters as a good friend of Fannia, he consulted first with Anteia, perhaps because she was the wife of Helvidius II and the mother of his children. He sent her a message, asking her to come to his home (*Letter* 9.13.4). It seems unusual to request that the person to be consulted come to one's own home. One would have expected Pliny to undertake the inconvenience of traveling through the city. It may have been even more unusual if the person to be consulted was a woman. Pliny explained, however, that his wife had recently died and he was confined to his home in accordance with rituals of mourning.[169] Although Anteia was now involved in a new marriage, she accepted Pliny's invitation, indicating that she remained concerned about the reputation of her previous husband. We do not know the circumstances of the meeting, and in particular whether Anteia was accompanied to Pliny's home by someone who served as an escort and/or an advisor, but nothing in Pliny's narration of events in *Letter* 9.13 suggests that it was improper for him to extend, or for her to accept the invitation. At the meeting, Pliny told Anteia that he had decided not to allow Helvidius II to remain unavenged. He asked her to convey this information to Arria and Fannia and to consult with them about whether they wished to be part of this action. He assured her that he did not need an associate, but he was not so desirous of his own glory as to begrudge them a share in it.

Anteia conveyed the message to the two women, and, without delay, they responded affirmatively. Pliny's narration of the events implies that the women had been unaware until that moment that Pliny had been planning to avenge Helvidius II's death. That scenario seems unlikely, however. We know that Pliny had been in contact with Arria Y and Fannia during their exile because, in *Letter* 7.19.10, he boasts that he was their solace during their relegation (and their avenger when they returned). It is more probable that they had known about Pliny's intentions for some time. Indeed, it is even conceivable that Fannia had planted the idea in Pliny's mind and encouraged its implementation. However, in recounting the story of the prosecution of Publicius Certus, it served Pliny's self-promotional interests to depict his own role as that of the person who initiated and developed the plan.

We do not know the precise nature of the charges that Pliny made against Publicius Certus at the Senate meeting which took place just a couple of days after he had obtained the approval of the women to pursue the case. Nor do we know what role Fannia, Arria Y, and Anteia played or expected to play in the prosecution. Women were not permitted to act as prosecutors, except in a few exceptional circumstances, but the women of Helvidius II's family may have appeared or wished to appear before the Senate as witnesses, or the evidence they provided may have been presented by Pliny. He reports that, at one point during the Senate meeting, one senator, Avidius Quietus, declared that it was very unjust to refuse a hearing to the complaints of aggrieved parties, and that therefore Arria's and Fannia's right of complaint should not be denied. A person's rank was not the issue, he added, but rather what case s/he had (*Letter* 9.13.15). Avidius Quietus' connections with the family went back a long way. And like Cornutus Tertullus (whom Anteia had chosen as guardian for one of Helvidius

II's daughters), his loyalty could be counted on. He had been a friend of Arria Y's husband, Thrasea Paetus (*Letter* 6.29.1) and apparently remained concerned about his descendants.[170] It is curious that Anteia, who had certainly been harmed by the death of her husband, is not mentioned as one of the aggrieved parties. The omission of her name may simply be a slip by Pliny or Avidius Quietus. Or perhaps she had withdrawn her support from Pliny's case. It is possible that her new husband persuaded her that it was dangerous to antagonize a man protected by so much influence and so many friends (*Letter* 9.13.11).

Pliny provides no information about what prompted Avidius to argue that Arria Y's and Fannia's right of complaint should not be denied. However, his comment seems to be a retort to a proposal that the Senate need not hear this case because the women, not being senators, had no standing in that body. After Avidius spoke, Cornutus Tertullus, the man who had been appointed as guardian to one of the daughters of Helvidius II, announced that he was conveying the very modest wish of Arria Y and Fannia. (Again, Anteia's name is absent.) They were content to remind the Senate of the bloodstained obsequiousness of Publicius Certus and to ask that, if no penalty were imposed for his very blatantly disgraceful deed, he at least be branded with an expression of censure (*Letter* 9.13.16). Cornutus's remark implies that he was speaking on behalf of the women – that is, that they were not expecting to plead their own case. We can do no more than speculate on whether Pliny had intended to present them as witnesses to his case.

At the Senate meeting, several senators expressed to Pliny their dismay that he wanted to reopen old wounds. They cried out: "Let those of us who survived (Domitian's reign) now be safe and secure" (*Letter* 9.13.8). They warned Pliny that he would be in danger if he persisted in this attack on such a powerful man. Even Bittius Proculus, the stepfather of Pliny's recently deceased wife, defended Publicius Certus (whose colleague he now was in the prefecture of the treasury of Saturn) (*Letter* 9.13.13). Pliny eagerly reveals to his readers his brave response to the warnings: he was willing to pay the penalty for a very honorable deed as long as he punished a very shameful one (*Letter* 9.13.12). Despite the initial opposition to Pliny's plan, his speech was, he reports, well-received and persuasive. Almost every senator heaped praise on him for being concerned about the public good, even at the risk of making personal enemies.

It is unclear, however, what action Pliny proposed or what the result of the Senate hearing was. Pliny states that Certus was punished by not being selected to the consulship of 98 CE and by having his term as prefect of the treasury of Saturn terminated (along with that of Bittius Proculus, Pliny's stepfather-in-law) (*Letter* 9.13.23). (It is notable that Pliny and Cornutus Tertullus assumed these very positions in 98.) Certus died in 98 CE, shortly after Pliny published his speech. We do not know, however, whether his term as prefect had been terminated or had naturally expired, or whether his failure to be selected for the consulship was indeed a result of Pliny's prosecution. Perhaps his illness, which led to his death, was a factor in his withdrawal from public office. In any case, if Helvidius II's family and friends had hoped for the imposition of a severe penalty, they were disappointed. Fannia and Arria Y had conveyed, through their spokesman, Cornutus Tertullus, the message that an expression of censure was the minimum punishment they wanted. Pliny, however, makes no mention of any formal expression of censure. He admits, in fact, that the emperor, Nerva, declined to make a response to the proceedings – that is, he did not allow an official decision in the case (*Letter* 9.13.22).[171] In Pliny's opinion, however, he had proved himself to be the champion of the women, the aggressive avenger of Helvidius II, and the courageous advocate of justice.[172] The women undoubtedly had hoped for a more decisive judgment against Certus and an explicit admission by the senators that their actions under Domitian had been cowardly. Nonetheless, they would have been pleased that Pliny had brought to public attention the fates of Helvidius II and, by extension, of Herennius Senecio and Arulenus Rusticus, and had, by the publication of his speech, preserved a record of the injustice done to their family.

Fannia (con.)

Pliny provides no information about Fannia's activities in the ten year period between the Senate hearing of 97 CE and the composition of *Letter* 7.19, about 107. In this letter, he discloses that Arria Y is deceased, and that he is very concerned about Fannia's ill health. It is notable that he opens his letter with phrasing which, once again, is designed to highlight both his close relationship with Fannia and his professed solicitude as a friend. *Angit me Fanniae valetudo*. "It distresses me, this ill health of Fannia."[173] The use of "me" is emphatic.

Fannia had contracted an illness while she was dutifully nursing Junia, one of the Vestal Virgins. She had first undertaken this task voluntarily, because she was a relative of Junia, but later she was requested to do so by the Pontiffs (priests of the Roman religion). Pliny explains that, when Vestal Virgins were forced to leave the compound of Vesta (which was in the Forum) because of illness, they were remanded to the care of other women.[174]

Junia, the Vestal Virgin

We do not know what the kinship was between Fannia and the Vestal Virgin, Junia, whom she nursed. (This Junia will henceforth be identified as Junia VV.) The word which Pliny uses to represent this kinship is *adfinis*, which does not denote a specific family relationship, although it frequently refers to a relative by marriage. Junia VV's name suggests that she may have been related by blood to the Junius brothers who were prosecuted in 93 CE along with Fannia. However, the connection is not incontrovertible; there were other Junius families. We cannot determine even an approximate age for Junia VV. Vestal Virgins, who were the priestesses of Vesta, the goddess of the hearth fire, were selected for service at a very young age, when they were between six and ten years old. They were expected to serve for a period of 30 years. At the end of that period, they were free to leave the unit and even marry if they wished. Some Vestal

Virgins, however, remained within the priesthood. It would have been daunting for a woman who had been separated from her family at so young an age, and had enjoyed the privileges and endured the restrictions of being a Vestal Virgin, to leave the compound and adjust to quite a different life. Tacitus reports that a Vestal Virgin named Occia served, with the utmost moral purity, for 57 years.[175] Thus, at the time of the composition of *Letter* 7.19, about 107 CE, Junia VV may have been anywhere from six to sixty or more years old. Sherwin-White proposes that she was a sister of Junius Arulenus Rusticus and Junius Mauricus.[176] This is certainly possible. However, she might also have been a daughter of one of these men. Or, as noted earlier, she may not have been related to them at all. Although it is tantalizing to posit a kinship between Junia VV and Fannia which would also connect Fannia and the Helvidii by blood or marriage to the Junius brothers, who so closely shared their fates, we have no conclusive evidence.

The children of Arulenus Rusticus

Pliny does not provide information about a wife or children for Junius Mauricus, who had been sentenced to relegation at the time that his brother, Junius Arulenus Rusticus, had been sentenced to death. Mauricus seems to have taken over the care of his brother's children after Rusticus' death in 93 CE. In *Letter* 2.18.4, Pliny praises Mauricus for his diligent care of these children, and adds: "I would call them your children except that you already love them more." The statement is obscure. Does it mean that Mauricus loved his brother's children more than his own, or that he loved them as if they were his own ("you could not love them more if they were your own")? I suspect that the latter interpretation is the correct one. If Mauricus had a wife and children, it would be odd that Pliny never refers to them.

We know that Mauricus' brother, Arulenus Rusticus, had at least two sons and at least one daughter (presumably named Junia, the feminine form of her father's family name, Junius). (See Genealogy Chart 2.) Although Rusticus was well into his 60s at the time of his death, his children were probably not yet in their teens. From Pliny's letters, we learn that, around 97 or 98 CE, the sons were still of school age (*Letter* 2.18), and a daughter was not yet married (*Letter* 1.14). Their youth implies that there was a considerable age gap between Arulenus and his wife, Gratilla, and that she therefore may not have been his first wife.[177] It is possible that Junia VV was a second daughter of Rusticus. If so, since, as noted earlier, it is impossible to determine her age, she may have been a daughter with Gratilla or with a previous wife.

Upon Arulenus' death, Junius Mauricus, being his closest agnate, would have been expected to assume the task of looking after the interests of his young children. Mauricus, however, was banished from Rome at the same time that the execution of Arulenus was ordered. Their mother, Gratilla, was also relegated in 93 CE. We do not know who looked after the children in their absence. However, when their paternal uncle, Mauricus, returned to Rome in 97, he likely took them into his household. In addition to providing his brother's children with a home and becoming a surrogate father, Mauricus was probably appointed official guardian for one or more of them. He may also have officially adopted one or more of them. He made major decisions about their futures, asking Pliny to recommend an instructor for Arulenus' sons (*Letter* 2.18) and a husband for a daughter (*Letter* 1.14).

Gratilla

We do not know the fate of Gratilla. We do not know on what charges she was convicted in 93 CE, where or with whom she spent her banishment, or whether she saw her children during the more than three years that she was banned from Rome. We do not even know if she survived the period of exile. Perhaps she died in exile. If she had taken her own life at the time her husband died, surely Pliny would have recorded it. Still, he makes no mention of her having returned to Rome when Fannia and Arria Y did, of joining in the prosecution of Publicius Certus, or of participating in decisions about her children. Her name is not brought up in *Letter* 1.14, Pliny's letter about the choice of a husband for her daughter, although it was customary for mothers to play a role in the selection of spouses for their children. However, the absence of a reference to her in this letter is not conclusive proof that she was no longer playing a role in her children's lives. The letter is addressed specifically to Junius Mauricus and pertains to a request made by Mauricus. Perhaps Pliny felt no need to mention Gratilla. Moreover, if the widowed Gratilla did return to Rome in 97, she may have remarried and started a new family. If so, her children by Arulenus Rusticus would have acquired a stepfather and perhaps stepsiblings, but perhaps not lived in the same household with them. Gratilla would not necessarily have lost contact with Arulenus' children, but they probably lived in the household of their closest agnate, Junius Mauricus.

Junia the bride

When Junius Mauricus, after his return to Rome in 97 CE, asked Pliny to recommend a husband for his niece, Pliny was very happy to oblige. It would be his pleasure, Pliny states, to be on the lookout for a husband for Arulenus' daughter. "With good reason do you impose this task on me above all. You know how much I looked up to and loved that outstanding man. He supported me with his advice when I was a young man, and, by his praise, he made me become worthy of praise. There is no duty which you can delegate to me which is more important or more pleasing, none which can be more honorable for me to assume than to choose the young man by whom it is fitting that the grandchildren of Arulenus Rusticus are created" (*Letters* 1.14.1 and 2). Pliny's remarks imply that he was the only person whose advice was solicited. It is likely, however, that Mauricus requested recommendations from several people. Pliny used the occasion of Mauricus' request to write and publish a letter which advertises that his relationship with the Junius brothers has been close and long-standing. Mauricus may have solicited advice from Pliny not just because they were friends, but also, as Sherwin-White suggests, because Pliny, about 36 years old in 97, was acquainted with many elite (and therefore suitable) young men through his political and legal activities.[178] Mauricus, being older than Pliny and having been out of Rome for several years, would be less familiar with the available bachelor pool. Pliny might also have a better idea than Mauricus about how the conviction and execution of the girl's father might affect her marriage prospects. In addition to bearing the stigma of a condemned father, the girl might not have received an inheritance if Arulenus' property had been confiscated. Her financial position would be an important consideration for any man contemplating a marriage arrangement. Of particular interest would be the size of her dowry, to which perhaps her uncle Mauricus was contributing.[179] Pliny could make discreet inquiries about the dowry expectations of a prospective husband. His task might also include ascertaining whether, with the death of Domitian, people were no longer afraid of forming marriage alliances with Domitian's enemies, and might even welcome the connection in order to demonstrate their solidarity with those who suffered under Domitian.

Sherwin-White makes the intriguing suggestion that Mauricus may have hoped that Pliny would recommend himself as a bridegroom.[180] He was available. He reports in *Letter* 9.13.4 that his wife had died about the time that Fannia and Arria Y, and presumably Mauricus, had returned to Rome. The 20 year or so age gap between Pliny and Arulenus' daughter would not be considered problematic. Indeed, when he was in his 40s, Pliny married a teenage girl. In 97, however, newly widowed, he was content to recommend a husband, not to be one. Despite his claim to be in the debt of the Junii, he was apparently not willing to repay their many favors by marrying Arulenus' daughter.

The name of the daughter for whom a husband was being sought is never revealed in *Letter* 1.14. Since her father was a Junius, she would traditionally receive at birth the feminine form of the family name, Junia, and this is the name by which commentators refer to her. She will henceforth be identified as Junia B – that is, the Bride, to distinguish her from Junia VV, the Vestal Virgin. We have seen, however, in the cases of Arria Y (whose paternal family name was Caecina) and Fannia (whose paternal family name was Clodius) that daughters were not always known by their family names. Not only is the daughter not named in the letter, but also no information is given about her age, her character, or her interests. In the relatively long letter, there is merely one general reference which might be applied to her. While remarking on the good looks of the recommended young man, Pliny comments a bit apologetically that this point needed to be included because the good looks of a bridegroom are the reward, so to speak, for the chastity of girls (*Letter* 1.14.8). Pliny assumes, first, that girls in general are satisfied with their family's choice of a husband as long as the groom is handsome, and, second, that Junia B is just like any other nubile (and, by implication, silly) girl.

The reference to chastity may inform us that Junia B has not been previously married and is therefore in her mid-teens.[181] It was quite usual for girls to enter marriage when they were about 14 or 15 years old. The high rate of infant and child mortality, which has been mentioned in Chapter 1, meant that a couple would need to have several pregnancies if they hoped to have even one or two children survive to adulthood. Thus girls were married soon after they began to menstruate and were able to become pregnant. Another reason for placing girls in a marriage when they were in the early teens was to avoid the possibility of their becoming sexually active outside of a marriage. A bridegroom would insist that a bride be a virgin if she had never been married. (However, a man might prefer a woman who had previously been married and produced healthy children because she had proved herself fertile.) The fact that Pliny makes only a brief and oblique allusion to Junia B is evidence that he does not know her well, or perhaps at all, despite his frequent assertions of being a close friend of her father and uncle. Additional evidence is the fact that he omits her name, as if he is ignorant of whether she is familiarly called Junia or something else. Admittedly, the letter is addressed to Junia's uncle, who does not need to have his niece described to him. Nonetheless, Pliny's letter leaves us with the impression that the prospective bride played little or no role in the arrangement of the marriage.

It is not surprising that Junia's happiness and preferences are accorded little importance in Pliny's letter. Roman marriage arrangements were not "love matches." Families cared, of course, whether their members were happy, but marriages were not arranged on the basis of personal attraction. In any case, it is unlikely that Pliny knew the girl well enough to learn what qualities she wanted in a husband. Moreover, girls were expected to come to a marriage not with the dream of having their own wishes catered to, but with the commitment to adapt to the situation and to accommodate themselves to the needs and interests of their husbands. Many girls would have spent very little time before the wedding with the husband chosen for them by their parents (or, in Junia B's case, by a surrogate father; we cannot ascertain what, if any, role her mother Gratilla played in the selection process). Girls were raised to believe that they must trust their parents and accept that their parents' choice was in their best interest. Families, in turn, were expected to choose wisely. Seneca the Younger commented that "a man who marries his daughter to someone who is abusive or who has been divorced several times does not look after her well."[182] Nonetheless, it must have been a frightening situation for many teenage brides to be handed over to a man who was older, often much older, and who was like a stranger. Roman wedding celebrations included a ritual in which the bride was forcibly removed from her family by men in the groom's party.[183] Although the custom of the forcible removal was intended to be harmless, at many weddings the bride's fear and unwillingness to leave her family must have been quite real.[184] Seneca comments that "with regard to matrimony, you will recommend how a man should conduct himself with a wife whom he married as a virgin, and how he should conduct himself with a wife who previously experienced marriage to another man."[185] Presumably most families would want to find for their daughter a husband who would treat her kindly, but the major criteria for choice included the financial stability and good reputation of the groom's family and, among elite families, the groom's social standing and political prospects.[186] (The groom's family would have similar concerns about the bride's family; hence the difficulty perhaps of arranging a marriage for Arulenus' daughter while Domitian was still alive.)

The purpose of marriage was not to find happiness – although that may have happened – but to produce children and secure the perpetuation the family.[187] As Pliny states at the opening of *Letter* 1.14, his task is to "choose the young man by whom it is fitting that the grandchildren of Arulenus Rusticus be created." His observation later in the letter that the recommended bridegroom is handsome and has a healthy complexion is included not just for the interest of Junia. Good looks and good health were indications that the groom was virile and capable of begetting children.[188] In addition, Pliny may have been concerned not simply with finding someone to father grandchildren for Arulenus, but to father children who would possess the virtues and interests of Arulenus. In earlier generations, Caecina and Thrasea both seem to have placed a premium, when selecting husbands for their daughters, on the compatibility of the bridegroom with their own personal values and political philosophies. Caecina chose Thrasea as a husband for his daughter Arria Y, and Thrasea chose Helvidius Priscus as a husband for his daughter Fannia. It was not a coincidence that both these sons-in-law perpetuated the tradition of political dissent.

The man whom Pliny recommended to Mauricus was Minicius Acilianus. Although we cannot be certain that Junia B did, in fact, marry him, commentators assume that she did. It would be odd for Pliny to include in his published collection a recommendation for someone with whom a match was not made. We know nothing about Acilianus beyond what Pliny tells us. The first quality for which Pliny recommends him is one that focuses attention on Pliny himself. Although Acilianus is only a few years younger than Pliny (he would therefore be about 15 or more years older than Junia B), he treats Pliny with respect and desires to be molded and instructed by him as Pliny was by the Junius brothers. Like Pliny, Acilianus originated in northern Italy which, according to Pliny, retained much of the modesty, frugality and rustic simplicity of the good old days. His father was Minicius Macrinus, a man of equestrian rank who chose not to pursue a political career although he had been invited to by Vespasian.[189] Acilianus' mother is not mentioned. Perhaps she is deceased.[190] However, the virtues of her family are mentioned prominently (although these relatives would not be the bridegroom's agnates). Perhaps Pliny was better acquainted with the mother's family than the father's. He informs his readers that Acilianus' maternal grandmother is Serrana Procula, a model of austerity (*severitas*). His maternal uncle, Publius Acilius, is a man of dignity, good judgment, and exceptional integrity.[191] Pliny assures Mauricus that the values of Acilianus' family are those of the Junius brothers.

It is striking that Pliny places so much emphasis on the moral uprightness of these people. Clearly he believed that these qualities were important to the bride's uncle, Junius Mauricus, to whom the letter is addressed. The letter was also intended, however, for a larger audience once Pliny selected it for publication. And, in selecting his letters for publication, Pliny presumably chose those that he thought would appeal to the concerns of his readers. In this case, he believed that readers would be interested in learning that several generations of these families still adhered to traditional moral principles. Pliny's contemporaries, the poets Juvenal and Martial, paint a picture of Roman society which is decadent, but, in this and other letters, Pliny indicates that many Romans admired and aspired to virtuous conduct.

The remainder of the letter focuses specifically on the qualities of Acilianus. He is, Pliny assures Mauricus, a man of very great energy and diligence, but also modesty. He has already held the offices of quaestor, tribune, and praetor. Thus – and this is a major selling point – Mauricus will not need to expend money and time helping him campaign for these offices. However, the praetorship was not the highest of the political offices. The consulship was – but not every man who was praetor could hope to become a consul. Even with the institution of suffect consulships, only about half of senators reached the office of consul.[192] It is not certain whether Pliny's comment means that Acilianus will probably not advance beyond the praetorship, or that Mauricus will need to be involved in only one campaign, the one for the consulship. The former seems too bluntly negative a prediction in a letter of recommendation.

The fact that Acilianus had advanced as far as the praetorship may suggest that he had been previously married.[193] Young men with ambitions for a political career often married in their early 20s, to take advantage of the benefits which the Julian laws offered to married men with legitimate children.[194] The age gap between Junia B and Acilianus may have been similar (about 15 years) to that between Fannia and Helvidius I, who had been previously married and had at least one child at the time he married Fannia. Pliny provides no information about whether Acilianus had fathered children in an earlier marriage. It is quite possible, however, that the young Junia became a stepmother.

Acilianus had, Pliny relates, the looks of a nobleman, a ruddy complexion, a handsome build, and the refinement of a senator. Only at the end of the letter does Pliny, with perhaps feigned hesitation, broach a topic that would be very significant in any marriage arrangement. He adds that Acilianus' family is wealthy: "I don't know whether I should add that his father has substantial means. When I envision you and your brother, for whom I am seeking a son-in-law, I think that I should be silent about the wealth."[195] The rationale for Pliny's statement is uncertain. Perhaps he believed that Mauricus' philosophic principles admonished against an interest in wealth. Pliny points out, however, that it is important to consider the children who will result from the marriage. By this he means that money will be needed to support their careers and social commitments and to provide suitable dowries. The children of this marriage would, of course, be formally part of the husband's agnate family. While Acilianus' father, Minicius Macrinus, was still alive, he would be their *paterfamilias*. Although Mauricus would have no legal jurisdiction over the children of his niece, he would not be absent from their lives. He would retain a social and emotional attachment to Junia B, whom he had raised as his own daughter, and, as Pliny's letter indicates, he had an interest in seeing the bloodline, if not name, of his brother continued.[196] If he was still alive when the grandsons began their careers, he would be expected to offer appropriate assistance. The importance of a wife's family is indicated by the importance which Pliny attaches to Acilianus' mother's family in his letter.

Acilianus may, or may not, have been a paragon of virtue. It was conventional for prospective bridegrooms to be lauded for having an excellent moral character, energy, wealth, and a respectable and successful family.[197] We would be very interested in knowing the qualities for which Junia B was commended when Mauricus approached Acilianus' family (perhaps through Pliny) about a match. The qualities of the ideal wife are discussed in Chapter 3. Undoubtedly Mauricus described Junia B as modest, diligent, affectionate, prudent, thrifty, obedient, and healthy (that is, fertile). Her virginity would be assumed, and therefore perhaps not mentioned explicitly. The high moral standards of her family would also be selling point. Depending on the political views of the family of the prospective bridegroom, the involvement of the Junius brothers in protesting imperial rule over several decades may or may not have been an issue. Dowry would be an important element in the final arrangements for the marriage, but perhaps at the early stages the matter was approached delicately. Mauricus must have been willing and able to provide a substantial dowry for Junia B, or Pliny would not have approached a wealthy family about a marriage match. We don't know whether the property of the Junius brothers had been confiscated at the time of their convictions in 93 CE, as it seems that Fannia's was (*Letter* 7.19.6). If so, the property may have been restored to the survivors after Domitian's death.

In *Letter* 2.16.1, Pliny reports the death of a man whom he names as Acilianus. We also learn that Acilianus had left part of his estate to Pliny. Because Pliny does not supply the man's *nomen*, we cannot know with certainty that this is the same Minicius Acilianus whom Pliny recommended as a husband in *Letter* 1.14.[198] The letter may have been written about 100 or 101 CE, about three years after the composition of *Letter* 1.14. If the Acilianus of *Letter* 2.16 is indeed the Acilianus of *Letter* 1.14, and if Junia B had indeed become his wife (admittedly many "ifs"), she may still have been a teenager at the time of her husband's death. Did she return to the household of her uncle as a very young widow? Was she close to her brothers? Did she remarry? And, if so, to whom? Did she ever produce the desired grandchildren of Arulenus Rusticus? Her fate is unknown.

Fannia (con.)

We do not know whether Fannia recovered from the illness reported in *Letter* 7.19. At the time that Pliny wrote his letter, Fannia's cough was becoming worse, and her fever was persistent. She was extremely thin and extremely weak. Only her mind and spirit remained strong, a mind and spirit most worthy, Pliny states, of her husband Helvidius I and her father Thrasea. The rest of her was slipping away. Although Fannia was still alive, her death apparently seemed imminent to Pliny, and his letter resembles a eulogistic obituary, albeit an obituary in which the author focuses much attention upon himself. In *Letter* 7.19.4, Pliny expresses his fear and grief that this outstanding woman is being removed from the sight of the community and that her "like" may never be seen again. He makes this point about her uniqueness several times in the letter. Then, as if to characterize her "like," he states that she possessed purity, integrity, dignity, and steadfastness.

Pliny goes on to recount the courageous behavior of Fannia at the trial in 93 CE. Under the menacing interrogation of the prosecutor, she fearlessly acknowledged that she had commissioned Herennius Senecio to write a biography of her husband Helvidius Priscus I and had lent him her husband's diaries. Pliny uses direct quotations from Fannia to help create a vivid portrait of her, just as he did in his depiction of Arria. As Carlon observes, however, Fannia's terse statements in the Senate meeting are quite different from the aphoristic utterances of her grandmother Arria E 50 years earlier.[199] In the situation of a trial, the brevity of Fannia's responses – just one word for each answer – revealed her steely resolve and perhaps her disdain for the interrogator. Fannia did not wither under the pressure of the interrogator. Her conduct, both at the trial and in preserving the banned books, was as intrepid as that of any brave man. However, she had not crossed any gender boundaries; her actions were performed on behalf of the men in her family, not herself.

Having established that Fannia had proved herself as stalwart as a man, Pliny nonetheless felt obligated also to assure readers that she possessed the virtues desirable in a woman. She was, he writes, good-natured and pleasant (*iucunda*), affable (*comis*), and she inspired not just respect, but even affection, a quality which, Pliny emphasizes, is granted to few people. Pliny's recital of Fannia's feminine virtues serves to suggest to the reader that Pliny is close enough to the family to have "insider information" about Fannia's private behavior. The public might be aware only of her dignified and resolute conduct under prosecution. Her friends – and Pliny considers himself one – know that she is also a kind and approachable person.

Pliny's description serves other functions, as well. In a modern portrait, the author might be said to be "softening" or "humanizing" the subject. Pliny's intent is somewhat different. He wants to show that Fannia conformed to the traditional norms of female behavior. Is he perhaps responding to criticisms that she inappropriately exhibited a masculine boldness and aggressiveness?[200] Pliny provides evidence – her periods in exile, her interrogation in court, her preservation of banned books – that she was indeed equal to a man in fearlessness, but he constructs his report in such a way that she seems to have acted only to promote the welfare of her family. Pliny does not conceal the fact that it was she who took the initiative to commission a book about her husband and presumably his anti-imperial activities, but he does not portray this initiative as an action overtly hostile to the emperor. As Carlon observes, Pliny seems "to cleanse Fannia's actions of any treasonous intent ... and to draw the reader instead to an assessment of her character based on familial devotion."[201] In order for Pliny to convince the reader both that Fannia had not taken on a masculine persona and that she had not deserved punishment for treason, it was essential that he indicate that she cultivated the qualities expected of a woman. And these were the qualities of a loyal helpmeet, a supporter whose duty was to encourage and comfort. Pliny describes Fannia as cheerful and gracious and states that therefore, while she was respected for her defense of her family, she was also loved. Like "Turia," Fannia had emerged into public prominence, but her actions were justified because they had been motivated by the female virtues of wifely devotion (*pietas*) and loyalty (*fides*). As Hemelrijk comments about "Turia," so too was Fannia's behavior an "acceptable extension of her domestic tasks."[202] From Pliny's description, she seems indeed to be the perfect woman – strong when strength is needed, but also amiable, accommodating, and utterly devoted to the interests of her family. In fact, Pliny designates her as a living model of admirable behavior, asking: "Will there be any woman in the future to whose example we can direct our wives? Will there be any woman from whom even men may take a model of fortitude? Will there be any woman whom we can admire, like the women described in books, but while we can still see her and hear her?" (*Letter* 7.19.7).

Although Pliny would consider both Fannia and her grandmother, Arria E, to be suitable models for emulation, his portraits of them differ substantially. Arria E, of course, had been long dead when Pliny developed into a letter the information about her given to him by Fannia (*Letter* 3.16). His presentation is therefore a report compiled from second-hand information about a woman with whom neither he nor any of his readers would be personally familiar. In the anecdotes which Pliny retells, Arria E appears as an *exemplum* of unwavering self-sacrifice who helped her ailing husband by suppressing her own grief and feigning cheerfulness even though her son was dead. However, Pliny mentions this behavior not to illustrate Arria's general "good nature," but rather to emphasize her willingness to subordinate her own needs to those of her husband. She is portrayed as an impressive, but not particularly likeable person. Readers might be inspired by her courage and devotion, and even by the aphoristic sayings attributed to her, but few would want, or need, to imitate her ultimate sacrifice. (Neither her daughter nor granddaughter followed her example, but, of course, they did not need to; their husbands did not hesitate to meet death.)

Fannia, on the other hand, was still alive, though fading, and was known personally to many of Pliny's contemporary readers. He therefore had available much information about her personality. Although he could not stray too far from the truth or exaggerate her virtues too much, he was able to create a laudatory, yet credible image of a woman who combined feminine complaisance with the toughness that is sometimes required to defend one's family. In Pliny's portrait, Fannia appears to be both respected and loved, exceptional, yet imitatable. Thus, in a culture which preferred to learn morality through exempla, rather than precepts, Fannia, even more than her grandmother, provided a perfect model.

Certainly Fannia must have had faults which Pliny does not mention in his eulogy, and her detractors would surely have quibbled at his presentation of her character. What we have received, in his letter, is the biased perspective of a friend. However, there is no reason to doubt that Fannia, whose strength of character is not in question, also often appeared gracious and pleasant. Admittedly, we cannot recover from Pliny's portrait the private thoughts of Fannia or ascertain whether she was "really" a pleasant person. We can learn only how Fannia presented herself to the people around her. In this respect, however, I suggest that we are viewing something real about Fannia because we are seeing the image that Fannia wanted to project.

Having despaired that Romans would no longer have a living model of behavior, Pliny next expresses concern that an illustrious family is dying out. "The very house is tottering; shaken to its very foundations, it seems about to collapse" (*Letter* 7.19.8). Although it may yet have descendants, their virtues and deeds may not be great enough to ensure that Fannia, at her death, is not the last of a line. Pliny is conflating several ideas here. Fannia was, of course, the last direct descendant of Caecina Paetus, Thrasea Paetus, and the two Arrias. She had no children and seems not to have had any siblings. The "house" to which Pliny refers is the house into which Fannia married, that of Helvidius I, her deceased husband. Their marriage connected the houses of Paetus and Helvidius, but did not produce any children. Helvidius I's one son by a previous marriage, Helvidius II, died in 93 CE. He and Anteia had one son and two daughters – Fannia's step-grandchildren. However, by the time *Letter* 7.19 was written, about 107 CE, the two daughters had died in childbirth (*Letter* 4.21), leaving behind two new-born daughters who would formally belong to the families of their fathers. Thus Helvidius III was the only direct descendant of Helvidius I who would pass on the family name. The bloodline of the great Thrasea Paetus was going to die out with Fannia, and even the continuation of the bloodline of Helvidius I was in peril.[203] Pliny is concerned that there are so few family members left that the family line (the house) of Helvidius (and, by step-relation, Paetus) is in danger of becoming physically extinct. He is also concerned, however, that the family members who do survive may not possess the qualities necessary to sustain the family tradition of courageous political action. Thus the tradition, if not the physical family, will die out. The meaning of Pliny's Latin phrase, which I have translated as "although it may yet have descendants," *licet adhuc posteros habeat*, is ambiguous. I interpret the "yet" to convey the meaning that an exemplary house is close to becoming extinct, but that there is still a chance that descendants may be born in the future.[204] But who are the "descendants," whether we assume that they are now alive or may be in the future? And was Pliny's concern that the family tradition of courage was in jeopardy just a rhetorical exaggeration, or was he suggesting that Helvidius III did not exhibit the virtues of his father and grandfather?

Pliny laments that Fannia's critical condition has reminded him of the death of her mother, Arria Y, and has reopened the painful wound of that loss. Fannia, he says, is so much like her mother that losing her will be like losing Arria Y again (*Letter* 7.19.9). At Fannia's death, the world would be deprived of two exceptional women. Pliny then asserts that he loved them both equally, and made his help available to them in times both of prosperity and of adversity. He was, he claims, their solace during their banishment, and their avenger when they returned. It is curious that he then adds, as a reason for hoping that Fannia recovers, that he has not yet returned all the favors that she and her mother did for him. Curious, because elsewhere Pliny emphasizes that he has done them great favors. Consider, by way of contrast, how openly and often he admits that he is indebted to the Junius brothers. We do not know what sort of debt Pliny believes he owes to Fannia and Arria Y. It cannot be financial because Pliny was a wealthy man. Sherwin-White conjectures, perhaps correctly, that Pliny's confession of indebtedness is an oblique admission of his guilt about his inaction during the years 93 – 96 CE.[205] Since Fannia and Arria Y were in a better position to do favors for Pliny prior to 93 CE, and especially in the mid-80s, when Helvidius II was consul, possibly the favors involved helping Pliny with the early stages of his political career. Pliny's debts to the Junius brothers seem to have extended back to this period.

We do not know if Fannia died as a result of the illness reported in 7.19. Pliny provides no further information about her.

The children of Helvidius II

As already mentioned, Helvidius II, who was the stepson of Fannia and was married to Anteia, left behind three children when he was executed in 93 CE. There was one son, Helvidius (here identified as Helvidius III) and two daughters, both presumably bearing the family name, Helvidia (plural: the Helvidiae), and one having Cornutus as a guardian (*Letter* 9.13.16). We do not know their exact ages at the time of their father's death, but we can speculate, on the basis of their probable age at the time of their marriages, that they were quite young. They and their brother were probably born not much before 90 CE. In *Letter* 4.21, written about 105 CE, Pliny sadly reports the deaths of the daughters of Helvidius II. Both died in childbirth, both having given birth to infant daughters who survived them. Of the Helvidiae, Pliny laments that death snatched away these very virtuous and fertile girls (*puellae*) in the flower of their youth. His choice of words – the flower of their youth – leads to the conclusion that the Helvidiae were in their teens, had probably been recently married, and died during their first pregnancy. Their sad fate is a reminder that childbirth was in the ancient world (and unfortunately still is in some parts of the modern world) a dangerous situation and a cause of very painful death for many young women. One second century CE epitaph, for example, memorializes the death of Aeturnia Zotica, who lived for 15 years, 5 months, and 18 days. She died 16 days after giving birth to her first child, a son, who survived her. The epitaph was commissioned by her husband.[206] Primitive medicine was certainly a major reason for the frequency of such deaths, but the youth of the mothers was also a factor, especially among slaves and the free poor whose diets were inadequate in quantity and quality and who were burdened with hard labor. The Helvidiae were members of the elite class and therefore less likely to have suffered from poor nutrition or over-exertion. Nonetheless, the hazards of childbirth claimed their lives. Their infant daughters may have been surgically removed from their bodies. If a mother died during childbirth, an attempt was made to save the child by Caesarean section.[207]

We do not know who the husbands of the Helvidiae were. It would certainly be interesting to learn whether they were politically aligned with the families of Helvidius I and the Junii. The now-motherless infant girls (henceforth identified as "the cousins") would belong legally to their fathers' families and would take the names of their fathers. Nurses, probably slaves, would be employed to nourish them with breast milk.[208] Because of the penalties imposed by the Julian laws, it is quite likely that their fathers remarried and thus brought into the households stepmothers for their motherless daughters (as Helvidius I had brought Fannia into his household as a stepmother for Helvidius II.) Additionally, because of the privileges granted to men with three children, the fathers of the cousins probably wanted to have at least two more children. The cousins would thus find themselves members of a blended family, sharing a home with half-siblings. We do not know whether the cousins remained in social contact.

In *Letter* 4.21, Pliny expresses his grief for the infant cousins, deprived of their mothers, for the husbands of the Helvidiae, deprived of their wives, and for himself.[209] It is surprising that he does not include in his lament Anteia, the mother of the dead women and the wife of their father, Helvidius II. Again, Pliny is not hesitant to shine the spotlight on himself in order to establish his credentials as a friend of the family. He declares that his love for their deceased father has been abiding, giving as evidence for this love his legal action against Publicius Certus (*Letter* 9.13) and his publication of the speech given at that time.[210]

Pliny points out that only one child of Helvidius II now survived, and that this son was the sole prop and support for the family (*Letter* 4.21.3). The two motherless daughters (the cousins) are not counted in Pliny's calculation of the descendants of Helvidius II, perhaps because, being infants, their survival was so uncertain. As noted earlier, the mortality rate for young children was very high in the ancient world. Or perhaps they are not included in the calculation because they had been absorbed into the families of their fathers. It is curious, however, that Pliny, who was never hesitant to advertise his friendship with Fannia, did not take this opportunity to mention her as the step-grandmother of Helvidius III. We do not know the age of Helvidius III at the time this letter was written. Since Pliny does not express a hope that Helvidius III will soon successfully produce off-spring to continue the family line, I suspect that he was younger than his sisters and not yet married. That he was not yet an adult may also be implied from Pliny's assertion that his anguish will ease if Fortune were to keep Helvidius III strong and healthy, and an equal to his father (Helvidius II) and grandfather (Helvidius I). Now, because he has become the sole survivor of his generation, Pliny is all the more concerned about his health and his character. Again Pliny raises the point that the end of a family might result from a failure to propagate physically, or might mean a failure to reproduce and transmit the spiritual virtues of earlier generations. When Pliny wrote his encomium on Fannia (*Letter* 7.19) about two years after this letter, he was still worried that the house (that is, the family) seemed about to collapse and disappear. "The very house is tottering; shaken to its very foundations, it seems about to collapse" (*Letter* 7.19.8). The hoped for descendants had not (yet) arrived. Nor was Pliny entirely confident that they would possess the qualities necessary to sustain the family tradition of courageous political action. It was this tradition that Arria E, Arria Y, and Fannia had so resolutely supported over several generations.

Figure 3 Pompeia Plotina (c. 60 – c. 122 CE), wife of the emperor Trajan. Museo Nazionale Romano. Photo © Vanni/Art Resource, NY.

3   Pliny's wives*

In his published letters, Pliny devoted considerable attention to the behavior of wives. The previous chapters have examined his accounts of the behavior of Arria the Elder and Fannia. Both these women acted courageously to support husbands who had chosen to make public their criticisms of the emperors. Through Pliny's eyes, we view Fannia as a model of feminine virtue because she was an amiable woman and devoted wife who used her strength in the service of her family. She thus won, he remarks, both the affection and the respect of others. This chapter will investigate Pliny's comments about other wives, and particularly his description of his own wife, and will explore his notions of the ideal wife. Although these women were not called upon to make the sacrifices that Arria E and Fannia had made, they exhibited, in Pliny's view, similar qualities of character and presumably could have risen to challenges even as Arria E and Fannia had. Pliny's focus is primarily on publicizing admirable behavior, and therefore he rarely mentions in his letters wives whose conduct was reprehensible. However, the few examples he provides will also be discussed.

The qualities for which Pliny commends wives are those which had traditionally been considered desirable in Roman culture. His interest in publishing stories about virtuous women – and his audience's interest apparently in reading them – may seem in jarring contrast to the writings of his contemporaries, Tacitus, Juvenal, and Martial, who were attracting audiences with accounts of outrageously shameless and self-indulgent conduct by women. However, earlier authors had also, like Pliny, chosen to draw attention to the selfless behavior of wives.[1] Praise for virtuous wives had, moreover, a long tradition in Roman funerary compositions. Of course, epitaphs, like obituaries, rarely present a completely accurate account of a person's character. Survivors are reluctant to speak negatively of the deceased, not only out of respect for them, but also, in some cases, because they wish to leave for posterity a portrait of family relationships which is rosier than reality. Epitaphs tend, moreover, to be formulaic. Yet, it is precisely for this reason that epitaphs are appropriate sources of information about ideals and norms. Conventional expressions presuppose a general agreement about the value of the qualities mentioned. And when the same words and phrases are repeated century after century, they "underscore the persistence of the model."[2] Although many of the women about whom Pliny published letters were still alive when he was writing, the qualities for which he applauded them were the same as those for which women were memorialized in epitaphs. It is therefore instructive, before examining Pliny's portraits, to look briefly at evidence from epitaphs in order to understand what qualities were attributed to the ideal Roman wife and how Pliny's portraits conform to these conventions.

Wives in epitaphs

One brief second century CE inscription, commissioned by a husband, encapsulates the wifely virtues. According to the husband, Marcus, his wife, Amymone, was an excellent and very beautiful woman who was a skilled worker of wool, dutiful (*pia*), modest (*pudica*), thrifty, chaste (*casta*), and content to stay at home.[3] The epitaph of "Turia," which was mentioned in Chapter 2, also provides information about wifely virtues. Because other funerary epitaphs in which husbands record the loss of a wife are quite brief, the lengthy "Turia" inscription is particularly important to our understanding of Roman marriages. In it, the husband recorded details about his wife's character and behavior, and about his feelings for her. It is not surprising that the portrait of "Turia" which emerges from the inscription is of a woman with many virtues and no faults. Funerary epitaphs were (and are) expected to provide flattering statements about the character of the deceased. Nonetheless, the inscription provides specific details of "Turia's" conduct which substantiate her husband's contention that she was a remarkable person.

We learn that the couple in the "Turia" inscription had been married for 40 years. The husband comments that it was rare for marriages of such long duration to be ended by death, not divorce. (It is striking that Pliny never mentions divorce in his letters. Since divorce appears to have been as common in classical Rome, at least among the elite, as it is in modern American society, his failure to mention it was likely a deliberate exclusion. He apparently believed that any reference to divorce would detract from his largely positive portrait of Roman society.)[4] "Turia's" husband also expresses a regret that he had not died first, since it would have been more just for him, who was older, to do so. He enumerates his wife's virtues: wool-working skills, modesty (*pudicitia*), obedience (*obsequium*), affability (*comitas*), obligingness (*facilitas*), simplicity of dress, and family dutifulness (*familiae pietas*).[5] With regard to the last element, he comments that "Turia" cared for his mother as much as for her own parents.[6] He adds, however, that she shared these virtues with other honorable Roman matrons.[7] This statement is significant because it informs us about what qualities were conventionally expected of a good wife. What set "Turia" apart, according to her husband, were the courage, competence, initiative, and resourcefulness she demonstrated when confronted by enormous challenges. From his description of events, we learn that she had, on several occasions, been forced by circumstance to enter the public sphere and to confront public officials (that is, to take on a man's role) in order to ensure that her family was treated justly. "Turia's" husband relates that, on the day before her wedding (when she was probably still in her teen years), her parents were murdered. Although it was highly unusual for a woman to initiate an indictment in a capital case, "Turia," an orphan with no brothers, considered it her duty to avenge her parents.[8] She diligently orchestrated the prosecution and punishment of their killers. And, when her relatives tried to have her parents' wills, which left their estates to her, invalidated, she again fought and won her case. She then used her inheritance to provide dowries for female kinfolk. When her husband's life was in imminent danger during the proscriptions of 43 and 42 BCE, and he was contemplating rash actions, she counseled him wisely and arranged for him a safe place of refuge outside of Italy. She also gave him her gold and gemstone jewelry so that he might purchase slaves and provisions to make his exile comfortable. Remaining in Rome, she lobbied his enemies for a pardon for him. When she prostrated herself before one of them, the triumvir Lepidus, he had her dragged away like a slave. And yet, though covered with bruises, she unflinchingly continued her plea for a pardon and revealed publicly the insults and injuries she had received in order to expose Lepidus' misdeeds. And she successfully defended her house against a gang of violent enemies who tried to break in and plunder it. Her courageous deeds are all the more impressive when we remember that she performed them when probably still in early 20s. And, although she had exhibited the aggressiveness of a man, her behavior was justified and admirable, as was Fannia's, because it was motivated by loyalty to her husband.[9]

During her husband's flight from Rome, the couple had, in a sense, experienced a reversal of roles, with "Turia" being the one to speak out in public places. However, she cast aside her masculine behavior once peace was restored after Octavian's (Augustus') defeat of Antony, and her husband returned to Rome. The couple resumed their domestic life. Her husband records that they longed for children, but fate denied them, and finally advancing age put an end to their hopes. "Turia" was depressed about *her* infertility and in anguish that her husband was without children. As society would expect of her, she blamed herself for the childlessness. Perhaps surprisingly, the couple did not adopt. In a remarkable display of self-sacrifice, "Turia" not only talked about divorce and yielding her place to a fertile woman (again placing the blame on herself), but also even offered to arrange a new marriage for her husband, to love the children of that marriage, to perform the duties of a sister or mother-in-law, and to leave the management of her estate in the control of her husband.[10] Her husband was stunned by her generosity, but refused to divorce her, saying that only death would end their marriage. "How could you even conceive of any reason why you should cease to be my wife, you who remained so faithfully with me when I was in exile? How could the desire or need for having children be so great that I would break faith with you?"

"Turia's" husband ends his address to her with the remark that her death has left him overwhelmed by sorrow and longing for her.[11] He finds consolation, however, in contemplating her fame. And it is, of course, he who ensures that her fame will endure by composing the eulogy and commissioning the tombstone to record her remarkable qualities and actions. Like Pliny's letters, the eulogy inscribed on stone has the power to grant undying glory.

This poignant story of "Turia's" self-sacrifices and her husband's grief at her death is evidence that strong bonds of affection existed between some husbands and wives even in a society where marriages were arranged, where husbands were often much older than their wives, and where husbands were not expected to be sexually faithful to their wives.[12] Pliny, too, records in his letters the existence of affective bonds in marriage. In particular, he reveals a strong emotional attachment to his wife in his letters to and about her. Of course, like the "Turia" inscription, Pliny's letters offer us only a male point of view. It is therefore difficult to ascertain how satisfying marriages were for the wives he mentions. This chapter will discuss the contexts of the marriages which Pliny records and will consider what the experience of marriage may have been like for the wives.

The women Pliny married

After the death of Domitian in September of 96 CE, Pliny resolved to initiate a Senate hearing into the conduct of Publicius Certus during the trial and conviction of Helvidius II in 93 CE (*Letter* 9.13). Before proceeding with his plan, he decided (as noted in Chapter 2) to confer with Helvidius' widow, Anteia. He contacted her and invited her to meet with him at his home (*Letter* 9.13.4). It might have been more usual and more courteous for the person requesting the conference to offer to travel to the other person, but Pliny explains that he asked Anteia to come to his home because his wife had died recently, and he was confined there in compliance with the customary period of mourning. He also remarks that he was greatly saddened by his wife's death. The period of mourning to which Pliny refers is the *feriae denicales*, a nine-day period following the funeral during which the bereaved family members secluded themselves, grieved, and purified their house.[13]

The meeting with Anteia took place near the beginning of 97 CE, when Fannia and Arria Y had already returned from the exile to which they had been sentenced in 93. We can therefore conclude that Pliny's wife died in late 96 or early 97. At some point, Pliny remarried, but there is uncertainty about whether this new wife was his second or third, and whether the wife who died in 97 was his first or second. In *Letter* 10.2, written in early 98 CE, Pliny thanks the emperor Trajan for granting him, although he was childless, the privileges accorded to a man with three legitimate children.[14] As noted in Chapter 1, the Julian legislation gave to men with legitimate children preference in career advancement. Pliny expresses his gratitude to Trajan for having made this decision one of the first actions of his very felicitous reign, and writes: "Now I desire all the more the children whom I wanted to have even in that very dismal period, as you can surmise from my two marriages." By "that very dismal period" Pliny means the reign of Domitian. Sherwin-White argues, and I agree, that the statement implies that the two marriages of which Pliny writes in *Letter* 10.2 occurred prior to Domitian's death in September 96 CE, that the wife whose death is recorded in 9.13 was a second wife, and that a marriage to a woman named Calpurnia, first mentioned in Book 4, is a third marriage and should be dated to after 100 CE.[15] Carlon, however, maintains that there were only two marriages and that Pliny was already married to Calpurnia at the time that *Letter* 10.2 was written in 98.[16] One problem with this theory is that it assumes that within one year, from the death of a wife in early 97 to the letter to Trajan in early 98, Pliny found a new wife and was already disappointed enough in her inability to produce a child that he mentioned this disappointment to Trajan. The question of two or three wives is unfortunately insoluble, but I continue to believe that there were three wives.

About Pliny's first and second wives we know almost nothing, not even their names or ages. Pliny was born about 61 CE and, if he followed the custom for elite young men, may have married for the first time when he was in his early to mid 20s – that is, about 85 CE. It would not be surprising to learn that he chose a bride from his own region of northern Italy. And perhaps the person who arranged the match wrote for him a letter similar to that which he wrote recommending Minicius Acilianus as a husband for Junia (*Letter* 1.14).[17] Pliny remained on good terms with at least one of his mothers-in-law (of whom there is discussion in Chapter 5) even when his marriage had been ended by the death of her daughter. He addresses *Letter* 1.4, written probably in 97 CE, to a woman named Pompeia Celerina, whom he identifies as his mother-in-law, presumably the mother of his second wife (who would have been dead at the time the letter was written).[18] Raepsaet-Charlier tentatively suggests that Pompeia Celerina may have been married to Lucius Venuleius Montanus Apronianus who was suffect consul in 92 CE.[19] If this supposition is correct, then the name of Pliny's second wife might have been Venuleia. In *Letter* 9.13.13, the letter in which Pliny reports his prosecution of Publicius Certus in 97 CE, which took place shortly after the death of his second wife, he reports that one of the senators who defended Certus was Bittius Proculus, the stepfather of that wife. Thus, if Venuleius was indeed the father of Pliny's second wife, he had either died or been divorced from her mother at some time before her death. And this is all we know about this wife: that she had a stepfather (who did not share Pliny's eagerness to avenge the death of Helvidius II), that she died in late 96 or early 97 CE, and that Pliny was greatly saddened by her death. About Pliny's first wife, we know nothing.

Calpurnia (Part 1)

We know considerably more about Pliny's third wife. In *Letter* 4.1, Pliny addresses a man named Lucius Calpurnius Fabatus and writes: "You are eager to see your granddaughter, and me as well, after such a long time. Your eagerness gratifies both of us, and is mutual." The granddaughter of this man is Pliny's third wife. (See Genealogy Chart 3.) The occasion of the letter is to inform Calpurnius that Pliny and his wife, Calpurnia, are preparing to visit him. "We are already packing our bags and planning to travel as quickly as the condition of our route allows." Calpurnius lived in Comum (modern Como) in northern Italy, which was also the home town of Pliny. It was thither that he and Calpurnia were headed on the journey mentioned in *Letter* 4.1. When Pliny had sought a new wife, after the death of the wife reported in *Letter* 9.13, he apparently wanted someone who was native to the same area as he was and someone recommended by old friends. Perhaps he was also looking for someone who shared with him the northern Italian values which he extolled in *Letter* 1.14, his letter recommending Minicius Acilianus as a husband.[20] As for Pliny's own qualifications for marriage, his wealth and successful political career would stand him in good stead, although prospective fathers-in-law might be concerned that his two previous marriages had failed to produce children.

As already noted, the date of Pliny's marriage to Calpurnia is controversial. If this is the second marriage mentioned in *Letter* 10.2, it began sometime between early 97 and early 98 CE – that is, not long after the death of the previous wife, and Pliny was, within a few months, already expressing disappointment about its barrenness. It is perhaps odd, however, that Pliny does not mention this new marriage in a letter earlier than Book 4. We might expect a reference to it in letters that appear to be written in the period between 98 and 100. In addition, Pliny seems to have been too busy between 98 and 100 to have embarked on a search for a wife, particularly if it had required that he travel out of Rome. He was occupied with his duties as a prefect of the treasury of Saturn and, in addition, served as an advocate in two high profile legal cases.[21] In fact, he considered his duties for the treasury so demanding that, when he was first appointed by Trajan, he put his legal work on hold (*Letter* 10.3.1) and was required to request from the emperor a leave of absence to travel to Tifernum (in Etruria) to initiate the construction of a temple which he was financing (*Letters* 10.8.2–6 and 3.4.2). He agreed only reluctantly to participate in the two high profile cases (*Letter* 3.4.3). In September and October of 100 CE, he served as suffect consul.[22] Given the constraints on his time during the period between 98 and 100, it seems to me more likely that the marriage to Calpurnia is a third one and that it began sometime after 100 CE.

In 100 CE, Pliny was about 40 years old. His new wife was probably in her mid-teens. From several letters, we infer that Calpurnia was raised by her grandfather and her paternal aunt (her father's sister), Calpurnia Hispulla, rather than by her parents.[23] Her father, the son of Calpurnius Fabatus, was also named Calpurnius (and will henceforth be identified as Calpurnius II). He was deceased (*Letter* 4.19.1), as was presumably also her mother, whose name and family are unknown. It is possible, of course, that her mother was alive, but had moved on to a new marriage, following either the death of or divorce from Calpurnius II, and that Calpurnia had remained in Comum with her father's agnate family, to which she legally belonged. Her grandfather, Calpurnius Fabatus, was her *paterfamilias*. Her paternal aunt, Calpurnia Hispulla, was also her agnate. (See Genealogy Chart 3.) In *Letter* 4.19.1, Pliny praises the aunt for loving her orphaned niece as if she were her own daughter and showing her the affection not only of an aunt, but also even of the father she had lost. He adds that Calpurnia has turned out to be worthy of her father, her grandfather, and her aunt. This comment is intended as a compliment to Calpurnia Hispulla on her skills as a surrogate parent. She has produced a young woman who bears the same admirable traits as her father and grandfather and who can therefore be depended upon to carry on the moral traditions of the family. The importance of perpetuating these traditions was discussed in Chapter 2 with reference to the family of Fannia and Helvidius I.

Calpurnia's family was wealthy, but considerably less distinguished than Pliny's. Her grandfather was a man of equestrian rank who had an honorable military career. In 65 CE, however, he was charged by Nero with complicity in a treasonous plot, although he escaped punishment because his role had been minor.[24] He served as a local magistrate in Comum, but was never a member of the Roman Senate. He owned estates in the Comum area and also in Etruria and Campania. It is striking that Pliny, despite his political ambitions, did not seek a marriage alliance with an illustrious Roman family, but was content, rather, to marry into a respectable but relatively unknown Italian family. In *Letter* 4.19.7, in a letter to Calpurnia's aunt, he writes: "You revered my mother as if she were your own and were accustomed to guide and praise me from the time I was a boy." We may infer that there were close ties between the Calpurnii and Pliny's maternal family, the Plinii, and that the marriage arrangement between Pliny and Calpurnia was a result of this family connection. (Pliny's paternal family was Caecilius and thus, at birth, he was given the name Caecilius, but he acquired the name Plinius when he was adopted by his mother's brother after the death of his father.) Calpurnius Fabatus appears to have been a prickly old man, and the relationship between him and Pliny after the marriage was sometimes strained. In *Letter* 6.12, Pliny replies to his grandfather-in-law's very blunt letters which rebuked him for a perceived failure to carry out a request. Pliny assures him that he appreciates the frank tone of the letters because he knows that the old man is treating him like a son. It is most likely that Pliny's comment is simply a polite attempt to defuse an awkward situation. However, we are reminded that Pliny's father had died when he was a youngster, and that the maternal uncle who adopted him died in the eruption of Vesuvius in 79 CE, when Pliny was only about 18 years old. Perhaps he truly did welcome a father figure, even a brusquely critical one. In *Letter* 7.23.2, Pliny writes to Fabatus that he reveres him as a parent (*parentis loco*). This is the same phrase which Pliny uses to describe the relationship between his own mother and Calpurnia's aunt in *Letter* 4.19.7.[25]

Since Pliny was of an age to be Calpurnius Fabatus' son, we may infer that he was old enough to be his wife's father. In *Letter* 7.11, Pliny responds to Fabatus' criticism of a real estate transaction he had made. Fabatus was upset that Pliny had sold the property for less than he might have asked. Perhaps he was concerned that Pliny was careless about money that Calpurnia and the children they expected her to produce should inherit. Nonetheless, he was willing to entrust to Pliny the inspection of his agricultural properties throughout Italy (*Letters* 6.30 and 8.20.3). The marriage between Pliny and Calpurnia was thus of benefit to Calpurnius Fabatus beyond the expected production of heirs. The grandson-in-law was able to assume the duties of property management which would have been the responsibility of the son were he alive.

We don't know how often Calpurnia may have seen Pliny when she was a girl in Comum. During her childhood, he lived primarily in Rome where he was busy establishing his legal and political career. And when he returned to Comum for visits, he would have had little time or attention for a young girl. He would be occupied with inspecting his own income-producing agricultural properties, scrutinizing account books, and listening to the complaints of the farmers who rented or share-cropped his land. Since his wealth was derived largely from his real estate holdings, he needed to pay close attention to how these holdings were managed.[26] He would also spend much of his time fulfilling his duties as a town patron. As one of the wealthiest landowners in the area and one who had competed successfully in Roman politics, he was expected to help the citizens of his hometown with advice and, more importantly, with financial support for community projects. When he was in attendance in Comum, people would flock to his door with requests. In return for providing advice and funding, Pliny would be acclaimed as a "local hero" and treated with great deference.

It was customary for those of a lower social status to indicate their respect for a patron by appearing outside his door; the more important the patron, the more crowded was the street in front of his home. Sometimes an attendee was invited into the reception area of the home for an audience with the patron. In *Letter* 4.13, written a short time after the visit to Comum which he is planning in *Letter* 4.1, Pliny reports to his friend, the historian Tacitus, that, when he was recently in his hometown, a man with a young son came to his home to pay his respects. When he learned from this man that there was no school in the town, he pledged to provide one-third of the costs of establishing a school.[27] We know from an inscription that Pliny was a generous patron to Comum, funding, for example, public baths, maintenance of a library, an annual dinner for citizens, and welfare support for boys and girls.[28] And he was generous not just to Comum. As noted earlier, Pliny relates in *Letters* 3.4.2 and 10.8.2–6 that he had offered to finance a temple in Tifernum and, in 98 or 99 CE, had taken a leave from his duties in Rome to attend the initiation of its construction. In *Letter* 4.1, composed about 104 CE, he writes to his grandfather-in-law that, on his way to Comum, he and Calpurnia will spend a few days in the town of Tifernum, which is close to one of the family estates in Etruria that he must inspect. The residents of that town adopted him as its patron when he was still very young.[29] He adds: "They celebrate my arrivals, regret my departures, and rejoice in my successes. In order to reciprocate their good will, I authorized the construction, at my own expense, of a temple in that town. Since it has now been completed, it is disrespectful to delay any longer its dedication. We will therefore be in Tifernum on the day of the dedication, which I have arranged to celebrate with a public banquet."[30]

Because his visits to Comum were occupied with so much business, it is not likely that Pliny had spent much, or any, time with Calpurnia when she was a child. A comment that he makes at the end of *Letter* 4.19 suggests that she, like other young girls, especially of the elite class, led a sheltered life. While living in the same household as her aunt, Pliny writes, Calpurnia saw only what was pure and honorable (*Letter* 4.19.6). Perhaps she attracted his attention as a teenaged girl, or perhaps they were largely unknown to one another at the time the marriage was arranged. The people who recommended her to Pliny – and it seems that her aunt had played a lead role in suggesting the match (*Letter* 4.19.8) – undoubtedly claimed that she had the qualities which the "Turia" inscription suggests were common to all honorable Roman matrons: modesty (*pudicitia*), obedience, affability, obligingness, simplicity of dress, and family piety. (There is no mention, however, in Pliny's letters of whether Calpurnia was skilled in wool-working.) She may also have been lauded for possessing the same virtues which Pliny saw in a 13-year-old girl who was engaged to be married. In *Letter* 5.16, which is discussed in Chapter 6, Pliny describes this girl's virtues as amiability, good judgment, sweetness, modesty, and dignity.[31] Calpurnia's virginity would be assumed. Her youth and good health would be emphasized, to assure Pliny that she would produce the children he wanted so desperately. The moral standards of her family might also have been mentioned (as were those of the family of Minicius Acilianus in *Letter* 1.14). A dowry would be discussed and settled on. Perhaps Pliny did not need to "sell" himself since he was a family friend and such a prominent person in the community. He might, as he did for Minicius Acilianus, have pointed out that Calpurnia's grandfather would not incur any expenses helping him campaign for public office because he had already held those offices. Calpurnius Fabatus was Calpurnia's *paterfamilias*, and his approval of the marriage arrangement was essential. As is clear from statements in other letters – "May he make you a grandfather as soon as possible" (*Letter* 6.26.3) – a man's fertility was a major concern to the family of a prospective bride. Pliny's inability to produce children in his two previous marriages may have caused Fabatus, who had no sons and apparently no grandsons, to hesitate before granting his approval. We don't know what arguments convinced Fabatus to put aside concerns he may have had about Pliny's childlessness. Certainly Pliny's wealth and political successes would be potent persuaders.

It must have been intimidating for Calpurnia to learn that she, who had grown up in a small town, sheltered from the unpleasant aspects of life, was to be married to a man more than twice her age, to leave her grandfather and aunt, who seem to have been her only agnates, and to move with her new husband to Rome where he was ardently engaged in the activities of a senator, activities about which she knew little. *Letter* 4.1, announcing to Calpurnius Fabatus that his granddaughter is coming to visit with her husband, hints at Calpurnia's joy in the anticipation of seeing her family again, and their desire to see her. "You are eager to see your granddaughter, and me as well, after such a long time. Your eagerness gratifies both of us, and is mutual. For we, in turn, are possessed by such an incredible longing to be with you." It is not difficult to imagine the excitement of a young woman – a teenage girl, in fact – who will be reunited with her family and friends after several months, or perhaps even a few years, of adapting to life in a strange and large city, as the wife of a middle-aged senator.

The discrepancy in the ages of Pliny and Calpurnia was not unusual. Minicius Acilianus and Helvidius (I) had, when they were already established in their careers, married girls – Junia and Fannia respectively – who were half their age. It is difficult to comprehend what the relationship was like, particularly in its early stages, between couples of such disparate age, education, and experience. Certainly the differences were such that the husband would consider himself superior in several respects and entitled to assume a dominant role. A comment by Quintilian, a scholar of oratory and one of Pliny's teachers[32], offers some insight into how men perceived their young wives. Quintilian's wife died when she was only 18 years old. She had already borne two sons. The younger died just a few months after his mother, at the age of five. Thus Quintilian's wife must have married him when she was only 12 years old, the minimum legal age for marriage.[33] He was in his 40s. Writing about her death, he reflects that "in age, she was like a girl, especially compared to my age, and her loss could be counted like the loss of a child."[34] It is unfortunate that we have no statements from the young women, expressing their feelings about being wed to men who surely seemed like father figures, while they were required to assume the duties of a wife and a mother. The stresses of adjusting to this situation were undoubtedly great.

In his letters, Pliny describes Calpurnia as having adapted well to her role as his wife. *Letter* 4.19, which is addressed to Calpurnia's aunt, Calpurnia Hispulla, provides our first glimpses into the young bride's behavior. The aunt, who was probably about the same age as Pliny and had been a friend since childhood, had been instrumental in the arrangement of the marriage: "You have given her to me, you have given me to her" (*Letter* 4.19.8). *Letter* 4.19 is, in essence, a thank-you note and a progress report, in which Pliny expresses his gratitude to the match-maker, Calpurnia Hispulla, for arranging the marriage, and reassures her about the welfare of her niece. He confirms that Calpurnia Hispulla's judgment has been excellent and that therefore the match has been very successful. Of course, since Pliny chose to publish this letter, it serves purposes beyond that of a polite "thank you" to a family member. Most importantly, it preserves a record of Pliny's marriage from his point of view and immortalizes him, Calpurnia, and her aunt. The power of Pliny's letters to produce enduring fame has been discussed in the previous chapters. Here, in *Letter* 4.19, Pliny repays Calpurnia Hispulla's favor to him by publicizing her devotion to her orphaned niece and her wisdom in choosing a suitable husband. Both the opening and the close of the letter highlight her contributions to producing so fine a young woman. And the proof of Calpurnia Hispulla's devotion (*pietas*) and wisdom is the success of the marriage, as Pliny describes it in the main body of the letter.

In her excellent analysis of *Letter* 4.19 and the three letters which Pliny sent to his wife (which will be discussed shortly), De Pretis explains that there is a circular motion to a letter. The addressee is not present, but is "re-created" in the mind of the letter-writer. The writer is influenced by the image which he holds of the addressee, which, in turn, influences the image of himself which the writer fashions as he composes his letter.[35] The letter-writer crafts the letter, and his image, to have an impact on a specific person. In composing *Letter* 4.19, Pliny was influenced both by his image of Calpurnia Hispulla, the addressee, and of his wife, Calpurnia, who is the subject of the letter. The Calpurnia Hispulla whom Pliny praises at the opening and close of the letter is depicted as a dedicated caregiver, a woman who had raised her orphaned niece and had also played a role in guiding Pliny's development. Although Calpurnia (his wife) is the subject of the letter, Pliny utilizes the letter also to create a positive portrait of her aunt.

The writer who knows that his letter will be published is also influenced by the image he has in mind of the reader of his published work. Pliny's decision to publish a portrait of his marriage reveals a desire to inform the world that he is happy and has found a wife whose behavior conforms to the expectations that he and honorable men like himself have of marriage. In the process of selecting and editing his letters for publication, Pliny had the opportunity to release only information which he, upon careful reflection, wished to be made public. Not surprisingly, therefore, he appears in the letters as a wise counselor, a respected author, a generous friend, and a loving husband. If we accept that his overall intention was to leave to posterity a flattering self-portrait, we are faced with the question of whether the Pliny we meet in the letters is a *persona* he created for himself. In the specific case of his letters to and about his wife Calpurnia, we must consider whether he is providing a portrait of his marriage as he actually experienced it, or a portrait of his marriage as he wished it to be known. We cannot be sure whether he was, in reality, a happily married man, or whether he adopted the *persona* of a happily married man. (We might compare the situation with the Roman poets, Catullus and Propertius. We do not know whether they were truly unhappy lovers, or whether they assumed this *persona* in their poetry.) We have no reason to suspect that Pliny was a miserably unhappy man, posing in his letters as a happy husband and fabricating stories about the joys his wife brought him. Nonetheless, his description of his marriage may be a presentation of an idealized situation. He is, in a culture obsessed by models, presenting the picture of a model marriage. And he portrays Calpurnia as exhibiting the behavior for which Roman women were conventionally praised. We can understand, of course, why he would paint a glowing picture to send to Calpurnia Hispulla. It is curious, however, that, when he was creating a flattering self-portrait for his contemporaries and posterity, he apparently believed that a necessary element of that portrait was a blissfully happy marriage. Recall that, in *Letter* 9.13.4, he had declared himself greatly saddened by the death of his second wife, another indication of his desire to present himself as a happily married man. As mentioned earlier, Pliny wanted the approval of his readers and therefore addressed topics that would interest them. He would not have emphasized the contentment of his marriage unless he believed that his readers would respond favorably.

Although we cannot know beyond a doubt that Pliny was truly pleased with Calpurnia, we can learn from his letters that Roman men thought that a harmonious marriage was a desirable situation. This is not surprising, of course. Even if marriages were not love matches, a marriage free of acrimony would certainly be more desirable than a rancorous one. In the late republican period, Cicero had expressed dismay at the constant wrangling between his brother and sister-in-law.[36] Nonetheless, their unhappiness was a concern only for the family. However, during Augustus' reign, the merits of harmonious marriages and virtuous wives were widely publicized by the emperor, whose subjects were encouraged to emulate the concord and contentment of Augustus' own (third) marriage. In a speech referred to in Chapter 1, in which Augustus praised men who were fathers, he also posed this rhetorical question: "What can be better than a wife who maintains self-control, stays at home, manages the household, raises your children, cheers you when you are well and tends you when you ail, is your companion in good fortune and encourages you in bad fortune?"[37] In the imperial propaganda, constructing a stable home life was officially advocated as a public duty. Augustus' successors, however, were less successful in creating models of marital bliss. The outrageous behavior of imperial wives like Messalina and Agrippina the Younger (wives of the emperor Claudius) served instead as a reminder that a man who cannot control his wife cannot govern the state well. When Trajan became emperor in 98 CE, he sought to revive Augustus' promotion of marital concord and to present his own wife, Pompeia Plotina, as a model of appropriate behavior.

Pompeia Plotina

Plotina (see Figure 3) was the daughter of Lucius Pompeius, and had been raised in Neumasus (modern Nimes, France).[38] We do not know the year of her birth;[39] her death occurred between 122 and 129 CE. We have no information about how or when her marriage with Trajan had been arranged, but it was prior to his accession to imperial rule. When he became emperor (98–117 CE), she continued to live modestly. Dio writes that "Plotina conducted herself during Trajan's entire reign in such a manner that she incurred no reproach."[40] In *Letter* 9.28.1, Pliny describes her as a woman of highest moral integrity (*sanctissima femina*). She and Trajan did not have any children. About 87 CE, Trajan became guardian of Publius Aelius Hadrianus (the future emperor Hadrian) whose parents had died when he was about 10 years old. Trajan and Hadrian shared a blood relationship; Trajan's father and Hadrian's maternal grandmother were brother and sister. Plotina became very fond of Hadrian and played an instrumental role in the development of his career. When her husband, Trajan, was dying in 117 CE, she persuaded him to adopt Hadrian as his son and heir. It is perhaps not surprising that Pliny, following the emperor's lead, should choose to publicize the laudable qualities of his own wife and marriage. Even before marrying Calpurnia, however, Pliny had documented the exemplary nature of the marriage of Trajan and Plotina in the *Panegyricus*.

The *Panegyricus* is a revised version of a speech which Pliny delivered in the Senate when he was suffect consul in 100 CE. It is the only one of his many speeches which has survived.[41] In it, Pliny celebrated Trajan for his wisdom, diligence, and integrity, and thanked him for restoring confidence to the state and honor to the Senate after the terror of Domitian's reign.[42] A prominent theme of the speech is that Trajan had returned Rome to its former glory by inspiring a renewed appreciation of ancestral values. Toward the end of the speech, Pliny focused on the relationship between Trajan and his wife Plotina, assuring his audience that an inspection of this emperor's private life was quite pertinent to a discussion of his glory because his conduct in his own home was as outstanding as his conduct in public. [*P* 83.1] Pliny expands on the idea that there should be no distinction between a man's public and private life, and asserts that only a man who can control himself and his family is fit to control the state. Pliny comments, moreover, on the importance of the head of the household keeping not just himself, but also his household members free of every contagion of vices. [*P* 83.2] He adds that many distinguished men have been disgraced by a wife either chosen unwisely or kept in check too mildly. These men had less authority in public affairs because they were less successful as husbands. [*P* 83.4] Trajan, in contrast, had made a wise choice of a wife, and wise decisions about monitoring her behavior. His success as a husband, far from being an insignificant element of his life, therefore enhanced his reputation. In his marriage, as in every other aspect of his behavior, he is (according to Pliny) a model for elite Roman men.

The *Panegyricus* was composed as a speech which Pliny delivered in public, in the presence of Trajan. Pliny would not have included in it any remarks of which Trajan would not have approved. As Roche points out, the speech "reflects the propaganda of Trajan's administration dutifully."[43] The portrait of the emperor which Pliny presented "concurred with the official line of the emperor's public image."[44] And that image included his ability to elicit virtuous behavior from his wife (and his sister, Ulpia Marciana, who is also mentioned, though not by name; see Figure 2). Thus the praise of Plotina redounds to the emperor's glory.

Trajan's wife, Pliny informs us, is his equal in honor and glory. [*P* 83.4] No one has greater moral integrity than Plotina, no one is a better example of ancient virtues. [*P* 83.5] Although her husband is now the most powerful man in the world, she asks nothing for herself except the pleasure his success gives her.[45] She and Trajan behave the same way they did before he assumed the position as emperor. [*P* 83.6] Plotina is still modest in her dress, unpretentious in her retinue, and unassuming in her manner of travel. [*P* 83.7][46] When Pliny reports that, in her simple lifestyle, she imitates her husband [*P* 83.8], he is suggesting that wives are malleable, and that, had Plotina had a less virtuous husband to imitate, she, too, might have been less virtuous. His remark informs us that Plotina's virtues are not innate or self-initiated. Her admirable conduct, asserts Pliny, is the work of her husband who instructed and trained her. He adds that, for a wife, a reputation for obedience (*obsequium*) is sufficient glory. [*P* 83.7][47]

In the *Panegyricus*, Pliny has clearly delineated the roles of husband and wife: the husband is responsible for domesticating his bride, the bride is to follow her husband's instructions cheerfully. We do not know whether Plotina was, like Calpurnia, still a girl when she became a bride. It was perhaps easier for a man to train a young bride to conform to his ways than a woman who had been previously married. In *Letter* 1.16.6, which is discussed later, Pliny writes about a man who molded the girl he married into an elegant wife.

Trajan was sensitive to concerns about the role of the women in his family. The establishment of the imperial form of government, 100 years prior to his accession to the position of emperor, had caused the diminishment of the authority of senators, but had also given the women of the emperor's family the potential to acquire considerable influence in public matters. During the republican period, the wives (and also mothers, sisters, and daughters) of senators might be presumed to have had some influence over the political decisions of their menfolk, but power in the state was not concentrated in one man. In the imperial government, however, one man – the emperor – held supreme power for a lifetime. His wife correspondingly had many opportunities, over a long period of time, to involve herself in affairs of the state. As Fischler has commented, "when the reins of the state were in the hands of only one man, then it became far easier for those without a constitutional office to have an effect on state decisions."[48] Many senators, already stung by their own loss of authority, resented what they perceived to be undue interference by the emperor's wife.[49] Although Livia, the wife of the first emperor, Augustus, was known to be her husband's close advisor in public matters and therefore a potent intercessor,[50] her husband had her portrayed as a woman whose focus was, in accordance with tradition, on family matters. At the same time, however, Augustus promoted his role as the pater (father) of the state, implying that Livia was the mater (mother) of the state and therefore duly concerned about public matters. He created, moreover, an ideology in which the security and interests of the state and the imperial family were intimately bound together. The issue of the appropriate role for an emperor's wife was not resolved in Augustus' lifetime. Many of the wives of his successors are depicted by Roman historians as transgressing traditional boundaries for female behavior. In turn, judgments about the effectiveness of their husbands as rulers were made, in part, on the basis of whether the men could control their wives.[51]

Pliny's depiction of Trajan as an emperor who insisted that his wife (and sister: see Figure 2) abide by traditional standards of behavior should be evaluated in the context both of contemporary concerns about the role of imperial women and of Trajan's desire to construct himself as an emperor who was returning Rome to its former glory as an austere and pious society. Like Augustus, he presented the harmony of his marriage as a model to be emulated, but also as an element important to the stability and success of the state. In choosing to write about, craft portraits of, and publish letters about virtuous women Pliny was affirming the values of Trajan's ideology. Trajan promoted a society in which women adhered to conventional roles and were praised for doing so, and in which men earned distinction for guiding their wives to accept these roles. Pliny's writings created symbolic capital both for himself and for the men about whose wives he wrote.[52]

The obedient wife

Pliny's approbation of obedience in a wife may shed light on a point made in Chapter 1, that Arria E's request to her husband's captors, that she be allowed to take on the role of a slave in order to comfort her husband, was laudable because she was fulfilling a wife's duty.[53] For a woman of any class, subservience to her husband was a desirable quality. An epitaph for a man who died at the age of 71 records that he had had two marriages, the first of 15 years, the second of 28. Both his wives were, according to the inscription, very obedient.[54]

The ideal Roman wife apparently agreed with her husband in all matters. She may, in fact, have promised at her wedding "to regulate her own behavior in the interest of her husband," "to accommodate her will to his will." The Latin phrase is *viro morem gerere*.[55] Dionysius of Halicarnassus claimed that a law of Romulus required Roman wives to conform to the personalities of their husbands.[56] The adjective *morigerus* is used in early Latin exclusively to describe wifely and filial obedience (and then almost disappears from use), as if a man might expect the same subservient behavior from both his wife and his children.[57] In one Roman comedy, the father of a woman who wants to divorce her inconsiderate and unfaithful husband responds unsympathetically to his daughter: "How often have I pointed out to you that you must accommodate yourself to your husband?" The Latin for the last part of the sentence is *viro ut morem geras*. The father agrees to help his daughter only when he realizes that his family wealth is being squandered by her husband.[58] In Livy's version of a speech which Cato the Elder gave in 195 BCE, condemning the actions of women who were protesting the Oppian law noisily in public, Cato admonishes Roman husbands to keep their wives under control, as they would an irrational animal like a horse.[59] He maintains that there is no possibility of shared governance or compromise in a marriage. If wives ever became equal, they would assume the position of superiors. Cato tried to link the stability of the state to the maintenance of marriages in which wives yielded to the authority of husbands. Despite his efforts, the Oppian law was repealed. However, its repeal did not signal a willingness by men to grant a measure of political power to women. Two centuries later, Valerius Maximus interpreted the controversy about it as an issue not of women demanding a voice in legislation, but of women seeking to squander money on personal adornments.[60]

Cato's speech focused on a traditional expectation that a husband was to assume responsibility for curbing the inappropriate impulses of his wife. During the reign of Augustus, the Julian legislation, which closely associated the behavior of women with the well-being of the state, moved tradition into law. It legally bound husbands to report and punish adulterous wives and thereby to regulate the private behavior of their wives. Furthermore, the Senate discussions, mentioned in Chapter 1, about the conduct of wives accompanying their husbands to provinces, offer additional evidence of the continuing conviction in Roman society that a husband must educate and monitor his wife and ultimately be culpable for her misbehavior. When, in 21 CE, Aulus Caecina Severus proposed legislation that governors be prohibited from taking their wives to provinces, one senator, who opposed the legislation, nonetheless asserted that if a wife exceeded the bounds of propriety, the blame belonged to her husband.[61]

Marriage and *manus*

The Latin word *manus* means "hand" (as in "manual" labor). It was also used metaphorically to denote "control" or "power." During the early and middle republican periods, a woman, at marriage, entered into the hand or control of her husband: *in manum*.[62] She left the control of her natal *paterfamilias* and came under the authority of her husband's *paterfamilias*. She had been transferred, as it were, to her husband's agnate family and acquired a status similar to that of a daughter. If her husband's *paterfamilias* was deceased, and he was therefore independent (*sui iuris*: "under his own regulation"), she had the same inheritance rights vis-à-vis him as a daughter. However, by the later republican period and on through the imperial period, it was more common for a woman, at marriage, *not* to enter *in manum* of her husband. She remained a daughter of her natal *paterfamilias*, and therefore under his authority, and an agnate to her siblings. However, she was not then an agnate of her own children. As mentioned in Chapter 2, the dowry which a wife not *in manu* brought to her marriage was in a sense on loan to her husband and had to be returned to her family in the case of divorce or death. Throughout the marriage, separate accounts were kept of "his" property and "hers."[63] The aim of this system was not to empower women, but to safeguard the property of a woman's agnate family. However, this system allowed Roman women to enjoy a degree of financial independence which has been rare for women until recently. Nonetheless, Roman wives were expected to defer to their husbands.

The anonymous wife of Macrinus

Letter 8.5, which was written about 107 or 108 CE, offers insight into a man's view of an ideal marriage. In this letter, Pliny praises the wife of Macrinus, although he does not give her name. In addition, because he refers to her husband by only one name, Macrinus, we are not able to identify him with certainty. In *Letter* 1.14.5, there is a reference to a Minicius Macrinus. He was the father of Minicius Acilianus, the man whom Pliny recommended as a husband for the daughter of Arulenus Rusticus. However, it is doubtful that he and his wife are the same people spoken of in *Letter* 8.5. In *Letter* 1.14, written in 97 CE, Acilianus' father is mentioned, but not his mother. Instead, Pliny reports that his maternal grandmother and uncle are recognized as models of the ancient integrity for which northern Italians were well-known (according to Pliny, himself a northerner). The omission of any reference to Acilianus' mother, while including praise for her kin, suggests that she is dead. If the couple was separated by divorce, praise for her kin, but not for her would seem inappropriate. On the other hand, the Macrinus mentioned in *Letter* 8.5, which was written about ten years later than *Letter* 1.14, had just recently lost his wife to whom he had been married for 39 years. He may be the Caecilius Macrinus to whom Pliny addressed *Letter* 3.4. Five other letters are addressed to a Macrinus, whom Sherwin-White conjectures was the same man.[64] Since four of the six letters contain details about trials for extortion, Sherwin-White also speculates that this Macrinus was not of senatorial rank, and therefore not present at the trials; hence the reason for Pliny to describe the events.

Letter 8.5 provides no information about Macrinus other than that he was a dear friend of Pliny and had been married to the same woman for many years. Her recent death was, Pliny reports, a grave trauma for him. He describes her as a wife of singular example, *uxor singularis exempli*, who would have been considered exceptional even in times past (that is, in the "good old days" when, according to

Pliny, people were more virtuous). The same phrase, "a wife of singular example," occurs also in *Letter* 3.1.5 in reference to a woman whom we know from other letters was named Cottia. (She is discussed later.) As noted in regard to Pliny's commendation of Arria E and Fannia, he considered it the highest praise for a woman to write that she could be presented as an example to others. He reports with approval, moreover, that Macrinus lived with his wife for 39 years without a quarrel (*sine iurgio*) and without annoyance (*sine offensa*). Pliny goes on to say that this woman deserved the greatest respect because she showed such respect to her husband. She brought together and combined in her own character so many and such important virtues, acquiring them at different times during her life. This comment suggests that a man who married a very young woman – someone today considered a girl – would not initially expect his bride to act like an older woman, but would anticipate that her personality would develop even as she matured physically. He would hope, of course, that, especially with his guidance, she would consider it of prime importance to cultivate qualities which would make her the perfect wife. Pliny then remarks that Macrinus, has a substantial consolation: he possessed such a treasure for so long. And yet, her loss was therefore all the more painful because the grief of being deprived of someone increases according to the pleasures enjoyed in the past. Pliny ends his letter with an expression of hope that time and diversions will assuage Macrinus' sorrow.

Letter 8.5 offers testimony, as does the "Turia" inscription, that, in a culture where marriages were arranged unions rather than love matches, and where brides and grooms did not enter a union with romantic expectations of their life together, husbands and wives nonetheless might develop feelings of deep affection. We have no reason to doubt Pliny's account that Macrinus was emotionally devastated by the death of his wife. The publication of the letter indicates, moreover, that Pliny believed that his readers would be pleased to learn about a lengthy marriage which had brought joy to a husband and would sympathize with Macrinus' plight. Pliny's revelation that Macrinus had enjoyed his relationship with his wife is intended to be to the credit of the grieving husband.

What we do not learn from the letter is what the wife's feelings had been toward her husband or what her role was in the marriage. She was, according to Pliny, a woman of sterling character who continued to cultivate virtues throughout her life. Although Pliny does not specify which virtues, we may perhaps infer that he means that she acquired age-appropriate virtues as she – and the marriage – matured. If she had married at about 15 years of age, she was about 55 years old when she died. Perhaps Pliny saw in her the type of woman he hoped his wife Calpurnia would develop into as she grew older. He does not remark, as he does in the case of Trajan's wife, Plotina (in the *Panegyricus*) and Saturninus' wife (*Letter* 1.16.6), that her husband had trained her well. However, the omission of such a remark does not mean that Pliny would not have given Macrinus the same credit for refining his young bride. The comment about the wife's cultivation of virtues implies, furthermore, that Pliny may have believed that marriage offered a woman the opportunity to have her potential developed. For a wife, however, the achievement that was worthy of favorable notice was moral development, not intellectual development. As will be discussed later, the emphasis, even among those men who recommended an education for women, was on improving their moral conduct so that they would be better wives.

Although Pliny does not include the word *concordia* in *Letter* 8.5 – the word which he used to characterize the harmony of his own marriage in *Letter* 4.19.5, and which he cited Arria as having used in reference to her marriage in *Letter* 3.16.10 – he nonetheless depicts Macrinus' marriage as a union of perfect harmony. Pliny relates that Macrinus lived with his wife for 39 years without a quarrel. It seems impossible that the couple never quarreled, in 39 years of marriage. Perhaps Pliny has exaggerated the situation. Nevertheless, Roman wives were often praised in funerary epitaphs for living with their husbands without dissension or strife. In one inscription, a husband records that his "incomparable" wife had lived with him "without any contention," *sine ulla controversia*. A wife memorialized in another inscription had lived with her husband "without any anger," *sine ulla iracundia*. Yet another inscription preserves the information that a woman who had married at the age of 14 had lived with her husband for 30 years "without cause for complaint," *sine querella*.[65] Of course, it is a convention of funerary inscriptions to present a portrait of the deceased which is often idealized. The inscriptions may tell us more about the situation which was desired, rather than the situation as it really was. It is noteworthy, however, that the epitaphs of men do not praise them for living with their wives without disagreements. We may conclude that the burden of keeping the marriage peaceful and harmonious fell mainly to the wife. The absence of anger and complaint, noted in the inscriptions already mentioned, seems to have meant not that both husband and wife were always blissfully content, but that the husband had no reason to be angry or to complain. And if there was no quarrel or contention in the marriage, the perfect harmony was likely achieved by the wife's willingness to defer to her husband on all occasions, rather than by a mutual effort to work out compromises.

In any case, *Letter* 8.5 is not a funerary inscription. Pliny is presumably relating to his addressee the words which Macrinus used to describe to friends his wife and his marriage. Although a grief-stricken husband's recollection of his marriage may be rosier than the marriage actually was, it may offer a more honest and personalized portrait than does a commissioned inscription. Looking back at his marriage, the widowed Macrinus apparently recalled that he had lived with his wife for 39 years *sine offensa*. *Offensa* means "grating" or "annoyance." Apparently, Macrinus' wife did not, in modern terms, "grate on him" or "rub him the wrong way." The two "very obedient" wives of the man who died at age 71 (see earlier) were recorded in the inscription as having lived with him *sine offensa*.[66] The phrase *sine offensa* occurs also in the "Turia" inscription which records another long marriage. Apparently, "Turia," like Macrinus' wife, had lived with her husband for several decades without "getting on his nerves."[67] Plutarch tells the story of a man who divorced a beautiful, wealthy wife because she irritated him like a pinching shoe. Plutarch concludes that small, but constant daily annoyances and petty disputes are as destructive to a marriage as major disagreements, and that therefore wives should always take care not to be obstinate and vexatious, but rather to be accommodating, pleasant, and agreeable toward their husbands. He puts the burden of keeping the peace on the wife; he makes no recommendation to husbands about avoiding churlish behavior.[68]

Did Macrinus' wife also view their marriage as free of irritation? Did she find it pleasurable, or stressful, to develop the characteristic of being always agreeable? The information is not available.

Calpurnia (Part 2)

Pliny expected and undoubtedly received warm applause for his comments in the *Panegyricus* about Plotina's virtues and Trajan's role in training her. He would similarly have expected that his own marriage, as he describes it in *Letter* 4.19, would earn him the respect of his readers and that he would enhance his reputation by publicizing his own wise decisions in the choice and training of his wife. Her successful adaptation to the role of a good wife would reflect well on him. Absent, unfortunately, from the evidence available to us are Calpurnia's thoughts about her marriage and her husband. Was she as content with the situation as Pliny claims that he was? Although we do not have Calpurnia's own words, it is possible to glean from Pliny's comments information which helps us understand how she adjusted to the role of wife and created a marriage which Pliny judged to be happy. Thus, in addition to learning Pliny's assessment of his marriage, we catch glimpses of Calpurnia's contributions to the union. These glimpses reveal (as also does *Letter* 3.16, the letter about Arria's sacrifices) something which Pliny himself seems not to have recognized: that the task of creating a harmonious marriage (or the illusion of one) rested primarily with the wife. However, this circumstance did not escape the notice of Pliny's friend, Tacitus, who observed about his parents-in-law that they had lived in remarkable harmony (*concordia*), because of their mutual affection (*caritas*) and the willingness of each to put the other first. But, Tacitus adds, a good wife receives greater praise even as a bad wife receives more blame.[69]

Letter 4.19 offers a catalogue of Calpurnia's virtues. Pliny commends her first for her frugality and her good judgment. In a few words, he is informing his readers that the young Calpurnia has learned how to manage well the household (which would include the oversight of many slaves). Implicit in his statement is the suggestion that he deserved credit for her training in this important area of wifely duties.[70] Pliny was proud of his own thriftiness (*Letter* 2.4.3), and boasted of the frugality of his (and Calpurnia's) native northern Italy (*Letter* 1.14.4).[71] In the *Panegyricus*, he pointed out that Plotina had imitated the simple lifestyle of her husband, Trajan. He is therefore pleased to reveal here that Calpurnia has imitated his pattern of thriftiness. There are other reasons, however, why he chose to laud her frugality. We might be surprised that a man as affluent as Pliny would expect his young wife to worry about expenses, but being a prudent household manager was an indication that a woman was continent in other ways as well. Thriftiness was associated with temperance and sexual restraint; extravagance with promiscuity. Sallust criticized Sempronia, a woman who supported the revolutionary

Catiline in 63 BCE, for lusting after men and squandering both her money and her reputation.[72] He also reports that women attracted to the Catilinarian conspiracy had extravagant spending habits which they supported by prostitution.[73] In contrast, Pliny's contemporary, the poet Statius, notes with approval that a friend's wife, Priscilla, remained careful with money even after her husband became wealthy.[74] And, as noted earlier, in the *Paengyricus*, Pliny commends Trajan's wife, Plotina, for continuing to live modestly even when empress.[75] Praise for a wife's thriftiness was, moreover, a convention of funerary tributes, as can be seen by its frequent appearance in epitaphs.[76]

Pliny's second comment about Calpurnia is: "She loves me, which is an indication of her chastity (*castitas*)." The noun *castitas* and the corresponding adjective *castus* have a general meaning of moral purity and, in this sense, can be applied to both men and women. In fact, in the *Panegyricus*, Pliny uses both *castitas* and *castus* in reference to the emperor Trajan.[77] When applied specifically to women, however, the words usually denote sexually purity or sexual fidelity.[78] For example, when Pliny wrote, in *Letter* 1.14.8, that the good looks of a bridegroom are the reward for the *castitas* of the bride, he was referring to the bride's virginity or sexual inexperience. However, when Martial described Arria E as *casta*, he was indicating that she had been sexually faithful to her husband.[79] Both these definitions – sexual inexperience and sexual fidelity – are appropriate in the context of *Letter* 4.19. Calpurnia came to the marriage as a virgin and is now sexually faithful to Pliny. Furthermore, the Latin verb *amare*, like the English verb "to love," has several meanings and can signify both emotional and physical experiences. Pliny's statement – "She loves me" – informs the reader that Calpurnia has found in him both emotional and physical satisfaction. She is (he believes) delighted by his company and has developed a fondness or emotional attachment to him. She also (he believes) finds sexual pleasure with him. Pliny's situation is the reverse of the plight of the republican period Roman love poets. For him, Calpurnia's love is proof of her purity and fidelity, her *castitas*. For Catullus and Propertius, the lack of *castitas* – the infidelity and promiscuity – of Lesbia and Cynthia was proof that their mistresses did not love them.

The comment "She loves me" is intended, however, to allude to more than Pliny's delight in his wife's fondness for him. He is informing Calpurnia Hispulla in a discreet manner that the sexual aspect of his and Calpurnia's marriage is good, and that they therefore can be expected to produce children. As noted in Chapter 2, the purpose of marriage was not to find happiness (although clearly it was gratifying to Pliny and his contemporaries to be happy in their marriages), but to produce children and secure the perpetuation of the family. In *Letters* 1.14.2 and 9 and 6.26.3, for example, Pliny raises the issue of grandchildren. There was enormous pressure on Pliny and Calpurnia to have children. He was the only survivor of his family. Calpurnia and her aunt, Calpurnia Hispulla, were her grandfather's only heirs, and Calpurnia Hispulla was apparently unmarried at the time of the letter and, since she was older than Pliny (*Letter* 4.19.7), probably past child-bearing age. All hope of the continuation of both families therefore rested in Pliny and Calpurnia. Calpurnius Fabatus may have had misgivings about marrying his granddaughter to a man who had been previously twice married and not fathered children. In *Letter* 4.19, Pliny is trying to reassure his wife's family that they will soon have the heir they so earnestly desire.

Most of *Letter* 4.19 is taken up with Pliny's third reason for happiness with his wife: she has devoted herself to his activities. Because of her affection (*caritas*) for him[80], she has become interested in the study of literature and reads and re-reads his writings, which she even knows by heart. She experiences great anxiety, moreover, when he is about to plead a case in court, and great joy when he has finished, and she even arranges for messengers to report to her what assent and applause he received and what verdict he won. When he gives a recitation, she listens very eagerly to the praise he garners, though modestly concealing herself behind a curtain.[81] And, finally, she sings his poems while accompanying herself on the lyre, taught by no musician, but rather by love itself.[82] Because of her devotion to his interests, Pliny is convinced that the *concordia*, the harmony of their union, will grow stronger every day and endure forever.[83]

Pliny's final comment about Calpurnia's wifely virtues is instructive. According to the middle-aged Pliny, his teen bride cared not about his age and physical appearance, which in any case deteriorate, but found attractive his *gloria*, his renown. Although the letter purports to be an enumeration of Calpurnia's virtues, it also serves to draw attention to Pliny's accomplishments. He lets his reader know that he wins acclaim for both his forensic work and his literary compositions. If the suggestion is correct, that Pliny constructs an image of himself in response to the image he creates of his addressee (who in this letter is his wife's aunt), perhaps Pliny believed that Calpurnia's family would be pleased to learn that he is so successful. Perhaps his reference to his *gloria* was meant as a compliment to the matchmaker aunt. However, his manner of interjecting comments favorable to himself in a letter about his wife leaves modern readers with an impression that he was not aiming for: that he is self-absorbed and immodest.

Similarly, most modern readers are either amused or annoyed by Pliny's self-centered observation that the marriage will be harmonious because his wife is so enthusiastic about *his* interests and so devoted to *his* pursuit of renown. Perhaps Pliny believed that a letter to his wife's aunt was not the place for him to mention whether he, in turn, had shown any concern for his wife's interests. Nonetheless, he seems quite unaware that she may have interests other than him and his activities. However, Pliny's preoccupation with himself was not unusual for a man of the Roman elite. His contemporary Statius expressed delight in his wife's listening to him as he composed and sharing the triumphs and disappointments of his literary career. (Unlike Pliny, however, Statius admitted that there were also disappointing moments.)[84] And Arria E clearly regarded a harmonious marriage as one in which the wife devoted herself to her husband's interests and welfare.

As already noted, a wife's good behavior was interpreted as an indicator of her husband's character. Thus Pliny had praised Trajan in the *Panegyricus* for his excellent job of training his wife, Plotina. In *Letter* 1.16.6, moreover, Pliny informs a friend that Pompeius Saturninus had turned the girl he married into a well-educated wife. We might therefore have expected Pliny to give himself more explicit credit in *Letter* 4.19 for molding his young wife into a suitable marriage companion. Perhaps he restrained his usual tendency to boast because this letter is, after all, intended to praise and thank Calpurnia Hispulla for *her* success in preparing the orphaned Calpurnia to be amenable to Pliny's training. Thus Pliny ends the letter by commenting that Calpurnia's exemplary behavior as a wife befits someone trained by Calpurnia Hispulla and guided by her teaching. While living in the same household as her aunt, Pliny writes, Calpurnia saw only what was pure and honorable (*Letter* 4.19.6). And she grew accustomed to love Pliny as a result of her aunt's recommendation.

In acknowledging the role of Calpurnia Hispulla in the development of Calpurnia's character, Pliny makes it clear that the aunt has produced a girl who possesses the qualities that Roman husbands found most desirable in their wives: tractability, compliance, and a willingness to adopt her husband's interests as her own. In Pliny's case, his driving interest was a desire for enduring fame, as both a doer and an author. Although readers may be amused by his delight in his wife's memorization of his literary works and her concern about his legal cases, what better proof could he offer of his wife's *pietas* (devotion) than her fascination with his work, both in the courts and as a writer, and her excitement about his achievements? Pliny had not suffered political persecution or exile. Calpurnia had therefore not been called on to display the heroic self-sacrifice of Arria E and Fannia or of "Turia." Nor had she been married long enough to rival the dedication of the wife of Domitius Tullus, who had admirably nursed her very disabled husband (*Letters* 8.18.8–10). Nonetheless, Pliny's description of Calpurnia is designed to indicate that her *pietas* was in no way inferior to that of women whose devotion had been tested by adversity. Statius explicitly makes this point when he says of a Priscilla, a friend's wife, that, if a critical situation had required her courage, she would gladly have endured armed bands, lightening, and storms at sea on behalf of her husband. But fortunately adversity never tested her devotion.[85]

The picture of his marriage which Pliny presents to Calpurnia Hispulla and to his readers is a portrait of harmony and contentment. Whether he is describing the reality of his own marriage, or whether he has embellished his account, he is offering a model of a happy marriage. However, *Letter* 4.19 reveals more than just Pliny's notion of a happy marriage. It also records Calpurnia's adaptation to the role of wife, and her transformation from girl (*puella, virgo*) to wife and matron (*uxor, matrona*), and it thus provides insights into a situation which was common in the Roman world: a teenage girl's adjustment to an arranged marriage to a middle-aged man whom she barely knew. On her wedding day, she put aside the self-centeredness which is characteristic of children, and assumed the burden of managing a household, and, though still young herself, the pressure to bear children (and, in cases like Fannia's, to look after stepchildren). She was, moreover, required to ascertain her husband's interests and needs, and devote herself to them. Calpurnia has fulfilled this responsibility remarkably well. Realizing that Pliny's interests are writing and speaking, she has taken an interest in reading and listening. He is active, she is passive. If she sings, the words are his. She listens to his literary works with an appreciative (rather than a critical) ear. In essence, Calpurnia chose to occupy herself with activities which focused attention on her husband's accomplishments. She was like the moon reflecting the light of the sun or revolving around the earth: her activities had value only in relation to those of her husband. (The same might be said of the quite different activities of Arria E and Fannia.)

The education of Roman girls

Calpurnia's activities should be looked at in the context of Roman attitudes to the education of women. We cannot expect her to have been as learned as her husband Pliny, who had spent his life studying and practicing rhetoric. Calpurnia's schooling would have been much more limited than his. Most Roman girls of wealthy families probably did receive an elementary education. (There was no publicly funded education system, and therefore lower-class children, especially girls, had few educational opportunities.) The quality of an elite girl's education would be determined both by her family's willingness to educate its daughters and by the location of her family's home. There were, for example, more teachers available in a large city than in a small town, such as Calpurnia's hometown of Comum. In Comum, even boys had only limited access to teachers, as Pliny's offer to help finance a school indicates (*Letter* 4.13). Even where schools existed, however, it was rare for girls to attend them; they were usually taught at home by private tutors. In *Letter* 5.16.3, we learn that Fundanus' daughter had instructors, but this probably means that tutors came to her home. Hemelrijk suggests that Pliny's use of the plural – instructors (*praeceptores*) – implies that Fundanus' daughter received specialized instruction in several fields. However, it may also mean that she had a succession of instructors, none of them specialized.[86] There was, moreover, no standardized curriculum. Each tutor chose the content of the lessons, no doubt in consultation with the pupil's father. A girl's education would also be of a much briefer duration than that of a boy of the upper-class. Fundanus' daughter, after all, was on the brink of marriage at the age of 13, an age when boys of her social class were just beginning more advanced studies.[87] Similarly Calpurnia's formal schooling would not have continued past her early teens, when she married Pliny.

The advanced studies which upper-class boys pursued, during their teen years and often into their early 20s, provided rigorous training in rhetoric, oratory, history, law, philosophy, and mathematics. This education was considered to be of practical value since it prepared them to assume positions of authority in the state. Since girls could not aspire to public careers, it could be argued that they had no need of a similar education. And, because the costs of hiring instructors were paid for by the families, many families would be unwilling to expend much money to educate their daughters. Nonetheless, wives of elite men were required to manage large households and, when their husbands were out of town, they were responsible for keeping them informed about matters important to the family (as is evident from the letters of Cicero discussed in Chapter 2). In addition, some fathers might consider the financial ability to hire instructors for their daughter(s) a type of status symbol. Perhaps, moreover, the education of daughters was valued more by fathers who had no sons. It is possible that Fannia, who seems to have been the only child of Arria Y and Thrasea Paetus, received more attention than was usual in families with sons and that she learned as a child the importance of preserving historical documents. However, it is difficult to imagine that Calpurnia's cantankerous grandfather would have been persuaded that educating her was a wise use of money. Some education was, nonetheless, considered suitable for girls of the upper-class, and, in their few years of schooling, they probably learned to read, write, and do arithmetic at a basic level, although they were not required to read widely, to analyze, or to create and compose. With regard to Calpurnia's reading skills, Pliny's letter informs us only that she reads *his* compositions; there is no mention of other authors. Although some scholars have used Pliny's letter as proof that Roman women, of the upper-class at least, were well-educated, in reality the letter tells us nothing about Calpurnia's formal education, about the breadth of her reading, for example, or her ability to comprehend what she had read, or to formulate and articulate ideas.

Learning to play the lyre might be a part of a girl's education at home, though perhaps it was not for Calpurnia. Pliny's words, "taught by no musician" (*Letter* 4.19.4), imply that her musical skills are self-taught. Moral instruction, which would include the reading of exemplary stories about virtuous Romans, occupied a prominent place in the curriculum of both girls and boys. Perhaps Calpurnia was required to learn about the heroic suicide of Arria E. The moral instruction might be entrusted to a family member, rather than a tutor. In *Letter* 4.19.6, Pliny notes that Calpurnia was trained by her aunt's precepts. Although fluency in Greek was essential for any man aspiring to a political career, it seems unlikely that many girls, especially those in a small town like Comum, learned Greek.[88] There was thus a great discrepancy between the educational levels of men and women of the elite class, a discrepancy of which men approved. Ovid, for example, lamented that few women appreciated poetry. However, he was not concerned that few women wrote poetry or, if they did, had it published.[89]

The education of elite Roman women

Elite men were content to marry girls with some education, but they did not want wives who were their rivals in erudition and eloquence. Men generally believed that women were intellectually inferior to them and lacking in emotional control. As noted in Chapter 1, guardians were assigned even to adult women because of the supposed weakness of their minds.[90] Roman men worried, moreover, that, if women acquired masculine skills, they would be unable to use them judiciously. For example, when Sallust related that Sempronia, Catiline's supporter in 63 BCE (whose squandering of both her money and her reputation was noted earlier) had read widely in both Greek and Latin literature, was witty and articulate, and could write poetry, his words were not intended as praise.[91] He was rather signaling to his readers that, although Sempronia had acquired the intellectual skills of a man, she was to unable to suppress her feminine emotions. Therefore, when she tried to act like a man, she behaved like the worst of men, ultimately becoming sexually promiscuous and supporting the overthrow of the state. Sallust's antagonism toward Sempronia was rooted in his conviction that a woman should not intrude into male spheres, and particularly not into the world of politics. He also disparages her for other behaviors inappropriate to a Roman matron, criticizing her for playing the lyre and dancing more elegantly than was necessary for an honorable woman. A Roman woman might learn to play the lyre, but only discretely and with modest success. Sempronia, however, had apparently offended Sallust by making her considerable talents conspicuous. Her dancing was especially egregious because this was an activity associated with lower-class women of questionable morality, as both Pliny and his contemporary Martial make clear.[92] In keeping with the moralizing tone of his work, Sallust mentions Sempronia's talents in order to cast doubts on her character and to intimate that she is sexually promiscuous.[93] In contrast to Sallust, the erotic poets of the late republican and early Augustan periods delighted in flaunting their relationships with women who refused to conform to society's expectations for the behavior of respectable women. Propertius, for example, frequently and favorably mentions that Cynthia was a skillful musician, dancer, poet, and conversationalist, and that she not just listened to, but also evaluated his poems.[94] Of course, Cynthia was also the dominant partner in the relationship, as it is described by Propertius. Thus his attraction to a talented and educated woman is as much a part of his own defiance of conventions as his willingness to be dominated by such a woman.[95] Many members of his society would have considered his willing bondage a kind of moral depravity. And few men would have tolerated such an inversion of traditional gender roles in their marriages. And perhaps Propertius did not tolerate it in his own marriage; Cynthia was his lover, not his wife.

One wife who was able to enjoy her education without giving offence was Cornelia, Pompey's fifth wife, whom he married in 52 BCE.[96] Plutarch reports that she was knowledgeable in literature, music, geometry, and philosophy. He adds, however, that she had "a nature that was free from that unpleasantness and meddlesomeness which such learning inflicts on young women." Plutarch's comment implies that education was acceptable in a woman provided that it did not cause her to become overbearing or to interfere in male concerns. Another Cornelia who was both a respected and educated woman was the mother of Tiberius and Gracchus, a woman whose sterling reputation as a *univira* has been mentioned in Chapter 1.[97] Her eloquence and erudition – she even studied Greek – were praised by later generations, but not because she utilized them to indulge herself (as Sallust suggests that Sempronia did). She is commended rather because, as a widow, she devoted herself to supervising the education of her sons and ensuring that they developed into excellent orators and statesmen. She had thus used her knowledge to undertake a role appropriate to a widow.

Sempronia and the two Corneliae are examples drawn from the republican period. Our evidence from the imperial period indicates that hostility continued toward educated women who appeared to be intruding into male spheres. Pliny's contemporary, Juvenal, was not reticent about admitting that men simply did not want to be confronted by women better educated than they, and he railed against women who openly displayed their learning and eloquence, especially if they were more learned and eloquent than the men present. "Don't marry a woman who speaks like an orator – or knows every history book. There should be some things in books which she doesn't understand. I hate a woman who knows all the laws and rules of correct speech and who quotes verses I've never even heard of. ... A husband should be allowed an occasional 'ain't'."[98] Another of Pliny's contemporaries, Martial, maintained that he did not want a learned wife because she would be quarrelsome.[99]

Nonetheless, we also have evidence from the early imperial period that some men considered an educated wife to be beneficial to a marriage. The first century CE Stoic philosopher, Musonius Rufus, who was an acquaintance of Pliny, believed that women possessed the same ability to reason as men, and he recommended that daughters receive the same education as sons, and that women study philosophy.[100] However, he did not suggest that the purpose of educating women was to enable them to take on the roles of men.[101] He asserts rather that an educated woman could better fulfill the traditional role of managing the household. Her study of philosophy would, moreover, make her a more virtuous woman and therefore a wife who was loyal, chaste, and self-restrained – the traditional desirable virtues. There also developed during the first century CE a conviction that a harmonious marriage could be created if a husband took responsibility for educating his wife. For example, Pliny's contemporary, Plutarch, recommended that a husband be his wife's guide and teacher in intellectual and moral matters. His reason for the recommendation, however, was that, if wives did not receive instruction from their husbands, they were liable to entertain foolish ideas and emotions.[102] It appears, from the comments of both Musonius and Plutarch, that the emphasis, even among those men who recommended an education for women, was on improving the moral conduct of women rather than on enhancing their intellectual abilities. The portrait which Pliny paints of the marriage of Trajan and Plotina, which has already been discussed, suggests a situation where the husband has molded his wife's behavior to meet his expectations. Both in the *Panegyricus* and in his letters, Pliny makes it clear, as Carlon aptly explains, that "a good wife does not simply arrive at a man's doorstep on the day she is led into marriage with him. Praiseworthy wives must be carefully selected and cultivated by their husbands, trained by each man to behave in ways that accord with his character and ambitions." The result of the training is "a seasoned matron whose chief concern will be the enhancement of her husband's reputation."[103]

Hemelrijk points out that the motif of a husband reading to his wife became popular in funerary art of the late second and early third centuries CE.[104] Such images may be intended to represent the desirable companionship of a marriage where a couple studies together, but they also demonstrate that the husband is the superior partner in the relationship. It is he, after all, who does the reading, presumably from material which he has chosen. The wife is in the position of a student and a subordinate. Still, many men did not want a wife with much education, and among them was the father of Seneca.[105] The younger Seneca wrote to his mother, Helvia: "Although you do not have a comprehensive grasp of all the liberal arts, you have nevertheless come into contact with them, at least as much as the old-fashioned severity of my father permitted you. I wish that my father, the best of men, had surrendered less to the custom of our ancestors and had been willing for you to be well-informed rather than merely acquainted with the teachings of philosophy."[106] It would be interesting to know what educational opportunities Seneca the Younger allowed to his wife, Paulina, who dutifully attempted suicide with him. Considerable attention has already been given to Pliny's praise of Trajan for his training of Plotina. And while her husband was alive, the self-effacing Plotina remained very much in his shadow. After his death, however, she revealed her interest in philosophy, especially Epicurean philosophy. In 121 CE, she wrote to then emperor Hadrian, whom Trajan had adopted shortly before his death, encouraging him to support the school of Epicurus in Athens.[107] As was true with Cornelia, mother of the Gracchi, a wealthy widow-hood allowed Plotina more freedom to engage in activities that interested her, without any loss of dignity.

The anonymous wife of Pompeius Saturninus

Nowhere does Pliny display the vitriol of his contemporary, Juvenal, with regard to educated and talented women. It is evident, however, that he assumed that wives would not only enter a marriage with considerably less education than their husbands, but also have less natural ability and be intellectually inferior to men. He may have believed that Calpurnia was not capable of learning more than how to appreciate his writing. And she, in turn, eager to fit his image of her, may have hesitated to learn more. In *Letter* 1.16.6, Pliny expresses skepticism about a claim made by his friend Pompeius Saturninus, who was a very talented composer of orations, histories, and poetry. Saturninus had read aloud to Pliny some letters which he claimed that his wife (Saturninus') had composed. (Pliny does not provide the name of the wife.) Nonetheless, the style of writing was so elegant that Pliny suspected that the letters had in reality been composed by Saturninus himself. However, Pliny does not claim to detect a gender distinction or suggest that the style of the letters was too masculine to be that of a woman. In any case, shrugs Pliny, the husband deserves commendation, either for writing the letters or for turning the girl he married into a wife who was so cultivated and refined. However, Pliny's skepticism may prompt readers to wonder why it was important to Saturninus that his friends think that his wife was an elegant writer. Was he a rare example of a husband who sincerely applauded his wife for accomplishing something of which few men were capable? Or, was he casting for compliments on his selection and training of his wife?

Pliny's comment, that the excellent style of the letters could be attributed to the husband, provides several critical pieces of information. Like his remark in the *Panegyricus*, that the admirable conduct of Trajan's wife was the result of her husband's instruction and training, this comment discloses a belief that it was the responsibility of a husband to mold his bride into the kind of wife he desired. It also suggests that, at the time of her marriage, a young bride would have only a rudimentary education and would require further instruction from her husband in order to read and write well – if, in fact, he desired a wife with literary skills.

Calpurnia (Part 3)

It seems that, for his own marriage, Pliny preferred a wife who could be educated by him only so far as to appreciate his work, but not to imitate and certainly not to compete with him. Compare his laudatory report on Fannia in *Letter* 7.19.5 and 6. He praises her for recognizing the value of her husband's activities and writings, for commissioning a biography about him, and for risking her life to preserve his memory. There is no suggestion by Pliny that Fannia could or should have written the biography herself. Fannia was forced by unfortunate circumstances to play an active role in producing a record of her husband's achievements. Calpurnia, however, was married to a man who had gained the favor of Trajan and whose life and work were therefore not in danger. Her admiration of his work could thus remain a private matter. Pliny's words in *Letter* 4.19 describe her as a model of propriety and submissiveness. Rawson contends that "Pliny's young wife must have been only one of many who attended literary readings, participated in literary discussions, and probably wrote for their own enjoyment."[108] However, Pliny's letter gives us quite a different picture, stating that, when he was entertaining guests with a recitation at his home, Calpurnia listened attentively to his words, but concealed herself modestly behind a curtain. She was neither seen nor heard. If she did not reveal her presence in her own home, it is unlikely that she attended, much less spoke up at recitations outside of her home.

As far as Calpurnia's musical skills, she had apparently learned just enough as was necessary to shine the spotlight on her husband. (Or, if she had expanded her repertoire beyond his poems, she was careful to conceal this information from him.) Pliny seems particularly pleased that her musical skills have been taught to her by no musician, but rather by love itself. One wonders if he was reluctant to allow a music teacher into his home because he feared that he might be opening the door to seduction.

Whatever the extent of her formal schooling may have been, *Letter* 4.19 reveals that, as a young wife, Calpurnia had learned one thing very well: that she could please her husband and persuade him of her *pietas* by exhibiting an interest in his work. What the letter does not reveal is whether her interest was genuine or a remarkably good pretense. Pliny, of course, had no doubt that it was genuine. Calpurnia ascertained that emphasizing her delight in her husband's work could please him in other ways as well. In *Letter* 1.14.8, Pliny had asserted that the good looks of a bridegroom are the reward for the chastity of the bride. Perhaps he was a bit concerned that his own young bride might not find his middle-aged appearance physically attractive. However, Calpurnia was an astute girl; she assuaged his fear by convincing him that he need not worry about their age difference because his renown was more appealing to her than a youthful body. Foucault offers the

Pliny-Calpurnia marriage as evidence that, by the imperial period, marriage had developed into a relationship of mutual solicitude and shared interest. He considers it significant that "Pliny likes Calpurnia to keep informed of his public activity, to encourage him, and to rejoice in his successes," and he maintains that Calpurnia does so because she is "inspired by the tenderness she feels for her husband."[109] We cannot know whether Calpurnia did indeed feel tenderness, or whether she was only playing the role of the good wife. It is obvious, however, that the relationship was one-sided. If the solicitude seems to Foucault mutual, if the interest seems shared, if Pliny enjoys their *concordia*, it is because Calpurnia has learned how to live harmoniously with Pliny.

The published collection of Pliny's letters includes three addressed to Calpurnia: *Letters* 6.4, 6.7, and 7.5. As De Pretis observes, "Calpurnia's replies to Pliny's letters (like those of all his correspondents) are not included in the collection, but this does not prevent them from affecting Pliny's text."[110] The absent person – in this case, the addressee, Calpurnia – is "present" in the creation of the letter. (In *Letter* 4.19, she was present as the subject of a letter addressed to her aunt.) As he composed his letters to her, Pliny was influenced by the letters which she had written to him. He had in mind an image, or construct, of her which, in turn, determined the image of himself that he wanted to present in his letters. However, Calpurnia, too, had been crafting an image of self in her letters. Husband and wife – each was responding to an image presented to them in the other's letter. In particular, each seems to have responded to the other's declaration that their separation was very difficult. We do not have Calpurnia's letters, but it is likely that she portrayed herself in a way which she believed he would find pleasing.

As author of his letters, Pliny controlled the content, and yet he reveals aspects of Calpurnia's behavior of which he himself seems not to be aware. In *Letter* 6.7 we find another indication of Calpurnia's perceptiveness in determining that she could win her husband's affection by expressing appreciation of his literary work. Pliny wrote the letter to Calpurnia when he was in Rome, occupied with senatorial duties, and she was in Campania recovering from an illness. He is replying to one of her letters in which she has written that she is very distressed by his absence and finds solace only in holding close his literary compositions, often even setting them in his stead by her side.[111] He writes: "I am gratified that you miss me and that you find comfort with such remedies" (*Letter* 6.7.2). It is curious that he does not mention that she reads the compositions, only that she embraces them, as one might hold close an article of clothing of an absent lover. Had Calpurnia failed to mention that she reads his work, or did Pliny simply overlook that aspect? Was her ability to read less gratifying to him than her fascination with his writing as extensions of himself? Calpurnia had apparently ascertained that Pliny would be delighted to hear that she cherished his compositions as substitutes for his physical presence. He had earlier been persuaded that his young wife found pleasure in his *gloria* and was not concerned about his age and appearance (*Letter* 4.19.5). She confirmed his conviction in her letter from Campania by intimating that his literary genius was so fundamental an aspect of his attractiveness that his compositions could be embraced as she would wish to embrace him.

In his response, Pliny attempts to flatter her by saying something which he himself would wish to hear: that he is captivated by her letters – that is, by *her* literary compositions. "I read your letters over and over, and pick them up again and again as if they were brand new" (*Letter* 6.7.2). He adds that her letters, so full of charm (*suavitas*), remind him that her conversation is so full of sweetness (*dulcedo*), and make him even more eager to be with her. Although "charm" and "sweetness" might seem to connote a feminine graciousness, and Pliny so uses it in *Letter* 5.16.2, when he writes that Fundanus' daughter, Minicia Marcella, was possessed of "girlish charm," elsewhere he uses these terms to describe the work of male authors whom he admires. In *Letter* 3.1.7, for example, he reports that Vestricius Spurinna composes very learned lyric poetry which exhibits remarkable *dulcedo* and *suavitas*. In *Letters* 1.16.4 and 5, he comments that the historical writings of Pompeius Saturninus are pleasing, in part, because of their *suavitas*, and that Saturninus' poetry is full of *dulcedo*. (Saturninus is the man who claimed that his wife had written very elegant letters.) About Voconius Romanus, Pliny reports that there is remarkable *suavitas* in his conversation and voice (*Letter* 2.13.6). And in *Letter* 5.8.10, he argues that historical writing pleases him because of its *suavitas* and *dulcedo*. Thus when Pliny declares to Calpurnia that her letters are full of charm and her conversation is full of sweetness, he is paying her a high compliment, and one which he himself would like to receive.

The letter in which Pliny expressed doubts about the literary talents of Saturninus's wife (*Letter* 1.16) predates this letter to Calpurnia by several years. One wonders, when reading his praise for the style of her letters, whether Pliny is simply, but insincerely trying to humor Calpurnia, or whether marriage to her has altered his opinion about the aptitudes of women, or whether perhaps he believed that he could take credit, in a letter he chose to publish, for doing what he lauded Saturninus for: turning the girl he married into a wife who was so cultivated and refined.

Letter 6.7 offers interesting insights into their marriage. Calpurnia, though considerably younger, correctly determined what words would please Pliny. He, on the other hand, simply assumed that she wished to hear what he wished to hear: praise for writing well. We cannot, of course, establish the sincerity of Calpurnia's affection, or hope to recover her personality from the few references about her in Pliny's correspondence. She may well have been happy with her marriage and her husband. She was probably trained, like countless other Roman girls, to be cheerful, obedient, amiable, and docile. However, *Letters* 4.19 and 6.7 suggest that it was Calpurnia who made most of the adaptation in this marriage. She worked hard and successfully to master that most essential of wifely skills: devotion to the interests of her husband.

Calpurnia's reward for her devotion was (in addition to the enduring fame Pliny created by publishing letters about her) the love of her husband. In *Letter* 6.7, Pliny uses the vocabulary and imagery of Latin love poetry to describe his emotions when he reads Calpurnia's letters. "I burn all the more with desire for you. ... Write as often as possible, even though your letters, which bring me such joy, also cause me such torture." *Letter* 6.7, as well as *Letters* 6.4 and 7.5, which were also written to Calpurnia during her recuperation in Campania, are remarkable because they are love letters from a husband to a wife, letters which express not simply fondness, but even passion. As Foucault points out: "Love is carefully differentiated from the habitual sharing of existence, even if both rightfully contribute to making the presence of the wife precious and her absence painful. ... . Behaviors that belong to the classic and negative image of passion are presented in a positive light; ... the fact that (Pliny) is ruled by his desire and his sorrow are offered as positive tokens of conjugal affection."[112] We do not have certain dates for the composition of these letters; Sherwin-White conjectures that they were written in mid-107 CE, which would put them still in the early years of the marriage. In *Letter* 6.4, Pliny reveals the distress which Calpurnia's illness and their separation produce in him.[113] Never before has he so much resented the work that forces him to remain in Rome. (In *Letter* 7.5, however, he confesses that the only time he is free of the torment of missing her is when he is exhausted by his activities in the Forum and law courts.) "Even if you were healthy, I would miss you and be anxious. To hear nothing about someone whom you love very ardently causes apprehension and trepidation. ... I beg you to relieve my fear with one or even two letters a day. I will feel more carefree while I am reading them, although I will immediately fear again when I have finished reading" (*Letters* 6.4.3–5). In *Letter* 7.5, the most erotic of the letters, Pliny describes the anguish he is experiencing. "It is unbelievable by what an enormous desire for you I am possessed." At night, he lies awake, haunted by her image; by day, his feet, of their own accord, draw him to her room – which he finds empty. Sick and melancholic, he withdraws from the doorway of the vacant room like, he writes, a lover who has been denied entry. Here he conjures up an image prominent in Augustan love poetry, that of the *exclusus amator*, the lover excluded or locked-out by his mistress.[114]

In Roman literature, wife and mistress were two very different women. Similarly, affection and passion belonged in separate categories. However, when Pliny employs the vocabulary, imagery, and conventions of Latin love poetry, he invites his reader to compare his relationship with his wife to the relationship between the love poet and his mistress.[115] He implies, moreover, that his and Calpurnia's marriage is a more blissful relationship than any enjoyed by love poets such as Catullus and Propertius because he has discovered in Calpurnia the woman for whom Catullus and Propertius yearned in vain: a woman who inspired passion, but remained constant and chaste. Like the love poets, Pliny is captivated by the object of his desires, but, unlike the poets, he is rewarded by his wife's loyalty and affection. In *Letter* 4.19.1, he confidently and publicly announces: "She loves me which is an indication of her chastity." Of course, Pliny was not an excluded lover, a man whose mistress has shut him out both physically and emotionally, but a husband who has been separated from his wife by her illness. The misery he experiences during her absence therefore serves as evidence not that she tortures him with her infidelity, but that she is normally nearby when he wants her. And she reciprocates his love, unlike the mistresses of the love poets, and proclaims that she is extremely distressed by his absence (*Letter* 6.7.1). Pliny's revisionist employment of the conventions of Latin love literature can be seen as another aspect of his determination to leave a record of an ideal marriage. And yet, Roman men did not, in published writing at least, describe their wives in terms which the love poets reserved for their mistresses. Cicero's letters to his wife, Terentia, during his exile of 58–57 BCE and Ovid's verse epistles to his wife during his banishment from Rome in 8 CE have been discussed in Chapter 2. Since both men were writing from exile, they certainly had reason to want to endear themselves to their wives. Their letters therefore express affection – not, though, passion. Cicero, for example, addresses Terentia as "most loyal and best wife," *fidissima atque optima uxor*.[116] Ovid, who describes his wife as "dear" (*cara*), "best" (*optima*), and "devoted" (*pia*), speaks of being haunted by an image of his wife, but also by images of familiar sights of his homeland.[117] In addition, both men, unlike Pliny, include references to domestic matters and family welfare, as we would expect from someone in exile. Perhaps the letters of Cicero and Ovid are also less passionate than Pliny's because they had been married longer. Pliny's contemporary, Statius, reveals that he is devoted to his wife of many years, but his words do not suggest infatuation.[118] Pliny's willingness to admit, and to admit in published letters, that he is infatuated with his young wife, and emotionally dependent on her, is remarkable.

It is possible that *Letter* 7.5 is "fictitious," – that is, a literary composition written specifically for publication – rather than a real correspondence. If the letter were indeed fictitious, then the forlorn husband would be a *persona*. The debate about whether Pliny's letters are real or fictitious has no objective solution. There is nothing in *Letter* 7.5 which would prove that it was not written for and sent to Calpurnia. As a "real" letter, it would demonstrate Pliny's love and affection for his wife. But even a "fictitious" letter (or a "real" letter that was insincere) would be illuminating because it would indicate that Pliny wanted his readers to believe that his marriage was both physically and emotionally satisfying. In other words, either he truly believed that his own marriage provided physical and emotional comfort, or he embraced an ideal that marriage could and should be so. The acknowledgment of either sentiment is unusual in Latin literature.

Pliny's decision to write to his wife, and later publish, love letters which imitate the style, but contradict the theme of Latin love poetry prompts the question of whether Pliny ever attempted to immortalize his passion for Calpurnia in verse. In several letters, he makes reference to his versifying, although nowhere does he mention poems specifically to or about his wife. He claims that he has composed poetry in a variety of meters, and was able to do so quickly and well (*Letters* 7.4.1, 4.14, 4.18), and that he finds relaxation in the process (*Letters* 4.14; 7.9.8–14).[119] He even admits that a few of his poems may shock readers because of their bawdy topics (*Letter* 4.14.4). In his defense, he cites the precedents set by many famous Roman authors (*Letter* 5.3). And some of his poems, he announces, are being set to music and sung by other men (*Letter* 7.4.9). It may well be that Pliny did write love poems, as well as love letters, to and about his wife. And perhaps these were the poems that Calpurnia set to music. However, none of his poetry has survived except for fragments embedded in *Letters* 7.4 and 7.9.

Although Pliny's letters to Calpurnia express an erotic passion which we do not find in the letters from exile of Cicero and Ovid, his expressions of distress are reminiscent of the letters of his predecessors. For Cicero and Ovid, so far from home and from the people, places, and activities dear to them, and so despairing of ever returning to Rome, their anguish was real and acute. For reasons both of personal consolation and of practical concerns, it was essential for them to retain the loyalty of their wives through the only means available to them: written communication. We might imagine that letters similarly expressing fondness, anxiety, and despondency were written by Helvidius I to Fannia during his banishments in the 60s and 70s CE, and by the four people, including Fannia, who were banished in 93 CE. Pliny's three letters to Calpurnia resemble letters from exile in the sense that Pliny describes himself as feeling desolate and fearful because of the separation (and Calpurnia, in her letters, evidently made similar comments). But, of course, neither he nor Calpurnia was in exile when the letters were written. In fact, he had remained in Rome and was fully occupied with his familiar senatorial activities. And Calpurnia was being well cared for in a Campanian villa. Thus, although Pliny represented their separation as a situation as painful as that endured by spouses during exile, in reality he had been deprived of nothing except the attentions of his wife for a few weeks. As noted already, neither Pliny nor Calpurnia had been called upon to exhibit the courage and self-sacrifice of people who had suffered political persecution, but Pliny was keen to establish that, had they been so tested by adversity, they would have proved capable of meeting the challenges. His published account of the anguish that he and his wife feel at their separation is intended to persuade the reader not only that they love one another, but also that they have experienced and survived a suffering similar to that of couples who were separated by banishment.

The purpose of marriage was to produce a new generation of family members.[120] In *Letter* 1.14.2, Pliny, when asked to recommend a husband for the daughter of Arulenus Rusticus, replied that he was happy to "choose the young man by whom it is fitting that the grandchildren of Arulenus Rusticus be created."[121] Pliny, who was the sole survivor of his family, must have been acutely aware of his failure to fulfill this duty.[122] His first two marriages had not resulted in children, but he remained optimistic that he and his young bride Calpurnia would have children. They never did. At least once she conceived, but miscarried. In *Letter* 8.10, which Sherwin-White dates to 107 CE, Pliny reported the miscarriage to Calpurnia's grandfather. He knew that news of the miscarriage would be a devastating blow to the grandfather because he had no other descendants of child-bearing age and was dependent on Calpurnia to perpetuate the family line. The wording of this letter and the following one, *Letter* 8.11, suggest that this was Calpurnia's first pregnancy. Scholars who propose that Calpurnia was Pliny's second, not third wife, and that the wedding took place in 97 CE, must assume that the family waited ten years for this pregnancy. If the wedding took place about 104 CE, as Sherwin-White argues, the wait was about three years. The references in this letter, and also in *Letter* 8.11.2, to Calpurnia's girlish age suggest that she is still a teenager – that is, that she and Pliny had been married fewer than the ten years which a marriage in 97 would require.

The careful wording of *Letter* 8.10 reveals that Pliny was anticipating that Fabatus would be angry at both him and Calpurnia and accuse them of denying him an heir.[123] Did Pliny suspect that Fabatus might regret marrying his grand-daughter to a man who had not produced children in two previous marriages? (Had Pliny had difficulty securing a bride in Rome and thus "settled" for a local girl?) Pliny carefully states that Calpurnia, being still a girl (*puellariter*), did not even know that she was pregnant, and therefore failed to take proper care of herself. Calpurnia has, moreover, paid a heavy price for her ignorance because she became critically ill. Pliny reminds Fabatus that, although it is distressing to hear that his old age has been deprived of a descendant who had been conceived, he should be grateful that Calpurnia herself did not die. The death of the fetus saved her life and preserved her for future production of children. Pliny is sure that this will happen because her pregnancy has proved that she is fertile. Nowhere in the letter does Pliny suggest that Fabatus might be worried about his granddaughter's health simply because he loved her and would be devastated at losing her. From Pliny's comments, we might conclude that Fabatus considered Calpurnia mainly as a producer of heirs and was frustrated rather than grieved by her loss of the fetus. So self-centered is the reaction which Pliny expects from Fabatus that he must even remind him that he, as the husband, wanted children just as fervently as Fabatus wanted descendants. (Being a tad self-centered himself, Pliny also reminds Fabatus that the hoped-for children will be the descendants of both of them, and that he, Pliny, will bequeath to them an easy avenue to public office, more widely celebrated names, and well-known ancestors.)

In *Letter* 8.11, Pliny reports the miscarriage to his wife's aunt, Calpurnia Hispulla. Once again, the wording of the letter reveals the reaction which Pliny anticipates. From Calpurnia Hispulla, who was both a close friend to him and like a mother to Calpurnia ("your affection for your brother's daughter is more gentle than a mother's tenderness," *Letter* 8.11.1), they can expect sympathy and concern for Calpurnia's health. He is certain that Calpurnia Hispulla, unlike Fabatus, will respond to the news with anxiety about Calpurnia's health. He therefore immediately assures her that Calpurnia is out of danger, but he is concerned that the aunt will be horrified by the thought of the life-threatening situation Calpurnia was in. He reports that Calpurnia, her life spared, is reco-vering well and is once more cheerful (*hilaris*) (*Letter* 8.11.2). Nonetheless, even to Calpurnia Hispulla he feels that he must explain that the miscarriage was not the fault of Calpurnia, but rather could be attributed to her age and inexperience, which made her unaware that she was pregnant. He acknowledges that Calpurnia Hispulla was hoping for the arrival of a grandson or granddaughter of her deceased brother, and remarks that the fulfillment of this hope has only been delayed, not denied. (It is interesting that Calpurnia Hispulla would apparently have been pleased by the arrival of either a girl or a boy infant. Calpurnia's grandfather was undoubtedly hoping for a male descendant.) Pliny ends the letter with a plea to Calpurnia Hispulla to explain to Fabatus that the miscarriage was an accident. Pliny was evidently still fretting about Fabatus' response to the disappointing news. It is curious that, in both letters, Pliny seems to feel obligated to stress that the loss of the pregnancy was not Calpurnia's fault. Abortions were attempted in the ancient world[124], but it is difficult to imagine that Calpurnia would have tried to abort a child which she knew that her husband and family so desperately wanted. Perhaps Pliny means only to inform Calpurnia's family that she had not knowingly engaged in any activities that would have caused a miscarriage.

As discussed earlier, the Julian laws bestowed privileges on men who produced legitimate children. Pliny apparently believed that he had been held back in his career goals because of his failure to have offspring (*Letter* 7.16.2). However, in early 98 CE, as we learn in *Letter* 10.2, Trajan granted him the "three-children privilege." Henceforth he was eligible for the career advancements and inheritance rights enjoyed by men with progeny. However, as he states in *Letter* 10.2, he now desired all the more the children whom he wanted to have even during the dismal period before Trajan became emperor. The political and financial "perks" of fatherhood were not the only, or even the main reason why elite men wanted children.[125] Men were anxious to leave behind descendants who would reproduce family traditions and maintain family values. It is quite clear from *Letters* 8.10 and 8.11 that Pliny and the family of Calpurnia were very conscious of the fact that she provided the last opportunity to save the two families from extinction. The pressure on Calpurnia to provide the families with descendants must have been enormous. And yet miscarriages and infant deaths were very common in the ancient world.

Soranus noted that hysteria was frequently a reaction to miscarriage.[126] This correlation between hysteria and miscarriage should not surprise us. Consider the emotional strain on a teenage girl like Calpurnia when her loss of a child prompted blame from family members and when her own grief and physical pain received little sympathy. Many of Pliny's correspondents were without children or without sons.[127] In a family with no sons, a daughter became very important as a producer of heirs, and may have been more pampered as a child than a girl with brothers. As noted earlier, daughters in families without sons may have received more attention and more education. However, we should not assume that such daughters were allowed a greater say in the direction of their lives. Indeed, they may well have had less control since they were looked on as prize breeding stock, and made aware not only that they had a duty to perform for the family, but also that the affection of family might be withdrawn if they failed to perform.

Calpurnia's miscarriage is the one dark cloud in the sunny picture which Pliny paints of their marriage. His portrayal of the harmony of their relationship has led Foucault to use this union as confirmation of his theory that the concept of marriage changed from the Greek, through the Hellenistic, to the Roman (particularly imperial) period. Foucault suggests that men in the imperial period viewed marriage not exclusively as a practical matter – that is, the acquisition of a housekeeper and child-bearer – but as an affective relationship and a partnership dependent on mutual understanding.[128] As evidence for this change, he cites

Stoic philosophers of the first century CE, particularly Musonius Rufus, who promoted the concept of marriage not simply as an institution to produce legitimate offspring, but as a relationship of companionship and reciprocal care.[129] Musonius' views on the education of girls and women have already been mentioned. Although he advised that girls receive the same type of instruction in the liberal arts as boys, he nonetheless believed that the practical function of such an education for a woman was not to make her competitive with men, but to make her better able to fulfill a traditional role as a manager of the household and a virtuous wife. With regard to marriage, he wrote that husband and wife had separate but complementary duties, and, in performing these duties and striving toward the same goal, they formed a unity.[130] However, although Musonius declared that the best union was one in which the partners had common interests and pulled together, like two animals yoked together, side by side, in reality most couples were harnessed in tandem: marriage was a happy unity if the wife followed where her husband led.

Musonius' opinions are similar to those expressed by Plutarch, a Greek writer who also lived in the first century CE. In his work, *Conjugalia Praecepta* (Conjugal Precepts), Plutarch speaks often of marriage as a companionate relationship, in which the partners should be affectionate toward and respectful of one another and should mingle together like liquids or intertwine like ropes. Nonetheless, he clearly believed that the husband should be the dominant partner, as the following quotations indicate.[131] "Whenever two sounds become harmonious, the lower sound (the baritone: Greek *baruteros* = "lower") produces the melody. Thus, every activity in a well-controlled household is done with both husband and wife in agreement, but reveals the leadership and choice of the husband. ... A wife is unsatisfactory and inept who is sullen when her husband is eager to be playful and cheerful, or who is playful and laughing when he is serious. One is an indication of an unpleasant character, the other of a disrespectful character. ... A wife should not have any emotion of her own, but should share in the seriousness and playfulness and anxiety and laughter of her husband. ... A wife should not rely on her dowry, or family lineage, or beauty, but rather on those things by which she especially affects her husband – that is, her conversation, her character, and her companionship. Day by day, she should present these as not harsh or vexatious, but rather accommodating, inoffensive, and agreeable. ... The small and continual and daily frictions between husband and wife divide and damage married life."[132] Plutarch was a Greek writer, and we must consider that his opinions were shaped by his Greek environment, in which, even in the first century CE, women were more restricted in their behavior than were Roman women. Nonetheless, he was writing for a Roman as well as a Greek audience, and his words reflect traditional beliefs in both cultures. We may applaud both Musonius Rufus and Plutarch for promoting the ideal that marriage partners should strive to create a comforting and affectionate relationship, in contrast to Juvenal, who viewed marriage as a vexatious affliction for men. At heart, however, the philosophers and the satirist are saying the same thing: the happiness or unhappiness of a marriage was dependent on the behavior of the wife. Our evidence suggests that the goal toward which married couples worked was usually determined by the husband's interests. Even a woman's decision to live or die might be made by her husband, or with her husband's reputation in mind, as we have seen in the stories of Arria E and of Seneca's wife Paulina. The Pliny-Calpurnia marriage seems so obvious an example of a tandem relationship that it is surprising that Foucault would theorize that it was a partnership based on mutual understanding. Although Pliny may, in his letters, express an affectionate tenderness toward his wife, he gives no indication that it has even occurred to him that she might entertain interests other than his. Considering the burden placed on Roman wives to be agreeable and accommodating, perhaps some Roman wives might have said what Nora said in the final scene of Ibsen's "Doll's House": "I was never happy. I was cheerful."

The anonymous wife of Maximus

In *Letter* 6.34, which was perhaps written about 106 or 107 CE, Pliny again lauds a deceased wife (as he did the wife of Macrinus, mentioned earlier, in *Letter* 8.5) and again without providing her name. This letter is addressed to Maximus, a man whose identity is unknown.[133] In the letter, Pliny commends Maximus for having sponsored a gladiatorial show for the people of Verona (whom Pliny, who was born in northern Italy, calls "our people"). Verona was the hometown of Maximus' deceased wife, a woman whom Pliny describes as very virtuous and very dear to her husband. We know nothing more about this woman. It was appropriate, Pliny remarks, that Maximus pay for either a public building or a public celebration to honor her memory.[134] Maximus decided to provide a gladiatorial show, which was a particularly fitting choice. By "fitting," Pliny is probably alluding to the belief that gladiatorial shows had originated as displays produced at the funerals and memorial services of elite people. We cannot, of course, be certain that Maximus truly held his wife dear, or that she was truly virtuous. Similarly, when Pliny divulges that a reluctant Maximus had been pressured into paying for a show by the many requests of the townspeople, we cannot necessarily assume that the townspeople truly felt a strong affection for his wife. They may have been grieved that the community lost a gracious woman – or they may simply have used her death as an opportunity to lobby for entertainment. In any case, Pliny deftly compliments Maximus on having made the townspeople's requests an occasion to display his generosity and good nature.[135] In doing so, he encourages Maximus to realize that his expenditure of funds on the gladiatorial show will earn him the respect and favor of the community. An additional reward, of course, though Pliny does not mention it, is the permanent and widely read record of his generosity which Pliny provides by publishing this letter. It is therefore notable that Pliny believed that he would enhance his portrait of Maximus by including the comment that his wife was very dear to him, implying that the marriage had been satisfying for him. Once again, we have evidence that, for many Romans, the perception that a man had been happily married contributed to a positive image of him.

Calpurnia (Part 4)

It is unfortunate that we have no words from Pliny's wife, Calpurnia, and therefore no way of learning how she felt about the people and events in her life. We must be mindful, of course, that, even if she could speak to us, she might disappoint our expectations, if, that is, we expected her to express frustration and dissatisfaction. She may have been quite content. She had, after all, been prepared since birth to accept the husband chosen for her and to make the best of marriage to him. She was, moreover, married at a young age, when she had scarcely had time to form interests of her own. The portrait which emerges from the information provided in her husband's letters is of a girl who is coping well with marriage to a family friend much more than twice her age. She has won the heart of her husband by her flattering attentiveness to his interests. The marriage cannot be viewed as an equal partnership. Pliny was at the height of his political career when he married Calpurnia; she entered adulthood and marriage at the same time.[136] Pliny's love letters provide the valuable information that Pliny believed (or wanted us to believe) that their relationship was mutually satisfying. We are in the dark about Calpurnia's true feelings.

After the letters reporting Calpurnia's miscarriage, which may date to about 107 CE, we learn little more about her. In *Letter* 8.19, which may date from approximately the same period, Pliny reports that he has recently been distressed by the ill-health of his wife and the maladies of his household slaves, some of whom have died. The life-threatening illness of one slave is revealed in *Letter* 8.1, and the deaths of others are announced in *Letter* 8.16. We do not know if the cause of all the maladies mentioned in the three letters was the same, or whether Calpurnia's "ill-health," to which Pliny refers in *Letter* 8.19, can be attributed instead to the miscarriage reported in *Letters* 8.10 and 8.11. We do know that Calpurnia overcame the debilitation of her ill-health and was well enough a few years later to undertake an arduous journey to Asia Minor. That trip is discussed later.

Pliny mentions Calpurnia again briefly in *Letter* 9.36.4, in which he describes his activities while staying at his villa in Etruria. He reports that, if he is dining with his wife or a few friends, a book is read aloud to them during the meal. After the meal, they are entertained by scenes from a comedy or by a lyre-player. (The lyre-player would be not be Calpurnia, but an entertainer of a much lower class, possibly even a slave.) Pliny's intent in this letter is to convey to his audience that his life outside Rome is productive, but simple, unhurried, and filled with contentment.[137] We might wonder whether a woman as young as Calpurnia found such activities as enjoyable as Pliny claims he did.

The anonymous wives of Bruttius Praesens and Calpurnius Macer

In several letters, Pliny reveals that he and his friends would agree that contentment includes the presence of a wife. In *Letter* 7.3, for example, written about 104 CE, he amiably chides Gaius Bruttius Praesens, who was about the same age as the ambitious Pliny, but who had abandoned the hectic busy-ness of senatorial duties in Rome to live in his native southern Italy with his wife, who was also a native of that region (she of Campania, he of Lucania). There, Pliny reports, Praesens indulges in a pleasurable life of leisure, not even donning a toga (the "business suit" of the senator).[138] We do not know the name of the wife. We have inscriptional evidence that Praesens was married to a woman named Laberia. However, this woman appears to have been not from the region of Campania, but from Lanuvium, a town only about 20 miles south-east of Rome. Raepsaet-Charlier has concluded that Laberia was a second wife, and that the anonymous wife of Pliny's *Letter* 7.3 was the first wife.[139] If her conclusion is correct, Praesens was separated from this first wife by either divorce or death.[140]

Another senator who found pleasure in life outside Rome was Publius Calpurnius Macer. In *Letter* 5.18, Pliny wrote to him from his own villa in Etruria, expressing his satisfaction in hearing that Calpurnius was with his wife and son, enjoying themselves at their beautiful villa near the sea. The wife's name may be Atilia.[141] She accompanied him to the province of Moesia when he became governor there about 109 CE.

Cottia

Pliny's account in *Letter* 9.36.4 of the dinner entertainment that he and Calpurnia enjoy at their villa in Etruria is reminiscent of a dinner he describes in *Letter* 1.15 where he notes that he was planning to have a reading or a performance by comic actors or a lyre-player.[142] It is also reminiscent of his account, in *Letter* 3.1.9, of meal time at the home of Titus Vestricius Spurinna, where dinner was often enhanced by scenes from comedies. Pliny's enumeration in *Letter* 9.36 of his other activities at his villa in Etruria – the dedication to study and literary composition, the exercise routine, the conversations with friends – also mirrors his account in *Letter* 3.1 of the daily life of Vestricius Spurinna. Spurinna was 78 years old when the letter was written (about 101 CE), and Pliny divulges that he aspires, when he grows old, to emulate the model of Spurinna's serene, but still active and engaged retirement (*Letter* 3.1.1). There is no mention in *Letter* 3.1 of the presence at dinner of Spurinna's wife, whose name was Cottia. However, we learn in section 5 that she often accompanied him on his regular carriage rides. These letters provide us with brief glimpses of the moments that Roman husbands and wives spent together and indicate that some Roman husbands enjoyed the company of their wives. However, we cannot ascertain the feelings of the wives.

Titus Vestricius Spurinna, the subject of *Letter* 3.1, was a distinguished senator who had held the consulship three times. He seems to have been a mentor to Pliny.[143] Cottia, his wife, whom Pliny describes in *Letter* 3.1.5 as a wife of singular example, *uxor singularis exempli*[144], may have derived from the Alpine area of northern Italy and may have counted among her ancestors a proconsul of Baetica (modern southern Spain) during the Augustan period.[145] Her family background is, however, speculative. We do not know when Spurinna and Cottia married, but she may have been quite a bit younger than he. We do know that their son was *iuvenis* and *adulescens* (*Letters* 2.7.3 and 5) when he died about 97 or 98 CE. These adjectives mean "young," but could be applied to men up to about the age of 40. For example, Minicius Acilianus, the man whom Pliny recommended as a husband for the daughter of Arulenus Rusticus, was also described as *iuvenis* and *adulescens* (*Letters* 1.14.3 and 10), but he had already held the praetorship and therefore was presumably in his mid to late 30s.[146] However, there is no mention in Pliny of Spurinna's son having held public office, and he was therefore probably younger than 30 at the time of his death. Spurinna was then about 75 years old. Cottia may have been the same age as he, and thus borne her son when she was in her 40s, but it seems more likely that there was a considerable age gap between husband and wife, and that her son had been born when she was a young woman. There is no information about other children.

The name of Vestricius Spurinna and Cottia's son is given by Pliny as Cottius (*Letter* 2.7). Presumably the *nomen* (family name) he received at the time of his birth was Vestricius, and Cottius was his *cognomen*, derived from his mother's family. His nomenclature is yet another example of the importance which Roman families attached to preserving the names of the mother's, as well as the father's, family.[147]

Pliny refers to the death of Cottius in *Letter* 2.7, which was written about 98 CE. He gives no information about the cause of the death, but deaths of young men and women were not rare in the ancient world.[148] Pliny reports that the Senate, on the recommendation of the emperor, had decreed a triumphal statue for Vestricius Spurinna in recognition of his valorous military service in northern Germany. In addition, a statue was approved for his son, Cottius, who had died while his father was away from home.[149] Pliny admits that a statue for a young man was an unusual event, but had been granted for three reasons: to honor Cottius' fine character, to console his grieving father, and to inspire, by its grant of immortality, other young men to cultivate virtues, and older men to produce children. Pliny does not mention Cottia in *Letter* 2.7. However, her grief at her son's death was undoubtedly as devastating as her husband's grief. Compounding her suffering was the fact that she received the news of her son's death when her husband was away from home. As an image of a sorrowing Roman mother, we might recall Pliny's report in *Letter* 3.16.5 of Arria overwhelmed by tears at the loss of her son.

Letter 3.10 was addressed to both Cottia and Spurinna. Cottia was thus one of only seven women to whom Pliny sent a letter that he later published.[150] In the letter, Pliny announces to Cottia and her husband that he has composed a biography of their deceased son and presented it at a recitation.[151] He is now planning to expand the composition and publish it, and has written to invite them to suggest additions, alterations, or omissions. He acknowledges that this is a difficult topic for them in their time of sorrow, but he assures them that he is aiming, with their guidance, to produce a likeness of their son that will be both accurate and immortal. It is significant that Pliny has included Cottia in this request for information, thus acknowledging the trauma which her son's death has been to her.

We don't know when Cottia died. Spurinna was still alive and well over 80 years old in about 105 CE when Pliny addressed *Letter* 5.17 to him.

Calpurnia (Part 5)

After *Letter* 9.36, in which Pliny describes the dinner entertainment that he and Calpurnia enjoyed at their villa in Etruria, we hear about Calpurnia only once more. A few years after her illness, which he reported in *Letter* 8.19, she was healthy enough to travel with him to the province of Bithynia-Pontus (the area which is now northern Turkey). At some point between 109 and 111 CE, Pliny was sent there with an appointment as the emperor's representative.[152] His assignment was not an easy one. Trajan admitted in a letter to Pliny that he had posted him to that province because "many things in it appeared to need to be corrected" (*Letter* 10.32.1). The province was prosperous, but plagued by political intrigue and financial mismanagement fueled by corruption among civic officials.[153] In addition, there were acrimonious factional feuds among the upper-class and bitter rivalries between the cities. Enormous sums of money had been spent wastefully and extravagantly on public building projects. Pliny's assignment was to make annual tours of the province, stopping in each major city to examine its financial records, identify areas where funds had been misadministered or misappropriated, and reorganize the public finances. He was also required to hear and decide on criminal cases that local magistrates could not deal with. This part of his assignment was especially irksome because residents had become accustomed to use the Roman governor's court as a venue to conduct factional vendettas. Corruption had not, moreover, been limited to the local administration. Two previous governors, Julius Bassus and Varenus Rufus, had been indicted by the Bithynians for extortion and for cruelty (*saevitia*) in the commission of extortion. At both trials, Pliny presented the case for the defense.[154] Trajan may have chosen Pliny as governor of Bithynia-Pontus because he had acquired considerable knowledge of the province while preparing these cases. In addition, Pliny had held several financial posts in the imperial administration and had the financial skills required to do the job which Trajan wanted done. Book 10 of Pliny's published correspondence covers a period of about three years and is a series of letters between Pliny and the emperor Trajan, dealing with a wide range of issues which Pliny confronted as he worked conscientiously to reform the financial administration of the cities. (However, the first 14 letters of Book 10 were written between 98 and 102 CE, well before Pliny's appointment to the province.) Calpurnia is mentioned as being present in the province in the final letters of Book 10, *Letters* 120 and 121. We do not know why we do not have any letters beyond 10.120 and 121. It is generally assumed that Pliny died shortly after writing those letters. We also have no information about who collected and published the letters contained in Book 10.

We do not know how Calpurnia, now perhaps in her mid-20s, responded to Pliny's news that he was being sent on official business to such a far-off territory. Although senatorial wives had usually stayed home during the republican period, it had become common in the imperial period, as discussed in Chapter 1, for wives to accompany their husbands to government postings. Was Calpurnia happy to travel to an area on the eastern edge of the Roman Empire and was she looking forward to new adventures there? Or would she have preferred to remain in Italy where she had family and friends?

It would be understandable if Calpurnia felt some trepidation about making the trip to Asia Minor. Such a long journey would be physically grueling, even for people like Calpurnia and Pliny, who could afford the finest transportation and accommodations and who, because they were traveling on official and high level government business, had access to opportunities not available to the average traveler. Pliny does not reveal whether Calpurnia traveled with him, although that seems more likely than that she traveled to Bithynia separately. Perhaps the fact that the letters about his journey and his activities in the province are essentially reports addressed to the emperor Trajan prevented him from including casual references about his wife. We are not told when they left Rome and whether they boarded a ship at Ostia (Rome's port) and thence sailed down the west coast of Italy before heading east toward Asia Minor, or whether they first traveled by land southeast to the eastern Italian port of Brundisium to sail across the Adriatic. Such a land journey might well take over a week, but would make the sea portion of the trip shorter.[155] Land travel in horse or mule drawn carriages was uncomfortable (consider the absence of rubber tires, springs, and upholstered seats), but travelers paused each night to rest, often in the villas of friends, where they could expect fine hospitality. In fact, a few years before he had married Calpurnia, Pliny had written a thank-you note to someone whose villas he had stayed in while traveling. In the note, he complimented her on the excellent treatment he received. He remarked: "Your slaves receive me with more care and attention than my own slaves do" (*Letter* 1.4).[156]

Sea travel was also uncomfortable, and there was always an element of uncertainty about how long a voyage might take. The unpredictability of the weather made planning difficult and travel hazardous. Pliny's uncle states that the voyage from southern Italy to Alexandria, Egypt, could be done in seven days.[157] However, this was true only when the winds were favorable and the sea calm, usually only in the summer when the prevailing winds were northerly. The return voyage, on the other hand, from Alexandria to Rome, could take two months or more, since the winds were adverse, forcing ships to battle headwinds and take roundabout courses. In addition, storms could cause seasickness in passengers and, not rarely, shipwrecks. In the New Testament, Acts 27, we read of a sea voyage which the apostle Paul made when he was being transported from Caesarea (in Palestine) to Rome to stand trial. He first traveled in a ship which headed east to the coast of Asia Minor. There, at Myra (on the mainland, opposite Cyprus), he was transferred to a freighter carrying a cargo of grain which was en route from Alexandria to Rome (by a roundabout course). For several days, the ship made little progress westward because of strong adverse winds. When it was off the coast of Crete, a storm approached, and the ship was tossed about for several more days. To lighten the load, Paul and the other prisoners and passengers helped the crew throw the cargo of grain overboard. Near Malta, the ship ran aground, and the prisoners were allowed to escape. The frightening journey from Myra to Malta had taken about two weeks.

In *Letter* 10.15, Pliny reports having sailed by Cape Malea, the southernmost promontory of Greece, and then traveling on to Ephesus, a major port on the west coast of Asia Minor. Some travelers from Italy, after rounding Cape Malea, sailed into Piraeus, the port of Athens, before continuing on to Asia Minor. Cicero, for example, when he was traveling to Cilicia (in southern Asia Minor) to take up his position of governor in the summer of 51 BCE, set sail from Brundisium, on the east coast of Italy, at some point between June 4 and 10 and reached Actium, on the north-west coast of Greece on June 14. From there Cicero arrived in Athens on June 24. He remained there for ten days and set sail again on July 6. The voyage from Athens to the island of Delos took six days. On the way, the ship may have stopped overnight at some of the other Aegean islands to pick up provisions and perhaps to allow passengers and crew the opportunity to sleep on solid ground. Securing fresh food and water was one of the main chores of the retinue of slaves which elite passengers like Cicero and Pliny took with them. Cloudy weather caused Cicero to delay on Delos for several days. Ancient mariners navigated by the sun and the stars, and therefore clear weather was essential. Cicero remarked: "Traveling by sea is no light matter, even in July." Cicero finally arrived at Ephesus on July 22. "Our voyage was free from danger and sea-sickness, but rather slow."[158]

Pliny and Calpurnia traveled during August (of perhaps 109 or 110 CE), one of the hottest months in the Mediterranean year. Unlike Cicero, Pliny does not document his and Calpurnia's journey to Ephesus. Nor does he mention a visit to Athens or any rest stops on Aegean Islands, although both seem probable. He also does not state the duration of the journey, although he informs Trajan that he, "along with all his people," reached Ephesus, but that the voyage had been delayed by adverse winds (*Letter* 10.15). Nonetheless, he had remained healthy (*Letter* 10.17). Pliny had planned to travel northeast from Ephesus to his province in part on land, by carriage, and in part by sea, on coastal vessels (*Letter* 10.15). The sea travel would be slow, he says, because of the adverse winds[159]. Land travel would be faster, but subject travelers to the very oppressive heat. Pliny and his entourage traveled as far as Pergamum by land vehicles, but there transferred to a ship both because of the heat and because he was assailed by a fever. Adverse winds impeded their progress, and Pliny and Calpurnia finally arrived in Bithynia on September 17, a date later than he had hoped. Sherwin-White conjectures that the journey from Italy to Bithynia took three to four weeks.[160]

To fulfill his duties as governor, Pliny needed to travel around the province, visiting all the main cities and towns. We don't know if Calpurnia traveled with him, or remained in the capital, Nicomedia. In either case, she may have found the companionship of other Roman women who were the wives of Roman businessmen in the province. It is unlikely that she was as isolated as the military wives, mentioned in Chapter 1, who accompanied their officer husbands to postings on the less civilized northern frontier. Calpurnia may also have developed friends among the women of the Bithynian elite, although the language difference would have presented a challenge. Since Bithynia was in the Greek-speaking part of the Roman Empire, the language of these women would have been Greek. However, perhaps Calpurnia had studied Greek, or perhaps some of the elite women had studied Latin. And, of course, she had undoubtedly been accompanied from Italy by a staff of trusted slaves who would provide her with company. Nonetheless, settling into a foreign country could be a trying and lonely experience for a young woman raised in a small northern Italian town.

We might imagine the resourceful Calpurnia setting up a household in Bithynia-Pontus and learning what behavior was expected there of a Roman official's wife. There is no inkling in the letters that Calpurnia did not behave with the utmost propriety. And Pliny paid scrupulous attention to making sure that no scandal attached to his appointment. In *Letter* 10.120, he wrote to Trajan, reporting that his wife's grandfather had died and that she had been anxious to return to Italy as quickly as possible to comfort her aunt. Pliny acknowledges that he had issued to her a travel pass to facilitate her journey. A travel pass allowed the bearer to use transport provided by the imperial courier system, a system designed to provide rapid movement between Rome and the provinces. Its use was limited to imperial messengers, state officials, and soldiers on special duty. The purpose of Pliny's letter is to explain to Trajan why he has violated policy by allowing his wife to take advantage of the system, and to request permission after the fact. Necessity, he writes, caused him to break the rules for he knew that the kindness inherent in the duty of providing comfort to a bereaved family member depends on the swiftness of fulfilling it. He also thought that Trajan would approve the journey because it was undertaken out of family devotion. Pliny adds that, had he waited to consult with and receive approval from Trajan, he would have acted too late. In his reply, Trajan assures Pliny that he had acted correctly and that it was fitting for his wife to increase the kindness of her visit to her aunt by arriving speedily (*Letter* 10.121). It is Trajan, then, who has the last word in the published collection of Pliny's correspondence. We do not know if Calpurnia reached Italy and consoled her aunt, nor do we know whether she later returned to Pliny in Bithynia-Pontus. Her eagerness to undertake a journey which, even by imperial transport, must have been grueling, and to undertake it without her husband, speaks to her deep affection for her aunt. Perhaps we might also speculate that she was home-sick, and happy to have a reason to return to Italy. Since the published correspondence breaks off here, we are left wondering whether Pliny died while Calpurnia was back in Italy. Our knowledge about their lives ends with Pliny's apology to the emperor for issuing a travel pass to Calpurnia.[161]

The wife of Domitius Tullus (perhaps Dasumia Polla)

The portrait of Calpurnia which emerges from Pliny's words is that of an astute young woman who learned early in her marriage how to please her husband. Pliny's letters to and about Calpurnia inform us both of the behavior which Roman men valued in a wife and also of the reward which an exemplary wife could expect: the affection of her husband and, for Pliny's wife, the immortalization which publication can confer. To his readers, Pliny offers, in his portrait of Calpurnia, a model of the type of ideal marriage which Musonius and Plutarch recommended, a union in which the husband is the dominant partner, and where it is mainly the efforts of the wife that produce the desired harmony. Calpurnia demonstrated the same unwavering devotion to her husband that Arria E, Arria Y, and Fannia had demonstrated, though she had fortunately not been tested as these other women had.

In *Letter* 8.18, which may date to the end of 108 CE, Pliny lauds the selflessness of another woman, the wife of Domitius Tullus. As with the wife commended in *Letter* 6.24 for committing suicide with her terminally ill husband at Lake Como, Pliny does not provide the name of this woman. He has, however, granted her enduring glory by choosing to report her behavior in a published letter. Some scholars have speculated that she was Dasumia Polla, a woman whose name appears as one of the beneficiaries in a very long and complex will, parts of which have been fortuitously preserved for us in an inscription.[162] Unfortunately, the part of the will giving the name of the testator has not been preserved.

The will was inscribed in the summer of 108 CE on a large marble monument which was placed alongside the Via Appia, a main road leading south from Rome.[163] It was customary for Roman families to locate their family tombs alongside major thoroughfares and thus give prominence to their memorials. Nevertheless, such a conspicuous display of a will, especially such a lengthy one, was unusual. Only three fragments of the marble copy of the will have been discovered, providing a total of about 15% of the information in the original. Scholars at first conjectured that the will belonged to a man named Dasumius, and the document was thus labeled "The Will Of Dasumius." However, since about 1978, following the discovery of the third piece, the prevailing hypothesis has been that the testator was Domitius Tullus, the man whose will Pliny discusses in *Letter* 8.18. The document is now generally referred to as "The So-called Will of 'Dasumius'." One of the four primary heirs announced in the beginning of the will is a woman named Dasumia Polla, to whom 1/12 of the estate is bequeathed. The identification of Dasumia Polla as the wife Domitius Tullus is admittedly speculative and based upon conjectures that the unknown testator of the will was indeed the Domitius Tullus mentioned in Pliny's *Letter* 8.18. Although the identification has not been proved beyond a doubt, the name Dasumia Polla will be used in the discussion later in reference to Tullus' wife, whom Pliny does not name.

The subject of Pliny's *Letter* 8.18 is the excitement which the publication of the will of the very wealthy Gnaeus Domitius Tullus has generated in Rome.[164] Pliny announces: "Tullus is all the talk of the town" (*Letter* 8.18.11). There is nothing in Pliny's letter that definitively corroborates the conjecture that the will of Domitius to which he refers is the same document as the will inscribed on marble. However, it is reasonable to speculate that the appearance of the marble monument would have caused the kind of excitement that Pliny reports. Pliny relates in *Letter* 8.18 that everyone who learned of the will was stunned to find out that Domitius Tullus had acquitted himself well with respect to looking after his family and friends. Pliny's opening line is: "That popular belief is certainly false, that a man's will is a mirror of his character, for Domitius Tullus appeared much better in death than in life." Apparently, Domitius Tullus' behavior while alive had been contemptible. He redeemed himself only after his death when it was revealed that he had acted honorably after all and made his family members his beneficiaries, rather than leaving his fortune to the *captatores*, the legacy-hunters, whose attentions he had apparently encouraged.[165] Pliny comments that Tullus' distributions were completely in accord with *pietas*, devotion to family, and were, for that reason, all the more unexpected (*Letter* 8.18.2). His primary heir was his adopted daughter, whose life is discussed in Chapter 6. At *Letter* 8.18.7, Pliny states that "the will was all the more praiseworthy because family devotion, loyalty, and a sense of decency created it. In it, Domitius Tullus expressed his gratitude to all his relatives for the services each had performed. He also expressed his gratitude to his wife. She received several very beautiful villas and a large sum of money." We cannot establish whether Tullus' wife received free and clear title to the villas – that is, became the owner of them and was able to bequeath them in turn when she died – or whether she received only usufruct of them. (Latin *usus* = "use"; *fructus* = "enjoyment.") It was not uncommon in the ancient Roman world for a man to provide for his widow by stipulating that she could enjoy the use of property for the rest of her life, but that, at her death, the property would revert to an agnate of her husband.[166]

We do not know how long Tullus and Dasumia Polla had been married. From Pliny's letter, we learn that she had been previously married and had borne children. Syme hypothesizes that her first husband was Publius Tullius Varro[167], who had twice been suffect consul, the second time in 98 CE, and that she had borne at least two sons in that marriage, Publius Tullius Varro and Publius Dasumius Rusticus. If the latter, who was consul in 119 CE, was indeed her son, his *nomen* (Dasumius, rather than Tullius) may indicate that he had been adopted by a brother of Dasumia. At the time of her marriage to Tullus, however, Dasumia had, Pliny says, been long widowed and was declining toward old age. (An argument against her having been married to Tullius Varro is the fact that he was consul in 98. Even if he had died shortly after his consulship, could Dasumia be said to be "long widowed" if she had married Domitius Tullus a few years before his death in 108?) The situation of widows, the suspicion with which they were regarded, and the pressure on them to remarry have been discussed in Chapter 2. However, at the time of her union with Tullus, there had, Pliny reports, been comments that it was quite inappropriate for an aging widow, who was a woman of noble birth and blameless character, to pursue marriage to a wealthy old man who was so ravaged by disease that he could become disgusting even to a wife whom he had wed when he was young and healthy. Pliny's comment implies that Tullus had been previously married, and that his earlier wife had found his incapacitation intolerable. We do not know whether that marriage ended because of divorce or death. Nor do we know why Dasumia Polla agreed to marry the very ill Domitius Tullus. Pliny's phrase, that she was "once a mother" (*Letter* 8.18.8) implies that she was past child-bearing years and therefore exempt from the Julian legislation on remarriage. Gossipmongers apparently believed that she was after his money. Pliny comments, however, that she was an excellent wife and a very patient one, and deserved good treatment from her husband all the more because she had been criticized for marrying him. Domitius Tullus was deformed and crippled in every limb. Even in bed, he could change position only if moved by others. He was fed and bathed by slaves, and suffered the indignities of infirmity. Yet, Pliny says, he continued to live, and wanted to live, sustained chiefly by his wife, who, by her perseverance, had turned the aspersions cast when the marriage began into renown (*gloria*) (*Letters* 8.18.8–10).

Domitius Tullus' primary heir was his adopted daughter. We don't know if she was adopted before or during the marriage to Dasumia Polla. In any case, Dasumia Polla proved to be not only a sterling wife, but also a good stepmother because she did not cajole her husband into leaving the bulk of his fortune to her.[168] (We learn at *Letter* 8.18.2 that her stepdaughter was herself a grandmother and thus probably about 40 years old.) We don't know when Dasumia Polla died. Syme hypothesized that she married for a third time after the death of Domitius Tullus, to Lucius Catilius Severus, a man who was twice consul (in 110 and 120 CE) and served several times as a provincial governor.[169] If this hypothesis is correct, it is perhaps surprising that she would have remarried. She was presumably well into middle age at the time of Tullus' death and had surely been exhausted by her duties of caring for him. She would have been financially secure because of the property he had bequeathed to her. It would be interesting to know why and by whom the marriage – to a man about 10 years younger than she – was arranged, and whether the aging Dasumia Polla traveled with Catilius to the overseas postings he held in Asia and Africa. Although widowhood had its attractions, especially after serving as a caretaker to a bedridden husband, it could be socially isolating. Perhaps Dasumia desired to enter a new marriage in order to be part of a social network. Or perhaps she believed that marriage to a man like Catilius Severus would be advantageous to the political careers of her sons. Her wealth (and possibly also her reputation for devotion) would have attracted the attention of men who were looking for a wife and who did not need (more) children. She may, however, have been pressured by her family members to settle into another marriage. Family members may have wanted to use a union to create an alliance with a prominent family. Or, if we think less charitably, they may have wanted to free themselves from the burden of caring for Dasumia Polla as she aged. If indeed Catilius did marry Dasumia, older than he by about ten years and past child-bearing, his motivation may well have been her wealth. Certainly his career blossomed in the years between 110 and 120 CE, aided perhaps by her financial support.[170]

Catilius was a friend of Pliny's. He was the recipient of *Letter* 1.22, discussed later, in which Pliny relates that Titius Aristo had been very ill and had discussed suicide with his wife, daughter, and friends. Catilius also received *Letter* 3.12, Pliny's reply to a dinner invitation. We do not know if Pliny's wife, Calpurnia, and Dasumia Polla were acquainted, but it is quite likely because "The So-called Will of 'Dasumius'" reveals that Pliny and Dasumia's husband, Domitius Tullus, had several mutual friends.[171] In any case, Calpurnia undoubtedly heard glowing reports of Dasumia's conscientious care of her ill husband. If the widowed Dasumia did indeed later marry Pliny's friend Catilius Severus, Pliny and Calpurnia would not have had many opportunities to socialize with them because they left for Pliny's posting in Bithynia around 110 CE.

Pliny, by his narration of her devoted care to her second husband, preserves for posterity a portrait of a woman who willingly undertook the challenges of caring for an invalid husband, ignored the malicious gossip about her motives, and performed her duties so remarkably well that she encouraged him to desire to stay alive. (The gossipers may have assumed that a "gold-digger" would try to hasten his death.) The behavior of the anonymous wife of *Letter* 6.24 presents an instructive contrast. She, realizing that her husband's painful illness was terminal, urged him to kill himself, and then contrived and accompanied him in the suicide, thus giving up her life for his sake. Dasumia Polla (also an anonymous wife in *Letter* 8.18), recognizing that her husband's condition, though painful, humiliating, and grave, was not terminal, dedicated herself to providing him with the support that would persuade him to continue to live. In each case, the wife exhibited a selfless devotion which Pliny believed was worthy of the *gloria*, the renown, which he could grant, and as equally deserving of emulation as was the much more dramatic gesture of Arria E.

Hispulla

In *Letter* 1.12, written in 97 or 98 CE, Pliny provides a third example of a wife dealing with the debilitating illness of her husband. He identifies her as Hispulla, the wife of Quintus Corellius Rufus (*Letter* 1.12.9). The name by which Pliny identifies her is the same as the *cognomen* of Pliny's aunt-in-law, Calpurnia Hispulla. It is a rare name, and perhaps we can conclude that Hispulla, like Pliny and his in-laws, was of north Italian origin. In fact, some scholars have suggested that Hispulla was a relative of Pliny's wife and therefore related to him by marriage.[172] Unfortunately we have no information about Hispulla's parents. It is possible that the wife of Pliny's grandfather-in-law, Calpurnius Fabatus, was also a Hispulla. More will be said on this topic in Chapter 4. (See Genealogy Chart 4.)

Corellius Rufus (born about 30 CE) had served as suffect consul in 78 CE and had been governor of Upper Germania (modern south and central west Germany) about 82 CE. It is quite possible that Hispulla accompanied him to this posting. If so, her experiences would have differed considerably from those of Calpurnia who accompanied Pliny to his posting in Bithynia-Pontus. The latter was a peaceful province, and Pliny was not called upon to deal with military actions. Upper Germania, however, was a territory in the unsettled northern part of the Roman empire where the Romans had been fighting Germanic tribes along the Rhine for decades. In fact, in 83 CE, the emperor Domitian launched a major offensive in that area and constructed a continuous fortified border. If Hispulla had indeed accompanied her husband, she may have found herself spending much of her time in an army camp, with few female companions and with far fewer of the "creature comforts" that the eastern parts of the empire offered.

Because there is no record of Corellius' having held other offices during Domitian's reign, his career seems to have been checked by Domitian. (Was Domitian unhappy about Corellius' performance in Upper Germania?) Pliny, who calls Corellius a witness (*testis*), guide (*rector*), and mentor (*magister*) of his life (*Letter* 1.12.12), also describes him as a man of the highest integrity, the highest renown, and the greatest authority (*Letter* 1.12.3).[173]

We do not know when Corellius and Hispulla had married. They had at least one child, a daughter, Corellia Hispulla, whose name is given in *Letter* 3.3, which Pliny addresses to her. The addition of the cognomen, Hispulla, to her agnate *nomen*, Corellia, would indicate that she was the daughter, not the stepdaughter, of Hispulla. In *Letter* 3.3, written about 100 CE, Pliny is replying to Corellia Hispulla's request to recommend a teacher of Latin rhetoric for her son. Boys began this level of intense rhetorical training in their early teens, a time when girls were preparing to be married. Thus, since the daughter of Corellius and Hispulla was already, in the years around 100 CE, an adult with a son entering his teen years, we may speculate that Corellius and Hispulla had been married in the mid-60s CE, and that, at the time that *Letter* 1.12 was written (97 CE), Hispulla was about 50 years old. Pliny provides little information about Hispulla (and we have no other sources of information about her), but he does report that she was very capable of keeping any secret her husband shared with her (*Letter* 1.12.7). This comment informs us not only about Hispulla's discretion, but also about her husband's willingness to confide in her and about the intimacy of their marriage.

Corellius had been afflicted by gout at the age of 32 (*Letter* 1.12.4). Although he tried to alleviate the symptoms by a strict diet, the condition worsened as he grew older, and he suffered torturous pain and (like Domitius Tullus of *Letter* 8.18) the indignities of being bedridden. As age exacerbated the agony of the disease, Corellius contemplated suicide, but, Pliny reports, resisted this option, realizing that he had many reasons to stay alive, including his wife, daughter, grandson, and sisters.[174] Corellius also confided to Pliny that he had endured such great pains for so long because he was determined to outlive the hated emperor Domitian, if only by a single day. Soon after Domitian's death in 96 CE, Corellius, who was now 67 years old, decided to end his pain by committing suicide by starving himself.[175] Though his wife and daughter begged him not to, he was resolved. As he grew weak, Hispulla sent a message to Pliny, asking him to intervene. However, Pliny arrived too late. Like Domitius Tullus' wife, Hispulla had supported her husband through his lengthy, crippling, and agonizing chronic ailment. Unlike Tullus' wife, she was not able, despite her efforts, to prevent him from carrying out his own death.

Thus Hispulla found herself a widow at approximately 50 years of age, and also probably deserving of the designation of *univira*, since she seems to have married Corellius at an early age. Undoubtedly her husband had made provisions in his will for her to live comfortably. She had, moreover, a daughter and grandson to offer company and support. Given the affection and gratitude felt by Pliny for her husband, one expects that he maintained ties with the widow. However, we hear nothing more about her after *Letter* 1.12, nor do we have other sources of information than Pliny. Therefore, we do not know if she remarried. Given her age, she was not bound by the Julian laws to do so. Pliny did not abandon the family, however, after Corellius' death. His services to the daughter and sisters will be discussed in chapters below.

Corellius' death raises again a topic discussed in Chapter 1: self-inflicted death. Our earlier discussions focused on the responses of wives to situations in which a husband was forced, by the threat of execution, to consider suicide. Arria E inspired in her husband the courage to kill himself by mortally wounding herself. Her daughter, Arria Y, also wanted to die with her husband, but was persuaded by him not to. In both these situations, the husbands were apparently healthy, but had been condemned to death for political reasons. The willingness of the wives to die with them could be viewed as a political statement, indicting the emperors for causing the loss to society of good and brave – and innocent – women.[176] In *Letter* 6.24, Pliny tells the tale of another female suicide who, like Arria, both encouraged and accompanied her husband in death. In her situation, however, the incentive for the husband's suicide was an incurable illness, and thus a personal, not a political reason. The situation of Hispulla in *Letter* 1.12 was similar to that of the unnamed wife of *Letter* 6.24, in that both women were caring for husbands with incurable and unremitting ailments. What is quite different, of course, is that Hispulla exhorted and persuaded her husband to remain alive, as had the wife of Domitius Tullus in *Letter* 8.18. And there is no report in Pliny as to whether, when Corellius decided to seek release from his excruciating pain by taking his own life, Hispulla offered to accompany him in death.

The anonymous wife of Titius Aristo

In *Letter* 1.22, written about 97 CE – that is, about the same time as *Letter* 1.12 – there is another mention, here a very brief one, of a wife and daughter pleading with a man not to commit suicide. Pliny reports that he has been delayed in Rome because of the lengthy and persistent ill health of his dear friend Titius Aristo. We do not know the nature of his ailment, but Pliny reports that it caused pain, thirst, and fever. Aristo had decided to take his own life if the illness was incurable, but to remain alive if it was merely difficult and long. He said that he owed it to his wife's pleas, his daughter's tears, and his friends' hopes. Fortunately, the doctors predicted a favorable outcome. We know that he survived because he is the recipient of two of Pliny's *Letters*, 5.3 and 8.14, written perhaps about 105 CE.

One interesting feature of *Letters* 1.12 and 1.22 is their revelation of how freely Roman men discussed their possible suicides with family members and sought counsel from friends. Arria E, too, debated the subject with her daughter and son-in-law (*Letter* 3.16.9–12), and Thrasea Paetus informed his wife, Arria Y, of his plans when he persuaded her not to kill herself. As Pliny reports in *Letters* 1.12, 1.22, and 8.18, the wishes of family members were a critical element in the decision-making process. Corellius Rufus listened to the entreaties of his wife, Hispulla, and his daughter, but was nonetheless determined to die (*Letter* 1.12.9). Titius Aristo, on the other hand, was swayed by the pleas of his wife and the tears of his daughter to remain alive (*Letter* 1.22.9). Similarly, Domitius Tullus' will to live was encouraged chiefly by his wife (*Letter* 8.18.10). Pliny relates stories of both personal and political reasons for men to want to commit suicide. He also records a variety of reactions that wives had to their husbands' contemplation of suicide, and a variety of responses that the husbands made after consulting with their wives. Whatever the outcome, in each of the stories, the wife is portrayed as demonstrating devotion to her husband. In Pliny's presentations, both the wife who nurses and sustains her ill husband, and the wife who devises an honorable death for her husband and herself are models of self-sacrifice.

The anonymous wife of Asinius Rufus

The prime duty of a wife was, of course, to produce offspring. And the Julian laws made this traditional duty a civic duty. The reproduction of the family – both physically and culturally – was important to many Romans. It was not rare for a marriage to end in divorce when it failed to produce children (although Pliny nowhere in the letters mentions divorce for this reason). As noted already, "Turia's" husband revealed that she offered him a divorce when she did not bear any children. He gallantly refused, but was nonetheless willing to allow her to accept the blame for their infertility. He was simply following the traditional belief that the wife was responsible if a marriage was barren. We hear nothing in Pliny's letters about the effect on a marriage of the success or failure to have children. This would be a sensitive subject for Pliny who, in three marriages, had not fathered a child, and who therefore, even before his third marriage, requested from Trajan a "three-children privilege."[177] We have discussed the anguish apparent in the letters he wrote to Calpurnia's grandfather and aunt about her miscarriage, letters in which he discloses that the grandfather might raise a question about the young Calpurnia's responsibility. The barrenness of his marriage does not, however, seem to have altered Pliny's feelings for Calpurnia, or, in any case, changed the portrait that he was creating of his marriage. Scholars conjecture that Calpurnia's convalescence in Campania, documented in the "love letters" 6.4, 6.7, and 7.5, was a result of her miscarriage. If this is true, Pliny appears to have remained enamored of his young wife despite the disappointment of an unsuccessful pregnancy. Pliny was not alone, however, in having a childless, but satisfying marriage. The marriage of Trajan and Plotina, for example, did not result in offspring. Pliny states in *Letter* 8.10.3 that he ardently desired children. He was aware, nonetheless, that some couples preferred to be childless.[178] Others, in contrast, had large families. In *Letter* 4.15.3, he reports that Asinius Rufus had several children. "He thus fulfilled the obligation of the best of citizens because he was very willing to make use of the fertility of his wife, in an era in which the rewards of childlessness make even one child seem to many to be burdensome." Pliny's phrasing reduces Asinius Rufus's wife to the category of a brood mare whose only value lies in her ability to produce offspring. Missing from the account is any mention of her role in the marriage as a companion.

The name of Asinius Rufus's wife may have been Pomponia, and she may have been the daughter or sister of Quintus Pomponius Rufus who was proconsul of Africa in 109–10 CE.[179] We do not know the total number of children that she bore. From Pliny's letter, we can ascertain that there was at least one daughter (presumably named Asinia) who was married to a man, otherwise unknown, named Saturius Firmus (*Letter* 4.15.3).[180] At the time the letter was written, about 106 CE, this marriage had produced one child. Asinius and his wife also had at least one son, Asinius Bassus, who had been selected for the quaestorship of 107 CE. Indeed, the purpose of Pliny's letter was to request from the addressee, Minicius Fundanus, that he be a mentor to this son and, if he (Minicius) should be selected as consul for 107, chose him as his assistant.[181] Nothing more is known about Asinius Rufus's wife: she was fertile, and a grandmother by 106 CE.

The anonymous wife of Junius Avitus

Letter 8.23, written about 108 or 109 CE, prompts us to consider again the high mortality among young people and the plight of widows, in this case a very young widow. In this letter, Pliny announces the death of Junius Avitus from an unspecified illness which struck suddenly and killed quickly. Avitus seems to have been his protégé, and Pliny confesses that the death has been a very heavy blow to him. Like most young men with senatorial aspirations, Avitus had served as a military tribune, in his case in 98 CE in Germany, under the command of Lucius Julius Ursus Servianus.[182] He was probably about 20 years old at the time. A few years later, with Pliny's help, he was selected for the office of quaestor and became a member of the Senate.[183] In the first century CE, the minimum age for holding the quaestorship was 25 years (reduced from the minimum age of 30 during the republican period). During Avitus' year in this office, he performed with diligence and modesty, according to Pliny. A year or two later, probably in 107 CE, he campaigned, again with Pliny's assistance, for the office of aedile. He was selected for this position, but died before he could serve his term. Avitus was probably about 27 or 28 years old at the time of his death. Pliny, who refers to him as still in *adulescentia* (*Letters* 8.23.3 and 7), believed that Avitus would have had a promising political career.[184]

Pliny laments the misfortune of the relatives he left behind: an aging mother, a wife whom he had married as a virgin only a year before, and an infant daughter (probably named Junia) whom he had just recently welcomed into the family. Avitus had married just prior to embarking on his campaign for the aedileship. The birth of a daughter within a year of his marriage was a boon to his political career because the Julian marriage laws allowed fathers to stand for office earlier than men without children.[185] We learn, for example, in *Letter* 7.16, that Pliny's friend and coeval, Calestrius Tiro, reached the office of tribune earlier than Pliny because of the privilege granted to fathers. Perhaps we can assume that Pliny had also married for the first time at about 24 years, but, unlike Avitus and Tiro, had not been blessed with the birth of a child to advance his career.

Because there is no mention of Avitus' father as one of the bereaved relatives, we may assume that he was dead, and that his mother was therefore a widow. She may have been living with her son. We know nothing about the two widows – Avitus' mother and his young wife – beyond this brief mention in Pliny.

The wife, whose name Pliny does not supply, had been a virgin at the time of her marriage a year prior (*Letter* 8.23.7) and was therefore probably in her mid-teens when she wed this promising young political figure who was her senior by about ten years. She must have anticipated a comfortable, perhaps even happy future. Within a year of marriage, she had given birth to a daughter – but then lost her husband. As Pliny commented, "One day nullified so many hopes and so many joys." This young woman had undergone several momentous upheavals in the span of only a year, moving from her father's home and the status of a daughter, to her husband's home and the status (and responsibilities) of a wife, and soon a mother, and then tragically a widow.

We do not know whether Avitus' wife wanted to remain a *univira*. Her relatives undoubtedly tried to arrange a new marriage for her as quickly as possible, not just because the Julian laws encouraged this, but because she provided them with the opportunity to form a valuable new alliance. Because she had produced a child within months of being married, her fertility and youth made her an attractive prospect as a wife.

However, her child, a Junia, legally belonged to Avitus' *familia*. Since Avitus' father was dead, the infant Junia did not have a grandfather to take her in, as Pliny's young wife Calpurnia had when her father died. Perhaps Junia was fostered by one of Avitus' agnates, such as a paternal uncle (if there was one), as seems to have been the case with another Junia, the daughter of Junius Arulenus Rusticus, who was condemned to death in 93 CE. Or perhaps Avitus' infant daughter was fostered by a paternal aunt, as was the case with Calpurnia. Or possibly she remained with her mother, as Pliny himself had done after the death of his father, and as Avitus perhaps did. If Avitus' widow relinquished her child to her husband's agnates, remarriage would have provided her with the opportunity to form a new family. However, it is not likely that she would forget her first-born child. If she retained care of the infant Junia, but later remarried, her first child probably grew up with half-siblings and step-siblings.

If, as seems probable, Avitus' father was dead, Avitus was *sui iuris* ("under his own regulation"), and had had control of the family estate that he had presumably inherited. We may assume that he had a will – most wealthy Roman men did – but we do not know whether he left anything to his wife, or whether she had to depend on her own agnate family for financial support during her widowhood. The plight of Avitus' widowed mother is also unknown. Although Pliny refers to her as old, she may have been in her late 40s or early 50s. She may have had an estate that descended to her from her agnate family, and she may also have received an inheritance from her late husband. It is likely, moreover, that Avitus provided for her in his will.

It is a curious coincidence that Junius Avitus was a beneficiary of two pounds of gold in "The So-called Will of 'Dasumius'," which has been discussed earlier in this chapter. It is assumed that Avitus died after the summer of 108 CE, because the will of "Dasumius" is dated to between May and August of 108. It is, of course, possible that Avitus died earlier, but that his name had not yet been removed from the will. In this will, Julius Servianus, who was Pliny's friend and had been Avitus' commander when he was a military tribune in Germany, was entrusted with making arrangements for the funeral. In addition, Servianus' daughter, Julia Paulina, was named as an alternate heir to Domitia, the daughter of the testator, as well as being named a beneficiary of five pounds of gold.[186] We do not know what the personal relationship was between Servianus and the testator, who is considered by many scholars to have been Domitius Tullus of *Letter* 8.18, nor do we know why the testator selected Julia Paulina as an alternate for his daughter. It is surprising to discover that Servianus, whom Pliny described as a most scrupulous man (*Letter* 8.23.5), who was the brother-in-law of Hadrian and advisor of Trajan, was also a trusted friend of the vile Domitius, and that their daughters may have been friends. We are also ignorant of Pliny's relationship with the testator, although we may suppose that they were at least close acquaintances since so many of Pliny's friends appear as beneficiaries in the will.[187] It seems likely that Pliny's wife, Calpurnia, moved in the same social circles as Julia Paulina, the daughter of Servianus, and Domitia Lucilla, the daughter of Domitius Tullus.

Julia Paulina

It was not unusual for aspiring politicians, like Junius Avitus, to marry in their early 20s. We learn in *Letter* 6.26, written about 106 or 107 CE, that the above-mentioned Julia Paulina, the daughter of Servianus, had recently been betrothed to Gnaeus Pedanius Fuscus Salinator. Her name is not provided by Pliny, but appears in "The So-called Will of 'Dasumius'." As already noted, the will can be dated to the summer of 108 CE. In it, Julia is recorded as the "daughter of Servianus" rather than as the wife of Fuscus. Her listing as a daughter rather than as a wife may indicate that her marriage to Fuscus had not yet taken place, or that the will was drawn up before her marriage, or that the deceased was favoring her with a legacy because she was the daughter of his good friend, Servianus, to whom the funeral arrangements were entrusted. Although Pliny does not mention Julia's mother (and Servianus' wife), we know from other sources that she was Domitia Paulina, a sister of Hadrian, the man groomed by Trajan and Plotina to succeed as emperor at Trajan's death in 117 CE.[188] Julia, with her close connections to the imperial palace, was undoubtedly an attractive marriage prospect for an ambitious young man. In addition, Fuscus' family, like those of Servianus, Hadrian, and Trajan, was from Spain. The families of the bride and groom had both apparently sought to make a match from their home region. We might compare Pliny's choice of Calpurnia, a bride from his region of northern Italy.

Fuscus, like Junius Avitus, had turned to Pliny for mentoring (*Letter* 6.11.2), and, in *Letter* 6.26, Pliny was fulsome in his praise for him. Indeed, *Letter* 6.26 resembles *Letter* 1.14, in which Pliny recommended Minicius Acilianus as a husband for Junia: Fuscus' family is patrician, his father is very distinguished, his mother is equally deserving of praise, and he has already proved to be an eloquent speaker. However, since the betrothal has already been arranged, Pliny's *Letter* 6.26 is not a recommendation, but an approbation of Servianus' wise decision to select

Fuscus as his future son-in-law. Unlike Minicius Acilianus, whom Pliny notes had already held several high offices, there is no mention in this letter that Fuscus has held any public office. We may conclude that he was in his early to mid-20s at the time of the betrothal and wanted to marry in order to qualify for the privileges granted to married men, and particularly married men with children. And Julia was probably, like Avitus's young bride, in her mid-teens when she married. *Letter* 6.26 ends with the wish: "May he make you a grandfather as soon as possible." Again we are made aware of the pressure on young brides to produce children and to assume the duties of mother, as well as wife, when they themselves were still in their teen years. Julia and Fuscus had at least one child, a boy, also named Pedanius Fuscus, who was born in 118 CE (the same year that his father was selected to be consul, sharing the office with his uncle-in-law, Hadrian, who was now emperor). If this was their first child, Servianus had waited over ten years to become a grandfather. However, they may well have had other children earlier, not reported in our sources.[189] Julia Paulina and her husband, Pedanius Fuscus Salinator, are not heard of after 118 CE. It therefore seems likely that they both died soon after that date, although we have no information about their deaths.

In addition to *Letter* 6.26, Pliny addresses to Servianus *Letter* 3.17, in which he calls Servianus a very dear friend and expresses concern for his well-being because he has not received any news from him recently. Although Pliny was the junior by about 15 years, he represents as close his friendship with Servianus, the brother-in-law of the future emperor, Hadrian. Furthermore, in *Letter* 10.2.1, sent to then emperor Trajan, Pliny records that the person who successfully recommended him to Trajan for the "three-children privilege" was Servianus. In *Letter* 9.28.1, moreover, Pliny alludes to having access to Trajan's wife, Plotina, and being able to deliver a message to her. [Pliny's praise of Plotina as an ideal wife is discussed earlier in this chapter.[190]] His comments suggest that he moved in the highest circles of Roman society, but it is not unreasonable to wonder whether he has portrayed his relationship to the imperial family as more intimate than it actually was.

The anonymous wife of Ummidius Quadratus

In *Letter* 7.24.3, written about 107 CE, we find another instance of a politically ambitious man marrying in his early 20s. Pliny briefly mentions the marriage of Ummidius Quadratus, another young man whom he had mentored (*Letter* 6.11.2).[191] In *Letter* 7.24.3, Pliny reports that Ummidius had married at the age of 23, and would have become a father if god had so granted it. The statement is puzzling (with its pluperfect subjunctive in the Latin). It may mean only that Ummidius had not yet become a father when the letter was written. It could, however, mean that the marriage had not produced a child and had ended, which would imply a divorce or the death of the wife. The word "wife" is not used at all in this passage, perhaps another reason to suspect that Ummidius was not married at the time of the letter.

The wife of Regulus (perhaps Caepia Procula)

As noted earlier, several of the beneficiaries of "The So-called Will of 'Dasumius'" were women. If their *paterfamilias* was no longer alive, they held legal possession of any property they inherited, although their disposal of their wealth was subject to the oversight of a *tutor*. *Letter* 4.2, composed about 104 CE, offers interesting insights into issues which might arise because of the Romans' custom of allowing wives to hold property separate from their husbands. It is one of several letters in which Pliny immortalizes the egregious behavior of a fellow senator, Marcus Aquilius Regulus.[192] Pliny portrays Regulus, who had been a *delator* (informer) during Nero's reign, as a shameless scoundrel or, in Champlin's words, as "a monster of all possible depravity" and "an offender against good taste."[193] We may well question Pliny's objectivity as a reporter. Indeed, even he reluctantly reveals in some of the letters that Regulus had quite a few influential friends and supporters.[194] However, since Regulus had apparently been instrumental in securing the convictions of "the Seven" in 93 CE, and since Pliny (after the death of Domitian) had been intent on establishing his credentials as a friend of "the Seven," it served his purpose to paint Regulus as a detestable arch-enemy. We might also see Regulus, as depicted by Pliny, as a foil: the former's deplorable behavior makes the latter's honorable behavior even more commendable.[195] Nonetheless, despite their lack of impartiality, Pliny's anecdotes about Regulus' conduct provide valuable information about Roman society.

In *Letter* 4.2, Pliny makes a brief reference to Regulus' wife, but without providing her name. Sherwin-White and Raepsaet-Charlier believe that she may have been Caepia Procula, named in an inscription as the wife of a Regulus.[196] If so, she may have been either the sister or daughter of Eppuleius Proculus Caepio Hispo who is mentioned in *Letter* 4.9.16 and who was perhaps a suffect consul in about 101 CE.[197] We do not know how long Regulus and Caepia (assuming that was her name) were married, but they seem to have had only one child, a son. That they had only one child is suggested by Regulus' excessive grief at his death, Caepia's testamentary plans, and the *captatores* (legacy hunters) who flocked around Regulus when his son died.[198] Pliny describes the boy as having a sharp, but unreliable intellect (*Letter* 4.2.1). It is quite possible that Pliny's appraisal of the son was negatively influenced by his hostility toward Regulus.[199]

As was the case for Roman women of this period, Caepia had possession of property in her own name and held it separately from her husband. (Terentia's ownership of real estate and slaves is discussed in Chapter 2.) She had probably not entered into the *manus* (see earlier) of her husband Regulus upon marriage. She remained an agnate of her father and siblings, not her husband, and when her *paterfamilias* had died, she had presumably inherited from him. She evidently wanted her son to be the primary heir of her estate when she died. However, the boy belonged to the agnate family of his father, not his mother and, as long as the boy's *paterfamilias* – that is, Regulus – was alive, the son remained in *patria potestate* – that is, "under his father's authority" – and would not have legal control of any estate bequeathed to him.[200] Under Roman law, the *paterfamilias* – that is, the ascendant male agnate – held legal possession of and management over all the property of the agnatic *familia* (to which, in a marriage without *manus*, the wife/mother did not belong). The only way that Caepia could ensure that her son would inherit and hold possession of her estate was if he were released from the *patria potestas* – that is, from Regulus' paternal authority.

Pliny does not provide any information about the circumstances of this family ("family" here denoting "the father-mother-child triad," not "the agnatic group"). Caepia seems to have anticipated that she would die before her husband. Perhaps she was ill for a long period. About her age at the time of her death, we can only speculate that she may have been in her early 30s, if she married for the first time, as was customary, in her mid-teens, and her son was still a boy when she died. Of course, she may have been married previously or have had other children. However, the fact that only one child is mentioned as her heir may argue that her marriage to Regulus was her first, and that the son mentioned in the letter was her only (surviving) child. She seems to have been unwilling to allow her husband to gain possession of her estate, as he would have if their son had inherited it while still in *patria potestate*. She therefore persuaded Regulus to formally release the son from his control. We do not know when the "release" occurred. Perhaps Caepia had made the release a condition in her will, stating that the son would inherit her estate only if he had been emancipated. If this was the case, the release, or emancipation, of the boy may have occurred after her death.

In accordance with the emancipation process, the boy would have been sold ceremonially by his father three times to a third party, who would then have released him from his "ownership."[201] (Among the legal powers of the *paterfamilias* was the power to sell one's children into slavery.) Although Pliny uses the story of the emancipation to discredit Regulus – even his wife distrusted him! – the existence of formal rules to regulate such arrangements argues that emancipation processes were not rare.[202] In fact, in *Letter* 8.18, Pliny reports another case (which is discussed in Chapter 6) of the release of a child, a daughter, from the *potestas* of her *paterfamilias*. This situation, too, involved the desire of one family member to prevent another from gaining control over an estate. In *Letter* 8.18, however, Pliny makes it clear that the stipulation of emancipation was prompted by animosity between in-laws. In *Letter* 4.2, he does not provide any information about why Caepia was intent on Regulus' not gaining access to her estate through their son. Was she concerned that he would squander it? As the *paterfamilias*, it was his legal right (unless formally declared incompetent) to manage, in any way he chose, the property of his *familia*, including property inherited by his son. From our modern viewpoint, it might seem to us that a marriage in which one spouse was intent on denying the other access to her estate would be a marriage fraught with distrust, tension, and hostility. However, elite Roman families were accustomed to the practice of keeping the financial accounts of husband and wife separate, and therefore perhaps Caepia's request did not seem unusual. Perhaps many Roman couples maintained affectionate and harmonious relationships while nonetheless contriving to keep their property separate.

(The women mentioned in Pliny's letters were almost exclusively from wealthy families and therefore in a position to acquire estates. It is important to keep in mind that the vast majority of people in the Roman Empire were poor, and that the vast majority of women therefore had possession of little or no property. They were financially dependent on their husbands and, even more than upper-class women, constrained by necessity to conform to their husband's expectations of a good wife. Few fathers, moreover, would support a daughter's request for a divorce because they would not want to become responsible again for her maintenance. In any case, because the average age of mortality was so low, many women would not have a father still alive to whose home they could return if divorced – or widowed.)

To return to Caepia, we might consider that she may have had siblings who pressured her to ensure that the estate that she possessed, which had been derived from her agnate *familia*, went directly to her son. He was, of course, not an agnate member of that *familia*, but he was at least a blood relative, which Regulus was not. Since, by Roman laws of succession, agnates received primacy in the inheritance of estates of people who died without wills, many people were careful to make wills, precisely because they wanted to leave their estates to non-agnate relatives [often referred to as "cognates"[203]]. The desire to provide for non-agnate relatives reflected the fact that people developed affectionate attachments with kin related by blood, such as a maternal uncle or a sister's children, or kin related by marriage, such as a wife's brother or nephews. Pliny himself, for example, was very close to his maternal uncle (by whom he was ultimately adopted). And, had Pliny and Calpurnia succeeded in having children, it is quite likely that her grandfather, although not an agnate of the children, would have wanted his estate to pass to them. Of course, the strongest bonds of affection between non-agnates were those between mothers and children, and it seems natural that Roman mothers, like Caepia, would have wanted the estates that they inherited to pass to their own children (rather than, for example, their brothers' children).[204] For reasons that we cannot ascertain, Caepia felt that she needed to protect her estate by requiring her husband to emancipate their son.

Still, the ideal marital situation (at least from a man's point of view) may have been one like that depicted in the "Turia" inscription, where the husband records: "Together we diligently saved the whole inheritance which you received from your parents' estate. For you did not worry yourself about keeping possession of what you handed over in full to me. We shared the responsibilities so that I acted as the custodian of your fortune, and you undertook to serve as protector of mine."[205] And, when her husband's life was in imminent danger during the proscriptions of 43–42 BCE, "Turia" gave him her gold and gemstone jewelry so that he might purchase slaves and provisions to make his exile comfortable.[206] Of course, "Turia" and her husband did not have children. Perhaps she would have been less willing to hand over her estate to her husband if she had been concerned about leaving her children well-settled. In any case, although Pliny portrays Regulus' situation in an unfavorable light, commenting that people gossiped that it was just like Regulus to sell his son (*Letter* 4.2.2), we cannot draw any conclusions from the emancipation about whether the marriage of Regulus and Caepia was happy or unhappy.

Their son was still a boy when his mother died. Pliny identifies him in *Letters* 4.2 and 4.7 as *puer*. As an emancipated child, he was no longer a member of Regulus' agnatic *familia*, but he may have continued still to live with his father and to be regarded socially and emotionally as part of the domestic unit. However, if he was not yet of the age of majority, as seems likely, presumably a *tutor* had been appointed to oversee, on his behalf, the estate he had inherited from his mother. That *tutor* may have been a member of his mother's agnate *familia*. In order to maintain a relationship with his emancipated son, Regulus was now in the position of having to win his affection, since he no longer had any legal authority or financial control over him. According to Pliny, he attempted to ingratiate himself by a pretense of fondness which was both disgusting (in Pliny's view) and unusual for a parent.[207] Unfortunately the son died. We don't know if he had been ill for some time before his death. Is it possible that Regulus had been ingratiating himself because he hoped that the son, now endowed with his mother's estate, would include him in his will? Pliny reports – and this is the main topic of *Letter* 4.2 (and also *Letter* 4.7) – that Regulus once again exhibited quite inappropriate behavior by grieving his son's death very ostentatiously. Pliny adds that Regulus was now attended by throngs of people who, in reality, detested him, but pretended that they loved him. (Again we may question Pliny's objectivity.) Perhaps Regulus had thwarted his wife's plan and had, by his extravagant displays of affection, induced his emancipated son to make him the heir to Caepia's estate. Pliny implies that the people who were flocking around Regulus were doing so because they hoped that he, now being without a son, would include them in *his* will. Even if he had not gained possession of his wife's estate, Regulus was a very wealthy man, having accumulated a fortune both as a *delator* (informer) and as a *captator* (legacy hunter).[208] In *Letter* 2.20, Pliny reports with disgust that, when Regulus was inveigling one wealthy and very ill woman, he swore on the life of his son that he was honest and credible. Pliny adds: "This is the man who accepts inheritances and legacies as if he deserved them." In *Letter* 4.2.4, Pliny snidely comments that the hypocrites who flocked around Regulus after his son's death were simply imitating his own loathsome behavior.

At the end of *Letter* 4.2, Pliny reports that Regulus said that he wanted to marry again, and comments that, as in all other matters, Regulus was wrongheaded. Since he was still grieving for his son (and perhaps also his wife), it was too early for him to remarry. However, since he was an old man, it was also too late, in Pliny's view, for him to remarry. We do not know how old Regulus was at the time of his son's death in about 104 CE. He had been active as an informer under Nero (who died in 68 CE) and therefore he may have been in his late 60s or early 70s at the time of his son's death. One wonders whether Pliny, who himself, in his 40s, had married a teenage girl and hoped to have children, would have been so critical of a friend who, having lost his only son, chose to remarry at an advanced age. We might also consider whether Caepia was Regulus' first wife. The significant age difference between them (as already mentioned, she may have been in her early 30s at the time of her death) suggests that he may have had a previous marriage.

Verania Gemina

The despicable character of Regulus is also the subject of *Letter* 2.20 in which Pliny describes his activities as a *captator*, or chaser of legacies. Regulus went to the home of an elderly and gravely ill woman, named Verania, and feigned concern for her health. He did an astrological calculation and declared that she would recover. He then confirmed his prediction by examining the entrails of a sacrificed animal.[209] Because Verania was so anxious about her fate, she believed him. Perhaps out of gratitude for his good news, she amended her will and added a codicil in Regulus' favor. However, her condition soon worsened. As she lay dying, she cried out that Regulus was a treacherous liar, and worse than a perjurer because he had sworn an oath to her on the life of his son. Pliny adds that Regulus frequently called down the anger of the gods on the head of his unfortunate boy. (This is presumably the same boy at whose death he later grieved so mightily, as reported in *Letters* 4.2 and 7). At the end of the letter, following two more stories about Regulus' legacy chasing, Pliny states that Regulus had made a fortune by preying on vulnerable people, a behavior which Pliny terms "the most immoral type of fraud" (*Letters* 2.20.13 and 14).[210]

Regulus' impudence in approaching Verania, and his success in deceiving her, were all the more astounding to Pliny (and worth recording in a letter) because Regulus had been a very bitter enemy of her husband (deceased long before the letter was written) and had been very much hated by her. Verania Gemina was the daughter of Quintus Veranius, a man who had a distinguished political career.[211] He served as governor of the provinces of Lycia and Pamphilia (an area in the southern part of what is now Turkey) about 43 to 48 CE, and was accompanied to his posting by his two daughters, Verania Gemina and Verania Octavilla.[212] Unfortunately we have no information about their ages at the time that they traveled so far from Italy, or about their experiences in the provinces. The journey they made would have been similar to the journey which Pliny and Calpurnia made to the province of Bithynia over 50 years later. Veranius was selected *consul ordinarius* for 49 CE[213] and then served as governor of the province of Britain. He died in that province about 58 CE.[214] Since Verania was probably already married at this time, it is unlikely that she accompanied him to this posting. We know nothing about her mother. Her sister died at the age of six years and ten months.[215] Her father was also noteworthy for having played a major role in the prosecution of Gnaeus Calpurnius Piso who, along with his wife Plancina, was accused in 20 CE of murdering Germanicus.[216] The tale of Plancina's self-serving abandonment of Piso during the trial, and his subsequent suicide were discussed in Chapter 1.

Verania, in contrast to Plancina, remained loyal to her husband, even at great risk to her own life. She was married to Lucius Calpurnius Piso Frugi Licinianus (henceforth: Calpurnius Piso). Despite the similarity of names, Verania's husband was not a close relative of Plancina's husband, Calpurnius Piso. However, he had an impeccable aristocratic family lineage. He was a descendant, on his father's side, of Marcus Licinius Crassus, and on his mother's side (her name was Scribonia) of Gnaeus Pompeius Magnus, the two powerful men who had shared power with Julius Caesar in the First Triumvirate during the 50s BCE. Calpurnius Piso's father (Marcus Licinius Crassus Frugi) had been consul in 27 CE.[217] Verania had married into a family which became well-acquainted with the vicissitudes of senatorial life under the emperors. Calpurnius Piso's parents had been fortunate in their production of children: at least five of their children – four sons and a daughter – reached adulthood. Calpurnius Piso's brother (named Gnaeus Pompeius Magnus after their famous ancestor) formed an excellent marital alliance by his marriage to Antonia, daughter of the emperor Claudius. The father and the brother had joined Claudius on his expedition to Britain in 43 CE, but they subsequently fell out of favor and were executed on Claudius' orders about 46 CE.[218] Another brother, a man named Marcus Licinius Crassus, was consul in 64 CE, but executed by the emperor Nero between 66 and 68 CE because of information brought against him by Pliny's bête noire, Regulus.[219] His wife, Sulpicia Praetextata, brought her four children to a Senate meeting early in Vespasian's reign, seeking vengeance for her husband's death.[220] Verania's husband, Calpurnius Piso, spent a long period in exile during Nero's reign, for reasons unknown to us.[221] Perhaps his enmity with Regulus began in this period and stemmed from the damage which Regulus' activities as an informer (*delator*) had caused his family. There is no record of where Calpurnius Piso spent the exile or whether Verania accompanied him, even as Fannia – the two women were about the same age – had accompanied her husband, Helvidius I into exile. In any case, anxiety and sorrow must have become familiar to Verania in her married life. Her husband is said to have endured much adversity.[222] Undoubtedly the same could be said about Verania.

We do not know when Calpurnius Piso and Verania were married or whether they had children. Calpurnius Piso was born about 38 CE.[223] The date of Verania's birth is unknown, but if this was her first marriage, and if she was about five years younger than her husband, she may have been born about 43 CE. It is worth noting that, in Pliny's account in *Letter* 2.20, Verania seems to have complete freedom to amend her will as she chooses. Unless she had borne three children, she would have required the approval of a *tutor* to create and change a will. Perhaps we can deduce from Pliny's account that Verania had indeed borne three children and therefore been relieved of the need to consult with a *tutor* about her will. Or perhaps Pliny, in order to keep his story brief, has simply omitted a reference to a *tutor's* involvement. We might, however, have expected a *tutor* to oppose any gifts to Regulus if he was indeed as notorious a legacy chaser as Pliny depicts him to be.

Verania's husband, Calpurnius Piso, seems not to have held any significant political or military offices. Perhaps he was deterred from a public career because of the unfortunate fates of his father and brothers. Or perhaps his long exile had removed him from Rome during the period when he would otherwise have been engaged in a political career. The fact that he was sent into exile under Nero indicates that he had been involved in some activity by which the emperor felt threatened. After Nero's suicide in June of 68 CE, chaos engulfed the Roman world as several powerful military generals vied to ascend to the imperial throne. The first to seize power, in the summer of 68, was Galba. His brief reign was plagued with mutinies by disgruntled soldiers, particularly in Germany. Much to the surprise of even those closest to him, and to the consternation of his sometime ally Otho, who had expected to be named heir, Galba decided to adopt Calpurnius Piso as his son and heir to the imperial throne.[224] Piso's distance from the political world may have made him attractive to Galba in part because he had made neither allies nor enemies in the Senate, and in part because he was not likely to engage in plots to overthrow the emperor. In addition, Galba could not be accused of choosing one close colleague over another. We do not know what Verania's response was to the adoption – that is, whether she was pleased or distressed that her husband had agreed to accept the very perilous position of Galba's second in command. When announcing his decision, Galba emphasized Piso's sterling character, his old-fashioned strictness, and the fact that he had not been corrupted by flattery or ambition. Indeed, although our ancient sources do not make this comparison, Piso seems to have had a stern character similar to that of Thrasea Paetus and Helvidius I. It would be interesting to know if Verania's life with such a paragon of virtue resembled that of Arria Y and Fannia.

Not everyone, however, was impressed by Piso's character. Galba's announcement angered many senators and also the Praetorian Guard. Within a few days, the supporters of Otho stormed through the streets of Rome, intent on removing Galba and replacing him with Otho. On January 16, 69 CE, Galba and Piso fled from the imperial palace toward the Forum. Galba was killed first by the murderous mob. Piso reached the Temple of Vesta in the Forum and was hidden inside by a slave, but Otho's men savagely dragged him out and slew him at the door of the temple. Both Galba and Piso were beheaded. Tacitus preserves a report that no other murder gave Otho greater joy than Piso's, and at no other head did he stare with such insatiable eyes.[225] He also records that, at a Senate meeting in 70 CE (the meeting mentioned earlier, which was attended by Sulpicia Praetextata, the widow of Piso's brother), Curtius Montanus reminded his colleagues that, after the murders, Regulus had given money to Piso's assassins and savagely torn at Piso's head with his teeth.[226] If the story is true, it is no wonder that, as Pliny writes in *Letter* 2.20.2, Verania hated Regulus, but it is even more surprising that she would have allowed him into her presence when she was ill and added him to her will.

We have no reports about Verania's activities in the days leading up to her husband's assassination, but we can conjecture that her life was fraught with fear and anxiety. There is, however, a record of her courage in the tumultuous aftermath. The heads of Galba, Piso, and at least one other man were displayed on poles in the Forum, while their headless bodies were left on the ground. Their killers proudly displayed hands covered with their victims' blood. Despite the danger of confronting these frenzied assassins, Verania and one of Piso's brothers negotiated with them to recover the body, pay a ransom for the head, and provide Piso with an appropriate final resting place.[227] The body of Galba was mutilated, but eventually given to Helvidius I, husband of Fannia, for sepulture.[228] Nowhere in his correspondence does Pliny mention a friendship between Piso and Helvidius I, but it seems likely that the two men shared similar views of the political situation in Rome. And, after the suicide of Nero, Helvidius I energetically tried to prosecute men like Regulus, who had served as informers under Nero and been responsible for the exiles and deaths of several senators, possibly including members of Piso's family. Perhaps their wives, Verania and Fannia, who were about the same age, were also well-acquainted. Certainly both acted bravely in perilous circumstances and were very loyal to their husbands.

At the death of her husband, Verania, when about 25 years old, became a widow. Despite the pressure on young widows to remarry she seems to have remained a widow and thus earned the designation of *univira*. She was apparently a wealthy woman (and therefore a target of Regulus' predation). Verania survived Calpurnius Piso by about 30 years, but, when she died, her remains were placed in an urn next to his.[229] There is no evidence of whether or not Verania promoted her husband's story as assiduously as Fannia seems to have promoted the story of her husband, Helvidius I.

Aurelia

In *Letter* 2.20, Pliny mentions a second female victim of Regulus' predatory behavior. Aurelia had appeared at the signing and sealing of her will dressed in very splendid clothing.[230] Regulus, who had showed up for the signing, persuaded her to amend her will on the spot and bequeath those clothes to him. (Presumably he would make money by selling them.) Again there is no reference to a *tutor* overseeing the creation of a woman's will. We do not know anything more about Aurelia, or her family, or her relationship to Regulus. In *Satire* 5.97 and 98, Juvenal mentions a woman named Aurelia who was the target of a *captator*. He bought gifts in order to ingratiate himself with her – and she promptly sold the gifts. Her money-making scheme was the reverse of Regulus'. The Aurelia of Juvenal may be a fictitious character, or may be the same person mentioned by Pliny. Pliny's Aurelia was still alive when he wrote the letter, around 100 CE.

Pliny also records in *Letter* 2.20 that Regulus tried to manipulate a man, Velleius Blassus, a wealthy former consul, into leaving him a legacy. However, Velleius Blassus, unlike Verania Gemina and Aurelia, was not taken in by Regulus' pretense of concern for his health. He left Regulus nothing. Pliny's choice of anecdotes makes women appear more naïve than men and therefore more vulnerable to unsavory characters like Regulus. It would have reinforced in the minds of readers the belief that women were less competent than men and needed someone to oversee their financial affairs.

Rectina

In *Letter* 6.16, Pliny replies to his friend, the historian Tacitus, who had asked him to provide an account of his uncle Pliny's death during the devastating eruption of the volcano, Mount Vesuvius, in August of 79 CE. The Elder Pliny had been stationed at Misenum, a town on the northwest end of the Bay of Naples, as prefect of the Roman naval fleet there. The Younger Pliny and his widowed mother, Plinia (sister of the Elder Pliny), were staying at the Elder Pliny's villa in Misenum. When the family observed an enormous cloud of smoke rising over the eastern part of the bay, the scientifically curious Elder Pliny decided to sail (or, more likely, be rowed) toward it to investigate (*Letter* 6.16.7).[231] A ship was made ready, but just as the Elder Pliny was leaving the house, he received a letter from a woman whom the Younger Pliny identifies by the name Rectina (*Letter* 6.16.8). She wrote that she was terrified by the danger threatening her because her villa lay at the foot of Vesuvius, and there was no escape except by ship. She begged the Elder Pliny to rescue her from the approaching destruction.

The Elder Pliny immediately changed his plan, and what he had begun as a research mission he now undertook as a heroic rescue mission. He set out eastward with several ships to bring help not only to Rectina, but also to the many others who lived on that part of the Bay of Naples. Ash and pumice stone were falling thickly as the ships approached the east shore. The Elder Pliny discovered that the shore was blocked by debris from the volcanic activity. However, rather than turning back to Misenum, he gave the order to head for the villa of Pomponianus, which was at Stabiae, about 10 miles south of the volcano. He reached Pomponianus' villa, but died several hours later, overcome either by the poisonous gases emitted by the volcano or (as some modern scholars suggest) by a heart attack.

We know nothing with certainty about Rectina. Pliny identifies her as the wife of Tascius (or perhaps Tascus). Some scholars have suggested that her husband was the Pomponianus at whose villa Pliny the Elder died. If this were true, his full name may have been Tascius Pomponianus, he may have been the birth son of Pomponius Secundus, who had been a friend of the Elder Pliny (*Letter* 3.5.3), and he may have been adopted by a man named Tascius, thereby changing his birth nomen, Pomponius, to Tascius Pomponianus.[232] Pliny's letter, however, suggests that Rectina was in a different location from Pomponianus, and was therefore not his wife. It seems more likely that Rectina's villa was closer to Mount Vesuvius, perhaps in the area of Herculaneum. Pliny the Elder was being rowed toward her villa, but discovered that landing was impossible because the shore was blocked by debris. He then appears to have changed course and headed south toward Stabiae where he was able to land (but, once landed, was unable to leave because of the turbulent water). Another factor that seems to argue against identifying Rectina as the wife of Pomponianus is that the letter requesting rescue came to the Elder Pliny from Rectina, not Pomponianus. If a couple needed assistance, and the husband was a friend of the Elder Pliny, one would expect the letter to have been written by him.

Another suggestion about the identity of Rectina is that the manuscript reading of Tascus is an error for Cascus, and that her husband was Gnaeus Pedius Cascus, who was a suffect consul in 71 CE.[233]

Rectina is a rare name. Interestingly, the wife of one of the Younger Pliny's friends was married to a woman named Popillia Rectina who died when she was only 18 years old.[234] The name of the friend was Gaius Licinius Marinus Voconius Romanus.[235] He and Pliny were schoolmates and thus he, like Pliny, was only about 17 years old at the time of the eruption of Vesuvius, and would not have been married yet. The two Rectinas would not be the same woman. They may, however, have been related.

All we really know about the Rectina of Pliny's *Letter* 6.16 is that she, like thousands of other people living under the erupting volcano in August of 79 CE, was terrified and desperate to escape. We do not know her fate.

Roman wives of foreigners: Arrionilla, Musonia, Pompeia

In *Letter* 1.5.5, written about 97 CE, Pliny reports that he had, several years earlier, appeared in the Centumviral Court on behalf of Arrionilla, the wife of Timon. He did so at the request of Junius Arulenus Rusticus. Presenting the case against Arrionilla was Pliny's arch enemy, Regulus. The focus of *Letter* 1.5 is Pliny's account of his long-standing hostile relationship with Regulus. Writing the letter shortly after the death of Domitian in 96, Pliny implies that he is considering prosecuting Regulus for his involvement in the deaths of Arulenus Rusticus, Helvidius II, and Herennius Senecio in 93 CE. He is waiting, however, for the return of Junius Mauricus (brother of Arulenus Rusticus), who was exiled in 93 CE along with Fannia, Arria the Younger, and Gratilla, to consult with him about such a prosecution. (Since Pliny does not, in later letters, mention undertaking such a prosecution, we may conclude that Junius Mauricus advised against it.) The case involving Arrionilla had taken place before 93 CE because Arulenus Rusticus was still alive to request of Pliny that he represent her in court. Pliny tells us virtually nothing about the nature of the lawsuit, not even recording its outcome. One area of jurisdiction of the Centumviral Court was wills and inheritances, but this case may have had another focus.[236] From the brevity of his account, it is clear that Pliny did not have a strong interest in her and her case. He mentions her only because, as Carlon comments, his "naming of Arrionilla and her benefactor offers the only direct link in the letters between Pliny and Rusticus while the latter was alive."[237] By publicizing Arulenus Rusticus' personal request of a favor of him, Pliny is subtly informing his readers that he was a trusted friend of Domitian's opponents at a time when it was dangerous to be so.

We know nothing about the identity of Arrionilla outside of this letter. Her name is unique among our extant sources. Sherwin-White speculates that she may have been related to Arria the Younger.[238] However, if her name had been derived from the family name Arrius, we would expect it to be spelled Arrianilla, not Arrionilla. Syme noted the existence of the name Arria Arrianilla in an inscription, but this person cannot be connected to the Arrionilla of *Letter* 1.5.[239]

Nor do we know anything about Arrionilla's husband, whose name Pliny records as Timon. The name may suggest a non-Italian origin; it is possible that Timon was not a Roman citizen. Sherwin-White speculates that he was a philosopher friend of Arulenus Rusticus, but there is no conclusive evidence for this theory.[240] In two other letters, Pliny also mentions, albeit briefly, situations in which Roman women had husbands who were apparently foreigners and non-Roman citizens (*peregrini*). These situations call attention to the issue of what constituted a legal marriage under Roman law.

In Roman society, corroboration that a couple had formed a legally valid marriage, *iustum matrimonium*, did not depend, as it does today, on the performance of a ceremony conducted by public or religious officials. A man and woman who demonstrated their "intent to be married," *affectio* (or *affectus*) *maritalis*, by living together as a couple could be considered partners in a legal marriage, provided that they met certain criteria that will be discussed shortly.[241] Of course, elite families devoted considerable attention to the arrangement of betrothals and dowries, and considerable expense to wedding celebrations. And both the betrothal and wedding festivities might be used as verification that the families indeed had a marriage in mind. In addition, a document specifying the dowry arrangements, and thus confirming the willingness of one *familia* to entrust some of its property to another *familia*, would serve as evidence that marriage was intended. However, the essential element of confirmation – the presumptive proof of the existence of a marriage – was simply the couple's co-habitation.[242]

Recognition of a marriage thus rested, not on any marriage certificate, but on observation by the community that the couple was behaving as if married. Nevertheless, to form a legally valid marriage, certain criteria needed to be met.[243] Both the bride and the groom needed to have reached puberty. For girls, the age of reaching puberty was considered to be 12 years.[244] (Recall that Quintilian's wife married him at the age of 12.) In addition, both the bride and groom needed to give their consent to enter into a marital union.[245] (One cannot but wonder at how the "consent" of a 12-year-old girl might be obtained.) The bride and groom could not, moreover, be close relatives.[246] And, most importantly, under Roman law, a marriage was valid only if both parties had the "legal capacity," *conubium*, to enter into a valid marriage with one another.[247] A Roman citizen had the capacity, *conubium*, to form a legal marriage only with another Roman citizen. There existed, of course, unions between a Roman citizen and a non-citizen, unions in which the partners could be observed as being intent on maintaining a life together and therefore appearing to be a married couple. However, they did not have a legally valid Roman marriage because they did not have *conubium*. Such unions might be called "mixed marriages," or "irregular unions," or "quasi-marital unions."[248] The importance of having *conubium* rested in the citizenship status of the children produced in the union. A marriage with *conubium* legitimized a child's identity as a member of a Roman family and his/her status as a shareholder in the state. Only children born into a legal marriage – that is, where both parents were Roman citizens – received Roman citizenship. Under the Lex Minicia (Minician Law), a child born to a "mixed marriage" received the status of the non-Roman parent.[249] In rare cases, *conubium* might be granted as a privilege to a non-citizen. However, even in this case, by the Lex Minicia, children born to a marital union between a Roman woman and a peregrine man were not Roman citizens.[250]

One letter in which a mixed marriage is referred to is *Letter* 3.11, although the topic is of minor importance in its context. Written after the death of Domitian, the letter is a vehicle for Pliny to explain how he behaved in 93 CE when others were being executed or banished.[251] Pliny opens the letter with an expression of (perhaps feigned) embarrassment that a philosopher named Artemidorus, who suffered banishment in 93, has been so vocal in praising him for his heroic assistance at that time. In the course of the letter, Pliny mentions that Artemidorus is the son-in-law of Gaius Musonius Rufus. Musonius has been referred to earlier in this chapter, in connection with Roman opinions about the education of women.[252] He was a Roman citizen of a wealthy family, born about 30 CE. He became a celebrated teacher of Stoic philosophy who attracted disciples with his system of practical ethics. Like Thrasea Paetus, Musonius cultivated an austere life and avoided the excesses of some of his contemporaries. Many of his views, however, were very progressive. For example, he was an advocate for the education of women, arguing that Nature had endowed women with the same ability to reason as men and with the same inclination toward virtue.[253] He also believed that marriage should provide more than simply a situation in which to bear and raise legitimate children. He argued that companionship and mutual affection should be present in a marriage.[254] Nevertheless he did not encourage women to aspire to the same occupations as men. He adhered to the conventional division of spheres, believing that a woman's main responsibility was the care of her husband and children and management of the household. Pliny's references in *Letters* 3.11.5 and 7 to Musonius as the father-in-law of Artemidorus informs us that he had at least one daughter, presumably named Musonia. It would be interesting to know whether he practiced what he preached with regard to his wife and daughter.

Musonius was first banished from Rome in 65 CE, accused of participation in the Pisonian conspiracy.[255] He returned to Rome after the death of Nero in 68. In 71, when the emperor Vespasian banished other philosophers from Rome, he exempted Musonius, but finally did banish him about 75 CE. Musonius spent his period of banishment in the Roman province of Syria, and returned to Rome sometime after the death of Vespasian in 79 CE.

In *Letter* 3.11.5, Pliny writes that he has admired Musonius for a long time. His profession of affection for the philosopher follows immediately upon his statement that his services to Artemidorus in 93 CE do not deserve the extraordinary renown which Artemidorus is proclaiming for them. Pliny modestly states, "I believe that I was only avoiding disgrace. For I have loved and respected Artemidorus' father-in-law, Musonius, since I was a young man." The "for" introduces the reason for Pliny's willingness to help Artemidorus, despite the (alleged by Pliny) significant dangers to him personally: Artemidorus was the son-in-law of a friend. However, the "for" also encourages the reader to conclude that Pliny adhered to the ethical system taught by Musonius and therefore readily assisted a friend in need. Since Pliny just previously in the letter had listed and described "the Seven" who were prosecuted in 93 CE as his friends, he thus subtly insinuates that he is connected to them by a long-standing interest in Stoicism.

Having established the link between himself and Musonius, Pliny then records that he became a close friend of Artemidorus when he (Pliny) was serving as a military tribune in the Syria (about 82 CE) (*Letter* 3.11.5).[256] We know nothing about Artemidorus outside of this letter. His name is Greek, but we may assume that he was Syrian. (The Roman province of Syria was at that time part of the Greek-speaking world.) It is likely that he had not acquired Roman citizenship.[257] Pliny praises Artemidorus as a truly wise man, a philosopher of great integrity and honesty (implying that he was not likely to lie about the magnitude of Pliny's assistance in 93 CE), and a person of exceptional physical endurance and mental strength. His virtues are so numerous that, Pliny states, he was deservedly chosen by Musonius, from all the suitors of every rank, to be his son-in-law.

Musonius' willingness to marry his daughter to a man who we surmise was a non-Roman was noteworthy. As noted earlier, the children of "mixed marriages" received the status of the non-Roman parent. Considering the importance that elite Roman men attached to having an heir to carry on not just the family name, but also the family tradition of participation in civic affairs, it is not surprising that most wealthy Roman parents wanted to arrange legal marriages for their children who would then produce Roman grandchildren. Of course, Musonius Rufus, who had devoted himself to the study and teaching of Stoic philosophy, had never followed the conventional pattern of behavior among wealthy Romans. When choosing a husband for his daughter, clearly he valued Artemidorus' accomplishments as a philosopher over the achievements or family lineage of other suitors. (By contrast, we might recall the reasons for which Pliny recommended Minicius Acilianus as a husband in *Letter* 1.14.) Nonetheless, it was possible for a Roman father to find a Roman son-in-law who held the same philosophical views that he did. That was certainly the case with Caecina Paetus and Thrasea Paetus, and with Thrasea Paetus and Helvidius I. Of course, we lack information about whether Musonius had, in addition to his daughter, sons who had married Roman citizens and produced the desirable Roman grandchildren. If this were the case, his choice of Artemidorus as a son-in-law would be less remarkable. We also need to realize that Artemidorus may have been a member of a wealthy and distinguished Syrian family, and a desirable "catch" for that reason.

We do not know when Musonius first met Artemidorus or when the marriage was arranged, but it is likely that they first became acquainted about 75 CE when Musonius traveled to Syria during his second exile. Nor do we know whether Musonia, presumably in her mid-teens at that time, had also traveled to Syria then, or whether she first met Artemidorus in Italy. Also unknown is whether the couple lived primarily in Italy or Syria and whether Musonia followed her husband into exile in 93 CE. And we have no information, unfortunately, about whether Artemidorus followed his father-in-law in advocating education for women and affection between marital partners.

Letter 1.10 (written about 98 CE) is a letter in which Pliny praises the character and talents of a philosopher and orator named Euphrates who was a native of Syria and, since he is identified by just his Greek name, probably not a Roman citizen.[258] As was true with Artemidorus, Pliny had become well-acquainted with Euphrates when he (Pliny) served as a young military tribune in that province about 82 CE (*Letter* 1.10.2). At some point, Euphrates had studied under Musonius Rufus (possibly when Musonius was in Syria after his exile in about 75 CE) and traveled to Rome. Sherwin-White conjectures that Euphrates left Rome in 93–94, when Domitian imposed an order of expulsion on philosophers (which also caused the departure of Artemidorus), but returned to Rome after the death of Domitian and was living there at the time that Pliny wrote *Letter* 1.10.[259] Pliny's account of his association with Euphrates implies that he had studied with the philosopher when he was in Syria as a young tribune and had maintained a close relationship with him in Italy, frequently turning to him for philosophic advice. Pliny's account is designed to inform readers not only of the considerable virtues of Euphrates, but also of Pliny's abiding interest in philosophy and his support of philosophers.

Pliny records that Pompeius Julianus chose Euphrates to be his son-in-law (*Letter* 1.10.8). We know nothing about Pompeius Julianus or his daughter (perhaps named Pompeia) outside of this letter. Pliny describes him as well-regarded and a leading figure in the province, the province presumably being Syria. However, his name suggests that he held Roman citizenship. He might therefore have belonged to a Roman family which had become established in Syria, or he might have been a Syrian who received a grant of Roman citizenship. In any case, his prominence in the province and his Roman citizenship would mean that he could have arranged a very lofty marriage for his daughter. And he had, in fact, considered several such offers. Pliny comments, however, that, to his credit, Pompeius Julianus chose a son-in-law outstanding not for his political successes, but for his philosophical interests (*Letter* 1.10.8). Not everyone was as impressed as Pliny by Euphrates' character. Apollonius, who was a harsh critic of Euphrates, denounced him for cultivating the wealthy and hanging tenaciously around the doors of aristocratic houses only in order to enrich himself.[260] However, Sherwin-White comments that most of the well-known foreign philosophers were themselves members of wealthy families.[261]

Pliny says nothing about the fact that, if Euphrates was not a Roman citizen, the union between him and Pompeius Julianus' daughter was a "mixed marriage." We do not know whether the marriage was a happy one for the daughter. It was certainly successful in terms of fertility. At the time that Pliny wrote *Letter* 1.10, she and Euphrates had three children, two sons and one daughter (*Letter* 1.10.8). Hoffer comments that, by dwelling on Euphrates' domestic life, Pliny creates a picture of a quite Romanized and "tamed" (despite his long hair and beard, *Letter* 1.10.6) eastern philosopher, married into a good Roman family and fulfilling the obligation of producing three children, two of them sons.[262] However, if Euphrates was not a Roman citizen, the children would also not be Roman citizens.

We do not know whether the Roman wives, Pompeia and Musonia, knew one another, although that seems likely, or whether they followed their Syrian husbands into exile in 93 CE.[263] Nor do we know if Pliny's young wife, Calpurnia, became acquainted with these women after she married him.

Casta

Almost all the wives on whose conduct Pliny comments are identified by him as virtuous. Almost all. He characterizes the vast majority of men and women who appear in his correspondence as people of integrity and good will, thus creating a picture of a society whose members conscientiously abided by high standards of moral and social behavior. The very few portraits of dishonorable people – among whom the contemptible Regulus stands out – may have been included as the exceptions that prove the rule, or at least emphasize the truth of Pliny's depiction of his society as basically trustworthy and principled. Among the wives whose conduct Pliny chooses to record, he presents only two whose actions he judged to be shameless and unlawful. Interestingly both of these wives misbehaved while in the provinces. This next section thus returns to a topic addressed in Chapter 1: the conduct of wives who accompanied their husbands to official postings in the provinces.

In *Letter* 3.9.19, Pliny informs a friend about a Senate hearing of 99 or 100 CE in which he prosecuted a woman named Casta for misconduct while her husband, Caecilius Classicus, was governor of the province of Baetica (modern Andalusia, Spain).[264] At the time of Classicus' appointment to Baetica in 97 CE, his political career had advanced as far as the office of praetor. Baetica would have been a desirable assignment for a man of his rank. In contrast to many of the other provinces in the western part of the Roman Empire, Baetica was stable, prosperous, and quite Romanized.[265] The Iberian peninsula had become Roman territory as a result of Rome's victory over Carthage in the Second Punic War (218 – 202 BCE). During the next few centuries, although resistance to Roman rule continued in the north, the southern portion of the peninsula quietly developed a thriving economy. When Augustus reorganized the administrative structure of the Iberian peninsula in 14 BCE, he divided it into three provinces. The southern portion became the province of Baetica and, because it was so peaceful, Augustus placed it under the control of the Senate (rather than retaining it under imperial control) and did not station a permanent legion there. Baetica was richly endowed with silver mines and with fertile land producing bountiful crops. Olive oil, wine, grain, and fish sauce were exported throughout the Mediterranean world. Economic opportunities attracted Italian families who invested in agriculture and mines or grew wealthy as merchants. The riches of Baetica became the foundation for the large fortunes of several Roman senatorial and equestrian families. And, as more Italian families settled in Baetica, Latin gradually became the predominant language. Among the notable Roman authors who were born in Baetica were the elder Seneca, the younger Seneca, Lucan, and Pliny's friend, the poet Martial.[266] Herennius Senecio, one of "the Seven," was a native of Baetica. And Trajan, who was emperor at the time that Pliny was involved in the case against Classicus, was also a native of Baetica, as was the family of the future emperor, Hadrian.

Casta and her husband, Caecilius Classicus, had therefore not been sent to a backwater or to a dangerous part of the empire. Relations between Rome and Baetica were long-standing and peaceful. The governor and his wife would enjoy not just fine weather, but, more importantly, the company of many wealthy and well-educated Latin-speaking people, and would have available the same comforts that Rome offered. Nor would Classicus be required to engage in any military action. The life of Casta and Classicus would therefore be far more pleasant than that of a couple assigned to a posting on an unsettled northern frontier or in a Greek-speaking province. (We might consider how isolated Calpurnia may have felt when she took up residence with Pliny in Greek-speaking Bithynia-Pontus. In contrast to the western province of Baetica, in which Latin was widely used, the people of the eastern provinces, such as Bithynia-Pontus, continued to use their native Greek language during the Roman period.)

Unfortunately, Classicus and Casta may also have thought that a posting in such a prosperous province would provide excellent opportunities to enrich themselves through extortionate activities which Roman law had declared illegal, but which had, over the centuries, tempted so many Roman officials, in so many provinces. As noted in Chapter 1, it was not until the end of the republican period that senatorial wives began to accompany their husbands to overseas postings. However, the behavior of wives in provinces became an issue which occupied senators in the first part of the first century CE. In 21 CE, in the aftermath of the Piso and Plancina affair, Aulus Caecina Severus had proposed that the Senate pass a ruling that a man going to the provinces on official business be forbidden to take his wife with him. As noted in Chapter 1, he argued that wives were physically and morally frail, encouraged extravagance, and meddled in government affairs. He also alleged that, when a government officer was charged with extortion, often the wife had instigated it.[267] His proposal was defeated. A few years later, however, in 24 CE, Gaius Silius (a military commander on the Rhine frontier) and his wife Sosia Galla were charged with treason and extortion (although the focus of the trial was the charge of treason).[268] He pre-empted condemnation by his suicide. She was sentenced to exile, and part of her estate was confiscated, although the remainder was allowed to pass to her children.[269] After this incident, the Senate passed a resolution that Roman officials be held accountable for the harm that their wives did in the provinces.[270] Modern scholars have debated the interpretation of this decree. Did it make the husband alone liable for extortion committed by his wife? Or, did it make the husband and wife jointly liable?[271] The events surrounding the indictment of Caecilius Classicus in 99–100 CE suggest that the decree of 24 CE made wives jointly liable.[272] In fact, not only was his wife Casta put on trial, but so also was their daughter (presumably named Caecilia) and their daughter's husband, Claudius Fuscus. Caecina's failed proposal of 21 CE had been directed at preventing wives from traveling to the provinces. In subsequent decades, however, senators like Classicus had apparently taken not just their wives to the provinces, but also adult children and their spouses, and even nephews.[273] However, this is the only attested case of a daughter being involved in a prosecution with her father for extortion.

We cannot ascertain whether Caecilia was Casta's daughter, or Classicus' daughter by a previous marriage.[274] It is quite probable, however, that Casta was her mother. Because Caecilia was already married when Classicus was governor of Baetica, she was probably about 16 years or older. If Classicus had married, as was common for men of the senatorial class, in his early or mid-20s, and had fathered a daughter soon after marriage, he would therefore have been about 40 at the time of his tenure as governor. The age of 40 is a reasonable conjecture.

To be eligible for a governorship, he would have previously served a term as praetor in his 30s.[275] The mother of the daughter was likely Casta; he married her in his 20s – when she was probably in her mid-teens. If this speculation is correct, she would have been in her mid-30s at the time of the Senate hearing described in *Letter* 3.9.

We know about Casta and Caecilius Classicus only from Pliny's letters. He says nothing about Casta's family or origin. From his comments, we can ascertain that Classicus was a senator of African origin who served as governor of Baetica in 97–98 CE. Pliny describes him as a vile and evil man who had acted violently and disgracefully during his tenure of office (*Letter* 3.9.2). His conduct was so corrupt that the people of the province, the Baetici, decided to request of the Roman Senate that he be prosecuted in Rome. From Pliny's account of the proceedings (*Letters* 3.4 and 3.9), it appears that they filed a charge not simply of extortion, but of extortion with violence (*saevitia*). This more serious charge was considered a capital offence because it involved executing or causing severe physical damage to innocent people during extortionate activities.

Under Roman law, the charge of extortion was referred to as *res pecuniae repetundae* (often abbreviated as *res repetundae*), "a matter of seeking back one's money." Extortion is the crime of obtaining the property of another person through threats or the use of violence. The Latin verb *extorquere* (from whose participle – *extortum* – the English word "extortion" is derived) means "to wrest away, to obtain by force." In the Roman world, charges of *res repetundae* referred specifically to extortionate activities in the provinces by people in positions of authority.[276] The scope of offences covered by the law was quite extensive. Prosecutable offences included not just obtaining money and property through violence, but also taking bribes, accepting gifts, receiving payment for services, and investing in local financial transactions.[277] Cicero described a wide range of corrupt practices in his speeches in which he prosecuted Verres in 70 BCE. Originally only governors of provinces were liable to prosecution, but, by the first century BCE, liability had been extended to members of the governor's staff, and, by Pliny's time, it had, as noted earlier, been extended to the governor's wife and children.

Since one of the main functions of a governor was to hear and pass judgment on legal cases in his province, he might be tempted to accept money to make a ruling favorable to the briber. Pliny records examples of such conduct in *Letter* 2.11. In January of 100 CE, he and Tacitus were appointed by the Senate to prosecute a case against Marius Priscus, who had been governor of Africa in 97–98, the same period in which Caecilius Classicus had been governor of Baetica. By interesting coincidence, Marius Priscus was a native of Baetica who served as governor in Africa, while Caecilius Classicus was a native of Africa who served as governor in Baetica. Pliny reports that the Baetici drolly lamented: "We gave an evil man, and received an evil man in return" (*Letter* 3.9.3). Priscus, whom Pliny relates had acted with cruelty and violence (*Letter* 2.11.2), had, in one case brought before him, taken a large sum of money to sentence a Roman equestrian[278] to exile and to execute seven of his friends, and, in another case, had taken an even larger sum of money to allow a Roman equestrian to be beaten with clubs, condemned to work in the mines, and finally executed by strangulation.[279] Although Pliny does not provide information about the specific charges laid against Casta's husband, Classicus, it is likely that they were similar to those against Priscus. We do not know the circumstances by which wives, like Casta, or daughters might extort money from provincials. Perhaps they accepted bribes to influence decisions made by their husbands or fathers. If, moreover, they meddled in provincial affairs, as Aulus Caecina Severus had suggested that wives did, they undoubtedly found willing accomplices, since few people would be prepared to offend the governor by refusing to co-operate with his wife or children.

The people of a province (the provincials) had the right to seek to recover their property by filing a charge in Rome. However, money which had been given to a Roman official as a bribe was not returned to the briber. It was instead placed in the public treasury, the *aerarium Saturni*, of which Pliny served a term as a prefect.[280] By Pliny's time, a case of extortion was heard by a court of five senators serving as judges. If the defendant was convicted, his penalty was limited to restitution of what he had taken. However, capital cases of extortion with violence (*saevitia*), such as those against Classicus, were heard by the full Senate and, if the defendant was convicted, he was liable to a capital penalty of exile or relegation.[281]

In *Letter* 3.4, Pliny reports that the Baetici asked the Senate to appoint him to represent them in their case against Classicus. Although he at first wanted to decline, and his colleagues at the *aerarium Saturni* testified that he should be excused because of the burden of treasury duties[282], Pliny was swayed to accept the task of prosecuting Classicus when the Baetici spoke of him as their patron, and reminded him of the honorable conduct he had displayed on their behalf in their case against Baebius Massa in 93 CE.[283] Clearly the Baetici had appealed to Pliny's sense of self-importance.[284] He relates to his addressee that he agreed to take the case against Classicus because of his desire to uphold the time-honored tradition of prosecuting injustices even against foreigners, and because he did not want the glorious memory of his dangerous prosecution of Baebius Massa to be overshadowed by a refusal to help now. He adds that another attraction of the case was that the defendant, Caecilius Classicus, had died, and that he, Pliny, could therefore do a favor while not incurring the wrath of a fellow senator.[285] Since (and as noted earlier), the emperor Trajan was a native of Baetica, we might speculate on whether Pliny's decision to accept the case was also influenced by his desire to please Trajan.

Pliny comments that Classicus circumvented the accusations against him by a death that was either fortuitous (that is, natural) or voluntary (that is, suicide) (*Letter* 3.9.5). He adds that, although it seemed credible that Classicus had wanted to depart from life, since he could not be defended, it nonetheless seemed remarkable that he had escaped the shame of condemnation by dying when he had not been ashamed to commit crimes that were deserving of condemnation. Despite Classicus' death, the Baetici were determined to continue with the prosecution. They announced, moreover, that they were including Classicus' allies and staff in their indictment (*Letter* 3.9.6). The proceedings were conducted in three stages. In the first, the evidence against Classicus was presented. It was easy,

Pliny remarks, for him and his co-prosecutor, Lucceius Albinus, to prove that Classicus was guilty because the governor had left behind accounts, written in his own hand, of how much he had received and for what reason. He had also sent boastful letters to a certain female friend in Rome (whose identity is unknown to us) about the money he had made in the province (*Letter* 3.9.13). Pliny reports that Classicus wrote to her, "Hurrah! Hurrah! I am coming to you a free man. I have sold a good part of the Baeticans, and made four million sesterces."[286]

The outcome of the hearing about Classicus' misconduct was a judgment tantamount to a verdict of guilty. The Senate decided that everything that he had possessed before going to Baetica should be consigned to his daughter[287], and the rest should be given to the people he had robbed. At the same time, two of his subordinates were relegated for five years, although they claimed that they had simply been carrying out his orders (*Letters* 3.9.14–17).

At a second set of hearings, Claudius Fuscus, the husband of Classicus' daughter, was indicted, as well as a tribune on his military staff. Pliny does not reveal why Classicus' son-in-law may have been in the province or what the charges against him (or the tribune) were. The husband was acquitted, but the tribune was convicted and sentenced to a two-year banishment. Pliny provides no clue about why the judgments were so different or whether he believed that the husband deserved an acquittal.

At a third set of hearings, Classicus' wife, Casta, and his daughter (Caecilia) were indicted, along with a large number of people who, according to Pliny, were much less important than Casta. However, before the case against Casta was presented, an accusation of collusion (*praevaricatio*) was brought forward (*Letter* 3.9.29). Pliny notes that this was a reversal of the customary order, whereby Casta's case would have been conducted before the collusion hearing. Curiously, however, he does not mention the accusation of collusion until after mentioning that Casta seemed guilty but was not convicted. Norbanus Licinianus, who was one of the men retained by the Baetici to collect evidence, was charged with colluding with the counselors defending Casta. Pliny describes Norbanus as a wicked man who had been retained by the Baetici only because he was an enemy of Classicus (*Letter* 3.9.31). He was hated in Rome for several reasons, but particularly, Pliny notes, because he had profited during the reign of Domitian. The Senate, swayed perhaps by anti-Domitianic sentiment, convicted Norbanus and assigned a punishment of relegation to an island.

Pliny provides no information about the nature of the collusion or how Norbanus' actions would have weakened the prosecution's case against Casta. Nor does he explain what the charges against Casta were. Even at the trial, he apparently said little about her conduct in Baetica. He admits that, when he argued for the prosecution, the point he pressed most strenuously was that the man retained to accuse her had been convicted on a charge of *praevaricatio* (*Letter* 3.9.34). He also mentions that, although she was suspected of being implicated, there was not enough evidence to convict her (*Letter* 3.9.19). He adds, however, that it was quite unusual and unexpected for a defendant to be acquitted when her accuser had been condemned for collusion. Pliny thus insinuates that Casta was indeed guilty, and his narration of the case is designed to persuade readers of her guilt. However, because he presents no evidence, we readers might not be easily persuaded.

In stark contrast to his handling of Casta, Pliny reports that no suspicion of wrongdoing was attached to Classicus' daughter (Caecilia), even though she had been included among the defendants (*Letter* 3.9.20). He decided that the most honorable course was not to treat her harshly since she did not deserve such treatment. (Are we to conclude that Casta did deserve harsh treatment?) Pliny even sought the advice of the Senate about whether he should use his eloquence (modestly stating: "if I have any") like a weapon aimed at the throat of an innocent woman (*Letter* 3.9.21). His lack of enthusiasm, as the prosecuting attorney, for attacking the daughter probably swayed the Senate to judge her favorably. Strangely, however, Pliny does not announce whether the daughter was acquitted, although he certainly leads us to believe that she deserved to be.

Since Pliny supplies no information about what behavior on the part of Casta and Caecilia had induced the Baetici to want them indicted, we are in the dark about whether the wife's conduct was indeed deserving of condemnation or whether Pliny's implication of her guilt was driven by a personal animosity toward her. Carlon makes the intriguing suggestion that "Pliny's assessment of Casta has more to do with her character than it does with any indictable behavior on her part. Pliny convicts her of failing her husband, by choosing to live after he had died."[288] Unlike Arria the Elder, who chose to commit suicide along with her husband, Casta decided to face her accusers and await the court's decision. Carlon argues that Casta therefore acted as treacherously as Vibia, the wife of Scribonianus, whom Arria had chided with words "Scribonianus died in your arms – and yet you are still alive?" (*Letter* 3.16.9; the proximity of *Letters* 3.9 and 3.16 in the published collection may be pertinent to our interpretation of Casta's behavior.) Since Pliny admits that it was unknown whether Classicus' death was natural or self-inflicted, we cannot ascertain whether Casta's actions might be construed as a betrayal of her husband. In any case, Pliny did not criticize Arria the Younger or Fannia for not dying with their husbands. Perhaps his animosity toward Casta derived from the collusion with Norbanus, whom Pliny asserts was hated by most senators because of his activities under Domitian. Indeed, he devotes considerably more attention to vilifying Norbanus than to explaining the charges against either him or Casta. The question of Casta's involvement in extortion in the province of Baetica remains a mystery. As Pliny states, the Baetici cast a wide net in their accusations, and received more convictions than acquittals (*Letter* 3.9.22). We cannot ascertain whether Casta was a guilty person who escaped justice, or an innocent person who escaped injustice.

Adultery

In *Letter* 6.31, Pliny reports on his participation in a judicial hearing concerning a woman named Gallitta, who had been charged with adultery. In the ancient Roman world, adultery (*adulterium*) was defined as a situation in which a man, either married or single, and a "respectable" married woman (not his wife) had sexual relations in a domestic setting (as opposed, for example, to a brothel).[289] A respectable woman was one who was not a slave, freedwoman, prostitute, actress, or even a woman who ran a shop.[290] Clearly two types of double standard existed in the definition of adultery. One was an instance of the pervasive Roman social stratification whereby a person of higher rank (and, inevitably, greater financial worth) was deemed to be more honorable and more worthy of consideration than a person of lower rank. The other double standard was the distinction between the behaviors of men and women. A married woman was guilty of adultery if she had sex with any man other than her husband. A man was guilty only if his partner was a "respectable" married woman. [A man who had sex with a respectable woman who was unmarried, widowed, or divorced might be accused of debauchery, *stuprum*. The debaucher was guilty of offending her *paterfamilias* by challenging his right to control the sexual activity of his daughters. Again, the social status of the woman was a key element.[291]] Thus a married man with a sexual partner of low social status did not risk an accusation of adultery, or even infidelity. It was indeed quite common in ancient Rome for married men to demand sexual gratification from slaves and to keep mistresses (behaviors about which Pliny makes only brief mention).[292] Roman wives accepted such behavior as normal. Male sexual behavior was an issue only if it compromised the integrity of another (respectable) man's *familia*. (We do not know the social status of the "certain female friend" to whom Classicus exclaimed triumphantly that he had made a fortune through extortion in Baetica.)

The main concern about adultery was that the married woman might bear a child who had not been fathered by her husband and who therefore did not belong to his agnatic *familia*. One Roman jurist suggested that the word *adulterium* was derived from a phrase meaning "child fathered by another."[293] The verb *adulterare* acquired the meaning not only "to commit adultery," but also "to corrupt," "to falsify," "to counterfeit." An adulterous wife might corrupt her husband's *familia* by bearing counterfeit children.[294] (However, theoretically a chaste wife would not be upset about her husband's adultery because any infant produced by his adultery would be the concern of the other woman's husband.) Adultery was problematic, in addition, because it defied the authority of both the wife's husband and her *paterfamilias* to regulate her actions, and it threatened the security of the household into which an unwelcome intruder had entered.

Throughout early Roman history, down to the end of the republican period, the punishment of adultery was a private matter, left to the woman's family. Both her husband and her *paterfamilias* would discuss the matter with a family council and decide upon an action. Her *paterfamilias*, whose power (*potestas*) included the power of life and death over his children, had the right to execute her. Scholars have debated whether either the husband or the *paterfamilias* had the legal right to kill her sexual partner with impunity if he was caught in the act, in the home. Treggiari concludes that, while there may not have existed a legal right for a husband or *paterfamilias* to kill an adulterer, the killer would probably not have been convicted of a murder which occurred in a moment of understandable anger and could be justified as the defense of the household against an intruder.[295] She adds that, although we hear in our ancient sources about the possibility that an adulterous couple might be killed by her relatives, there is, in fact, no evidence to document that such killings were the usual outcome. Most families would want to avoid the bad publicity such a killing would create, and most situations were probably resolved by a divorce and financial settlements, whereby the disgraced woman's family did not demand the return of all her dowry and the adulterous man made a payment to the husband for causing him distress. To the end of the republican period, the suppression of adultery remained a private matter.

A momentous change occurred early in the imperial period when Augustus made adultery a public matter. Under the Julian Laws, sponsored by him in 18 BCE and 9 CE, adultery became a criminal offence that could be prosecuted in and punished by a court.[296] Personal sexual morality now became liable to state oversight. There was discussion in Chapter 1 of those provisions of the Augustan legislation which were designed to encourage people to marry, stay married, and produce legitimate children. The intent of this legislation was to promote the stability and integrity of families and, with this intent in mind, it also penalized adultery. Augustus claimed that the Civil War had produced a decay of traditional morality and that his aim was to restore the Romans to the probity of their ancestors.[297] His solution, however, was far from traditional. Rather than simply advocating a set of moral standards, he imposed legal sanctions on adultery. He thereby took the radical step of inserting the government into family matters, in the same way that his laws concerning marriage and procreation intruded into family matters. As Severy comments, "the ways in which Augustus legislated these areas of private life changed in some critical ways the conceptual relationship of the family to the state."[298] In a sense, Augustus constructed a model of the state as a family writ large. And, having assumed for himself (and his successors) the title of *pater patriae*, "father of the fatherland," he also endowed himself with the moral authority that the *paterfamilias* had traditionally had to regulate the marriages, procreation, and sexual behavior of his children, and to exercise discipline over them. In an unprecedented move, the emperor took on oversight of the affairs of his "family" of citizens. Behavior within families, moreover, was now linked ideologically with the health of the state. Augustus promoted the idea that it was the deterioration of private morality (not the personal political ambitions of men like Octavian/Augustus himself) that had caused the collapse of the *res publica*, the state, in the first century BCE. Citizens were instructed that, in order for the state to prosper, it was necessary for them to avoid adultery and raise large families. It also became the duty of citizens to monitor and report the aberrant behavior of others. Harries aptly comments that the Julian law on adultery "introduced new thinking on what was 'criminal' in the sense of being a threat to the public good. What consenting adults did in private was made the concern of the community." She also observes that "in the dominant ideology of the Augustan period … the body of a woman was at the service of her family and of the state."[299]

The Julian Laws established punishments for adultery. Although they preserved a role for the husband and the *paterfamilias* of the adulterous woman, they dictated the terms by which the husband and *paterfamilias* must respond to adultery. Essentially it became more difficult for families to deal with such matters privately. If a *paterfamilias* caught an adulterer in the act, in his house, or in the house of his son-in-law, he could kill both the daughter and her partner with impunity, provided he acted at the moment of discovery.[300] A husband could kill with impunity an adulterer he caught in his own home, in the act, provided the adulterer was a man of low social status, such as a pimp, actor, stage performer, gladiator, wild beast fighter, or a freedman or slave of the family.[301] However, the husband could not kill his wife.[302] It is unknown how many men may have chosen to kill the adulterers. It is possible that this sanction of what is essentially revenge-killing was written into the adultery laws mainly to deter potential offenders. The husband was required to divorce his wife.[303] In addition, he or her *paterfamilias* was required to initiate a public prosecution of the adulterer and the wife.[304] If the family did not pursue prosecution within 60 days, outsiders or third parties were allowed to bring forward the prosecution.[305] And, if the husband chose not to proceed with prosecution, he was liable to a charge of pandering – that is, selling his wife's sexual services.[306] Perhaps the intent of this provision of the law was to discourage the husband from accepting a payment from the adulterer to avoid prosecution. If convicted of adultery, the penalty for the wife was relegation to an island and confiscation of one-half of her dowry and one-third of her property. For the adulterer, the penalty was also relegation to an island (not the same one to which the wife had been sent) and confiscation of one-half of his property.[307] Not incidentally, the confiscations enriched the state treasury. In keeping with the double standard of adultery definitions, a wife could not, at least not directly, bring a charge of adultery against her husband. She might, of course, persuade a family member or friend to do so. Women could press criminal accusations only in cases where their own interests were at stake. As noted already, her interests were not at stake if her husband introduced a "counterfeit" child into someone else's agnatic family.

We do not know whether the Julian Laws were successful in curbing adultery. Two poets who lived during the period in which the laws were enacted had quite different responses. Horace praised Augustus' laws for creating a moral environment in which homes were not polluted by debauchery, and wives produced children who looked like their husbands.[308] Ovid, on the other hand, defied Augustus' moral revival program and celebrated adultery in his poetry. He was punished by exile to the hinterland of the Roman empire.[309] Augustus' wife, Livia, carefully cultivated a public image of being chaste and modest. However, his daughter, Julia, was discovered to be guilty of adultery and relegated to the island of Pandateria in 2 BCE.[310] And when his granddaughter, Julia, was also found guilty of adultery in 8 CE, Augustus relegated her to the island of Trimerus.[311] Although banished women were sometimes allowed to return to Rome, both Julias died in exile.

Augustus' successor Tiberius may have been less rigid in his enforcement of the adultery laws. And yet, it was during Tiberius's time that some elite Roman women took the drastic step of officially registering as prostitutes or becoming stage performers (that is, non-respectable) so that they would not be liable to the penalties of the adultery laws. The Senate soon (19 CE) passed a decree outlawing such loopholes.[312] Despite having registered as a prostitute, Vistilia, a woman of the upper-class, was condemned to banishment to an island. An inquiry was held into her husband's failure to report her adulterous activities within 60 days, but ultimately he was not penalized.[313]

Prosecution of women for adultery continued throughout the first century CE.[314] Sometimes the charge of adultery was filed in conjunction with accusations of other crimes. In 37 CE, for example, Albucilla, who Tacitus records was notorious for her many love affairs, was indicted for adultery and treason. Several of her lovers were indicted at the same time. Having been convicted, she attempted suicide unsuccessfully. She was consigned to a prison where she died.[315] In 39 CE, charges which apparently included adultery were filed against Cornelia. Her misconduct had occurred in the province of Pannonia[316], at the time that her husband, Calvisius Sabinus, was governor there. The accusations against Cornelia were that, prompted by a lust to see the military camp, she had entered it at night disguised as a soldier, had acted shamelessly toward the sentries, and had had sex in the general's headquarters. She and her husband were both convicted, he perhaps of failing to control the behavior of his wife (and thereby endangering the entire camp) and of failing to report her adultery. In anticipation of a capital penalty, husband and wife both committed suicide. Cornelia's sexual partner in the general's headquarters was also convicted and punished.[317]

When Tacitus provided a synopsis of lamentable conditions in the Roman Empire in the mid-first century CE, he included a comment that there were notable adulteries.[318] We have no way of ascertaining, however, whether the incidence of adultery had increased or decreased. Enforcement of the laws may have depended to a great extent on the will of the emperor.[319] Pliny was writing about 100 years after the enactment of the Julian laws on adultery. When Trajan became emperor in 98 CE, he apparently promoted, as Augustus had, a revival of a stringent moral code. Certainly his wife, Plotina, was careful, as noted earlier, to project an image of purity and spousal loyalty. And Pliny's letters reveal an interest in the promotion of a society in which husbands and wives cherished the notion of harmonious marriages.

The existence of the Julian Laws on adultery meant that women had to be cautious about their behavior. Although the punishments for adultery were similar for both men and women, suspicion of adultery was a heavier burden for women. If a divorced woman remarried, she might find herself charged with adultery in her previous marriage if evidence was presented of her involvement with the new husband when she was still married to the former husband.

Because the Roman legal system allowed third parties to bring forward accusations of adultery, it created a situation which encouraged outsiders to monitor other people's private behavior. Tacitus relates that informers accused Aemilia Lepida of adultery with a slave (in 36 CE).[320] She committed suicide rather than face a trial. Some accusers may have been motivated by an honest desire to see moral legislation enforced. (Tacitus states that there was no doubt about her guilt.) Others, however, may have been motivated by a desire for revenge against her family, or for a pay-off. Even among people who were not adulterous, the realization that some acquaintances were willing to be informers may have made it difficult to trust anyone.[321] An accusation of adultery, even if finally judged by the court to be unfounded, wrecked the lives of many innocent people. The court demanded that evidence of sexual contact be presented. The most likely witnesses to a relationship would be slaves in the household. And it was mandatory under Roman law that slaves be tortured while questioned for evidence.[322] Many slaves died or were permanently injured by the torture of the interrogation process.[323] In 20 CE, during the trial of another Aemilia Lepida (not the same woman who was just mentioned above), the slaves both of Lepida and of the ex-husband who had accused her of adultery were tortured.[324]

The trial of this second Aemilia Lepida reveals some of the complications which a charge of adultery might entail. As a child, she had been betrothed to Lucius Caesar, the grandson of Augustus.[325] Lucius died in 2 CE, at the age of 19 (hence born in 17 BCE). Taking into account the marriage patterns of the Roman elite, perhaps we can conjecture that Lepida was about five years younger than he – that is, born about 12 BCE. After the untimely death of Lucius, Lepida was married to Publius Sulpicius Quirinius, who had been consul in 12 BCE and was therefore considerably older than she, perhaps by about 35 years.[326] After a divorce from Quirinius, she married Mamercus Aemilius Scaurus and gave birth to a daughter. According to Tacitus, the charges brought against Lepida in 20 CE by her previous husband, Quirinius, were: falsely claiming to have borne his child, adultery, poisoning, and consultation of astrologers regarding the imperial family (which could be interpreted as treason, but this charge was dismissed by the emperor Tiberius).[327] Unfortunately, we have no further information about Lepida's alleged assertion that she had produced a child for Quirinius, or about the accusation of adultery. If she had recently divorced Quirinius, then quickly married Aemilius Scaurus, and given birth before her new marriage was nine months old (to the daughter mentioned by Tacitus), it is possible that she had said that the child she bore was fathered by Quirinius.[328] Quirinius may have countered by claiming that the child was fathered by Aemilius Scaurus before the divorce and that Lepida had therefore been guilty of adultery when married to him. The divorce had apparently been acrimonious. Tacitus reports that Lepida, although herself reprehensible, had won sympathy because of Quirinius' hostility toward her after the divorce.

Lepida was represented in court by her brother, Manius Aemilius Lepidus. The trial was interrupted for several days so that participants could attend the Games[329] During that time, Lepida, accompanied by other distinguished women, entered the Theater of Pompey and, with much lamentation and weeping, invoked her ancestors, especially Pompey, whose great-granddaughter she was and whose statutes were within view of everyone.[330] The crowd was so moved to pity her that it burst into tears and shouted insults at Quirinius. Spectators complained that Lepida was being sacrificed on account of a childless old man from a very obscure family. However, when her slaves were tortured for evidence, they exposed her crimes. At the trial, Lepida was convicted and sentenced to banishment.[331] Suetonius, who records only the charge of poison, which he states had taken place 20 years before Quirinius filed the charge, remarks that Lepida's condemnation was intended to gratify Quirinius.

Gallitta

Pliny's one mention of adultery, in *Letter* 6.31, concerns a situation which, like that of Cornelia (who entered the military camp in Pannonia), occurred in the provinces. He reports that, in 107 CE, he took part in a judicial hearing about a case of adultery. He had been invited by the emperor Trajan to serve on an imperial council (*consilium*). These councils were not standing judicial committees, but rather advisory groups composed of men whom the emperor selected to offer him counsel about specific issues as a need arose.[332] It was, of course, an honor to be chosen by the emperor, and Pliny notes that he took great pleasure in the invitation (*Letter* 6.31.1). He had served on such councils on at least two previous occasions (*Letters* 4.22 and 6.22). On this occasion, the council was asked to evaluate three cases. The second case concerned a woman named Gallitta who was accused of adultery. Since this gathering was a consultation, not a trial, the accused Gallitta would not have been present. We know nothing about her, or the men in her life, except what Pliny tells us. It is curious that Pliny supplies her name, but not that of her husband or lover. In so many letters, he omits the names of women of whose conduct he approves, yet here he publishes the name of a woman whose behavior must have been an embarrassment to her family.

Gallitta's husband was a military tribune. Military tribunes were young men from elite families, in their early 20s, who were posted with a Roman army unit as junior officers in order to acquire a bit of experience of military service. It was common for a young man who aspired to a senatorial career to serve as a military tribune for about a year (or less) before embarking on his first campaign for political office in Rome. Pliny himself had served as a military tribune in Syria about 81 CE, when he was about 20 years old.[333] Like the young Pliny, Gallitta's husband intended to campaign for political office (*Letter* 6.31.4). It is unusual that he was married at the time of his military tribuneship. Most young men who had ambitions for political careers waited until they were settled back in Rome before marrying. It is possible that Gallitta's husband was about 20 at the time of their marriage, that she was about 15 or 16 years old, and that they had not been married long. We do not know in what province he was posted, or whether she had accompanied him from Italy or was perhaps from a Roman family residing in that province. Nor do we know the social status of Gallitta's family, although we can conjecture that she, like her husband, was from an elite family, because people rarely married outside of their own social and economic rank.

Pliny's report provides us with additional information about the conduct of some Roman wives in the provinces. He recounts that Gallitta had stained her own honor (*dignitas*) and that of her husband by having a love affair with a centurion (*Letter* 6.31.4). A centurion was the commanding officer of the smallest unit of the

Roman army, a "century." As opposed to a military tribune, he was a professional soldier, and therefore his social rank was considerably lower than that of a military tribune. Perhaps Gallitta's adultery was deemed especially shameful because her lover had been a man of lower social status. Since a soldier became a centurion by working his way up through the ranks, it would seem that Gallitta's lover would have been quite a bit older than she or her husband.

Her husband reported the adulterous affair to the governor of the province, whose title Pliny gives as that of consular legate. Because the crime committed was not a capital offence, the governor had the authority to make a judicial ruling in the province. (A Roman citizen charged with a capital offence would be transferred to Rome for trial.) However, he chose to refer the case to the emperor in Rome. His referral suggests that the governor was wary of offending important people and is perhaps confirmation that Gallitta and her husband were both from elite families. Having reviewed the evidence, the emperor ordered a dishonorable discharge for the centurion and relegated him, probably before he summoned the advisory council (*Letter* 6.31.5). The issue on which Trajan sought advice was how to deal with Gallitta and her husband. As Pliny states, adultery was a crime of two people, and therefore both (that is, Gallitta, as well as the centurion) had to be punished (*Letter* 6.31.5). And, as already noted, it was the responsibility of the husband to prosecute his wife – or risk an accusation of pandering.[334] Gallitta's husband, however, hesitated, both because he loved his wife and because he blamed himself somewhat for tolerating the affair. In fact, even after the adultery had been exposed, rather than divorcing Gallitta, as the law required, he had allowed her to remain in his home, as if he was content simply to have removed his rival. Having been warned that he must complete the prosecution, he did so, though unwillingly. Pliny comments that it was necessary that the wife be condemned, even if her accuser (her husband) was unwilling (*Letter* 6.31.6). The advisory council met with Trajan for a day to discuss the case, but Pliny does not inform his reader on what specific points Trajan requested their counsel, or whether he and his colleagues debated the possibility of allowing Gallitta to go unpunished. He simply states that Gallitta was condemned and sentenced to punishment in accordance with the Julian Laws (*Letter* 6.31.6). Presumably she was relegated, and some of her property was confiscated.

Pliny concludes this section of his letter by stating that Trajan attached to his report on the sentencing the name of the centurion and a comment about military discipline. His intention in so doing was presumably to register his displeasure about a slackness in the military discipline and to indicate that the decision reached in this case was a precedent to be applied in other cases. Trajan thus appears to have wanted to avoid having subsequent cases of a similar nature referred to him. In any future case, an adulterous wife was to be divorced and punished, despite the resistance of the husband.

It is not clear why this case was referred to Trajan in the first place, or why he felt the need to consult with a council. We may perhaps assume that the unnamed husband was of a powerful family and that both the governor of the province and Trajan himself believed that the matter required delicate handling.

But were there other, perhaps extenuating, considerations? Was the husband's desire to remain married to Gallitta so unwavering that Trajan wanted to give special attention to the case?

Pliny exhibits no sympathy for either Gallitta or her husband. It is possible that he wanted, in this published letter, to leave an unambiguous record of being uncompromising about moral legislation because he believed that this was Trajan's position. His account of the case displays a rigid approach to the issues. His assessment of the situation is that the law states unequivocally that a husband must both divorce and prosecute an adulterous wife, and that the law must be enforced. Gallitta is a rarity among Pliny's letters, where wives are generally mentioned (though often unnamed) only if they are worthy of praise. In Pliny's eyes, Gallitta deserved censure because she was selfish and stained the honor of her husband. And her husband was an object of reproach, not pity, because he was unable and unwilling to control the behavior of his wife. Modern readers may look at the situation from a different angle. The couple was very young. They were in a strange land, far from home and their families. The husband loved his wife and was willing to forgive her. However, the letter of the law allowed no room for a compassionate resolution. Despite Pliny's apparent comfort with the decision reached, the case prompts several questions. The first is whether the involvement of the state in this very personal matter served the intent of the law. Although the Julian Laws may have been created to strengthen marriages, the result in this case was the unwilling separation of a married couple. Another question is the fairness of the discrimination against women. Had Gallitta's husband had a sexual relationship with a woman of lower status (and he may have), there would have been no charge of adultery. One Roman jurist, Ulpian, who lived about 100 years after Pliny, recommended that adultery courts investigate whether the husband had set a good example for his wife by himself living virtuously.[335]

The fact that there was a provision in the law specifying that a husband must divorce his wife if he caught her in an adulterous act suggests that this situation – of a husband who was willing to forgive his wife – was not unique and that other husbands, in similar situations, had also desired to stay married. *Letter* 6.31 offers a brief glimpse into the complications and the hardships imposed by the Julian Laws on adultery. Although earlier emperors may have been less insistent on a rigid application of the laws, Trajan seems to have been determined to renew Augustus' campaign to raise moral standards. And Pliny was an enthusiastic supporter of this campaign. Many of his letters offer his readers positive examples of virtuous behavior. For his subjects, the reward for good conduct was the enduring commemoration that his letters provide. In *Letter* 6.31, however, he delineates the consequences of behavior that was considered both immoral and illegal. His letter serves as a warning to readers that such behavior deservedly ends in a harsh punishment – and the everlasting shame of being named, as Gallitta was, in a letter.

Figure 4 Biographical Sarcophagus, probably c. 176–93 CE. This sarcophagus relief presents a picture of a mother, seated on the right, watching as a nurse, on the left, bathes her infant child. The three female figures in the background may be the Three Fates. A more extensive relief, on the long side of the sarcophagus, depicts a man (presumably the sarcophagus contained his remains) as a victorious soldier.

The child in the above relief may be this man as an infant, or the child of this man. Los Angeles County Museum of Art, LA, USA. Photo © 2012 Museum Associates/ LACMA, Licensed by Art Resource, NY.

4 Mothers, nurses, and stepmothers

The focus of this chapter will be on the mothers mentioned by Pliny in his letters, and also the women who took on the maternal care of children who were not their own. Pliny unfortunately tells us very little either about the interactions between mothers and their children or about the affective relationship between them. It is a common assumption that mothers universally love their children and want the best for them. However, the factors which influence the relationship between a mother and her child vary from family to family. The nature of the relationship is, moreover, determined by the social environment in which the mother and child live. In our modern society, women marry at a later age than they did in ancient Rome and have fewer pregnancies. They anticipate that they will develop strong mutual bonds of affection with their children, beginning right from the child's infancy. And, given current life expectancy statistics, they also anticipate that their relationship with their children will continue for many decades. Although we have evidence from the ancient Roman world that mothers cared deeply for their children, they faced challenges which, fortunately, relatively few mothers in today's developed world face. In particular, the result of the high rate of infant and child mortality – perhaps 30% of children died within their first year – was that many women experienced the death of one or more of their young children.[1] In addition, the high rate of mortality among people in their 20s and 30s meant, first, that middle-aged mothers not infrequently lost children who were young adults, and, second, that often young mothers died, leaving behind children who needed to be placed in the care of other women. There are several examples in Pliny's letters of women who took on the role of surrogate mothers and, correspondingly, of children who were raised by women who were not their birth mothers.

The frequency of infant mortality in the ancient world has prompted scholars to consider whether parents, in an effort to protect themselves from emotional distress, avoided making a sentimental investment in their infants, and waited until the child had survived her/his first two or three years before trying to establish an affective connection.[2] By delaying their emotional commitment, the parents might hope to reduce their anguish if their child died. Some parents may have practiced such emotional detachment from their children, but there are certainly examples of parents who were devastated by the deaths of their infants and very young children. For example, in an essay which Plutarch, who lived about the same time as Pliny, wrote to his wife, he reveals that she grieved intensely the death of their two-year-old daughter. (They had previously suffered the deaths of two of their four sons.)[3] Nonetheless, although he is sympathetic to her distress, he praises her for being so outwardly restrained in her display of mourning. People in the ancient world seem to have believed that the death of an infant was of less consequence than death at a later age. Perhaps they needed to cling to this belief in order to cope with the all too common infant deaths. Or perhaps, because infants seemed to have only purely physical needs and to exhibit little indication of intellectual or social development, they were seen as not yet integrated into their community. Cicero, for example, comments that many people were of the opinion that the death of a small boy should be accepted with equanimity, and that the death of an infant, who was not yet old enough to have developed intentions or aspirations, should not be mourned at all.[4] Seneca chided his friend Marcellus for reacting too emotionally to the death of his little son, a child still too young, suggests Seneca, to show promise for the future.[5] The belief that infants were not yet capable of being accepted as part of the human community may explain why the exposure or abandonment of newborn infants was an accepted practice in the ancient world.[6]

If indeed ancient parents considered the activities of infants to have little relevance to their future development, their lack of interest in these activities may have produced an emotional distance between mother and child. A lack of interest might also explain, at least in part, the widespread use of wet-nurses in elite families. The role of wet-nurses, who were mother surrogates, will be examined here.

Pliny's nurse

In *Letter* 6.3, Pliny thanks his friend Verus for agreeing to assume management of the small farm which he, Pliny, had given to his nurse. We know nothing more about the nurse than the bit of information which Pliny provides in this letter. We do, however, have knowledge about the functions of nurses in Roman society, and can speculate about the role which Pliny's nurse played in his life.

The Latin word for "nurse" is *nutrix*. It has the same root as the Latin verb *nutrire*.[7] The basic definition of *nutrire* is "to nourish by suckling." However, the extended meaning of the verb may include "to care for and support" in ways other than just the supply of food (or "nutrients"). Similarly the word *nutrix* was applied to a woman who suckled an infant with her breast milk and was therefore specifically a "wet nurse." She probably also, however, had the responsibilities of a "nursemaid" – that is, of keeping the infant clean, healthy, and happy. And these responsibilities may have continued well beyond the time that the child was weaned.

Letter 6.3 was written about 106 CE, when Pliny was about 44 years old. The nurse to whom he gave the small farm was not someone employed to provide the middle-aged Pliny with medical care, but rather a woman who had nursed him with her breast milk when he was an infant and attended to his needs as he progressed through childhood to adulthood. That the adult Pliny had bestowed such a significant gift as landownership upon his nurse – who was presumably now older than 60 years – suggests that he had continued to regard her with affection long after his childhood. Perhaps she had continued to work for his family in capacities other than child-rearing, as a housekeeper or maid, for example.

Pliny's decision to publish a letter advertising his affection for this woman implies that he believed that his readers would approve of his generosity and not think it peculiar. Certainly Pliny's upper-class readers would have been familiar with the practice of having infants breastfed and cared for by women who were not their birth mothers. In the ancient Roman world, it was common – perhaps even the norm – for wealthy women *not* to breastfeed their own infants, but rather to assign this vital responsibility to other women. My focus here is on the decision of elite women not to breastfeed. Slave women and impoverished free or freed women may also not have breastfed, but out of necessity, rather than choice. If their owner or employer compelled them to return to work soon after giving birth, the feeding of the infant had to be left to another woman (a slave whose job might be to nurse several infants each day). A slave owner who was in the business of breeding slaves might refuse to allow his slave to nurse because he wanted her to conceive again as quickly as possible.[8] For many wealthy women, however, the use of a wet nurse was a personal choice.

There were, of course, circumstances when the birth mother might not be available to nurse her infant. For example, the two Helvidiae had died in child-birth, leaving behind infant daughters who would have needed suckling in order to survive.[9] Or, if an infant's parents divorced, and the infant, who by law belonged to the father's *familia*, remained with the father, a wet nurse would be required. And some mothers may have been so weakened by the birth process as to be unable to nurse their own infants. However, in the majority of cases in which an infant of an elite family was not nursed by her/his own mother, the reason was apparently the mother's unwillingness to take on this task. Nursing was considered a demeaning job, as were the cleaning of, and tending to, a child. In the minds of upper-class women, this was purely physical labor that should therefore be delegated to slaves or lower-class women. Writing about the same time as Pliny, the satirist Juvenal scornfully remarked that poor women had to endure the drudgery and discomfort of nursing, but wealthy women were able to avoid it.[10] Roman moralists referred back to an unspecified era of "the good old days" when all Roman mothers nursed their own children. Plutarch, for example, noted about Cato the Elder, the paragon of conservatism whose life spanned the third and second centuries BCE (not Cato the Younger, of the first century BCE, whose suicide is referred to in Chapter 1), that his wife breastfed their son and also bathed and swaddled him herself.[11] And Pliny's contemporary, Tacitus, writing about 102 CE, constructed a conversation taking place about 75 CE in which Vipstanus Messala said: "In the good old days, every child born to a virtuous mother was raised not in the tiny cell of a slave nurse, but rather in the bosom and lap of his mother. ... But nowadays, an infant, as soon as it is born, is handed over to some wretched little Greek slave girl."[12] And, in the *Germania*, a book in which Tacitus lauds the Germans for exhibiting the virtues which he believes the

Romans had once possessed but then abandoned, he praises German women for suckling their own infants rather than leaving this task to slaves and nurses.[13]

Although Tacitus and Pliny were close associates, perhaps even friends[14], Tacitus, quite in contrast to Pliny, paints a picture of Roman society in which many people have rejected the values of their ancestors. The failure of mothers to breastfeed their own children seemed to Tacitus to be just one example of the decadence of the imperial period. It is impossible, however, to establish when elite Roman women first began to delegate the nursing and cleaning of their infants to women of the lower classes. When Roman mothers of the republican period are commended for their strong, positive influence on their children, it is their role in educating their children and developing their moral values that wins attention from ancient authors, not their assumption of the menial, physical tasks of feeding and cleaning. For example, the late republican period writer, Cicero, comments favorably about Cornelia, mother of the Gracchi, who lived in the mid-second century BCE (that is, about 250 years earlier than Pliny and Tacitus), that her children were raised not so much in the lap of their mother as in her speech.[15] By providing them with her own example of excellence in speaking, Cornelia produced sons who, as adults, won acclaim for their oratorical skills. Cicero's statement does not, of course, tell us whether Cornelia did or did not breastfeed her children, but it does reveal that the important duty of the birth mother, at least in the case of upper-class women, was thought to be her participation in the moral and intellectual development of her children, rather than her attendance to their physical needs. Tacitus, too, applauds Cornelia for supervising her sons' education with discipline and strictness and thereby training them to be both virtuous and eloquent.[16]

Few ancient authors address an issue which receives considerable attention in our own time: the development of strong bonds of affection between mother and child through tender physical interaction during infancy. Aulus Gellius, however, writing in the mid-second century CE, attributes to the philosopher Favorinus the recommendation that Roman mothers nurse their own children.[17] Favorinus cautioned that the love which a mother should naturally have for her child waned if she did not breastfeed. In turn, the infant's love was directed toward the wet nurse, not her/his mother. Favorinus' concerns were not, however, limited to the absence of the development of a maternal bond. Most wet nurses were slaves.[18] Many were women already owned by the family. They were lactating because they had recently given birth to their own children, but they were forced to undertake the nursing of their master's child, which may have meant neglecting their own child. Some may have been lactating women purchased specifically for this function. We do not know the fate of the children to whom they had given birth – that is, whether the infant was purchased along with the mother, or left behind with the slave dealer.[19] In some cases, a family might hire a poor freed or free woman to serve as a wet nurse. It is likely that a hired nurse was dismissed once the child was weaned, as opposed to a slave who might be retained in the household and assigned other tasks (although she apparently continued to be referred to as a *nutrix*). Whatever the situation, a wet nurse was a woman of the lowest social status and might well be someone of foreign birth, transported to Italy as a slave. As noted earlier, Tacitus described a nurse as "some wretched little Greek slave girl." Favorinus believed that the character of a wet nurse influenced indelibly the character of a child. He expressed concern that the low and alien moral standards (as judged by the Roman elite) of wet nurses would have harmful effects on Roman children. He even believed that such nurses could transmit the worst qualities of their degenerate cultures (again, from a Roman point of view) in their breast milk.

Quintilian, a professor of rhetoric and one of Pliny's teacher, urges parents to select a nurse who is not only of good character, but also speaks correctly since it is the nurse whom the child will hear first and whose words he will try to imitate. Quintilian adds that first impressions are persistent, and a child should therefore not become accustomed while an infant to a pattern of speech which he will later have to unlearn.[20] Quintilian's advice is sound, but idealistic. Because nurses were drawn from the lowest strata of society, most would have been poorly educated. It is perhaps puzzling that Roman parents of the elite class were so willing to entrust their children's earliest intellectual, social, and emotional development to women whom they considered very much inferior to themselves. Apparently, ancient Romans (as opposed to modern researchers) believed that infants learned very little during their first year or two and that close contact with an uneducated woman would therefore not harm them.

Quintilian also recommended the selection of a nurse with good character. However, it would be a mistake to imagine that all nurses doted on their nurslings and provided them with patient and loving attention. Surely some nurses resented being compelled to suckle the child of another woman, particularly if doing so meant depriving their own children of milk. If the nurses were slaves, their own infants may have been removed from them and given to another slave for care or possibly even left to die. We should not assume that all nurses were kindly and devoted care-givers. Some may have been negligent or even cruel. Soranus, a medical doctor who practiced in Rome about 100 CE, commented that "some wet nurses are so lacking in sympathy for their nursling that they give it no attention even when it cries for a long time."[21] Galen, another medical doctor practicing in Rome in the second century CE, discovered the reason for one baby's crankiness: the nurse had not cleaned him or his bedding.[22] Favorinus, in Aulus Gellius, similarly warns that a nursling might be incorrectly swaddled or might suffocate in a nurse's bed. A Roman law of the fourth century CE declared that nurses whose service had been abominable were to be punished by having hot molten lead poured down their throats.[23]

On the other hand, some, perhaps many of the nurses did provide attentive and compassionate care to their nurslings. And the early intimacy between the wet nurse and the infant sometimes developed into an enduring bond of affection as the nurse became a nanny for the maturing child, and then a loyal and trust-worthy attendant for the adult. In 68 CE, when Nero received the devastating news of Galba's revolt, his nurse – the author uses the diminutive *nutricula*, his "little old nurse" – was at his side, trying to console him when he had been abandoned by his "friends."[24] One indication of the lasting affection which some nurslings had for their nurses is the existence of funerary inscriptions commemorating the death of a nurse and paid for by the former nursling.[25] Some former nurslings provided material support for their nurses while the latter were still alive. Pliny's gift of a farm – and its revenue – to his nurse is one example. Another is the bequest given in "The So-called Will of 'Dasumius'" to the nurse Dasumia Syche.[26] [The fact that the former nurse, Dasumia Syche, could inherit property – that is, own property – meant that she was no longer a slave. She had been given her freedom by her former owner – a generous gift in itself – and was now a freedwoman. Slaves, being themselves property, were not legally able to have possession of property.[27]] And, in one of his poems, Propertius crafted a scenario in which his mistress Cynthia dies, and her ghost asks him to see that her nurse, who is now in her waning years, is provided for.[28]

Favorinus, in Aulus Gellius, expressed concern that a mother and child might not develop a close emotional attachment if the child's feeding and care were relegated to a nurse. The effect of the Roman practice of wet-nursing on a child's relationship to her/his mother has piqued the interest of modern scholars. The lack of parental contact would seem likely to produce an emotional distance between the mother and child which modern parents would find undesirable. However, ancient parents appear not to have worried that physical detachment would result in emotional distancing, and moreover they were able to envisage care of a child's physical needs as a separate, and less important category than education. In any case, it was expected, as noted earlier, that a mother would be closely involved in supervising, if not actually participating in the care of her children. Favorinus' observation that an infant was likely to direct its affection towards the nurse rather than the mother would have been correct for the first few months after birth. And undoubtedly the infant, in this early period, associated her/his identity with that of the nurse. Soon, however, the child would learn that s/he was akin to the parents and belonged to their social group, while the nurse belonged to a much inferior social group. It was quite likely the responsibility of the mother to instruct the child about her/his social status and about duties and loyalties to one's family. It may also have been her role to discipline the child, since it would be increasingly difficult for a nurse to impose discipline once a child became aware of her/his superior social status. Although the nursling may have retained an affection for the nurse, especially if the nurse had been indulgent, s/he would have recognized from an early age that they were separated by a considerable social distance.

As the nursling matured and became less and less dependent on the nurse to cater to her/his needs, the nurse became more dependent on the good-will of the nursling and the family. Ungrateful or thoughtless families discarded nurses once their nurturing was no longer needed – selling them if they were slaves or firing them if they had been hired. We do not know whether the disappearance of a nurse was a trauma for a child. Some families, however, retained the nurse in the household, assigning her different tasks. This seems to have happened in Pliny's household. Moreover, at the time that *Letter* 6.3 was written, the nurse had already been granted an important gift: she had been manumitted. We know that she was a freed person because a slave would not have been able to receive a gift of property. Her manumission may have been arranged many years previously by Pliny's parents, or it may have been his benefaction, a reward to her for her devoted and loyal service. Unfortunately, manumission was not always desirable from the slave's point of view. An old or physically incapacitated slave would have found it difficult to survive without the food and shelter provided by an owner. As a freedwoman, especially an elderly freedwoman, Pliny's nurse would have been hard-pressed to support herself. She was fortunate that her nursling, Pliny, was a generous man.

Pliny informs the addressee of *Letter* 6.3, Verus, that the little farm (Pliny uses the diminutive *agellum*) that he gave his nurse had once been valued at 100,000 sesterces.[29] It is possible that the property was about 40 or 50 acres in size, and therefore, in the ancient world of non-mechanized agriculture, not so "little" a farm.[30] Pliny, however, probably hoped that Verus would think well of his modesty in describing the gift as "little." In any case, a farm of 50 acres was certainly "little" in comparison to the vast estates which Pliny himself owned. The land had previously been quite productive, but the level of productivity had declined under bad management, and its value had correspondingly depreciated. It is not likely that the nurse lived on the farm or played an active role in its oversight. (Some of Pliny's activities as a landowner, as discussed in Chapter 3, included dealing with hail damage and finding buyers for his grape harvest. In *Letters* 1.21 and 3.19, he writes about the purchase of slaves.) In *Letter* 6.30.4, Pliny describes farm life as "dreary solitude." The elderly nurse probably lived in an urban area and depended on the sale of the farm's products to provide her with an income. As the level of productivity declined, so did her income and her welfare. Hence Pliny's concern to find a good manager who would insure that the cultivation of the land would be profitable for his nurse. He was also concerned about his reputation. As noted earlier, he would not have publicized his gift by writing this letter unless he believed that his readers would approve of and be impressed by his generosity. It was therefore important to him that his gift continue to serve its recipient well. He thus admonishes Verus, whom he has hired to rehabilitate the farm: "Remember that I am entrusting to you not just the fruit trees and the land, but also my little gift (again Pliny uses the diminutive). It is as important to me, the donor, as to the recipient that it be as productive as possible."

Several questions remain unanswerable. Did Pliny give the nurse free and clear title to the land? Perhaps she had been given only usufruct, in which case the land would revert back to Pliny when she died.[31] In any case, the land might well have reverted back to Pliny even if he had given her free and clear title to it. Legally, slaves were considered not to have families – no parents, no children. Owners of slaves were their *patresfamilias*, and children born to them during their slavery were the property of their owners. When Pliny's nurse was emancipated, she became his freedwoman, and he became her patron and thereby her *tutor legitimus*, or "legal guardian," from whom she needed consent to draw up a will. If the nurse died intestate (and if Pliny refused consent to drawing up a will, she would be intestate), Pliny, as her patron (and former *paterfamilias*) would be her heir. If she wanted to make a will, she would have needed his consent as her *tutor*. She could only be free of this consent requirement if she had given birth to four children after her emancipation.[32] Children born before manumission were not included in the count. If she were already middle-aged when manumitted, it seems unlikely that she would have later had four children. With fewer than four post-manumission children, she would have needed Pliny's approval to bequeath something to them. What about children she may have had while still a slave? Presumably, since she had been assigned the task of nursing Pliny, she had already given birth to at least one child, but this child (or children) would have been the property of Pliny's family and may have been sold and thus permanently separated from her/his mother. Although a nurse might be well-treated by the people she served, there remained with her the sadness of not being able to protect, or possibly even to know, her own children.[33]

Roman mothers

While it is true that, in today's society, many working mothers leave their children for a good part of the day in the custody of day-care workers and baby-sitters, perhaps a closer comparison to the ancient practice of using servants for child care would be the employment by wealthy families of nannies who co-habit with the children and are responsible for their care 24 hours a day. However, although elite mothers may have been free of the drudgery of feeding and cleaning their children, many nonetheless paid close attention to their children's activities and spent considerable time with them, especially as they emerged from infancy.[34] A mother was undoubtedly required to discipline a misbehaving child, a task which a nurse would find harder to perform as the child grew older and became more cognizant of the nurse's inferior social position. However, it was believed that mothers were generally more indulgent than fathers. Seneca wrote: "Don't you see how fathers treat their children one way, and mothers another way? ... Even on holidays, fathers don't allow them to be idle, and they wring sweat and sometimes tears from them. But mothers want to hold their children on their laps and keep them in the cool shade. They want them never to be made unhappy, never to weep, and never to be in distress."[35] In another passage, Seneca wrote: "It is of the greatest benefit that children be raised in the correct manner even if this means harsh discipline. ... For the child who has never been denied anything, whose tears an anxious mother has always dried, who had his own way with the pedagogue[36] – this child will be unable to cope with the harsh realities of life."[37] Some scholars have suggested that the high infant and child mortality rates may have made Roman mothers, in order to protect themselves from the trauma of loss, less emotionally attached to their children than modern mothers. It is quite possible, however, that the loss of several infants may have made Roman mothers very protective of their surviving children. Since we do not have extant any literature written by mothers, revealing their thoughts, we cannot know with certainty how they felt about their surviving children. Seneca imagines the mother of an absent son saying: "I miss the embrace of my dear, dear son. I cannot enjoy his countenance or his voice. Where is he at the very sight of whom my sad face softens? Where is he in whom I confided all my cares? Where are the conversations, of which I was insatiable? ... Where is that boyish glee that always appeared when he saw his mother?"[38] In this passage, Seneca portrays the eagerness for a visit to be mutual. The son's face lights up when he catches sight of his mother.

Ideally a mother was responsible for her children's early moral education. Marcus Aurelius, who was emperor of the Roman world from 161 to 180 CE and an ardent disciple of Stoic philosophy, notes the importance of his mother, Domitia Lucilla, to his moral training[39]: "From my mother, I learned reverence for the gods, generosity, and abstinence not only from doing evil, but even from thinking it."[40] In the *Consolatio ad Helviam*, Seneca praises his mother, Helvia, for her unceasing devotion to him, not only in childhood, but also in the advancement of his career as an adult. He encourages her to become involved in the upbringing of her motherless granddaughter, Novatilla[41] – that is, to take on the role of a mother. "Now is the time to form her moral character and mould her. Those precepts sink in most deeply which are imprinted in the tender years. Let her become accustomed to your conversation. Let her be shaped to your standard."[42]

The moral education of a child remained a concern to a mother, even as she considered the child's academic training outside the home. In *Letter* 3.3, Pliny writes to Corellia Hispulla, recommending a *rhetor*, a teacher of advanced studies, for her son. Corellia Hispulla was the daughter of Quintus Corellius Rufus who had been Pliny's political mentor. After her father's death, which Pliny describes in *Letter* 1.12 (see Chapter 3), she and Pliny maintained a friendship. They may have been relatives by marriage (an issue discussed later). When the time came for her to hire a *rhetor* for her son, Pliny was happy to provide advice, no doubt to repay the many significant favors her father had done in promoting his political career. Pliny declares that, up to this point, the boy had remained in his mother's company because of his young age. He had had teachers at home, where there was little or no opportunity for problems to occur. Presumably Pliny means that Corellia Hispulla, executing the responsibilities of a good mother, kept a close watch over her son and his teachers. Now, however, it was time for his studies to be expanded beyond the threshold of his home and for a teacher of rhetoric to be sought out.[43] Nonetheless, this man's instructional program must, Pliny insists, include strictness (*severitas*), propriety (*pudor*), and above all moral purity (*castitas*).[44] Pliny recommended Julius Genitor, a man from whom her son would hear nothing inappropriate.[45] Pliny is assuring Corellia Hispulla that, if the right instructor is selected, her son's moral education, on which she focused her attention while he was at home, will continue even as he enters upon his advanced rhetorical training.

Tacitus, as already noted, applauded Cornelia, the mother of the Gracchi, for supervising her son's education in the second century BCE with discipline and strictness, and decried the declining attention paid by mothers of his own time to their children. (Corellia Hispulla's concern about her son's education would seem to prove Tacitus wrong.) He considered the upbringing of his father-in-law, Agricola, to have been exemplary, but implies that such maternal care was not common in the first century CE. "His mother, Julia Procilla, was a woman of exceptional moral purity (*castitas*). Agricola spent his boyhood and adolescence at her side and in her tender care being trained in every aspect of honorable achievement."[46] Although Tacitus' comments suggest that most mothers of his (and Pliny's) period did not devote enough attention to their children, and that the distancing began in infancy with the use of wet nurses, we should be cautious about accepting his moralizing comments as indication that detached mothers were the norm.[47] It is true that Roman literature preserves few personal memories of affectionate moments between mothers and children, but this absence probably reflects literary convention rather than reality (and the fact that the Latin literature preserved for us was written by men, not mothers). Marcus Aurelius provides a rare and charming insight into the type of warm and relaxed relationship that a young adult Roman son might have with his mother. In a letter to a friend, he wrote: "I chatted for a long time with my dear mother, who came into my room and sat on the edge of my bed."[48]

Roman children were taught from an early age to satisfy the demands of *pietas*, and this included respect for one's mother. Yet passages such as the previous one from Marcus Aurelius indicate that many children had a relationship with their mothers that was affectionate, and not simply a performance of duties. It was also Marcus Aurelius who delineated the distinction between actions inspired by a sense of formal obligation and those inspired by genuine affection. "If you had a stepmother and a mother at the same time, you would treat your stepmother with respect, but you would constantly return to your mother."[49] (This statement suggests a scenario where a child's parents were divorced, but the child still had frequent contact with her/his mother.) The close bond that could develop between a nurse and her nursling has already been discussed, but an epigram of Publilius Syrus asserts that the loss of a child was a greater blow to the mother than to the nurse.[50]

Although we do not have any accounts written by women about their children, we do not lack evidence that the loss of a child was a major trauma for a mother. The impact of a daughter's death on Plutarch's wife has already been referred to. Marcus Aurelius' friend and correspondent, Fronto (who had himself lost five children), informed Marcus by letter of the death of a young grandson (his daughter's son). He provides a very touching description of his son-in-law's attempts to comfort the grieving mother. "Her husband, the best of men, will comfort her by weeping alongside, sighing when she does, speaking when she speaks, and being silent when she is silent."[51]

Seneca addressed an essay of consolation to a woman named Marcia, who has been mentioned in Chapter 2 in connection with her preservation of the writings of her father. Seneca wrote the consolation because Marcia had been mourning the death of her son for over three years. Marcia had apparently been paralyzed by her grief. (Her son was about 20 years old at the time of his death.)

In *Letter* 3.16, discussed earlier, Pliny describes the poignant situation of Arria the Elder, whose son died at the same time that her husband was very ill. Despite being afflicted by grief, she forced herself to conceal the death of her son from her husband lest the news cause his illness to worsen. She arranged and attended the funeral without his knowledge. Suppressing her anguish, she assumed a happy and comforting countenance when she entered his bedroom, and pretended that their son was still alive and even recovering. Only when she left the bedroom did she allow herself to dissolve into tears. Since she chose to conceal her grief, she did not receive the kind of husband's comfort that had eased the pain of Fronto's daughter.

The anonymous mother of Calpurnius Piso

Several of Pliny's letters offer brief references to the activities for which mothers were praised. In *Letter* 5.17, which is addressed to Vestricius Spurinna, whose "model wife," Cottia, has been discussed in Chapter 3, Pliny reports that he had attended a recitation at which Calpurnius Piso read aloud his poem titled "Elevation to the Stars."[52] We do not know who this Calpurnius Piso was, but Pliny lauds him for his talent both in composing poetry and in reciting it. From Pliny's comments about him, we can conclude that he was a young man from a family which had been senatorial for many generations. Pliny expresses his delight in seeing a member of the old nobility accomplish something worthy of his ancestors, and thus pass on to his descendants the torch which he had received. These remarks suggest that Pliny, who was the first (and last) in his family to reach the exalted ranks of senatorial membership, believed that his contemporaries from the old noble families had achieved little and been content to bask in the reputations of their ancestors.[53] He was impressed that Calpurnius displayed modesty and even nervousness during his performance, qualities which Pliny found more appropriate than self-confidence. At the conclusion of the performance, he embraced Calpurnius Piso affectionately and used praise to inspire him to further achievements. He then congratulated his brother (who is not named) who, Pliny states, deserved no less credit for his familial *pietas* than Calpurnius Piso deserved for his eloquence. Pliny recounts that the brother's anxiety was very noticeable when Calpurnius Piso first began his recitation, but soon was replaced by joy. Pliny also congratulated the mother (who is not named) of the two brothers, describing her as "an excellent mother" (*Letter* 5.17.5). However, he does not elaborate and tell his reader why he thought her "excellent." Surely it must be because she had trained her sons well, teaching them to be supportive of one another, to be appropriately modest, and to strive to distinguish themselves by their own accomplishments, not simply their family name. She had also apparently arranged for them to receive very good educations which enabled one at least to do a creditable job at writing and performing poetry.

It is not clear from Pliny's letter whether the mother was present at the recitation, which seems to have taken place at the family home. He wrote, "I congratulated his excellent mother. I congratulated his brother who (exited) from the auditorium."[54] We know that the mother had made an appearance because Pliny was able to congratulate her. Perhaps she was also in the auditorium, quite visible to the other attendees. Or, perhaps like Pliny's young wife, Calpurnia, she listened to the recitation, sitting close by, but concealed by a curtain (*Letter* 4.19.3). Although Pliny writes several letters about recitations, he nowhere else mentions the presence of women at them. Rawson suggests that many women attended literary readings and even participated in the discussions.[55] Hemelrijk takes a more conservative view, with which I agree: recitations were, as a rule, all-male affairs.[56] If women were present, they were probably relatives of the author, at whose home the recitation was occurring, or relatives of the host who had made his home available for the recitation. Women were present for dinner entertainment by musicians, dancers, and actors, whose status was lower-class, but these types of performances were considered of quite a different nature from a recitation by an author of senatorial status.[57] Nonetheless, although it was probably unusual for women to attend recitations, Pliny believed that it was appropriate for a mother to be acknowledged for raising a son who was well-educated and virtuous.

We do not know who this woman's husband was. Presumably he was a Calpurnius. Since he is not mentioned in the letter, he was probably deceased.[58]

The anonymous mother of Gnaeus Pedanius Fuscus Salinator

In *Letter* 6.26, Pliny writes to congratulate Julius Servianus on the engagement of his daughter to Fuscus Salinator. (These two men and the fiancée, Julia Paulina, are discussed in Chapter 3.)[59] The prospective bridegroom's family is, writes Pliny, patrician. His father is very honorable (*honestissimus*), and his mother deserves equal praise. This is all we know about the mother. Pliny's words are most likely a reference to the high rank of the mother's family. In the next sentence, however, Pliny extols the virtues of her son. He is studious, well-read, and a good speaker. He has the openness (*simplicitas*) of a child, the affability (*comitas*) of a young man, and the dignity or seriousness (*gravitas*) of an older man. A reader of the letter will conclude that Fuscus combines the virtues of each age group, and, importantly, possesses the mature wisdom of an older man. Perhaps the proximity of Pliny's favorable comments to the references to Fuscus' father and mother denotes a subtle compliment to them for raising so fine a young man.

Pliny's mother

Pliny tells us very little about his mother, but we are able to extract some information about her from his letters and from our knowledge about her brother, Gaius Plinius Secundus (Pliny the Elder).[60] Although her name is never revealed, we assume that it was Plinia, the feminine form of the family *nomen* Plinius. She was born into a wealthy equestrian-order family whose hometown was Comum in northern Italy. There is no record of siblings other than her brother, who was born about 23 CE. The year of Plinia's birth is unknown, but, considering the year of her son's birth (61 or 62 CE), I speculate that she was quite a bit younger than her brother. It is possible that she was born in the mid-30s CE. She married a man named Lucius Caecilius, also from a wealthy Comum family. If this was her first marriage and, following custom, she married in her mid-teens, the marriage may have taken place in the early or mid-50s. We do not know how many pregnancies she may have had. Since her son, Pliny the Younger, does not write about any siblings, we assume that he was the only child who survived her. She may also have had a daughter, Caecilia, who pre-deceased her.[61]

We know nothing about Plinia's parents or about her education.[62] Her parents had sent her brother to Rome to ensure that he received the type of advanced education which young men of the elite class were expected to have. Throughout his life, he remained enthusiastic about learning and published voluminously on such diverse topics as natural history, military practice and history, biography, and grammar and rhetoric.[63] If his parents had inspired his love of learning at an early age, perhaps they had also considered it important to provide a good education for their daughter, Plinia. She, however, would have remained close to home (or even in home) for her lessons, and her formal schooling would probably have ended at the time of her marriage.

Her husband, Lucius Caecilius, is unknown to us except for several inscriptions in which he is mentioned as the father of "our" Pliny, who was born a Caecilius, but became a Plinius by adoption. It is from these inscriptions that we learn that the agnate family *nomen* was Caecilius and that the father's *praenomen* was probably Lucius.[64] He may be the Lucius Caecilius who served as a senior magistrate in Comum and initiated the building of a temple to the Eternity of Rome and Augustus in the name of his daughter Caecilia.[65] We have no way of knowing how old Caecilius was at the time of his marriage to Plinia, whether this was his first marriage, or whether he had children from a previous marriage. Nor does Pliny give us any inkling of what his relationship with his father was like. Perhaps he was still too young at the time of Caecilius' death to have formed memories. Caecilius died before Pliny reached the age of 14 (before 76 CE), perhaps well before then. We know this because, at his death, Pliny was young enough to require the appointment of a *tutor* (guardian).[66] The *tutor* whom Caecilius had nominated in his will was Verginius Rufus. Verginius, who did not have a son of his own, displayed toward Pliny "the affection of father" (*adfectum parentis*) (*Letter* 2.1.8). Even after Pliny reached the age of maturity, Verginius continued to advise him and to support his political career, just as his father would have done, had he been alive.

Since we do not know the cause of Caecilius' death, we cannot speculate about his age, or whether there was as large a difference in age between him and Plinia as there was, for example, between his son and his son's third wife, Calpurnia. If he died much earlier than 76 CE, Plinia became a widow when her son was still a young child. The situation of widows has been discussed in Chapter 2. Because her family was wealthy, and Plinia had demonstrated her fertility by the birth of a son, she may well have had suitors for her hand, but there is no mention in Pliny's letters of another marriage or a stepfather. Although Pliny belonged legally to the family of his father rather than his mother, we do not learn in the letters about any close paternal relatives who were involved in raising him. (Consider, by contrast, the situation of Pliny's wife Calpurnia, who was raised by her paternal grandfather and aunt after her father's death.) Perhaps his father had been an orphan without siblings. It is likely that the son continued to live with Plinia in Comum after the death of Caecilius. She may have devoted the same attention to his education – both moral and academic – that Corellia Hispulla, mentioned earlier, did with her son. Since there was no instructor of rhetoric in Comum, he was sent to Rome for his advanced studies.[67] We don't know if Plinia accompanied him there. Neither she nor her son had financial concerns. Caecilius had left his son well-provided for, and Plinia had inherited property from her family.[68] In accordance with Roman law, she was allowed to hold the property in her own name. Nonetheless, even though she was an adult woman, she would have been assigned a *tutor* to oversee the management of her finances when her *paterfamilias* died. Perhaps her brother was her *tutor*. If not, she may nonetheless have turned to him for advice and for emotional as well as material support as she raised her son. He seems not to have had children of his own and may therefore have taken an interest in the activities of his sister's son, particularly his education.

During the son's (Pliny the Younger's) childhood, his uncle served as an imperial procurator in, successively, the provinces of Gaul, Africa, and Spain. We have no evidence that his widowed sister and nephew accompanied him as he traveled outside of Italy. About 76 CE, the elder Pliny was appointed prefect of the Roman naval fleet at Misenum, a town on the northwest end of the Bay of Naples. He was joined there by Plinia and her son, although we do not know in what year or for how long. His sister and nephew may have moved in with him, or may simply have been visiting. They were at his villa in Misenum when the volcano, Mount Vesuvius, erupted in August of 79 CE. The younger Pliny noted, in a letter which he wrote to Tacitus almost 30 years after the eruption (*Letter* 6.16), that Plinia was the first to observe the enormous ash cloud that had formed across the Bay. She summoned her brother and son, both of whom had been busy reading, to come and see it. The elder Pliny, in his capacity as prefect, hastily assembled several ships and sailed (or, more likely, was rowed) to the east side of the Bay in an attempt to rescue people. He invited the younger Pliny to accompany him, but the nephew declined, stating that he preferred to continue the reading assignment which his uncle had given him (*Letters* 6.16.7 and 6.20.2). Several hours after landing near Stabiae (a town about four miles south of Pompeii), the elder Pliny died, overcome either by the poisonous gases emitted by the volcano or (as some modern scholars suggest) by a heart attack. He was about 55 years old.

In his will, the elder Pliny adopted his 17-year-old nephew as his son and heir, a process known as testamentary adoption (as opposed to adoption while the adopter was still alive).[69] In *Letter* 5.8.5, the younger Pliny refers to him as "my maternal uncle and also my father by adoption." Upon adoption, the man who wrote the letters we are examining changed his name from Lucius Caecilius to Gaius Plinius Caecilius Secundus.[70] By this adoption, the elder Pliny thus secured a blood relative (though not an agnate) to carry on his and Plinia's family name. The younger Pliny, in turn, inherited his uncle's fortune.[71]

Nowhere in the letters does Pliny mention that he had an affectionate relationship with Plinia's brother. Nonetheless, the childless uncle seems to have taken a paternal interest in his orphaned nephew, even though the formal adoption occurred only after the uncle's death. And, in turn, in *Letter* 6.16, in which the younger Pliny describes his uncle's actions during the eruption of Vesuvius, he reveals a deep admiration for his courage. In *Letter* 3.5, moreover, he provides a laudatory account of his uncle's literary activities, energy, and dedication to scholarship, noting in addition that his uncle was remarkably prolific for a man also so involved in public service. The inclusion in this letter of many details about Pliny the Elder's daily routine suggests that the younger Pliny spent a considerable amount of time with his maternal uncle. His decision to publish the letters also implies that he was determined to honor and preserve the memory of a man he considered a model Roman: brave, capable, self-sacrificing, dedicated to public service, and devoted to literary pursuits. In *Letter* 6.16.1 and 2, Pliny urged Tacitus to include his account of his uncle's heroic rescue mission and death in the history book he was writing because his uncle would then be assured immortal fame. In *Letters* 5.8.1 and 2, a reply to a friend who had suggested that Pliny write a history book, he comments that it seems to him a particularly noble thing not to allow to fade from memory those to whom immortality is owed. He then adds, however, that it is noble to expand the fame of others (that is, of those one writes about) along with one's own fame (that is, as an author). "Nothing stimulates me as much as the love and desire for enduring fame. This is the most worthy goal for a man." As to the choice of writing history, rather than oratory or poetry, he claims that a family example impels him toward this pursuit: his maternal uncle (also his father by adoption) wrote histories (*Letters* 5.8.4 and 5). We may perhaps speculate from the yearning for personal recognition which is obvious in these and other letters that the younger Pliny looked to his mother's brother as a role model and was driven by a desire to emulate his uncle's ability to "do things worth writing about and to write things worth reading" (*Letter* 6.16.3).

Pliny's quest to appear the equal of his uncle/adoptive father may have influenced the manner in which he documents his own activities and those of his mother, Plinia, during the eruption of Vesuvius. After receiving *Letter* 6.16, the account of the elder Pliny's activities, which had been written at his request, Tacitus asked the younger Pliny to provide a report on his own response to the disaster. *Letter* 6.20 is this report, and it is designed to portray the author, the younger Pliny, then 17 years old, as a calm and collected agent during the terrifying events. It is therefore difficult to determine what role his mother, Plinia, played in the decisions made about their actions. After his uncle set sail, Pliny continued his reading, which, he reminds us, was the reason he declined to join his uncle. That night, he slept fitfully because of the violent earth tremors. His mother burst into his bedroom, but he was already getting up to wake her. Fearing the collapse of the building, they sat outdoors. He calmly read and took notes. He does not tell us what his mother did, but a friend from Spain scolded Pliny for ignoring the danger, and his mother for allowing him to do so.

In the morning, it seemed advisable to leave the town. Although Pliny does not state who proposed the plan to depart, he does record that he and his mother were followed by a panic-stricken crowd of people who preferred to leave the decision-making to someone else. In his narrative, Pliny emerges as the decision-maker. The crowd of refugees jostled them from behind. Once they were clear of the structures of the town, Pliny and Plinia stopped. The ground was shaking, the sea had retreated, and the dark sky was filled with flashes of flames. Their Spanish friend urged them to flee the danger, saying that their brother and uncle would want them to be safe. They – and Pliny does use the plural here – replied that they would not consider their own safety while his (the elder Pliny's) fate was unknown. Soon afterward, the spreading dark cloud of ash obliterated every landmark. Plinia begged, exhorted, and ordered her son to flee in any way he could. He was, she said, a young man and could do so. She, on the other hand, was weighed down by her years and her aging body. She would die at peace if she had not been the cause of his death. He, of course, refused to find safety without her. Grasping her hand, he forced her to quicken her pace. Reluctantly she obeyed, though chiding herself because she was delaying him. As the blinding black cloud of ash moved closer, "spreading over the earth like a flood" (*Letter* 6.20.13), Pliny decided that they should turn off the road in order that they not be knocked down and trampled by the crowd. They paused to rest in the utter darkness, and heard the shrieks and moans and wailing of those around them. They were soon coated with thick ash. Nonetheless, Pliny boasts, not a groan or a cowardly word escaped him in the midst of such grave dangers. He does not state whether Plinia was similarly brave. The next day, the cloud dispersed, and, in the weak, but welcome daylight, their trembling eyes perceived that everything was buried by deep snow-like ash. They returned to Misenum, where they remained, despite the continuing earth tremors. Pliny states that, although they had experienced dangers and were expecting more, they – and again he uses the plural – had no intention of leaving until they received news about the elder Pliny.

Pliny's publication of *Letter* 6.20 serves the purpose of immortalizing his mother, although this was not its main function. There are surprisingly few insights, however, into the nature of the relationship between the mother and son. The picture of Plinia that emerges from Pliny's narration is, first, of an indulgent mother who was willing to leave the crucial decision-making to her 17-year-old son, allowing him to continue to read while other people were recommending flight. Of course, we do not know what really happened on that fateful day. We must take into account, however, that the function of this description may be to enhance Pliny's self-portrait, making him appear to have been a very mature, wise, and unflappable young man with a tenacious dedication to scholarly matters. Perhaps Plinia played a larger role in the decision-making than Pliny has admitted.[72]

A second element of the picture is that Plinia was a mother who was willing to sacrifice her own life to save that of her son. Again, we do not know what she actually said, but it is not difficult to believe that a mother urged her child to abandon her and save his own life. Pliny, moreover, wanted to leave for posterity a record that each was willing to die for the sake of the other. In ancient Roman terms, their willingness would serve as an outstanding example of *pietas*. In modern terms, it would be considered a "greater love." We again face the problem which arose in interpreting the relationship between Pliny and his wife, Calpurnia. We do not know whether Pliny and his mother truly loved one another, or whether they did not, but he wanted his reader to think that they did. His inclusion of this episode in his published correspondence indicates that he expected his readers to respond favorably to a portrait of him as a loving and loved son. It also reinforces our perception that the Romans valued a strong bond between mothers and children. While Pliny may have invented the offers of self-sacrifice, it seems quite plausible that his mother, in this apparently hopeless situation, pleaded with him to save himself, and that he refused to leave her. I am willing to believe that we can accept that there existed a strong emotional bond between them. It was noted in the discussion earlier that some ancient authors believed that the use of wet nurses weakened the bond between a birth mother and her child. This does not seem to have been the case with Plinia and Pliny, who, as we have seen, had a wet nurse with whom he retained a sentimental attachment even as an adult. As already noted, mothers demonstrated their love for their children in ways other than providing for their physical needs when they were infants, and children responded favorably to the attention which their mothers bestowed on them.

There are very few references in Pliny's letters to people's physical appearance.[73] In her exhortation to Pliny to flee, Plinia apparently said that she was weighed down by her years and her body, meaning that she would slow him down. Some commentators have taken the word "body" (Latin *corpus*) to suggest that Plinia was fat. She may have been. Her brother is described in *Letter* 6.16.13 as snoring loudly because of the amplitude of his body. Perhaps bodily heaviness was a trait of the Plinius family. However, in Plinia's case, *corpus* might also imply, as I have translated it, "aging body." She feared that she would retard her son's flight because she was not physically able to move as quickly as he. Nonetheless, we should not form a picture of a very elderly woman. It is likely that Plinia was only in her early 40s in 79 CE.

One other element of Plinia's character that emerges from her son's description of events is her devotion to her brother. The siblings, both unmarried at this point, may have had a particularly close relationship if, as it appears, they had no other near relatives than the younger Pliny. Although Pliny attributes much of the decision-making during this terrifying event to himself, he shares with Plinia the decision to remain at Misenum until they have learned the fate of the elder Pliny.

We do not know when Plinia died. Since Pliny makes no mention of any involvement by her in his activities as an adult, perhaps she died not long after her brother (79 CE), and well before the younger Pliny began the correspondence which he published. This is only speculation. If it is correct, perhaps the younger Pliny remained close to his nurse because she was the only person left with whom he could share memories of his childhood.

Plinia is mentioned briefly in several other letters, written at a time when she was deceased (and her son had inherited her property). In *Letter* 1.19, Pliny announces to the addressee, Romatius Firmus, that he is offering him a gift of a very substantial amount of money: 300,000 sesterces.[74] This gift, when added to the 100,000 sesterces which Romatius already possesses, will make him eligible for enrollment in the equestrian order.[75] Pliny gives several reasons for his willingness to bestow so generous an amount on Romatius. He is a fellow townsman (presumably of Comum), and they were students together and friends from an early age. In addition, Romatius's father was a friend of his mother and uncle. In *Letter* 2.15, Pliny reports to a friend that the property that he inherited from his mother is not treating him well.[76] Presumably he means that the land has not produced much income. He adds, however, that he enjoys the property precisely because it was his mother's.

In *Letter* 4.19.7, a letter written to Calpurnia Hispulla, the paternal aunt of his wife, Calpurnia, Pliny writes: "You revered my mother as if she were your own (*parentis loco*) and were accustomed to guide and praise me from the time I was a boy." And in *Letter* 7.11, addressed to his grandfather-in-law, he explains why he approved the sale of some land near Comum, at below market or tax-assessed value, to a woman named Corellia.[77] He states that he feels affection and respect for Corellia because she was a sister of Quintus Corellius Rufus, who had been Pliny's mentor, as well as the wife of Minicius Justus, with whom Pliny had long-standing ties, and the mother of a man with whom Pliny's ties had been especially strong. In addition, Corellia herself had been a very close friend of his mother. These brief references to Plinia (*Letters* 1.19, 2.15, 4.19, and 7.11) provide some additional information about Pliny's feelings for his mother and suggest that, even years after her death, fond memories of her influenced his decisions. He seems to have had a sentimental attachment to the property he inherited from her and from his father, although nowhere does he reminisce about happy times spent with his parents on these estates. Nor does he, in the correspondence, describe estates in Comum with the loving and familiar detail with which he describes his Laurentine villa (*Letter* 2.17) and the villa in Etruria (*Letter* 5.6). The properties inherited from his parents were essentially farms, worked by tenants and slaves, which provided the Plinius and Caecilius families with much of their income and investment wealth. Pliny's attachment to them seems then to have developed not from personal experiences on the estates, but rather from the fact that they were a part of his mother's history and that his subsequent ownership of and concern for them continued to connect him to her even though she was now deceased. We must also consider that his commitment to tending to his mother's property – and his mother's friendships – was an aspect of *pietas* and that Pliny felt bound by familial obligations.

Pliny appears to have considered it important to honor and maintain relationships established by his mother (and his maternal uncle). His generosity toward Romatius Firmus (*Letter* 1.19) was prompted not only by their own long-standing friendship, but also by the friendship which Plinia and the elder Pliny had enjoyed with Romatius' father. It is worth noting that Pliny's phrasing implies that Plinia and the elder Pliny were equally friends of Romatius' father – that is, that Plinia had cultivated male friendships. It is possible that the amity between the Plinius and Romatius families had begun in an earlier generation and that Plinia had known Romatius' father when they were both children in the Comum area. By the generation of the younger Pliny, the Plinius family was clearly much wealthier than the family of Romatius. There is, in fact, a patronizing attitude apparent in Pliny's letter. Pliny reminds Romatius that he is obligated to be forever grateful for the gift and to conduct himself, in his new, higher social rank, in a way which will not embarrass his benefactor. Pliny seems to be speaking here in the role of a patron rather than a friend.[78] Nonetheless, the letter demonstrates his commitment to nurturing associations formed by his mother and her family. (It is curious that Pliny does not, in the correspondence, write about friendships that his father may have had.)

Pliny's generosity toward Corellia was similarly motivated, he asserts, by long-standing friendships – his with her brother, husband and son, hers with his mother, Plinia. The friendship between the two women may, in fact, have been the basis of Pliny's other connections to Corellia's family. It is regrettable that Pliny's letters provide so little evidence of the importance that Roman society attached to friendships between women. In letters by other authors, we can detect a desire among men to confirm that the women of their families were fond of the families of their addressees. These men apparently believed that their own male friendships benefited when the women also were (or were perceived to be) friends. For example, in a letter to Atticus, Cicero writes: "Terentia (*Cicero's wife*) loves you and your sister and your mother very much. And my sweet little Tullia (*Cicero's daughter*) wishes you the best of health."[79] In a letter which Marcus Aurelius wrote to Fronto, he recounts a conversation which he had with his (Marcus') mother who had come, as related earlier, to sit on the edge of his bed. "She asked me, 'What do you think my friend Gratia (*Fronto's wife*) is doing?' And then I asked, 'What do you think sweet little Gratia (*Fronto's daughter*) is doing?' ... We were playfully arguing about which of us two loved which of you three the best."[80] Although Pliny never offers such explicit examples of the development of affection between the female family members of friends, female friendships may have been a significant element in the Roman system of requesting and granting favors.

If the friendship between Pliny's mother and Corellia was the basis of Pliny's other connections to Corellia's family, then Plinia may have played a pivotal role in the development of her son's successful legal and political career. We have already noted that elite Roman mothers were involved in the early education of their children and in the choice of advanced teachers as their sons grew into their teens. For the families of elite boys in their mid to late teens, who were planning a senatorial career, it was customary to secure the assistance of an established public figure to serve as a mentor. A young man, serving an internship as it were, accompanied his mentor for several years and learned by observation how to negotiate the arenas of power. The mentor facilitated his building of a network of political alliances by introducing him to other influential people and eventually allowing him to help with legal cases. Cicero, for example, when he was still in his teens, was entrusted by his father to Quintus Mucius Scaevola for guidance.[81] In turn, once Cicero's career had been established, he took on the role of mentor to several young men.

The securing of a mentor was the responsibility of a boy's father, who would use his own personal connections to persuade a prominent and powerful public figure to assume the time-consuming task of mentoring. Pliny's father, however, had died when his son was young and had apparently left no brothers who might, as paternal uncles, have taken upon themselves the responsibility of ensuring that Pliny received the assistance he needed to forge a successful political career. His maternal uncle, the elder Pliny, had not held any senatorial magistracies, but had a distinguished record of military service, which may have been what brought him to the attention of the emperor Vespasian.[82] The younger Pliny records in *Letters* 3.5.7 and 9 that his uncle had a friendship with the emperor and used to visit Vespasian before dawn. Apparently, both men began work when it was still dark.[83] The elder Pliny's access to the imperial family might have been of considerable benefit to his nephew. As Carlon observes, "the ambitious needed to cultivate relationships with those men most closely associated with the *princeps*."[84] But the elder Pliny died in the eruption of Vesuvius when the younger Pliny was just 17 years old, leaving the nephew without a strong male figure on the maternal side of his family. His father had arranged for Lucius Verginius Rufus, a distinguished senator from northern Italy (the home region of the Caecilius and Plinius families), to serve as his son's *tutor* upon his death (*Letter* 2.1.8). Fortunately for Pliny, Verginius Rufus showed him the affection of a father (*adfectum parentis*) and went well beyond the financial oversight responsibilities of a *tutor*, which would have ended once Pliny reached the age of majority. Verginius Rufus supported him as he advanced in his career. Nonetheless, the responsibility of plotting out Pliny's future seems to have fallen to a great extent to his mother, Plinia. And the task of gaining the assistance of an influential man of senatorial rank would have been difficult because Pliny's family, though wealthy, was not senatorial. His father had not served in even the lowest-ranking of Roman magistracies and had not developed the network of senatorial allies that most ambitious elite young men could call upon. In the eyes of many senators, Pliny would have been an outsider trying to break into an exclusive club.

Despite these disadvantages, Pliny acquired as his mentor a man named Quintus Corellius Rufus.[85] Corellius Rufus, born about 30 CE, had served as suffect consul in 78 CE when Vespasian was emperor. He was relatively old (about 48 years) to be selected for this magistracy. Perhaps he was also an outsider who had had difficulty finding acceptance by the more established senatorial families. About 82 CE, during the reign of Domitian, he served as a legate in Upper Germany.[86] He seems not to have held any further offices under Domitian, which suggests that he had angered the emperor in some way. His hatred of Domitian was not a secret, at least not to his friends. As noted in Chapter 3, in the discussion of his wife, Hispulla, Pliny reports that Corellius Rufus had been plagued by a painful physical ailment for decades, but was determined to outlive "that bandit" (as he called him), Domitian, even if just by one day (*Letter* 1.12.8). (Of course, in the post-Domitianic period when Pliny published his letters, it suited his self-promotional interests to record that his mentor had been an enemy of Domitian.) In the end, Corellius survived Domitian by more than a day, and was appointed to a land commission by the next emperor, Nerva. Nevertheless, in 97 or 98 CE, he decided to end his physical torment by suicide, despite the pleas of his wife, Hispulla, and his daughter. Hispulla summoned Pliny to their home, but, like them, he was unable to dissuade Corellius Rufus.

In several letters, Pliny pays glowing and loving tribute to Corellius Rufus, describing him as a man of the highest integrity (*conscientia*), highest renown (*fama*), and greatest influence (*auctoritas*) (*Letter* 1.12.3; cf. *Letters* 3.3.1 and 4.17.4). Letters in which Pliny praises Corellius Rufus appear throughout the published correspondence, from Books 1 to 9.[87] Clearly he felt that he owed an enormous debt to this man whom he identifies as his witness, guide, and teacher (*Letter* 1.12.12). In *Letter* 4.17, Pliny records the support which Corellius Rufus gave him, beginning from the time that Pliny was a very young man.[88] His narrative informs us about the responsibilities of a mentor. "He was my sponsor (*suffragator*) and witness (*testis*) when I was campaigning for public offices, my champion (*deductor*) and companion (*comes*) when I entered these offices, and my counselor (*consiliator*) and guide (*rector*) when I served in them. ... How greatly he built up my reputation, both public and personal, and even with the emperor" (*Letters* 4.17.6 and 7).[89] Because our only evidence for Corellius Rufus' character and career is derived from Pliny's letters and two inscriptions, we cannot be certain that he was as powerful a political figure as Pliny makes him out to have been.[90] However, the success of Pliny's career seems to be testament to Corellius Rufus' abilities as a mentor. In fact, he once told the emperor Nerva that Pliny did nothing without his advice (*Letter* 4.17.8).[91] On one occasion, however, Pliny formulated a plan without consulting Corellius Rufus. It was the plan to avenge the prosecution of Helvidius II by raising the topic at a meeting of the Senate. Pliny's involvement of Fannia, Arria Y, and Anteia in his plan has been discussed in Chapter 2. Pliny writes in *Letter* 9.13.6: "I always consulted Corellius Rufus about everything because I knew that he was the wisest and most perceptive (*providentissimus*) man of our age. However, on this occasion, I was comfortable with my own judgment, and I was afraid that he might veto my plan since he was by nature rather hesitant and cautious." Why did Pliny on this one occasion not seek the advice of his long-time mentor? Perhaps, despite his admiration and affection for Corellius Rufus, Pliny wanted the glory of being Helvidius's avenger to redound only to him. His reference to Corellius Rufus' cautiousness encourages the reader to conclude that Pliny, in contrast with his mentor, was bold and independent in righting wrongs and avenging friends.[92]

Corellius Rufus had been an excellent choice as a mentor for Pliny. But whose choice was he? In *Letter* 7.11.3, Pliny reports that Corellius Rufus's sister, Corellia, had been a very close friend of his mother (*matri meae familiarissimam*). They may have known one another since childhood. Plinia's family was from the Lake Comum area, and a phrase in *Letter* 7.11.5 (discussed later) suggests that Corellia, too, was well-acquainted with that area. It is possible that the mentorship arrangement came about through this friendship. The widowed Plinia may have prevailed upon Corellia to persuade her brother to assume the task of guiding and promoting Pliny's career. As a woman, she was denied the right to run for public office, or even to vote, but Plinia may have had ambitious plans for her son and been willing to exploit her friendships to promote his career.

Plinia's friendships seem also to have played a role in Pliny's choice of a third wife, and to have produced a marriage which may have brought him into a familial connection with the Corellius family. In *Letter* 4.19.7, Pliny makes reference not only to Calpurnia Hispulla's kind guidance of him when he was a boy, but also to the fact that her relationship with Plinia had been like that of a daughter and mother ("you revered my mother as if she were your own" – *parentis loco*). In this case, the close relationship between Plinia and Calpurnia Hispulla seems to have been a factor in Pliny's choice of Calpurnia (Calpurnia Hispulla's niece) as his third wife. In his search for a new wife, Pliny returned to his hometown and sought advice from someone who had loved and been loved by his mother. In turn, Calpurnia Hispulla, who had assumed the role of surrogate mother to Calpurnia, was undoubtedly pleased that she could repay the kindness of *her* surrogate mother, Plinia, by arranging the marriage of her niece to Pliny. That it was Calpurnia Hispulla who was responsible for the arrangement appears evident from Pliny's comment at the end of the letter: "We owe you thanks, I because you gave her to me, and she because you gave me to her" (*Letter* 4.19.8).

Pliny's marriage to Calpurnia seems to have been a consequence, at least in part, of his mother's close relationship with Calpurnia Hispulla. It may, in addition, have connected him to the Corellius family. (See Genealogy Chart 4.) The name of the wife of Pliny's mentor, Corellius Rufus, was Hispulla (*Letter* 1.12.9). The name Hispulla (and the masculine forms Hispo and Hispullus) was very rare, an indication perhaps that family members had difficulty continuing the family line.[93] Those who did reproduce may have been anxious to preserve the family name through female members.[94] The daughter of Corellius and Hispulla carried the names of both her parents: Corellia Hispulla. (She was the woman to whom Pliny recommended a rhetor in *Letter* 3.3.) The only other person we meet in Pliny with the name Hispulla is Calpurnia Hispulla, the aunt of Pliny's third wife. She was the daughter of Lucius Calpurnius Fabatus and an anonymous wife. Because the daughter bore the double name Calpurnia Hispulla, it is possible to conjecture that the name of Calpurnius Fabatus' wife was Hispulla, and furthermore that she was related to – perhaps even a sister of – the Hispulla who was the wife of Corellius Rufus. If they were sisters (although it is safer to conjecture only that they were "relatives"), then Corellia Hispulla and Calpurnia Hispulla would have been maternal first cousins. Pliny's wife, Calpurnia, would have been the grandniece of the Hispulla who was married to Corellius Rufus, and Pliny would, by his third marriage, have become a distant in-law of his now-deceased mentor and of the Corellia who was a close friend of his mother. In addition to Pliny's testimony that his mother, Plinia, was a very close friend of Corellia, we have his statement that Plinia had been like a mother to Calpurnia Hispulla. It is therefore reasonable to conjecture that Plinia was also close to Hispulla, wife of Corellius, and the putative Hispulla, wife of Calpurnius Fabatus. If the conjecture about Pliny's marriage connection to the Corellius family is correct, then all of the female recipients of his published letters, but one (out of seven), would be relatives.[95] Still, the fact that he never mentions such a connection in the letters casts some doubt on the intriguing theory about his in-laws. At the time that *Letter* 7.11 was written, about 106 or 107 CE, Pliny had been married to Calpurnia for about six years. However, he does not mention, as one of the reasons for his generosity toward Corellia, that she was a relative by marriage.

The two women from the Corellius family to whom Pliny addresses letters deserve closer attention. Because one was a friend of Pliny's mother, and both were themselves mothers, as well as wives and daughters, their stories are appropriately discussed in this chapter.

Corellia

In *Letter* 1.12.3, Pliny recounts that his mentor, Corellius Rufus, had chosen to commit suicide despite the fact that he had many reasons for living, including his wife, daughter, grandson, and sisters. One of these sisters was the Corellia of *Letters* 7.11 and 7.14. About the other sister(s), we know nothing. Nor do we have any information about the parents of Corellia and her brother, Corellius Rufus. The name Corellius is uncommon. Pliny's uncle, the elder Pliny, makes a passing reference to a Corellius of equestrian rank from the town of Ateste.[96] Perhaps this bit of information indicates that Corellia's family, like Pliny's family, had roots in northern Italy.[97] At the time of his suicide, Corellius Rufus was 67 years old – that is, he was born about 30 CE. We do not know if Corellia was older or younger than he. When *Letter* 7.11 was written, about 107 CE, she was healthy and alert enough to be engaged in the purchase of property. Perhaps she was younger than her brother, and in her early 70s in 107 CE. In any case, she was a member of the generation prior to Pliny's, the generation of his mother, Plinia, whose good friend she was.

Corellia was married to Minicius Justus. His family was an important family in the north Italian town of Laus Pompeia, which Syme suggests might also have been the hometown of the Corellius family.[98] During the chaotic year after Nero's suicide in June of 68 CE, Minicius was a supporter of Vespasian, who emerged from the fray as emperor in December of 69 and held the position until his death in 79 CE. In 69 CE, Minicius held the rank of Camp Prefect (*praefectus castrorum*) for the troops in northern Italy who were fighting against Vespasian's rival, Vitellius. The Camp Prefect was a senior officer, and someone who had worked his way up the ranks.[99] We may therefore theorize that Minicius was in at least his mid-30s at the time, putting him (like his wife Corellia) in his mid-70s when Pliny wrote *Letter* 7.11. Minicius was a harsh disciplinarian, and his troops were relieved when he was sent to a location closer to Vespasian.[100] Although we know nothing more about his career, it is likely that his early support for Vespasian served him well once Vespasian became emperor. Nonetheless, we do not know whether he held any magistracies and became a member of the Senate. He may have devoted himself to an equestrian rather than a senatorial career.[101] We cannot determine whether he and Corellia lived primarily in Rome (as a senator would) or elsewhere in Italy, perhaps in the north where they both had family roots.

In *Letter* 7.11, Pliny explains to his grandfather-in-law, Calpurnius Fabatus, why he approved the sale of some land near Comum, at below market or tax-assessed value, to Corellia. (Recall that Calpurnius and Corellia may have been related as in-laws, through Hispulla's family.) Pliny states that he has both affection and the greatest respect for Corellia (*Letter* 7.11.3).[102] In *Letter* 7.11.4, Pliny adds: "I have

long-standing ties with Corellia's husband, Minicius Justus, an excellent man."
We do not know the origin or nature of the relationship between these two men.
Had it developed separately from Pliny's relationship with Corellia? Or, do we
again detect the influence of Plinia, through Corellia? We hear about Minicius
again in "The So-called Will of Dasumius'" (108 CE), where it is stated that two
pounds of gold were bequeathed to him.[103] No information is given in the will
about why Minicius Justus was a beneficiary. Another recipient of two pounds of
gold was Junius Avitus, an aspiring young man whom Pliny had mentored.[104] We
do not know how or whether Minicius Justus and Junius Avitus were associated
with one another. The will provides a tantalizing glimpse, but only a glimpse, at
the intricacies of elite Roman social relationships.[105]

Corellia and Minicius Justus had at least one child, a son, who is mentioned in
Letter 7.11.4. Pliny does not provide his name, but he is thought by some scholars
to have been Lucius Minicius Rufus, a man who was *consul ordinarius* for 88 CE.[106]
If this admittedly disputed identification is correct, the son had carved out for
himself a successful senatorial career, and one which would have made his mother
(and uncle Corellius Rufus) proud. In addition to (and prior to) his consulship, he
had served as a praetorian legate in Gallia Lugdunensis (now part of France).
Later, but prior to Domitian's death, he had served as a governor of Bithynia, the
same province to which Pliny was sent about 110 CE. Indeed, our knowledge of
this posting is gained from a letter which Pliny wrote to Trajan from Bithynia.
In *Letter* 10.72, Pliny makes reference to correspondence sent by Domitian to
Minicius Rufus at an earlier date, concerning the legal status of children in that
province who were born free, but had been enslaved. Although the consulship of
Minicius Rufus occurred during the reign of Domitian, whom his maternal uncle
despised, we need not conclude that the family was split in its opinion of the
emperor, the uncle hating him and the nephew approving of him. As noted in
Chapter 2, many men of the senatorial class concealed their disapproval of the
emperor and tried to collaborate with him, whether selfishly to protect their own
positions and wealth, or selflessly to try to work on behalf of the good of the state.

In 7.11.4, Pliny states: "My ties with Corellia's son were especially strong, in
fact, so strong that, when I was praetor, he presided over my games." Pliny's
praetorship may be dated to 93 CE.[107] In the imperial period, the task of organizing public entertainments ("games"), such as chariot races, was assigned to the
praetors.[108] For most praetors, the opportunity to preside over the games and win
applause from a grateful audience were welcome compensation for the efforts and
often personal expenditures that organizing the games demanded. Pliny gives us
no indication about why the younger Minicius, rather than he himself, presided
over his games.

Minicius Rufus, the putative son of Corellia, was several years older than Pliny.
In 88 CE, when Pliny was about 26 years old, Minicius, as consul, would
have been over 30. We don't know when their relationship began, but they may
have known one another since boyhood if their mothers were close friends. It
was certainly to Pliny's advantage to have ties to a man of consular rank when he was
beginning his political career. When *Letter* 7.11 was written, however, Corellia's

son seems to be deceased. In reference to him, Pliny uses a past tense: "My ties were especially strong." In contrast, when speaking of his father, Minicius Justus, Pliny writes in the present: "My ties are long-standing." Corellia had thus outlived her son.

Although in her 70s, Corellia retained an active interest in property investment. The land which Pliny sold to her at below market or tax-assessed value was a piece which Pliny and several other people had inherited jointly from someone whom Pliny does not name. Although it was customary for co-heirs to consult with one another about the disposition of jointly inherited property[109], Pliny had ratified his freedman agent's agreement to sell his portion of it (5/12) to Corellia, and at a reduced price, without discussing it with the others or participating in an auction. Calpurnius Fabatus had apparently written to express his displeasure about the sale, concerned no doubt that his grandson-in-law was making unsound financial decisions that would imperil his granddaughter, Calpurnia, and the ardently hoped for great-grandchildren.[110] He seems also to have been surprised by Pliny's failure to co-operate with his co-heirs, which might be considered a breach of good manners or even an unwise political move. Pliny does not apologize for the sale, but instead seeks to explain that he dissociated himself from his co-heirs because of a greater obligation than any he had to them. He then lists his reasons: he has both affection and the greatest respect for Corellia because she was the sister of Quintus Corellius Rufus, the wife of Minicius Justus, and the mother of his friend. And Corellia had also been a very close friend of his mother. (It is notable that he does not, however, refer to a connection of marriage between Corellius, who had married a Hispulla, and Calpurnius Fabatus, who may possibly have married a Hispulla.)

Pliny adds that, during a recent visit to the Comum area (where the grandfather-in-law lived), Corellia had told him that she wanted to purchase land near Lake Como. His statement suggests that Corellia was in the same area, at the same time he was. She may, of course, have simply been visiting, but perhaps her family already owned property there, though not near the lake. In any case, Pliny told her that he would sell her any piece of property that he owned, at the price she wanted, except for those that had belonged to his mother and to his father.[111] Although Pliny does not specifically mention that the properties of his parents had sentimental value, he writes: "I cannot relinquish them even to Corellia" (*Letter* 7.11.5). When Pliny learned that he had been bequeathed 5/12 of a property, he sent Corellia a message, via his freedman, Hermes, announcing that the property would be coming up for sale. However, Corellia insisted that Hermes arrange an immediate sale of Pliny's share to her, and Hermes obeyed her. Pliny then explains his response to the situation: "You see how I must ratify the decision which my freedman made and which is so in accordance with my own character." He ends the letter by pointing out that his co-heirs do not have the ties with Corellia that he does. "Therefore they can consider their own financial interests. For me, friendship took precedence over profit" (*Letter* 7.11.8). In Pliny's Latin, the word *amicitia* ("friendship") receives great emphasis because it is placed at the very end of the sentence, and is the last word in the letter.[112]

When Corellia learned that Pliny had allowed the land to be sold to her at a reduced rate, she apparently offered to pay Pliny the market value. We do not have a copy of her letter to Pliny, but his *Letter* 7.14 is a response to her. Pliny opens this letter, unusually, with a personal pronoun: *tu* ("you").[113] By his use of the emphatic pronoun, he brings to the fore his friendly relationship with Corellia. He also, however, gives her an immediate hint that he will not be complying with her wishes. Reading the "you," she would expect a "but I" (which does, in fact, appear later). Pliny continues his opening sentence with the complimentary "you have acted very honorably." Then he defines her honorable behavior: "you earnestly both ask and insist that I give instructions that the payment accepted from you for the land be not the 700,000 sesterces (*agreed by the freedman*), but the 900,000 (*the value assessed by the tax collectors*)." For the word "insist," Pliny uses the same verb here (*exigere*) as he did in *Letter* 7.11.6 of Corellia's insisting that Hermes arrange a sale. Apparently, she had a very insistent personality. Pliny's choice of words offers a glimpse into the behavior of wealthy women who had grown up surrounded by privilege and were accustomed to being obeyed by people who were their inferiors in age or social status. Most of the women in Pliny's letters appear in the context of their birth families or marriages, where they are portrayed as submissive to their *paterfamilias* or husband, and affable to their social peers. We need to keep in mind, however, that they might have strong opinions about matters pertaining to the interests of their families and that they were capable of ensuring that these interests were attended to.

We don't know if "both ask and insist" were words used by Corellia in her letter to Pliny, but he repeats them in *Letter* 7.14.2 to emphasize the earnestness of his decision to decline her offer: "I both ask and insist that you consider not only what is fitting for you, but also for me, and that you allow me, in this one matter, to oppose you with the same spirit with which I am otherwise accustomed to obey you in all matters."[114]

Pliny's final words in the letter, "I am otherwise accustomed to obey you in all matters," indicate that his relationship to her was usually one of a subordinate, perhaps because she was older than he, but perhaps because his debts to her family were so numerous. Pliny may have agreed to give Corellia an advantageous price on the land (an arrangement made initially by his freedman) in order to offset his unwillingness to sell her properties that he had inherited from his parents. His comment to his grandfather-in-law in *Letter* 7.11.5 suggests that Corellia had set her sights on his ancestral property. He does not state in *Letter* 7.14, as he did in *Letter* 7.11, the reasons for his generosity to Corellia: his ties to her brother, husband and son, and her friendship with his mother. Perhaps the letter he published is an abbreviated version of one in which he did make clear to Corellia that he owed her and her family a debt of gratitude. In any case, *Letter* 7.14 is a very carefully designed epistle, revealing an interesting struggle for control in a social relationship. Pliny had acquired "social capital" by his beneficence. Corellia, having figured out that she would now be in Pliny's debt for his selling the land at a lower price (and that it was now public knowledge that she had prevailed upon his freedman), has insisted on paying the higher amount. Was her insistence motivated strictly by a sense of integrity and a desire not to take advantage of her friend Plinia's son? Or, was she concerned that, if she acquiesced in the lower price, she would now become obligated to Pliny. Perhaps she did not want to lose the upper hand in their relationship by accepting Pliny's benefaction. For his part, Pliny's refusal to take the additional 200,000 sesterces she has offered suggests that he wanted to repay his debts to her family and to create a more balanced relationship with her.[115]

His publication of *Letters* 7.11 and 7.14 is designed to enhance his self-portrait as a loyal and generous friend, ever cognizant of his obligations to family and friends.[116] We do not know the resolution of this story – that is, whether, in the end, Corellia paid 700,000 sesterces or 900,000 sesterces for the property near Comum. What emerges from *Letters* 7.11 and 7.14, however, is an image of Corellia as a shrewd elderly woman with an interest in and good instincts for real estate investment. She had successfully pressured Pliny's freedman, who had been sent to her only as a messenger, to arrange for the immediate sale to her of property involved in a joint inheritance. The sale had raised eyebrows because it had circumvented the usual custom of consulting with the other heirs and perhaps also because it had been arranged by a freedman. When the consternation of the other heirs and the anxiety of Pliny's in-laws became known to her, she offered to pay the market value, thus preserving a reputation for integrity while also avoiding too much indebtedness to Pliny. We do not know whether Corellia was as attentive to the management of her estates as Pliny was of his – that is, whether she visited them regularly, checked the account books, and concerned herself with sales of products and purchase of equipment. I suspect she may have been.

Incidentally, Corellia's ability to purchase property again raises the topic of guardians for adult women. Since we do not know whether she had more than one child, we do not know if she was free of the requirement to obtain a guardian's approval for large purchases, or whether she had a compliant *tutor*. We should also keep in mind that her husband's name on a will published in 108 CE probably means that he was still alive when *Letters* 7.11 and 14 were written. Although she may have discussed her real estate dealings with him, she held her property separate from him. It would be interesting to know, since the son mentioned by Pliny seems to be dead by 107 CE, who the beneficiaries of her will were.

Corellia Hispulla

Corellia Hispulla was the daughter of Hispulla and Pliny's mentor, Corellius Rufus. She was also the niece of the earlier-mentioned Corellia and a cousin of Corellia's son, Minicius, with whom Pliny, by his own admission, had very strong ties (*Letter* 7.11.4). If, moreover, the conjecture is correct that her mother's sister was the wife of Calpurnius Fabatus, she was a first cousin of Calpurnia Hispulla, the aunt of Pliny's wife, Calpurnia (and also a first cousin of Calpurnia's father). There is no evidence that Corellia Hispulla had siblings. We first meet her briefly in *Letter* 1.12, in which Pliny reports the suicide of her father Corellius Rufus in about 97 or 98 CE. There Pliny states that, among Corellius Rufus' reasons for living, were his daughter and grandson. There is no mention of other children or grandchildren. In *Letter* 3.3, written about 101 CE, we learn that Corellia Hispulla's son is now ready to be put in the charge of a *rhetor* and therefore about 14 years old. If Corellia Hispulla had married at the age of 15, she may have been in her early to mid-30s when *Letter* 3.3 was written, and thus several years younger than Pliny. Pliny does not provide the name of her son, and his identity is not certain. He is conjectured to have been Lucius Neratius Corellius Pansa, who was *consul ordinarius* in 122 CE.[117] This identification is based mainly on the fact that Corellius was a rare *nomen*, and that someone with that *nomen* would probably have been related to Pliny's mentor, Corellius Rufus.[118] If indeed this person was the son of Corellia Hispulla, he certainly carved out an impressive career for himself, having reached the distinguished position of *consul ordinarius* when in his early 30s.[119]

The identity of the husband of Corellia Hispulla has been a topic of some dispute. Pliny does not provide his name. If the son was Lucius Neratius Corellius Pansa, her husband's *nomen* was presumably Neratius (but the addition of Corellius is another example of the preservation of the name of the mother's family). In *Letter* 3.3.1, Pliny states that her son's paternal grandfather was renowned and esteemed, and that his father and uncle have also garnered illustrious praise. The several conjectures about the identity of Corellia Hispulla's husband are set forth by Raepsaet-Charlier and Carlon.[120] The most likely candidates seem to be the brothers Lucius Neratius Marcellus, who was suffect consul in 95 CE (and *consul ordinarius* in 129), and Lucius Neratius Priscus, who was suffect consul in 97 and a respected jurist. The two brothers with the *nomen* Neratius would fit the terms "father and uncle" used by Pliny.[121] Raepsaet-Charlier argues that the husband of Corellia Hispulla is Lucius Neratius Priscus. She contends that, because the other brother is known from epigraphical evidence to have had a wife named Domitia Vettilla who commissioned his funerary epitaph (that is, she was his last wife)[122], we would have to imagine that he had divorced Corellia Hispulla after the birth of their son, and then – quite against Roman custom – had given custody of the son to her (since we learn in *Letter* 3.3.3 that he was raised in he company of his mother). Raepsaet-Charlier's argument is persuasive. It is more plausible that Corellia Hispulla's husband was the jurist Lucius Neratius Priscus and that they remained married.

Carlon proposes that evidence from Pliny may support the identification of Corellia Hispulla's husband as the famous jurist.[123] Pliny addresses four letters to someone whom he identifies only by the *cognomen* Priscus (*Letters* 2.13, 6.8, 7.8, and 7.19). The identity of the addressee(s) has not been resolved, but the addressee may be the jurist Neratius Priscus.[124] If this identification is correct, it would strengthen the argument that he was the husband of Corellia Hispulla. We might conclude that Pliny corresponded with him in order to maintain his ties with her family, but also used his ties to the Corellii as a means to cultivate a beneficial relationship with this politically successful man. Nonetheless, there is no conclusive evidence of a close connection between Pliny and Corellia Hispulla's husband. However, in *Letter* 3.8, Pliny writes to his friend, Suetonius Tranquillus, the biographer, about a position as military tribune which he had obtained for Suetonius from the "very distinguished senator" Neratius Marcellus. This Marcellus was the brother of Neratius Priscus and was governor of Britain beginning about 102 CE. Presumably Suetonius was to have served his term as tribune with the governor in Britain. This letter indicates that Pliny was on good enough terms with the Neratii to ask Marcellus for the favor of appointing his friend as tribune.[125] And, in *Letter* 2.13, addressed to Priscus (perhaps Neratius Priscus) Pliny requests a military appointment for his friend, Voconius Romanus.

Like his brother, Neratius Priscus had an illustrious career. After a term as consul suffect in 97 CE (the same year that Tacitus was a consul suffect), he was governor of the province of Pannonia (perhaps 102–6 CE).[126] At some point, perhaps prior to his consulship, he was a prefect of the treasury of Saturn, a position which Pliny also held.[127] He left an impressive legacy, preserved in the *Digest*, as a jurist. When Hadrian tried cases, he had in his council not only friends and members of his staff, but also jurists, in particular jurists such as Neratius Priscus.[128] Moreover, there was a report that Trajan, with the approval of many of his friends, had planned to appoint as his successor not Hadrian, but Neratius Priscus.[129]

We do not know when Corellia Hispulla and Neratius were married. If he was about 37 years old at the time of his consulship in 97 CE, he was born about 60 CE – that is, just a year or two before Pliny. He may have married Corellia Hispulla about 83 CE, at which time she may have been about 15 years old. As already conjectured, she may have been in her early to mid-30s when her son was ready to be sent to a *rhetor*. Since her father was a member of the Roman Senate from the 70s until his death, she had probably spent much of her childhood in Rome, in a household in which senatorial affairs were discussed. She would therefore have been better prepared for marriage to a politically ambitious man such as Neratius Priscus than was, for example, Pliny's third wife, Calpurnia, who seems to have grown up in northern Italy. (One wonders if a match between Pliny and Corellia Hispulla had ever been entertained.) She would also have been well-informed about the education which their son needed if he were to be successful in a senatorial career (which ultimately he was). We do not know if Corellia Hispulla accompanied her husband to his posting as a governor. Pannonia was a very militarily unsettled province during the early years of Trajan's reign and would not have been as comfortable a place for a senatorial wife as was, for example, Spain (to which Casta accompanied her husband: Chapter 3), or even the province of Bithynia-Pontus to which Pliny and Calpurnia traveled a few years later.

If Neratius Priscus was indeed Corellia Hispulla's husband, his posting to Pannonia would have occurred about the same time as their son was ready to be handed over to the instruction of a *rhetor*. *Letter* 3.3 (already discussed), in which Pliny recommends a *rhetor*, has raised questions about Neratius Priscus' whereabouts and involvement in his son's life because it is addressed only to Corellia Hispulla. Perhaps the husband/father was out of the country at the time that Pliny wrote the letter and had delegated the choice of a *rhetor* to his wife.

Letter 3.3 is one of only ten letters in Pliny's collection addressed to a woman. (There are only seven different female addressees.) It is not clear from *Letter* 3.3 whether Corellia Hispulla had asked Pliny to recommend a *rhetor*, or whether Pliny had simply assumed this task. He had already, just a few years earlier, spent quite a bit of time visiting schools in order to find a suitable *rhetor* for the sons of Junius Arulenus Rusticus, one of the men condemned to death in 93 CE.[130] He describes these search activities in *Letter* 2.18. At that time, he had been invited to embark on a search by Arulenus' brother, Junius Mauricus. Certainly, there is a difference in the tone between *Letter* 3.3 and *Letter* 2.18, addressed to Junius Mauricus, where Pliny opens with the statement: "What more pleasing task could have been imposed on me by you than to search for a teacher for the children of your brother."[131] In *Letter* 2.18, there is no doubt that Pliny's help was solicited. By contrast, in *Letter* 3.3, Pliny makes no mention of a request by Corellia Hispulla. Indeed, there is not even a direct reference in the first section of the need for a teacher. The letter begins instead with praise of Corellius Rufus, Pliny's mentor and the father of Corellia Hispulla, and an assertion by Pliny that he is obligated to hope and to strive as much as he can that Corellia Hispulla's son may grow up to be like his maternal grandfather. Pliny's feeling of obligation is motivated, he says, by his love and reverence for Corellius Rufus and by his special affection for Corellia Hispulla, which in turn arises both from the remembrance of her father and from the respect which she herself deserves. Pliny's statement explaining his fondness for Corellia Hispulla seems rather formal and also deferential.[132] It suggests perhaps that, although he and Corellia Hispulla may have been well acquainted with one another (he must have been a frequent visitor in the house of his cherished mentor), they were not close friends. There is none of the jocular style that we find, for example, in *Letter* 1.4, which is addressed to Pliny's mother-in-law (and will be discussed later), a style that suggests a warm and relaxed relationship. If the conjecture about a family relationship between the families of Calpurnius Fabatus and Corellius Rufus is correct, we might expect a more "familiar" letter. Perhaps the letter was edited before publication. Or perhaps the marriage of Pliny and Calpurnia occurred after the composition of the letter.

Pliny continues his letter with an acknowledgment that the boy's father, uncle, and paternal grandfather are also prominent and well-regarded. (With respect to the issue raised earlier, of which of the Neratius brothers might be Corellia Hispulla's husband, these flattering references to the father and other close paternal relatives suggest that Corellia Hispulla and her husband were married – not divorced – at the time of the letter, and that the husband would then be Neratius Priscus, not Neratius Marcellus.) Only then does Pliny state that the boy will mature to resemble all of his distinguished male relatives only if he is instilled with an honorable education, and that the person from whom he receives his education is therefore a matter of the greatest importance. The boy, by the way, is never named in the letter. We may wonder how well Pliny was acquainted with him. Perhaps, however, it was customary not to give the names of children, particularly in published letters. Recall that, in *Letter* 1.14, Pliny did not provide the name of the daughter of the deceased Arulenus Rusticus for whom he was recommending a husband.

As already noted, Pliny recounts that, up to this point, the boy had remained in his mother's company, and had teachers at home, where there was little or no opportunity for problems to occur and where presumably his mother kept a close watch (*Letter* 3.3.3). Now, however, it was time for him to be put in the charge of a teacher of rhetoric, but one whose instructional program included strictness, propriety, and, above all, moral purity. Curiously, Pliny remarks that this young fellow – he uses the term *adulescens*[133] – possesses, in addition to his other endowments, an exceptionally handsome body (*eximia corporis pulchritudo*), and therefore, at this precarious time of his life, a person must be sought who would be not only a teacher, but also a guardian (*custos*) and a guide (*rector*) (*Letter* 3.3.4). Pliny's reference to the boy's good looks is one of the few references in his letters to physical appearance, and it is certainly not specific.[134] The same phrase – *corporis pulchritudo* – is used in *Letter* 1.14.8 in reference to a prospective bridegroom. In that context, the phrase was included to alert the addressee discreetly that the recommended man was healthy, without physical restrictions, and capable of siring healthy children. In the context of *Letter* 3.3, however, Pliny's reference implies that sexual impropriety was not a rare occurrence at Roman schools, and that parents might be anxious about their sons' sexual vulnerability to their teachers.[135] It suggests, moreover, as do other comments in the letter, that Corellia Hispulla was a woman much concerned about moral behavior and the possible corruption of her son. Also striking is Pliny's reference in *Letter* 3.3.4 to the son as "*our* young fellow." Pliny quite unexpectedly (to the reader) insinuates himself into the family of his mentor, referring to himself as if he were a close male relative of Corellia Hispulla. The contrast between the formality of *Letter* 3.3.1 and the use of *our* here is rather jarring.

At this point, Pliny finally advances the name of a *rhetor*: Julius Genitor.[136] He is, Pliny says, a serious man, without faults, although a little too severe and unyielding in comparison with the excesses of the times. Again we can perhaps discern that Pliny is appealing to a morally conservative mother. Pliny assures her that Genitor's rhetorical expertise is well-recognized, but asks her to accept him, Pliny, as the guarantor that there are no dark secrets in Genitor's life. Her son will hear nothing inappropriate from him. Moreover, the boy will be reminded by Genitor no less often than by his mother and by Pliny ("by you and by me") of the great names he bears and of the burden he has to match the reputations of his ancestors (*Letter* 3.3.6). Once again, with his inclusion of himself in the sentence – "by you and by me" – Pliny implies that he shares with Corellia Hispulla the task of guiding her son's future. Carlon comments that Pliny employs first-person verbs frequently in the letter and that their collective effect "serves to emphasize Pliny's personal stake in the boy's future and his sense of duty to the family of his mentor."[137] Perhaps his phrase "by you and by me" is meant only to reassure her that his gratitude to her father and his loyalty to her family are unfailing. We might wonder what the boy's father and uncle thought of Pliny's injection of himself into their family matters. Since both the Neratius brothers may have been in their provinces or on their way to their provinces at this time, Pliny's concern for the boy may have been welcome. Pliny ends the letter with a statement that one cannot learn eloquence without first learning moral conduct.

All in all, we learn little from *Letter* 3.3 about Corellia Hispulla's character or her feelings about Pliny. We might conclude that she was very protective of her son and concerned about his moral development, but perhaps no more so than other Roman mothers. Pliny strives to give the impression that he is like a family member or at least that he is undertaking the responsibilities of a family member. However, there is a certain formality about the letter which suggests not only that he and Corellia Hispulla were not close friends (that is, friends to whom one wrote amusing letters), but also that Pliny approaches her as someone still much in debt to her family and trying, by his favors, to achieve a level of parity with her. Romans of the elite class engaged in an elaborate system of accumulating and repaying obligations which, as is apparent from this letter, continued through several generations and applied both to men and women. The person with the fewest obligations to repay was in a superior position. The situation in *Letter* 3.3 appears to be similar to that revealed in *Letters* 7.11 and 14, where Pliny seems anxious to erase his debt to Corellia (the aunt), and even to put her in *his* debt by selling his property to her at a low price. We wish we knew Corellia Hispulla's response to Pliny's letter. Was she pleased to receive his advice and did she send her son to Julius Genitor (who would now be indebted to Pliny for recommending him)? The answer is probably "yes" because it seems unlikely that Pliny would publish a letter containing advice which his addressee decided to ignore. Whomever Corellia Hispulla chose as her son's *rhetor*, she apparently made a wise choice. If her son was indeed the Lucius Neratius Corellius Pansa who was *consul ordinarius* in 122 CE, he had reached the high point of a senatorial career – *consul ordinarius* – at the minimum age requirement. An excellent education would have been an advantage to his career plans, but equally important would have been the support of his mother. One question raised by Pliny's recommendation of Julius Genitor remains unanswerable: did Corellia Hispulla feel that Pliny was now a bit less in debt to her family?

Pliny continued his attempts to balance his account book of obligations. In *Letter* 4.17, written in 105 CE, about four years after his letter to Corellia Hispulla about the *rhetor*, he reveals that he has undertaken to support her in a legal case. Unfortunately for us, who are trying to learn about the lives of the women mentioned in his letters, Pliny provides no details about the case. In his opening sentence, he refers to "the case of Corellia in her absence against Gaius Caecilius, a consul designate."[138] In the last sentence, quoting his addressee (Clusinius Gallus), he refers to "a legal action which is novel perhaps because it is directed against a woman." This is the only information that he gives about the case, and it is information which simply leaves us with many questions. We can surmise that Gaius Caecilius had brought a charge against Corellia Hispulla when he was a private citizen since he did not become suffect consul until September. He may have initiated a criminal or a civil suit. However, since Pliny spends no time explaining the charge, perhaps we can speculate that it was a civil matter of little general interest or importance and with no hint of scandal. Nor does Pliny explain why Corellia Hispulla was absent – that is, whether she was simply out of town, whether she was in Rome but chose not to attend (perhaps to avoid embarrassment), or whether she was precluded from appearing in court for reasons unknown to us.[139] Particularly puzzling is Pliny's reference to the legal action as being perhaps novel because it was directed against a woman. As noted in Chapter 3, it was not unusual for women to be charged in both civil and criminal suits. However, the nature of the case against Corellia Hispulla remains a mystery.

It is disappointing that Pliny chose not to reveal the nature of this case. Elsewhere in his published collection, he is quite effusive about providing details relating to legal cases in which he was involved. In *Letter* 3.9, for example, a letter discussed in Chapter 3, he describes at length the high profile prosecution of the family of Caecilius Classicus, including at least two women, his wife, Casta, and his daughter. However, the focus of *Letter* 4.17 is not Corellia Hispulla or her legal problem. As Carlon skillfully demonstrates, the purpose of the letter is "to delineate his deep connections to the family (*of Corellius*) and particularly to explain how his bonds to Corellius now obligate him to those left behind after his death."[140] Pliny uses the letter – and Corellia's legal problem – as an opportunity to showcase his virtues as a loyal friend and to create an enduring record of how he continued to fulfill his obligations, even after the death of his mentor. The letter is carefully crafted. The addressee, Clusinius Gallus, had apparently written to urge Pliny to undertake the defense of Corellia Hispulla. Pliny replies that he is insulted by the inference that he might not do so, because not to do so would be very shameful. How could he, he asks, hesitate to support the daughter of Corellius Rufus? Nonetheless, Pliny then sets forth the reasons why he might consider not becoming involved: the charge is being brought forward by a friend (although not a close one), a man of high status, and one who will soon hold the office of suffect consul, an office which, Pliny reminds his addressee, he himself held.[141] His phrasing implies that these reasons, on any other occasion, would be sufficient to decline involvement, but he dismisses them now as weak when he reflects that it is the daughter of Corellius whom he will be defending.

Pliny then makes a transition to an account of his relationship with Corellius Rufus. Several elements of this account have already been discussed. Corellius was, in Pliny's opinion, a man of outstanding dignity, integrity, and perceptiveness with whom, over the years, he developed a very close relationship. He sponsored Pliny when the latter began his career and campaigned for office, and counseled him when he served in office. He built up Pliny's reputation, both public and personal, and even with the emperor. Pliny relates the anecdote that Corellius told the emperor Nerva that Pliny did nothing without his advice (*Letter* 4.17.8). Pliny considered this comment a compliment because it indicated that he always acted very wisely since he followed the advice of a very wise man.[142] "By his use of the same superlative (*very wise*) to describe his actions and Corellius' character, Pliny becomes a perfect reflection of his most intimate friend and mentor."[143] Pliny encourages the reader to view him as a man as admirable as Corellius Rufus and therefore his equal – his "replacement" perhaps – in his social community.

Pliny returns to Corellius' daughter but only to relate another anecdote. He reports that Corellia Hispulla often remarked that, as her father was dying, he said: "During my rather long life, I have acquired many friends for you, but Secundus and Cornutus are very special" (*Letter* 4.17.9).[144] Pliny declares that when he remembers these words, he knows that he must work hard so that he not appear in any way to have abandoned the trust which that very prudent man, Corellius Rufus, had in him. "Very prudent" is a translation of Pliny's word, *providentissimus*, which conveys the meaning that Corellius Rufus saw far into the future (*pro* = "in front," *videre* = "to see") and made careful plans ("pro-visions") to prepare for what he believed would happen.

Having publicly revealed the confidence which Corellius had placed him, Pliny asserts that he will energetically support Corellia Hispulla (whose name appears here in 4.17.11 for only the second time in the letter) and will not be reluctant to incur resentment. Nevertheless, he closes the letter with an admission that he expects to win not just pardon, but even praise from Corellia Hispulla's accuser if he says more fully during the court case the things expressed here in the limited space of the letter. Presumably he planned to speak at length about his admiration for and obligations to Corellius, and his own commitment to honoring those obligations.

Letter 4.17 is not about Corellia Hispulla. Pliny uses the occasion of replying to a friend as a ploy to publicize his own behavior. There are some similarities between this letter and *Letter* 7.11, in which Pliny delineates for his grandfather-in-law the reasons why he sold property to Corellia (aunt of Corellia Hispulla) for a low price. In both letters, Pliny uses his explanations to enhance his self-image as a man loyal to his friends. In *Letter* 7.11, however, we can imagine that the grandfather-in-law was truly concerned about the financial loss to the family and deserved an explanation. In *Letter* 4.17, on the other hand, Pliny uses an inquiry from his addressee as an excuse to articulate arguments against becoming involved with the case, but only to reject them and thus create an opportunity to expound on his relationship with Corellius Rufus. When we reach the end of the letter, it seems apparent that Pliny had nothing to lose and much to gain by supporting Corellia Hispulla – and then publishing the letter.

Although we learn nothing about the particulars of Corellia Hispulla's legal problem, the letter nonetheless provides a glimpse at how a Roman father, especially a *providentissimus* one, might utilize the complicated system of social obligations to ensure that his family would be protected after his death. In *Letter* 4.17.9, we learn that Corellius Rufus, by his own admission, had purposively acquired many friends for his daughter. The Latin verb which Pliny uses for "I acquired" is *paravi*, which also has the meaning of "I prepared" and "I purchased." Corellius "purchased" friends by his good services toward them, being Pliny's mentor, for example. (His friends would also expect to receive bequests in his will, although the bulk of his estate was undoubtedly inherited by his daughter.) The friends performed their duties by attending upon him, but their obligations did not end with his death. Pliny's letter makes it clear that an honorable man continued to help his friend's family. If Corellius Rufus had had a son, Pliny would have assisted him in his political career. For his daughter, Pliny's services included a recommendation for a *rhetor* and support in a legal action. Corellia Hispulla surely had a *tutor* assigned upon the death of her father. We have no evidence of who that man was, but his responsibilities would have been mainly oversight of her financial affairs. Corellius Rufus' friends – the honorable ones, at least – would have provided his daughter with other kinds of service and protection. The obligation to look after a friend's family extended even to the friend's siblings, as *Letters* 7.11 and 14 indicate. One might assume that a man would also want to ensure protection for his wife. However, there is no mention in Pliny about the activities of Corellius Rufus' loyal and trustworthy wife, Hispulla, after his death, or about any help Pliny provided to her. He may, of course, have simply not published any references to his services to her. Or perhaps she remarried, or received sufficient assistance from her agnate family. Her agnate family had apparently thought well of her marriage to Corellius Rufus, and wanted its name, Hispulla, joined to his when a daughter was born. However, we do not have information which would allow us to speculate about the relationship between Hispulla and her daughter, Corellia Hispulla, and whether they remained close after the death of Corellius Rufus. In any case, the daughter, Corellia Hispulla, was "bequeathed" a network of friends by her father. We have no way of knowing her thoughts about these friends, or whether she kept in regular contact with them and enjoyed their company. As noted earlier, although she and Pliny were of a similar age and had presumably been acquaintances for many years, his approach to her in *Letter* 3.3 seems deferential, not intimate. Their relationship nonetheless demonstrates how connections made in one generation – the close friendship of Pliny's mother, Plinia, with Corellia (7.11.3) – affected the lives of men and women in successive generations.

The anonymous mother of Varisidius Nepos

In *Letter* 4.4, Pliny provides another example of a man who benefited from his mother's connections. The letter, written sometime after 99 CE, is addressed to Quintus Sosius Senecio, a man who was consul in 99 and 107 CE.[145] After his term as consul in 99, he apparently received a proconsular command in a province. The purpose of Pliny's letter is to request that Sosius Senecio grant a military tribuneship of six months duration to a man named Varisidius Nepos.[146] Pliny is willing to vouch for the good character of Varisidius, who he says is industrious, honest, and eloquent. However, an equally important element of the recommendation is the information that Varisidius is the son of the sister of Calvisius Rufus, whom Pliny describes in this letter and in *Letter* 1.12.12 as his *contubernalis*[147] and the addressee's friend. Pliny states pointedly that he is making the request for the tribuneship, which will enhance the standing of Varisidius Nepos, for the sake both of the young man and of his maternal uncle. He adds that, by granting him (Pliny) the favor, Sosius Senecio will also be granting a favor to their friend, Calvisius Rufus, and that the young man, Varisidius Nepos, will henceforth be in Sosius Senecio's debt no less than Pliny himself is.

The closeness and duration of the friendship between Pliny and Calvisius Rufus is attested by the fact that Pliny published seven of his letters to Calvisius (one of them, *Letter* 3.19, describing Regulus' vile behavior as a legacy-hunter), and that these letters extend over many years, from Books 1 to 9. Calvisius and Pliny were both natives of the Comum area (*Letters* 5.7.2 and 3). Perhaps Pliny had been a close friend of Calvisius Rufus since childhood, and an acquaintance of his sister (who is not named in the letter, but may be a Calvisia). In any event, *Letter* 4.4 offers interesting insight into the functioning of the Roman patronage system and indicates that women, especially mothers, could play a significant role in the career advancement of men. The mother of Varisidius Nepos may have spoken to her brother, Calvisius Rufus, about the benefits to her son of a military appointment. He, in turn, approached their fellow-townsman, Pliny, who had carved out a successful senatorial career. Or, perhaps the mother, if she had been acquainted with one of her brother's best friends since childhood, felt that she could approach Pliny directly. Pliny then wrote to his acquaintance, Sosius Senecio, who had recently been given a provincial governorship and, with it, the prerogative of choosing military tribunes. In return, Pliny, Calvisius, and Varisidius would be indebted to Sosius Senecio. There is no mention of the mother also assuming a debt of gratitude, but she was clearly a link in the system.

Mothers of the opposition

Several mother–child relationships have been considered in previous chapters, particularly relationships in families which criticized the emperors. The grief of Arria E, for example, at the death of her son has been noted (*Letter* 3.16.5), as well as her recommendation to her daughter that she share the fate of her husband, even if it meant suicide (*Letter* 3.16.10). The circumstance under which Arria E made that recommendation sheds a small light on the affective ties of that family. Arria E's daughter and son-in-law, with whom she was apparently living in the days before her and Caecina Paetus' suicides, tried to dissuade her from killing herself and then, having failed in their pleas, became even more vigilant in trying to prevent her death. Their behavior argues for an emotional bond between Arria E and her daughter, and between the daughter and her husband. Nonetheless, the tales of Arria E's heroism, as told by Pliny, produce a portrait of a woman whose first priority was her husband. Of course, it is possible that her suicide could be interpreted as a sacrifice to guarantee the welfare of her daughter. Had she not induced Caecina Paetus, by her own example, to commit suicide, had he instead been executed, his estate might have been confiscated, leaving his daughter without an inheritance. Whatever the reasons why Arria E stabbed herself – devotion to her husband, a desire to preserve his estate, a yearning for eternal fame – her daughter was left an orphan.

This daughter, Arria Y, when faced with the same dilemma that her mother had faced – dying with her husband or living for her daughter – chose the latter option, with her husband's encouragement. Perhaps she wanted to spare her own daughter, Fannia, the pain of losing both parents in the same moment. Arria Y and Fannia remained close over the years, sharing a determination to preserve and promulgate stories of their family's opposition to tyranny and, because of these activities, also sharing time in exile. After their return from exile, although she was now probably in her 70s, Arria Y continued to treat her daughter's concerns as her own and became involved in Pliny's efforts to bring to justice the senators responsible for the death of Fannia's stepson, Helvidius II. Fannia had no children of her own, but was a devoted stepmother. Her relationship with the children of Helvidius II will be discussed later.

Anteia was the wife of Helvidius II and probably the mother of his children, a son (Helvidius III) and two daughters (both formally named Helvidia). She had apparently remarried after his death, but was still involved in decisions about the welfare of the children. We do not know if the children remained in her care after the death of their father and her remarriage, or went to live with an agnate relative. However, we learn in *Letter* 9.13.16 that she and her new husband had requested of the consuls that they appoint Cornutus Tertullus as *tutor* (guardian) for one of the daughters.[148] This request implies that Anteia (with her new husband) had remained responsible for care of the children, perhaps because there were no surviving close agnate relatives. (Recall that Pliny was apparently raised by his mother.) Unfortunately, we know nothing about how the marriages of the two daughters were arranged, or what part their mother may have played. Sadly, they both died in childbirth (*Letter* 4.21). If Anteia was still alive at this time, the untimely (and undoubtedly very painful) deaths of her daughters must have been a crushing blow. They had both given birth to infant daughters who survived them, but were probably placed in the care of their fathers' families, not their grandmother Anteia. We have explored in this chapter the relationships between birth mothers and their children, but some children, like the infants of the Helvidiae, never knew their birth mothers.

Among "the Seven" who were punished in 93 CE was Verulana Gratilla, wife of Arulenus Rusticus. He was sentenced to death, she was sent into exile. They had several children. The only information that Pliny provides about Verulania Gratilla is that she was exiled at the same time as her brother-in-law (her husband's brother), Junius Mauricus (*Letter* 3.11.3). We don't know even if she returned from exile, or, if she did, whether she remarried. It is probable that custody of her children was given to their agnate uncle, Junius Mauricus. It was he who solicited Pliny's assistance in recommending a husband for his brother's daughter (*Letter* 1.14) and a teacher for his brother's sons (*Letter* 2.18). It was not uncommon for a mother to be separated from her children upon the death of or divorce from their father. We do not know whether or how such mothers might remain in contact with their children. A statement by Marcus Aurelius, cited earlier, suggests that some mothers, though divorced, kept in close touch with their children. "If you had a stepmother and a mother at the same time, you would treat your stepmother with respect, but you would constantly return to your mother."

Cottia, the mother of Cottius

Pliny tells of several mothers, in addition to Arria E, who suffered the death of sons. He wrote *Letter* 3.10 to inform Cottia and her husband, Titus Vestricius

Spurinna, that he had composed a biography of their deceased son. The letter is addressed jointly to the couple, but Cottia was one of only seven women to whom Pliny addresses a published letter, and perhaps the only female recipient to whom he was not related. We do not know where or how her son died. In *Letter* 2.7.4, written about 98 CE, Pliny relates that the son had exhibited clear evidence of natural talent and was a young man of integrity, dignity, and influence (*sanctitas, gravitas, auctoritas*).[149] He was therefore well-deserving, Pliny states, of the honorific statue which the Senate had decreed for him. His commemoration would, moreover, inspire virtue in other young men and encourage older men to produce children. Pliny admits, however, that the decree of a statue for so young a man – and one who seems not yet to have held any public offices – had been approved mainly to ease the grief of his father. There is no mention in *Letter* 2.7 of the grief of his mother, Cottia, but surely we can conjecture that she, too, was devastated by her son's death. She seems to have lost him when he was just embarking on a career and showing great promise for success. She may, moreover, have had to make the funeral arrangements without her husband because he was away from home at the time of the death. She would not have had the comfort which Fronto's son-in-law provided for his bereaved wife when he wept alongside her. Although Cottia was apparently quite a bit younger than her husband (who was in his mid-70s when their son died), she was probably past her child-bearing years. By including Cottia as an addressee of *Letter* 3.10, recognizing the depth of her grief, and inviting her, as well as her husband, to comment on and amend his literary portrait of their son, Pliny brings to his readers' attention the trauma which she has endured and the pain which her memories caused.

In *Letter* 2.7, Pliny identifies the son by the name Cottius. Presumably the *nomen* (family name) he received at the time of his birth was Vestricius, the *nomen* of his father's family, and Cottius was his *cognomen*, derived from his mother's family. His nomenclature, Vestricius Cottius, provides yet another example of the importance which many elite Roman families placed on preserving the names of the mother's, as well as the father's family. Perhaps the attachment of a name from the mother's family also indicated a desire on the part of the mother's family to form and maintain a strong affective attachment with the child. Although a child was not an agnate member of his mother's *familia*, he was certainly a blood relative to her kin. It was quite likely that Cottius' mother would have left to him, had he survived her, at least part of her estate (even as Regulus' wife made provisions for their son to inherit her estate). And if her siblings had no children, he might have inherited also from them, as Pliny had inherited from his maternal uncle. By including the name of her agnate family in her child's name, a mother tried to ensure that the property of her *familia* descended to someone with the *familia* name. Unfortunately for Cottia, her son predeceased her.

The anonymous mother of Julius Avitus

Pliny reports the deaths of several other young men who, like Cottius, were survived by their mothers. In *Letter* 5.21, written about 105 or 106 CE, he commiserates with a friend about the passing of Julius Avitus. We know nothing more about this young man than what Pliny tells us here. He had served a term as quaestor in a province (Pliny does not say which one) and died on board a ship during the return voyage. Since the minimum age for holding the quaestorship during the imperial period was 25 years, we can assume that Julius Avitus was about 25 or 26 years old. He had so much natural talent that he would, Pliny assures his readers, have attained the highest offices had his virtues had time to mature. That he died so far from those who loved him distressed his family – his brother, sisters, and mother, none of whom are named (although it is likely that the siblings carried their agnate family names: Julius and Julia). Because of the breadth of the Roman empire, young men aspiring to senatorial careers could expect to be sent to regions far from home. (Recall that Pliny served as a military tribune in Syria when he was about 20 years old.) One can imagine the anxiety that a mother must have felt when her son departed for a posting overseas and while he was far away. For Julius Avitus' mother, unfortunately, her fears became a reality when he died before returning home.

Since there is no mention of a father as one of the survivors, we may assume that he was dead, and that the mother was therefore a widow. At least she had a remaining son and more than one daughter to comfort her and provide support in the future.[150]

The anonymous mother of Junius Avitus

In *Letter* 8.23, written about 108 or 109 CE, Pliny announces the death of Junius Avitus, who died of an unspecified illness which apparently struck suddenly and killed quickly.[151] Pliny's grief was especially sharp because Junius Avitus had been his protégé and, with Pliny's assistance, had won selection to the offices of quaestor and then aedile. He was an aedile-elect at the time of his death and was probably about 27 or 28 years old. (Pliny's mentorship of this young man mirrors Corellius Rufus' mentorship of him.) He had married just a year earlier and already produced a daughter. Pliny laments the misfortune of his wife and infant daughter, and also of his aging mother, now bereft of her son. (She may have been in her late 40s, and not much older than Pliny at the time the letter was written.) Again, we may assume that the son's father had predeceased him because there is no mention of a father as one of the survivors. Nor does Pliny report that Junius Avitus had siblings. He describes the unnamed mother as *orba*, which can mean "childless."[152] Junius Avitus' death would have been an enormous blow to his widowed mother if it left her without any children to help her in the future. She may have had an estate that descended to her from her agnate family, and she may also have received an inheritance from her late husband. However, as she aged, she no doubt wanted and needed more than just material support. We do not know if she maintained a relationship with her son's young bride and infant daughter, who was likely her only grandchild. The young bride may well have remarried and become part of a new family.

The anonymous mother of an anonymous son

There seems to have been no doubt that the deaths of Cottius, Julius Avitus, and Junius Avitus, though untimely and lamentable, were natural. However, in *Letter* 7.6, written about 106 or 107 CE, Pliny tells an anecdote about a death that was alleged to have been a murder. A mother whose son had died had brought charges of forging or falsifying a will and of poisoning against his freedmen (that is, his ex-slaves), who happened to be coheirs with her of his estate.[153] We may infer that she suspected that the freedmen had killed her son and altered his will to their benefit. We may also assume that her accusation was motivated by a desire to avenge her son's death and to punish those whom she believed had wrongly gained possession of part of his estate. However, Pliny provides no information about the circumstances of the case or the identities of the accuser, the defendants, and the deceased. Nor do we learn whether the mother and the freedmen were the only heirs listed in the will. If that were so, we might consider that the son was not married and had no children or siblings, and that his father was dead. We may have another situation where the mother who lost her adult son was a widow. In this case, she was fighting to gain control of her son's total estate.

Both offences – falsifying a will and poisoning – were considered "public crimes" (*crimina publica*). At a time when it was difficult to keep food from spoiling, many accidental deaths may have been misinterpreted as deliberate poisoning. On the other hand, deliberate poisoning would have been a charge difficult to prove.[154] With regard to forgery, Champlin maintains that it was also an "all-too-convenient charge to hurl at one's enemies."[155] The charges were capital and usually were adjudicated by a standing jury court (*quaestio*). The plaintiff would bring the charge to the attention of a magistrate who would then refer it to a *quaestio*. However, there were several unusual elements about the case which Pliny records. That the plaintiff was a woman was certainly exceptional. Women were permitted to bring forward capital charges only in a case involving the death of their parents or children.[156] The mother in *Letter* 7.6 was within her rights in making an accusation about the death of her son, but it was nonetheless unusual that she, rather than a male family member, made the accusation. In addition, she may have overstepped her boundaries by making an accusation about the forging or falsifying of his will, a public crime, but not involving the death of a family member. Moreover, the law excluded multiple accusations – that is, accusations of more than one crime or against more than one person – from being adjudicated in a *quaestio*.[157] However, according to Pliny's account, the mother brought the charges not before a magistrate, but to the emperor himself, who acceded to her request that Julius Servianus judge the case.[158] Of course, we would love to know how it was that the mother was able not only to approach the emperor, but even to ask for a specific judge – and why the emperor granted her request. We may speculate that her family was very prominent and had close connections to the imperial family. However, and unfortunately, Pliny does not provide any information about her identity.

Nonetheless, Pliny does imply that this was a high profile case. Indeed, he terms it a *causa notissima*, a case that was very well-known, which attracted a huge crowd and engaged the talents of very illustrious men on both sides. Pliny was one of these illustrious men, pleading the case for the defendants. He reports that the *quaestio* put an end to the investigation with a decision which favored the defendants. Pliny's words are frustratingly confusing. We cannot determine whether he has used the term *quaestio* loosely to mean simply "court" (in this instance, the judge, Julius Servianus), or whether he actually means that Julius Servianus reviewed the materials for the case and, finding that it had merit, then turned it over to jury court. What Pliny is clear about, however, is that the judgment favored the defendants.

The mother nonetheless persisted. She again approached the emperor – how did she gain access? – and declared that she had discovered new evidence. Sextus Attius Suburanus was instructed to reexamine the case if the mother did indeed produce any new evidence. The reopening of a case after an acquittal was highly unusual.[159] Again we are left to wonder who this woman was and what leverage she had. The mother engaged a talented young speaker to present her case. Pliny, who scoffed that the young speaker was not all that clever, again agreed to speak for the defense. He ends his story about the mother's lawsuit by reporting that he humiliated the mother's young lawyer and won applause from the audience by a brief but cutting reply. Curiously, he does not state the outcome of the hearing – that is, whether Suburanus concurred with the original acquittal or determined that there was indeed enough new evidence to warrant a retrial. Thus we do not know whether the mother was successful in her attempt to prosecute her deceased son's freedmen and gain possession of his estate.

Another anonymous mother of an anonymous son

Another anonymous mother of an anonymous son is the wife of Publius Calpurnius Macer. She is given passing reference in *Letter* 5.18 where Pliny expresses his pleasure that Calpurnius is at his seaside villa with his wife and son. (See Chapter 3.)

The mother of Regulus' son (perhaps Caepia Procula)

Another of Pliny's stories about a mother, a son, and a will has been discussed in a Chapter 3. In *Letter* 4.2, Pliny reports on the death of the son of Marcus Aquilius Regulus and on Regulus' not unexpectedly loathsome (as portrayed by Pliny) behavior both before and after his son's death. At *Letter* 4.2.2, Pliny relates that Marcus Aquilius Regulus emancipated his son – that is, released him from the *patria potestas* – so that he could gain control of his mother's estate. We know very little about the mother, who may have been a woman named Caepia Procula.[160] Her death seems to have occurred just a few years before that of her son, who was still a boy at the time of *his* death. (Pliny identifies him in *Letter* 4.2 and again in *Letter* 4.7 as *puer*.) If this was her first marriage, she was perhaps in her early 30s (or even late 20s) when she died. It is possible, of course, that she had been previously married and borne other children who remained with their father after a divorce. Even if this were so, her age at death, considering the youth of her son, would probably still not be more than 50. However, at the time that *Letter* 4.2 was written, about 104 CE, her husband Regulus may have been in his late 60s or early 70s. There was apparently a considerable gap in age between these spouses, and it is unlikely that this was Regulus' first marriage, though it was probably the only marriage which produced a child. Their son, whose *nomen* was presumably that of his father, Aquilius, appears to have been the only (surviving) child of the couple. No other children are mentioned in Pliny's letters, or by the poet Martial.[161] Additional evidence that the son was an only children might be Regulus' ostentatious mourning, as described in *Letters* 4.2 and 7, and the flocks of legacy hunters who besieged Regulus (*Letter* 4.2.4). Legacy hunters preferred to target elderly childless people.

Caepia (if that is her name) seems to have inherited property from her agnate family and, as was customary, held it separate from her husband. We may conclude from Pliny's brief account that she wanted her son to be the primary heir of her estate when she died. However, as long as the boy's *paterfamilias* (that is, Regulus) was alive, the son remained *in patria potestate* (that is, "under his father's authority") and would not have legal control of any estate bequeathed to him. The only way that Caepia could ensure that her son would inherit and hold possession of her estate was if he were released from Regulus' paternal authority. We do not know how long Caepia was ill, but she seems to have anticipated that she would die before her husband, and to have been unwilling to allow her husband to gain possession of her estate. She therefore persuaded Regulus to formally release the son from his control. Caepia may have made the release a condition in her will, stating that the son would inherit her estate only if he had been emancipated. If this was the case, the release, or emancipation, of the boy may have occurred after her death. (The emancipation process has been discussed in Chapter 3.) Pliny gives us no hint about why Caepia was so determined that her husband not have access to her estate. Regulus was, according to Pliny, a very greedy man, who had risen from poverty to enormous wealth through unsavory behavior such as legacy hunting (*Letter* 2.20.13). His lucrative activities as an informer during the reign of Nero are mentioned by Tacitus, who also reports that Regulus' early poverty was a result of his father's loss of the family estate.[162] The estate had been confiscated during the father's exile and then claimed by creditors. Caepia may have feared that her husband's greed and lingering insecurity about his finances would make him inclined to devise a way to keep her son's inheritance for himself. Or perhaps she feared that he might decide to bequeath it to someone else. Her fear was not unreasonable. In *Letter* 6.33, which is discussed later, Pliny records a situation in which a woman was disinherited by her octogenarian father just ten days after he remarried. At *Letter* 4.2.6, Pliny reports that Regulus had been saying that he wanted to marry again. Undoubtedly Caepia's agnate relatives would have wanted the property derived from their agnate *familia* to descend to a blood relative (even if he were non-agnate), not to Regulus' new wife or any children she might bear. Caepia may have requested that the boy's *tutor*, who would oversee the inherited estate until the boy reached the age of majority, be a member of her agnate family.[163]

Clearly Caepia wanted the best for her son. We can imagine the distress she felt when she knew that she was dying and leaving her young son motherless. She tried to make arrangements that would protect him. Unfortunately, she was not able to ensure good health for him, and he died not long after her, from causes not stated by Pliny. Pliny leaves the reader with the impression, moreover, that Regulus may have thwarted his wife's plan. He states that Regulus tried to win his now emancipated son's affection with lavish gifts and a pretense of affection. He then comments that, since his son's death, Regulus has been the target of legacy hunters, perhaps implying that Regulus may have persuaded the son to make him, Regulus, the beneficiary of his will and bequeath to him the estate to which Caepia had tried to deny him access. In any case, if the boy died without a will, his father, although he had emancipated him, could make a claim as a legal heir.[164]

Pomponia Galla

We are treated to another anecdote about a mother, a son, and a will in *Letter* 5.1. Wills were of considerable importance to people of the elite class. The poor – that is, the vast majority of the population – had few possessions to worry about passing on. The wealthy, however, had vast amounts, and the posthumous distribution of these possessions was a matter of intense concern, both to the owner and to his/ her family and friends. Indeed, Pliny spends what seems to modern tastes an inordinate amount of time reporting on the arrangements which people made for the disposal of their estates.[165] Champlin offers several reasons for the seeming obsession of the elite class.[166] Certainly wills were of great economic significance because inheritance was a primary method of transferring wealth. People were interested in wills because they enriched the people included in them. In addition, however, wills provided the testator with his/her last opportunity to express feelings about family members, friends, and acquaintances – and perhaps the only opportunity to express them candidly. As the title of Champlin's book signifies, a will made known the testator's "final judgments" about the people in her/his social milieu. Inclusion in a will was public recognition that one had been regarded by the testator as a dutiful family member or a true friend. Indeed, in *Letter* 6.22.3, Pliny relates that a man produced in court another man's will as evidence that they had been close friends. The opening of a will must have been attended with some apprehension on the part of people eager to know not just whether they would be receiving property, but also whether they had earned the affection and respect of the testator.

Pliny was proud to have been appointed an heir and to have been the recipient of many legacies because his good fortune indicated that his friends valued him.[167] For a non-family member to be named an heir, rather than simply a legatee, was a considerable honor. To be nominated as a legatee – that is, to receive a legacy – meant that one received a posthumous gift, with no obligations. To be nominated as an heir, however, meant that one was asked to take on several important obligations. Heirs were entrusted with the responsibility of making sure that the estate was disposed of according to the wishes of the deceased. Heirs took control of the total estate, but then distributed portions of it to the legatees, in the amounts specified in the will. However, heirs also had the responsibility of paying out of the estate any and all debts which the deceased had accumulated. They retained only the amount of the estate that remained after satisfying debts, distributing legacies, manumitting slaves named in the will, and paying funeral expenses. If the estate was heavily encumbered with debt, a person might decline nomination to the position of heir.[168] Nonetheless, appointment as an heir was a signal that the deceased considered you a person of integrity. In order not to disappoint trustworthy friends or inadvertently to reward disloyal people, it was critical to keep one's will up to date. In *Letter* 5.5.2, Pliny laments that Gaius Fannius died before making out a new will, and thus omitted some people whom he loved very much, while enriching others with whom he had become displeased.[169] If a will was up to date, a family member or acquaintance who was excluded from it suffered the humiliation of public exposure that s/he had been deemed by the deceased to be unworthy of consideration. By the same token, a will allowed the survivors to pass a final judgment on the deceased. A testator who was generous to his/her family members and friends would be honored and remembered as someone who had fulfilled his duties. In *Letter* 8.18, which is discussed in Chapter 3, Pliny reports that, when the will of Domitius Tullus was opened, he appeared to have redeemed himself, in fact "appeared much better in death than in life," because he had made his family members his beneficiaries, rather than leaving his fortune to the legacy-hunters, whose attentions he had encouraged.

Because wills were so important both to the distribution of wealth and to the functioning of social relations, there was anxiety about people gaining inclusion in wills through forgery, tampering, fraud, or legacy hunting (*captatio*). In *Letter* 7.6, discussed earlier, Pliny reports on a mother's accusation that her son's will had been falsified. Anecdotes about Regulus' flagrant legacy hunting were mentioned in Chapter 3. Pliny was outraged that Regulus accepted legacies as if he deserved them – that is, as if he had had been a true friend (*Letter* 2.20.11). Pliny comments that Regulus had risen from poverty to wealth by preying on vulnerable people, a behavior which Pliny terms "the most immoral type of fraud" (*Letters* 2.20.13 and 14). Pliny depicts his own behavior as quite opposite to that of Regulus. Several times in the letters he suggests that both how a testator arranged his/her will, and how an heir or legatee earned and then accepted a bequest were important indicators of character. He portrays himself not only as deserving the legacies he has gained, but also as someone who honors wills. In *Letter* 2.16.2, he writes, in reference to a situation in which the codicils of a friend (which incidentally included a bequest for him) were declared invalid: "I have established my own rule: that I should protect the wishes of the deceased as though perfectly expressed, even if they are deemed under the law to be insufficient."[170]

The disposition of an estate is the topic of *Letter* 5.1, which was written about 104 or 105 CE. Here we encounter another anecdote about a mother, a son, and a will. However, the relationship between the mother and son was very different from that between Regulus' wife and their son (*Letter* 4.2). Pliny opens the letter with an announcement to his addressee that he has received a legacy which is modest, but very gratifying. In the rest of the letter, he explains why it is gratifying: its bestowal was an acknowledgment on the part of the testator that Pliny was an honorable man. (Not surprisingly, the letter focuses on Pliny's behavior.)[171] The circumstances surrounding his being given this legacy were unusual. The testator was a man named Asudius Curianus. Some years before his death, his mother, a woman named Pomponia Galla, had died. Her death is conjectured to have occurred between 93 and 96 CE, the final years of the reign of Domitian, because Pliny mentions "the fear during those times," and the concern that some men had that their friendship with Arulenus Rusticus and his wife Verulana Gratilla might be held against them (*Letters* 5.1.7 and 8).[172] We know nothing about Pomponia Galla and Asudius Curianus other than what Pliny tells us. Pomponia Galla may have been the daughter or sister of Gaius Pomponius Gallus Didius Rufus, a man of senatorial rank who had served as governor of Crete and Cyrene in the late 80s.[173] From her son's name, we may conclude that she was married to a man whose family *nomen* was Asudius.

Pliny relates that Pomponia Galla had disinherited her son, and left as her heirs Pliny, another man of senatorial rank, named Sertorius Severus, and several distinguished men of equestrian rank. Nowhere in the letter does Pliny state Pomponia Galla's specific reasons for disinheriting her son, or for choosing to leave her estate to Pliny and the other men. It seems probable that Asudius Curianus was her only child and, since she chose non-family as heirs, that she had no surviving agnates – brothers, sisters, fraternal nephews, fraternal nieces – who might expect to receive a portion of her estate, most of which likely descended to her from their common *paterfamilias*. Disinheritance of a child was a serious breach of convention in ancient Rome. Deeply embedded in the traditions of Roman society was a presumption that parents would pass their estates – or at least part of their estates – down to their children. Any parent who disinherited a child risked accusations of disregarding the demands of *pietas* – that is, of parental moral duty. If a child was omitted from a will, the testator generally was careful to state the reasons why, both in order to maintain his/her reputation as a duteous person and to avoid challenges to the will by the disinherited child.[174] Reasons for disinheritance might include bringing dishonor to the family by criminal activity or being unduteous – that is, neglecting the duties which a child owed a parent.

The legal system reflected the traditions of Roman society, at least in regards to fathers. If a man died intestate (that is, without a will), his property was divided equally among his children as heirs. If a will had been made, Roman law, in the form of the Lex Falcidia, permitted a testator to give out as much as three-fourths of his estate in legacies to non-family members, but required that one-fourth be reserved for each of his children – unless a good reason could be presented for disinheritance.[175] Of course, the testator might leave the whole estate, or any portion above one-fourth to his child. The rules of succession and legal claims on the distribution of a woman's property are more difficult to determine. In marriages without *manus*[176], which most marriages at Pliny's time were, the mother was not the agnate of her children. Therefore, if she died intestate, her children had no legal entitlement or civil law rights of inheritance of her estate. Nonetheless, there was a social expectation that a mother would, by creating a will, either designate her children as her heirs or leave them legacies.[177] The first century BCE funerary inscription of a woman named Murdia praises her because she made all her sons equal heirs and gave her daughter a share, probably as a legacy. "Her maternal love was evident in her affection for her children and the equal size of the portions (of her estate)."[178] Valerius Maximus criticizes as mad the will of a mother with two daughters who made only one of her daughters an heir, despite the fact that both were equally virtuous.[179] By Pliny's time, the legal system reflected the expectation that a mother would provide inheritances or legacies for her children: it allowed a child who had been excluded from a mother's will to file a complaint.[180]

As already stated, Pliny does not explain the reason why Pomponia Galla disinherited her son, Asudius Curianus. He does tell us, however, that the son believed that he had been unjustly disinherited. He asked two things of Pliny. First, he requested that Pliny give him the share of the estate that he (Pliny) had received, but he promised that he would, by a tacit understanding, keep that share safe. What Pliny's phrasing seems to mean is that Asudius Curianus promised Pliny that he would, in the future, return the amount of the inheritance to Pliny, but that, for the time being, he wanted the proposed arrangement kept secret. Asudius Curianus' second request was that Pliny assist him in a *praeiudicium*. The word *praeiudicium* has several meanings.[181] Here the meaning seems to be a preliminary inquiry (a "pre-judgment," *prae-judicium*) to determine questions of status and rights. Asudius Curianus was apparently intending to challenge his mother's will if the *praeiudicium* established that he had a case. He may have been planning to file a *querela inofficiosi testamenti*, a "complaint of unduteous will" (that is, a complaint that the testator had not been observant of the moral duties owed to one's children or close agnates).[182] In his complaint he would undoubtedly have tried to prove that it was his mother, not he, who had disregarded the demands of *pietas* and been unduteous. A main reason for filing a *querela inofficiosi testamenti* was, of course, to gain possession of the estate of a close relative. If the complaint was deemed justified by the court, the will was then set aside. The deceased was considered to have died intestate, and all legacies specified in the will became void. If Pomponia Galla's will became void, her entire estate may have reverted to her son, her closest cognate, because, as noted earlier, she seems to have had no close agnates.

Financial gain was a main reason for filing a complaint. There was, however, another reason. If a person created a will in which he omitted a child, this would be an indicator that the child had engaged in behavior of which the testator disapproved and which society deemed unacceptable. Omission from a parent's will was, in a sense, a signal of dishonorable conduct. In order to restore one's honor, it was necessary to file a *querela inofficiosi testamenti* and have the will declared null. The usual grounds for having a will declared null was a charge that the testator had not been mentally competent. However, in proceeding with a case and attempting to gain the estate and to gain back a good reputation, the complainant publicly brought the deceased parent's character and competence into question. All in all, the proceedings of a *querela inofficiosi testamenti* must have revealed some unpleasant aspects of the relationship between the parent and the child(ren). In the specific case of the mother and son in *Letter* 5.1, we can assume that Pomponia Galla thought carefully about whether to omit her son, Asudius Curianus, from her will, knowing that he might file a *querela inofficiosi testamenti* and tarnish her reputation. Her disapproval of him, however, was apparently strong enough that she was willing to take that risk.

It is possible, however, that Asudius Curianus may have hoped to recover his mother's estate by invoking the *Lex Cincia*, a law concerning gifts and presents. This law ruled that gifts over a certain value (the exact amount is unknown) could be given only to persons within the fifth degree of kinship to the donor (which Pliny and the other heirs were not).[183] However, the statute did not contain criminal penalties or render void donations in excess of the ceiling amount. Moreover, the provisions of the law were rarely enforced, probably because the wealthy men who controlled the justice system did not themselves want to be restricted in their gift-giving or gift-receiving. In any case, from the little information which Pliny provides, it seems more likely that Asudius Curianus was attempting to file a *querela inofficiosi testamenti* and to have his deceased mother's judgment scrutinized.

Pliny replied to Asudius Curianus that he was not willing to do anything dishonorable, but Asudius Curianus was persistent and asked Pliny to conduct an informal and possibly private investigation, presumably about whether his mother, Pomponia Galla, had been justified in disinheriting him. Pliny relented, but warned that he would pronounce in favor of the mother if that was where honesty led him. To conduct the investigation, Pliny brought in as advisors "two men whom the state esteems very highly" (*Letter* 5.1.5), Quintus Corellius Rufus, about whom much has already been said, and Sextus Julius Frontinus, a man who was consul three times.[184] The three men listened as Asudius Curianus presented his case, and then Pliny responded with a few words because there was no one else present who might defend the honor of the deceased Pomponia Galla. Finally, he pronounced his judgment: that Asudius Curianus' mother seemed to have had good reasons for being angry with him. We are left to wonder, however, what behavior of the son had so infuriated the mother that she did something that few Roman parents did: she disinherited her son, who seems to have been her only child.

Despite Pliny's pronouncement, which favored the mother, Asudius Curianus made it known that he was applying to the Centumviral Court for an indictment of all the heirs but Pliny.[185] However, Pliny brokered a deal between the heirs and Asudius Curianus. The heirs, including Pliny, offered to give him one-fourth of the shares of the estate that had been bequeathed to them. As Pliny reminded Asudius Curianus, one-fourth was the minimum portion which the law granted to descendants who had been included in a will. Although this settlement netted him only one-fourth of the estate, rather than the whole, perhaps Asudius Curianus was willing to accept it because he thought that it was unlikely that the Centumviral Court would rule in his favor. Pliny offers no explanation of why the heirs approved of a settlement in which they lost one-fourth of their shares, except to comment, as noted earlier, that there was fear during those times, and that some of his co-heirs were concerned that their friendship with Arulenus Rusticus and his wife Verulana Gratilla might be held against them (*Letter* 5.1.7 and 8). Perhaps his co-heirs feared that the Centumviral Court would rule in favor of Asudius Curianus and that they would then lose everything, or that, even if it ruled against him, the emperor Domitian might overturn the ruling.[186]

Asudius Curianus died a few years after this incident, and his will revealed that he had left to Pliny a legacy of the amount (that is, the one-fourth) that Pliny had given to him in accordance with the out of court settlement.

In *Letter* 5.1, Pliny's intent is to depict himself as a man of great integrity, but did his defense of Pomponia Galla's will, by which he profited, not seem a matter of promoting his own interests? Despite his pronouncement in *Letter* 2.16.2 that he had established his own rule, which was to protect the wishes of the deceased (again in reference to a case in which he stood to gain if the will was judged valid), in the end, Pliny did *not* protect Pomponia Galla's last wishes and her final judgment. He brokered a deal which gave one-fourth of her estate to the son at whom she was very angry.

Letter 5.1 provides interesting insights into the evolution of a child's entitlement to inherit from a mother. At the time that Pliny wrote the letter, children did not yet have a civil law right to inherit their mother's estate, but society expected a mother to provide for her children at the time of her death, and the legal system allowed disinherited children to challenge a will as unduteous. Less than 100 years later (178 CE), the *senatusconsultum Orphitianum* put children (perhaps even illegitimate children) first in the order of succession, even over the mother's agnates. From then on, "all children had essentially the same level of priority in inheriting on intestacy from their mothers as from their fathers."[187]

Although both *Letter* 4.2 and *Letter* 5.1 make brief mention of two mothers who died just a few years before their only sons, there is a sharp contrast between the two situations. In *Letter* 4.2, the mother tried to protect her estate so that only her son would have access to it. In *Letter* 5.1, the mother was determined to exclude her son from her estate.

The anonymous mother of Asinius Bassus

This unnamed woman was the mother of several children and already the grandmother of at least one child, at the time that *Letter* 4.15 was written, about 105 CE. We learn at *Letter* 4.15.3 that her husband, Asinius Rufus, "had fulfilled the obligation of the best of citizens because he was very willing to make use of the fertility of his wife, in an era in which the rewards of childlessness make even one child seem to many to be burdensome." We have no way of knowing his wife's thoughts about her numerous and healthy pregnancies and her brood of children. Many people, among them Pliny, Calpurnia, and the family of the

Helvidiae (*Letter* 4.21), would have considered her fortunate to be so fertile, to have survived the dangers of childbirth, and to have lived long enough to see the birth of grandchildren.

Hispulla

Hispulla is mentioned in *Letter* 1.12 as the wife of Pliny's mentor, Corellius Rufus (see Chapter 3). She was also the mother of their daughter Corellia Hispulla, and the grandmother of Corellia's son, for whom Pliny, in *Letter* 3.3, suggests a *rhetor* (see earlier). Because the daughter bore Hispulla's name as her *cognomen*, we assume that Hispulla was the birth mother, and not a stepmother. We might also speculate that her agnate family had not been very fertile, and in particular had not produced many male descendants, and was therefore interested in having the family name carried on as a *cognomen* by a female descendant. Although Hispulla seems to have had only one child who reached adulthood, she was, like the woman just mentioned, fortunate to have lived long enough to see a grandchild. Hispulla and her daughter tried unsuccessfully to dissuade Corellius Rufus from suicide (1.12.9).

The anonymous wife of Titius Aristo

Letter 1.22 offers a similar story, but with a happier conclusion. The prayers of the anonymous wife of Titius Aristo (see Chapter 3) and the tears of his daughter convinced him to abandon his plans for suicide (*Letter* 1.22.9). We cannot be sure, however, that the wife was the birth mother, rather than the stepmother of the daughter. In neither *Letter* 1.12 nor *Letter* 1.22 do we learn anything about an affective relationship between mother and daughter. Pliny records only that they were united in their attempts to preserve the lives of the husband/father.

Casta

Another mother and daughter appear in *Letter* 3.9, which contains Pliny's report on the prosecution of the family of Caecilius Classicus, a senator of African origin, for malfeasance in the province of Baetica. (See Chapter 3.) Again we cannot know with certainty that Casta was the birth mother. Nor do we know whether she had other children or whether her relationship with her daughter was close. The daughter (presumably named Caecilia) was already married at the time the letter was written in 100 CE, and she and her husband seem to have spent time with her parents in Baetica since they were included in the charges of malfeasance.

The anonymous wife of Cocceianus Dio

In *Letter* 10.81 (addressed to Trajan), we learn that the orator, Cocceianus Dio (known to us also as Dio Chrysostom; see Chapter 7) had inappropriately buried his wife and son in a building containing a statue of the emperor Trajan. Nothing else is known about this mother and son. The family lived in the city of Prusa, which was in the province of Bithynia to which Pliny had been sent as governor.

The anonymous mother of Voconius Romanus

In *Letter* 10.4, addressed to Trajan, we meet a mother who was willing to expend an enormous amount of money to further the career of her son. One of Pliny's oldest friends was a man named Voconius Romanus.[188] The family of Voconius Romanus was located in the province of Hispania Tarraconensis (north-eastern Spain).[189] However, like Pliny, Voconius Romanus had apparently been sent to Rome to be educated. Pliny comments that they had been schoolmates and close friends from an early age (*Letters* 2.13.5, 10.4.1.).[190] Their friendship continued through their adulthood. Eight of the published letters, spread out from Books 1 to 9, are addressed to Voconius Romanus: *Letters* 1.5, 2.1, 3.13, 6.15, 6.33, 8.8, 9.7, and 9.28. In addition, he is the subject of two other letters: *Letters* 2.13 and 10.4.

From inscriptional evidence, we may conjecture that Voconius Romanus had married at least once, to a woman named Popilia (or Popillia) Rectina, who unfortunately died at the young age of 18 years.[191] She shared her *cognomen*, Rectina, with the woman who had, during the eruption of Mount Vesuvius in 79 CE, sent a message to the Elder Pliny, imploring him to come and rescue her (*Letter* 6.16.8; see Chapter 3). We do not know if or how the two women may have been related.

Although Pliny praises his friend as an excellent speaker in court and a talented writer (*Letters* 2.13.6 and 7), Voconius Romanus was apparently less successful than Pliny in establishing a political career and was dependent on Pliny's help in this regard.[192] In *Letter* 2.13.4, Pliny gives only one indication that his friend had as yet held a public office, and it was not one in Rome or even in Italy: he oversaw the operation of the imperial cult in eastern Spain.[193] *Letter* 2.13 is addressed to a Priscus, a man whose identity is unknown to us, although he may have been Neratius Priscus, the conjectured husband of Corellia Hispulla (see earlier.) From the letter, we learn that he had command of a large army in one of the provinces. Pliny requests a favor from him: that he give Voconius Romanus a post as an officer in his army. In the same letter (*Letter* 2.13.8), we learn that Pliny had requested and acquired from the emperor *ius trium liberorum*, the "three-children privilege" for his friend.[194] (We don't know if Voconius Romanus remarried after the death of Popilia Rectina. Perhaps, like Pliny, he had remarried, but still not produced children.) In 9.28.1, we discover that Voconius Romanus had asked Pliny for another favor – to deliver a letter from him to the empress Plotina.[195] Pliny replied that he was happy to do so. In *Letter* 10.4, Pliny publishes a record of yet another favor that he has done for his friend, a favor also involving the mother of Voconius Romanus.

We do not know the name of his mother. Presumably her birth family resided in Spain as did her husband's. Pliny describes her as coming from one of the "first families" – that is, from one of the most distinguished families (*Letter* 2.13.4).

Inscriptional evidence suggests that she had married Voconius Placidus,[196] whom Pliny identifies as a prominent member of the equestrian order (*Letter* 2.13.4), and given birth to at least one son, Voconius Romanus. Her husband died, but we do not know whether her son was still a child at the time. Nor do we know how long she was a widow. In any case, she remarried, to a man whose name we can deduce from the inscriptional evidence was Licinius Macrinus (or Marinus). She was fortunate in her second marriage. Not only was her second husband an even more prominent member of the equestrian order than her first, but also he acted more like another father than a stepfather to her son, succeeding to the title of "father" because of his devotion to him (*Letter* 2.13.4). Step relations were common in the ancient Roman world because of the high mortality rate among young adults, but they were not always happy. The mother of Voconius Romanus was lucky to have entered into a second marriage in which her son was treated well by his stepfather. At some time, Licinius Macrinus adopted the son, at which point the son acquired additional names (recorded in the inscription), becoming Gaius Licinius Macrinus Voconius Romanus. Voconius Romanus had inherited his father's estate (*Letter* 10.4.4) and would presumably also be the heir to the estate of his step/adoptive father.

We should not assume that the son was a child at the time of the adoption. The adoption of adults was a common practice in ancient Rome.[197] What is interesting in this situation is the closeness between the mother and the son, and the son and her new husband. Since a child formally belonged to the family of his father, not of his mother, the Voconius family might have claimed custody of Voconius Romanus if he had been a child when his father died. However, since he seems to have remained with his mother, we might speculate that he was already an adult at the time of his father's death (and able to make decisions for himself), or that there were no Voconius relatives to ask for custody. In any case, his mother continued to protect his interests even as he advanced into middle age. *Letter* 10.4 contains a record of one of her attempts to promote his career.

As already noted, Voconius Romanus, despite his rhetorical talent and wealth, had been less successful than Pliny in achieving public distinction. Both men were about the same age and had attended the same schools in Rome, and both had arisen from equestrian families. By the time that he was about 28 or 29 years old, Pliny had been selected to the office of quaestor and thus gained lifelong membership in the Senate and admittance to the senatorial order. Admittance to the senatorial order had, however, eluded Voconius Romanus. About 97 CE, Pliny agreed to petition the emperor Nerva to advance his friend to the senatorial order. It was within the power of the emperor either to admit a person directly into the Senate or to select him as quaestor, in which case his admittance to the Senate would be automatic. However, there was a property qualification for membership in the senatorial order. A man of senatorial rank was required to have a property rating of at least one million sesterces.[198] In comparison, the property qualification for membership in the equestrian order was much lower: 400,000 sesterces.[199] Of course, even 400,000 sesterces was a sum which would make a person very wealthy, but it was substantially less than the senatorial requirement. Voconius Romanus had inherited his equestrian father's estate, but apparently this was not enough to fulfill the senatorial requirement. His mother therefore arranged to transfer to him a very large amount from her estate – real property (not cash) to a value of four million sesterces, or four times more than the minimum amount required for senatorial rank. (Her willingness to give him so large a gift may imply that he was her only child, or that she was extremely wealthy.) She had stipulated this amount in a document which she sent to Nerva. However, she had not yet completed all the necessary legal formalities before Nerva died. In *Letter* 10.4, Pliny petitioned the next emperor, Trajan, to approve the promotion of Voconius Romanus to the senatorial order. The fact that the appeal had first been filed when Nerva was emperor suggests that this letter was written in 98 CE, not long after his death. At this time, Pliny and his friend were about 36 years old, and the mother may have been in her mid- to late 50s. The "legal formalities" which had not been completed apparently involved procedures for the transfer of agricultural land within Italy when the land was intended as a gift to a family member, rather than a sale to a non-family member. Pliny states that the mother, upon his advice, "emancipated" some of her farms. Apparently, she emancipated the farms – that is, she released them from her possession by a ceremonial (fictitious) sale.[200] At this point, her son then gained possession of them, although we do not know the details of the transfer. (We might compare Regulus' ceremonial "sale" of his son during the process of emancipating him and freeing him from *patria potestas*; see Chapter 3.)

Although we do not know the name of the mother of Voconius Romanus, we can deduce that she was a very wealthy woman who took a very active interest in her son's career and was willing to pay handsomely for his advancement. If she had, as it seems, fewer than three children, she would have had a *tutor* to oversee her distribution of her wealth. If so, she was able to convince him that her large transfer of property to her son was a worthwhile plan. We have seen, in Corellia, for instance, other examples of women who managed their estates with considerable independence. However, we cannot know if the mother of Voconius Romanus was disappointed that he had been less successful than other men of his age and education, and that he had not produced grandchildren.

Stepmothers

In *Letter* 6.33, Pliny presents another report on a family dispute about a will. This letter also offers a glimpse at what might happen when a man with children remarried and introduced a stepmother to his children. As already noted, step-relations were quite common in the ancient Roman world, both because of the high mortality rate among people of child-producing years and because of the ease of divorce. When a woman with children died or was divorced, the children usually remained with the father since they were members of his (not her) agnate family. Of course, there were always exceptions, when, for example, a father died and left no close relatives to take in the children. This seems to have been the situation with Pliny, who remained close to his mother, with Voconius Romanus, who was adopted by his stepfather (*Letter* 10.4), and with the children of Helvidius II and Anteia, who apparently remarried after Helvidius II's death (*Letter* 9.13.16). More often, however, the children stayed with their father, who would be likely to remarry, both to secure a custodian for his children and household and to avoid the penalties for celibacy which Augustus had established. The entrance into the household of a woman who would take over the position of a child's mother was undoubtedly as fraught with potential problems as it is today. The Latin word for stepmother, *noverca*, is based on the Latin word for "new," *novus* (compare the English word "novelty"). The "newness" of a *noverca* caused her to be viewed by household members with the suspicion that she was a disruptive intruder. Adding to the reluctance of children to welcome a stepmother was the fact that a middle-aged man might marry a woman much younger than himself (consider the difference in age between Pliny and Calpurnia), and that the stepmother might therefore be the same age – or even younger than – his children.

The wicked stepmother was a familiar figure in Classical literature and rhetoric.[201] In contrast, there were few representations of stepfathers as evil. The difference may be attributable to the reality that, after a divorce, children were more likely to live with their father and a stepmother than with their mother and a step-father. It was widely believed that a stepmother would put her own interests ahead of the interests of her husband's children, and this anxiety was com-pounded if the stepmother brought to the household her children by a previous husband, and especially if she bore children to her new husband. His children would be apprehensive that their half-siblings and step-siblings would be rivals for their father's affection – and estate. They might also fear that their stepmother might try to remove them from the household, either by coaxing their father to disinherit them or, in the most frightening of nightmares, by killing them. The poets Vergil and Ovid were among the literary figures who perpetuated a stereotype of the scheming villainous stepmother who tries to eliminate her stepchildren with "noxious plants and baleful spells" and "ghastly poisons."[202] The stereotype was present also in Roman declamations. In his collection of rhetorical exercises, the Elder Seneca cites several fictitious scenarios in which a stepmother was accused of poisoning a stepson.[203] There is no evidence that deliberate poisonings by stepmothers were a common occurrence, but, in an era when the preservation of food was difficult and when accidental food poisoning was therefore frequent, it is easy to imagine how suspicion of malevolence would fall on a stepmother.

The anxiety about the evil that a stepmother might do apparently haunted not only children but also their birth mothers. Ovid imagines that the mythical Medea, who was divorced by Jason and exiled from her children, implores Jason to think about their sons: "a dreadful, vile stepmother will treat them cruelly."[204] Propertius portrays Cornelia, speaking from beyond the grave, as urging the children she left behind to be cautious with regard to their stepmother, but to be patient and speak well of their father's new marriage. She advises them not to praise their mother too much or offend their stepmother by making comparisons, but to win her over by their good behavior.[205] The younger Seneca noted that his mother, Helvia, had lost her mother during childbirth, and had grown up with a stepmother. Their relationship had been a good one, but was so, Seneca maintains, because Helvia had converted the stepmother into a "mother" by her own exceptional obedience and *pietas*, as great as can be displayed in a daughter. He thus leads his reader to conclude that, when a step relationship was harmonious, the credit belonged to the child. Indeed, he asserts that "even a good stepmother is a great burden."[206] Marcus Aurelius, in a passage cited earlier, portrays a child's relationship to his stepmother as dutiful and cordial, as opposed to his warm affection for his birth mother (from whom he was presumably separated by divorce). "If you had a stepmother and a mother at the same time, you would treat your stepmother with respect, but you would constantly return to your mother."[207]

There were, nonetheless, a few reports of benevolent stepmothers. One was Octavia, born about 69 BCE, and the sister of Octavian, who became the first Roman emperor, Augustus. She had three children, two daughters and a son, with her first husband, Gaius Claudius Marcellus. He died in 40 BCE. Soon after his death, Octavia remarried, to Mark Antony, who was at this time still an ally of her brother. Their marriage was intended to strengthen this political alliance. Octavia was Antony's fourth wife. (One of the four is recorded only by Cicero.) He brought to the marriage two sons from his third wife, Fulvia (who died in 40), and Octavia thus became a stepmother. Octavia and Antony subsequently had two daughters. Their household was thus a blended family of siblings, step-siblings, and half-siblings. Within a few years, however, the alliance between Antony and Octavian/Augustus had begun to crumble. In addition, Antony did not end his relationship with the Egyptian queen, Cleopatra, with whom he had three children. Octavia and Antony divorced in 32 BCE, and he and Cleopatra committed suicide in 30 BCE, after their defeat by Octavian's naval forces at Actium. After his death, Octavia continued to look after all of Antony's children. (One of his sons with Fulvia was killed in 30 BCE.)[208] She was commemorated as an exemplum of a noble and selfless Roman woman, who harbored no bitterness toward her husband, despite his scandalously insulting behavior, and who devoted herself to the welfare of her children and her stepchildren, even including her Egyptian stepchildren.[209]

Reports of generous behavior by a stepmother are, however, an exception. The anxiety that a stepmother would try to gain possession of the estate of her husband, and thus deprive his children of it, was deep-rooted. This scenario is expressed in several places in Roman legal commentaries. "It must not be allowed to parents to cause harm to their children by their wills. They do this most often when they make a spiteful judgment against their own blood, having been taken in by the charms and enticements of stepmothers."[210] (It is noteworthy that stepmothers, but not stepfathers are blamed.) In another passage, a stepmother is admonished thus. "If your husband appointed you as his sole heir in his will, and disinherited the daughter whom he had in his *potestas* (legal control) and left her nothing, this disinheritance will not be permitted because she did not give him any just cause for being offended. If she should complain that her father's will was unduteous, there is no doubt that she could obtain the entire estate."[211]

Pliny does, by implication, record a couple of positive stepmother situations. Fannia, for example, was a stepmother to Helvidius II and, from what we can surmise from Pliny's references, remained close to him after her husband's death and was very supportive of his political activities. Additionally, in *Letter* 8.18 (which has been examined in Chapter 3) Pliny reported to a friend on the will of Domitius Tullus. He had – quite properly, according to Pliny – made his adopted daughter his heir. Elsewhere in the letter, Pliny extols the virtues of Domitius Tullus's wife (perhaps named Dasumia Polla) who had dutifully cared for her invalid husband and to whom he left a substantial legacy. The wife was the stepmother of his daughter, but apparently had not tried to entice him to disinherit her. In *Letter* 6.33, however, Pliny describes a situation in which a child was deprived of an estate because of a stepmother.

Attia Viriola

Letter 6.33 was addressed to Voconius Romanus, the friend for whom Pliny requested the "three-children privilege," a military commission, and, from the emperor, admission to the senatorial order (*Letters* 2.13 and 10.4). Voconius Romanus was also the man who was adopted by his stepfather, who, even before the adoption, treated him with the kindness of a father (*Letter* 2.13.4). Perhaps a deliberate juxtaposition was not intended by Pliny, but a reader acquainted with Voconius Romanus' experience with a benevolent stepfather might see a contrast with the sinister stepmother mentioned in *Letter* 6.33. Pliny's letter was a cover letter attached to a copy of a speech which he had recently delivered before the Centumviral Court.[212] He commented that he and his friends considered this speech one of the best that he had ever composed. The reason for sending the speech and the letter was to provide Voconius Romanus, who had not been present at the court hearing, with the pleasure of reading Pliny's masterpiece. However, the purpose of publishing this cover letter was probably to provoke the curiosity of readers of the correspondence and entice them to request copies of the speech.[213] In any case, the letter unfortunately provides only a sketchy account of the legal case in which Pliny was involved.

He announces at the beginning of the letter that he composed the speech on behalf of a woman named Attia Viriola. We know about her only from Pliny's letter. He describes her, in *Letter* 6.33.2, as a woman "splendidly born," *femina splendidus nata*. Elsewhere Pliny employs the adverb *splendidus* and the adjective *splendidus* to denote equestrian rank.[214] Although her family may have been equestrian, she had married well, to a man who, at the time that the letter was written, had reached the office of praetor (*Letter* 6.33.2). Later in the letter, Pliny writes that a man named Suburanus was also a plaintiff (*Letter* 6.33.6). Scholars have assumed that he was a kinsman of Attia, and also of the Sextus Attius Suburanus Aemilianus who was prefect of the Praetorian Guard from 98 to 101 CE (which was an office of equestrian rank), and then consul in 101 (at which time he must have been admitted to senatorial rank) and again in 104 CE. A Suburanus is mentioned elsewhere in Pliny as the judge appointed to examine the new evidence presented by the anonymous mother who had charged her son's freedmen with his murder (*Letters* 7.6.10 and 11). We do not know if this was the same person or a relative.[215]

Pliny informs his reader that the speech was noteworthy because of the distinction of the person involved, the rare nature of the case, and the magnitude of the court (*Letter* 6.33.2). Attia Viriola had been disinherited by her octogenarian father within eleven days of his introducing to her a stepmother for whom he had been captivated by love. The Latin words which Pliny uses for "captivated by love" are *amore captus*. Perhaps he wanted to prompt the reader to think of the word *captatio*, and to associate the stepmother with "legacy chasers" like Regulus.[216]

Attia Viriola applied to the Centumviral Court – presumably by a *querela inofficiosi testamenti* – to recover her father's property. We may assume that her disinheritance was revealed in his will after his death. Pliny does not supply these details, nor does he tell his reader anything about the identity, character, or age of the stepmother. We are left to speculate that she was a conniver who had schemed to have an old man become infatuated with her and to leave her his estate. The truth may be something else. Pliny's description of the events of the trial is quite limited, perhaps because he assumed that someone wanting more information would read his speech. We learn that all the 180 judges of the Centumviral Court met together to hear the case. This was apparently an uncommon event – hence Pliny's earlier reference to the "magnitude of the court" – because the judges were usually divided into four smaller panels. Perhaps the smaller panels were regularly used for other cases. Or perhaps such a division was used when there was more than one plaintiff or one heir to one estate. The procedure is not clear. There were also, Pliny remarks, a large number of advocates and assistants on both sides. (Whoever the stepmother was, she was not without supporters.) In addition, there was a densely packed ring of onlookers who surrounded the very broad courtroom with a circle several persons deep. The tribunal was also crowded, and, in the upper gallery of the Basilica[217], men and women hung over the edge in their eagerness to hear (which was difficult) and to see (which was easy). Great was the anxious anticipation, Pliny reports, of fathers, of daughters, and even of stepmothers. It was not unusual for men to congregate in courthouses to observe legal proceedings, but this case had attracted many women as well, and particularly daughters and stepmothers, apprehensive, no doubt, about how the verdict might affect them personally. Pliny constructed a very dramatic description of the setting in which he delivered his magnificent (in his judgment) speech on behalf of Attia Viriola. As he admits, he wanted to set the stage, as it were, so that Voconius Romanus would feel, as he read the speech, that he was actually in the courthouse (*Letter* 6.33.7).

Pliny's account of the verdict is unfortunately confusing. He reports that the result was not uniform, and that he and his colleagues were victorious in two of the panels, but defeated in the other two. He comments that such a great divergence was remarkable in the same case, with the same judges and advocates, and at the same time. Because Pliny seemed earlier to recount that the four panels of the Centumviral Court – that is, all 180 judges – had assembled together (*Letter* 6.33.3), we do not know why four separate decisions were made. It is at this point in the letter, moreover, that we learn that the stepmother had been an heir to only one-sixth of the estate. Pliny says clearly, nonetheless, that she lost the case. If, as it seems, there was more than one heir to the estate, Attia Viriola may have brought a suit against all of them, but received a favorable verdict in only two of the suits. Also a loser was Suburanus, mentioned here for the first and only time in the letter. Pliny discloses that he had been disinherited by his own father and did not dare to sue for that estate, but now, with unparalleled impudence, was claiming the estate of someone else's father. Pliny's words imply that Suburanus, like Attia Viriola, had filed a *querela inofficiosi testamenti*. However, the outcome of the hearing remains a mystery. The hearing may have involved multiple suits, claims, and persons, and Pliny chose to focus only on those elements of the case in which he was an advocate. We can perhaps conclude, nonetheless, given Pliny's delight in his performance, that the outcome had been favorable for Attia Viriola, and unfavorable for the anonymous stepmother.

Another mystery is the presumed kin relationship between Attia Viriola and Suburanus.[218] If indeed he filed a *querela inofficiosi testamenti*, he must have been in the direct line of intestate succession, and therefore closely related to Attia Viriola. Conjectures about their relationship are numerous. She may have been the daughter of Sextus Attius Suburanus Aemilianus, the praetorian prefect and consul mentioned earlier (and perhaps the judge in *Letter* 7.6.10). The Suburanus mentioned in this letter may have been her brother. One problem with this theory is that the father lived into his 80s (the word "octogenarian" appears in *Letter* 6.33.2). If he were the praetorian prefect and then consul in 101 and 104, he would have held the office of consul for the first time when well into his 70s, a situation which would have been highly unusual. Moreover, if Attia Viriola and the Suburanus mentioned in the letter were sister and brother, Pliny's statement about Suburanus' having been disinherited by his own father and claiming the estate of someone else's father would be puzzling (*Letter* 6.33.6). Possibly the octogenarian had been the father of the prefect/consul Suburanus, and Attia Viriola had been the sister of the prefect/consul (who was now deceased and disinherited his son). If the Suburanus mentioned in the letter were the son of the prefect/consul, he would have been Attia Viriola's nephew (and the grandson of her father). Or, both Attia and Suburanus may have been cousins – that is, the grandchildren of the same *paterfamilias* and in direct line of succession. In this scenario, the fathers of Attia and Suburanus would have inherited from the grandfather. Suburanus' father died before Attia's father, and had disinherited Suburanus. Another conjecture is that Attia was the niece of Suburanus.[219] The nature of the kin relationship cannot be solved with the scanty information available to us. Since our focus is on learning about the lives of the women in Pliny's letters, we would like to have more definitive knowledge about who her relatives were. Unfortunately, the most we can conclude is that she was, in some way, related to Sextus Attius Suburanus, whose successful career indicates that he had won the favor of the emperor Trajan. The Suburanus mentioned in the letter was probably not the prefect/consul because it seems unlikely that Pliny would bring such negative attention to a friend of Trajan. He may, however, have been a son of the prefect/consul. In any case, Attia Viriola's family was distinguished enough and well-connected enough that, although of equestrian rank, they were able to marry her to a man of praetorian rank – that is, a senator. We do not know who her husband was, or whether she had children. We do know, however, that she had a stepmother who she believed had cheated her out of an inheritance. Undoubtedly, in his speech on behalf of Attia Viriola, Pliny had spoken with great rhetorical flourish about the proverbial evils of stepmothers.

Figure 5 Julia (c. 64 – c. 91 CE), daughter of the emperor Titus and niece of the emperor Domitian. Traces of paint on the marble indicate that Julia's hair was reddish in color. Her elaborately curled hair style was fashionable in the late first century CE. The diadem which she is depicted as wearing was undoubtedly inlaid with precious gems. Photo © The J. Paul Getty Museum, Villa Collection, Malibu, California.

5   Grandmothers, aunts, and mothers-in-law

The focus of this and the following chapter will be women identified by Pliny in family roles other than those of wife and mother. The previous chapter included discussion about women who, in their positions as nurses and stepmothers, served as surrogate mothers. This chapter will begin with a continuation of the discussion about surrogate mothers and a look at the situation of grandmothers in Roman families.

Grandmothers

A Roman grandmother might be quite young in comparison with the image of grandmothers in our own society. If a girl married, as was common, at the age of 15, and bore a daughter by the time she was 17, and this daughter, in turn, produced a child at the age of 17, the grandmother would be 34 years old. Were life expectancy the same as it is today in the western world, the 34-year-old grandmother might reasonably assume that she would live to see great-grandchildren and even great-great-grandchildren. However, as noted earlier, life expectancy was very low in the ancient Roman world, and deaths both of children and of young adults were all too common. Many of these young adults were mothers who did not live to see their children grow up and produce grandchildren. In *Letter* 4.21, for example, Pliny reports the deaths of the two Helvidiae, the daughters of Fannia's stepson, Helvidius II. They were probably in their late teens or early 20s when they died while giving birth to daughters. We do not know how long these daughters lived or whether they married and had children. If they did, their children would not have known their maternal grandmothers, the Helvidiae. In fact, relatively few Roman children had the experience of knowing their grandmothers.

Women who survived to an advanced age might consider themselves fortunate, especially as they watched several younger generations grow up. However, the early mortality of others might leave a long-lived person with few or no close family members. Pliny's friend, Quintilian, lost his 18-year-old wife and their two young sons within a few years time.[1] (We do not know if he remarried.) Marcus Aurelius' teacher, Fronto and his wife, Gratia, lost five children and at least one grandchild.[2] The younger Seneca relates that his mother, Helvia, experienced the deaths of three grandchildren.[3] Living a long time was a blessing only if one had financial resources and the support of family members. Ancient states offered no safety net of social services for the sick, disabled, and/or elderly. A wealthy childless person would have slaves as attendants and might also receive assistance from *captatores* who were hoping to be included in the person's will.[4] However, an old and poor person who had outlived her/his descendants was in a very precarious situation. A poignant inscription from the grave of a two-year-old boy notes that he had (that is, by dying first) cheated his grandmother because he used to say that he would care for her and be her support in her extreme old age.[5]

The life of Seneca's mother, Helvia, exemplifies the mutability of Roman family situations. Like the Helvidiae, her own mother died giving birth to her.[6] Thus, from her earliest moments, she never knew her mother. Nor did her sons know their maternal grandmother. She was, fortunately, raised by a benevolent stepmother. (See Chapter 4: Helvia had converted the stepmother into a "mother" by her own exceptional obedience and *pietas*.) Unlike her mother, she had the good fortune to live at least well into middle age (we do not know when she died) and see her sons mature. However, several of her grandchildren died well before she did. And Helvia was called upon to raise an orphaned grandchild. As already mentioned, her son Seneca urged her to become involved in the upbringing of her motherless granddaughter, Novatilla.[7] (And Novatilla's mother, in turn, provides an example of a woman who died as a young adult.)

When the mother of young children died (or was divorced), responsibility for raising the children fell upon their father and his family. Helvia's father remarried, and she was cared for by a stepmother. This was also the situation for the son of Helvidius I. When Helvidius I married Fannia, he introduced a stepmother to his son. In some cases, however, a grandmother took on the care of children without a mother in the household. After the death of Quintilian's 18-year-old wife, his two young sons were cared for by their grandmother (as well as nurses).[8] We have other evidence of children who were raised by grandmothers, for example, a funerary inscription commemorating a woman who is described as a very dear grandmother and a very sweet nurturer (or: rearer, *educatrix*).[9] The inscription was commissioned by her grandson.

Several women in Pliny's letters can be identified as grandmothers. He mentions that Serrana Procula was the maternal grandmother of Minicius Acilianus, the man whom he recommended as a husband for the daughter of the deceased Arulenus Rusticus. (*Letter* 1.14; see Chapter 2.) About her, Pliny writes that she was from the township (*municipium*) of Patavium – that is, from the general region of northern Italy of which he also was a native. He describes her as a model of stringency in a region known for its moral strictness. "You know the moral code of that place. But Serrana is a model of austerity even to the Patavians" (*Letter* 1.14.6). Elsewhere in the letter, we learn that Minicius Acilianus' father is still alive, but there is no mention of his mother, and we therefore assume that she was dead. The reference to his maternal grandmother was therefore intended to provide the information that both of Minicius Acilianus' parents came from families which valued moral integrity. Pliny's comment instructs us that the character and social standing of a person's maternal family, and not just of his/her agnates, was considered of importance. Because his father was still alive, it is not likely that he lived in the household of his maternal grandmother, but Pliny's words suggest that she might nonetheless have played a substantive role in a child's moral education.

About Hispulla (*Letter* 1.12.3) and the anonymous, but fertile wife of Asinius Rufus (*Letter* 4.15.3), we know nothing with regard to their activities as grandmothers, but we do know that their children were also alive – that is, that the grandmothers had not been required to take on the role of caregivers for their grandchildren. Nonetheless, a grandmother might well desire to remain close to her child and grandchild. This would be particularly true if the parent of the grandchild was one's daughter, as was the case with Hispulla, whose daughter (Corellia Hispulla) had borne a grandchild. (On Hispulla and Corellia Hispulla, see Chapters 3 and 4.) Dixon comments that mothers would help their daughters through childbirth and would visit them and the grandchildren regularly.[10] In Chapter 4, reference was made to an essay by Aulus Gellius in which he presents the views of the philosopher, Favorinus, about the virtues of breastfeeding. The occasion of that discussion was a visit which Favorinus made to the home of a friend whose wife had just given birth. There he met the young wife's mother who had apparently been present during the travail. When Favorinus suggested that the young woman breastfeed the infant, her mother rebuked him, saying that she had been through a long and difficult labor and needed to rest.[11] The solicitous concern of a maternal grandmother was probably common in Roman families, even though the grandchild belonged to his/her father's family. We do not know to what extent a paternal grandmother – such as the anonymous wife of Asinius Rufus (*Letter* 4.15.3) or the anonymous mother of Junius Avitus (*Letters* 8.23.7 and 8) – would be involved when the mother (her son's wife) was alive, but it is not unlikely that she, too, would want to see her grandchildren often. Pliny makes no reference to a grandmother's eagerness to see her grandchildren, but he does write to his wife's paternal grandfather, "You are eager to see your granddaughter" (Pliny's third wife, Calpurnia; *Letter* 4.1.1). There is no reason to think that grandmothers – maternal and paternal – would not be similarly eager.

When Calpurnia's father died, she moved into the custody of her paternal grandfather (her *paterfamilias*). There is no mention in Pliny of her mother or grandmothers; it is likely that they were deceased, though divorce is a possibility. In *Letter* 8.23, we learn about Junius Avitus, whose father had died when he was quite young. Unlike Calpurnia, Junius Avitus seems not to have gone to live with agnate kin, but to have stayed with his mother. He may have been her only child to reach adulthood. He married, and within a year of his marriage, a child was born. However, he died shortly after the birth of his daughter. We do not know whether his mother was able to maintain contact with what may have been her only grandchild. Her son's agnate family, if any members were still alive, may have claimed the infant girl (as Calpurnia's grandfather had claimed her). Or, if the child was left with her mother (Junius Avitus' young wife), the mother may have remarried and moved the child to a new household.

Ummidia Quadratilla

We find in Pliny's published correspondence only one account of a grandmother's interaction with her grandchildren. In *Letter* 7.24, which was written about 107 CE, Pliny announces the death of a woman named Ummidia Quadratilla.[12] She had, he reports, died just short of completing her 80th year. We can conclude that she was born about 27 CE, during the reign of Tiberius, and had lived to see the accession to power of 11 more emperors (Caligula, Claudius, Nero, Galba, Vitellius, Otho, Vespasian, Titus, Domitian, Nerva, and Trajan) and to experience considerable changes in the political and social environment of the Roman world. Ummidia Quadratilla was more fortunate than most of her coevals; she had lived a long life and was vigorous up until her final illness. And she was wealthy. In a rare departure from his silence about the physical attributes of people[13], Pliny notes that her body was compact (*compactum*) and sturdy (*robustum*) even beyond the matronly norm.[14] It is not certain, however, what Pliny's words mean, and whether we should assume, as some scholars have, that Ummidia Quadratilla was, like the nursery song teapot, short and stout. What is clear is that she enjoyed remarkably good health to an enviable old age.

Her *nomen*, Ummidia, was not common, and suggests a kinship with a man named Gaius Ummidius Durmius Quadratus.[15] He may have been the father of Ummidia Quadratilla. Syme conjectures that he had at least three children (perhaps by two wives): Gaius Ummidius Sallustius, Gaius Ummidius Quadratus, and our Ummidia Quadratilla.[16] (See Genealogy Chart 5.) He was a man from a wealthy family in the south Italian countryside who rose to political prominence in Rome. Because of the addition of the *cognomen* Sallustius for one of the men presumed to be a son, Syme conjectured that Gaius Ummidius Durmius Quadratus was married to a hypothetical Sallustia. (However, the nomenclature could indicate an adoption.)[17] He connects her by marriage to the imperial family, as the sister of Gaius Sallustius Passienus Crispus, who was married to Julia Agrippina (Agrippina the Younger), who was mother of Nero (and great-granddaughter of Augustus). If Syme's conjecture about a Sallustia is correct, Gaius Ummidius Durmius Quadratus may have owed his political success to the patronage of the emperors Tiberius, Caligula, Claudius, and Nero. He was quaestor in 14 CE, and then served as aedile and praetor, and reached the office of suffect consul about 40 CE. Ummidia Quadratilla may therefore have spent at least part of her childhood in Rome and may perhaps have become acquainted with members of the imperial family. Ummidius Durmius Quadratus apparently served as a governor in Lusitania around 37 CE[18], in Illyricum after his consulship,[19] and in Syria, where he died in 59 or 60 CE.[20] We don't know if he took his family with him to his provincial postings, as did, for example, Caecilius Classicus (*Letter* 3.9). It is possible that Ummidia Quadratilla spent some time as a child in Lusitania. By the 50s, however, when Gaius Ummidius Durmius Quadratus was in Syria, she was about 30 years old and probably married and raising a family of her own.

The Ummidius family seems to have had its roots at Casinum, a town about 80 miles south-east of Rome.[21] The Roman author Varro, who lived in the first century BCE and had a villa at Casinum, passes on a story about a Ummidius at Casinum who suffered the insult of having an aristocratic Roman dinner guest spit out the fish served to him because it was a river fish. (Apparently, only ocean fish were acceptable to this snob.)[22] The poet Horace, also of the first century BCE, relates an anecdote about a very rich and miserly man named Ummidius, who was killed with an ax by a freedwoman.[23] We do not know if this Ummidius was a resident of Casinum. However, several inscriptions referring to the Ummidius family have been found there.[24]

One inscription records that Ummidia Quadratilla funded the construction of an amphitheater and temple for the people of Casinum.[25] Substantial remains of the amphitheater still exist, but no evidence of the temple has been found. Clearly she was a very wealthy woman and a generous patron of her hometown.[26] We don't know the source of her family's wealth, but her benefactions to the community would have made her a person of considerable influence. Also existing on a slope nearby are the remains of a theater. In close proximity is a vaulted mausoleum built of large stone blocks and today referred to as the Tomba di Ummidia Quadratilla. It is quite likely the mausoleum of the family, but we do not know if the remains of Ummidia Quadratilla were placed there. Pliny's *Letter* 7.24 suggests that she had spent a good part of her life in Rome. And there has been discovered in Rome a piece of lead pipe bearing the name Ummidia Quadratilla.[27] Although the precise location where the pipe was found is not certain, the discovery seems to be evidence for a home of the Ummidius family in Rome. Like other wealthy Italian families, the Ummidii probably maintained homes in several locations. They depended for income on their agricultural properties, which they visited occasionally, and remained generous to residents of their hometowns, but enjoyed living in Rome, the political and cultural capital.

An inscription found in the theater at Casinum informs us that Ummidia Quadratilla renovated the building in honor of her father.[28] Another inscription found just outside the main entrance to the amphitheater records the name Ummidia Quadratilla Asconia Secunda, daughter of Gaius.[29] The addition of the name Asconia may indicate that Gaius Ummidius Durmius Quadratus was married another time (in addition to the hypothetical Sallustia), to a woman from the Asconius family. Ummidia Quadratilla Asconia Secunda may be the full name of the woman of Pliny's *Letter* 7.24. Or she may be a sister or half-sister of Pliny's Ummidia Quadratilla. Raepsaet-Charlier gives her a separate listing.[30] She might even be the daughter of another Gaius Ummidius Quadratus. Syme suggests, however, that we "let the identity stand" – that is, assume that the woman of this inscription is the woman of Pliny's letter.[31] If her mother was of an Asconius family, it may have been the Asconius family from Patavium, in the same general area of northern Italy from which Pliny hailed.[32] If this is true, the Ummidia Quadratilla of *Letter* 7.24 was distantly related to several prominent Asconii living in the same period as she: the scholar Quintus Asconius Pedanius, Nero's courtier Asconius Labeo, and the politician and epic poet Silius Italicus, whose full name was Tiberius Catius Asconius Silius Italicus.[33]

Since we "meet" Ummidia Quadratilla as a 79-year-old grandmother whom Pliny describes as unusually compact and sturdy, it is difficult to form images of her as a child, a young woman, a sister, a wife, and a mother. We don't know whether she was raised primarily in Casinum or Rome, with a politically ambitious father, or whether, as a child, she traveled to a province where her father was a governor. Her generous donations to Casinum suggest that she was familiar with and fond of that community, and perhaps that she had spent much of her youth there. As a member of a very affluent and locally prominent family, her childhood experiences would have included a luxurious lifestyle, the ministrations of many slaves, and the deference of more humble neighbors for whom she would, as an adult, serve as a patron. We might imagine a similar childhood for Pliny in northern Italy, although his formal education would undoubtedly have been more rigorous and more extensive than Ummidia Quadratilla's. It is noteworthy that both their families instilled in them a commitment to use their wealth and status to provide benefits to their hometowns. (We might contrast the apparent reluctance, reported in *Letter* 5.11, of Pliny's grandfather-in-law to spend money on a community project to honor his deceased son.) We do not know at what stage of her life Ummidia Quadratilla supplied the funds to construct the amphitheater and temple and to repair the theater at Casinum.

Two very important pieces of information about Ummidia Quadratilla's life are unfortunately missing: the identities of her husband(s) and her child(ren). We may assume that she married in her mid to late teens, but we do not know to whom, or how long the marriage lasted, whether it was ended by death or divorce, or whether this marriage was her only one. It is not unreasonable to assume that her family would have chosen for her a husband (or husbands) similar to her father and brothers – that is, someone wealthy, interested in political advancement, and with good family connections. (We might compare the qualifications which Pliny outlines for the prospective bridegrooms of *Letters* 1.14 and 6.26.) Because Pliny mentions a grandson and granddaughter, we know that Ummidia Quadratilla had at least one child, and perhaps more than one, who lived to adulthood. The grandson and granddaughter may, or may not have issued from the same parents. Pliny does not provide the name of the granddaughter ("I scarcely know the granddaughter": *Letter* 7.24.2), but he does tell us that the grandson was one of his protégés, Gaius Ummidius Quadratus. His name creates more confusion about the identity of his family. As already noted, a child received at birth the *nomen gentilicium* of his/her father's family. Thus Minicius Acilianus of *Letter* 1.14 was the son of Minicius Macrinus. (The *cognomen* Acilianus may have been derived from his mother's family *nomen*.) Corellia Hispulla of *Letters* 3.3 and 4.17 was the daughter of Corellius Rufus. (The *cognomen* Hispulla was acquired from her mother.) A son of Ummidia Quadratilla would have received the *nomen* of his father (her husband), but the identity of the father is unknown to us. In turn, the son would have passed on to his son (her grandson) the *nomen* of her husband. A daughter of Ummidia Quadratilla would also have received the *nomen* of her father (Ummidia's husband), but her son (Ummidia's grandson) would have received the *nomen* of *his* father. Why the grandson is identified as a Ummidius is a mystery. Syme posits several solutions.[34]

Ummidia Quadratilla's son may have been the suffect consul who died in office in December of 93 CE. We do not know whether the cause of his death was natural or whether he was one victim of the many executions and assassinations of that year.[35] He would have, at birth, received the name of his unknown father (Ummidia's husband). On the basis of inscriptional evidence, Syme conjectures that Ummidia's husband was a Sertorius; their son would therefore have received the name Sertorius. Raepsaet-Charlier identifies him as Sertorius Severus.[36] However, the *nomen gentilicium* of Ummidia's family may have been appended, and he may have decided to use that name primarily, instead of his father's. He would, however, be polyonymous – that is, "a man with many names" since he would also retain his father's name. Syme comments on "the liberties the aristocracy took with *nomina*, annexing or discarding them. Nobody could stop them."[37] Perhaps Ummidia Quadratilla's husband had died when the son was young, and she had encouraged her son to assume (in Syme's terms, "annex") *her* family name. It is also possible that the son was formally adopted by one of her brothers and formally received the Ummidius name as a result of the adoption (even as our Pliny, though born a Caecilius, assumed the name Plinius after his adoption by his uncle).

If there was an adoption into the Ummidius family, the Gaius Ummidius Quadratus of *Letter* 7.24 would have received that name at birth.[38] If, however, his father had retained the name Sertorius Severus, he would have been named Sertorius Severus at birth, but would have been given or have assumed the *nomen* of his grandmother's family as an addition, and may have preferred to use that one. Syme theorizes, on the basis of inscriptional evidence, that he was governor of the province of Lower Moesia in the early 120s and that his complete name was Gaius Ummidius Quadratus Severus Sertorius.[39] A Sertorius Severus is mentioned in *Letter* 5.1.1 as a co-heir to the estate of Pomponia Galla (who had disinherited her son; see Chapter 4), but we have no solid grounds for connecting him to the family of Ummidia Quadratilla.[40]

Of course, as Syme recognizes, the Gaius Ummidius Quadratus of *Letter* 7.24 could be the son of a daughter of Ummidia Quadratilla. He would have been given the *nomen gentilicium* of his father (perhaps a Sertorius Severus) at birth, but also at some point have acquired the *nomen* of his grandmother's family, and have preferred to use it (and to be polyonymous).

Syme favors the first alternative, that the Gaius Ummidius Quadratus of *Letter* 7.24 was the son of Ummidia Quadratilla's son, and that his name included Sertorius Severus (or Severus Sertorius), although he was commonly known as Ummidius. Whatever the process of his acquisition of the name Ummidius, his preference for that name indicates it was respected among the elite.

Despite the lack of evidence about who his father, mother, and grandfathers were, information provided by Pliny's letters and by inscriptions indicates that the Gaius Ummidius Quadratus of *Letter* 7.24 (Ummidia Quadratilla's grandson) had been well-educated and, with family financial support, had successfully pursued a senatorial career. He was a suffect consul in 118 CE, sharing the office with

Hadrian who had, just months previously, become emperor.[41] The probability that he was governor of Lower Moesia in the early 120s has been previously mentioned. Inscriptional evidence also suggests that he served as a governor of Africa in 133 or 134.[42]

When *Letter* 7.24 was written, however, in 107 CE, Ummidia Quadratilla's grandson was just beginning his career. We learn from the letter that he had married before the age of 24. He was thus born about 83 CE. His marriage was perhaps timed to allow him to benefit from the incentives of the Julian Laws regarding the acceleration of political candidates who were married and had children. The possible identity of his wife will be discussed later. Our focus here is Ummidia Quadratilla.

The first two words of *Letter* 7.24 are her name: Ummidia Quadratilla. The opening sentence continues with the announcement that she has died. A reader could be excused for jumping to the conclusion that the subject of the letter was going to be Ummidia Quadratilla and that Pliny had produced an obituary for her. However, Pliny curiously does not express any personal grief or any sadness that the community had suffered a loss with the passing of this woman. We might contrast this letter with his sorrowful reaction to the grave illness of Fannia in *Letter* 7.19. Nor does Pliny offer words of consolation to family members, as he does, for example, in *Letter* 3.10, addressed to Vestricius Spurinna and Cottia about the death of their son. In fact, the absence of any statements of personal distress or of consolation suggests that the death of Ummidia Quadratilla is not the main subject of the letter. And indeed, it becomes clear as the letter proceeds that the main subject is the deceased woman's grandson, Gaius Ummidius Quadratus. In fact, the letter ends not with a reference to the grandmother, but with a prediction of future greatness for her grandson. He will become as impressive an orator as Cassius was a jurist, that Cassius whose former home, we learn, had become the property of Ummidia Quadratilla (*Letters* 7.24.8 and 9).[43]

Pliny is not a detached reporter. His fondness for the young man is apparent in the phrase "my Quadratus" (*Quadratus meus*) which appears at the end of the letter (*Letter* 7.24.9).[44] The reader of *Letter* 7.24 is informed that Ummidia Quadratilla had entrusted to Pliny supervision of the education of her grandson (*Letter* 7.24.5). In Letter 6.11, moreover, Pliny boasts that Ummidius Quadratus and Fuscus Salinator, whom he describes as young men of the greatest promise and ability as public speakers, and possessing admirable honesty and a healthy strength of character, looked upon him as their guide, mentor, and model.[45] In *Letter* 7.24, as in *Letter* 6.11, Pliny's praise of his protégé serves a function beyond drawing attention to the accomplishments of a young man. The publication of the letters also offers Pliny the opportunity to enhance his own reputation because the reader is reminded that it is Pliny who played a major role in the development of the young man's fine character and skills.

The reader might expect that Ummidia Quadratilla would be given some of the credit for her contributions in raising her grandson, and she is. For the most part, however, Pliny depicts her as having been a potentially bad influence and uses her as a foil, leading the reader to the conclusion that the grandson turned out well *despite* being raised in her household. In Pliny's careful crafting of the tale, the emergence of Ummidius Quadratus into adulthood as an industrious and self-disciplined person can be ascribed largely to his own natural character traits and, of course, to Pliny's mentorship. Ummidia Quadratilla is constructed in *Letter* 7.24 almost as an obstacle to her grandson's moral development – and to Pliny's education of him. The rhetorical design of the letter requires that the flaws of the grandmother who raised Ummidius Quadratus must be disclosed in order to convince readers that he experienced moral challenges in his childhood. Nonetheless, Pliny needed to strike a balance. He could not publish a devastatingly unflattering and thus offensive portrait of the grandmother of a close friend, particularly since the grandmother and friend bore the same name. We must therefore be wary of accepting Pliny's portrait of Ummidia Quadratilla as accurate or complete. He includes only elements that reflect positively on her grandson, even if they reflect negatively on her. Nevertheless the letter offers insights about her activities and about what behavior was expected of elderly Roman women.

Near the beginning of *Letter* 7.24, Pliny reports that Ummidia Quadratilla had died leaving a very honorable will (*honestissimum testamentum*). He immediately explains what he means by "honorable": she had designated her grandchildren as her heirs, leaving two-thirds of her estate to her grandson and one-third to her granddaughter. It was not unusual for a female heir to receive a smaller portion than a male heir. She may have already received part of the family estate as her dowry. There has been discussion in previous chapters about the traditional assumption in Roman society that people would leave their estates primarily to close relatives, and especially to their children. Pliny's comment about Ummidia Quadratilla's will is reminiscent of his remarks about the will of Domitius Tullus, who had made his daughter his heir, left legacies to his grandchildren and a great-granddaughter, and made generous provisions for his wife (*Letter* 8.18). In that letter, Pliny conveys the impression that Domitius Tullus' will caught people by surprise. Because he had apparently encouraged the hopes of fawning *captatores*, his exclusion of them from his will was quite unexpected. And his arrangements were all the more unexpected because they revealed the highest attention to *pietas* – that is, to devotion to his family (*Letter* 8.18.2). In fact, Pliny opens the letter with the comment that the "popular belief is certainly false, that a man's will is a mirror of his character, for Domitius Tullus appeared much better in death than in life."

Pliny does not so blatantly disparage Ummidia Quadratilla's character in his report about her honorable will, but there is an implication that some people (though perhaps not Pliny himself) may have expected her to short-change her grandchildren and enrich folk less worthy of her generosity. Like Domitius Tullus, she had been courted and flattered by people hoping to be rewarded in her will. Pliny describes one occasion when, in a theater, people who were strangers to her tried to win her favor by enthusiastically and wildly expressing their approval of the performances she had funded (*Letter* 7.24.7). She dashed their hopes, however, by leaving them only very small bequests.

Having reported briefly on her death and her will, Pliny immediately turns to a very favorable description of the grandson, Ummidius Quadratus, whom he asserts that he cherishes as a very good friend (*Letter* 7.24.2). Pliny explains that this remarkable young man is well-loved, and not just by people to whom he is related by blood. Is this statement meant to suggest that Ummidius Quadratus' character is so endearing that his grandmother could not help but love him? Perhaps Pliny wants the reader to conclude that Ummidia Quadratilla might have been a less generous and conscientious grandmother had her grandson not possessed a rare combination of virtue and winsomeness. He had, in other words, made her a better person.[46] Towards the end of the letter, Pliny writes of Ummidia Quadratilla that he is delighted by the *pietas* revealed by her will (*Letter* 7.24.8). Again we might recall Pliny's comment about Domitius Tullus's will, that it disclosed an unexpected attention to *pietas*. Pliny does not, in *Letter* 7.24, state explicitly that Ummidia Quadratilla's *pietas* was a surprise, but there is an implication that devotion to family had been inspired in her by her grandson.

Ummidius Quadratus appears in Pliny as a paragon of virtue, someone after whom readers would do well to model themselves. Although conspicuous for his handsomeness as a boy and as a young man, he escaped all the gossip of malicious people (*Letter* 7.24.3). This rare remark about physical appearance is reminiscent of Pliny's comment to Corellia Hispulla in *Letter* 3.3.4, that her son had an exceptionally handsome body. (See Chapter 4.) In that letter, attractive appearance was mentioned as a potential liability for the boy, probably in his early teens, and about to leave his mother's protective custody to attend rhetorical school. Pliny's comment implies that boys, especially handsome boys, were vulnerable to seduction into inappropriate sexual activities. Ummidius Quadratus, however, had apparently avoided all such situations and thus provided no fodder for rumormongers. And yet, unlike Corellia Hispulla's son, whose mother had sheltered him from salacious situations, Ummidius Quadratus had had access to them right in his grandmother's home because, as Pliny remarks, Ummidius Quadratus lived in the home of a pleasure-loving grandmother.[47] Nonetheless, he lived very austerely, though very courteously (or, very obediently; Latin *obsequentissime*: *Letter* 7.24.3). The addition of the word *obsequentissime* gives the impression that Ummidius Quadratus possessed, even at a young age, an innate disdain for frivolous pastimes, but was very courteous in his refusal to engage in them. Pliny draws a clear contrast between the grandson and the grandmother: she was by nature pleasure-loving, he was abstemious (but not censorious). In a sense, their roles had been reversed, with the younger generation providing a model of decency and restraint for the older. Pliny then presents a specific reason why activities in Ummidia Quadratilla's household might have corrupted a boy of lesser moral strength: his grandmother owned a group of pantomime performers and she doted on them more extravagantly than was appropriate for a woman of high rank.

Pantomime was a very popular form of scenic entertainment in imperial Rome.[48] As in modern ballet, the performers conveyed the events of the drama (usually a mythological theme) through gestures and dance movements to the accompaniment of music. Unlike modern ballet, the gestures of the pantomimes were apparently often sexually explicit and designed to titillate spectators. Juvenal carped that women (whom he judged to be more susceptible to impulses than men) became sexually aroused while watching pantomime performances and even became quite inappropriately enamored of pantomime dancers.[49] The second century CE physician Galen reported on a case where an upper-class woman became ill as a result of her infatuation with the dancer Pylades.[50] At the time of the emperor Tiberius, there were complaints that pantomime performers debauched women and caused riots.[51] The performers were mainly slaves and freedmen and therefore among the lowest classes of society. Hence the inappropriateness of women (or men) becoming enamored of them. Many were also foreign-born and thus subject to the Roman prejudice against non-natives. In addition, the risqué nature of some of their performances led people to believe that, even off-stage, the performers were libidinous. It was widely assumed that performers, both male and female, were also prostitutes. These negative associations made them the targets of the suspicion and contempt of Rome's upper classes. The Julian Laws forbade the marriage of senators and their children to women and to the children of women who had engaged in the occupation of acting.[52] The emperor Domitian is reported to have divorced his wife (although they later remarried) because she fell in love with an actor named Paris.[53]

In 15 CE, Tiberius initiated regulations forbidding senators from entering the houses of pantomime performers, and banning performances in any location other than a theater.[54] In 24 CE, the emperor banished pantomime performers from Italy, alleging that the licentiousness of their performances was subversive of public order and private morality.[55] However, the next emperor, Caligula, recalled them at the beginning of his reign in 37 CE.[56] Imperial attitudes toward pantomime actors (and other performers) continued to fluctuate, although popular interest in them never seemed to diminish, and they continued to attract audiences from all classes. When audiences became unruly, emperors instituted measures to maintain civil order. The emperor Domitian forbade actors (apparently not just pantomimes) to appear on stage, although he allowed them to give performances in private homes.[57] His successor, Nerva, lifted these restrictions, but shortly after Trajan became emperor, he, too, imposed restrictions on pantomimes.[58] In praising Trajan's decision, Pliny condemned pantomimes as "improper for this age" – a reference to the age of moral propriety which Trajan had claimed to be ushering in. It is amusing to witness Pliny's careful tap dance in section 46 of the *Panegyricus*. He characterizes Domitian's suppression of pantomimes as an action which the populace endured unhappily, but Trajan's similar restrictions as a measure which they welcomed as beneficial. And, at the same time, he lauds Nerva's reinstatement of pantomimes as a necessary countermeasure to the evil Domitian. Nonetheless, despite Pliny's commendation of Trajan for elevating the moral environment, Trajan lifted his own restrictions within a few years, perhaps bowing to public demand and desiring to curry favor with the Roman populace.[59]

Trajan's reversal indicates how popular pantomimes were, despite the disdain expressed by moralists like Pliny. The restrictions imposed by first Tiberius and then Domitian had opposite effects, the former limiting the viewing of pantomimes to a public theater, where officials could monitor the actors and the crowd, and the latter limiting the viewing to private homes and thus removing potentially arousing material from the public sphere. However, both restrictions suggest that it was not uncommon for wealthy people to hire pantomime dancers to perform at private parties, offering a more salacious kind of entertainment than Pliny provided at his parties. Pliny's choice of dinner entertainment was the reading aloud of a literary work or comedy, or a music concert.[60] He acknowledged, nonetheless, in *Letter* 9.17, that other people might find them boring. In that letter, he chided Julius Genitor – yes, the same Julius Genitor whom he had, in *Letter* 3.3.5, approvingly described to Corellia Hispulla as "a little too stern and unyielding, at least for the licentiousness of our time" – for his complaints about being disgusted by the vulgar entertainers at a dinner party. He recommended that they should tolerate such behavior in order that their preferences also be tolerated. Pliny's comments reveal perhaps a wish not to offend powerful people who were fans of pantomime. Yet, even fans of pantomime would admit that the performances were far from morally uplifting.

Because people associated pantomimes and their performers with immorality and corruption, Ummidia Quadratilla's fondness for them may have made her seem a person less concerned than she should have been about her own reputation and about the proper upbringing of her grandson.[61] Pliny relates, however, that Ummidius Quadratus never watched pantomime performers, either in his grandmother's home or at a theater, nor did she insist that he do so. Pliny uses the Latin verb *exigere*, "to insist" (*Letter* 7.24.4). This is the same verb that he used in *Letters* 7.11.6 and 7.14.1 and 2 to convey the forcefulness of Corellia's demands that Pliny's freedman sell land to her and that Pliny accept the market price for it. Pliny's use of *exigere* in *Letter* 7.24.4 emphasizes two points: that the grandson was virtuous by nature, and that the grandmother possessed at least one good quality, in that she did not force him to adopt her habits. In fact, she acknowledged to Pliny, when she was entrusting to him the supervision of her grandson's education, that during those hours of leisure that, according to Pliny, women have, she was accustomed to relax by playing board games or watching her pantomime performers. However, when she was about to do either, she always instructed her grandson to go and study. Pliny then adds a surprising comment: "She seemed to have done this out of reverence for him as much as love." Again a picture emerges of a self-indulgent and frivolous grandmother who is bemused by, but tolerant of her grandson's austere character.

Pliny does not explain why the care of the grandson, and perhaps also the granddaughter, had fallen to her. Nor can we ascertain whether the grandson and granddaughter were brother and sister. Presumably both parents of Ummidius Quadratus had died, and Ummidia Quadratilla was his closest surviving relative. If his father was, as conjectured, the consul who died in 93 CE, he would have been about ten years old at the time of the death. We know nothing about his mother. If the boy entered Ummidia Quadratilla's home in 93 CE, she would have been about 66 years old. The responsibility of raising a young boy (and perhaps also a young girl) must have required considerable adjustment in her life. Fortunately she enjoyed good health, and the wealth to employ a large household staff, including nannies and teachers to attend to her grandson's needs. She lived a life that lower class women – who formed the vast majority of Roman women – must have envied. Free of the mundane tasks of cooking, cleaning, and child care, she had many idle hours during which she was, by her own admission to Pliny, accustomed to relax by playing board games or watching her pantomime performers. Pliny characterizes women as having idle hours, but only wealthy women would enjoy much leisure. Most women were too occupied with the dreary tasks of family survival to have idle hours.

Elite women had fewer options for leisure activities than men, but for both men and women, playing board games and watching pantomime performances were considered decadent activities. The association of pantomimes and profligacy has been discussed earlier. Board games were denounced because they generally involved gambling. In the *Panegyricus*, Pliny contrasted Trajan's laudable leisure activities, such as hunting, which required strenuous physical exertion[62], with the dissolute activities of previous emperors who squandered their relaxation time on dice games, *stupra* (debauchery), and *luxus* (vulgar self-indulgence). "It is a man's pleasures by which one best judges his dignity (*gravitas*), integrity (*sanctitas*), and self-control (*temperantia*). ... We are betrayed by our leisure" (*Panegyricus* 82.8 and 9). Among moralists, it was a serious charge against a man that he squandered his leisure with unproductive or unedifying activities. Leisure hours were not supposed to be idle hours. Pliny was careful to publicize that his pleasures included recitations, writing poetry, and after-dinner readings of plays. In *Letter* 9.6, he proudly reports that he was delightfully occupied with literary pursuits while other people were enthralled by the publicly sponsored chariot races. "On the days which other men squander on the most idle pursuits, I very gladly fill my leisure with literature." At all other times, he was industriously engaged in work. The Latin word *negotium* can be translated as "work" or "busy-ness." It means an absence (*neg-*) of *otium*, which means "leisure." Men were expected to devote themselves primarily to *negotium*. Pliny assumed that (wealthy) women had much *otium* because they were free (or, in other terms, barred) from the onerous responsibilities of a senator. However, since they received considerably less education than men, they apparently did not occupy themselves with such enriching leisure activities as recitations. Nonetheless, they – even more so than men – were expected to avoid activities that society judged to be decadent. Pliny's chaste wife, Calpurnia, read his literary works and set his poems to music (*Letter* 4.19.2–4). Ummidia Quadratilla clearly did not conform to the convictions of men like Pliny about the appropriate conduct of women.

Of course, Ummidia Quadratilla had grown up in an era quite different from that in which Calpurnia had matured. She was born during the reign of Tiberius and was a young and then middle-aged woman during the reign of Nero, an emperor (54 – 68 CE) with an unabashed love of scenic arts, sensuous entertainments, and wanton pleasures. Pliny portrays her as a product of this period of unrestrained self-indulgence among the Roman elite, and her grandson, in contrast, as a product of the post-Julio-Claudian period, when frugality, modesty, and self-control were advocated by the emperors. The type of abstemious behavior espoused by Thrasea Paetus, the husband of Arria Y, behavior which was denounced by the Neronian court and was ultimately responsible for his death (see Chapter 2), now became the fashion. Vespasian, who emerged as emperor in 69 CE in the violent aftermath of Nero's death was a champion of this new morality or, rather, as its proponents called it, this return to the stern morality of the ancient Romans. In particular, elite Italian families from outside Rome regarded themselves as the conservators of traditional austerity and pristine virtue.[63] According to Tacitus, the change in attitudes among the Roman elite was fostered in part by the arrival into the Senate of men from communities outside of Rome, men who had not been ruined by the luxurious lifestyle that had spoiled the traditional Roman nobility. "New men from the Italian towns and even from the provinces were often admitted into the Senate, and they brought with them their native frugality. Although most had arrived at a wealthy old age through good fortune or hard work, their old mind set remained with them. The most conspicuous advocate of this strict morality was Vespasian himself, with his old-fashioned manner and mode of life."[64]

Pliny was a prime example of a senator who brought to Rome the more conservative values of his small northern community. He wrote proudly of these values in his recommendation of the north Italian Minicius Acilianus as a husband for the daughter of Arulenus Rusticus: "our region of Italy still preserves much of its modesty, frugality, and even old-fashioned rusticity" (*Letter* 1.14.4). Pliny was delighted by the accession to power in 98 CE of Trajan, who promoted a culture of simplicity, industry, and temperance, and, even in his personal life, followed a pattern of austerity that he encouraged for others. As noted in Chapter 3, moreover, Pliny reports that Trajan's wife, Plotina, following his model, remained "modest in her dress, unpretentious in her retinue, and unassuming in her manner of travel" even after he became emperor (*Panegyricus* 83.7). According to Dio, "she conducted herself during Trajan's entire reign in such a manner that she was incurred no reproach."[65]

A woman like Ummidia Quadratilla, as she is defined by Pliny at any rate, seems a striking contrast to Plotina. Of course, Plotina belonged to a younger generation and one which had adopted a more sober lifestyle than that of its predecessors. Yet Ummidia Quadratilla's behavior, again as it is reported by Pliny, was also quite different from that of Serrana Procula, the grandmother of Minicius Acilianus (*Letter* 1.14.6), although the two women may have been about the same age. However, Serrana may have spent most of her life in northern Italy in a family which did not aspire to a place in the politics of Rome, and thus she may have retained the "modesty, frugality, and even old-fashioned rusticity" of that region. Ummidia Quadratilla, although perhaps born in Casinum, may have spent much of her childhood and her years as a wife in Rome where she was influenced by the *mores* of the Julio-Claudian period. In any case, it served Pliny's purpose, in his recommendation of Minicius Acilianus, to focus on the high moral standards of his family. On the other hand, he had reasons to emphasize the distinction between the behaviors of Ummidia Quadratilla and her grandson and perhaps even to exaggerate the differences. By drawing attention to just one aspect of Ummidia Quadratilla's life, her penchant for pantomimes, and reporting that her grandson, in contrast, was impervious to their attraction, Pliny underscores his moral integrity. Her weakness for foolish and dissolute pleasures is a foil to his strength of character. Ummidius Quadratus saw his grandmother's pantomime performers for the first time when he was in his 20s, and then only because the troupe was performing at a public event which, as an aspiring politician, he could not afford to miss. His disinterest on that occasion was a striking contrast to the enthusiastic response of people who were trying to ingratiate themselves with his grandmother (*Letter* 7.24.6 and 7). Pliny's mention of Ummidia Quadratilla's activities also indirectly reminds his reader that, under Trajan's positive influence, Rome was enjoying a revival of the moral standards of its ancestors and that the youngest generation of senators, represented by Ummidius Quadratus, had shown itself to be capable of acting with propriety.

At the end of the letter, where Pliny predicts that Ummidius Quadratus will become as impressive an orator as Cassius was a jurist, we learn that the young man had inherited from his grandmother the former home of Cassius. We do not know whether this was the house in which Ummidia Quadratilla raised her grandson. If so, underlying the glorification of the grandson is more criticism of Ummidia Quadratilla even though she is not mentioned. In the final sentence of the letter, Pliny expresses confidence that Ummidius Quadratus will be a fitting occupant of the house and will restore its ancient dignity, renown, and glory (*Letter* 7.24.9). Pliny's words imply that the house had lost its dignity when Ummidia Quadratilla occupied it and been entertained there by pantomimes and board games. Of course, his prediction of success as an orator for Ummidius Quadratus also brings favorable attention to him since he had been asked by the grandmother to supervise the young man's studies.

Thus Pliny's portrait of Ummidia Quadratilla is crafted to shine a very positive light upon her grandson and, by extension, the regime of Trajan. It was not Pliny's intent to produce a eulogy for her and, by using her as a foil for her grandson, he has left a portrait of an idle, self-indulgent woman with decadent tastes, and one whose commitment to her family seems to have been doubted by those who expected her to leave her wealth to strangers. Nonetheless, readers of the letter can distinguish some of Ummidia Quadratilla's admirable qualities. Her willingness to assume, at an elderly age, the role of a surrogate mother and take in and raise her orphaned grandson (and possibly granddaughter also) was evidence of *pietas*. And perhaps Ummidia Quadratilla should be credited with remarkable tolerance if the grandson was as priggish as a child as Pliny makes him seem. Pliny's portrait of Ummidius Quadratus is entirely favorable, but it is possible that he and his grandmother were so different in character that there were tensions between them, tensions which led some people to suspect that she would bequeath much of her estate to non-family.

However, Ummidia Quadratilla did "the right thing," and not just in her will. In some respects, she displayed the same attentive care as a surrogate mother as Pliny attributes to Corellia Hispulla, the mother in *Letter* 3.3. When she informed Pliny that, during hours of leisure, she was accustomed to relax by playing board games or watching her pantomime performers, her statement was not a confession of weakness, but rather an assurance that she had insisted that her grandson occupy himself with his studies. Both Ummidia Quadratilla and Corellia Hispulla were concerned about the moral development of the children in their care and tried to shelter them from corrupting influences. Both were concerned, moreover, that the children receive excellent educations. And certainly Ummidia Quadratilla's solicitation of Pliny to serve as her grandson's mentor would be considered, by Pliny at least, as an indication of very sound judgment. And she may also have helped finance her grandson's political career. Of course, as heir to his father's estate and perhaps also his mother's, he probably had a considerable estate of his own.

Perhaps Pliny's comment, at the beginning of the letter, about her remarkable good health, is intended to assure readers that she had not suffered the ravages of a self-indulgent lifestyle despite appearing to have frittered away her time on morally questionable activities. Or perhaps Pliny was subtly informing his reader that she had, in fact, led a life which was far from idle and unprofitable. David Sick has developed an intriguing and plausible theory that Ummidia Quadratilla's interest in pantomimes was not an idle past time, but rather a lucrative business venture.[66] Evidence from inscriptions suggests that the Ummidius family of Casinum, which is located about halfway between Rome and Naples, had long been involved in the for-profit ownership and promotion of pantomimes. For example, Actius Anicetus was a very popular pantomimist whose troupe performed throughout Campania (which includes the Bay of Naples area). He is known to us from graffiti discovered in Pompeii and Herculaneum (two of the cities buried by the 79 CE eruption of Mount Vesuvius in which the Elder Pliny perished).[67] There has also been discovered at Pozzuoli (ancient Puteoli), another town in the Bay of Naples region, an inscription which records a pantomimist named Gaius Ummidius Actius Anicetus.[68] If, as seems likely, this is the same man as the pantomimist in the Pompeii graffiti, the addition of Ummidius to his name suggests that he had once been a slave of the Ummidius family, but then freed. (Recall that, upon manumission, freed slaves received the family name of their former owners.)[69]Another inscription, discovered at Ostia Antica (the ancient port of Rome), records the commemoration of a Ummidia Quadratilla by a man named Dionysius.[70] This is a Greek name and, because it lacks a Roman family name, suggests that the man was a slave. Dionysius was not an uncommon name for an actor. The Ummidia Quadratilla who is commemorated may well be the pantomime owner of *Letter* 7.24. Several other inscriptions referred to by Sick, as well as the inscription already mentioned about the renovation of the theater at Casinum, support his conjectures about the ownership of acting companies (and the slave actors) by the Ummidius family.

The involvement of the Ummidius family, and of Ummidia Quadratilla in particular, in maintaining troupes of performers could well be a business venture. In the Roman world, troupes were maintained not just, or even primarily, for private amusement. They were hired out to towns or individuals who wanted to provide shows. The owner received a rental fee, from part of which he would pay those members of the troupe who were freedpersons. Members of the troupe who were slaves probably did not receive any pay. Thus ownership of the troupe was an income-producing investment. We learn, for example, from one of Cicero's speeches (*Pro Quinto Roscio Comoedo*) about two men, Roscius and Fannius, who had purchased a slave with the intention of training him to act, and then sharing the income he made. In *Letter* 7.24.4, Pliny reports that Ummidius Quadratus never watched his grandmother's pantomimes, either in the theater or at home. The inclusion of the phrase "in the theater" implies that Ummidia Quadratilla's pantomimes performed in public to large audiences – that is, that they were rented out. This supposition is reinforced by the information that the grandson first saw her freedman perform at the Sacerdotal Games, a public event (*Letter* 7.24.6). The magistrate (in the imperial period, usually a praetor) who was responsible for securing the entertainments for a public event would negotiate rental contracts with the owners of the troupes of performers (such as actors, dancers, musicians, chariot-drivers, and gladiators).[71]

It was not just the rental fee that was a source of income to the owner of a troupe. The performers themselves, if they were slaves, were valuable property. The selling price of a slave increased substantially if s/he were trained in a trade or skill. Roscius and Fannius were depending on this when they purchased their slave. Unfortunately, their plans went awry when the slave was murdered. In the court case to determine the compensation settlement from the murderer, their lawyer, Cicero, argued that there was a substantial difference between the sale price of an untrained *vs* trained slave. Plutarch tells us that the Elder Cato added to his income by lending money to his slaves, money with which they, in turn, purchased other slaves.[72] They trained these slaves, sold them at a nice profit, and then repaid the crafty Cato who had undoubtedly charged them a very high interest rate on the loan. The economic success of Cato's and his slaves' ventures depended on the fact that the price of a trained slave was much more than the price of an untrained one. Another way an owner might profit would be to offer to manumit a slave provided that the slave paid a purchase price. If the owner had trained the slave, s/he could demand a higher purchase price than s/he had paid initially. The Elder Pliny reports that some pantomimists paid more than 700,000 sesterces to purchase their freedom.[73] Of course, manumitting a trained performer meant a loss to the owner of the income which his/her performances brought in, but not a total loss. Freedpersons were expected to work, without charge, for their patrons (former owners) several days each year.[74] On those days, a patron would presumably retain the payment for a freed actor's performance.

Sick's theory invites us to look at Ummidia Quadratilla from a perspective quite different from the one which Pliny employs. Her ownership of a troupe of pantomime performers may be evidence not that she was a dissolute person, but rather that she was a clever businesswoman. (We do not know if she had a guardian. Perhaps as an elderly, but hale and hearty woman she still conferred with a guardian about her investments.) If she was indeed a skillful investor, we might compare her with Corellia (*Letters* 7.11 and 14) who successfully manipulated Pliny into selling her a nice piece of property at a nice price. Of course, Corellia had purchased real estate, the most venerable type of investment for the senatorial class, whereas Ummidia Quadratilla had purchased purveyors of pleasure to the public. As Sick observes: "(O)wning a company of performing slaves is a distinction Ummidia Quadratilla shares with one of the most decadent characters of Roman literature – Trimalchio."[75] Perhaps she was utilizing an investment strategy which modern financial advisors give to clients: invest in some activity that interests you personally. Or perhaps she was continuing a family tradition. Whatever motivation she may have had, this type of investment, though less estimable than real estate, would have nonetheless resulted in financial profits and perhaps also social influence. Members of the Roman elite harbored an ambivalence about public entertainments. They knew that they were popular and that aspiring politicians could therefore gain favor with the masses by producing them. Even the emperor, or perhaps especially the emperor, needed to provide shows in arenas and theaters in order to keep the masses content. Recall that Trajan, that champion of moral revival, had placed restrictions on actors at the beginning of his reign, but soon lifted them, perhaps fearing the resentment of the populace. Nevertheless, some members of the elite believed that they should not be too closely associated with spectacles they criticized as vulgar and degrading. It is possible that, because of the stigma attached to public entertainments and entertainers, men of senatorial rank avoided investing in them, and thus left investment opportunities open to women and wealthy freedmen like Trimalchio. And Ummidia Quadratilla may not have been the only wealthy woman to take advantage of these opportunities. Sick provides names of other women who did so.[76] It is amusing to consider that Ummidia Quadratilla's grandson, so disapproving of pantomimes, inherited an estate which may have been enriched by investment in pantomimes. In any case, however much elite men may have voiced disapproval of the spectacles, they still needed to offer them to the masses and they relied on the owners of troupes to supply them with performers and equipment. For a shrewd owner, even a woman, there might therefore be social and political profit to be gained from the competent provision of entertainers. The business of supplying entertainers undoubtedly enabled troupe owners to do favors for – and to request favors from – men of the highest ranks.

Ummidia Quadratilla's family made friends in high places, perhaps even marrying into imperial families. Pliny informs us in *Letter* 7.24.3 that her grandson, Gaius Ummidius Quadratus (Severus Sertorius), had married at the age of 23, and would have become a father if god had so granted it. I speculated in Chapter 3 that the statement might mean that the marriage had not produced a child and had ended, which would imply a divorce or the death of the wife. Syme[77] has conjectured, however, that Ummidius Quadratus had a wife (was she a second wife?) who was a daughter of Marcus Annius Verus who had been consul in 97 CE (and served as consul twice more). If this conjecture is correct, the name of this wife/ daughter would have been Annia. And her brother would have been the documented Marcus Annius Verus who married Domitia Lucilla the Younger, daughter of the Domitia Lucilla the Elder about whom Pliny writes in *Letter* 8.18 (and who is discussed in Chapter 6).[78] (See Genealogy Chart 5.) This conjecture would make Ummidia Quadratilla a distant relative by marriage of Domitius Tullus who, though apparently otherwise loathsome, also wrote a good will. (See Chapter 3.) Domitia Lucilla the Younger and Marcus Annius Verus had at least two children, a daughter, Annia Cornificia Faustina, and a son, known to us as Marcus Aurelius, who was emperor 161–80 CE. Although Pliny reports in *Letter* 7.24.3 that Ummidia Quadratilla's grandson had not yet produced children, Syme also proposes that Ummidia Quadratilla's grandson and his conjectured wife, Annia, eventually had a son, named Ummidius Quadratus Annianus Verus. He further proposes that this Ummidius Quadratus Annianus Verus and Annia Cornificia Faustina, who would have been first cousins if his hypothesis is correct, married. And, if this were the case, Ummidia Quadratilla's great-grandson would thus have been the brother-in-law of the emperor Marcus Aurelius. Looking even beyond her great-grandson, Syme conjectures that her great-great-grandson was *consul ordinarius* of 167 CE, her great-great-great grandson was involved in a conspiracy against Commodus (emperor 180–192 CE, and Marcus Aurelius' son), and a few generations later, one of Ummidia Quadratilla's descendants married Elagabalus (emperor 218–22). Syme speculates that the last identifiable descendant of Ummidia Quadratilla was Pomponia Ummidia, wife of a consul in 270 CE.

Returning to Ummidia Quadratilla's grandson, we suspect that he was a member of the emperor Hadrian's inner circle of friends. His grandmother's care and influence had served him well. He was a suffect consul in 118 CE, sharing the office with Hadrian who had, just months previously, become emperor. However, he incurred the anger of Hadrian at some time in the years between 135 and 138 CE.[79] We don't know if he survived Hadrian or was forced to commit suicide, as was Julius Servianus, the brother-in-law of Hadrian and the father-in-law of that Pedanius Fuscus who is mentioned in *Letter* 6.11 as, like Ummidius Quadratus, having had Pliny as a mentor.[80]

Aunts – Calpurnia Hispulla

Like Ummidius Quadratus, Pliny's third wife, Calpurnia, was raised in the household of a grandparent. The death of her father brought her to the home of her paternal grandfather and *paterfamilias*, Lucius Calpurnius Fabatus, in Pliny's hometown of Comum. The woman who assumed the role of her surrogate mother was her paternal aunt, Calpurnia Hispulla. We know very little about Calpurnia Hispulla. Her father was the above-mentioned Calpurnius Fabatus. We do not know who her mother was although, given that the *cognomen* Hispulla was attached to Calpurnia's name, the mother may have been a Hispulla. And, as discussed in Chapter 3, she may have been related to the Hispulla who was the wife of Corellius Rufus, Pliny's mentor (*Letter* 1.12.9). As noted in Chapter 3, Calpurnia Hispulla's father, Calpurnius Fabatus, had not risen to senatorial rank in Roman politics. Nonetheless, as the daughter of a wealthy family located in a rural north Italian town, Calpurnia Hispulla would have been raised in a grand style enjoyed by few other families in her community. We do not know what manner of formal education was provided to her, but she would have been aware that she was a member of the community's gentry. She had at least one brother, who had married and produced a daughter before his death. There is no mention in Pliny that she had other siblings. Calpurnius Fabatus' longing for a new descendant, as revealed in *Letter* 8.10, suggests that he had (remaining) only one daughter, now past childbearing years, and one granddaughter (Pliny's third wife). We do not know if Calpurnia Hispulla had ever married, although it seems quite likely that she had because it would have been very unusual for a Roman woman not to marry. Nor do we know whether she had children. Again, her father's longing for descendants suggests that, if she had had children, they were deceased. Since it seems from Pliny's letters that Calpurnia Hispulla had raised her niece in the household of the *paterfamilias* Calpurnius Fabatus, perhaps she had been married, but lost her husband either to death or divorce, and returned to her father's home to live.

From a comment in *Letter* 4.19.7, we may surmise that Calpurnia Hispulla was about the same age as Pliny, who was in his early to mid-40s at the time that *Letter* 4.19 was written. Perhaps she was a bit older, since his description of her behavior is like that of a doting older sister. He notes that she had been accustomed to guide and praise him from the time that he was a boy. Because Pliny and Calpurnia Hispulla had been close friends since childhood, it seems likely that Pliny was also a friend of her brother, who became the father of Pliny's third wife. The friendship between Pliny and Calpurnia Hispulla may have arisen simply because their wealthy families would, in a small community, be socially linked. We might compare the friendship of Pliny's mother and uncle with the father of Romatius Firmus (*Letter* 1.19.1). However, Pliny also records in *Letter* 4.19.7 that Calpurnia Hispulla revered his mother as if she were her own mother (*parentis loco*). Pliny's comment does not, unfortunately tell us specifically that Plinia had taken Calpurnia Hispulla under her maternal wing after her own (Calpurnia's) mother had died, but that seems a reasonable interpretation of the comment. Plinia may have undertaken this task because she was a friend not only of the Calpurnius family of Comum, but also of the Corellius family. We learn in *Letter* 7.11.4 that Plinia and Corellia (the sister of Pliny's mentor, Corellius Rufus) were very good friends. Corellia's sister-in-law was Hispulla. The mother of Calpurnia Hispulla may also have been a Hispulla, and thus Plinia, in showing a concern for Calpurnia Hispulla, may have been fulfilling the obligations of friendship with two families. (See Genealogy Charts 3 and 4.)

When her brother died, Calpurnia Hispulla took over the raising of his daughter, Calpurnia. We do not know for certain whether the girl's mother had died. When her father died, the girl may have been taken from her mother because legally she belonged in the custody of her *paterfamilias*, who was her grandfather, Calpurnius Fabatus. In his home, the duties of a surrogate mother fell to the paternal aunt, Calpurnia Hispulla. The orphaned girl apparently developed strong ties of affection with her agnate family. In *Letter* 4.1.1, in which Pliny announces that he and his young wife are returning to Comum for a visit, he reveals that Calpurnia is as eager to see again her grandfather and aunt as they are to see her. And in *Letter* 10.120, we learn that Calpurnia hastened home from far-off Bithynia to comfort her aunt on the death of the *paterfamilias*. According to

Pliny, the aunt had done an excellent job of raising her niece, and training her to be his wife. *Letter* 4.19 is both a thank you note, expressing gratitude to Calpurnia Hispulla for arranging the marriage between Pliny and her niece, and a progress report, relating how well the young Calpurnia was adjusting to her role as wife. Pliny's report confirms that Calpurnia Hispulla's judgment has been excellent and that therefore the match has been very successful. And, as discussed in the Chapter 3, the publication of the letter was an additional gift of gratitude because it publicized and immortalized Calpurnia Hispulla's wisdom and devotion to her family. Although most of the letter is occupied by Pliny's account of the young Calpurnia's virtues, in the opening and closing sections, Pliny compliments Calpurnia Hispulla on her admirable contributions to the development of her niece's character. Pliny describes Calpurnia Hispulla as a model of family devotion (*pietas*) who loved and was loved by her brother, who loved his daughter as if her own daughter, and who has shown toward her the affection not just of an aunt, but even of her deceased father. She will therefore be delighted, he adds, to learn that the young Calpurnia has turned out to be worthy of her father, her aunt, and her grandfather (*Letter* 4.19.1). The aunt has produced a young woman who will carry on the moral traditions of the family.

Pliny attributes his wife's exemplary behavior to the fact that she was trained by Calpurnia Hispulla and guided by her teaching. He writes that, while living in the same household, *contubernium*,[81] as her aunt, Calpurnia saw only what was pure and honorable (*Letter* 4.19.6). Like Corellia Hispulla (to whom she may have been related by marriage) and Ummidia Quadratilla, both of whom also raised children *in contubernio*, Calpurnia Hispulla had focused on the child's moral education and on shielding the child from what might corrupt. Also like a mother, she had undertaken to arrange a marriage for the child entrusted to her. Pliny expresses his gratitude to her for choosing Calpurnia for him, and him for Calpurnia, and for preparing Calpurnia to love him (*Letter* 4.19.6–8). The ties of old friendship were strong for Pliny. As a wealthy and politically successful widower, he must have been considered a "good catch" to elite families in Rome, but when he was seeking a new wife, he returned to his hometown and a trusted childhood friend for a "match." And Calpurnia Hispulla did not disappoint him.

Pliny chose to publish another of his letters to Calpurnia Hispulla and again bring to public notice her willingness to act as a mother to her orphaned niece. In *Letter* 8.11, he announces to her the sad news that the young Calpurnia had suffered a miscarriage. He begins the letter with the comment "your affection for your brother's daughter is more gentle than even a mother's tenderness." Pliny is certain that she will respond to the news with anxiety about Calpurnia's health and he therefore immediately assures her that Calpurnia is out of danger and recovering well. Nonetheless, even to Calpurnia Hispulla he feels that he must explain that the miscarriage was not the fault of Calpurnia, but rather that it could be attributed to her age and inexperience. He acknowledges that Calpurnia Hispulla's loss of her beloved brother made her hope for the consolation that the arrival of his grandson or granddaughter would bring, and he assures her that the fulfillment of this hope has only been delayed, not denied. Pliny ends the letter with a request that she explain to her father (the young Calpurnia's grandfather) that the miscarriage was an accident. The careful wording of the previous letter (*Letter* 8.10), addressed to Calpurnius Fabatus, reveals that Pliny was anticipating that he would be angry at both him and Calpurnia and would accuse them of denying him an heir. (See Chapter 3.) His lack of sympathy may have strained relations between him and his granddaughter and grandson-in-law. In *Letter* 8.11, Pliny turns to his old trusted friend Calpurnia Hispulla to smooth the situation and restore peace in the family.

Pliny assigned to Calpurnia Hispulla the task of mollifying her father's distress at the loss of a child he surely hoped would be a replacement for his deceased son and an heir to carry on family traditions. He may even have hoped that the child would be given his name, Calpurnius, as well as Pliny's name. One wonders what distress Calpurnia Hispulla might have felt, since she had apparently failed to provide him with an heir. He seems to have been a man quick to place blame and not hesitant to express it (*Letters* 6.12 and 7.11). Did he often remind his daughter that she had not given him an heir? Perhaps her own heartache was exacerbated by the news of the young Calpurnia's miscarriage. We can only imagine what her life was like as an unmarried woman in the household of her crotchety father. Materially, she enjoyed the comforts of the life of the gentry. However, it is reasonable to assume that the departure from Comum of her niece, upon her marriage to Pliny, was a sorrowful event for the woman who had raised her as her own daughter and become accustomed to her company. She probably cherished the visits which her niece made, but Pliny does not state this specifically. One such visit is announced in *Letter* 4.1, where Pliny writes to Calpurnius Fabatus that he and his wife "hope to find you and your daughter hale and hearty" (*Letter* 4.1.7). In *Letter* 5.14.8, Pliny informs his addressee that he was visiting his wife's grandfather and aunt (as well as inspecting his real estate holdings in that area).

When Pliny and Calpurnia were in Bithynia, they received word that her grandfather had died. Calpurnia bravely undertook the grueling journey back to Italy in order to be with her aunt at this time of bereavement. Her wish to reach her aunt as quickly as possible was the reason why Pliny had violated official rules by equipping her with a travel pass to facilitate her journey without advance authorization from the emperor. (See Chapter 3.) He wrote *Letter* 10.120 to report the violation to Trajan, ask for the emperor's indulgence, and explain that its cause was a matter of *pietas*, family devotion. In his response (*Letter* 10.121), Trajan assures Pliny that he has acted correctly and that it was fitting for his wife to increase the kindness of her visit to her aunt by arriving speedily. The young Calpurnia's desire to undertake the journey, without her husband, is evidence of a deep affection between her and the aunt who had loved her like a mother.

The two letters which Pliny addresses to Calpurnia Hispulla also offer a glimpse into the relationship between these two, which in turn might instruct us about the possibility of comfortable friendships between men and women in the Roman world. We can conjecture that Pliny and Calpurnia Hispulla shared many childhood experiences and developed a strong trust in one another. As they approached their teen years, they set out on quite different paths. Pliny left Comum to advance his rhetorical training and then embark on a public career in Rome. Calpurnia Hispulla probably married at a young age and either remained in Comum or returned there when her marriage ended. Her life was much more circumscribed than his. Nonetheless, during the many years that they were separated in distance and activities, they seem to have retained the warmth and trust that they had enjoyed as children.

Mothers-in-law: Pompeia Celerina

In *Letter* 1.4, one of the earliest letters in Pliny's published collection, he writes to a woman named Pompeia Celerina, whom he identifies as his mother-in-law (*socrus*). Pompeia Celerina's father may have been Lucius Pompeius Vopiscus Arruntius Catellius Celer (a very polyonymous man!) who was suffect consul around 77 CE and a governor of Lusitania.[82] We know nothing about her childhood, although we can surmise that she was raised in a wealthy senatorial family which owned property in Etruria and Umbria, and undoubtedly elsewhere as well. Like most of the women whom we meet in Pliny's letters, she enjoyed a life of privilege. We do not know whether she accompanied her father to his position in Lusitania. Her age is difficult to estimate. We are accustomed today to a situation where husbands and wives are about the same age, and therefore mothers-in-law are about twice the age of their sons-in-law. In the ancient Roman world, however, a husband might well be twice the age of his wife, and therefore about the same age as his mother-in-law. Thus Pompeia Celerina may have been about the same age as her son-in-law, Pliny. (Consider that Pliny's aunt-in-law, Calpurnia Hispulla, was probably about the same age as he.) However, if Pliny married her daughter when he was in his early 20s, she may have been two decades older than he.

During her lifetime, Pompeia Celerina married at least twice. From *Letter* 9.13.13 we learn that, in 97 CE, she was married to a man of senatorial rank named (Quintus Fulvius Gillo) Bittius Proculus who was a prefect of the treasury of Saturn in the year prior to Pliny's appointment there, was suffect consul in 97 or 98 CE, and served as proconsul of Asia at some time after 99 CE. We do not know if Pompeia Celerina accompanied him to that assignment. In *Letter* 9.13.4, in which Pliny refers to events which took place in late 96 and early 97 CE, he writes that he had at that time recently lost his wife. At 9.13.13, he identifies Bittius Proculus as the stepfather of his deceased wife. We thus learn that the father of Pliny's anonymous wife must have been a previous husband of Pompeia Celerina. We do not know his identity or whether the marriage was ended by death or divorce. Raepsaet-Charlier speculates that he was Lucius Venuleius Montanus Apronianus, who was consul in 92 CE.[83] If this speculation is correct, the name of Pliny's wife may have been Venuleia. Raepsaet-Charlier further conjectures that Pompeia Celerina and Venuleius may also have had a son, Lucius Venuleius Apronianus Octavius Priscus, who was consul in 123 CE. If this is correct, then Pliny also had a brother-in-law, although he never mentions him.

The issue of how many women Pliny married has been discussed in Chapter 3. For reasons stated there, I agree with Sherwin-White that Pliny married three times (Calpurnia being his last wife), and that the daughter of Pompeia Celerina was his second wife. We do not know how long he and "Venuleia" were married. In *Letter* 1.18, addressed to Suetonius Tranquillus, the biographer of the emperors[84], he recounts that he once had a dream that his mother-in-law came to him on bended knee and begged him not to take on a case which was going to be heard in the Centumviral Court.[85] Pliny does not tell his reader explicitly why he imagined his mother-in-law might have made such a request, but it seems that his opponents in the case were friends of the emperor, whereas he, by his own admission, was at the time "still a young man" (*adulescentulus; adulescentulus* is the diminutive of *adulescens*). Perhaps fear of embarrassing himself by a bad performance, and anxiety about offending powerful men had caused him to have such a dream. As noted earlier, the term *adulescens* might denote a man in his early 20s and at the beginning of his career – or in his early 40s.[86] Pliny relates, however, that his defense of the accused was successful, bringing him to the attention of others and opening doors for him (*Letter* 1.18.4). This comment implies that he was, at the time of the dream, just starting to establish a reputation as a speaker. If this is true, and if the mother-in-law about whom he dreamed was Pompeia Celerina, then he had married her daughter when he was in his early or mid-20s, and the marriage had endured until his wife's death in 96 or 97 CE (when Pliny was about 35 years old). And yet, if this was his second marriage, then he had been married previously and briefly, at an even younger age. We have no idea who the first bride or her parents may have been, or whether the marriage was ended by death or divorce. It is possible that Pliny is referring in *Letter* 1.18 to his first mother-in-law and in *Letter* 1.4 to his second mother-in-law, Pompeia Celerina. Most scholars, however, believe that all the references in his letters to a mother-in-law are to Pompeia Celerina.[87] As already noted, the mother of his third wife, Calpurnia, is presumed to have died before the marriage.

Mother-in-law jokes have been popular fodder for comic writers in our own period, but the topos of the meddlesome mother-in-law extends back to antiquity. Indeed, the Latin playwright Terence, who lived from about 190 to 158 BCE, produced a comedy titled *The Mother-in-Law* (*Hecyra*). Earlier in this chapter, reference was made to the story of the philosopher Favorinus and his visit to the home of a friend whose wife had just given birth. The friend's mother-in-law had intervened when he was recommending breastfeeding and had insisted that her exhausted daughter be allowed to rest. Favorinus had resented what he perceived to be exasperating interference on her part.[88] However, some readers, especially women readers, would consider the mother's protection of her daughter and grandchild to be very appropriate. In contrast to negative literary portrayals, Pliny's relationship with his (second) mother-in-law was a good one, and continued after her daughter's death and even after his marriage to Calpurnia. Nor was his situation unique. Recall that Antonia and Turia went to live with their mothers-in-law after the death (Antonia) or exile (Turia) of their husbands. In Pliny's published correspondence, letters either addressed to or containing references to his former mother-in-law appear from Books 1 to 10, a testament to the enduring nature of their friendship. Since it was Pliny who selected the letters that were published, the question arises about his motives. Why was it so important to him that their close association be publicly recognized? Since the knowledge we have about Pompeia Celerina's family is both conjectural and scant, we cannot determine how important she and her relatives may have been to Pliny's political ambitions. Based on the information which Pliny provides about her real estate holdings, her family was at least as wealthy as his. The wealth of a bride's family was an important consideration because in-laws were expected to help finance a man's political career. Their ability and willingness to do so would be an issue for discussion in arrangements for a marriage. In *Letter* 1.14.7, for example, Pliny informs his addressee, Junius Mauricus, that Minicius Acilianus, the man he is recommending as a husband for Junia, has already held the positions of quaestor, tribune, and praetor, and that Junius Mauricus has therefore been released from the need to campaign for him. (See Chapter 2.) His statement is meant to assure Junius Mauricus that he will not be required to contribute large sums of money to the advancement of an in-law's career.

Letter 1.4 is addressed to Pompeia Celerina and, in it, Pliny thanks her for allowing him to stay at four of her villas, located at or near the towns of Ocriculum, Narnia, Carsulae, and Perusia. (Her ownership of these four villas is but one indication that she was a very wealthy woman.) The first three were located in Umbria, along the Via Flaminia, the great Roman road which led northeast from Rome to the Adriatic coast. Travelers heading to the Po Valley, and towns like Comum (Pliny's hometown), would take the Via Flaminia. However, the fourth villa was at Perusia (modern Perugia) which was in Etruria and to the west of the Via Flaminia. Pliny's itinerary suggests that he had been traveling to the properties at Tifernum Tiberinum in Etruria which he had presumably inherited from his uncle/adoptive father. Several of his letters indicate that he had also inherited his uncle's role as patron in the area of the estates (*Letters* 3.4.2, 4.1.3, and 10.8.1). The purpose of the journey he outlines in *Letter* 1.4 may have been to inspect the properties at Tifernum Tiberinum and make sure that they were being managed well. A landowner concerned about the profitability of his/her estates and a conscientious community patron would often be on the road, visiting his/her property. In Chapter 3, there was comment on Pliny's activities during sojourns in Comum. In *Letter* 3.19, he mulls over the purchase of land which adjoins his Tifernum Tiberinum estate. One advantage of such an acquisition, he writes, is that he could inspect two properties in one trip (*Letter* 3.19.2). He means that he could cut down on some of the time and effort of traveling. Even for the wealthiest people, travel could be grueling, as noted in Chapter 3. And yet, Pliny admits, there is a great deal of pleasure in traveling between estates and experiencing a change of climate and location (*Letter* 3.19.4).

With respect to *Letter* 1.4, it is quite possible that Pliny was planning to journey on to his hometown of Comum after his visit at Tifernum Tiberinum. This would be the same itinerary that he revealed to his grandfather-in-law in *Letter* 4.1. It was common for elite folk to stay at the villas of friends and family when they were traveling, rather than at inns, which catered to a lower class of traveler and offered, as we learn from Horace's *Satire* 1.5, rough accommodation. The primary reason for possessing rural properties was, of course, to garner income from the agricultural production or from rental fees. However, the properties often had on them a fine residence to accommodate the owner when s/he came on inspection visits.[89] By allowing friends to use the residences when traveling – that is, by doing them a "favor" – the elite built up that all-important social capital.

The residences had staff who kept them ready for use and were prepared to cater to visitors. (Among the advantages outlined by Pliny in *Letter* 3.19 regarding his purchase of adjacent property was that he would need to maintain only one residence in the area and invest in only one set of slaves and equipment.) Pompeia Celerina had sent a brief written message to the staffs of her villas, alerting them that Pliny had her approval to stay at them. Pliny's remark at *Letter* 1.4.1, that her brief letter to the staff was *vetus* – that is, "old" or perhaps "previous" – may imply that she had once written a message that he was welcome on any occasion and that therefore he did not require a new letter for each visit. If this is true, it seems that Pompeia Celerina placed great trust in him. His next comment, that he feels that her villas are his own, adds to an image of a very comfortable relationship with his mother-in-law. The initial writing of the letter, and its subsequent publication, were intended to show Pliny's gratitude to his mother-in-law by bringing attention to her generosity. We should keep in mind, however, that the publication was also intended to highlight Pliny's ability to build such trust and deserve such generosity.

Nothing in *Letter* 1.4 informs us unequivocally whether or not Pompeia Celerina's daughter (Pliny's second wife) was alive when the letter was written. Pliny uses the plurals "our" and "us" several times – for example, "you will enjoy our properties" (*Letter* 1.4.3) – which may mean that the daughter was still alive. However, it was not unusual for Latin authors to use the plural when referring only to themselves. If the daughter/wife were now deceased, Pliny's letter to Pompeia Celerina may have been intended to keep the relationship strong (and to indicate to readers that it remained strong) despite the formal termination of the family tie. Pliny would not have been the first person to maintain a bond of affection with a former in-law. Cicero, for example, described the relationship between Publius Sestius and his wife's father, Gaius Albinus. "The death of his daughter removed the title of father-in-law from Albinus, but did not remove the affection and good-will of this connection. Still today he loves Sestius."[90] In this case, there were two children, who would have remained, after their mother's death, with their father, Sestius, their closest agnate. Albinus, the maternal grandfather, may have remained on good terms with Sestius in order to see his grandchildren. Pliny did not have any children and thus his good relationship with Pompeia Celerina was not dependent on her wanting to preserve a bond with her daughter's children. However, we do not know if Pompeia Celerina had other children (and grand-children). She is another example of a person whose adult child had predeceased her. As noted earlier, Raepsaet-Charlier conjectures that Pompeia Celerina and Venuleius may have had, in addition to a daughter, a son (Lucius Venuleius

Apronianus Octavius Priscus) who was consul in 123 CE. This remains conjecture. If Pompeia Celerina had no other children, perhaps she was interested in maintaining contact with Pliny because she still regarded him as "family." If, as seems likely, Pliny's marriage to Pompeia Celerina's daughter had endured for more than ten years, he and his mother-in-law may have developed a warm relationship. And since Pliny's own mother seems to have died when he was a young man, perhaps he looked on Pompeia Celerina as a surrogate mother.

In his thank-you note to Pompeia Celerina, which is both courteous and cordial, Pliny compliments her on the many amenities of her villas and particularly on the attentiveness of her servants. He claims that they treat him more solicitously than do his own servants. He then encourages Pompeia Celerina to visit his villas so that she may "enjoy our properties" and so that his own servants, who treat him negligently, may finally bestir themselves. Pliny then ponders the phenomenon that servants lose their fear of kindly owners because they grow used to them, but are roused to action by new visitors. They strive, he says, to win the approval of their owners through their service to the owners' guests rather than to the owners themselves.

The tone of the comment is light-hearted and suggests an easy familiarity between the two. It is not clear, however, what message Pliny intends to convey, first, to Pompeia Celerina, and then to his readers, by his comments on the attentiveness of her servants and on the propensity of servants to cater with more care to guests than to owners. Perhaps she had complained to him about the slackness of her slaves, and he wrote to reassure her that they had treated him very well. Or perhaps it was customary for well-mannered guests to praise the comfort and service they received as a way of praising the villa owner for her/his selection and training of slaves. We do not know how often Pompeia Celerina was able personally to inspect her several villas. Perhaps she was depending on her son-in-law to provide her with a report about activities there, even as Calpurnius Fabatus seems to have depended on his grandson-in-law to give him reports. (See *Letter* 6.30.) Pliny's remark about slaves losing their fear of kindly owners implies that he believed that both he and Pompeia Celerina treated their slaves well. Nor does he suggest that they change their ways and become harsher owners. He simply muses on the situation. Nevertheless, his willingness not just to tolerate the carelessness and lackadaisical attitude of his slaves, but even to reveal it to his readers, is puzzling. Presumably he thought that his readers and his mother-in-law would be in sympathy with his views. Elsewhere in his letters as well, he depicts himself as a humane slave-owner.[91]

Letter 1.18.3, where Pliny discloses the dream in which his (unnamed) mother-in-law asked him to refuse a court case, has already been discussed. The passage informs us that Pliny was married when he was at the beginning his career and that his mind created a dream that his mother-in-law was concerned about his future. It adds little to the portrait of Pompeia Celerina. Much more interesting is the reference to her in *Letter* 3.19.8, written about 100 CE – that is, three or four years after the death of her daughter. *Letter* 3.19, concerning the purchase of property adjacent to Pliny's Tifernum Tiberinum estate, is addressed to Calvisius

Rufus, a good friend (*contubernalis: Letters* 1.12.12 and 4.4.1) of Pliny's from Comum and the recipient of several letters. (It was Calvisius' nephew whom Pliny recommended for a six-month stint as military tribune in *Letter* 4.4; see Chapter 4.) Pliny's opening sentence – "I am sharing with you, as usual, my real estate plan" – informs us that he regularly consulted with Calvisius, whom, at the end of the letter, he lauds for his experience and wisdom. One advantage of this purchase has been mentioned earlier: consolidation of the two properties would result in reductions in the costs of equipment and slaves and in the amount of personal travel time. Another advantage – and this is the major one – is that the land is fertile and well-watered and produces a variety of products which yield a modest, but steady income. The property, which may have been about 2500 acres[92], was leased out in small parcels to peasant farmers by the previous owner, who did not manage the system well. The profitability of the land consequently declined, and it was now on the market at a substantial price reduction from five million sesterces to three million.

Pliny anticipates that Calvisius will ask whether he, Pliny, can easily raise three million sesterces. He acknowledges that almost all his capital is tied up in real estate, and some in loans, but that it will not be difficult to borrow money. He announces, in addition, that he will obtain money from his mother-in-law, whose wealth he uses as his own (*Letter* 3.19.8). His statement about his access to his mother-in-law's wealth is surprisingly blunt, and gives the impression of a man who is very confident about the solidness of his relationship with her. The statement is all the more surprising because their formal relationship had been terminated three or four years earlier by the death of her daughter. In addition, we learn from *Letter* 9.13.13 that, in 97 CE, the man who was the stepfather of Pliny's late wife and the husband of Pompeia Celerina, Bittius Proculus, spoke in the Senate in opposition to Pliny when he tried to instigate an inquiry into the prosecution and death of Helvidius II. (See Chapter 2.) His opposition does not necessarily mean that the two men were hostile toward one another, but their political loyalties were apparently divergent. Pompeia Celerina had nonetheless continued to provide Pliny with emotional and financial support.

There is no reason to speculate that Pliny took undue advantage of her generosity. In fact, we may want to consider whether *Letter* 3.19 offers information about Pompeia Celerina's financial acumen. She had in her possession several estates which she may have inherited from family members. Or, she may have acquired them herself as real estate investments. Recall that Corellia, even in her senior years, had an active interest in land acquisition (*Letters* 7.11 and 14). We do not know how profitable Pompeia Celerina's real estate holdings were, but it is notable that she had ready access to a very large amount of liquid capital, perhaps as much as the three million sesterces that Pliny needed to purchase the land described in *Letter* 3.19. Pliny seems quite certain, moreover, that he will receive money from her. It is possible that he and Pompeia Celerina had discussed the property before he wrote to Calvisius and that she had assessed it as a good investment for both her and her former son-in-law. Presumably she would provide him with the money as a loan, not a gift, and therefore make a profit from the interest he paid. It is even possible that the purchase of the property would be a joint venture, and that she would share possession with Pliny. Perhaps we should consider whether the relationship between Pliny and Pompeia Celerina endured because it was to the financial benefit of both. He gained a wealthy investor, and she gained someone to scout out investment opportunities and to inspect properties that she owned.

Raepsaet-Charlier speculates that Pompeia Celerina may have had a son. Pliny, however, never mentions having a brother-in-law. His silence is not definitive evidence that the Venuleius about whom Raepsaet-Charlier speculates was not a son of Pompeia Celerina. We may wonder, however, why, if she had a son, she continued to participate in real estate ventures with her former son-in-law, and how the son may have responded to her willingness to allow Pliny to use her money as his own, especially when there was no longer a family tie. It would, after all, have been his inheritance that Pliny was using. We do not know who Pompeia Celerina's *tutor* (financial guardian) was.

In *Letter* 6.10, Pliny reports to his addressee that he had visited another of his mother-in-law's villas, this one at Alsium. Alsium was on the west coast of Italy, about 20 miles northwest of Rome. Since it was on the coast and within a day's journey from Rome, it was a desirable location for villas of the elite. Pliny may have arranged a stopover there while he was traveling from Rome to Centum Cellae (modern Civitàvecchia), a town about 50 miles northwest of Rome, to which he had been summoned by the emperor Trajan to serve on an advisory council. In fact, he may have been traveling to Centum Cellae to discuss the case of Gallitta, the woman discussed in Chapter 3, who, while in a province with her military tribune husband, had had an adulterous affair with a centurion (*Letter* 6.31).

Pliny relates that Pompeia Celerina's villa at Alsium had previously been owned by Verginius Rufus. In *Letter* 2.1.8, we learn that Verginius Rufus was native to the same area of northern Italy as Pliny, and that their family properties were adjacent. When Pliny's father died, Verginius Rufus was appointed his *tutor* and showed him the affection of a parent. He continued over the years to take a personal interest in Pliny's education and career. *Letter* 2.1 is, in fact, an emotional eulogy of Verginius Rufus, who died in 97 CE, at the age of 83 years, shortly after assuming the office of consul for the third time. In *Letter* 6.10, Pliny provides the information that it has been ten years since Verginius Rufus' death. We can therefore date the letter to 107 CE. We also learn that Verginius Rufus was accustomed to call the villa the "little nest" of his old age (*Letter* 6.10.1). It is reasonable therefore to assume that Verginius Rufus owned the villa until the time of his death. His heirs apparently then sold it. To whom? Perhaps it changed hands several times, or perhaps Pompeia Celerina purchased it the first time that it came on the market. In any case, we have evidence of a real estate transaction by her. It is worth speculating on Pliny's role in this transaction. Although the property came on the market in the period after the death of his wife, and the consequent severing of his formal connection to Pompeia Celerina, the former in-laws may have discussed the purchase of the property. Pliny had a strong sentimental attachment to the place because of visits there while his *tutor* and political patron was alive and because it was now the site of his tomb (*Letters* 6.10.1 and 2). Perhaps it was he who approached Pompeia Celerina and suggested that she invest in the property. As mentioned earlier, the mother-in-law and the son-in-law may, during the years of Pliny's marriage, have developed not just a bond of affection, but also a financial arrangement which his wife's death did not terminate. Of course, by 107 CE, he had been married to Calpurnia for several years. This new marriage, however, had apparently not weakened his relationship with his former mother-in-law.

The main topic of *Letter* 6.10 is Pliny's disappointment that construction of the tomb of Verginius Rufus had not yet, even after almost ten years, been completed. The fault lies, he remarks, with the inertia of the person to whom the task had been entrusted. Pliny is not here placing any blame on his former mother-in-law. Responsibility for construction and maintenance of the tomb belonged to Verginius Rufus' heirs.[93] The letter ends with a lament by Pliny that the deceased are quickly forgotten and that nowadays people must take on the task that rightly should be done by their heirs and must make their own arrangements for the disposition of their remains (*Letter* 6.10.5).

The final letter in which Pliny mentions his mother-in-law is *Letter* 10.51. He was now in Bithynia-Pontus, in his capacity as imperial legate. Because we do not know the exact year in which Pliny traveled to the province, the date of this letter is uncertain, but it was probably written after 110 CE – that is, more than 13 years after the death of Pompeia Celerina's daughter. Nevertheless, the bond between the mother-in-law and son-in-law remained strong. In *Letter* 10.51, Pliny thanks Trajan for arranging the transfer to Bithynia-Pontus of Caelius Clemens, whom he identifies as the *adfinis* of his mother-in-law. The word *adfinis* is a general term for "relative" or "kinsman."[94] We know nothing more about Caelius Clemens, the nature of his kinship to Pompeia Celerina, or the arrangements of the transfer. It seems, however, that Pliny had made a request to Trajan that Caelius Clemens be allowed to leave a post in one province and move to Pliny's. Perhaps Caelius Clemens was unhappy in his post and appealed to his kinswoman, Pompeia Celerina, to use her influence with Pliny to find a more agreeable situation. He may have been serving a term as a military tribune, which he would complete in Bithynia-Pontus, under Pliny's supervision. Whatever duties Pliny may have assigned to Caelius Clemens, for our purposes the important aspect of *Letter* 10.51 is that Pliny's mother-in-law (and he identifies her as such, not as his *former* mother-in-law) still felt comfortable about asking him for a favor, even 13 years after her daughter's death. Also notable is the indication that, although Pompeia Celerina may well have been in her "golden years" by this time, she remained actively involved in the Roman system of trading in social currency. She seems as remarkable as Ummidia Quadratilla. Both provide images of indomitable elderly women whose wealth gave them power. If we had more information about them, there might have been a chapter in this book titled *Successful Businesswomen: Pompeia Celerina, Ummidia Quadratilla, and Corellia.*

Figure 6 Minicia Marcella, died c. 105/106 CE. This inscription on her tombstone reads: *D(is) M(anibus)* ("to the divine spirits"), *Miniciae Marcellae* ("of Minicia Marcella"), *Fundani F(iliae)* ("daughter of Fundanus"), *V(ixit)* ("she lived") *A(nnos) XII* ("12 years"), *M(enses) XI* ("11 months") *D(ies) VII* ("7 days"). Museo Nazionale Romano. By kind permission of the Ministero per i Beni e le Attività Culturali – Soprintendenza Speciale per i Beni Archeologici di Roma. Photo © Rebecca Bush.

6   Daughters and sisters

Previous chapters have identified women as wives, mothers, grandmothers, and aunts. All of the women mentioned by Pliny were, of course, also daughters, and some were sisters. Calpurnia Hispulla, for example, was the daughter of Calpurnius Fabatus, as well as being the sister of the younger Calpurnius, and the aunt of Pliny's third wife. In several of his letters, Pliny provides information which enhances our understanding of the relationships between daughters and parents and between siblings. This chapter will explore these relationships.

Daughters

Most of the daughters referred to in Pliny's letters are adults when we meet them. A few of the letters, however, allow us a glimpse into the childhood of daughters. Several were orphans, not a surprising circumstance because the high mortality rate among young adults deprived many children of a parent. For example, the two neonatal daughters of the Helvidiae were left motherless as a result of their own births (*Letter* 4.21). We know nothing more about them, but presumably they grew up in the families of their fathers, perhaps with stepmothers. The Helvidiae themselves had lost their father, Helvidius II, as a result of his execution in 93 CE, when they were probably still toddlers. Their mother, Anteia had remarried, and the Helvidiae, along with their brother, Helvidius III, seem to have been raised with a stepfather. They also had been put under the financial oversight of guardians (*Letter* 9.13.16; see Chapter 2). Arulenus Rusticus was executed at the same time as Helvidius II, leaving behind a daughter of about ten years (who had at least two brothers; *Letters* 1.14 and 2.18). The mother of Minicia Marcella died before Minicia reached puberty (*Letter* 5.16). Pliny's third wife, Calpurnia, had lost both her father and her mother in circumstances unknown to us, and been taken in by her paternal grandfather and aunt. Junius Avitus' daughter had lost her father to a fatal illness when she was less than a year old and thus was left, according to Pliny, "not knowing her father" (*Letter* 8.23). We do not know her fate, or whether she was removed from her young mother to live with her father's agnates. A father's death might also mean that a child would suffer the additional trauma of separation from her/his widowed mother. Divorce, which Pliny never mentions, might also result in detachment from a mother. Although we are in the dark about the circumstances, the granddaughter of Ummidia Quadratilla seems to have lost one or both parents at an early age and been taken in by her grandmother (*Letter* 7.24). We don't know whether the granddaughter was the sister of Ummidius Quadratus, also taken in by his grandmother. The daughter of Domitius Lucanus seems to have lost her mother (*Letter* 8.18). These few, brief references in Pliny underscore the fact that family life could be unstable and unpredictable for many children, even those in the elite classes. A child might live in several different households before reaching maturity.

Even at the moment of birth, acceptance into one's agnate family was not guaranteed to an infant. The father had the option of lifting up the new-born infant, shortly after birth, and thus signifying that s/he had been received into the *familia* – or of declining to do so, and thereby indicating that s/he was not accepted.[1] In the latter case, the infant was then "exposed" – that is, removed from the home and abandoned out-of-doors, in an urban alleyway or garbage heap, for example, or a rural location. Although many of the exposed infants may have died from lack of nourishment, cold, or attacks by dogs or rats[2], the Romans did not consider exposure to be infanticide because they did not directly kill the child, through strangulation, for example, or drowning, or employing someone else to do so.[3] They convinced themselves that the infant would be picked up and cared for by someone else. However, if s/he was indeed rescued, the "savior" was often a slave dealer who raised the infant in order to profit by later selling him/her. In *Letters* 10.65 and 66 (also *Letter* 10.72), we have an exchange of letters between Pliny (in Bithynia) and the emperor Trajan which discusses people who, though free born, were exposed as infants, picked up by slave dealers, and raised as slaves. The immediate issues were whether these "foundlings" should be allowed to file a claim to regain their status as free persons and, if so, whether they should have to reimburse the dealers who raised them for the costs incurred in rearing them. Trajan's answers (which then established policy for Bithynia) were "yes" to the first question and "no" to the second.[4] We might well wonder, however, how people who were slaves would have the legal standing to make a claim, and would possess plausible proof of their free birth. Presumably their birth parents would make the claim, but it is unlikely that many birth parents would want or be able to keep track of their exposed child. As noted earlier, a slave was considered to have no parents or siblings, and to belong only to the *familia* of his/her owner, who was his *paterfamilias*.

There were several reasons why a father might decide not to accept an infant into the family. A child who was sickly or deformed might be exposed, or even become a victim of infanticide. In fact, the Twelve Tables assigned to a *paterfamilias* the power to kill quickly a deformed child.[5] However, healthy infants were also victims of infanticide and exposure. The custom of girls' marrying at an early age probably developed in order to allow as many pregnancies as possible in an era when the average age of mortality was about 27 years. However, women who were very fertile and long-lived might produce more children than the family wanted. Poor families might abandon children because they could not afford to raise them.[6] For people who lived at bare subsistence level, taking on an additional mouth to feed meant jeopardizing the lives of themselves and their other children.[7] Wealthy families might discard infants because they did not want to divide the family estate among too many heirs. The Stoic philosopher, Musonius Rufus, whom Pliny admired, criticized the practice of exposure whether it was done because of poverty or because of a desire to protect enormous wealth.[8] However, in an era when contraceptive methods were unreliable, and abortion was extremely dangerous, exposure was a method of limiting the size of one's family.[9]

Exposure had the advantage over contraception and abortion that the *paterfamilias* would know the sex of the infant before deciding whether to keep it. Many scholars believe that more female infants were abandoned than male infants.[10] Dionysius of Halicarnassus attributes to Romulus a law stipulating that a father was obliged to raise all his healthy sons, but only his first-born daughter.[11] The historicity of this legislation is debatable.[12] Our evidence suggests, moreover, that many Roman families in the late republican period, when Dionysius lived, did not rear all the sons born to them. Dionysius apparently believed that the legislation was authentic and archaic, but his report may reflect a concern expressed in the late republican period about the frequency of exposures. Nonetheless, the implication of the mandate he records, that at least one daughter not be exposed, is that some Romans would have preferred to discard all female infants. Although we cannot determine how many female infants were exposed, it is rare to locate an ancient Roman family with more than one or two daughters. Sons were considered more valuable to families than daughters because sons could carry on the family name and business[13] and could bring in an income and support elderly parents. (For elite families, however, the costs of a son's political career were substantial.) Daughters, on the other hand, were considered a financial drain on the family because they would not, as adults, be income-producers and because, as will be discussed later, they required a dowry at the time of their marriages – that is, the family was required to release part of its estate to the groom's family.[14] Although we do not have statistical or physical evidence to prove conclusively that infant daughters were more often exposed than sons, there is literary evidence of the preference for sons. For example, in a letter written in Roman Egypt about 1 BCE, a man instructed his pregnant wife: "If you have the baby before I return, and it is a boy, let it live; if it is a girl, expose it."[15] And the poet Ovid included in his *Metamorphoses* a fictional account of a man who told his wife as she was approaching labor: "I pray for two things – that you may have an easy labor, and that you may bear a male child. For a girl is too burdensome, and we just don't have the money. ... I say this with great reluctance – if you should bear a girl, we will have to kill her."[16] In another fictional passage, but also perhaps reflecting a widely known practice, Apuleius creates a situation in which a pregnant woman was ordered by her husband, as he was setting out on a long journey, to kill the infant when it was born if it was a girl.[17]

By the imperial period, the number of children being raised by citizen families in Italy was apparently so low that Augustus felt impelled to devise a combination of penalties and rewards for marriage and the production of children. These incentives, which have been discussed in Chapter 1, granted married men with children precedence in political careers, gave inheritance privileges to both men and women, and allowed women with three children (freedwomen with four children) release from having a *tutor*. The establishment of these incentives assumed that people were fecund, but intentionally limiting the size of their families, through methods which included exposure. Surprisingly, Augustus did not ban, nor, as far as we know, even censure the practice of exposure. We do not know whether his legislation, with its requirement of three children, encouraged parents to raise all the daughters born to them in order to make the complement.

A hundred years later, there were still concerns about the low number of children raised by citizen families. Pliny suggested in his letters that childlessness was for many people a deliberate choice.[18] However, his own inability to produce children, despite wanting them, indicates that not all childlessness was voluntary. In any case, the incentives of the Augustan legislation had more relevance to politically ambitious upper-class men than to lower-class families. The legislation did not address the concerns of the poor, who could barely eke out a living and simply did not have the financial resources to rear several children. One hundred years after Augustus, Trajan (who did not himself have children) realized that imperial exhortations and laws that affected inheritance and public careers were not sufficient incentives for poor people. He (and subsequent emperors) developed a more pragmatic system of encouraging the poor to raise their infants. Under the *alimenta*, which were programs to help provide nourishment for freeborn children, funds were made available to defray the costs of rearing children.[19] In his *Panegyricus* (28.5–7), Pliny applauded Trajan's program, which, according to Pliny, had, by 100 CE, already assisted the families of almost 5000 freeborn children, children who would grow up to be loyal citizens and, in turn, produce a new generation of productive citizens.[20] In his cloying speech before the Senate, Pliny declared: "For the poor, there is only one inducement to raise children: a good emperor. ... Under you, it is a pleasure and an advantage to raise children." (*Panegyricus* 26.5 and 27.1) He added that the security and prosperity which Trajan had brought to Italy were as much incentives to having children as the *alimenta*.[21]

In addition, Trajan and subsequent emperors encouraged private philanthropy by wealthy citizens. Pliny, for example, donated 500,000 sesterces to fund an alimentary program for the annual maintenance of freeborn boys and girls in his hometown, and he expressed hope that he would inspire others to accept the tedious hard work of raising children.[22] The evidence for the program – an inscription and two of his letters – does not specify whether Pliny arranged for the amount allotted for the maintenance of a girl to be as much as that for a boy. Some inscriptional records of alimentary programs delineate a distinction, granting boys a larger allowance and for more years.[23] However, Antoninus Pius, emperor 138–61 CE, commemorated his wife, Faustina the Elder, when she died by establishing a foundation to support girls.[24] We cannot ascertain whether the rate of exposure of infants, and particularly of female infants, decreased as a result of alimentary programs.

We might conclude that the Romans had a very callous attitude toward female infants.[25] And yet, if the *paterfamilias* accepted her into the family, a girl was often cherished.[26] For one family, the commissioning of a graffito at Pompeii, announcing the birth of a daughter, suggests that they were happy to welcome her. "Our daughter was born early in the evening on Saturday, August 2."[27] Plutarch records that his wife, Timoxena, had longed for a daughter after bearing four sons.[28] And when the longed-for daughter died at the age of two, her parents grieved. Indeed, Plutarch's consolatory letter to his wife reveals that she was crushed by the loss. Funerary inscriptions indicate that the untimely death of a daughter was mourned by parents, even though these same people may have had no qualms about discarding a second female infant. One inscription, which is accompanied by the carved image of a seated child with hands outstretched toward a basket, reads: "Telesphoris and her husband, the parents, to their very sweet daughter. One must lament for this sweet little girl. ... She lived half a year and 8 days. The rose bloomed and immediately wilted."[29] Another inscription, accompanied by the image of a young girl carved on the tombstone, reads: "Quintus Haterius Ephebus and Julia Zosime provided this memorial for their very unfortunate daughter Hateria Superba who lived one year, six months, 25 days."[30] Consider also: "Marcus Opinius Rufus and Gellia Neptilia, her parents, [*dedicate this memorial*] to Opinia Neptilia, aged 14 years, a virgin promised in marriage, who died when her wedding day was close."[31] Although, as noted in Chapter 4, there is scholarly debate about whether Roman parents allowed themselves to become emotionally invested in infants and young children, these epitaphs indicate that some parents did indeed become very attached to children, even daughters, as young as six months. Laws limiting the period of mourning for children and prohibiting mourning for infants under one year also suggest that parents were devastated by the loss of their children.[32]

When Cicero's daughter was about eight years old, he wrote: "My daughter is very close to my heart. ... For what has nature wanted to be more delightful and more dear to us [*than a daughter*]? What is a more worthy thing on which all our care and indulgence may be lavished?"[33] The name of Cicero's daughter was Tullia, the feminine form of his family name, Tullius (Marcus *Tullius* Cicero). Although sons received a *praenomen*, or "first name" (for example, Marcus), as well as the family name (*nomen gentile*), daughters received only the *nomen gentile*.[34] Two daughters would thus have the same name, and be distinguished by calling one Secunda ("Second") or Minor ("Younger"). Perhaps this discrimination in name-giving indicates that daughters were valued less than sons – or that most families did not accept more than one daughter and therefore did not need to worry about assigning different female names. However, in letters to friends, Cicero's warm feelings for his daughter are apparent in his frequent references to her by the affectionate diminutive, Tulliola, "my little Tullia."[35] Cicero's good friend, Atticus, also had a daughter (born in 51 BCE) and apparently kept Cicero informed of her activities. Cicero wrote in return: "I rejoice that your little daughter is such a delight to you."[36]

However, although Cicero was very fond of Tullia, he does not express any reservations about betrothing her in marriage at the age of about 11 years.[37] He announces to Atticus quite abruptly and briefly that his "little Tullia" is engaged.[38]

And if he had concerns about the sexual demands which a husband would make on his young daughter, he does not reveal them in a letter. Fathers may, however, have considered how frightening these sexual demands would be to a girl. We might recall a passage from Seneca the Younger that was cited in Chapter 2: "with regard to matrimony, you will recommend how a man should conduct himself with a wife whom he married as a virgin, and how he should conduct himself with a wife who previously experienced marriage to another man."[39]

Tullia married in 63 BCE, when she was about 14, to Gaius Calpurnius Piso Frugi (quaestor of 58 BCE) who was ten years or more older than she. Piso died in 57 BCE.[40] Tullia married twice more; both those marriages were ended by divorce. On what basis did fathers select husbands for their young daughters? As noted in previous chapters, the social standing and political achievements of the man's family were certainly important to elite families, but, in addition, a father might choose as a son-in-law a man who had interests and a temperament similar to his own, as Caecina and Thrasea seem to have done. (See Chapter 2.) Years after Tullia's first marriage, Cicero recalled that Piso had excelled in oratorical skills, diligence, self-discipline, and self-restraint, which must certainly have been qualities that Cicero himself strove to exhibit.[41]

Young brides, almost children themselves, were expected to produce children. The dangers of childbirth at a young age did not deter fathers from arranging marriages for daughters in their early teens. In *Letters* 1.14.2 and 6.26.3, Pliny announces his expectation that the marriages discussed in the letters will soon produce children. Surely Cicero had the same expectation for Tullia's marriage. And Pliny, of course, similarly hoped that his young wife, Calpurnia, would bear children.

Despite the many references to Tullia in Cicero's letters, we learn almost nothing about what sort of person she was. Seeing her through Cicero's eyes, she appears as a "daddy's girl" on whom he doted even as she grew into adulthood. Even after her marriage to Piso, she seems to have remained very close to her parents, an indication perhaps of the behavior of young Roman girls who were suddenly thrust into the role of wife and then mother at a very early age. Cicero's references to Tullia suggest that he was fond of her because she delighted him. We have noted in previous chapters that Roman wives were praised for being pleasant and accommodating. Perhaps they learned this behavior as young children in order to win the attention and affection of their fathers.

Cicero continued to refer to Tullia as his *filiola* (his "little daughter") even when she was married. And she continued to spend much of her time with her birth family. In a letter to Atticus, written in 60 BCE, when Tullia had been married about three years (but was about 17 years old), Cicero speaks of the respite from political turmoil that he finds in the company of his wife, "little daughter," and sweet little son.[42] He also reports that Tullia stayed with her family, apparently without her husband, at their residences both in Rome and at villas elsewhere.[43] Perhaps we can surmise that, although girls married when barely in their teen years, many did not move far – physically or emotionally – from their parents. (If this is true, the separation of Calpurnia from her family in Comum, when she moved to Rome after marrying the much older Pliny, must have been quite traumatic.) We should also consider that the Roman practice of husbands and wives keeping separate financial accounts might have made married daughters more financially dependent on their birth families than women today. In any case, Tullia was very supportive of her father when he was in exile in 58/57 BCE. (See Chapter 2.) He wrote to his brother that he missed Tullia very much. "What family devotion (*pietas*), what modest behavior, what intelligence she has! She is the image of me in face, conversation, and spirit."[44] After his return to Rome, Cicero again enjoyed his daughter's company. Years later, he reminisced that, when enjoying her conversation and sweetness, he unburdened himself of all his cares and sorrows.[45]

Cicero's little Tullia died in 45 BCE, shortly after giving birth to a son at the age of about 33. Custody of the infant was apparently taken by the family of her third husband, whom she had divorced before the birth. Cicero was devastated by her death. In his letters, he confesses to friends that he was paralyzed by grief and overcome by uncontrollable weeping.[46] Our knowledge about the relationship between Tullia and Cicero suggests that, although the rate of exposure of female infants may have been high, many fathers cherished the daughters whom they had accepted into the family.

Minicia Marcella

The death of a daughter is the subject of *Letter* 5.16, in which Pliny informs the recipient of the news that the daughter of their mutual friend, Fundanus, has died. The letter, written perhaps in 105 or 106 CE, serves a dual function, informing the reader both about the character of the deceased girl and the grief of her father.

The father was Gaius Minicius Fundanus, who was the recipient of several of Pliny's published letters.[47] The tone and topics of these letters suggest that Pliny and Fundanus were good friends. The latter may have, like Pliny, claimed Cisalpine Italy as his homeland.[48] Having held several lower-ranking positions, he was selected as suffect consul for 107 CE, and proconsul of Asia around 124 and 125 CE. The date of the consulship suggests that Fundanus was about seven years younger than Pliny, who was consul in 100 CE. In *Letter* 5.16.8, Pliny characterizes him as a learned and wise man who, from his earliest days, devoted himself to higher studies and the arts. Fundanus has been identified with the Fundanus who was a friend of the scholar Plutarch. In his essay "On the Tranquility of the Mind," Plutarch wrote: "Our friend Eros received a letter from that most excellent man, Fundanus."[49] In Plutarch's essay "On the Control of Anger," Fundanus is the principal speaker. At one point in the essay, Fundanus is recorded as saying: "I remember this precept of Musonius."[50] This Musonius is presumably Musonius Rufus, the Stoic philosopher whom Pliny admired.[51] Fundanus's statement of recollection is not enough evidence to label him as a Stoic, but it does indicate that he had an interest in Stoicism. The word *sapiens* which Pliny uses in *Letter* 5.16.8 to describe Fundanus may mean "wise" (as I have translated it), or specifically "a philosopher."[52] Pliny's friendship with Fundanus was such that he felt comfortable requesting favors of him (and undoubtedly expected to grant favors in return). For example, in *Letter* 4.15, Pliny informs Fundanus that a young man named Asinius Bassus has been selected as one of the 20 quaestors for the year.[53] Pliny asks Fundanus to choose Bassus as his assistant when he is consul. In *Letter* 6.6, Pliny requests of Fundanus that he support the political campaign of one of Pliny's protégés, a young man named Julius Naso whose father (and also a brother) was dead and who therefore lacked the type of help that a father (and brother) provided in the competition for political advancement.[54]

An inscription, which will be discussed later, seems to indicate that Fundanus was married to a woman named Statoria Marcella. She may also have been, like her husband, from a north Italian family.[55] In Plutarch's essay "On the Control of Anger," Fundanus refers to his wife and daughters.[56] From *Letter* 5.16.4, we can ascertain that he had two daughters. (We don't know the fate of surviving daughter.) He seems not to have had a son, which may be why Pliny thought that he might be willing to offer paternal assistance to the two young men mentioned earlier. The death of his younger daughter is the occasion for *Letter* 5.16.

Fortuitously, there has been discovered just outside of Rome a family tomb which includes two inscriptions which appear to refer to Fundanus' family. One commemorates the death of Minicia Marcella, who is identified as a daughter of Fundanus.[57] (See Figure 6.) The second is dedicated to Statoria Marcella who we may conclude was Fundanus' wife.[58] (If this assumption is correct, the daughter received, in addition to her father's family name, Minicia, the name of her mother, Marcella.) There is broad scholarly agreement that the Minicia Marcella and Fundanus of the inscription are the daughter and father discussed by Pliny in *Letter* 5.16, even though he does not provide the name of the deceased daughter.[59] There is one discrepancy between the two items. The tomb inscription records that Minicia Marcella lived for 12 years, 11 months, and seven days.[60] Today we might say that she was "12, going on 13." However, in the manuscript of Pliny's letter, it is stated that the daughter had not completed 14 (xiiii) years, a piece of information from which we would conclude that she was "13, going on 14" when she died (*Letter* 5.16.2). Since it seems unlikely that the family who commissioned the inscription would be mistaken about the girl's age, or allow a stonemason's carelessness to go uncorrected, the error may have occurred in the transcription and transmission of the manuscripts of Pliny's letters. Perhaps Pliny wrote xiii (13) years, but an inattentive copier wrote xiiii (14) years. Or Pliny himself may have been mistaken about the girl's age. Or perhaps Pliny intended not to provide a precise age, but rather to point out that she had not quite reached the age of sexual maturity – that is, 14 years. Bodel argues that Pliny was not saying that Minicia was 13 years old, but rather that she had not completed a recognized stage of life – childhood – which extended from infancy to 14 years, when puberty (and adulthood) began.[61]

The first sentence of the letter bluntly conveys the news that "the younger daughter of our friend Fundanus has died." However, the first word of the letter is *tristissimus* ("very sad"), and Pliny uses it to describe his own feelings about the girl's death: "very sad, I write to you."[62] As Carlon comments, *Letter* 5.16 is an "elegant and highly structured lament."[63] Although he writes to encourage his addressee to send a note of consolation to Fundanus, Pliny himself seems in need of consolation, so distressed is he about the death.[64] He does not provide the daughter's name, but he leads us to believe that he was well-informed about her character and activities. We don't know how frequently he may have visited the home of Fundanus, but Pliny reports that he never *saw* anyone more *festivus* or *amabilis* than the daughter, nor anyone more worthy not only of a longer life, but also almost of immortality. The verb *saw* (Latin: *vidi*) attests that Pliny observed the behavior of Fundanus' daughter, rather than simply being told about it, but does not apprise us of how often he saw the girl or whether he talked with her. Only here in the published correspondence does Pliny use *festivus* in reference to a person. In this context, the word seems to mean "jolly," "cheerful," or perhaps "good-natured." Today we use the term "a happy child." Cicero employs *festivus* to describe a young slave of whom he was very fond: *puer festivus*.[65] We can imagine that the slave pleased Cicero because he was good-natured and appeared always happy. *Amabilis* is the same word which Pliny used of Fannia in *Letter* 7.19.7. It means "amiable," "lovable," "inspiring affection." It was used also by Cicero in reference to the infant daughter of Atticus. In a letter, part of which was translated earlier, Cicero writes to his friend: "I rejoice that your little daughter is such a delight to you. I have never seen her, but nonetheless I love her, and I am certain that she is *amabilis*, lovable."[66]

It is not surprising that Pliny chose the same word to characterize both Fannia and Minicia Marcella. He has designed his portrait of each woman to serve as an *exemplum* of laudable feminine behavior, Fannia representing the virtues of a wife (and an adult daughter of Thrasea Paetus) and Minicia representing those of a young daughter and a girl on the brink of womanhood. It is notable that the first piece of information that we are given about Minicia is that she was good-natured and lovable. As we have observed in Pliny's portraits of other women, "agreeableness" was a desirable trait in a woman. And a girl was never too young to display a winning personality. Plutarch wrote of his deceased two-year-old daughter that she was by nature remarkably good-tempered, gentle, affectionate, and generous. As an example of her kindness, Plutarch relates that she used to ask her nurse to breastfeed not only other infants, but also even inanimate objects and toys.[67] (Plutarch does not report the nurse's response to the girl's generosity.)

Pliny continues his report about Minicia Marcella in *Letter* 5.16 by stating that she was not yet 14 years old when she died. However, as we now might say, she was 13 going on 30. She behaved with a maturity well beyond her years. In addition to a girlish sweetness and maidenly modesty, qualities perhaps not unexpected in a girl of her class, she possessed, so Pliny writes, *prudentia*, the wisdom and good judgment, of an elderly person, and *gravitas*, the dignity or seriousness, of a mature woman (*Letter* 5.16.2). Fannia, too, possessed *gravitas*, "dignity" (*Letter* 7.19.4).[68] What was unusual about Minicia was that she was serious and wise at such an early stage of her life. In *Letter* 8.5.1, Pliny commented about Macrinus' wife, "a wife of singular example"[69], that she "brought together and combined in her own character so many and such important virtues, acquiring them at different times during her life." It seems from this comment that a woman was not expected to exhibit every desirable virtue at a young age, but could acquire virtues gradually as she matured (and perhaps as she was educated by her husband). Minicia was remarkable in that, even before she had reached physical maturity, she had cultivated virtues which were usually not acquired until adulthood.[70]

Our first impression of Minicia is that she was a sweet, but serious little person. Pliny provides more details about her behavior. How she clung to her father's neck! How she embraced his friends (including Pliny) affectionately, but modestly! How she loved her nurses, pedagogues (attendants)[71], and teachers! How intently and intelligently she used to read! How sparingly and cautiously she used to play! With what restraint, patience, and resolve (*constantia*) she endured her last illness![72] She obeyed the doctors, comforted her sister and father (her mother had apparently predeceased her), and, when her physical strength left her, she sustained herself by the strength of her spirit. (We might consider whether she "played sparingly" because she lacked physical strength.) Pliny presents a portrait of a girl with exceptional inner resources, who faced her illness and impending death calmly and courageously. Despite her tender age, she displayed a fortitude in illness which Pliny also attributes to men such as Corellius Rufus and Titius Aristo, who had lived long and productive lives and earned his admiration.[73] However, her fortitude at so young an age was not unique. The words *constantia* and *gravitas* were also used by Quintilian to describe the courage of his ten-year-old son during his eight month terminal illness. He wrote that the boy, who exhibited great promise as a scholar and orator, displayed *constantia* and *gravitas* in the face of pain and fear, winning the admiration of his doctors. In his final moments, he consoled his father.[74] Quintilian's account of how his son coped with his affliction is similar in many respects to Pliny's account of Minicia. Perhaps it was a convention to describe terminally ill children as enduring their condition bravely in order to heighten the pathos of their deaths. Or, perhaps both these particular children were, in fact, remarkably valiant. If Minicia did truly endure her affliction without complaint and in a manner unusually resolute, we might ask whether she inwardly chafed at the role of "good patient" that she believed that she must play, or whether she was pleased to able to cope so well with her situation. In either event, she could see that her behavior won her the approval and affection of her family.

Both Minicia and Quintilian's son displayed evidence that they would have developed into well-respected adults. Minicia, of course, as a woman, could not have expected to achieve success in all the areas that a man might. Had she lived, her success would have been measured by her performance as a wife and mother. It is significant that, according to Pliny, even in her final days, Minicia's primary concern was to please those around her and put them at ease. In this regard, though still a girl, she had already learned the ideal conduct for a wife. She apparently concealed her own suffering as well as Arria the Elder had concealed her grief. It would be simplistic, however, to maintain that elite Roman girls grew up to be timid and self-effacing women. We would not, for example, describe Arria the Elder or her granddaughter Fannia as timid. As Hemelrijk observes, "(g)irls like Minicia Marcella were brought up to stand their ground in the complicated and sophisticated social life of the capital."[75] Elite women learned how to negotiate situations in order to promote the interests of their families. The focus of their efforts, however, was the family, not their own advancement. And their social skills were a matter of appearing agreeable and amiable. It is not difficult to imagine that a woman like Corellia acted with charm even as she managed to execute a favorable real estate transaction (*Letters* 7.11 and 14).

Pliny's phrase, "she endured her last (or: latest) illness," may indicate that Minicia's poor health had been chronic, and that she had been a "sickly" child (*Letter* 5.16.3).[76] He declares that her death was a sad and bitter occurrence – and an untimely one. She had recently been engaged to an outstanding young man. (His identity is unknown to us.) A date for the wedding had been set, and invitations had been sent (*Letter* 5.16.6). The arrangement of a marriage for a girl who had not yet completed her fourteenth year was not, of course, unusual. We may, however, wonder whether – and, if so, why – the arrangement was made at a time when Minicia was not healthy. Her death was "untimely" because it had deprived her of the opportunity to enter into adulthood, which, for a girl, was marked by the entry into marriage. Although girls were not infrequently married before the age of 14 (Quintilian's wife was 12 years old at the time of their marriage, and he was about 41), the age of 14 years was regarded as the usual age of sexual maturity for girls, the age at which they were ready to undertake the task allotted to them by Nature: the bearing and raising of children.[77] The onset of puberty prompted the arrangement of a marriage so that legitimate children could be produced. However, boys of the elite class (that is, of Minicia's class) would in contrast, at the age of 14, be beginning a period of higher education, followed by brief military service, and then, in their 20s, embarkation on a career in politics, law, and administration, and perhaps a marriage, which would facilitate their advancement in public office. Many opportunities awaited them for public recognition of their talents and virtues. Their "peak" might be a term as consul when middle-aged, or even the rank of elder statesman in old age. Girls, on the other hand, could look forward only to marriage and motherhood at a young age, and a plateau rather than a peak in these roles. Their achievements were measured within the confines of the few activities considered appropriate for women.

The death of a child is always "untimely" in the sense that we expect children to outlive their parents. This was true even in the ancient world, when mortality among young people was high. Parents anticipated that their children would bring honor and perhaps wealth to the family by their accomplishments, and would support them in old age. The death of a child meant the death of the hopes which the parents had had for the child. However, the expectations of achievement were different for sons than for daughters. In *Letter* 8.23, Pliny reports the death of his protégé Junius Avitus, who died of an illness shortly after having been selected to the office of aedile.[78] He had previously served as a military tribune and a quaestor. Like Minicia, he had a sterling character which portended a bright future. His death, like Minicia's, could be termed "untimely," and both had been cut off just before their prime. Junius Avitus' prime, however, would have been advancement to the highest political office, while Minicia's would have been marriage. Pliny mentions Junius Avitus' marriage and fatherhood only to complete the portrait of a young man who has successfully negotiated the career track. In contrast, he mentions the scheduled marriage of Minicia as the only promise for her future.

When a girl died before reaching the age of marriage, she was considered to have been robbed of the chance to excel in the role for which Nature and society had designed her. Plutarch's wife, for example, lamented that their deceased two-year-old daughter had died unmarried and without children.[79] However, the daughter was not old enough to have, at the time of her death, a concept of the adulthood of which she was being deprived or of the hopes which would be unfulfilled. Especially poignant was the situation of a girl like Minicia, who died on the brink of marriage, and who had come so close to entering upon her adult life. The pathos of such a situation was a familiar topos in Classical thought. An epitaph from southern Italy, commissioned by a grieving father, describes a situation very similar to that of Minicia. His daughter had completed twice six years and "she held out hope of marriage when death, coming too quickly, snatched away her maturing years."[80] Another epitaph, quoted also earlier, commemorates Opinia Neptilia, aged 14 years, "a virgin promised in marriage, who died when her wedding day was close."[81] In *Letter* 5.16, Pliny leads his reader to conclude that Minicia's fate was particularly grievous because she had, even as a child, displayed the qualities that would have made her an ideal wife.

In *Letters* 5.16 and 8.23, Pliny announces the deaths of two young people and catalogues their virtues. He then turns his attention to the plights of the family members left behind. For the mother, wife, and infant daughter of Junius Avitus, "one day nullified so many hopes and so many joys" (*Letter* 8.23.7). For Minicia's father, Minicius Fundanus, so much joy was transformed into so much grief (*Letter* 5.16.6). Pliny reports that he was heartbroken when he heard Fundanus giving instructions that the money that he had intended to spend on clothing, pearls, and jewels – presumably his daughter's trousseau – be instead spent on incense, ointments, and perfumes (to be used at her funeral).[82] Pliny then writes that, although Fundanus had been a student of philosophy for many years, and was a "learned and wise man" (*Letter* 5.16.8), in this trying situation he had renounced all philosophic principles[83] and devoted himself totally to *pietas*, to caring about his family. Pliny presents himself not as a stern and censorious philosopher, but as a generous and humane counselor.[84] Far from scolding Fundanus for abandoning his philosophic principles, Pliny explains that his grief is understandable because he lost a daughter who resembled him no less in character than in facial features. With remarkable similitude, she was a copy of her father in every respect. His comment is reminiscent of Cicero's remark to his brother, quoted earlier, that his daughter, the dear little Tullia, was his image in face, conversation, and spirit.[85] Both men were pleased and proud that their daughters had inherited both their personality and their physical appearance. Both seem to have had a genuine affection for their daughters. Neither man, however, expressed in his letters any discomfort about arranging marriages for them at such a young age.

Pliny ends *Letter* 5.16 with a request that his addressee write to Fundanus and offer him condolences for his loss, not criticism for his emotional response to it. However, Pliny himself had not been sympathetic about his adversary Regulus' immoderate (in Pliny's opinion) grief for his son in *Letters* 4.2 and 4.7, saying that he was mourning him insanely, and even casting doubt upon his sincerity: "this was not grief, but the affectation of grief" (*Letters* 4.2.3 and 4).[86] It is interesting that Pliny writes that Regulus' son might have turned out well, but he resembled his father (*Letter* 4.2.1). The verb which he uses, *referre* ("resemble") is the same that he uses in *Letter* 5.16.9 to state that Minicia resembled her father in character and looks. Pliny was obviously much more lenient with his friends than with Regulus, commiserating with Vestricius Spurinna and Cottia in *Letter* 3.10 on the death of their son Cottius. And because Fundanus was a good friend, Pliny finds it easy to recommend that he be given time to mourn for Minicia.

Pliny makes no mention of Fundanus' elder daughter, who was now his only surviving child. (Her name would also have been Minicia.) Since she was older than the girl who died on the brink of marriage, she may already have been married and perhaps even a mother. Fundanus' anguish may have arisen, in part, from his realization that he could now anticipate fewer grandchildren.[87] And perhaps he was especially fond of Minicia Marcella, who mirrored his character and his face, and might have passed these features on to his grandchildren.

Since Fundanus did not have a son, he may have been more willing to expend money on the education of his daughter(s). His own interests in learning may also have made him more open to providing good instructors – and more than one instructor – for his daughter(s). However, we have no way of knowing what his views were about the education of women. And Pliny's letter tells us only that Minicia Marcella loved her teachers and studied hard. It would be rash, on the basis of this small piece of information, to conclude that she was "well-educated" – especially since Pliny includes it not to illuminate the reader about her education, but primarily to make the point that Minicia was affectionate, obedient, and serious. Pliny's focus in the letter is not on the content of her lessons, but on her moral and social development. We have no idea what she studied, or how her education might have compared to that of a boy of a similar age and class.[88] In contrast, Quintilian, in writing about the death of his son, proudly tells the reader that the boy had already learned to speak well not only Latin, but also Greek.[89] Minicia probably had tutors who came to her house (or lived in her house) rather than her going outside the home for schooling. And her formal education may have ended at the time of her marriage. Even if her father had been more attentive to her schooling than other fathers were, and even if Pliny had stated that she was well-educated, the term would probably have been relative: well-educated, for a woman.

Our impression of Minicia Marcella must be derived solely from Pliny's description of her. It is unlikely, however, that he spent much time with her. His judgment was undoubtedly formed from observing her behavior when her father was present and from hearing comments made by her father. She certainly appears, from Pliny's words, to have been the perfect daughter – always cheerful, accommodating, and sensitive to the wishes of others. However, we cannot know whether she was truly a happy child, or whether she had developed an ability to play the role of a happy child. Perhaps she was content to have learned to play her role well. Certainly she had won the favor of her father. Was she a chronically ill child who realized that she could best gain his attention and affection by not complaining? Did she miss her mother? Was she pleased at the prospect of being married, or perhaps frightened by the expectation of leaving her family and home? We cannot retrieve from Pliny's letter her thoughts about her situation. In any case, even if we could, we might be surprised to discover that she was happy to have succeeded in fashioning herself into the perfect daughter – and in possessing the qualities that were desirable also in a wife. What we can retrieve from Pliny is the information that a father, Minicius Fundanus, was very fond of his daughter who matched his every expectation.

Fathers, marriage, and dowries

We do not know whom Fundanus had selected to be the husband of his beloved daughter. He may have been a young man in his early 20s (like Ummidius Quadratus), just embarking on a senatorial career and seeking the benefits, including political advancement, that marriage offered. Or, he may have been a middle-aged man, previously married (like Pliny). Although Pliny uses the word *iuvenis* ("young man"), to describe him (*Letter* 5.16.6), the Latin word could apply to a man up to the age of about 40.[90] If Minicia, at the age of about 13 years, had married a middle-aged man who was already a father, she would have become a stepmother to children who were not much younger than she. Undoubtedly, Fundanus had solicited from his friends recommendations for husbands, even as Junius Mauricus had asked Pliny to recommend a husband for his niece (*Letter* 1.14). When a prospective husband had been identified, negotiations about a dowry would begin between Fundanus and the groom's *paterfamilias*, or, if the *paterfamilias* was deceased, with the groom himself, who was now *sui iuris* ("under his own regulation").

The dowry was a critical element in the arrangement of a marriage.[91] A dowry might consist of cash, real estate, moveable property, or a combination of these. The bride's family transferred the dowry to the groom's family, but, if the marriage were not one in which the wife was *in manu* – and most wives in this period were not *in manu*[92] – the bride's family could recover the dowry whether the marriage was ended by divorce or death.[93] However, the groom's family, during the marriage, had control over the dowry, and could, for example, use the cash to purchase real estate, or alternatively could sell real estate to produce cash. If the husband's *paterfamilias* was still alive, he managed the dowry. If the husband was *sui iuris*, he was the financial manager. At the end of the marriage, however, the husband or his family was responsible for returning to the wife's family the original value of the dowry, though not necessarily the precise pieces of real estate or moveable property. The income produced by the dowry, however – that is, through real estate rentals, interest or capital gains on investments, or the sale of agricultural products – belonged to the husband's family, and they were free to use it as they pleased. Nonetheless, there was an expectation that the income from the dowry was intended to compensate the husband for the expenses he incurred by providing his wife with food, shelter, clothing, and, in wealthy households, such items as slaves, carriages, jewelry, and luxuries.[94]

As noted in previous chapters, in a marriage in which the wife was not *in manu*, the husband and wife kept separate accounts of the property that each owned. The wife's property (cash, moveable and immoveable items) would usually consist of what she had inherited from an agnate family member, particularly her *paterfamilias*. (She could legally own property only if her *paterfamilias* was dead, in which case she would be assigned a *tutor*.) She might, of course, use the cash, the sale of items, or the income from items to purchase more property (including slaves) which, in turn, would be kept in an account separate from her husband's property. Her dowry, however, was a different matter. As Dixon explains, in the compartmentalized view of matrimonial property, everything was "his" or "hers" except for the dowry, which was "hers" but "his to use for the time being."[95]

If the marriage was terminated by divorce, children produced during the marriage customarily remained with their father. If the divorce was initiated by the wife or her *paterfamilias*, the husband could retain one-sixth the original value of the dowry for each child up to a maximum of three children (a total which would constitute half the dowry). If, moreover, he could prove misconduct on the part of the wife, he might claim an additional portion of the dowry. However, if the wife could prove misconduct on the part of the husband, he could make no claim on the dowry, even for the children. It must be stated, however, that families were free to draw up arrangements about the recovery of the dowry which were suited to their particular circumstances.

A dowry might be paid in installments, usually three.[96] When Cicero's daughter Tullia married her third husband, Publius Cornelius Dolabella, in 50 BCE, Cicero agreed to pay the dowry in three annual installments, but he had considerable difficulty making the payments. Cicero even thought about initiating a divorce for Tullia (an action which would have nullified the dowry arrangement), in part because of the financial strain, and in part because of Dolabella's improprieties.[97] Then, in 47 or 46 BCE, Cicero and his wife, Terentia, divorced after about 32 years of marriage. The reasons for the divorce remain a mystery, but Cicero's letters reveal that the couple had been quarreling for several years about financial matters.[98] Cicero agreed to return her dowry, which had an original value of 400,000 sesterces (= 100,000 denarii), in three annual installments.[99] His difficulties in making these payments are documented in his letters.

There are, unfortunately, few references in our ancient sources to the size of dowries provided in the marriages of historical figures. Treggiari points out that, in literary sources from the early imperial period, "one million sesterces recurs several times as a conventional figure for a large dowry for the wealthiest class."[100] She believes nonetheless that one million was exceeded by some families, and that Pliny would have offered much more than a million if he had had a daughter. In 19 CE, the daughters of two senatorial families were presented for one vacancy in the college of Vestal Virgins. The emperor Tiberius selected one of the girls, but then awarded a dowry of one million sesterces as a "consolation prize" to the girl who had not been chosen.[101] By the first century CE, one million sesterces was also the minimum capital required for membership in the senatorial class. Because campaigning for public office and maintaining a lifestyle appropriate for a senator was very expensive, it is not surprising that men aspiring to a political career married in their early 20s. As noted earlier, marriage and the production of children gave a man priority in the selection for public offices. The dowry which accompanied marriage also brought an injection of financial resources to support a political career.

A large dowry was not always, however, an unqualified benefit for a husband. A man seeking a very obedient wife – and most men were – might feel that the dowry put constraints on his behavior, in the sense that he could not afford to offend his wife lest she seek a divorce – and the return of her dowry. A character in one of Plautus' plays comments that a wife without a dowry is under the control of her husband, but a wife with a dowry destroys her husband.[102] Juvenal lamented that a wife's dowry bought for her the freedom to do as she pleased.[103] And Cicero recounts that a man named Aris did not want to stay married to his wife because of her ugliness, but did not want to divorce her because of her dowry.[104]

A woman whose *paterfamilias* was dead, and who was therefore *sui iuris* (although having a *tutor*), would do her own dowry negotiations, presumably in consultation with her *tutor* and her close relatives. A teenage girl – consider Junia of *Letter* 1.14 – would presumably need to depend on the wisdom and experience of those older than she to make dowry decisions. However, a wealthy middle-aged widow or divorcee might have considerable power in dowry arrangements and then in her new marriage. This power is a factor to be taken into account in our appraisal of the situation of (wealthy) widows. We don't hear of dowry-chasers to the extent that we hear of legacy-chasers. Presumably, with the ease of divorce in the Roman world, a woman could divorce a husband who offended her, and take her dowry (and inheritance) with her. Courting a dying person to gain a legacy may have seemed a surer bet than courting a widow for a dowry.

Although Plautus' character expressed a preference for a woman without a dowry, it is quite likely that even poor families provided some dowry. For example, a peasant farmer might plant a tree at the birth of his daughter, and then cut it and sell the wood to produce a dowry when she was of marriageable age.[105] The offering and acceptance of a dowry was one indication that the couple's co-habitation was a legal marriage. As discussed in Chapter 3, the validity of a union between a man and woman, who both possessed *conubium* (the legal capacity to enter into a valid marriage or *iustum matrimonium*), did not depend on any ceremony of sanction performed by a religious or state official. The man and woman were considered to be partners in a legal marriage if they demonstrated their "intent to be married," *affectio maritalis*, by living together as a couple. Recognition of a marriage thus rested on observation by the community that the couple was behaving as if married – that is, as if husband and wife. An announcement of betrothal and then wedding festivities were not legally required, but they might be the first pieces of evidence that a legal marriage was intended. Similarly the transfer of a dowry from the bride's family and the acceptance of it by the groom's family could be presumptive proof of a marriage. If, as there might well be, there was a written contract, specifying and recording the arrangements for the dowry, it would be a solid piece of documentary evidence. The bride's family had conveyed part of its property to the husband's family. Thus, even among the lower class, families might consider a dowry essential.

We do not know if a woman from a wealthy, but undistinguished family required a larger dowry than a woman from an aristocratic family in order to attract a husband with elite ancestry. It seems likely. Conversely, an ambitious man whose family was wealthy, but inactive in Roman politics, might not be able to request a very large dowry from a family with a strong record of political success. It would be interesting to know the identity of Pliny's first wife, whom he likely married at the time when he was beginning his pursuit of political office in Rome. His north Italian family had the resources to finance his campaigns, but not perhaps the personal connections necessary to assist him. It is possible that he chose a wife who brought to the marriage a relatively modest dowry, but many senatorial kinsmen who could smooth his career path. The fact that a wife's kinsmen were expected to support her husband's political campaigns is alluded to in *Letter* 1.14.7. We have no idea what size dowry the Junia of *Letter* 1.14 may have brought to her marriage. Her father, Arulenus Rusticus, had been executed during the reign of Domitian, but she was to be married in the post-Domitianic period. Was her father's fate a liability or an asset? Did Junia require a very large dowry to compensate for her father's unpopularity with Domitian. Or, in the post-Domitianic period, was her father regarded as a hero, whose daughter a man would be proud to marry?

For some fathers, eager to advance their own social positions through a "good" marriage for their daughters, or perhaps simply wanting to see their daughters well-settled, it may have been tempting to offer a dowry larger than they could actually afford. It was apparently not uncommon for relatives and friends to make contributions towards a girl's dowry. Turia, for example, who was mentioned in Chapter 3, provided dowries for some of her female relatives.[106] An inscription found near Rome documents the many acts of generosity of a man named Marcus Aurelius Cotta Maximus toward his freedman (former slave), Zosimus. Among them, Cotta, acting like a father (*ut pater ipse*), provided dowries for Zosimus' daughters. (Cotta had earlier ordered Zosimus to raise – that is, not expose – the children born to him, and provided for their maintenance.)[107] And Cicero wrote that it was quite appropriate to help "settle" the daughters of friends.[108]

Calvina

"Help" with a dowry might involve a gift or a loan to the father of the bride. In *Letter* 2.4, addressed to a woman named Calvina (one of the seven female addressees), Pliny relates that he had made both a gift and a loan for her dowry. The letter was written perhaps sometime in the late 90s and apparently subsequent to her marriage, but we do not know how long she had been married, whether she was still married, or whether she had children. Pliny reports that his generosity was motivated by *adfinitatis officium*, the obligation of kinship. We may surmise that Calvina was an *adfinis*, a relative of his, although we cannot determine the nature of the relationship. (The same word was used to identify the relationship between Fannia and the Vestal Virgin, Junia, in *Letter* 7.19.1, and between Pliny's mother-in-law, Pompeia Celerina, and Caelius Clemens in *Letter* 10.51.) Her father borrowed an undisclosed amount of money from Pliny to assemble a dowry for her.[109] In addition, Pliny contributed a gift of 100,000 sesterces. (For comparison, Pliny gave his nurse a small farm valued at 100,000 sesterces: *Letter* 6.3.) The situation suggests that the size of the dowry was well beyond the financial resources of Calvina's father. We do not know if he was trying to "marry up" and make a connection with a more elite family, or whether his family was sinking in status, and he hoped to retain its prestige by making a good match for his daughter. Nor do we have information about whether the dowry was paid in one lump sum, or in several installments, and, if the latter, whether all the installments were eventually paid. We have already noted how troublesome the payment of a dowry could be even for a man as wealthy as Cicero.

Calvina's father seems to have had a problem finding enough money to cover his expenses, a problem which became hers when he died. She was apparently his only child. When he died, she was named his heir. If a deceased person was financially solvent, the heir would pay off any outstanding debts and take possession of the remaining estate.[110] If, however, the deceased had been deeply in debt, the entire estate would be turned over to his creditors, leaving nothing for the heir. The heir would, moreover, be responsible for administration of the debt payment, and creditors might dun the heir about debts which the estate did not cover. It is no wonder that people sometimes chose not to accept the designation as heir. In fact, by law, the person designated as heir needed to make a formal statement of acceptance.[111] In Calvina's case, her father had incurred so much debt that, upon his death, she was reluctant to agree to be his heir. Pliny admits that the situation would have been grave even for a man. His statement suggests that Calvina did not have any brothers. It is also a reminder that Roman men assumed that women were less capable than men of managing financial matters, and that tutors therefore needed to be appointed to them when the *paterfamilias* died. We do not know who Calvina's *tutor* may have been.

Pliny informs Calvina that he, prompted by the obligation of kinship, has already paid off all the other creditors, who were strenuously pressing their claims. However, he does not indicate whether he did this before or after her father's death, or whether the father owed him more than just the money he had borrowed for the dowry. In any case, Pliny emerged as her sole creditor. One purpose of the letter seems to be to persuade Calvina to accept the designation of heir. Apparently, her refusal would reflect badly on her family, to which Pliny was connected. He makes a pledge of good will, and instructs her to restore her deceased father's reputation and honor (*Letter* 2.4.2). To assist her materially in this endeavor, he says that he will forgive the entire amount of her father's debt. He adds, however, in a section amounting to about a third of the letter, an account of his own financial situation. Although the income from his properties is modest (or so he claims), his personal thriftiness enables him to display generosity to others.

There can be no doubt about the purpose of the final section of the letter. Pliny's published announcement that he will absorb all the debts incurred by Calvina's father creates an image of a man who is wise in the management of his own property, generous toward others, and possessing a strong sense of duty toward kin. Not coincidentally, thriftiness and generosity were traits promoted by the emperor Trajan and lauded by Pliny in the *Panegyricus* (that is, sections 25 and 49).[112] Pliny thus presents himself in the letter as one who follows the pattern set by Trajan, and himself serves as a model for others. On the other hand, despite his admonition to Calvina that she must repair her father's reputation and honor, Pliny has damaged the man's reputation by publishing *Letter* 2.4 and thereby exposing and immortalizing his inability to manage his financial affairs.

And what portrait of Calvina emerges in the letter? She was the daughter of a man who lived beyond his means and who arranged for her a marriage which her family could not afford in terms of a dowry. We do not know if her marriage survived. If her father was unable to complete payments on her dowry – the size of which was determined to a great extent by the generosity of Pliny – her husband may have sought a divorce. It is noteworthy that she seems to have faced the issue of her deceased father's debts without assistance from her husband. Pliny's intervention rescued her from a very difficult situation. However, his letter leaves us with the impression that he made Calvina feel like a "poor cousin" who must be eternally beholden to a wealthier relative. His remark that she need not fear that his gift would prove burdensome to him seems designed to impress upon her precisely that his dutiful care of his kin was, in fact, a burden – though one which he could bear, not because he was wealthy, but because he was thrifty (something her father had not been). There is a patronizing attitude in *Letter* 2.4, as there was also in *Letter* 1.19, which was discussed in Chapter 4. There Pliny reminds Romatius Firmus, to whom he was offering a gift of 300,000 sesterces, that he (Romatius) is obligated to be forever grateful for the gift and to conduct himself in a way which will not embarrass his benefactor. Perhaps Calvina's predicament was an embarrassment to her kinsman, Pliny, and it was this embarrassment which motivated him to clear her father's debts. We do not know whether Calvina harbored any resentment about her dependence on her wealthy kinsman.

The anonymous daughter of Quintilianus

Letter 6.32 is addressed to a man named Quintilianus. He was not the well-known professor of rhetoric who suffered the loss of his young 18-year-old wife and two young sons.[113] The Quintilianus of 6.32 had a daughter who was betrothed to Nonius Celer. Pliny does not give the daughter's name, but identifies her as the granddaughter of a man named Tutilius. Tutilius may have been the writer on oratory referred to by the rhetorician Quintilian and by the poet Martial.[114] Or he may have been the Stoic philosopher, Gaius Tutilius Hostilianus.[115] In any case, he was more likely the maternal, than the paternal grandfather of the betrothed girl. About the prospective bridegroom, Nonius Celer, we know nothing. Pliny opens *Letter* 6.32 by complimenting Quintilianus for being content with a simple life and for raising his daughter in a manner befitting her father and grandfather. (Did he, like Thrasea Paetus and Helvidius I, adopt an austere life-style?) Nonetheless, Pliny observes, she is to marry a very distinguished man (*honestissimus vir*) whose public duties require a certain display of elegance. As his wife, she must be fitted with clothing and attendants appropriate to her husband's position.[116] Pliny states that, since Quintilianus is a man with peace of mind, but limited resources, he wants to share the burden, as if a second father to the girl and contribute 50,000 sesterces, which he qualifies as a modest little gift, *medio-critas munusculi*.[117] We might compare Pliny's expressed desire to act paternally with the generosity of Marcus Aurelius Cotta Maximus who, acting like a father, provided dowries for the daughters of his freedman, Zosimus.

It is clear that Pliny believed that the girl should enter her marriage with a supply of stylish clothing and a retinue of slaves. It is not clear, however, whether the 50,000 sesterces were to be used to augment the dowry – that is, whether clothing and slaves valued at 50,000 sesterces would be calculated as part of the dowry administered by the husband's family, or whether the 50,000 sesterces worth of clothing and slaves would be gifts to the bride which would be calculated as her family's property, administered by her *paterfamilias*.[118]

Domitia Lucilla

In *Letter* 8.18, we learn of a daughter who was drawn by her father and uncle into a scheme to enrich themselves. The two men were brothers: Gnaeus Domitius Lucanus (the father) and Gnaeus Domitius Tullus (the uncle). Their birth father was Sextus Curvius Tullus, but they had been adopted about 41 CE by the distinguished orator Gnaeus Domitius Afer.[119] (See Genealogy Chart 6.) The reasons why Domitius Afer adopted them are unknown. However, his relations with their birth father apparently became strained, and Pliny reports that Domitius Afer was instrumental in having Curvius Tullus removed from the citizen roll (*Letter* 8.18.6), which presumably means that he was involved in a prosecution which led to his banishment. The relationship between the orator and his adoptive sons also soured, though again we do not know why. Domitius Afer was so unhappy with them that he took steps to have their birth father's property confiscated (*Letters* 8.18.5 and 6). Strangely, however, he failed to change his own will.[120] Therefore, when he died in 59 CE, they became his heirs.

The two brothers had successful public careers, both having achieved the rank of suffect consul sometime in the 70s, and both later serving as proconsuls of Africa. Domitius Tullus may have been consul a second time in 98. The brothers were very close. The epigrammist, Martial, records their affection for one another.[121]

Their bonds were perhaps more, however, than just affective. In *Letter* 8.18.4, Pliny uses the phrase *consors frater*, and Sherwin-White speculates that, when their adoptive father died, the brothers did not each, as separate heirs, take possession of half of the property, but rather formed a *consortium bonorum*, a "joint holding of the goods." They agreed, in essence, to co-own the entire estate.[122] Under this concept of co-ownership, the property of Domitius Afer remained unpartitioned, and each brother had an equal right in the enjoyment and administration of it. It was as if there was one household with two *patres familiares*.

Domitius Lucanus married a woman who was the daughter of Curtilius Mancia, suffect consul in 55 CE and then legate of Upper Germany. We do not know how or why the marriage between Domitius Lucanus and Curtilius' daughter (perhaps named Curtilia) was arranged, but Curtilius grew to detest his son-in-law (*Letter* 8.18.4). The couple seems to have had only one child who reached adulthood, a daughter named Domitia Lucilla.[123] And she may have been Curtilius' only grandchild. One might have expected Curtilius to designate his daughter as his heir. Because he did not, perhaps we may surmise that she predeceased him, and that he had no other remaining children. In any case, Pliny informs us that Curtilius planned to leave his estate to his granddaughter, Domitia Lucilla. However, since he loathed her father, he made the stipulation, presumably stated in his will, that she could inherit his estate only if she were released from the *patria potestas*, the paternal control, of her father (her *paterfamilias*), Domitius Lucanus. A similar situation has been discussed in Chapters 3 and 4, in connection with Regulus and his son. According to *Letter* 4.2, the boy's mother had apparently insisted that he could be her heir only if he had been emancipated. In both these situations, since the *patres familiares* of the children were alive, any property they inherited would have come under the legal control of the *patres familiares* unless they, the children, had been emancipated. Regulus complied with the mother's wishes, and formally released their son from his paternal control. The crafty Domitius Lucanus also released his daughter, but arranged to have her adopted by his brother, Domitius Tullus. The daughter, Domitia Lucilla, thus immediately returned under *patria potestas*, now of her uncle/adoptive father. We do not know how old she was at the time of the emancipation/adoption scheme, and whether she was a willing participant. A phrase at *Letter* 8.18.7 suggests that there was some tension among the brothers and Domitia Lucilla. According to Pliny, Domitius Lucanus, in his will, made his brother his heir, rather than his daughter, in order that there might be a reconciliation (*ut conciliaretur*). Pliny provides no details about that situation. In any case, once Domitia Lucilla had been released from the *patria potestas* of her father, she was free to inherit the estate of her maternal grandfather. However, the estate passed into the control of her uncle once he became, by adoption, her new *paterfamilias*. And, because the brothers Domitii seem to have formed a *consortium bonorum*, the estate of Curtilius came to be managed equally by the son-in-law he had detested. As Pliny explains: "The father emancipated, the uncle adopted. Thus the terms of the will were circumvented, and the brothers shared the estate. One, by the fraud of adoption, transferred into the control of his brother both the daughter he had emancipated and the very ample fortune she had inherited" (*Letter* 8.18.4).

After the death of Domitius Lucanus (the natal father), Domitius Tullus (the uncle/adoptive father) was solely in control of the family's vast fortune. When he died, his will was made public and its contents were the subject of Pliny's *Letter* 8.18. Pliny opens the letter with the comment: "That popular belief is certainly false, that a man's will is a mirror of his character, for Domitius Tullus appeared much better in death than in life." Since his behavior while alive had been contemptible, people were surprised to learn that he had, in the end, acted honorably and made his family members his beneficiaries, rather than leaving his fortune to the *captatores*, the legacy-hunters, whose attentions he had apparently encouraged. Pliny observes that Tullus' "will was all the more praiseworthy because family devotion (*pietas*), loyalty (*fides*) and decency (*pudor*) created it" (*Letter* 8.18.7). In Chapter 3, there was discussion of Tullus' generous bequests to his dutiful wife (perhaps his second wife and perhaps named Dasumia Polla), who nursed him when he was crippled and bedridden. His heir, however, was his adoptive daughter, Domitia Lucilla. (He seems not to have had any children of his own.) As commented in Chapter 4, his wife proved to be not only a sterling wife, but also a good stepmother because she did not cajole her husband into leaving the bulk of his fortune to her rather than to his daughter. And yet, as Pliny notes, he did not so much *leave* the wealth to his daughter as *return* it to her since it was through her that he came to acquire it (*Letter* 8.18.3).

The fact that the two wealthy and apparently unscrupulous brothers had, between them, only one child to serve as heir, is a reminder that many Roman families (and Pliny's was one) had difficulty producing descendants. And, of course, the brothers Domitii had been adopted by someone who had presumably not produced blood children. In addition, Curtilius Mancia, the father of Domitia Lucilla's mother, seems to have had only one child, a daughter, who reached adulthood. However, she may have predeceased him, leaving his only choice for a blood heir to be his granddaughter (and leaving the girl without a mother).

With the death of her uncle/adoptive father, Domitia Lucilla came into possession of a very large estate, comprised in part of the property of her maternal grandfather, Curtilius Mancia, and of her paternal grandfather by adoption, Domitius Afer. From Pliny's *Letter* 8.18.2, we learn that in 108 CE she was not only the mother of several children, but also the grandmother of one child (a girl), to all of whom Domitius Tullus dutifully left legacies. We may speculate that she was about 40 when she gained this inheritance. If she had at least three children, she would not have required a *tutor*. Among the many lucrative properties which she inherited was one or more brick and pottery factories.[124] Her name is preserved by the stamps on tiles from these factories. We do not know how active a role she may have played in the running of these factories, but her ownership of them (which she passed on to her daughter) is an indication that some wealthy women acquired opportunities to engage in business enterprises. Domitia Lucilla may have been as shrewd a businesswoman as we speculate that Ummidia Quadratilla (Chapter 5), Pompeia Celerina (Chapter 5), and Corellia (Chapter 4) may have been.

Publius Calvisius Tullus Ruso, who became *consul ordinarius* in 109 CE, is assumed to be the husband of Domitia Lucilla. He is recorded as the father of her daughter, also named Domitia Lucilla.[125] [Henceforth the mother – adopted by Domitius Tullus – will be identified as Domitia Lucilla E (the Elder, Maior) and her daughter as Domitia Lucilla Y (the Younger, Minor). We do not know why the daughter preserved the name of her mother's family – Domitius – rather than her father's – Calvisius.] Since the daughter herself bore a child in 121 CE, when she may have been about 17 or 18 years old, we may conjecture that her parents had been married since at least 103 CE.[126] However, Pliny tells us that Domitia Lucilla E already had a granddaughter in 108 CE and was therefore about 40 years old. If her husband, Publius Calvisius Tullus Ruso, became consul for the first time in 109 CE, he was probably in his early 30s then. If these speculations about their ages are correct, Domitia Lucilla E probably had been married previously, in her early teens, perhaps about 83 CE, and borne one or more children with that husband. It seems quite likely that her family would have wanted her married off and producing children at a young age. The granddaughter of Pliny's *Letter* 8.18.2 would have been the offspring of a child from her first marriage, which was ended either by death or divorce. Publius Calvisius Tullus Ruso, ready for marriage when he was in his early 20s – that is, about 100 CE – chose a bride who was several years older than he, but who had proved her fertility and was enormously wealthy. There is scholarly debate about whether Domitia Lucilla E was predeceased by Publius Calvisius Tullus Ruso, and married for a third time, to Catilius Severus to whom Pliny addressed *Letters* 1.22 (about the illness of Titius Aristo) and 3.12. Syme presents this suggestion, but also proposes that Catilius may have married the widow of Domitius Tullus (perhaps named Dasumia Polla) – that is, the stepmother of Domitia Lucilla E.[127] The possibility of this marriage, which would have been a third one for Dasumia Polla, is discussed in Chapter 3. (The speculations are based on a reference, which will be discussed shortly, about Catilius Severus's identification as a grandparent.) We do not know how many children and grandchildren in total Domitia Lucilla E had. Only one child has left a record, the daughter whose father was Publius Calvisius Tullus Ruso.

About 118 CE, Domitia Lucilla Y married Marcus Annius Verus whose family had ties to and property in Spain, but whose father was a Roman senator. One of his sisters, Annia Galeria Faustina the Elder, married Antoninus Pius, who was adopted by Hadrian and served as emperor 138–61 CE. Domitia Lucilla E's daughter (and Domitius Tullus's granddaughter) thus married into a family with prestigious political connections. The wealth of the Domitius family was undoubtedly an attraction in the arrangement of the marriage. Another of Marcus Annius Verus's sisters may have married Gaius Ummidius Quadratus, grandson of Ummidia Quadratilla, the woman whose death is reported in *Letter* 7.24 (and discussed in Chapter 5). If this conjecture is correct, Ummidia Quadratilla would have been related by marriage to the avaricious Domitius Tullus. Both these people redeemed themselves, according to Pliny, by writing good wills.

Domitia Lucilla Y and Marcus Annius Verus had two children, a son and a daughter, who lived to adulthood. The daughter, Annia Cornificia Faustina, married her (possibly) first cousin, the Ummidius Quadratus who was the son of Ummidia Quadratilla's grandson. The son of Domitia Lucilla Y and Marcus Annius Verus, who was born in 121 CE, became the emperor Marcus Aurelius (emperor 161 to 180). Domitia Lucilla Y's husband (and Marcus Aurelius' father) died at an early age, perhaps in 124 CE, before he had reached the rank of consul.[128] Her son was adopted by his paternal grandfather, Marcus Annius Verus (yes, the same name as his father) and apparently lived with him as he grew up. One of our sources records that Catilius Severus was the maternal *proavus* of Marcus Aurelius.[129] *Proavus* can mean either "grandfather" or "great-grandfather." If Catilius Severus had married Domitia Lucilla E (that is, been her third husband), he would have been the step-grandfather of Marcus Aurelius. However, had he, as Syme proposes, married the widow of Domitius Tullus, he would have been the step-great-grandfather.

Although Marcus Aurelius spent his childhood in the home of his paternal grandfather, he retained a strong emotional bond with his mother. The affection between them has been noted in Chapter 4. Marcus Aurelius also praised his mother for providing him with an excellent moral upbringing: "From my mother, I learned reverence for the gods, and charity, and abstinence not only from doing wrong, but even from thinking it, and simplicity in my way of life, and repudiation of a rich man's lifestyle."[130]

Marcus Aurelius was born well after the death of Pliny. He is mentioned here, in part, to indicate what a good marriage his grandmother, Domitia Lucilla E, had been able to make for her daughter, Domitia Lucilla Y. He is also mentioned, however, because his characterization of his mother may shed some light on the character of Domitia Lucilla E. We learn nothing about her character from Pliny's *Letter* 8.18. We might assume that a woman whose childhood was dominated by two avaricious brothers and who appears, in Pliny's letter, to have been used as a pawn in their scheme to enrich themselves, would have learned from them the behavior of greedy schemers, and would have passed this behavior on to her daughter. However, Marcus Aurelius' depiction of his mother leads us to a different conclusion. Admittedly, we must be aware that his depiction may not be unbiased, but it is striking that he emphasizes that she taught him charity and a scorn for wealth. Perhaps we may consider that Domitia Lucilla E, despite living with the brothers Domitii, developed a strong sense of moral conduct, and that she taught her daughter, who in turn taught her son (the future emperor Marcus Aurelius), to lead a good life. In addition, we learn from the letters of Fronto, who was the teacher and friend of Marcus Aurelius[131], that his mother, Domitia Lucilla Y, was fluent in Greek and very knowledgeable about Greek culture.[132] Perhaps we may speculate that her mother, Domitia Lucilla E, played a decisive role in ensuring that her daughter received a type of advanced education which few girls received. She may have inspired in her an interest in learning and in ethical behavior.

Attia Viriola

Unlike Domitia Lucilla, a woman named Attia Viriola was not well-treated by her father in his will. Pliny's *Letter* 6.33, addressed to his friend Voconius Romanus[133], was a cover letter attached to a copy of a speech which Pliny had recently delivered before the Centumviral Court. The court case concerned Attia Viriola's appeal of her father's will. The letter has been discussed in Chapter 4 and will receive only brief mention here. We know about Attia Viriola only from this letter of Pliny, which may have been written about 106 or 107 CE. The identities of her father and her husband are both unknown. We know that her family, which was apparently of equestrian rank, was well-connected and wealthy enough to marry her to a man who embarked on a political career and attained the office of praetor, but had not (yet), at least at the time the letter was written, been selected for the consulship (*Letter* 6.33.2). As praetor, he would have been about 30 years old, but may have been much older at the date of the letter. We cannot therefore use his age to speculate on Attia Viriola's age. And although her father was at least 80 years old, he may have been married several times. If Attia Viriola was the child of a second or third wife – that is, of a wife much younger than her husband – the age gap between her and her father might have been considerable. We do not know if Attia Viriola and her husband had children. The identity and fate of her mother are also unknown. If she was dead, her daughter may have inherited her property or been left a substantial bequest. Attia Viriola may have been related to the Sextus Attius Suburanus Aemilianus who was prefect of the Praetorian Guard from 98 to 101 CE, and then consul twice, in 101 and in 104 CE. (See Chapter 4.)

She was a woman of high enough rank and wealth to be able to bring her grievance before the Centumviral Court, and to enlist the assistance of Pliny. He states that his speech is important because of the distinction of the person involved and because of the rare nature of the case (*Letter* 6.33.2). Attia Viriola had been disinherited by her octogenarian father within 11 days of his introducing to her a stepmother for whom he had been captivated by love. Although Pliny states that the nature of the case was rare, the situation – disinheritance by a parent – was one which was examined in Roman legal commentaries. The topic was explored in Chapter 4, in the discussion of Pomponia Galla's exclusion of her son from her will. Roman jurists generally supported the tradition of a father choosing his children as his heirs. They cautioned in particular about the possibility of a stepmother persuading her husband to deprive his children of his estate. "It must not be allowed to parents to cause harm to their children by their wills. They do this most often when they make a spiteful judgment against their own blood, having been taken in by the charms and enticements of stepmothers."[134] In another passage, a stepmother is admonished thus. "If your husband appointed you as his sole heir in his will, and disinherited the daughter whom he had in his *potestas* and left her nothing, this disinheritance will not be permitted because she did not give him any just cause for being offended. If she should complain that her father's will was unduteous, there is no doubt that she could obtain the entire estate."[135] There was in Roman culture a deep-rooted fear that a stepmother, perhaps with her own children by a previous marriage, would gain possession of the estate of her new husband and deprive his children of it.

Unfortunately, Pliny provides no details about the circumstances surrounding the father's decision. Did the disinheritance come as a surprise to Attia Viriola, revealed only when her father died and his will was opened? Had her relationship with her father previously been loving? Was the 80-year-old father a silly old man, whose judgment was clouded by his infatuation for his new bride? Was the new bride the proverbial wicked stepmother who had seduced the old man into leaving his fortune to her? She may have been quite a young woman, the same age as, or perhaps even younger than Attia Viriola. There are no answers in Pliny's letter. It is possible, of course, that the father had a good reason for disinheriting Attia Viriola – that is, that she had given him just cause for being offended – even as Pomponia Galla had just cause for disinheriting her son (*Letter* 5.1). We learn only that Attia Viriola applied to the Centumviral Court – probably by a *querela inofficiosi testamenti* – to have her father's property transferred to her. As the legal passages cited earlier suggest, the courts seemed to be unsympathetic to stepmothers. Pliny's description of the proceedings are sketchy, but Attia Viriola seems to have won her case.

Although Pliny's letter gives us very little information about Attia Viriola's life, it provides an intriguing glimpse into the kind of complications that might arise when a man brought a stepmother into his household. Undoubtedly, in the speech which he presented before the Centumviral Court and was now sending to Voconius Romanus, Pliny spoke with rhetorical flourish about the wickedness of stepmothers. The only example we find in Pliny of what appears to have been a good relationship between a stepdaughter and stepmother is that between Domitia Lucilla and the wife who nursed her father so devotedly.[136] Admittedly, *Letter* 8.18 tells us nothing about how Domitia Lucilla and her stepmother got along. They may have spent little time together because Domitia Lucilla was occupied with her own children and even a granddaughter.[137] It seems, however, that the step-mother did not scheme to deprive Domitia Lucilla of her inheritance. Or perhaps her father recognized his duty toward his adoptive daughter and was adamant about leaving the bulk of his estate to her.

Daughters and stepfathers

There is not expressed in Roman literature the same anxiety about stepfathers. The Latin word for "stepfather" is *vitricus*, which does not, like *noverca* ("stepmother"), allude to the "newness" or "stranger-ness" (Latin: *novitas*) of a father's new wife. We might suppose that children would have the same apprehensions about a stepfather finagling to deprive them of a share of their mother's estate, or about step-siblings or half-siblings being rivals for their mother's affection and property. We might, moreover, suppose that children were as likely to fear abuse or murder by a stepfather as by a stepmother. However, angst about an evil stepfather was not encoded in popular folk tales and myths. The difference may be attributable in part to the fact that children were more likely to live with a stepmother than with a stepfather. Step-relations were common in the ancient Roman world, both because of the high mortality rate among people of child-producing years and because of the ease of divorce. When a woman with children died or was divorced, the children usually remained with the father since they were members of his (not her) agnate family. He would likely remarry, both to secure a manager for his children and household and to avoid the penalties for celibacy which Augustus had established. Even if it were the father, rather than the mother, who died, the children might be removed from her care and placed with an agnate relative. Of course, there were always exceptions, when, for example, a father died and left no close relatives to take in the children. This seems to have been the situation with Pliny, who apparently continued to live with his mother after his father's death, and to have been adopted by his maternal (that is, non-agnate) uncle. There is no record of Plinia having remarried and introduced a stepfather to her son. However, the doting mother of Pliny's friend, Voconius Romanus, seems to have retained custody of her son after her husband died, and to have remarried. This stepfather treated Voconius Romanus with the kindness of a father (*Letter* 2.13.4) and eventually adopted him (*Letter* 10.4).[138]

We can identify only two women in Pliny's published letters who had stepfathers. Pliny's second wife, about whom we know almost nothing, had a stepfather.[139] Her mother was Pompeia Celerina, to whom Pliny addressed *Letter* 1.4 and whom he mentions in *Letters* 1.18.3, 3.19.8, 6.10.1, 9.13.13, and 10.51. (Pliny's relationship with her is discussed in Chapter 5.) Her father is unknown, although Raepsaet-Charlier speculates that he was Lucius Venuleius Montanus Apronianus, who was consul in 92 CE.[140] If this speculation is correct, the name of Pliny's wife may have been Venuleia. We do not know whether Venuleia's parents were separated by death or divorce. We learn in *Letter* 9.13.13 that, by 97 CE, though perhaps much earlier, Pompeia Celerina had married again, to a man of senatorial rank named Bittius Proculus. We cannot ascertain whether, at the time of this marriage, "Venuleia" was living with her mother, or with her father's agnate family, or was already married to Pliny. If her mother's second marriage had taken place in the mid-90s, "Venuleia," who died in late 96 or early 97 CE, may have had little contact with her stepfather. As noted in Chapter 5, Pliny continued, after his wife's death, to have a close relationship with her mother, Pompeia Celerina.

The only other mention which Pliny makes of a daughter-stepfather situation occurs in *Letter* 9.13.16. There he writes that the mother and stepfather of Helvidius II's daughter had chosen Gaius Julius Cornutus Tertullus to be her guardian. (She was one of the two daughters who died in childbirth about 105 CE.) Because Helvidius II's wife at the time of his death sentence was Anteia, it is assumed that she was also the mother of his two daughters and one son. She remarried soon after his death, to a man whose identity is not known to us. Helvidius II seems not to have had any close agnate relatives[141], which may explain why Anteia and her new husband took on the responsibility of selecting a guardian for the daughter. Their involvement in this matter suggests that the girl, who was probably not yet a teenager, lived in their household. We have no information, however, about the relationship between this stepdaughter and stepfather.

The daughters of Titius Aristo and Corellius Rufus

The mention of the Helvidius family is a reminder of two other daughters who were discussed earlier, though mainly in their roles as wives: Arria the Younger and Fannia. (See Chapter 2.) Both women were married to men who shared their fathers' discontent with the conduct of the emperors. This is not surprising because most marriages were arranged by the father or *paterfamilias*, although in consultation with the mother, other family members, and friends. Both Arria Y and Fannia were already married when their fathers died. Any attempt to define these father-daughter relationships is speculation. Arria Y lost her mother (Arria E) at the same time as her father. Her attempts to prevent the suicide of her mother are recorded in *Letters* 3.16.10, and 11. After her mother's death, she seems to have taken on the task of publicizing Arria E's heroism. The mother-daughter relationship between Arria Y and Fannia was apparently close. Arria Y was persuaded by her husband, Thrasea Paetus, not to join him in death, but to remain alive for Fannia's sake. After Thrasea's death, mother and daughter may have lived in the same household and continued to promote the reputations of deceased family members and the careers of living family members. They both endured several years of exile in the mid-90s. We don't know if they spent it in the same location. Fannia's attempts, unfortunately unsuccessful, to protect her mother from prosecution, are recorded in *Letter* 7.19.5. Although we cannot ascertain whether mother and daughter loved one another, certainly their loyalty to one another and to their family is evident in their actions.

The bond between fathers and daughters receives brief attention in two letters. In *Letter* 1.22, written about 97 CE, Pliny reports to Catilius Severus[142] the grave illness of Titius Aristo and his contemplation of suicide. At 1.22.9, Pliny mentions that Titius Aristo was moved by his daughter's tears [and wife's pleas][143] not to act hastily, but to wait for the doctors' assessment of his chances for survival. Again, we have no way of knowing whether the daughter (whose name Pliny does not provide) was in tears because she loved her father deeply, or because she was expected to act thus. It is striking that the father revealed his suicide plans to his daughter (as Arria E revealed her plans to her daughter, Arria Y). In *Letter* 1.12, written about 97 CE, Pliny announces the suicide of Corellius Rufus. Unlike Titius Aristo, Corellius was impervious to the entreaties of his daughter and wife (*Letter* 1.12.9). At this time, his daughter, Corellia Hispulla (mentioned in Chapter 4), was married and had a son about ten years old. Nonetheless, she maintained a relationship with her father that included her participation in discussions about his plans for suicide. After her father's death, his friends, or Pliny at least, continued to demonstrate their esteem for her father by assisting her. In *Letter* 3.3, for example, Pliny recommends a teacher for Corellia Hispulla's son, stating that he loved and revered her father and now feels obligated to exert himself so that her son may grow up to be like his maternal grandfather. And, in *Letter* 4.17, he explains to his addressee his willingness to support Corellia Hispulla in a legal case. As discussed in Chapter 4, this letter serves to notify readers that Pliny was a loyal friend who continued to honor his deceased mentor, Corellius Rufus, by lending help to his daughter. Pliny reiterates his commitment several times. "I cannot hesitate to support the daughter of Corellius" (*Letter* 4.17.2). "All concerns (*about the distinguished status of her opponent*) are weak when I reflect that it is the daughter of Corellius whom I am to defend" (*Letter* 4.17.4). "When he was dying, he told his daughter, as she often proclaims: 'During my rather long life, I have acquired many friends for you, but Secundus and Cornutus are very special'" (*Letter* 4.17.9).

Letter 4.17 offers some insight into how a Roman father might utilize the complex system of social obligations to provide support for his children after his death. In Pliny's account, Corellius Rufus admits that he had purposively built a coterie of friends for the sake of his daughter. The Latin verb which he used for "I acquired (friends)" is *paravi*, which also has the meaning of "I prepared" and "I purchased." Apparently, he had done favors for them – being Pliny's mentor, for example – and expected them to reciprocate, even after his death. Pliny's letter makes it clear that an honorable man continued to help his friend's family.[144] We must remember that Corellia Hispulla was married at the time of her father's death, managing her own household, and could presumably depend on her husband for support and advice. Nonetheless, her bond with her father had remained strong, and he was concerned that she be adequately protected after his death. In a sense, he bequeathed to her a network of friends (as well, presumably, as his estate). Corellius Rufus' paternal concern for his daughter, even when she was married, was probably not unusual. Earlier in this chapter, there was mention of the apparent frequency with which Cicero and his married daughter, Tullia, spent time together. Perhaps fathers, who were willing to marry off their daughters when they were barely in their teens, nonetheless continued to think of them as vulnerable little girls. And perhaps the daughters continued to act, at least in the presence of their fathers, like "daddy's girls." A married woman, at least one from a wealthy family, would expect to inherit an estate from her father, and thus become financially independent of her husband. She had good reason to be affectionate toward her father. This is not to say that her affection might not be genuine, but it is worth keeping in mind that a daughter's dependence on her father, and his desire to protect her, did not end with her marriage. In contrast to Corellius Rufus' concern for his daughter's continued well-being, we might consider the plight of Attia Viriola of *Letter* 6.33, a married woman whose father had disinherited her soon after his remarriage.

The daughter of Caecilius Classicus (perhaps Caecilia)

Most of the fathers referred to in Pliny's letters were men with senatorial careers who would, at some point in their careers, have held appointments in the provinces. They may have been accompanied by their wives (as Pliny was accompanied to Bithynia by Calpurnia) and by their children. For example, as children, the sisters Verania Gemina (*Letter* 2.20) and Verania Octavilla, who are mentioned in Chapter 3, accompanied their father to his posting in the provinces of Lycia and Pamphilia. In *Letter* 3.9, Pliny mentions the presence in the province of Baetica (modern Andalusia, Spain) of the wife and daughter of Caecilius

Classicus. This letter was discussed in Chapter 3, where the question of whether the wife (Casta) was the biological mother of Caecilius' daughter is addressed. Caecilius Classicus was governor of the prosperous and very Romanized province from 97 to 98 CE, during which time he acted, according to Pliny, disgracefully (*Letter* 3.9.2). Within a year or so of his departure, the Baetici requested of the Roman Senate that Classicus be prosecuted in Rome on charges of extortion, and probably the more serious charge of extortion with violence, which was a capital offence. Pliny accepted the task of serving as one of the prosecutors and he discusses the case in *Letters* 3.4 and 3.9. Classicus died before the trial began ("by a death that was either fortuitous or voluntary", *Letter* 3.9.5), but he was tried nonetheless and convicted. The Senate continued with the prosecution of many other people who were suspected of having joined Classicus in his extortionate practices, including his wife, Casta, his daughter, perhaps named Caecilia (although Pliny leaves her anonymous), and his son-in-law, Claudius Fuscus (presumably the husband of "Caecilia"). We gain no idea of how old the daughter may have been, except that, since she was married, she must have been at least in her mid-teens. Unfortunately, Pliny provides no information about why Caecilia and Claudius Fuscus were in the province. Perhaps he had an official position on the staff of his father-in-law, the governor, or perhaps they were there simply as family members. Whatever the circumstances, we have another example of a daughter remaining close to her parents even after marriage. In this case, however, the bond between the father and the daughter caused her to be suspected of illicit activity. As noted in Chapter 1, there had been considerable discussion in the Senate in the early decades of the first century CE about the activities of wives in the provinces, and a decree of 24 CE apparently made wives liable for extortionate practices. However, Pliny's account of the Classicus affair is the only attested case of a daughter being indicted for extortion at the same time as her father. Pliny does not give details of the charges against Classicus's family members, but perhaps they were accused of encouraging bribes to influence the governor's decisions.

Several sets of hearings were held in the Senate, over several days. At the second set, Classicus' son-in-law, Claudius Fuscus, was prosecuted, along with a tribune on his military staff. In an interesting turn of events, the son-in-law was acquitted, but the tribune was convicted and sentenced to a two-year banishment. Pliny offers no clue about why the judgments were so different or whether he believed that the husband deserved an acquittal. At the third set of hearings, Classicus' wife, Casta, and his daughter, Caecilia, were prosecuted, along with a large number of people who, according to Pliny, were much less important than Casta. One might have expected Pliny to describe the charges against the women. Instead he only insinuates that Casta was guilty, and then admits that there was not enough evidence to convict her (*Letter* 3.9.19). She was acquitted (*Letter* 3.9.34). About Caecilia, however, Pliny reports that no suspicion of wrongdoing was attached to her (*Letter* 3.9.20). He decided that the most honorable course was not to treat her harshly and not to aim his eloquence like a weapon at the throat of an innocent woman (*Letter* 3.9.21). Curiously, however, he does not announce whether the daughter was acquitted, although he certainly leads us to believe that she deserved to be. It seems that all three of Classicus' family members were ultimately found not guilty of the charge of extortion. The truth about Caecilia's involvement cannot be recovered, but her story indicates how a daughter could be harmed by her father's wrong-doing.

Caecilius Classicus, though deceased, was tried in the early part of the proceedings and convicted. Since the charge was a capital one, his punishment would likely have been the most severe meted out to an elite person: exile with the confiscation of citizenship and property. Had such a punishment been imposed, Caecilia would have been deprived of her inheritance. However, the Senate decided to separate the property which Classicus had possessed before arriving in Baetica as governor from the property he acquired while governor, and to allow Caecilia to take possession of the former as his heir (*Letter* 3.9.17). As noted in Chapter 1, the Senate and even the emperor were often inclined not to ruin the lives of the children of convicted men by removing their patrimony. The property which Classicus acquired during his time in Baetica was to be given to the people he had robbed. We know nothing more about Caecilia's life.

The anonymous daughter of Publius Accius Aquila

Letters 10.106 and 107, written about 111 or 112 CE, reveal a military father's efforts to gain Roman citizenship for his daughter. *Letter* 10.106 was written by Pliny when he was governor of Bithynia, and it was part of his official correspondence with the emperor Trajan. It is, in fact, a cover letter, which accompanied a petition (not extant) which a soldier requested that Pliny forward to Trajan. We learn that the soldier, whose name was Publius Accius Aquila, was a centurion of *cohors sexta equestris*, the Sixth Cavalry Cohort. Nothing is known about this unit. Sherwin-White points out that its name lacks the usual ethnic designation (that is, *cohors prima Hispanorum* and *cohors prima Brittonum*), and that the word *equestris* is used instead of the more usual *equitata*.[145]

A cohort comprised about 600 men. A cavalry cohort was usually a mixed unit, containing a larger number of infantry than mounted soldiers, perhaps about a 4:1 ratio. Most importantly for our interests, cavalry cohorts were "auxiliary" units (*auxilia*), which means that their members were recruited from free men who lived in Roman provinces, but were not Roman citizens. (Enrollment in the Roman legions was reserved for Roman citizens.) There were, however, occasionally Roman citizens who joined auxiliary units, sometimes enlisting at the beginning of their military careers, sometimes transferring from a Roman legion after several years of service, perhaps in order to receive an appointment to a higher rank.[146] During Pliny's time, perhaps half of the centurions in the *auxilia* were Roman citizens.[147] For men without Roman citizenship, enrollment in the *auxilia* was attractive because of the benefits gained upon retirement. At the conclusion of 25 years of active service, an auxiliary soldier and his children were granted Roman citizenship. Soldiers were not allowed to marry during their years of service, but, upon retirement, they were granted *conubium*, a privilege which recognized the unions they had formed with non-Roman women as valid marriages.[148] This privilege, in turn, provided their children with intestate rights of inheritance. However, their wives were not granted Roman citizenship.

The centurion of *Letter* 10.106 was Publius Accius Aquila. His name suggests that he was a Roman citizen. We do not know why he had joined an auxiliary unit or why he was in Bithynia. Perhaps he had served in a Roman legion, but later transferred to an auxiliary cohort because such a transfer offered the opportunity to be appointed to the rank of centurion. Or perhaps he had arrived in Bithynia as a legionary, formed a union with a local woman, and then moved to an auxiliary cohort so that, upon his retirement, his children would receive Roman citizenship and intestate inheritance rights. In *Letter* 10.106, Pliny explains to Trajan that he is forwarding a petition from Accius Aquila. It is in *Letter* 10.107, which is Trajan's reply, that we learn the nature of the petition: Accius Aquila was requesting that Trajan grant Roman citizenship to his daughter. Since the girl would have received citizenship upon his retirement, he was, in effect, asking that the privilege be granted prematurely. But why? Wolff suggests that the girl was of marriageable age, and that Accius Aquila was negotiating a marriage for her with a Roman citizen.[149] She would be much more attractive to the prospective groom's family as a Roman citizen who could form a legally valid marriage with their son.[150]

In his cover letter, Pliny makes the point that Trajan has been accustomed to show great kindness to the requests of soldiers. And in his reply, Trajan announces that, moved by the centurion's pleas, he has granted Roman citizenship to his daughter. He sent back to Bithynia the original petition, with his decision written at the end of it. The document would provide the centurion's family with proof of the girl's status.

Flavia Julia

In *Letter* 4.11.6, a letter which was written perhaps about 104 or 105 CE, Pliny makes brief mention of the daughter of Titus who was emperor from 79 to 81 CE. Although he does not include her name, we know from other sources, both literary and epigraphical, that she was called "Julia."[151] (See Figure 5.) Her complete name probably included "Flavia," the family name of her father Titus (whose full name was Titus Flavius Vespasianus). She was born in September, possibly in 63 or 64 CE.[152] Her paternal grandfather, Vespasian, who became emperor in 69 CE, would, of course, have been her *paterfamilias* until his death. Her paternal uncle was Titus' brother, Domitian, who would rule as emperor 81 to 96 CE. Flavia Julia's mother may have been Titus' first wife, Arrecina Tertulla, or his second wife, Marcia Furnilla.[153] Arrecina Tertulla's family was not senatorial, but Suetonius reports that her father had been prefect of the praetorian cohorts. He also states that, after the death of Arrecina Tertulla, Titus married, but then divorced, Marcia Furnilla, a woman of very distinguished family, with whom he had a daughter.[154] Suetonius' account thus leaves open the possibilities that Flavia Julia was the daughter of Marcia Furnilla, or that she was the daughter of the earlier wife, Arrecina Tertulla, and thus had a half-sister.[155] In any case, Flavia Julia probably remained in the custody of her father's family after the death or divorce of her mother, living in the Flavian palace with her grandfather, father, and uncle. The name of her nurse was Phyllis, who had also been the nurse for her uncle Domitian, who was considerably younger than his brother, Titus, and about 12 years older than his niece, Flavia Julia.[156] Titus seems not to have had any sons, at least none that survived childhood. Domitian and his wife, Domitia Longina, had produced one son in 73 CE, but he died in childhood.[157] Thus Flavia Julia became a critical element in the dynastic plans of Vespasian and Titus. The situation was similar to that facing the first emperor, Augustus, about 100 years earlier. He had produced only one child, a daughter named Julia. In order to create a dynasty, he married her to his nephew (his sister's son), Marcellus, whom he began to groom to succeed him in the emperorship. Marcellus unfortunately died within two years of the marriage, without having produced children with Julia. Flavia Julia's father, and perhaps also her grandfather, wanted to marry her to her uncle Domitian. An uncle-niece marriage was not without precedent: in 49 CE, the emperor Claudius had married his niece, Agrippina, (the daughter of his very popular brother, Germanicus; see Chapter 1). However, such a union was illegal at the time. Consequently, Claudius went to the Senate and demanded a decree to legitimize the marriage of a man to his brother's daughter.[158] Claudius' choice of Agrippina (the Younger) as a wife was undoubtedly more political than romantic; it prevented her from marrying someone who might, using her support, emerge as a rival for imperial power. Titus' plan to consolidate the imperial power within the Flavian family by marrying his daughter to his brother had one flaw: Domitian was married to someone else. According to Suetonius, Domitian was asked several times to marry Flavia Julia, but he refused because he was devoted to his wife, Domitia Longina.[159]

Having been born in the early 60s, Flavia Julia was ready for marriage about 77 or 78 CE, when her grandfather Vespasian was still alive and holding the *patria potestas* to arrange family marriages. A match was arranged with Titus Flavius Sabinus, a grandson of Vespasian's brother and perhaps also a first cousin of Julia through her mother's family.[160] The marriage seems not to have produced any children (who survived to adulthood).

By 81 CE, Flavia Julia had received the honorific title "Augusta."[161] After the death of her father in September of 81 CE, her uncle Domitian acceded to the position of emperor. He was nominated as *consul ordinarius* for 82 and chose as his co-consul the man whom some might have considered to be next in line for the imperial throne: Flavia Julia's husband, Titus Flavius Sabinus. Soon afterward, however, perhaps in early 83, Domitian had Sabinus executed, allegedly because a herald had inadvertently referred to him at a consular assembly as emperor instead of consul.[162] Apparently, Domitian feared that Flavia Julia's husband posed a threat to his position. Flavia Julia lived for several years after her husband's execution. She died between 87 and 90 CE, and was deified shortly afterward.[163] At the time of her death, she was about 25 years old, a young woman whose family had arranged for her a marriage based on dynastic aspirations, and a widow whose husband had been executed on the orders of her uncle. Her thoughts about her situation were not recorded.

The information already given is not found in Pliny. His mention of Flavia Julia in *Letter* 4.11 is brief. The main topic of the letter is Domitian's decision to have a Vestal Virgin named Cornelia buried alive. The story of Cornelia will be examined in Chapter 7. In *Letter* 4.11.6, Pliny highlights the cruelty and hypocrisy of Domitian by noting that he condemned to death a Vestal Virgin for allegedly being unchaste (*incestum*), "even though he himself had not only defiled with incest but even killed his brother's daughter, because she, when a widow, perished during an abortion." The word which Pliny uses, *incestum*, is the source of our English word "incest" – meaning sexual activity between close relatives. The meaning of the Latin word, however, is broader than the English "incest." It means "not chaste," not *castus*, engaging in forbidden sexual activity. Recall that a young unmarried girl was *casta* if she was a virgin, and that a wife, like Arria, was *casta* if she was not adulterous. The Vestal Virgin, Cornelia had not engaged in incest, but was guilty of being unchaste – *incesta* – because she had sexual relations, which were forbidden to Vestal *Virgins*.

The sordid story of an incestuous relationship between Flavia Julia and her paternal uncle Domitian is related by two other authors, Suetonius and Juvenal, who, like Pliny, lived through the reign of Domitian, as well as by Dio Cassius and Philostratus, who wrote about 200 CE. Suetonius reports that, although Domitian had refused to marry his niece, he seduced her after she married another man. When her father and husband died, he did not conceal his passion for her. He caused her death, however, when he compelled her to abort a child conceived by him. Juvenal calls Domitian an adulterer and relates that Julia, using abortificants, "cast off lumps that resembled her uncle." Dio reports that Domitian, having divorced his wife (Domitia Longina) on the grounds of adultery with an actor named Paris[164], then lived openly with his niece, Julia, as husband and wife. He later remarried Domitia, but continued his relationship with Julia. Philostratus relates that Domitian planned to marry Julia.[165] In *Letters* 6.31.4–6, Pliny describes a hearing, in the presence of Trajan, of the case of a woman named Gallitta who was married to a military tribune, but committed adultery with a centurion. (See Chapter 3.) Julian Law required that the husband, though unwilling, divorce his adulterous wife. Trajan and his council of advisors were apparently adamant that this law be obeyed. The fact that Domitian, who also insisted on strict compliance with the Julian Law, divorced his (allegedly) adulterous wife, but subsequently remarried her, gave his detractors ammunition to accuse him of hypocrisy.

The fact that people who lived during the reign of Domitian relate the story of Domitian's incest does not, of course, make it true. Vinson and Jones present arguments that make the events unlikely and build a strong case to dismiss the story as malicious and false rumors invented by Domitian's enemies.[166] They note that tales of adultery and incest were commonplaces of political invective. In this particular case, the rumor of a forced abortion that resulted in death may have been added to create an even more sensational tale. The purpose of the rumors was to vilify Domitian and invalidate his regime. After his assassination in 96 CE, Pliny and other writers were eager to circulate stories which represented Domitian as an evil man and a dreadful ruler, and which therefore justified his overthrow. Pliny's brief account of Domitian's incestuous relationship with Julia is embedded in his report on Domitian's order to execute a Vestal Virgin for unchaste behavior. The rumor about Julia is inserted to emphasize the hypocrisy of Domitian, who was unable to control his own sexual urges, but insisted on the death penalty for similar behavior in others. Domitian had, moreover, taken a hard line on the enforcement of the Julian moral legislation. People who resented his harsh position may have spread rumors of his own failure to comply. Juvenal complains that the polluted adulterer Domitian revived the bitter laws that were feared by everyone.[167] In the period after his death, the defamation of Domitian also served to enhance, by contrast, the regime of Trajan. There has been discussion in Chapter 3 of Pliny's comment in the *Panegyricus* that it was appropriate to examine an emperor's private life because only a man who can control himself and his family is fit to control the state. There should be no distinction, Pliny asserts, between a man's public and private life. Pliny's *Letter* 4.11 is designed to highlight a disconnection between Domitian's private life and public posture, and expose him both as a hypocrite and as an individual too weak to rule. In *Panegyricus* 83.1–4, Pliny claims that a man who fails to monitor his wife's behavior is not good material for a ruler. The tale about the adultery of Domitian's wife, Domitia, with an actor, Paris, may have been a rumor invented to strengthen the picture of Domitian being unable to control his household. In *Panegyricus* 52.3, moreover, Pliny claims that, during the reign of Domitian, statues of the gods were defiled because they were placed in close proximity to statues of Domitian, "the incestuous emperor" (*incestus princeps*).

Because the purpose of the rumors, when they were first circulated, was to discredit Domitian, Julia appears in Pliny, Suetonius, and Juvenal as a victim of his lust, rather than a willing partner. The later accounts of Dio and Philostratus, however, suggest complicity on her part. We cannot recover the true story. She and Domitian may have been innocent of the charge of incest. The uncle and niece had both grown up in the household of Vespasian, in the Flavian palace. They both may have continued to live there after their respective marriages. It is easy to understand how malevolent people could spread rumors. To contradict these rumors, Jones points to an epigram of Martial which was written not long after Julia's death. Martial expresses the hope that Domitia will bear a son, and then predicts that Julia (now deified) will watch over him. Jones contends that Martial would not have written these lines if there had really been an affair between Domitian and Flavia Julia and especially if her death had occurred during an abortion of Domitian's child. He would not have risked his own life by embarrassing Domitian and Domitia Longina.[168] At about this same time, Helvidius II was sentenced to death because Domitian believed that he had composed a farcical play in which he used characters named Paris and Oenone to censure Domitian's divorce from Domitia Longina.[169]

It is possible, of course, that Julia was a willing sexual partner and became pregnant by Domitian. Still, her death may have been the result of a miscarriage rather than a forced abortion. The truth eludes us. Suetonius reports that, after Domitian's assassination in September of 96 CE, Phyllis, the nurse who had raised both him and Flavia Julia, recovered his corpse, cremated it on her property outside Rome, secretly carried the ashes to the temple of the Flavian family, and mingled them with those of Julia. If Suetonius' narrative can be believed, the nurse's actions might suggest that she believed that Domitian and Julia belonged together for eternity because of the love they shared during life.[170] Domitian's wife, Domitia Longina, outlived him by 30 or more years. The disposition of her remains is unknown.

Sisters

The relationships between women and their siblings was an important element in the lives not only of the women, but also of their children.[171] Women were the agnates of their siblings, but not of their children or their husbands. Thus, even when married, they remained formally, in one sense, in their natal *familia*. Both brothers and sisters, even as adults, continued to be financially dependent on their *paterfamilias* and expected to receive a portion of his estate upon his death. In an era when many people died at an early age and therefore when brothers and sisters might lose their father when they were still young, they depended on one another to provide assistance and maintain family ties. In Plautus' comedy, *Aulularia* ("Pot of Gold"), a woman says to her brother: "I want you to understand that I am speaking to you for the sake of my conscience and your welfare, as a sister has a right to speak. ... Brother, keep in mind this one thing, that I am your nearest relative, and you are mine. It is right that we should consider matters together and counsel and advise one another."[172] Women who were widowed or divorced undoubtedly looked to their siblings to offer material and emotional support. Siblings also counted on one another to provide help for their children, such as preparing them for careers, promoting them for positions, and arranging marriages. And again, the high mortality rate among young people meant that siblings were called upon more often than they are today to take on the raising of orphans of their agnates. Roman culture valued affection and loyalty among siblings, and one aspect of *pietas* was the undertaking of obligations towards one's siblings. Musonius Rufus maintained that "it is better to have many siblings than many possessions. ... Siblings are our strongest supporters."[173] And Festus, in his definition of the Latin word *amita* ("paternal aunt"), wrote that "sisters are usually more loved by brothers than brothers are loved by one another, clearly because of the difference in personalities. Sisters have less inclination to disagreement, and therefore less inclination to rivalry."[174] His words remind us that women were important to a family not because of what they themselves might achieve in the public sphere, but because of their efforts to stimulate and facilitate achievements by the men in their family. In *Letter* 4.19.7, Pliny expressed his gratitude to Calpurnia Hispulla thus: "You revered my mother as if she were your own (*parentis loco*) and were accustomed to guide and praise me from the time I was a boy." Calpurnia Hispulla was not the biological sister of Pliny (she was sister of his wife's father). However, Pliny's words suggest that she had looked upon his mother, Plinia, like a mother, and that she and Pliny had spent much time together as children and developed a brother-sister relationship. Note that her role in the "family" was to guide and praise her "brother." Brothers might engage in rivalry for status and power. Sisters, however, advanced the interests of the family by being supportive of their brothers.

Several of the women who have been discussed previously can be identified as having had roles as sisters. Unfortunately, however, Pliny provides very little information about the relationships between siblings. His own mother, Plinia, had apparently maintained close ties with her brother, Plinius. They shared at least one friend (*Letter* 1.19.1), and her brother was very solicitous of her and her son, especially, it seems, after the death of her husband. As a widow, she apparently looked to her closest agnate for comfort. The Romans had two words for "uncle," differentiating between a "mother's brother" (a non-agnate), *avunculus* (from which is derived our English word "uncle"), and a "father's brother" (an agnate), *patruus*. The Elder Pliny was the *avunculus* of our Pliny. Plinia and her son, the younger Pliny, were living with her brother at his villa at Misenum in 79 CE, at the time that Vesuvius erupted. Although Pliny does not state directly that the sister and brother were fond of one another, *Letters* 6.16 and 6.20 indicate that Plinia was very distressed that she and her brother had been separated by events of the eruption. Her brother's affection for her might be seen in his decision to adopt her son and designate him as his heir.

Calpurnia Hispulla was the sister of the Calpurnius who was the father of Pliny's third wife. In *Letter* 4.19.1, Pliny describes the relationship between these siblings as one of mutual fondness. "You cherished your excellent brother, who loved you very much, with equal affection." When her brother died, Calpurnia Hispulla took on the duty of raising his orphaned daughter, showing her the devoted attention not only of an aunt, but also of her lost father. The Romans had two words for "aunt" – differentiating between a "mother's sister" (a non-agnate), *matertera*, and a "father's sister" (an agnate), *amita*.[175] Calpurnia Hispulla was thus the *amita* of Pliny's wife. We cannot ascertain whether or not the brother and sister were truly fond of one another, but, in his letter, which is addressed to the sister, Pliny chose to represent their relationship as warm. Even if the truth were otherwise, Pliny's comments reveal to us what Roman expectations were of the ideal sibling relationship. And since the letter is addressed to Calpurnia Hispulla and meant to flatter her, Pliny must have assumed that she would be pleased to have her relationship with her brother publicized as affectionate. Pliny cites her devotion to her brother as a praiseworthy aspect of her character. Indeed, the letter opens with the remark that she is a model (*exemplum*) of *pietas*, and the first example given of this *pietas* is the mutual love of the brother and sister.

Siblings were expected to be supportive of one another, even when they were adults and had families of their own. In *Letter* 4.4, Pliny requests of Sosius Senecio that he appoint a young man named Varisidius Nepos to a six-month tribunate. The young man was the son of the sister of Pliny's friend Gaius Calvisius. (See Chapter 4.) Calvisius, probably in response to his sister's urging, had apparently lobbied Pliny to help him advance the career of his nephew. (He was an *avunculus*). Perhaps Pliny's own uncle had made similar efforts on his behalf. It indicates that children were helped not just by agnates – their father's family – but also by their mother's family. Pliny's request to Sosius Senecio also indicates that people were expected to do favors for the sisters of their friends. And in *Letter* 7.11, Pliny explains to his grandfather-in-law that he has sold some property at below market rate to a woman named Corellia. One of his justifications is that she is the sister of his mentor, Corellius Rufus (as well as having been a good friend of his mother; see Chapter 4).

Pliny gives just passing reference to several sisters. We learn in *Letter* 5.16.1 that Minicia Marcella, who died as a 13 year old on the brink of marriage, had a sister who survived her. And Julius Avitus of *Letter* 5.21, who died while traveling at sea, left behind sisters and a very loving brother. The brother may have been Julius Naso who is mentioned in *Letter* 6.6.7 as having lost an excellent brother and thereby having been deprived of the assistance which a brother would provide in a political campaign. The two daughters of Helvidius II had a brother who survived them after their deaths in childbirth (*Letter* 4.21). We don't know whether he played a role in the lives of his orphaned nieces. Arulenus Rusticus left behind a daughter and at least two sons (*Letters* 1.14 and 2.18). Pliny gives no information about the relationship between these siblings. Ummidia Quadratilla, of *Letter* 7.24, left her estate to two grandchildren: a grandson, Ummidius Quadratus, and an anonymous granddaughter. We don't know if the two were siblings and if the granddaughter was also raised in the household of the grandmother. Arria Y had at least one brother, who died as a child, as we learn from *Letter* 3.16.3. As discussed in Chapter 2, she may also have had a second brother who was adopted into another family and perhaps chose to sever his ties to his birth family. And it is possible that Pliny himself had a sister. However, this conjecture is based on an inscription, not on any statement in his letters.[176]

Trajan's sister, Ulpia Marciana (see Figure 2), is not mentioned in the letters, but is given brief mention in the *Panegyricus* 84. She lived in the imperial residence with her brother and his wife, Plotina.[177] We don't know if she had lived there while her husband was still alive, or had moved in after his death in about 78 CE.[178] She died – a *univira* – about 112 CE. Pliny states that she possessed the same virtues as her brother: integrity, restraint, and honesty. In addition, he praises both Ulpia Marciana and Plotina for living together so amicably and sharing a home without engaging in rivalry. "They respect one another and yield to one another, and, because they both love you enormously, they consider it of no importance which of them you love more." (*Panegyricus* 84.4)[179] The true situation in the imperial palace may not always have been so rosy, but Pliny's description enables us to discern what Roman men would consider the ideal family scenario. A woman could look to her brother for support, especially if widowed. In turn, a brother could expect that his sister would be on good terms with his wife, and that both wife and sister would give primary consideration to his interests.

Figure 7 Vestal Virgin. It was customary for Vestal Virgins to be depicted wearing a headband and with their hair covered by a veil. Museo Nazionale Romano. Photo © Alinari Archives-Anderson Archive, Florence.

7   Women outside the family

The topic of this chapter is the women who appear in Pliny's letters in roles other than those of family members. Almost all of Pliny's references to women place them in the context of family matters. Rarely do we see women engaged in non-family activities. In *Letter* 7.11, there is a brief glimpse of Corellia's shrewdness in negotiating the purchase of real estate (although Pliny uses "family friendships" as a justification for agreeing to a deal favorable to Corellia; see Chapter 4). And, in *Letter* 7.24, there is a hint perhaps that Ummidia Quadratilla's interest in pantomime (of which Pliny disapproved) was not a decadent pastime, but rather a lucrative business venture. (See Chapter 5.) Nonetheless, Pliny's emphasis in these letters remains on family ties. In a few letters, however, we find women whose lives and experiences were quite different from those of the Roman matrons (and matrons-in-training) who were more often the subject of his attention.

Cornelia, the Vestal Virgin

In *Letter* 4.11, Pliny recounts the execution of a Vestal Virgin named Cornelia. One other Vestal Virgin is mentioned by name in the published correspondence: Junia, a Vestal Virgin who, when gravely ill, was nursed by her kinswoman, Fannia (*Letter* 7.19.1). It is possible that Cornelia and Junia were Vestal Virgins at the same time.

The Vestal Virgins were the priestesses who tended the cult of Vesta, who was the spirit or deity of hearth fires. The hearth fire which warmed the residents of a house and cooked their food was critical to the survival of a household. Since the Roman state was constructed as the family writ large,[1] the state, too, possessed a hearth fire in a central location: the Roman Forum. That fire was contained in the *aedes Vestae*, Temple of Vesta, which, unlike other temples, was circular, perhaps to represent the round huts in which the earliest inhabitants of Rome had lived and lit their hearth fires.[2] (Remains of the Temple of Vesta and the residence of the Vestal Virgins can be viewed today by visitors to Rome.) In another departure from the design of other temples, the interior of the Temple of Vesta did not contain an image or statue of the deity. Instead of a statue, there was the fire on the hearth which in itself signified the presence of Vesta.[3] The fire, in turn, symbolized that the Roman state was healthy, stable, and prosperous. It was therefore essential that it burn continuously. The security, the permanence, indeed the very existence of the state, were thought to be closely linked to the fire, and any extinction of it was viewed as a portent of disaster. The main task of the Vestal Virgins was to maintain the flames so that they did not go out.

The Romans traced the institution of the Vestal Virgins back to the legendary second (after Romulus) king of Rome, Numa Pompilius, who was said to have ruled from about 717 to 673 BCE.[4] He is credited with building the Temple of Vesta and appointing two priestesses, and then two more, to tend it. The number of priestesses was raised by a later king to six, and not increased again. The priestesses were selected by the Pontifex Maximus (who, from the time of Augustus, was the emperor).[5] The requirements were that a girl be between six and ten years of age, and free of physical defects, and that both her parents be free born, alive, and not engaged in a vulgar type of business. In the early history of the institution, the girl's family had to be patrician. Later, girls from elite plebeian families became acceptable. During the time of Augustus, it became difficult to find suitable young girls whose families were willing to give them up, and Augustus therefore allowed the daughters of freedmen to be chosen, beginning in 5 CE.[6] Vestal Virgins left their families and lived together in an official residence located next to the Temple of Vesta in the Forum. They were supervised by the Pontifex Maximus who had the right to punish them for infractions.

A Vestal Virgin took a vow of celibacy, and served for a period of at least 30 years. At the end of the 30-year period, she could choose to continue in service, or leave the temple and even marry if she wished. Among the six Vestal Virgins who lived in the Vestal residence at any time, the gap in age might be as much as 50 years. From Tacitus we learn about a search in 19 CE for a replacement for a Vestal Virgin, named Occia, who had "presided over the rites of Vesta with the greatest moral purity for 57 years."[7] She apparently died in service. In the same passage, Tacitus relates that two fathers, Fonteius Agrippa and Domitius Pollio, offered their daughters to replace Occia. The emperor (and Pontifex Maximus) Tiberius thanked them both, but chose Pollio's daughter because Agrippa's house had been diminished in reputation by a divorce. Nonetheless, the emperor consoled the rejected girl by giving her a dowry of one million sesterces.[8]

The legal status of a Vestal Virgin was anomalous. Roman girls were subject to the *potestas* of their *paterfamilias* (father or, if alive, grandfather).[9] Even when adult and married, a woman remained *in potestate* until the death of her *paterfamilias*.[10] At this point, she passed out of *patria potestas* (that is, she became *sui iuris*, "under her own regulation"), but was assigned a *tutor* (guardian) who oversaw her expenditure of the funds which she had received mainly from her agnate family. In contrast, when a girl was selected to be a Vestal Virgin, she passed out of the *potestas* of her *paterfamilias*, but without the type of formal procedure of fictitious sale and emancipation which was required, for example, if a father released his son from the *patria potestas*.[11] Nor did the girl undergo a *capitis deminutio* (a change in civil status). She was not, for example, made a member of another family. She came under the supervision and discipline of the Pontifex Maximus, but he did not have ownership of her property and therefore seems not to have assumed the role of a surrogate *paterfamilias*. Nor was he her *tutor*, because the Vestal Virgins were exempt from *tutela*.

A Vestal Virgin was in a special category, separate from the usual female categories. Though her birth parents were still alive, she was no longer a daughter. Nor, at least for 30 years, would she be a wife or mother. Of course, she might well maintain affective ties with her "former" family. Cicero touches on the continuing emotional attachment between a Vestal Virgin and her brother in a speech defending a man named Fonteius.[12] Fonteius had been charged with extortion in Gaul and, if convicted, would have received the punishment of exile. In his speech, Cicero makes an emotional plea to the jury to consider the needs of his sister, Fonteia, who was a Vestal Virgin.[13] Cicero contends that a Vestal Virgin needs the comfort and protection which a brother can provide because she has neither children nor a husband with whom she shares her life. There is no one but her brother who can bring her joy. (He also warns the jury that the tears of the Vestal Virgin sister for her brother might douse the eternal flame of Vesta which she has vowed to maintain.)

Although a Vestal Virgin might continue to be emotionally close to her brother, she had nonetheless been formally removed from her *familia* and lost her right to intestate succession. She could, however, receive bequests or legacies from "former" family members and from friends. Similarly, if she died intestate, she had no legal heirs because she had no legal family members. Her estate went to the public treasury.[14] However, she could – and most Vestal Virgins probably did – draw up a will bequeathing her property to family and friends. In fact, Vestal Virgins, being exempt from *tutela*, enjoyed a right denied to other women: the right to make a will without the oversight of a man and to dispose of her property as she wished. The Vestal Virgins also had the right, unlike other women, to speak in court, perhaps because, having been severed from their families, they no longer had male relatives to speak for them.

A Vestal Virgin might accumulate an estate of considerable size during her 30 or more years of service. Augustus granted the Vestal Virgins the *ius trium liberorum*, the "three-children privilege," which exempted them from the restrictions on receiving legacies that his legislation had placed on unmarried and childless people.[15] However, a Vestal Virgin's estate was not acquired only from gifts and bequests. At the time that she entered the order of Vestal Virgins as a young girl, she was paid a stipend.[16] During the reign of Tiberius, the stipend was raised to two million sesterces.[17] When Tiberius gave Agrippa's daughter a dowry of one million sesterces as consolation for rejecting her as a replacement for Occia, he knew that Pollio's daughter would receive twice that amount as a Vestal Virgin. An amusing story related by Plutarch gives some indication of the wealth of a Vestal Virgin.[18] Marcus Crassus, a very rich and avaricious man who was a member of the First Triumvirate[19], was accused of consorting with a Vestal Virgin named Licinia. It turned out, however, that Crassus was always hanging around her and flattering her because she owned some nice suburban property which he was hoping to purchase for a low price. He was acquitted of the charge of corrupting a Vestal Virgin because of his reputation for avarice; jurors realized that it was greed, rather than sexual attraction, that had kindled his interest in Licinia. This story not only informs us about the general perception of Crassus' character, but also suggests that, as a Vestal Virgin and therefore without a *tutor*, Licinia was free to purchase and dispose of property as she wished. We do not know if she was as shrewd a businesswoman as Corellia (*Letters* 7.11 and 14).

It is not clear what the legal status was of a Vestal Virgin who left the order after her 30 years of service. Perhaps she returned to her birth family and re-entered the *potestas* of her *paterfamilias*, or, if he was dead, was assigned a guardian, a *tutor*.[20] If this were the case, her re-entry into her natal family would have meant a significant loss of independence. She could marry, and her personal wealth might make her an attractive marriage prospect, at least to a man who was not looking for a young bride who could bear many children. However, as a middle-aged woman who had been celibate for 30 years and had enjoyed considerable autonomy, authority, and public respect, she would face a difficult adjustment to the demands of pleasing a husband. Ancient sources maintain that few Vestal Virgins married after retirement, and those who did regretted having done so.[21] Since, however, we do not have any commentaries written by Vestal Virgins themselves, we do not know how they may have felt about retirement and marriage.

The severance of the Vestal Virgins from their families could be construed as a guarantee that they would remain impartial in affairs of state.[22] However, because of their prominent position in the state and their reputation for integrity, Vestal Virgins were able to influence matters well beyond the cult of Vesta, and to enjoy roles as patrons. From one inscription, for example, we learn that a Vestal Virgin named Campia Severina had obtained for Aemilius Pardalas the benefits of equestrian rank and an officer commission in an auxiliary cohort.[23]

When the Pontifex Maximus was removing from her family the young girl whom he had chosen as a Vestal Virgin, he uttered this formula: "I take you, Amata, to be a Vestal priestess who will perform the rites which it is correct for a priestess of Vesta to perform on behalf of the Roman people."[24] Having been separated from her family, the girl now served the Roman state. The duties of the Vestal Virgins included the all-important task of making sure that the fire in the Temple of Vesta did not go out. They were responsible, moreover, for cleaning the temple every day with water which had been drawn only from a particular spring, located at a considerable distance south of the Roman Forum, near the Porta Capena. Other duties included the preparation of *mola salsa*, the ground and salted spelt which was sprinkled on the heads of animals just prior to their being killed in sacrifices.[25] The Vestal Virgins also prepared the ashes of unborn calves that were used during the Parilia, a religious festival celebrated in April. In addition, they were responsible for safe-guarding wills that were deposited with them. Julius Caesar, Mark Antony, and Augustus, for example, deposited their wills with them.[26] Important documents, moreover, such as peace treaties, were sometimes placed in the care of the Vestal Virgins.[27] This practice indicates the trust that the Roman people had in the honesty and impartiality of the Vestal Virgins. As related in Chapter 3, when Calpurnius Piso, husband of Verania

Gemina (of *Letter* 2.20), was fleeing Otho's supporters in 69 CE, he sought and was given a hiding place at the Temple of Vesta. Nevertheless, Otho's men dragged him out and slew him.[28]

Although the Vestal Virgins were set apart from their fellow citizens both because of their unique legal status and because of their living arrangements, they did not live isolated lives. They were guests at dinner parties, and attended public ceremonies and public entertainments at which they were given seats of honor.[29] Their privileged seating arrangement had, however, the effect of dividing them from the rest of the audience and reminding others of their special status. From the beginning of the imperial period, moreover, the separation of the Vestal Virgins from the general population was clearly demarcated when they traveled outside of the Vestal residence. They were preceded by an attendant known as a *lictor*, and people were required to give them the right of way.[30] Lictors carrying implements of punishment (*fasces*) accompanied consuls and praetors and were the symbols of these magistrates' right to impose punishment for crimes. A consul was escorted by 12 lictors, a praetor by six. Only one lictor accompanied a Vestal Virgin, and his role may have been that of a bodyguard, rather than an enforcer of the law. Nonetheless, the presence of a lictor, a traditional signifier of authority, set the Vestal Virgins apart from the general public.[31]

Although there are quite a few artistic depictions of Vestal Virgins, including statues found in the residence or dormitory where they lived in the Forum, we have no certain description of how they may have been required to dress. (See Figure 7.) However, they were expected to be modest in appearance and behavior, and their clothing and hair style were meant to be a reflection of their moral purity. In 420 BCE, a Vestal Virgin named Postumia was put on trial for *incestum*, unchaste behavior, having fallen under suspicion because she dressed too elegantly and spoke more wittily than was proper for a virgin.[32] She was acquitted, but warned by the Pontifex Maximus to stop making jokes and to dress chastely, rather than stylishly.[33]

The Vestal Virgins were required to be *casta*, chaste. *Incestum*, unchastity, was punished severely. The fact that a girl was enlisted into the priesthood of Vesta between the ages of six and ten, and that she vowed to be celibate for at least 30 years of service, meant that she was required to refrain from sexual activity during the period when she was most fertile and most interested in sex. Scholars have offered several explanations for the celibacy requirement, but the issue has not been resolved. The prohibition on sexual activity set the Vestal Virgins apart from the experiences of male priests, who could marry, as well as from the rest of the population of Rome. Perhaps it was instituted to prevent the Vestal Virgins, whose family ties had been formally severed, from becoming pregnant and forming new families. Remaining childless enabled them to represent themselves as having concern for the interests of every member of the state rather than of a particular family. A restriction on intimate relations also helped them maintain a reputation for neutrality and impartiality. (Since this restriction was not imposed on priests, the Romans likely believed that men were better able than women to resist the temptation to do favors for a sexual partner.) There seems also to have been a symbolic element to the required virginity of a Vestal. Parker, who, like Staples, proposes that a Vestal Virgin was seen as an embodiment of the city and citizenry of Rome, argues that the "unpenetrated body (*of a Vestal Virgin*) was a metaphor for the unpenetrated walls of Rome. ... The Vestals' virginity was more than merely a symbol of the inviolability of Rome. It was also the guarantee."[34] The very existence of the state was tied to the continued celibacy of the Vestal Virgins. As long as they remained unpenetrated, so did Rome. Or, to state the opposite, if a Vestal lost her virginity, the whole state was threatened.

There was a considerable discrepancy in the expectations of behavior and reputation for male and female priests. "For male priests, the standard was set at a fairly low level."[35] Some priests were allowed to remain in their positions no matter how badly they behaved or how incompetently they performed. For a Vestal Virgin, on the other hand, the penalty for having betrayed her vows, for being unchaste and thus putting the state in danger was severe: death. Roman historians recorded several instances of Vestal Virgins being tried for *incestum*, unchastity. Perhaps not surprisingly, the accusations of unchastity were made primarily at times of crisis, when hysteria about threats to the state was high. In 483 BCE, for example, when the Romans were at war with the Volsci, a series of bad omens led them to believe that the gods were angry at them for some violation of the sacred. A Vestal Virgin was accused and convicted of *incestum*, and then buried alive. The two men who were accused of consorting with her were publicly whipped and then executed.[36] Subsequently favorable omens appeared, and the Romans were satisfied that the gods were no longer angry. In 472 BCE, a deadly plague descended upon Rome. A Vestal Virgin named Orbinia was accused and convicted of *incestum* and buried alive. Of the two men who were accused of consorting with her, one committed suicide and the other was publicly whipped and executed. After their punishments, the plague ceased.[37] The cessation of the plague and of bad omens would have satisfied people that the interment of the Vestal Virgins had repaired their relationship with the gods. In 216 BCE, in the aftermath of the disaster at Cannae, when the population of the city was in a panic, two Vestal Virgins, Floronia and Opimia, were accused and convicted of *stuprum* ("debauchery" or "sexual defilement"). One committed suicide, the other was buried alive. A priest who had been complicit was whipped to death. During this time of turmoil and fear, the Romans also buried alive two Greeks and two Gauls in a rite of human sacrifice.[38] In 113 BCE, after the destruction of Cato's army in Thrace, three Vestal Virgins, Marcia, Aemilia, and Licinia, were convicted of *incestum* and buried alive. About the same time, two Greeks and two Gauls were buried alive.[39] Parker contends that the executions of the Vestal Virgins in these tumultuous situations were both forms of human sacrifice intended to remove a suspected impurity or pollution, and also punishments for treason because the Vestal Virgins had harmed the state by betraying their vows.[40] It is curious that, although one ancient author, Dionysius of Halicarnassus, states that the extinction of the fire in the Temple of Vesta would be construed as a portent that the destruction of the city was imminent, neither he nor our other ancient sources report that the fire had actually gone out in the situations referred to earlier, when Vestal Virgins were suspected of unchastity.[41] Instead, the fact that the Romans were suffering a disaster apparently triggered a suspicion that a Vestal Virgin had been unchaste and had therefore been impure when performing her duties. The corroborating evidence of their guilt seems to have been testimony presented by or (in the case of slaves) extracted by torture from people close to them who might have witnessed inappropriate behavior. We will never know whether the executed Vestal Virgins were truly guilty of *incestum* (or whether, in times of no turmoil, the *incestum* of a Vestal Virgin was punished less severely). "(W)hen the political stability of the state was under threat the possibility that a Vestal might have been unchaste provided a convenient mechanism for averting the threat."[42]

Our ancient sources indicate that an accusation of *incestum* against a Vestal Virgin was heard by the Pontifex Maximus and the College of Pontiffs (all men, of course). If judged to be guilty, she was condemned to be buried alive. She was tied on to a funeral bier and covered with sheets to muffle any cries she might make. The bier was carried through the Forum, where spectators watched in silence, to the Colline Gate which was in the northeastern area of the city wall. At the gate, steps led down to a subterranean chamber. The veiled Vestal Virgin was untied and forced to descend into the chamber. In it were a couch, a lamp, and small portions of bread, water, milk, and oil. Once the Vestal Virgin was in the chamber, the steps were removed, and earth was heaped up to conceal the entrance.[43] Burial alive was not a usual form of capital punishment. Its use with the Vestal Virgins (and with the scapegoat Gauls and Greeks mentioned earlier) seems intended to signify that the Romans were removing from their community the source of pollution (as one might bury trash).[44] However, the fact that the chamber contained food and water suggests that they were absolving themselves of responsibility for the death of the Vestal Virgin. Perhaps they believed that they were leaving her ultimate fate to the will of Vesta. Another oddity about the punishment meted out to a condemned Vestal Virgin is that she was buried within the walls of the city. Interment within the city was prohibited to other residents. Perhaps the chamber in which she had been placed was not defined as a tomb because she had entered it when alive, and no one knew whether she was truly dead.

Following the deaths of the three Vestal Virgins in 113 BCE (there were 11 reported executions of Vestal Virgins from Rome's earliest history to 113 BCE), there are no reports of other burials until the reign of Domitian. There were several accusations of *incestum* during the first century BCE, but they resulted in acquittals. For example, in 73 BCE, Fabia, the half-sister of Cicero's wife, Terentia, was charged with having an affair with Catiline, but acquitted.[45] And, as noted earlier, Licinia was suspected of consorting with Crassus, until people realized that he was interested only in her property. During Domitian's reign, however, there occurred two instances in which Vestal Virgins were judged guilty of *incestum*. They were recorded by several authors, perhaps because punishments so harsh and so archaic shocked the community. Pliny, in *Letter* 4.11, reported on one incident, while his contemporary, Suetonius, recorded both. According to Suetonius, Domitian, soon after his accession, embarked on a program to curb corruption and immorality in the state and to restore respect for religion.[46] As one facet of this program, he decided to punish severely the *incestum* of the Vestal Virgins, to which, he believed, his father (Vespasian) and brother (Titus) had turned a blind eye. Perhaps he thought that both of these men, holding the positions of Emperor and Pontifex Maximus, should have provided stricter oversight of the conduct of these state priestesses. We do not know whether the Vestal Virgins of the second half of the first century CE were more neglectful of their vows of celibacy than earlier generations. At the beginning of his *Histories*, Tacitus describes the period which saw the rise to power of Vespasian as one in which sacred rites were defiled, but Tacitus is undoubtedly describing not just the behavior of the Vestal Virgins.[47] In any case, Domitian, who was Pontifex Maximus as well as emperor, resolved that they must adhere to the ancient rules and that those who did not must receive capital punishment. Early in his reign, in either 83 or 84 CE, he allowed three condemned Vestal Virgins – two of them sisters – a "free choice of death," *liberum mortis permisisset arbitrium*.[48] Presumably Suetonius' statement means that they were condemned to death, but permitted to commit suicide and thus avoid the agony of a burial alive. Their alleged sexual partners were, according to Suetonius, sentenced to relegation, a capital punishment, but one much less harsh than being whipped and executed. Dio provides a briefer account of this incident and reports that Domitian took pride in the fact that he did not bury the priestesses alive.[49] Apparently he wanted to enforce the ancient rules strictly, but not inhumanely. However, Dio also mentions that one of the pontiffs present at the hearings fainted because he was not able to tolerate the harshness of the examinations and the number of people accused.[50] (Slaves called upon to give evidence were routinely tortured.)

During the 80s CE, there were no crises comparable to, for example, the Roman defeat at Cannae, which might have triggered panic and a suspicion that the Vestal Virgins had offended the gods. Nor is there record of portents or bad omens. It seems that Domitian's decision to investigate and then punish the three Vestal Virgins was based on information that they were breaking their vows, and was motivated by a wish to return the priesthood to its traditional standards of purity. However, the punishments in the early 80s did not frighten all the remaining Vestal Virgins into remaining celibate. Suetonius writes that Cornelia, the chief or senior Vestal Virgin, the *Virgo Vestalis Maxima*, was later tried and found guilty. She had, he notes, been previously tried, but, on that occasion, acquitted. We do not know if the previous trial had been the one in 83 or 84 CE at which the three Vestal Virgins were condemned. In any case, as a result of the second trial, Cornelia and the men with whom she had been sexually active received capital penalties. She was buried alive, and they were whipped to death. It may be that Domitian's frustration at yet another scandalous case of Vestal misconduct had erased any desire to be humane. However, one of the accused men was allowed to go into exile because he admitted his guilt at an early stage of the investigation, when torture (presumably of slaves) had rendered no decisive evidence.

Pliny's *Letter* 4.11 is our other source of evidence about the trial and punishment of Cornelia.[51] He offers, however, a very different perspective on Domitian's behavior in pursuing the case. The letter is a prime example of Pliny's efforts with his published correspondence, first, to use the epistle form to construct historical narratives which would win him acclaim, and, second, to represent Domitian as a wicked man and deplorable emperor.[52] Although Pliny presents himself as an objective narrator, he manipulated the information available to him about the Vestal incident in order to vilify Domitian. Pliny's letter begins with an announcement that he is sending to his addressee, Cornelius Minicianus, some recent news[53]: Valerius Licinianus, a talented man who had reached the rank of praetor, was now reduced to being a rhetoric teacher in Sicily (*Letter* 4.11.1). The opening word, *audistine*, "have you heard," raises the expectation that the letter will convey information unknown to the addressee and thus conform to the function of letter-writing. However, Pliny soon adds the comment that Licinianus has sunk from being a senator to being an exile. Although the addressee may have been unaware of Licinianus' relocation to Sicily from an earlier place of exile, his sentence of exile was not current news, and was surely not unknown to the addressee. We know that the letter was composed after the deaths both of Domitian and of his successor, Nerva, because Pliny refers to Nerva at *Letter* 4.11.14 as *divus*, "deified."[54] Thus the letter may be dated to the reign of Trajan, perhaps to the early 100s, while Licinianus' sentence of exile was imposed between 89 and 93 CE.[55] The opening question, "have you heard" is therefore a rhetorical ploy to allow Pliny to introduce the topic of his historical narrative.

That the addressee was familiar with Licinianus' sentence of exile, and the reasons for it, is proved by Pliny's statement in *Letter* 4.11.4 that he anticipates that the addressee will reply that Licinianus deserved his fate because he committed *incestum*. It is apparent that Licinianus is the same man whose exile Suetonius recorded. However, Pliny fashions his narration so that Domitian appears as a villain, and the conviction of Licinianus and Cornelia is called into question. Having anticipated that the addressee had believed the story that Licinianus committed *incestum*, Pliny acknowledges that Licinianus did indeed confess to *incestum*. However, he immediately comments that it is not certain whether Licinianus confessed because the *incestum* was true, or because he feared more serious consequences if he denied it. Pliny thus adopts the pose of someone who wants to uncover the truth about the incident. He plants seeds of doubt about Licinianus' guilt, while at the same time he creates a portrait of an emperor who would terrify a senator into making a false confession to a capital crime. We learn later in the letter that the prosecution of Licinianus occurred after that of Cornelia. At this point, Pliny attributes Domitian's harsh treatment of Licinianus to his seething rage that people hated rather than praised him for his punishment of her (*Letter* 4.11.5).

Pliny's narrative then progresses to a dramatic account of the fate of Cornelia, the senior Vestal Virgin. He relates that Domitian wanted to bury her alive because he thought that his reign would gain luster from examples of this sort (*Letter* 4.11.6). Pliny thus constructs Domitian's desire to curb the violations of the Vestals' rules as a perverse scheme for glory rather than an honest attempt to improve the state. He thereby effectively moves the attention away from the charges against Cornelia. In contrast, moreover, to Suetonius, he does not mention that

Cornelia had been previously tried for *incestum* or that, in the earlier case, Domitian had granted the condemned women the option of suicide. (None of our sources report whether Cornelia was offered a "free choice of death," *liberum mortis arbitrium*.)

The Cornelia of Pliny's letter and Suetonius' report has been plausibly identified as the Cornelia Cossa who became a Vestal Virgin in 62 CE.[56] If this identification is correct, Cornelia was between six and ten years old in 62 CE. Her trial probably occurred between 89 and 93 CE. Thus she would have been between 33 and 41 years old at the time of her death. Pliny concedes that Domitian had the right, as Pontifex Maximus, to investigate the suspicion of *incestum*, but immediately adds that it was rather because of his cruelty as a tyrant and unfettered power as a despot that he summoned the college of priests. He thus obscures the fact that Domitian followed traditional procedure for both the investigation and the punishment. Pliny insinuates, moreover, that Domitian's decision to hold the inquiry at his Alban villa, rather than at the Regia in the Forum, was sinister and unprecedented. However, it was not uncommon for emperors to hold meetings outside the city.[57] In any case, there may not have been a "regular" place for such an inquiry because the investigation of *incestum* by a Vestal Virgin was so rare. To bolster his implication that Domitian acted like a tyrant, Pliny describes him several times in the letter as raging furiously. The result is a portrait of the stereotypical tyrant: a ruler who cannot control his own emotions and who savagely abuses his power.

Pliny next declares that Domitian, by a crime no less heinous than the one he appeared to be punishing, condemned Cornelia of *incestum* although she was absent from the proceedings and therefore unheard. Pliny adds that Domitian passed this judgment "even though he himself had not only defiled with *incestum*, but even killed his brother's daughter, because she, when a widow, perished during an abortion" (*Letter* 4.11.6). He is referring, of course, to the allegations of incest between Domitian and his niece, Flavia Julia, allegations which were discussed in Chapter 6. As noted in Chapter 6, Pliny uses the same word, *incestum*, "unchastity," to denote the sexual relationship between Domitian and his niece, Julia, and Cornelia and her partners. Although it is often translated more narrowly as "incest" in the former case, it is important to keep in mind that Pliny was, by using the same word, emphasizing the similarity between Domitian's actions and the charges he made against others: engaging in forbidden sexual activity. Pliny's motive in mentioning this story is to paint Domitian as a depraved hypocrite who piously preached moral uprightness and severely punished sexual transgression, but himself engaged in prohibited sexual activities. Since, moreover, there were rumors that his incest with his niece began when her husband was still alive, Pliny was perhaps reminding readers that Domitian was guilty of wanton disregard of the Augustan legislation which he claimed to be enforcing.[58] Under these laws, he himself should have been punished, not allowed to punish others. By including the allegation of Domitian's incest with his niece, Pliny emphasizes the disparity between the emperor's private life and his public policies. He thus depicts Cornelia and her partners as victims of an unscrupulous tyrant. He never states unequivocally that they were innocent. Instead he concentrates on creating the impression that the emperor was guilty of such depravity that he should not have been judging them. He thus impugns Domitian's moral revival program and casts doubt on the legitimacy of his regime.

The disparagement of the emperor, in a letter written, however, after his death, is consistent with Pliny's attempts to portray himself as a man who had always been critical of Domitian's policies and who enthusiastically endorsed the reign of the Trajan. By drawing a connection between the corrupt nature of Domitian's personal and public actions, Pliny suggests that he was unfit to rule and that his overthrow was therefore justified.[59] His cynical interpretation of the emperor's efforts to enforce moral rules clashes, however, with the more favorable perspective of Suetonius and Statius, and prompts the question of whether Pliny's bias prevents him from giving his reader an accurate assessment of Cornelia's guilt or innocence.

When Cornelia, who had been denied an opportunity to speak at her trial, learned of her sentence, she protested her innocence, or so Pliny relates, by calling upon Vesta and other deities, and exclaiming: "Does Caesar (that is, *Domitian*) think that I have been unchaste? And yet, while I was performing the sacred rites, he enjoyed victories and triumphs." Cornelia is, along with Arria and Fannia, one of only three women in *Letters* 1–9 whom Pliny allows to speak for herself.[60] We cannot, of course, be certain that the words he records are precisely those she spoke. Their inclusion in the letter vividly accentuates the pathos of Cornelia's situation, thus drawing the sympathy of the reader toward her plight and distracting attention from the legal and religious issues. In the statement attributed to her, Cornelia was alluding to the belief that the health of the state was contingent upon the Vestal Virgins remaining chaste and performing their duties. If the gods were satisfied with the conduct of the Vestal Virgins, the state would prosper. Since Domitian had continued to have success in war, it would be logical to assume that the Vestal Virgins were dutiful and undefiled. (None of our sources make mention of any divine signal of Vestal impropriety, such as the temple fire going out.) However, the logic of Cornelia's statement, repeated again and again as she was led to her doom, fell on deaf ears. Even Pliny was not ready to commit himself to an unambiguous declaration of her innocence. Instead he writes: "I don't know whether she was innocent. Certainly she acted as if innocent as she was led away" (*Letter* 4.11.8).

Cornelia's journey through the Forum to the underground chamber at the Colline Gate was undoubtedly similar to that described by Plutarch.[61] In fact, Plutarch may have been describing her journey, since he, as a contemporary of Pliny and Suetonius, may have witnessed the gloomy procession himself or heard about it from a witness. Pliny reports that, as Cornelia stepped down into the chamber, a man offered her a hand in assistance. "She turned away and shrank back and rejected the foul contact as if from a chaste and pure body, in a final act of holiness" (*Letter* 4.11.9). Pliny thus depicts her as descending with dignity into the chamber of death. Even in her final moments above ground, she appeared bravely confident that the gods would acknowledge her innocence. Pliny describes the man who offered assistance as a *carnifex*, "butcher," "executioner." Since a

Vestal Virgin was not technically executed, but rather removed from the world of the living, Pliny's use of the word *carnifex* is inaccurate, but designed to inspire sympathy for Cornelia, particularly if, as Vinson seems to suggest, the man referred to as *carnifex* was the Pontifex Maximus, Domitian himself.[62]

One of her alleged partners, Licinianus, had, as already noted, received a sentence of relegation. Pliny relates that another, named Celer, who was a man of equestrian rank, was whipped in public, perhaps to death.[63] He asked again and again: "What have I done? I have done nothing" (*Letter* 4.11.10). Again, Pliny encourages us to conclude that he was innocent, without actually declaring him so. Nor do we know if Crispinus, mentioned by Juvenal as another of Cornelia's partners, was punished.[64]

At the end of his letter, in a nice example of ring composition, Pliny returns to the news about Licinianus. He reiterates that Domitian, responding in typical tyrant fashion, was seething because his punishment of Cornelia had earned him a reputation for cruelty and injustice. He had apparently expected to win praise for his stringent crackdown on transgressors. Pliny's account places the arrest of Licinianus after the interment of Cornelia and attributes it to Domitian's petty but intense chagrin. (Suetonius' account suggests that he had admitted his guilt at an early stage of the investigation.) Pliny states that Domitian had Licinianus arrested for having hidden a freedwoman of Cornelia and thus prevented her from giving evidence. At this point, Licinianus confessed in order to avoid a public flogging, and withdrew from Rome. At *Letter* 4.11.5, Pliny stated that Licinianus had confessed to *incestum*, but may have been driven by fear into making a false confession. At *Letter* 4.11.11, Pliny leaves readers with the impression that the charge was simply one of concealing a potential witness. He thus insinuates that Domitian had unjustly destroyed the career of a successful senator who was guilty of a non-capital charge. However, a few lines later, in *Letter* 4.11.14, he relates that Domitian's successor, Nerva, had mercifully allowed Licinianus to move from his original place of exile to Sicily. The fact that Nerva did not nullify the sentence of exile, but simply allowed a change of location, seems to indicate that he agreed with his predecessor Domitian that Licinianus was guilty of a capital offence.

Licinianus' departure was announced to Domitian by Herennius Senecio, the man whom Pliny claimed as a friend and who was later sentenced to death by Domitian along with Arulenus Rusticus and Helvidius II.[65] Pliny's inclusion of Senecio's name is not casual. It allows him again to appear aligned with one of the most notable of Domitian's critics. Pliny then adds that Domitian was overjoyed by Licinianus' confession. It both proved that he had been right to conduct the investigation and absolved him of any blame for Licinianus' punishment. A relieved Domitian mitigated Licinianus' sentence as a reward, allowing him to retain some of his possessions before the rest were confiscated for the state treasury.[66] Pliny closes the letter with a statement of his reason for sending what is essentially an historical narrative: he was concerned that his addressee might have heard only that Licinianus had been relegated for *incestum* and been unaware of the circumstances surrounding the relegation order. However, despite his attempt to pose as an objective narrator, Pliny's carefully crafted report betrays the biases of the author. Pliny may have written the letter while having in mind the intent to publish it. His version of the circumstances was designed to leave a permanent portrait of the now-deceased Domitian as a maniacal, lustful, and cruel tyrant.[67] In the end, the letter tells us almost nothing about Cornelia other than that she was a senior Vestal Virgin who was buried alive after being convicted of *incestum*. Pliny's letter evokes in readers a sense of horror at the nature of Cornelia's punishment and elicits sympathy for her. However, he is not able to convince the reader beyond a doubt that Cornelia and her partners were innocent.

The Christian ministrae

Women who performed religious duties are mentioned again briefly in *Letter* 10.96. This is one of Pliny's best-known and much-discussed letters. It is included among the correspondence between the emperor Trajan and Pliny, when he was governor of Bithynia-Pontus.[68] Pliny's letter and Trajan's reply (*Letter* 10.97) contain the earliest non-Christian literary evidence about the nature and growth of Christianity in the Greek-speaking area of the Roman Empire and about the perceptions which Roman officials had of this new religion.[69] In his letter, which was written about 111 CE, Pliny requests guidance from Trajan about the appropriate procedure for dealing with people who are brought before him on the accusation of being Christians. Pliny acknowledges that he has never been present at any hearings about Christians and therefore does not know what is usually investigated or punished, or to what extent. As a senator and holder of high political offices, it is likely that Pliny would have attended such hearings if they were held in Rome. His declaration of not attending suggests that they were very rare, at least in Italy. He was not prepared for the situation he encountered in his province. One particular concern of Pliny is whether simply the name or designation of being Christian should be punished, even if the person had committed no crimes, or whether it is the crimes associated with the name that should be punished. Pliny does not state what crimes he believes were associated by non-Christians with the name of Christian. From other sources we learn that Christians were suspected of flagrantly depraved behavior such as incest and cannibalism during the practice of their religion.[70] The credibility of these charges must be gauged against the fact that the same charges were raised against adherents of other religious groups, most notably against the worshippers of Bacchus in 186 BCE.[71]

Pliny had already, at the time he wrote the letter, investigated and passed judgment on several people who had been accused of being Christian. As governor, one of his main duties was to travel throughout the province to adjudicate cases filed by local residents. The accusations against the Christians were made by their fellow provincials. There is no evidence in this letter of a systematic religious inquisition or persecution by the Roman state. It is even possible that the accusations were prompted by factors not directly connected to religion. The province of Bithynia-Pontus was plagued by inner-city rivalries and intra-city factionalism.[72] Pliny's contemporary, Dio Chrysostom, who was a resident of Prusa, a city in

Bithynia, mentions these problems frequently in his orations.[73] Indeed, Pliny began *Letter* 5.20, which he wrote several years before being assigned as governor to that area, with the exasperated exclamation: *Iterum Bithyni*, "the Bithynians again"! He was referring to the fact that the Bithynians were bringing, for the second time, charges of extortion against a governor. Pliny thus seems to have been well aware, before he accepted his assignment, of the contentiousness of the Bithynians. And the Bithynians were not hesitant to use the court of the provincial governor to assail one another in factional disputes. In fact, in *Letter* 10.81, Pliny reports to Trajan that Dio Chrysostom had been accused of mis-appropriating public funds and of placing a statue of the emperor in the same building in which the bodies of his wife and son had been buried. (See Chapter 4.) The latter action could be construed as showing disrespect toward the emperor. In his reply (*Letter* 10.82), Trajan interprets the accusation as a charge of treason – but a very frivolous charge, which he advises Pliny to dismiss. The incident indicates, however, how readily the people of Pliny's province brought against one another accusations which were motivated by personal enmity rather than real concern about wrongdoing. Thus factional or some other non-religious animosity may have instigated the litigation against the people referred to Pliny as Christians.

The issue is, however, very complex. At the end of the letter, Pliny informs Trajan that "the contagion of this superstition has spread not only to the cities, but also to the villages and even to the farms." As a result, the rites of the Roman religion had been neglected, and the sales of animals to be sacrificed at these rites had declined (*Letter* 10.96.9 and 10). Non-Christians may have been frightened by the changes that were occurring and by the potential obliteration of their ancestral customs. More importantly, they may have resented their Christian neighbors because they seemed to ignore the welfare of the community and to be defiantly engaged in behavior that would offend the gods and thus bring about the destruction of the state. To non-Christians, the Christians' refusal to worship the gods who protected the security and prosperity of the Roman Empire was a behavior that would anger the gods and turn them against the state. It was a behavior tantamount to both sacrilege and treason. The Christians, however, believed that they could not participate in the rituals of the Roman religion without offending their god.

The fact that the Christians could be identified as a group which seemed to promote contempt for the gods of the state, and even to be conspiring to weaken the power of Rome, left them liable to charges that they formed associations whose practices put the community in danger. In *Letter* 10.96.7, Pliny writes that he had, by edict, outlawed the existence of associations or clubs (*hetaeriae*) in accordance with a mandate from Trajan.[74] Trajan's mandate pre-dated the occurrence of accusations against the Christians and was probably intended as a general measure to bring stability to Bithynia-Pontus by curbing the political vendettas and violence among its residents. The conspiracies of the *hetaeriae* are mentioned by Dio Chrysostom.[75] Trajan's apprehension about associations can be seen in *Letters* 10.33 and 34. Pliny asked him for permission to establish an association (*collegium*) of firefighters in the city of Nicomedia where there had recently been a devastating fire. Pliny's proposal seems reasonable and was probably based on his acquaintance with firefighting units in Rome. Trajan denied the request, however, expressing concern that the proposed association might foment political unrest. In his reply to Pliny in *Letter* 10.34, Trajan warns: "Remember that your province, and particularly those towns, have been disturbed by factions of this kind. When people gather together for a common purpose – whatever name we may give them and whatever function we may assign them – they soon become *hetaeriae*." By *hetaeriae*, Trajan clearly means a group of people who promote political instability. Pliny does not state specifically that the people brought before him were charged with belonging to a forbidden association (*hetaeria*), but perhaps they were so described by their accusers.

Despite his reservations, Pliny seems to have punished the people brought before him simply for being Christian, rather than for specific crimes. During the initial hearings, he asked them if they were Christian, threatened punishment, and gave them two opportunities to deny it. If, upon being asked a third time, they refused to deny it, he ordered them to be punished, probably with execution. "For I had no doubt that, whatever the nature of their belief, their stubbornness and inflexible obstinacy surely should be punished." Refusal to comply with the wishes of a government official was interpreted as a kind of willful defiance which in itself deserved punishment. In *Letter* 10.57.2, a letter from Trajan to Pliny, the emperor recommended an increase in the punishment of a man because of his *contumacia* ("stubbornness"). However, Pliny did not punish Roman citizens in the accused group, but rather ordered them to be sent to Rome. Roman governors had supreme power over non-Romans in their provinces, but potentially capital cases against Roman citizens were by law to be referred to Rome for trial.[76]

At *Letter* 10.96.4, Pliny states that, as frequently happens, once the hearings began, the number and variety of accusations increased. A list of names was published anonymously, and other people were accused by an informer. Pliny set free those who denied they were now or had ever been Christian, prayed with him to the Roman gods, made offerings of wine and incense to Trajan's statue, and cursed Christ. He had been told that those who were truly Christian could not be forced to do any of those things (*Letter* 10.96.5). Some accused before him claimed that they had met together not for the purpose of plotting a crime, but rather to swear not to commit theft, robbery, or adultery, not to break their word, and not to cheat anyone of money. They sang hymns and shared a meal of food that was ordinary and innocent. (They apparently meant to repudiate a charge of cannibalism which arose from stories about eating the flesh and drinking the blood of Christ.) They had, however, ceased to do even this once Pliny issued his edict outlawing *hetaeriae*.

Uncertain perhaps about whether to accept the word of the accused, Pliny thought that it was necessary to investigate further. He therefore sought out the truth from two female slaves (*ancillae*) (*Letter* 10.96.8). And he used torture while questioning them. Pliny writes that the two slaves were called *ministrae*, which is a Latin word which means "servants" or "attendants." Since his province was in the Greek-speaking part of the Roman Empire, it is reasonable to assume that a

Greek word had originally been used to describe the two women, and that Pliny (or his interpreter) translated that word into Latin. The Greek word was probably *diakonissa*, the feminine form of *diakonos*, which are translated into English respectively as "deaconess" and "deacon." In ancient Greek, the words mean "servant" or "attendant." The terms evolved, however, in Christian usage, to mean a person who holds an office in the church, someone who "serves" the congregation. As early as the mid-first century CE, the apostle Paul used the term *diakonos* to identify a church official or leader, who, he insists, must be very virtuous.[77] In the New Testament, the term *diakonos* is first applied to a woman in Romans 16.1 and 2, in reference to a woman who worked for the church near Corinth, Greece. "I commend unto you Phoebe who is a *diakonos* at Cenchrea. ... She has been the benefactor of many and of myself also." However, the specific duties and rank of Phoebe are not stated. (In the Latin translation of the Greek New Testament, the word *diakonos* is translated as *ministra*.) Certainly we cannot ascertain from this biblical passage whether a female *diakonos* had liturgical or pastoral functions or whether her role was limited to serving as an assistant to male officers – and whether a *diakonissa* had the same functions as a female *diakonos*. Nonetheless, many scholars have assumed that the two *ancillae* were described to Pliny as *diakonissai* not because they were "servants" (the traditional meaning of the word *diakonissai*), but because they held official positions or leadership roles in the young church. This assumption rises from a circular argument: Pliny wanted to interrogate the women because they held influential roles in the church, and the women must have held influential roles in the church because Pliny wanted to interrogate them. The assumption that the *ancillae* had leadership functions has furthermore led scholars working on the social history of early Christianity to cite, perhaps too hastily, Pliny's letter as evidence that, in the first centuries, the traditional gender hierarchy was ignored, and women, and even slave women, were allowed to play leadership roles.

Harrill urges caution, however, about this interpretation of Pliny.[78] Recall that Pliny uses in his letter the Latin word *ministrae*, not the Greek *diakonissai*. Harrill argues that Pliny's employment of the word *ministrae* is informed by Roman religious terminology and institutions. He recommends that readers consider the significance of the word *ministrae* to Pliny and Trajan. In *Letters* 10.31 and 10.32, Pliny and Trajan use the words *minister* and *ministerium* to refer to the duties of slaves working for the local government. When Pliny uses the word *ministra* in *Letter* 10.96, he does not qualify it or explain to Trajan that its Greek equivalent, *diakonissa*, may have a special meaning to Christians of his province. He may not have realized that. *Minister* (the masculine form of *ministra*) was, however, a word used in the context of Roman religion. Inscriptions indicate that male slaves, called *ministri*, were employed in the service of the cult of the *Lares Augusti* (Guardian Deities of the Emperor's Family).[79] The worship of these deities, in order to protect the welfare of the imperial family, was conducted in all parts of the empire. The *ministri* were not leaders or officers or priests, but rather assistants or servants to the leaders. Moreover, there is no evidence for female slaves in this position. Thus Pliny's statement to Trajan is likely intended to convey to the emperor the information that the *ancillae* were servants working at menial positions in the church rather than that they had leadership roles. Although it would surely have made sense for Pliny to interrogate the women if he thought that they were officers of the congregation, there is no indication that he was aware that the word *diakonissa* may have acquired a special meaning of "officer" or "leader" in the young church, and certainly no indication that this particular congregation had female officers. We should consider instead that Pliny interrogated the *ancillae* because, as slaves attending to the needs of the church leaders, they would have access to information about the lives of those leaders which members of the congregation might not have. As Harrill points out, they were "best positioned to see, hear, and betray any monstrous crimes that their masters may have committed."[80] In addition, because they were slaves, they could be tortured and might, under torture, reveal information which other people would conceal.

It was customary in legal cases for slaves to be tortured before and while they gave evidence. The Romans, like the Greeks, believed that slaves would tell the truth only under torture.[81] Some slave-owners manumitted their slaves before a trial began, either to spare them the agony of torture and possible death, or to prevent them from revealing incriminating information. However, when Calpurnius Piso was accused of murdering Germanicus by having slaves put poison in his food at a dinner party (see Chapter 1), he asked that his slaves be tortured. He was apparently convinced that their evidence would acquit him. The story is told by Tacitus, and it is notable that he uses the word *ministri* to identify the slaves who had served the dinner.[82] As already noted, one of the pontiffs present at the hearings about the *incestum* of the Vestal Virgin, Cornelia, fainted because he was not able to tolerate the harshness of the examinations. Until the time of the emperor Hadrian (117–38 CE), all the slaves in a household where the owner had been murdered were tortured for evidence.[83] Cicero describes an interrogation in one of his speeches.[84] A cruel woman named Sassia wanted to investigate the death of her husband. She demanded that several family slaves be interrogated, including a slave who was known to have served her husband well. She invited friends to attend the interrogation. "It was carried out vigorously with every form of torture. ... Nevertheless the slaves said that they did not know anything. The interrogation was halted for the day, on the advice of friends. They were summoned back after a sufficiently long interval. The interrogation began again. No level of the most painful torture was omitted. The witnesses could scarcely bear it. ... When the torturer and even the instruments of torture were worn out, the cruel woman was not willing to call an end." The witnesses finally persuaded her to stop the interrogation. In another speech, Cicero acknowledges that his client, Milo, had manumitted all his slaves before his trial for murder began.[85] The prosecution insinuated that he had done so in order that they might not be tortured into supplying incriminating evidence against him. Cicero, however, claimed that Milo freed them out of sympathy, because he did not want his dear slaves to suffer.

Pliny provides no details about the interrogation under torture of the two *ancillae*. He informs Trajan that he discovered "nothing other than perverse and excessive superstition" (*Letter* 10.96.8).[86] We do not know whether the two slave women survived the torture and, if so, whether they were subsequently executed for being Christians.

Slaves

Slaves were ubiquitous in Roman society.[87] They were considered the property of their owners, like farm animals or machinery or tools. They were granted no moral standing, and could be treated as abusively as their owner might wish to. Ancient sources indicate that it was common for slaves to be beaten, both to punish them and to frighten them into being obedient. It was also common for slaves to be sexually assaulted by their owners. Slaves were employed in private urban residences, in factories, shops, and transportation, on public projects and in public offices and religious buildings, and in rural areas, on farms and in mines. The wealth of Rome's affluent citizens was generated, to a great extent, by the toil of slaves who labored on their properties. To sustain his senatorial lifestyle, Pliny depended for income, in part, on the sale of agricultural products raised by slaves on the many estates he owned. In *Letter* 1.21, he thanks a friend for his advice on the purchase of slaves, and in *Letter* 3.19, he asks a friend for advice on the purchase of agricultural land that will be worked by slaves.[88] Ummidia Quadratilla may have been the recipient of income produced by renting out her company of slave performers. (See Chapter 5.) Of course, both Pliny and Ummidia Quadratilla and their friends also enjoyed the luxury of being cared for by the many domestic slaves they purchased for use in their homes.

The comfort of every elite woman mentioned by Pliny in his letters depended on the services of a large number of slaves who labored in her household, cooked and cleaned, looked after her children, and attended to all her personal needs. In reflecting upon the lives of the elite women, we should not overlook their dependence on their many slaves who were involved in every aspect of their lives. The benefits of owning slaves, particularly slaves who lived in one's household and catered to one's personal needs, might, however, be accompanied by insecurity and anxieties.[89] The fear of being physically attacked by one's slaves will be discussed later. Owners might also suspect, whether or not with good reason, that they were being cheated or mocked by their slaves. In addition, owners might fear or resent the control which slaves ironically could have over the behavior of their owners. The best household slave was one who acted as a mere instrument of the owner's will. But to do so, the slave needed to anticipate the owner's thoughts and know her/him intimately. An intelligent and resourceful slave was both a blessing and a threat. Household slaves were silent witnesses to their owner's every word and action. The owner would hope, of course, that the slave would remain loyal and not expose secrets. However, perhaps one reason that owners so frequently lashed out, both literally and figuratively, at their slaves was because they wanted to reinforce their dominance over the lives of creatures whom they considered vastly inferior, but also very essential.

About the lives of the slaves who remain in the shadows of Pliny's letters, we know almost nothing. In legal terms, slaves had no family of their own and could not form marriages. Their *paterfamilias* was their owner, who could sell them – or their children, "spouse," parents, or siblings – at any time, for any reason, just as an owner of livestock could sell animals. Separation from blood relatives and "spouses" was a frequent occurrence in a slave's existence. And, as noted in Chapter 4, a lactating slave might be forced to abandon her own baby in order to nurse the infant of her owners. Can we learn anything in the letters about what the lives of Pliny's slaves were like? Although, in the case of the *ancillae* of the Christian congregation (*Letter* 10.96), Pliny followed the standard procedure of employing torture during the interrogation, he appears from his letters to have been a relatively kind slave-owner. His generosity to his old nurse, revealed in *Letter* 6.3, has been discussed in Chapter 4. In *Letter* 1.4, discussed in Chapter 5, he light-heartedly tells his former mother-in-law that he is so soft on his slaves that they take advantage of him. In *Letter* 5.19, he discloses to a friend (and, after publication, to all his readers) that he treats his slaves with indulgence and tries to act like the father figure (*pater*) that the role of *paterfamilias* implies. In *Letter* 8.1, he mentions his concern about the illness of a slave, Encolpius, who was Pliny's reader. (The Romans did not read silently to themselves, but rather had slaves read aloud to them.) And in *Letter* 8.16, he tells his addressee that he is distressed by the recent illnesses and deaths of some of his slaves. He finds some consolation in the fact that he manumitted those who were dying and allowed them to bequeath their "possessions" to other slaves in the household. Legally slaves could not own possessions because they themselves were property, not persons. More-over, any property within the household legally belonged to the *paterfamilias*. However, Pliny permits his slaves to act as if items they may have acquired (perhaps through gifts) were their possessions. About his response to their deaths, he writes, "I am crushed and shattered. ... Not that I would wish to be less compassionate" (*Letter* 8.16.3). We do not have the information that would allow us to ascertain what it was like to be a slave owned by Pliny. We do not know whether Pliny's slaves regarded him as a master who was kinder than average and felt fortunate to have been purchased by him. Perhaps they did not. Perhaps he was, despite his comment to his mother-in-law, as suspicious as other owners about being taken advantage of. It is noteworthy, however, that he wanted to leave a permanent portrait of himself as a compassionate slave-owner. He must have believed that his readers would regard his behavior as admirable. We read so frequently in Roman literature and legal texts about extremely cruel treatment of slaves that it is salutary to learn that there existed slave-owners who believed that, at least on some occasions, they should be sympathetic towards their slaves.

Slaves who worked closely with their owner, such as Pliny's readers and his nurse, and perhaps his wife Calpurnia's maid servants, might be treated more kindly than slaves who labored, for example, in the kitchen, or in a factory, or on a farm. Slaves in factories and on farms had little personal contact with their owners. They were expected to produce income for their owners, rather than attend to their personal needs. Their value lay in the work that could be extracted from their bodies, and they were therefore considered to be pieces of equipment, purchased to be used and then discarded when old or broken. It is unlikely that Pliny was as considerate toward the slaves who labored on his various estates, and whom he rarely saw or spoke to, as he was toward the slaves who served him in his home(s). Nonetheless, Pliny reveals that he did not employ the most brutal practices on his rural estates. On many farms, for example, slaves were chained together 24 hours a day. In *Letter* 3.19.7, however, in which Pliny discusses the possible purchase of a farm (with money borrowed from his former mother-in-law), he tells his addressee that neither he, nor other landowners in the area, keep their slaves chained. This was admittedly a very minor kindness, but a kindness nonetheless.

Pliny had no sympathy, however, for slaves who attacked their owners. Slave-owners, being always surrounded by slaves, even when they ate or bathed or slept, felt anxious about their vulnerability. And wealthy people, with the most slaves, were perhaps especially fearful. Pliny owned at least 500 slaves, employed both in Rome and on his rural properties.[90] An aphorism quoted by Seneca stated that "you have as many enemies as you have slaves."[91] Elsewhere Seneca wrote: "Consider the examples of those who perished through treacheries in their own homes, either by open violence or by deceit, and you will understand that the anger of slaves has killed no fewer people than the anger of kings."[92] In *Letter* 6.25, Pliny records two occasions on which men had disappeared while traveling. He offers as one theory about their disappearance that they had been attacked by their slaves. The Romans used threats of harsh penalties to keep their slaves from plotting against them. If a slave-owner was murdered, and one of his slaves was the suspect, all the slaves in the household, even though innocent, could be tortured and executed, often by crucifixion.[93] It was hoped that this practice would encourage slaves, who knew that others were conspiring to harm their master, to inform upon them in order to avoid being executed themselves. This threat of mass execution "betrays an underlying suspicion that slaves would gladly see their masters dead, and would never help to save them unless they were forced to."[94] Hadrian declared that a slave woman who might be too scared to call for help when her mistress was attacked must be executed. Her execution would be an object lesson to other slaves that they should always consider the safety of their owners more important than their own.[95] In 61 CE, the 400 slaves of a murdered slave-owner were executed, even though few had participated in the plot. Popular opinion was opposed to the execution of 400 innocent people. A spirited debate took place in the Senate, but, in the end, the senators voted for a mass execution. As one speaker argued, "we can live safely and securely, though one man among many slaves, if they are afraid."[96]

The execution of 400 slaves, most of them innocent of their owner's murder, was an event which shocked Roman residents. Some scholars have suggested that so harsh a penalty was rarely invoked. Aside from humane considerations, the execution of all the slaves in a household meant a great financial burden for the heirs of the murdered slave owner: they would now have to purchase a new set of slaves.[97] Gamauf argues, however, that the fact that there was so much discussion among jurists, as recorded in the *Digest* 29, about exceptions and loopholes to the legislation requiring execution (the *senatus consultum Silanianum*) is "ample evidence of its regular application."[98] He also maintains that slaves did indeed on occasion harm their owners and that Roman slave owners did indeed feel vulnerable. As Gamauf comments, Roman legislation was a response to the demands of the elite and was shaped by real cases, not theory or vague anxieties. It embodied the power of the elite, but also revealed their fears.

In *Letter* 3.14, Pliny reports that the slaves of Larcius Macedo, a man of praetorian rank, had attempted to murder him while he was taking a bath. He was beaten viciously, but rescued by his "more faithful" slaves. Nonetheless, he died a few days later. The treacherous slaves ran away, but were hunted down. Their executions were undoubtedly excruciatingly painful. Pliny says nothing about whether or not all the slaves in the household were executed. (The heirs of the murdered man might oppose their execution because the death of a slave – the destruction of property – meant a significant financial loss.) He admits that Larcius Macedo was an arrogant and savage master, who remembered too little – or perhaps too well – that his own father had been a slave (*Letter* 3.14.1).[99] Nonetheless, Pliny considers his murder an atrocious deed and one that needed to be widely publicized. In fact, to put emphasis on the vileness of the murder, he opens the letter with the words *rem atrocem*. However savage Macedo may have been, the actions of his slaves could not be excused because, as Pliny writes, "No one can feel secure, even if he is a lenient and kind master" (*Letter* 3.14.5). Pliny's account of the event has puzzled readers because of apparent inconsistencies in his attitude toward slaves.[100] He admits that Macedo was a cruel owner, which seems to provide an explanation for the slaves' actions and to suggest that the slaves were provoked by their owner's savagery. And yet he also laments that even a humane owner may fall victim to his slaves. "You see how many dangers, insults, and ridicules we (*slave owners*) are exposed to. ... Slave owners are murdered because of the wickedness, not the rational thought (*of their slaves*)" (*Letter* 3.14.5). Pliny's statement implies that he would attribute the actions of Macedo's slaves to their wickedness, rather than to an understandable response to their owner's cruelty. His statement also reflects the same haunting concern about the loyalty of slaves that he expresses in *Letter* 6.25, where he speculates not that travelers were attacked by bandits, but that they were killed by their own slaves. It is difficult to reconcile his declaration that all slave owners were vulnerable and all slaves were potentially wicked with his professions elsewhere about his affection for his slaves, his leniency with them, and his willingness, expressed a few letters later, in *Letter* 3.19.7, to allow his farm slaves to be unchained. Pliny's statement that "no one can feel secure" instructs us, however, about the anxiety under which both slaves and their owners lived – owners fearing that even a trusted slave might turn on them, and slaves fearing that even a kind owner might distrust them and consign them to torture and death.

Freedwomen and concubines

As Larcius Macedo's more faithful slaves came to his assistance, his concubines (*concubinae*) ran up, wailing and shouting (*Letter* 3.14.3). The Latin noun *concubina* is cognate with the verb *concubare*, "to lie together," "have sexual intercourse." The concubines were likely to have been freedwomen – that is, women who had been slaves, but had been freed or manumitted.

The Latin word *concubina* has a range of meanings.[101] In many situations, *concubina* refers to the female partner in a stable, long-term relationship of cohabitation. The relationship, the concubinage (*concubinatus*), was similar to a marriage, and is sometimes referred to by scholars as a *de facto* marriage or quasi-marriage. The male partner may have been prevented from forming a legal marriage with the woman because he was a soldier, or she was a non-citizen, or he was a senator and she was a freedwoman (*liberta*).[102] In some situations, a legal marriage was not forbidden, but the man was of a much higher social status than the *concubina* and perhaps under family pressure not to form a legal marriage. If he had children from a previous marriage, he might not wish to remarry (despite the Julian laws) and produce more heirs to his property. The children of concubinage were not legitimate heirs. Quite a few of the examples of concubinage involve a partnership between a freedwoman and her former owner. These examples suggest that the relationship was based on an emotional attachment that developed when the woman was still a slave and that her owner manumitted her because of his affection for her. These partnerships were asymmetrical, since the woman was usually of a lower social and economic class, but they were not considered dishonorable.[103]

In other situations, however, *concubina* refers to a woman who provides sexual pleasure for a man with no expectation of a permanent relationship or a shared life. Indeed, the man was quite likely married. Suetonius reports, for example, that Domitian was a man of enormous libido who had many concubines.[104] And Tacitus records that Tigellinus was in the midst of debauchery with his concubines when he learned of the order for his execution.[105] These concubines would be considered less respectable than a concubine in a *de facto* marriage. It is undoubtedly concubines of this nature that Pliny is referring to in *Letter* 3.14.3. His report of their rushing to the scene of the attempted murder suggests that they lived in the household. It was not unusual for freedpersons to continue to live in the household in which they had been slaves. And, although Pliny identifies them as concubines, these women may have had additional roles in service to the household. For example, a slave who had worked in the kitchen and been an involuntary sexual partner for the master might, after manumission, be retained as a freed kitchen worker and sexual partner. We do not know whether it was unusual for a man to keep at home several concubines to serve his sexual wishes. The stories about Domitian and Tigellinus indicate that some men did so. However, the references to these concubines seem designed to portray them as men of vile character and repulsive habits. Thus, by mentioning the presence of concubines in *Letter* 3.14.3, Pliny perhaps invites the reader to speculate that Macedo engaged in sexual practices which his peers deemed unacceptable. Some scholars, observing that the slaves who attacked Macedo pummeled his genitals, have conjectured that Macedo was a sexual deviant whose demands had driven his slaves to desperation.[106] However, Pliny offers no explicit information about the reasons for the attack (nor does he show any compassion for the murderous slaves).

Those of us who enjoy the considerable personal freedoms and financial independence of modern society might wonder why a freedwoman would remain in such a position. In ancient society, however, economic conditions kept many freedpersons dependent upon their former owners. We might also wonder why these women would bewail the attack on a man whom Pliny acknowledges was an arrogant and savage master. Again, the answer is economic dependence. However unpleasant the situation might be in the household of Larcius Macedo, these women were provided with shelter and food. They were bewailing the loss of this security.

Manumission – "sent from (*missum*) the hand or control (*manus*)" – was a common occurrence in ancient Rome.[107] In fact, it is an aspect of Roman society that sets it apart from other slave-owning societies. Very few slaves in the American antebellum South, for example, were manumitted by their owners. In Rome, however, slaves were not just freed, they were granted Roman citizenship. Manumitted slaves were identified as "freedpersons," *liberti* (singular: *libertus*, *liberta*), but their children (at least those born after the manumission) were free persons, who became assimilated into Roman society, with all the rights and privileges of Roman citizens. Manumission was undoubtedly the dream of all slaves. It was a reward for loyalty and excellent service.[108] Roman slave-owners controlled their slaves with a combination of threats of savage punishment and promises of rewards. The hope of manumission was an incentive for slaves to work hard and be obedient. As noted earlier, some owners freed female slaves with whom they had developed an emotional attachment, and some freed slave children in order to adopt them.[109] (The children may have been their own illegitimate children.) Manumission meant a loss of property for the owner, and therefore some owners made the manumission effective only at the time of their death by stating in their will that certain slaves were to be freed. The loss of "property," however, reduced the inheritance of their heirs. Other owners required that the manumitted slave pay for his/her freedom. The newly minted freedperson became the client of the former owner/*paterfamilias* who, in turn, became the patron (*patronus*). Although some freedpersons went into business for themselves, perhaps with financial support from their former owners, many continued to work for their former owners, and some even continued to live in the household. The relationship between an ex-slave and ex-master did not end with the manumission process.[110] Freedpersons had a legal obligation to provide several days of labor or service each year, even if they did not continue to live in the household. Freedwomen over the age of 50 were exempt from this requirement. Concubines living with their patrons were also exempt from providing (additional) services for them.[111]

Pliny's manumission of some of his slaves when they were on their death beds is not perceived by modern readers as a particularly magnanimous gesture (*Letter* 8.16). And he does not write in the published correspondence about freeing slaves on other occasions. However, we can ascertain from the letters that he had manumitted some of his slaves when they were healthy, and that he treated them well as freedpersons. The probable manumission of his former nurse, and his gift to her of a farm, have been discussed in Chapter 4. In *Letter* 5.19, he laments the illness of his freedman, Zosimus, who was one of his readers (like the slave Encolpius of *Letter* 8.1) and asks the addressee if he may send him to his country estate to recover. Pliny had previously sent him to Egypt for a lengthy recuperation. Here is a case of a freedperson who continued to live in the household of his former owner and apparently continued to do the same work. He was a well-educated individual who had close contact with Pliny and thus many opportunities to display his honesty, trustworthiness, and intelligence. It is nonetheless to Pliny's credit that he recognized and rewarded the man's talents and virtues. Slaves who worked in a household or small shop and interacted frequently with their owners had a better chance of gaining manumission than those utilized in factories, on farms, or on public projects. Slaves owned by wealthy people were perhaps more likely to be manumitted because the owner could better absorb the loss of property which manumission entailed. However, and as mentioned earlier, an owner might ask the slave to reimburse him for the loss. We do not know if female slave owners manumitted their slaves more or less often than male owners. We know from *Letter* 1.4 that Pliny's former mother-in-law, Pompeia Celerina, owned slaves, but not whether she ever manumitted any. A woman needed the approval of her *tutor* (guardian) in order to manumit slaves since she was, in essence, relinquishing part of her family's estate. A woman whose *paterfamilias* was dead may have inherited the family slaves or might purchase slaves with money she inherited. She would then own the slaves separately from her husband, as apparently Cicero's wife, Terentia, did. (See Chapter 2.) In the case of Pliny's wife, Calpurnia, however, since her *paterfamilias* (her paternal grandfather) was still alive, she would not have possessed any property in her own name.

It was not unusual for a patron to invite his freedmen (but perhaps not freed-women) to a banquet. Some hosts, however, served their freedmen food and wine of lesser quality than that served to the other guests, and thus made the class distinctions very apparent. In *Letter* 2.6, Pliny criticizes this practice and asserts that he serves all his guests the same fare, whether free or freed, "for I invite them for dinner, not for humiliation. ... I think of them as fellow diners, not freedmen" (*Letter* 2.6.3).

Letters 7.16 and 32 (written about 107 CE) are both addressed to Pliny's grandfather-in-law, Calpurnius Fabatus, and, in them, Pliny discusses the manumission of some of Calpurnius' slaves (slaves that would, if not freed, eventually have become the property of Pliny's wife, Calpurnia). A slave might be informally declared freed by his/her owner, but, in order for the slave to acquire the full citizen rights of a freedperson, it was necessary that a magistrate (a consul or proconsul, for example) be present for the manumission process. If this did not happen, the freedperson gained only partial rights of Roman citizenship. S/he was identified by the term Junian Latin, rather than Roman citizen. In *Letter* 7.16, Pliny informs his grandfather-in-law that one of his good friends, Calestrius Tiro, who was now a proconsul, will be traveling near Comum and would be willing to go to Calpurnius' home to manumit his slaves formally.[112] Pliny urges his grandfather-in-law to agree to this procedure. In *Letter* 7.32, we learn that the crusty Calpurnius did take advantage of the proconsul's visit to Comum to have many of his slaves manumitted. There is no information, however, about whether all the manumitted slaves were household slaves, or whether some were farm-workers, or what the ratio of male to female slaves may have been. Surprisingly, Pliny praises the manumission on the grounds that it increased the number of citizens in the area.

Another example of Pliny's advocacy of humane treatment is found in *Letter* 8.14 (written about 105 CE), where he requests the opinion of a friend about a Senate matter. The consul Afranius Dexter had died. It could not be determined with certainty whether his death was a murder committed by someone in the household, or an unassisted suicide, or a suicide with which his household staff – both slaves and freedpersons – had assisted. As noted earlier, it was customary for all the slaves in a household to be executed if their owner's death was suspicious. Even if an owner had pleaded with his slaves for assistance in suicide, they were considered guilty of a crime because the law required that slaves do everything in their power to prevent the death of an owner.[113] There was discussion in Chapter 1 about the impact of suicide on the family of an upper class person. For slaves and freedpersons, an owner/patron's suicide might have disastrous consequences. In 57 CE, the Senate had passed a decree that freedpersons living in the household were also to be executed.[114] (The ruling is a reminder that many freedpersons continued to live and work in their patron's household, and an indication that, for many of them, life after manumission may not have been substantially different than life as a slave.) At the investigation into Afranius Dexter's death, some senators proposed execution for all the slaves and freedpersons in the household. Others proposed relegation for the freedpersons. Pliny, however, argued that the freedpersons should be released unpunished (*Letter* 8.14.12). In the end, the pro-posal for execution was withdrawn. Pliny does not state, however, whether the freedpersons were acquitted or relegated, or whether any of the slaves were spared execution.

In *Letter* 9.21, Pliny advised his friend to forgive a young freedman who had angered him. We are not told what the freedman had done to provoke the ire of his former owner, but we need not assume it was a major offence. Freedpersons were expected to be obsequious, and therefore even a slight disagreement or assumed affront might be construed as disloyalty and ingratitude. Since freed-persons often depended on their patrons for financial and social support, a breach in the relationship could be devastating. The freedman had begged Pliny to make an appeal on his behalf, and Pliny agreed. He encouraged his friend to be mer-ciful and pointed out that, because he was a man of gentle nature, he would only cause himself pain by being angry.

The freedwoman of Cornelia the Vestal Virgin

In *Letter* 4.11.11, Pliny reported that Licinianus was arrested for hiding a freed-woman of the condemned Vestal Virgin, Cornelia, on his estate. He probably hid her so that she could not be interrogated for evidence which incriminated him. However, he may also have been trying to protect her from torture and even a cruel execution.

Sabina

In *Letter* 4.10, Pliny discusses the will of a woman named Sabina. The pre-occupation with wills among elite Romans has been discussed in Chapters 3 and 4. In several letters, Pliny states that he believes that the wishes of the deceased should be honored even if a strict interpretation of the law might nullify parts or all of a will. In some of these letters, Pliny had been designated as one of the heirs, which meant that he was required to oversee the distributions of bequests and legacies of the estate made in the will. His statement in *Letter* 2.16.2, that he believed that he "should protect the wishes of the deceased as though perfectly expressed, even if they are deemed under the law to be insufficient", might seem self-serving because, in that particular case, he stood to lose an inheritance if the law was strictly enforced. In other instances, however, he argued for satisfying the wishes of the deceased even when it meant a financial loss to him. In *Letter* 5.7, for example, addressed to his good friend, Calvisius Rufus[115], we learn that Pliny and Calvisius had been named co-heirs of Saturninus' estate. He therefore had the responsibility for distributing the bequests and legacies announced in the will. Saturninus (whose identity is unknown) had designated his municipality (appar-ently Pliny's hometown of Comum) as a recipient of a bequest amounting to 400,000 sesterces, or about one-quarter of his estate. Bequests to municipalities were, however, forbidden by law. Because the bequest would be nullified, the amount inherited by Pliny and his co-heir, Calvisius, would be increased by 400,000 sesterces. However, Pliny maintains that the intention of the deceased is more important than the law, and he suggests to his co-heir that they comply with Saturninus' intention by taking 400,000 sesterces from their inheritance and donating it to the municipality.

Pliny's advocacy for fulfilling the intentions of the deceased is apparent again in *Letter* 4.10, where we learn that Sabina had designated Pliny and Statius Sabinus (possibly her relative) as her heirs. We know nothing about Sabina except what Pliny tells us. In her will, she had left a legacy to someone named Modestus, with the notation, "To Modestus, whom I have ordered to be freed." However, she had not left specific instructions in the will that Modestus be freed. Thus, according to a strict interpretation of the law, Modestus was still a slave and therefore could not receive property. If the two co-heirs adhered to the law, they would receive a larger inheritance: they would inherit both the slave Modestus and the legacy which he could not receive. However, Pliny's object in writing the letter is to persuade his co-heir Sabinus to give up that income – that is, to agree that Sabina had, in fact, intended Modestus to be manumitted and had simply failed to state this unequivocally. To persuade Sabinus, Pliny uses flattery, and reminds him that he has always acted honorably and been scrupulous in obser-ving the deceased's wishes. If the co-heir agreed with Pliny, Modestus would win the freedom which his owner, Sabina, had promised him. However, we do not know the outcome of the situation. Nor do we know why Sabina had made so critical an omission in her will. Carlon posits that women had less experience and familiarity with the law and therefore needed to be very careful about whom they chose to assist with the writing and administration of their wills.[116] Although Sabina's advisor in the writing of the will had been negligent, she had, in designating Pliny as an heir, selected someone who was adamant about interpreting and complying with the deceased's intentions. By publishing the letter, Pliny portrays himself as a conscientious and honorable man. He also appears as someone who was sympathetic to the plight of slaves. It would have been easy to treat Modestus simply as disposable property and to ignore his expectations of manumission.

Antonia Maximilla

Several freedwomen and two female patrons are mentioned very briefly in Book 10. In *Letter* 10.5, written by Pliny to Trajan about 98 CE, Pliny appeals to the emperor to grant citizen rights to an Egyptian man, a physiotherapist named Harpocras, who had cared for him when he was gravely ill, and to (Antonia) Hedia and Antonia Harmeris, who were freedwomen of Antonia Maximilla, whom he describes as an excellent woman. Harpocras had been a slave of a woman named Thermuthis, wife of Theon. These names are Egyptian, but Harpocras was living in Italy when he nursed Pliny, and perhaps Thermuthis, who was dead at the time the letter was written, had also lived in Italy. Thermuthis had given Harpocras his freedom, perhaps stating in her will that she desired that he be manumitted. However, because Thermuthis was herself not a Roman citizen, Harpocras did not receive Roman citizenship upon his manumission. (We learn in *Letters* 10.6, 7, and 10 that Trajan granted Pliny's request.) In *Letter* 10.11, written about 99 CE, Pliny made another request to Trajan to grant citizenship rights to several foreigners, including one woman.

Antonia Maximilla, the patron of the two freedwomen, is identified by Pliny in *Letter* 10.6.1 as his *necessaria*, which might mean his kinswoman or his friend. We do not know the nature of this relationship or anything more about this woman. She had asked Pliny to request full Roman citizenship for these two freedwomen. (And Trajan granted the request, *Letter* 10.6.1.) Since Pliny identifies the two women as *libertae*, or freedwomen, it is not clear why they do not already have the Roman citizenship usually granted upon manumission. Antonia Maximilla seems to have manumitted them informally – that is, without the presence of a magistrate – and they thereby gained only the status of Junian Latins. Recall that Pliny's grandfather-in-law had also wanted to have some of his former slaves formally manumitted. Sherwin-White speculates that Antonia Maximilla may have acted without the consent of her *tutor* and therefore been legally prevented from establishing full Roman citizenship for her former slaves.[117] However, a Junian freedperson could attempt to obtain Roman citizenship by petition to the emperor.[118] Antonia Maximilla had apparently appealed to her friend/kinsman,

Pliny, to make this petition on behalf of her freedwomen. It was customary for slaves, upon manumission, to take on the family name of their former owner. Thus Hedia and Harmeris adopted the name Antonia.[119] (A male freedman would have adopted the masculine form of the name: Antonius.)

Furia Prima

Letter 10.58 was written to Trajan by Pliny from his province about 110 or 111 CE. A man named Flavius Archippus had asked to be excused from jury duty on the grounds that he was a philosopher.[120] Some people – his enemies presumably, in this province of bitter political rivalries and vendettas – used the occasion to declare that he was an escaped convict who should be returned to his punishment.[121] He had been convicted of forgery and condemned to work in the mines by Velius Paulus, who had been governor about 83 or 84 CE – that is, more than 25 years earlier. (Condemnation to the mines, rather than relegation, was a very harsh penalty for a man of the elite class. It was accompanied by the loss of civic rights.) Flavius Archippus could produce no document to prove that his civic rights had been restored (which, in turn, would attest to the voiding of his sentence). Instead he offered documents from the emperor Domitian (81–96 CE), which praised him as a man of good character, and from the emperor Nerva (96–98 CE), announcing that he would not rescind any benefits granted by Domitian. Pliny requested the advice of Trajan about the status of Flavius Archippus. *Letter* 10.59 is a cover letter to two documents which Pliny sent to provide Trajan with more information about the situation. One was a petition from Flavius Archippus himself. The other was a petition from a woman named Furia Prima, whom Pliny identifies as the accuser of Flavius Archippus.

The fact that the latter petition which was presumably intended to present the case against Flavius Archippus was sent by Furia Prima suggests that she had been the principal victim of his forgery. And, because the accuser was a woman, the forgery is likely to have been one involving a will. Falsifying a will was a "public crime," *crimen publicum*, dealt with under the *Lex Cornelia de falsis*, and the charge was capital, hence the severe penalty. As noted in previous chapters, women were not permitted to bring forward capital charges except in cases involving the death of their parents or children, or cases involving a falsified will.[122] Furia Prima was thus legally permitted to prosecute Flavius Archippus. Still, it was unusual that the plaintiff was a woman – that is, that she did not ask a male relative to make the accusation.

Flavius Archippus seems to have served his penalty in the mines for only a year or so before he broke free of his chains and escaped. The sentencing magistrate, Velius Paulus, was in Bithynia about 83 or 84 CE, and the governor to whom Domitian sent the letter praising Archippus was there about 85.[123] Archippus certainly did not act like a fugitive after he left the mine. He returned to playing a prominent role in the community and apparently to involving himself in factional intrigues. His enemies' complaint that he had broken out of his chains may have been metaphorical; in reality, he may have been released through the maneuvers of his friends who cultivated the good will of the next governor and even of the emperor Domitian. It is interesting to observe from the letters how bitter and persistent the factional vendettas of this community were. For Pliny, his time as governor must often have seemed like living in the proverbial hornets' nest. Furia Prima was apparently determined, even 25 years after the offence, to see Archippus punished. She may, however, also have brought forward a new charge or perhaps a modified charge. Recall that in *Letter* 7.6.10, also concerning a woman who made an accusation of will tampering, when the case was decided in favor of the defendant, the woman appealed, claimed she had new evidence, and won a new hearing of the case. In *Letter* 10.60, in his reply, Trajan states that he believes that Domitian had intervened favorably on Archippus' behalf. He also notes that residents of the town (Prusa) had set up many statues in Archippus' honor even though they were not unaware of the original "guilty" verdict. The implication of Trajan's words is that Pliny should not proceed with any prosecution of Archippus on the old charge. However, he also recommends that Pliny should treat any new charge with customary rigor.

The collection of Pliny's correspondence – a collection which happily has survived the vagaries of time and fortune for 2000 years – terminates with *Letters* 10.120 and 121, Pliny's apology to Trajan for issuing a travel pass to his wife Calpurnia without prior imperial approval, and Trajan's positive response. (See Chapter 3.) We do not know why there are no more letters extant. It is generally assumed that Pliny died in his province, Bithynia-Pontus, shortly after this exchange of letters. It is possible, of course, that Pliny did not die then, that he finished his term of office, returned to Italy, and was reunited with Calpurnia, that they lived long contented lives, but that his letters from these years have not been preserved. However, we have no evidence for his life after he wrote *Letter* 10.120. For us readers who are interested in the lives of the women in Pliny's letters, it is fortuitous that the collection concludes with information about Calpurnia and her family relationships: that she had been anxious to return from Asia Minor to Italy so that she might console her aunt after the death of her grandfather and that she had been willing to endure a long grueling journey in order to fulfill the dictates of *pietas*. It is, moreover, satisfying to learn that Pliny was sympathetic to his wife's grief and did not hesitate (or depicts himself as not having hesitated) to arrange safe and speedy passage for her.

Notes

Introduction: writing about lives

1 Plutarch, *Timoleon*, Preface 1.
2 Tacitus, *Agricola* 1.1.
3 Mayer (1991) p. 144.
4 Quintilian, *Institutio Oratoria* 12.2.30.
5 Seneca, *Letters* 6.5.
6 Mayer (1991) p. 165.
7 Dixon (2001a) pp. 8–18.
8 Dixon (2001b) p. xiv.
9 Barrett (1996) p. xiv.
10 Barrett (1996) p. xiv.
11 Ash (2003) p. 214. For an analysis of *Letter* 1.1, see Hoffer (1999) pp. 15–27.
12 On the chronology of the correspondence, see Aubrion (1990) pp. 315–323, and Sherwin-White (1966) pp. 20–41. I have followed Sherwin-White's suggestions for the dates of composition of the individual letters.
13 Henderson (2003) p. 116. Henderson suggests that Pliny wanted to generate a friendship with Tacitus because being mentioned in his historical works would guarantee immortality. Riggsby (1998) p. 88, comments that Pliny may have inflated the reputations of some of his friends as a means of raising his own standing in his community.
14 De Pretis (2003) p. 137.
15 Hutchinson (1998) p. 17.
16 Hoffer (1999) p. 133; Morello (2003) p. 187.
17 Hutchinson (1998) p. 16.
18 De Pretis (2003) p. 132.
19 Carlon (2009) p. 9.
20 Morello and Gibson (2003) p. 109.
21 In *Letter* 5.8.5 and 6, Pliny declares that he does not yet have time to write history because he needs to revise his speeches for publication. He assumed that his published speeches (only one of which survives) would outlive him and earn him everlasting renown. In *Letter* 5.5.2, having reported the death of Gaius Fannius, he comments that it was especially grievous that Fannius left behind an unfinished book manuscript. Several scholars point out the centrality of Pliny's oratorical activities to the picture that he presents of himself in his letters. He used his letters to generate and sustain public interest in them. See Riggsby (1995); also Mayer (2003) p. 227. Gamberini (1983) p. 150, asserts that epistolography was not the genre by which Pliny expected to win future fame; rather, he hoped that his oratory would survive.
22 Ash (2003) pp. 213 and 216.

23 On the popularity of "death scenes" in the literature of the early imperial period, see Ash (2003) pp. 222 and 223, and Edwards (2007) pp. 131–134.

24 Ash (2003) p. 221.

25 Henderson (2003) p. 115.

26 Shelton (1987).

27 Leach (1990) pp. 14–39. In *Letters* 7.33.2 and 3.10.6, Pliny compares the work of a sculptor, creating a likeness of a person, to the work of a biographer or historian who shapes words to produce a permanent portrait of a person. Henderson (2002) p. xiii, declares that Pliny "writes portrait sculpture."

28 Radicke (1997) pp. 461–466. See also Henderson's (2002) discussion of several letters in Book 3 and Hoffer's (1999) discussion of several letters in Book 1.

29 McNeill (2001) p. 5.

30 *Panegyricus* 95.3 and 4. Pliny was appointed suffect consul (*consul suffectus*; see Chapter 1, note 6) for September and October of 100 CE. As was customary, he delivered before the Senate a speech expressing gratitude to the emperor for his appointment. He then revised, expanded, and published the speech, after soliciting comments from friends (*Letter* 3.13.1). The extant speech is turgid with flattery of Trajan. When Pliny invited friends to a recitation of the written version, he spent three days reading it aloud (*Letter* 3.18.4).

31 *CIL* 5.5262 and 5.5667.

32 Tacitus, *Agricola* 42.

33 Edwards (2007) p. 131. For example, 35 senators lost their lives either by the command of or with the subsequent consent of the emperor Claudius (emperor 41–54CE). (See Suetonius, *Claudius* 29.2; Seneca the Younger, *Apocolocyntosis* 14.) If these numbers are representative for the period from Tiberius to Domitian, then every eighth senator had a violent end by imperial mandate. See Hahn and Leunissen (1990) p. 61.

34 In *Letter* 5.5.3, Pliny reports that the topic of the book that Fannius was composing at the time of his death (see note 21) was the people put to death or exiled by Nero.

35 Leach (1990) p. 31.

36 Hoffer (1999) p. 3.

37 Pliny, *Letter* 4.24.7: "It is my practice to share my thoughts with you and to advise you with the same precepts and examples with which I advise myself. This was the purpose of this letter." On Pliny's moral didacticism, see Griffin (2007).

1 Arria the Elder and the heroism of women

1 Shelton (1987).

2 Raepsaet-Charlier (1987) pp. 112–113, provides brief notices about Arria's known relatives and about the ancient sources by whom she is mentioned.

3 For example, the son of Vestricius and Cottia was known to Pliny as Cottius (rather than Vestricius) – that is, by a designation which preserved the name of his mother's family (*Letter* 2.7). Cottia and her son are discussed in Chapter 3.

4 Sherwin-White (1966) p. 267, on the age and career of Arrius Antoninus.

5 For brief biographical information about Aulus Caecina Paetus, see *PIR*[2] C 103. *PIR* (= *Prosopographia Imperii Romani*) provides information about most of the people mentioned in Pliny's letters.

6 Suffect consul or *consul suffectus*: With the establishment of the imperial constitution, the office of consul lost many of the powers that it had had under the republican constitution. Nonetheless, the title of consul was still very honorific. In order to enable more elite men to achieve this level of distinction, it became customary for the two consuls who had entered the office in January (each called a *consul ordinarius*) to resign after a few months and thus allow the appointment of other men who then held the office as suffect consuls. Pliny was a suffect consul in the autumn of 100 CE. The Latin word *suffectus* means "having been substituted."

7 *CIL* 6.31548 a and b = *ILS* 5929a and b. Raepsaet-Charlier (1987) p. 112, is confident that this man is Arria E's son.
8 *PIR²* C 104 and L 31 and 33.
9 The motivation for the adoptive father was to ensure that he had a son to carry on his name. However, some childless men waited until their deaths to make an adoption, and declared their intention to adopt in their wills (a testamentary adoption). They thus avoided while alive the considerable outlay of money that a son's political career might entail. In "The So-called Will of 'Dasumius'" discussed in Chapter 3, the testator designated a man to be his heir on the condition that he and his descendants would take his name. On reasons for adoption, see Corbier (1991).

   Pliny's rhetoric teacher, Quintilian, had two sons and had arranged to have the elder son adopted by a man of consular rank in order to give him a better chance to reach the highest political offices. Unfortunately both sons died at a very young age. Quintilian, *Institutio Oratoria* 6. Preface 13.
10 See note 50.
11 By coincidence, Pliny's career, several decades later, followed a similar pattern. He was suffect consul in 100 CE, curator of the Tiber River about 105 CE, and imperial legate to the province of Bithynia (in Asia Minor) about 111 CE.
12 Saller (1994) p. 23.
13 *CIL* 6.27556 = *ILS* 8473; *CIL* 6.8571 = *ILS* 1660; *CIL* 1.2.1211 = *ILS* 8403.
14 Plutarch, *Tiberius Gracchus* 1.3–5.
15 *CIL* 3.3572.
16 Suetonius, *Caligula* 7.
17 Quintilian, *Institutio Oratoria* 6. Preface 4–13.
18 Severy (2003) pp. 55–56.
19 These laws, as they appear in disparate sources, have been collected in Riccobono (ed.) *Acta Divi Augusti*. Much of our knowledge about them comes from later summaries and commentaries by jurists who tended to conflate the 18 BCE and 9 CE laws. In addition, the interpretations of these jurists were assumed to be part of the legislation. It is thus difficult to distinguish between the original Augustan legislation and later revisions and interpretations. The ramification of the laws is, however, clear: they authorized the intervention of the state in the structure of the family. For a good discussion, see Treggiari (1991) pp. 60–80.
20 Tacitus, *Annals* 15.19, reports that, during the reign of Nero (54–68 CE) there was a widespread practice of childless men acquiring sons through fictitious adoptions just before an appointment to office was to be made, and then releasing the person from adoption immediately after the appointment had been made. With reference to another type of fraud, Suetonius, *Tiberius* 35.2 records that a man married the day before an allotment of public offices and divorced his wife the day after. The emperor removed him from office.
21 Dio 56.2–5.
22 Suetonius, *Augustus* 34 and 45.1.
23 The Ara Pacis Augustae (the "Augustan Altar of Peace"), one of the best known monuments of Augustus' reign, was dedicated in 9 BCE to celebrate the era of peace which he claimed to have inaugurated. Although the inclusion of images of women and children had been very rare in monumental sculpture of the republican period, the Ara Pacis depicts three generations of Augustus' family attending a religious ceremony at which he is officiating. The images of the happy and pious family highlight Augustus' distinctive role as an exemplary father to both his immediate family and to his empire-wide "family." The fertility of his own family, moreover, is offered both as a model for emulation and as an assurance of the future stability of the state through the continuity of his dynasty. See Severy (2003) pp. 104–112; also Kleiner (1978) pp. 753–785.
24 Cf. Pliny, *Letters* 1.8.11 and 2.7.5.

25 Tacitus, *Annals* 3.25 and 28.3. Hoffer (1999) pp. 230–231, makes the interesting suggestion that being childless was an advantage in the securing of imperial patronage. "(A) politician with children to inherit his power after him would threaten to form an independent political base." Hoffer adds that the "neatest solution" was the loophole that allowed the emperor to grant the privileges of having three children to a childless man. Pliny received such a grant, *ius trium liberorum*, "the three-children privilege" (*Letter* 10.2). Although he expresses a yearning for children in *Letters* 8.10.3 and 10.2.2, Hoffer questions his sincerity.

26 For example, Augustus and the emperors who succeeded him emphasized the correlation between family values and civic stability through the use of portraits of imperial family members on coins, whose circulation guaranteed the wide dissemination of the message. See Beryl Rawson (2001) pp. 21–42.

27 Gardner (1986) p. 197. For the legislation, see Gaius, *Institutes* 1.145 and 194.

28 A child's *paterfamilias* might first be her/his paternal (agnate) grandfather (the oldest direct male ascendant). When the grandfather died, the father became the *paterfamilias*. However, if the father died before the grandfather, the grandfather continued to be the *paterfamilias*. This was the situation with Pliny's wife, Calpurnia, who will be discussed in Chapter 3.

29 "Cognate" was a more general term than "agnate" and could designate any blood relative within six degrees.

30 Gaius, *Institutes* 1. 145 and Plutarch, *Numa* 10.3. There is more discussion of the Vestal Virgins and their privileges in Chapter 7.

31 Junius Mauricus was also apparently *tutor* for the minor sons of his deceased brother (*Letter* 2.18). A male child, whose *paterfamilias* died, was assigned a guardian only until he reached the age of majority, about 14 years. We do not know how old Pliny was when his father died, but he was placed under the *tutela* of Verginius Rufus (*Letter* 2.1.8). On the legal sources for guardians, see Evans Grubbs (2002) pp. 23–46. The theory and practice of *tutela* are examined at length in Gardner (1986) pp. 5–26.

32 Not all men were content to assume the task of being a *tutor*. As noted in the chapter text, men with three children received the privilege of release from the burden of *tutela*. On guardians: Dixon (2001a) pp. 74–88.

33 Ulpian, *Rules* 11. 1, 27 and 28; Gaius, *Institutes* 1.144; *Digest* 22.6.9 pref. (Paulus); Cicero, *Pro Murena* 27; Evans Grubbs (2002) pp. 51 and 52.

34 Gardner (1998) pp. 220–233.

35 Gaius, *Institutes* 1.157 and 171.

36 See Chapter 3, note 14 on the *ius liberorum* and *ius trium liberorum*.

37 Raepsaet-Charlier (1982) pp. 56–69; Marshall (1975b) pp. 109–127.

38 Plutarch, *Antony* 33.3.

39 Tacitus, *Annals* 3.34.6. Severy (2003) pp. 150–152.

40 Suetonius, *Claudius* 2.

41 Suetonius, *Caligula* 7–9; Tacitus, *Annals* 2.54.

42 Phang (2001) pp. 2–4.

43 A letter discovered at Vindolanda gives a glimpse into the life of the wives of army officers on the northern frontier of the Roman Empire. Vindolanda was the site of an ancient Roman army camp along Hadrian's Wall in northern England (which must have seemed like the end of the world to a Roman). The letter, written about 100 CE, is an invitation from one officer's wife to another wife in another camp to attend a birthday party. An image and a translation of this letter, labeled as Vindolanda Tablet 291 (Vindolanda Inventory no. 85.057), are available at Vindolanda Tablets Online: vindolanda.csad.ox.ac.uk/

44 Tacitus, *Annals* 3.33. The *nomen* (family or gentile name) of the author of the proposal, Caecina, has led to speculation that he may have been Arria's father-in-law, but there is no conclusive evidence. For a discussion of this Senate debate, see Marshall (1975a) 11–18; he argues that Tacitus frames the debate to underline the decay of the moral

integrity of the Senate. See also Barrett (2005). Foubert (2011) p. 353, comments that a wife accompanying her husband overseas could be interpreted in ancient Rome as either an abandonment of Roman tradition that the *domus* ("household") must be the focus of a wife's activity, or conversely, as an extension of a woman's duty to be a wife and mother.

45 Tacitus, *Annals* 3.34. *Digest* 1.16.4.2 (Ulpian). Raepsaet-Charlier (1982) pp. 56–69, comments that, in Tacitus, criticism of governors' wives appears as an element of attacks on their husbands' conduct in office. Ginsburg (1993) pp. 88–96 and L'Hoir (2006) pp. 120–124 and (1994) pp. 12–17 contend that Tacitus has framed the debate of 21 CE to emphasize a theme prominent throughout Tacitus' writings: female usurpation of male power, and female intrusion into male physical, social, and moral spaces.

46 Tacitus, *Annals* 2.43 to 3.18.

47 Marshall (1990) p. 342. In addition to Tacitus' account of the fates of Piso and Plancina, we are fortunate to have discovered bronze tablets inscribed with a record of the resolutions passed by the Roman Senate concerning the trials of those two. For discussion of these inscriptions, see Potter and Damon (1999). For the most part, the inscriptions corroborate Tacitus' version of the trials. The bronze tablets record that Plancina was pardoned despite the "very many and very great charges" against her. In 34 CE, a few years after the deaths of Livia in 29 and Agrippina in 33, Plancina was charged with "notorious offences." She committed suicide. Tacitus, *Annals* 6.26, remarks: "Now that the hatred of Agrippina and the protection of Livia had vanished, justice prevailed. By her own hand, Plancina executed a punishment that was long delayed, but well-deserved."

48 Tacitus, *Annals* 4.20.

49 Tacitus, *Annals* 4.19 and 20. Rogers (1935) pp. 75–78; Marshall, (1990) pp. 343–344.

50 One of the incentives to commit suicide, rather than to wait for execution, was that one's property was not confiscated by the state. *Digest* 48.20.7 pref. (Paulus) and Tacitus, *Annals* 13.43. However, in an exception to this practice, Silius' estate was, in fact, confiscated. Nevertheless, Silius and Sosia's children were not left destitute. Roman women were legally empowered to own property (real and moveable) and to hold it separate from their husbands. Tacitus reports that, when Sosia was banished, part of her estate was confiscated by the state, but the majority was allowed to pass by inheritance into the hands of her children.

51 *Digest* 1.16.4.2 (Ulpian). On the interpretation of this legislation, see Marshall (1990) pp. 334, note 4, and 347. The debate is whether the 24 CE decree made the husband alone responsible for his wife's offences under extortion proceedings, or whether husband and wife were jointly responsible. There is more discussion on wives and extortion proceedings in Chapter 3.

52 Tacitus, *Annals* 6.29.

53 Seneca the Younger, *Consolatio ad Helviam* 19.6.

54 Other ancient sources on the conspiracy are Dio 60.15; Suetonius, *Claudius* 13.2; Tacitus, *Annals* 12.52 and *Histories* 1.89 and 2.75.

55 *Digest* 1.5.4 pr. and 1 (Florentinus): "*Libertas* is the natural opportunity of each person to do what he pleases, unless something is prevented by force or law. *Servitus* is a condition of universal law by which, contrary to nature, someone is subject to the dominion of another."

56 Parker (1998) pp. 152–173, discusses the conceptual parallelism between wife and slave.

57 Dio 60.16.

58 On suicide in the Roman world, see Hill (2004) pp. 182–212; van Hooff (1990); Grisé (1982); Plass (1995) pp. 81–134; Edwards (2007) pp. 78–160, 179–206; Griffin (1986) pp. 64–77 and 192–202. There is no one word in Latin that means "suicide." The word *suicidium* (from the Latin roots *suus*, "oneself" and *caedere*, "kill") is a neologism created in the seventeenth century; see van Hooff (1990) p. 136. The Romans used phrases such as *mortem quaerere*, "to seek death," *finem vitae suae imponere*, "to put an end to one's life"; van Hooff (1990) pp. 246–250.

59 Tacitus, *Annals* 11.3. Suetonius, *Tiberius* 54.2, reports on someone "forced into a voluntary death," *ad voluntariam mortem coactum*. Hill (2004) pp. 193–197, however, argues that a "free choice of death" would not have been a paradox to the ancient Romans because it offered the condemned the opportunity to demonstrate his awareness of the aristocratic code of behavior and to choose a worthy death.

60 Edwards (2007) p. 7.

61 Plass (1995) p. 85.

62 The accusations against Caecilius Classicus and his wife, Casta, are discussed in Chapter 3.

63 Tacitus, *Annals* 4.19.4.

64 Tacitus, *Annals* 6.29.1 and 2; Dio 58.15. 3 and 4. However, see also note 50.

65 Tacitus, *Annals* 14.59.1 and *Histories* 2.48.2.

66 Tacitus, *Annals* 12.52.

67 Plass (1995) pp. 116–134. Edwards (2007) p. 124, discusses situations in which the emperor, after the death of an opponent, laments that he would have been willing to be merciful and to exercise clemency, if only the opponent had waited for the verdict. The emperor "thereby exonerates himself of any guilt for the death. But, of course, such a retrospective offer can never be wholly convincing."

68 Hill (2004) p. 209.

69 Edwards (2007) p. 103.

70 Dio 60.16.7. One of the most telling (though unintended) reflections of the passivity of the senatorial class appears in Pliny's *Panegyricus* 66.4 where he expresses his gratitude to the emperor Trajan for ordering Romans to be free.

71 Edwards (2007) p. 154.

72 Tacitus, *Histories* 1.3.1. Cf. *Annals* 3.65.1: "It is the prime duty of writing history that virtues not be relegated to silence." Edwards (2007) p. 13, comments that Tacitus played a vital role "in vindicating the honour of Nero's victims by bearing witness to the nobility of their deaths." She also observes, pp. 113–114, that "(w)hile the motives of those who take their own lives must ultimately remain opaque, the fascination these deaths held for Roman elite authors and presumably their readers is evident in much of the literature of the early principate. The death of the individual can never be fully disentangled from the literary context in which it is recorded."

73 Tacitus, *Agricola* 42.3. I have translated the Latin phrase *ambitiosa mors* as "ostentatious death." Hill (2004) p. 10, discusses the meaning of the word *ambitiosa*.

74 Martial 1.8.5 and 6.

75 Martial 1.13.

76 Dio 60.16.1.

77 Dio 60.15.5 and 16.2.

78 Dio 60.16.6.

79 However, Vibia apparently did not escape punishment, but was sent into exile for her role in the conspiracy. After being allowed to return to Rome, she, along with her son, was accused in 52 CE of inquiring of astrologers about the emperor's death and sent again into exile. Tacitus, *Annals* 12.52.

80 Dio 60.16.6. In the brief mention of Arria in the *Vita Persii* ("Life of the poet Persius"), Oxford Classical Text of Aulus Persius Flaccus, pp. 31–34, it is stated that Arria died "before" her husband. The phrase used is *ante virum*. This could mean (as could the English translation) that Arria killed herself before her husband killed himself, or that she killed herself in front of him. Curiously, Edwards (2007) p. 259, n. 57, maintains that, in Dio's account, Arria apparently survives the stabbing, but succeeds in killing herself not long after her husband's death.

81 Dio 60.16.7.

82 Arria's statement was memorably translated by Timothy Kendall, *Flowers of Epigrammes* (1577), as "Trust me (said she) my goared gutts, doe put me to no paine."

83 Dio 60.16.6.

84   *CIL* 10.5920 = *ILS* 6261. In the funerary inscription, the deceased woman, Oppia, is commended to Arria and Laodamia, respectively the Roman and Greek *exempla* of wifely devotion. There are various accounts of Laodamia's death. In one account (Apollodorus, *Bibliotheca* 3.30) her husband, Protesilaus, was killed by Hector in the Trojan War. Laodamia mourned his loss mightily. Finally, Hermes brought him back from Hades for a visit, but when he was taken back to Hades, Laodamia, overwrought, stabbed herself to death.

85   Carlon (2009) p. 47.

86   Carlon (2009) p. 47.

87   Carlon (2009), p. 48.

88   Dio 60.15.6. Dio reports that Claudius even endorsed the torture of free persons (people who were not and had never been slaves). The torture of slaves and freedpersons is discussed in Chapter 7.

89   Livy 1. 57–60; Valerius Maximus 6.1.1; Seneca, *Consolatio ad Marciam* 16.2; Dionysius of Halicarnassus 4.64.68. Langlands (2006) pp. 80–96. Joshel (1992) pp. 112–130. Langlands (2006) p. 81, considers the story of Lucretia to be "the paradigm of paradigms for the Romans."

90   Pseudo-Quintilian, *Declamation* 3.11: Lucretia stabbed herself so that her pure soul (*pudicus animus*) might be separated from her defiled body (*polluto corpore*).

91   Seneca the Elder, *Controversiae* 6.4.

92   The story of Porcia's death is reported in Dio 44.13 and 14.1; 47.49.3; Plutarch, *Brutus* 13.3–11 and 53.5, and *Cato the Younger* 73.4; Valerius Maximus 4.6.5; Appian, *Civil Wars* 4.136. Plutarch, *Brutus* 53.6 and 7, discounts a claim that Porcia died of an illness before Brutus's suicide, although Cicero also seems to suggest this in his *Epistulae ad Brutum* 1.9.2. See Treggiari (1991) p. 487 on the controversy.

93   It is possible that her death was caused by carbon monoxide poisoning when she burned charcoal in an unventilated room. However, Seneca the Younger, *De Providentia*. 6.9, refers to swallowing fire as a method of suicide.

94   Martial 1.42.

95   Valerius Maximus 4.6.5.

96   Cicero, *Tusculan Disputations* 2.43.

97   Valerius Maximus 6.1.1.

98   Plutarch, *Brutus* 13.4 and 23.4.

99   More conventional choices of suicide for women were starvation, poison, and hanging. On starvation: Appian, *Civil Wars* 4.21 and 23. On poison: Seneca the Elder, *Controversiae* 6.4 (mentioned in the chapter text). On hanging: Seneca the Elder, *Controversiae* 8.1 and 10.3.

100   Velleius Paterculus 2.88.3.

101   Velleius Paterculus 2.26.3; Plutarch, *Pompey* 9.3.

102   Tacitus, *Annals* 6.29.1.

103   Tacitus, *Annals* 6.29.4.

104   Dio 58.4.5 and 6. Marshall (1990) p. 345. On the joint suicides of Gaius Calvisius Sabinus and his wife, Cornelia, prior to a trial during the reign of Caligula, see Dio 59.18.4 and Tacitus, *Histories* 1.48. He and his wife had just returned from the province of Pannonia where he had been governor. According to our sources, her behavior in the province had been scandalous. She had watched the soldiers at drill, dressed herself as a soldier in order to enter the camp at night, and had committed adultery. Marshall (1990) p. 351.

105   Plass (1995) p. 109.

106   Tacitus, *Annals* 15.60–64. Griffin (1976) pp. 367–388; Edwards (2007) pp. 157–159. L'Hoir (2006) p. 215: Tacitus portrays Seneca's death as a "piece of theater."

107   Rosenmeyer (1989) p. 48: "Stoic heroism is a planned, a highly contrived and intellectualized activity. It achieves its full meaning only if it draws attention to itself as the central spectacle in a crowded arena."

108 Tacitus, *Annals* 15.64.
109 Tacitus, *Annals* 16.10 and 14. 57–59. Marshall (1990) pp. 351–352. Tacitus states that Pollitta's husband, Gaius Rubellius Plautus, offended Nero because he openly imitated the ways of the ancient Romans (that is, he lived austerely) and he assumed the arrogance of the Stoics who were accused of plotting sedition.
110 In 66 CE, four years after her husband's assassination, Antistia Pollitta committed suicide along with her father and maternal grandmother when her father was targeted by Nero.
111 Dio 62.25.
112 Seneca, *Letter* 11.10.
113 Seneca, *Tranquillitate Animi* 16.1.
114 Latin *unus* = English "one"; *vir* = "man". See Cantarella (1987) 152. Men were not praised in epitaphs for marrying only once.
115 Valerius Maximus 2.1.3. Valerius Maximus, in 6.1.1, bestows on Lucretia the title of *dux* (leader, foremost) in Roman *pudicitia*. I have translated the Latin word *pudicitia* as "virtue." Langlands (2006) p. 1, translates it as "sexual virtue" and maintains that the word always refers to sexual behavior. Treggiari, (1991) p. 233, comments that *pudicitia* connotes "the conscience which keeps a person from shameful actions." It is often used in the same contexts as *castitas* which means "sexual purity" in reference to a virgin, and "sexual fidelity" in reference to a wife.
116 G. Williams (1958) pp. 23 and 24. Lattimore (1942) p. 278. Lightman and Zeisel (1977) pp. 19–32. Treggiari (1991) pp. 232–236.
117 Propertius 4.11. 36, 61–62, 68.

2 Arria's family and the tradition of dissent

1 On the unidentified origin of the name Arria, see Chapter 1.
2 For my speculations about the ages of the Arrias, see Chapter 1.
3 On the definition of "cognate", see Chapter 1, note 29. Information about the life of Persius and his relationship to Arria's family is found in the *Vita Persii*, Oxford Classical Text of Aulus Persius Flaccus, pp. 31–34.
4 On the translation of *ante*, see Chapter 1, note 80.
5 For brief biographical information about Publius Clodius Thrasea Paetus, see *PIR*[2] C 1187. PIR (*Prosopographia Imperii Romani*) provides information about most of the people mentioned in Pliny's letters.
6 Syme (1983) p. 104 (= RP p. 374).
7 On Stoicism and monarchy, Griffin (1984) pp. 171–177; Wirszubski (1950) pp. 143–147; and Rudich (1993) p. 163.
8 For example, 35 senators lost their lives either by the command of or with the subsequent consent of the emperor Claudius (emperor 41–54 CE). See the Introduction, note 33.
9 Rudich (1993) pp. xxii–xxx, on *dissimulatio*.
10 On *delatores* (informers) who spied on households and reported violations of the Julian laws, see Chapter 1.
11 Definitions of *libertas* are discussed in Chapter 1. For members of the senatorial class, *libertas* meant not just the possession of basic civic rights (the opposite of slavery), but freedom of expression and action in the pursuit of one's political ambitions.
12 Wirszubski (1950) p. 143.
13 Pliny was just a child at this time, but his uncle had apparently felt pressured to choose only "safe" topics for his literary endeavors, such as a book on grammar.
14 Wirszubski (1950) p. 124, characterizes Tacitus' *Annals* as having been conceived and executed as the story of the struggle to wrest *libertas* from the Principate.
15 Tacitus, *Annals* 14.48 and 49; 16.21.

16 Dio (Epitome) 61.15.3; Tacitus, *Annals* 14.12 and 16. 21.

17 Dio (Epitome) 62.26.3.

18 For more on Pliny's impressions of Thrasea, see *Letter* 6.29.

19 Plutarch, *Cato the Younger* 25.1 and 37.1. See Chapter 1 on Cato's suicide.

20 Juvenal 5.36 and 37. See Chapter 1 on the suicide of Brutus' wife, Porcia.

21 Compare Chapter 1, note 109: The husband of Antistia Pollitta, Gaius Rubellius Plautus, offended Nero because he openly imitated the ways of the ancient Romans (that is, he lived austerely) and assumed the arrogance of the Stoics who were accused of plotting sedition. Tacitus, *Annals* 14.57.

22 For discussion of the Stoic "opposition" to the Principate, see Carlon (2009) pp. 21 and 22; Rudich (1993) pp. 69 and 70, 163; Wirszubski (1950) pp. 143–145; also Wistrand (1979). Jones (1992) pp. 121–125, discusses the Stoic opposition during the period of Domitian, pointing out that critics were not punished just because they were Stoics.

23 Martial 1.8.1. For another reference to this epigram of Martial, see Chapter 1, note 74.

24 Tacitus, *Annals* 14.57. See note 21.

25 Rudich (1993) p. 164. Rudich analyzes the extent of Thrasea's involvement with Stoicism, concluding that Thrasea was not interested in philosophical ideology, and that his interests lay rather in constitutionalist principles (pp. 162–166).

26 Tacitus, *Annals* 13.49.

27 Dio (Epitome) 61.15.4.

28 Suetonius, *Nero* 37.1.

29 Tacitus, *Annals* 15.23.

30 Tacitus, *Annals* 16.22.

31 Tacitus, *Annals* 16.22; Dio (Epitome) 62.26.3.

32 Rudich (1993) p. 165. He adds that surveillance depends on the use of informers. The use of *delatores* by emperors is discussed earlier in this chapter.

33 On Seneca's suicide, and the attempted suicide of his wife, Paulina, see Chapter 1.

34 Tacitus, *Annals* 16.21.

35 Tacitus, *Annals* 16.22.

36 Thrasea's trial and final moments are described by Tacitus in *Annals* 16. 21–29, and 34 and 35. Also Dio (Epitome) 62.26.

37 Junius Arulenus Rusticus was one of the ten tribunes of the plebs for the year 66. The tribunes held office for a year and could veto an act of the Senate. (The Latin word *veto* means "I forbid".) Also one of the ten tribunes that year was Tacitus' father-in-law, Agricola. We do not know whether he spoke in the Senate in favor or in opposition to Thrasea Paetus.

38 Bauman (1974) pp. 153–156, examines how Thrasea's behavior could make him liable to a charge of treason.

39 Dio (Epitome) 62.26.1.

40 Tacitus, *Annals* 16.33. On "free choice of death," see Chapter 1. Thrasea's son-in-law, Helvidius Priscus, was banished from Italy.

41 The quaestor was a low-ranking magistrate who served for a year. The quaestorship was usually the first step in a political career. Election to the quaestorship ensured entry into and life-long membership in the Roman Senate.

42 See Chapter 1, note 107.

43 Edwards (2007) p. 145, urges us to consider how far the beautifully articulated death is the creation of the dying subject, and how far it is the composition of the author who recounts it.

44 Tacitus, *Annals* 16.34.

45 On this Cornelia, see Suzanne Dixon (2007).

46 Plutarch, *Tiberius Gracchus* 1.4.

47 Drusus was the stepson of Augustus and the brother of Tiberius. Antonia was the niece of Augustus (the daughter of his sister, Octavia, and her husband, Mark

Antony). As noted in Chapter 1, Antonia, accompanied Drusus to his military command in northern Gaul and, in 10 BCE, gave birth to a son who later became the emperor Claudius. On Antonia: Plutarch, *Antony* 87.3.

48 Valerius Maximus 4.3.3. He relates that Drusus, during his marriage, engaged in sexual activity only with his wife. This chaste behavior was unusual for a Roman husband (but expected of a wife). On the double standard of adultery, see Chapter 3.

49 McGinn (2008) pp. 8–11.

50 The rumor about Julia and Domitian is discussed in Chapter 7.

51 Valerius Maximus 4.3.3; Josephus, *Jewish Antiquities* 18.180.

52 The Latin word for such a person was *captator*, often translated as "legacy hunter" (and the practice of chasing after inheritances was termed *captatio*). *Captatores* preyed also upon old men, especially childless old men. Sherwin-White (1966) pp. 203–204, discusses *captatio* in the context of Roman notions of friendship.

53 Because her parents and her husband had committed suicide, thus pre-empting execution, their property (or most of it) was presumably not confiscated.

54 Suetonius, *Nero* 47–49.

55 Tacitus, *Histories* 1.4; Suetonius, *Nero* 57.

56 However, for more sympathetic views of Domitian, see Jones (1992) and Southern (1997).

57 On names from a female side of the family, see Chapter 1, note 3. Recall that Arria Y seems to have been called by the name of her mother, Arria E, rather than her father, Caecina. Syme (1983), p. 105 (= RP p. 375), claims the name Fannia was "no doubt" the name of Thrasea's mother.

58 Biographical information about Helvidius I is found in Tacitus, *Histories* 4.5 and 6, *Annals* 16.33 and 35, and *Dialogus* 5; Dio (Epitome) 66.12; 67.13; Suetonius, *Vespasian* 15.

59 Tacitus, *Histories* 4.5. The Helvidius mentioned in Tacitus, *Annals* 12.49.3 as a *legatus legionis* in Syria in 52 CE was probably not the same person. Men holding the rank of *legatus legionis* were senatorial.

60 Tacitus, *Histories* 4.5; Dio (Epitome) 66.12.

61 Tacitus, *Annals* 13.28.2. Although the manuscript suggests that Helvidius was tribune in 56, some scholars assume that a transposition occurred in the text and that the word quaestor, not tribune, was meant to follow Helvidius' name. The Scholiast on Juvenal 5.36 relates that Helvidius was a quaestor in Achaea. On the position of quaestor, see note 41.

62 Tacitus, *Histories* 4.5; Dio (Epitome) 66.12.

63 Ummidius Quadratus married at the age of 23: *Letter* 7.24.3. Calestrius Tiro was able to serve as tribune a year before Pliny because he already had a child: *Letter* 7.16.2.

64 Tacitus, *Histories* 4.5.

65 Dio (Epitome) 66.12.

66 Juvenal, 5.36 and 37.

67 Tacitus, *Annals* 16.33.

68 Tacitus, *Annals* 16.28.

69 Tacitus, *Annals* 16.29.

70 Tacitus, *Annals* 16.33 and 35.

71 Suetonius, *Vespasian* 15.

72 *Digest* 48.1.2 (Paulus). Kelly (2006) pp. 17–68. Also Braginton (1944).

73 *Tristia* 5.11.21 and 22. Ovid was much more precise about the terms of his own banishment than the historians or Pliny were about the banishments of other people.

74 The Scholiast on Juvenal 5.36 says Helvidius I spent his exile in Apollonia, but is perhaps not a reliable source. Also, there were several towns named Apollonia.

75 In *Histories* 1.3.1, Tacitus assured his readers that the period was not so barren of virtues that it did not produce some good examples. He included among his examples "women who accompanied their husbands into exile."

76 Valerius Maximus 6.7.3; Appian, *Civil Wars* 4.39.

77 Cicero, living in the republican period, had been banished in 58 BCE for executing Roman citizens involved in the Catilinarian conspiracy when he was consul in 63 BCE. However, Ovid, living at the very beginning of the imperial period, had been banished for offending the emperor. As early as the reign of Augustus, an alleged lack of respect for the emperor could culminate in capital punishment for treason.

78 The account is found in a long inscription (*CIL* 6.1527, 31670, and 41062 = *ILS* 8393) which was commissioned by her husband in the last decade of the first century BCE, perhaps about 5 BCE. This inscription is, in fact, the longest surviving Latin inscription erected by a private individual. Fragments of the stone on which the inscription was inscribed were discovered in different locations in Rome and painstakingly pieced together. As of now, only about half of the inscription has been found, providing us with 180 lines of text. It was intended to be the tombstone for the woman and may be a record of the funeral eulogy delivered by her husband. Unfortunately, the names of the husband and wife are not preserved in the surviving pieces. At one time, scholars identified the woman as the Turia mentioned by Valerius Maximus (6.7.2), but that identification now seems doubtful. Nonetheless, the woman is commonly referred to as "Turia" and the inscription as the "Laudatio Turiae," the "Praise of Turia." See Horsfall (1983) pp. 85–98; Gowing (1992) pp. 283–296.

79 Cicero, *Epistulae ad Familiares* 14.3.5; *Epistulae ad Quintum Fratrem* 1.3.3; Ovid, *Tristia* 1.3. 79–86. Grete (2003).

80 Ovid, *Tristia* 1.3.101–2. Cicero, *Epistulae ad Familiares* 14.3.5 and 14.4.3.

81 Cicero, *Epistulae ad Familiares* 14.1.4. Cicero uses the word *vicus*, which may mean a row of urban houses, or a village. In either case, it was an extensive piece of property.

82 Cicero, *Epistulae ad Familiares* 14.1.3; 14.4.4.

83 A husband had the right to manage his wife's dowry, but it remained, in a sense, on loan to him and had to be returned to her family in the case of divorce. Dixon (1986) p. 96, comments that the issue of whether a wife's dowry would be confiscated, if the husband's property was, is a "vexed question." She believes, however, that the slaves whom Cicero refers to as "yours" were part of Terentia's dowry – that is, not inherited or purchased by her during the marriage.

84 On married women and property, see Treggiari (1991) pp. 323–396.

85 Dowries are discussed more fully in Chapter 6. When Cicero divorced Terentia about 47 or 46 BCE, the return of her dowry caused him financial difficulty: *Epistulae ad Atticum* 12. 12, and 19–22; 16.6.3 and 15.5. On the size of Terentia's dowry, see Chapter 6, note 99.

86 *CIL* 6.1527, 6.41062, left hand column (Column I), lines 45 and 46.

87 See Gardner (1998) pp. 220–233 on mothers' wills.

88 Cicero, *De Domo Sua* 60 and 62; *Epistulae Ad Familiares* 14.2.

89 Ovid, *Tristia* 1.6.7–14.

90 *CIL* 6.41062, right hand column (Column II), lines 8–11.

91 Cicero, *Epistulae ad Familiares* 14.2.2.

92 *CIL* 6.41062, right hand column (Column II), lines 1–5.

93 Ovid, *Tristia* 1.3.82, 4.3.49, 5.11.2.

94 "Turia's" prosecution of the murderers of her parents was unusual because ordinarily women were not allowed to bring suits before criminal courts. However, exceptions were made in cases where they had a direct personal interest, such as the murder of a parent or child. *Digest* 48.2.1 (Pomponius) and 48.2.2 (Papinianus). See Evans Grubbs (2002) pp. 60–71, on the restrictions on women's rights to act legally. "Turia" seems not to have had a brother to fulfill this filial duty. Even though "Turia" may have initiated the suit, she would have enlisted the services of a senatorial rank man to present her case in court.

95 See, for example: Ovid, *Tristia* 5.2.35–38, *Epistulae ex Ponto* 3.1.31–42.

96 Hemelrijk (2004) pp. 189–190, in her analysis of the inversion of gender roles in the "Laudatio Turiae," observes that the husband and author of the inscription uses

military metaphors (the military being a distinctly masculine sphere) to describe his wife, and also admits that he has displayed some feminine qualities in his response to her death.

97 Ovid, *Tristia* 4.3.72; *Epistulae ex Ponto* 3.1.44.
98 Ovid, *Tristia* 4.3.81–82.
99 Cicero, *Epistulae ad Familiares* 14.1.4; Ovid, *Epistulae ex Ponto* 3.1.31 and 32, 65 and 66; 3.7. 11 and 12. Claassen (1999) explores the frustration and sense of social isolation experienced by exiles.
100 The Julio-Claudian emperors were men who were direct descendants of Augustus (the first emperor), whose family name was Julius, and his stepson Tiberius (the second emperor), whose family name was Claudius.
101 Tacitus, *Histories* 4.6 and 4.10.
102 Tacitus, *Histories* 2.91
103 Tacitus, *Histories* 4.4.
104 Tacitus, *Histories* 4.7. See Pigon (1992).
105 Tacitus, *Histories* 4.8.
106 Tacitus, *Histories* 4.40.
107 Tacitus, *Histories* 4.43.
108 Tacitus, *Histories* 4.44.
109 Tacitus, *Histories* 4.8 and 9; *Dialogus* 5.
110 Tacitus, *Histories* 4.6.
111 Dio (Epitome) 66.12.1 and 2.
112 Suetonius, *Vespasian* 15.
113 Arrian, *Discourses of Epictetus*, 1.2.19–21.
114 Dio (Epitome) 66.13
115 Suetonius, *Vespasian* 15. Bauman (1974) pp. 157–159, notes that Vespasian had abolished charges of treason (*maiestas*) and suggests that Helvidius was relegated on a charge of defamation and harassment of the emperor. See also Malitz (1985) pp. 231–246.
116 Suetonius, *Vespasian* 15.
117 Since Vespasian had rescinded, though too late, the order for Helvidius I's execution, he may not have confiscated his property. On the distinction between relegation and exile, see earlier in the text.
118 When her husband was forced to flee from Italy, "Turia" went to live with her mother-in-law, in order to preserve her reputation for virtue (*pudicitia*).
119 Dio (Epitome) 67.12.2. On Domitian's increasing intolerance of dissent, see Syme (1983).
120 Tacitus, *Agricola* 2.3. The definitions of *libertas* and *servitus*, as they were employed by the senatorial class, are discussed in Chapter I.
121 Jones (1992) pp. 119–125, discusses the conflicting reports in ancient sources about whether there was more than one expulsion of philosophers, and when they occurred.
122 As Jones (1992) p. 121, observes, none of the Seven were punished specifically for being Stoic. Syme (1991 c).
123 Tacitus, *Annals* 16.26, *Histories* 3.80, and *Agricola* 2; Suetonius, *Domitian* 10; Dio (Epitome) 67.13; Pliny, *Letter* 1.5; Plutarch, *De Curiositate* 15. On the dates of magistracies for this period, see Gallivan (1981).
124 Tacitus, *Histories* 4.40.4.
125 Dio (Epitome) 67.13.2; Pliny, *Letter* 7.33.
126 The precise year of his consulship has not been determined. See *PIR*^{2} H 60.
127 Pliny, *Letter* 5.1.8. Sherwin-White (1966) p. 748, suggests that she may have been the Verulana Gratilla who sided with Vespasian in 69 CE during one event of the civil war: Tacitus, *Histories* 3.69.
128 Rogers (1960) pp. 19–23. Domitian had reinstated charges of *maiestas* after their abeyance under Vespasian and Titus. There is debate about whether everyone in the group of Seven was charged equally with *maiestas*, or whether the three women and

Junius Mauricus, who were sentenced to exile, not death, received a lesser charge of abetting treason. Bauman (1974) pp. 159–162, discusses the charges, which he argues were charges of defamation.

129   Suetonius, *Domitian* 10.3; Dio (Epitome) 67.13.2.

130   Tacitus, *Agricola* 2.

131   Dio (Epitome) 67.13.2.

132   Bauman (1974) pp. 153–156.

133   Aquilius Regulus assisted in the prosecution of Arulenus Rusticus: Pliny, *Letter* 1.5.2. He is characterized in several of Pliny's letters as a despicable human being (that is, *Letters* 2.20 and 4.7).

134   Pliny, *Letter* 4.11.12.

135   Suetonius, *Domitian* 10.4.

136   Pliny, *Letter* 3.11.3, writes that they were relegated.

137   Tacitus, *Agricola* 2 and Dio (Epitome) 67.13.3 also mention the expulsion of philosophers. For the disputed date of the expulsion, see Sherwin-White (1966) pp. 239–242 and 763–765.

138   Dio (Epitome) 67.13.2 and 3.

139   Pliny, *Letter* 1.5.2 and 3. On Pliny's characterization of Aquilius Regulus, see note 133. Despite Pliny's sympathy with Stoic moral philosophy, he uses the label "Stoic" only here in the *Letters*; Griffin (2007) 476, n. 77.

140   Tacitus, *Histories* 3. 80 and 81. On Musonius Rufus, see note 144.

141   Tacitus, *Agricola* 45.

142   Pliny does, however, record in *Letter* 9.13.2, as one of the most shocking events of Domitian's reign, that one senator, presumably Publicius Certus, who was one of the accusers of Helvidius II in 93, had laid hands upon another senator, presumably Helvidius II, in the Senate house. We do not know the circumstances of this event.

143   Pliny apparently never did indict Aquilius Regulus. In *Letter* 1.5.10, 15 and 16 he states that he was awaiting the return from exile of Junius Mauricus, whom he describes as a prudent man. Perhaps Mauricus advised against an indictment, even though Regulus had participated in the prosecution that had resulted in the death penalty for his brother, Junius Arulenus Rusticus.

144   On Musonius Rufus: Dillon (2004). He was a Roman citizen and man of the equestrian class, a social class of people wealthy, but usually not competing for the highest political offices in the state. Pliny's father and uncle were equestrians. (On the equestrian order, see Chapter 4, notes 75 and 101.) Musonius Rufus became a well-known teacher of Stoic philosophy. His students included people of the senatorial class, and the Seven may have been among them. A friendship between Arulenus Rusticus and Musonius Rufus had developed at least as early as 69 CE (note 140). In 60–62 CE, Musonius accompanied one of his supporters, Rubellius Plautus, into exile in Asia Minor. Rubellius Plautus had offended Nero because of his Stoic demeanor (Tacitus, *Annals* 14.57–59). Musonius was present at the murder of Rubellius Plautus who was the husband of Antistia Pollitta. (See Chapter 1, notes 109 and 110.) After her husband was ruthlessly killed by Nero's henchmen, she kept his blood-soaked clothes, maintained a disheveled appearance, and ate very little. (See Chapter 1.) Musonius Rufus was banished for having participated in the Pisonian Conspiracy of 65 CE (when Seneca the Younger and his nephew Lucan were sentenced to death). After Nero's death in 68 CE, he returned to Rome and prosecuted a man who had been an informer under Nero. However, he was banished again by Vespasian in the mid-70s, and went to Syria where Pliny may have met him (*Letters* 1.10.2 and 3.11.5). In 79 CE, he was recalled by Titus. We do not know when or how he died. Tacitus, *Annals* 15.71; *Histories* 4.10 and 40; Dio (Epitome) 62.27.4 and 66.13.2; Philostratus, *Vita Apollonii* 7.16; Jerome, *Chronica*, 214th Olympiad.

145   For discussion of Pliny's interest in Stoicism, see Butler (1967), André (1975), and Griffin (2007). Griffin, pp. 472 and 474: Pliny deploys "the language and teaching of

moral philosophy to endorse a *consciously moral code*, admired at his level of society. ... His echoes of Stoicism reflect its dominance at Rome."

146 In *Letter* 4.22.3, Pliny praises Mauricus' resoluteness and honesty. In *Letter* 6.14, Pliny responds to Mauricus' invitation to visit his villa at Formiae. (Formiae – modern Formia – is a town on the western coast of Italy, about halfway between Rome and Naples.)

147 There is discussion of Arrionilla in Chapter 3. If there was a family connection with Arria, one would expect her name to be Arrianilla, rather than Arrionilla. There is record of an Arria Arrianilla in *CIL* 6.12404. Syme (1968 a), p. 146 (= RP 2, p. 712).

148 Tacitus, *Agricola* 2.

149 Suetonius, *Augustus* 35.2, *Tiberius* 61.3, *Caligula* 16.1; Seneca the Younger, *Consolatio ad Marciam* 1.2–5, and 22.4–7; Tacitus, *Annals* 4.34 and 35; Dio 57.24.2–4.

150 Tacitus, *Annals* 4.34–35.

151 Seneca, *Consolatio ad Marciam* 22.7.

152 Although we might expect that the daughter's name would be the feminine form of her father's, and thus Cremutia, she was known as Marcia. Compare Fannia, the daughter of Clodius Thrasea, and Arria, the daughter of Caecina Paetus.

153 Tacitus, *Annals* 4.34–35.

154 Edwards (2007) p. 140.

155 Dio 57.24.4 remarks that the books aroused much greater interest because of Cordus' unhappy fate.

156 Note Seneca's emphasis on the value of providing paradigms of brave and honorable behavior: *Consolatio ad Marciam* 1. 3 and 4. See Shelton (1995).

157 Bauman (1974) p. 160, contends that Fannia was charged as an "instigator." See *Digest* 47.10.5.9 (Ulpian) on prosecution for defamation.

158 Tacitus, *Annals* 16.14. Raepaset-Charlier (1987) p. 86, #68, conjectures that Anteia was a daughter. However, Sherwin-White (1966) p. 493, maintains that she "might be a connexion, but hardly a daughter."

159 Rogers (1960) p. 23.

160 Raepsaet-Charlier (1987) stemma XLVIII, proposes that Anteia may have been the sister of Anteia Rufina, who may have been the wife of Lucius Neratius Priscus. Their son, also Lucius Neratius Priscus, may have been the husband of Corellia Hispulla, to whom Pliny addresses *Letter* 3.3.

161 Gaius, *Institutes* 1.157, 168, 171. See Chapter 1.

162 On Pliny's relationship with Tertullus, see *Letters* 5.14, 7.21, 7.31, 2.11.19, 4.17.9. Although he was older than Pliny, perhaps by about 15 years (Sherwin-White (1966), p. 345), he later succeeded Pliny as governor of the province of Bithynia-Pontus.

163 Pliny's *Letter* 9.13, in which he describes his activities to initiate a hearing into the prosecution of Helvidius II, was addressed to Gaius Ummidius Quadratus, a protégé of Pliny, whose family will be discussed in Chapter 5. At the beginning of the letter, Pliny states that Quadratus had read the speeches which Pliny had composed on the vindication of Helvidius II and had requested from him more information about the hearing. By publishing a letter in which he mentions the publication of his speeches, Pliny perhaps hoped to generate and sustain interest in them. See note 21 of the Introduction. The speeches in vindication of Helvidius II are mentioned again in *Letter* 4.21.3. See also *Letters* 1.2.1, 1.8.2, 2.5.1, 3.10.1, 3.13.1, 3.18 (about Pliny's *Panegyricus* praising Trajan), 4.5, 8.3, and 9.4. It was not unusual for Roman senators to publish speeches which they had composed, especially in high profile cases. Publication offered the opportunity to revise and expand, and to immortalize one's words.

164 See note 94. Sherwin-White (1966) p. 493 and Marshall (1990) p. 356, believe that the three women's participation in the hearing was as witnesses. However, Bauman (1974) pp. 170 and 171, argues that the women lodged the accusation jointly with Pliny – that is, they were *subscriptores*. He contends that the charge in the case was one of senatorial misconduct amounting to treason, and that, although women were

usually denied the right to make accusations, they did possess it for charges of treason. See also Marshall (1989) on appearances by women in Roman civil courts.

165 Regulus had also prosecuted Arrionilla (*Letter* 1.5.5), who may have been related to Arria; see note 147.

166 Carlon (2009) p. 59, note 44, theorizes that, because Pliny never calls Publicius Certus a *delator* (informer), Certus' role in the trial of Helvidius II was "somewhat peripheral."

167 See note 142.

168 Bauman (1974) p. 171.

169 The family of the bereaved was required by custom to observe nine days of home seclusion after a death. See Toynbee (1971) pp. 50–51.

170 Avidius Quietus had served as suffect consul (Chapter 1, note 6) in 93 CE, the year in which the Seven were prosecuted (Syme (1958) pp. 639–640). He provides another example of a member of that circle who had achieved high office during the reign of Domitian. In *Letter* 6.29.1 (another letter addressed to Ummidius Quadratus), Pliny identifies himself as being loved by Avidius Quietus, thus drawing another connection between himself and the Seven.

171 Sherwin-White (1966) p. 498; Marshall (1990) p. 356.

172 In *Letter* 7.19.10, he writes that he was their avenger (*ultor*) when they returned from exile.

173 Curiously, in *Letter* 5.5.2, Pliny uses the same phrase, *angit me*, "it distresses me," to describe his reaction to Gaius Fannius' failure to update his will. (On Gaius Fannius, see Introduction, note 21.)

174 The Vestal Virgins are discussed in Chapter 7.

175 Tacitus, *Annals* 2.86. The year was 19 CE.

176 Sherwin-White (1966) p. 424.

177 That Arulenus and Gratilla were married is assumed from *Letter* 5.1.8.

178 Sherwin-White (1966) p. 117.

179 On Pliny's contribution to the dowry of a relative (*adfinis*), see *Letter* 2.4. "Turia" (note 78) used her inheritance to create dowries for her female relatives. For more on dowries, see Chapter 6.

180 Sherwin-White (1966) p. 117.

181 As noted in Chapter 1, the word *castitas*, "chastity," "sexual purity," can also refer to a wife's sexual fidelity to her husband. Thus Arria E was described in Martial 1.13 as *casta*, "chaste" However, in a reference to a prospective bride, *casta* and *castitas* are more likely to denote the bride's absence of sexual experience, rather than her fidelity to a previous husband.

182 Seneca the Younger, *De Beneficiis* 4.27.5.

183 Treggiari (1991) p. 166.

184 Catullus 61. 56–59.

185 Seneca, *Letter* 94.15.

186 In *Letter* 6.26, Pliny congratulates his friend Julius Servianus for arranging for his daughter to marry Fuscus Salinator, whose father and mother are both, Pliny states, of very distinguished standing.

187 Plautus, *Captivi* 889; Suetonius, *Julius Caesar* 52.3; Aulus Gellius 17.21.44. In *Letter* 6.26.3, where Pliny congratulates Julius Servianus, he ends with a wish that Fuscus will, as soon as possible, make Servianus a grandfather.

188 Musonius Rufus XIII B (Lutz (1947) pp. 90 and 91).

189 On the equestrian order, see Chapter 4, notes 75 and 101.

190 Contrast the praise for the virtues of both the mother and father in *Letter* 6.26.1.

191 The *nomen* (family or gentile name) of the prospective bridegroom is that of his father: Minicius. However, the *nomen* of his maternal uncle, Acilius, provides a clue to the origin of the bridegroom's *cognomen*, Acilianus. It probably derives from his mother's family name and was attached to inform people of his maternal family connections. The uncle may be the man to whom *Letter* 3.14 is addressed.

Regarding the possibility that Pliny was better acquainted with the family of the bridegroom's mother than his father, in *Letter* 2.16.1, Pliny records receiving an inheritance from someone named Acilianus, possibly the young man who is recommended here as a bridegroom. If this is correct, he left behind a young widow.

192 Hopkins (1983) pp. 124 and 149; Hoffer (1999) p. 181. On suffect consuls, see Chapter 1, note 6.

193 The minimum age for holding the praetorship in the imperial period was 30 (reduced from the minimum age of 40 during the republican period). The fact that Acilianus had already held the praetorship means that he was older than 30.

194 See note 66.

195 As noted in Chapter 1, under Roman law, all the property of the agnate *familia* rested in the control of the *paterfamilias*, in this case, Acilianus' father.

196 As stated in note 191, it was not uncommon for a woman's family to secure the perpetuation of their family name through the addition of a *cognomen* to her children. Perhaps Mauricus hoped that the family name, Junius, would be continued in a similar fashion.

197 Sidonius, *Epistles* 2.4.1.

198 He is assumed by Sherwin-White (1966) p. 185, to be the same person.

199 Carlon (2009) p. 55.

200 Hemelrijk (2004) pp. 191–193, points out that Mark Antony's wife, Fulvia, was fiercely loyal and supportive of him, but was criticized by her enemies for lacking feminine qualities.

201 Carlon (2009) p. 55.

202 Hemelrijk (2004) p. 197.

203 Did the bloodline survive? Sherwin-White (1966) 298, notes that the family names recur later in Lucius Valerius Helvidius Publicola and Lucius Valerius Messala Thrasea Priscus (consul in 196 CE). We cannot, however, trace the connections of these men securely back to Fannia and her husband Helvidius I.

204 Radice (1963) p. 198, translates the phrase as "even though she may leave descendants" – that is, descendants may yet be born. Walsh (2006) p. 176, translates as "though as yet she has descendants" – that is, there are now a few descendants. Radice and Walsh seem to have taken the subject of *habeat* as Fannia. I have taken it as *domus ipsa*, "the house itself."

205 Sherwin-White (1966) p. 426.

206 *CIL* 3.272 = *ILS* 1914.

207 *Digest*, 5.2.6 pr (Ulpian); 6.2.11.5 (Ulpian); 11.8.2 (Marcellus); 28.2.12 (Ulpian); 38.8.1.9 (Ulpian); 38.17.1.5 (Ulpian); 50.16.132.1 (Paulus).

208 Wet nurses are discussed in Chapter 4.

209 Carlon (2009) p. 50, comments on the oddness of Pliny composing a *consolatio* to himself.

210 On Pliny's publication of his speech vindicating Helvidius II, see note 163.

3 Pliny's wives

* Some of the material in this chapter is drawn from my article, "Pliny the Younger and the Ideal Wife," *Classica et Mediaevalia* 41 (1990), pp. 163–186. I thank the editors of *Classica et Mediaevalia* for their permission to use this material.

1 For example, Valerius Maximus 6.7.

2 Cantarella (1987) p. 132.

3 *CIL* 6.11602 = *ILS* 8402. On the meanings of *pudica* ("modest," "virtuous") and *casta* ("sexually pure and faithful"), see Chapter 1, note 115. Wool-working was considered one of the traditional duties of a Roman matron. Therefore, even upper-class matrons, who had slaves to labor for them, were praised for their skill and diligence in wool-work. Suetonius relates that Augustus had his daughter and granddaughters

taught wool-working (*lanificium*): *Augustus* 64.2. On wool-working and female virtue: Lovén (1998). In reality, however, most, if not all, of the wool-working in a wealthy household would have been done by slaves. Today women are not usually celebrated in their obituaries for household tasks. "Roman society, however, stressed the connection between women and housework even in the case of women unlikely to have performed any tasks of this kind": Hallett (1990) p. 141. Consider the second century BCE epitaph of Claudia, who "managed the household and spun wool": *CIL* 6.15346 (= *CIL* 1.2.1211 = *ILS* 8403).

4 In *Letter* 6.31.4–6, however, Pliny relates that a husband was censured for not divorcing his adulterous wife, Gallitta; the case is discussed later in this chapter.

5 Recall that Fannia, in *Letter* 7.19, was lauded for being dutiful, affable (*comis*), and good-natured (*iucunda*). On the definition of *obsequium*, Treggiari (1991) pp. 238–241, maintains that, in the context of marriages, the word meant obligingness, or accommodating oneself to one's husband's wishes, rather than the strict obedience expected of a slave.

6 *CIL* 6.41062, left hand column (Column 1), line 32. As noted in Chapter 2, note 118, after the death of her parents, in order to maintain propriety, "Turia" went to stay with her mother-in-law, to await the return of her husband. See also Chapter 2, note 51, on Antonia living with her mother-in-law, Livia.

7 A similar statement – about the virtues of individual women not being unique – is made about a woman named Murdia by her son, who commissioned an epitaph from about the same time period as "Turia's": *CIL* 6.10230 = *ILS* 8394. However, he goes on to commemorate Murdia's obedience (*obsequium*), moral integrity (*probitas*), virtuousness or modesty (*pudicitia*), wool-working, diligence (*diligentia*) and loyalty (*fides*).

8 *CIL* 6.41062, left hand column (Column 1), lines 3–9. On women seeking indictments in capital cases, see Chapter 2, note 94. "Turia" could do this because the charge involved the murder of her parents.

9 S. Braund (2002) p. 160: "Clearly 'Turia' had shrugged off the usual invisibility of Roman women to make a public intervention on behalf of her husband and this is expressed in masculine terms." See also Chapter 2, note 96.

10 *CIL* 6.41062, right hand column (Column 2), lines 47–48. As noted in Chapter 2, "Turia" and her husband shared responsibilities for managing one another's estates.

11 On his admission of feminine qualities, see Chapter 2, note 96.

12 "Turia" and her husband were of the elite class of Roman society, but the story of their loyalty to one another would resonate among people of all classes. It is interesting that we find a parallel to their marriage in Petronius' fictional account of the long-lasting marriage of the freedpersons, Trimalchio and Fortunata, who had risen from slavery to the heights of nouveau riche vulgarity. ("Freedpersons" – that is, freedmen and freedwomen – were people who had formerly been slaves, but had been freed.) When her husband suffered a business disaster, Fortunata sold her jewels and fine clothing to help finance a new enterprise (*Satyricon* 76.7), even as "Turia" used her jewels to support her husband in flight. And Trimalchio, like "Turia's" husband, rejected the idea of divorce when his wife did not bear children (*Satyricon* 74.15 and 16).

13 See Chapter 2, note 169.

14 *Ius trium liberorum*: the "three-children privilege." An emperor could formally grant to a childless man the privileges of a man with three legitimate children. (A man whose child died at an early age retained the privileges.) Pliny's early career had been slowed by his lack of children. In *Letter* 7.16.2, he relates that Calestrius Tiro had been able to serve as tribune a year before him because he had a child. Candidates for the several political offices (which each had a term of one year) were required to observe an interval of one year minimum between holding offices. However, an exemption from this interval was granted to fathers. This remission of one year could be invoked only once for each child, not at each stage. See Sherwin-White (1966) pp. 420 and 558. The full set of privileges was available to men with three children,

but a man with just one or two children was eligible for the one-year remission on holding office; this allowance was the *ius liberorum*, the "privilege of children."

15 Sherwin-White (1966) pp. 264 and 559–560, on the number and dates of Pliny's marriages.

16 Carlon (2009) pp. 104–105. She comments that Pliny provides information about the family members of only two wives, the one who died in 97, and Calpurnia, assuming that, if he had an earlier (that is, first of three) wife, he would mention her kinfolk. Perhaps, however, there was an earlier wife who had no close relatives. Or perhaps the marriage ended with a bitter divorce.

17 Acilianus, however, had already served terms as quaestor, tribune, and praetor when he was being recommended as a husband for Junia. He had therefore most likely been previously married.

18 Pompeia Celerina was one of only seven women to receive one of the letters which Pliny chose to publish. (One of the seven was a co-recipient with her husband: *Letter* 3.10.)

19 Raepsaet-Charlier (1987) pp. 507 and 508, #626 and 627. The evidence is slim. An inscription records the name of the wife of a Venuleius as Celerina: *CIL* 11.1735.

20 Treggiari (1991) pp. 107 and 108, remarks that seeking a spouse from the same locality as oneself had the advantage of ensuring a known background, strengthening local ties, and making compatibility more likely.

21 These were the cases of Marius Priscus and Caecilius Classicus, both of them charged with extortion in the provinces. The trial of Classicus is discussed later in this chapter.

22 Pliny's colleague in both the treasury of Saturn (98–100 CE) and the suffect consulship (100 CE) was Cornutus Tertullus (*Letter* 5.14.5), the man whom Anteia had chosen as guardian (*tutor*) for one of her and Helvidius II's daughters. (*Letter* 9.13.16). See Chapter 2, note 162.

23 Aunt and niece have the same name: Calpurnia. It was the feminine form of their family name, Calpurnius. Traditionally women received only one name. The aunt had an additional name, Hispulla, which may have been derived from her mother's family or her father's maternal family. The name Hispulla is discussed in Chapter 4.

24 On Lucius Calpurnius Fabatus, see *CIL* 5.5267 = *ILS* 2721. On equestrian rank: Chapter 2, note 144, and Chapter 4, notes 75 and 101. Tacitus, in *Annals* 16.8, reports that in the aftermath of the Pisonian conspiracy of 65 CE, charges were fabricated against Junia Lepida, whose husband and nephew were condemned for their alleged participation in the conspiracy to assassinate Nero. (On the Pisonian conspiracy and Seneca's suicide, see Chapter 1.) Junia was charged with magic and with incest with her brother's son. Lucius Calpurnius Fabatus, along with two senators, was charged with complicity. The three men escaped punishment by appealing to Nero, who was so preoccupied with larger crimes that they were, Tacitus remarks, saved by their insignificance. Tacitus' account implies that Calpurnius Fabatus was not guilty of any crime.

25 In *Letter* 5.14.5, Pliny says of Cornutus Tertullus (see note 22) that he revered him as a father, *ut parentem vererer*.

26 On Pliny's activities as a landowner, see *Letters* 3.19 and 6.3 (purchasing property); 4.6 (dealing with hail damage); 5.14.8, 7.30.3, 9.15.3, and 9.36.6 (inspecting properties, reviewing account books, listening to the complaints of farmers); 7.30.3, 9.37, and 10.8.5 (finding good tenants); 8.2 (finding buyers for a grape harvest); 8.15, 9.16, and 9.20 (dealing with a poor grape harvest).

27 There may have been in the town teachers who taught at an elementary level, but none who provided more advanced instruction for the town's boys.

28 *CIL* 5.5262 = *ILS* 2927.

29 Nichols (1980) pp. 368–370. Pliny inherited the agricultural property in the area from his maternal uncle, who died in the eruption of Vesuvius in 79 CE. His uncle had presumably been a patron of the town of Tifernum, and Pliny had inherited this role along with the property when his uncle died. Pliny was about 17 or 18 years old at

the time. Champlin (2001) p. 122, maintains that the villa at Tifernum was "second in his heart only to Comum."

30 An inscription preserves a record of the financing of a temple in Comum by a Lucius Caecilius Secundus, who may be Pliny's father, in commemoration of a Caecilia, who may be a deceased sister of Pliny: *CIL* 5, Supplementa Italica, #745. Pliny himself may have dedicated the temple. On Pliny's benefactions, see Nichols (1980) pp. 379–380. Even Pliny's grandfather-in-law, who seems to have been a tight-fisted individual, was persuaded to endow a colonnade in Comum, dedicated in the name of himself and his deceased son (Calpurnia's father and Pliny's father-in-law). In *Letter* 5.11, Pliny comments that he is delighted by this generous gesture because it brings glory to Fabatus, some of which is reflected on to Pliny because of his marriage relationship.

31 Fannia was also praised for her affability, amiability (ability to inspire affection), and dignity or seriousness (*gravitas*).

32 Pliny, *Letters* 2.14.9 and 6.6.3.

33 By law, the minimum age for marriage for girls was 12 years: Dio 54.16.7; *Digest* 23.1.9 (Ulpian), *Digest* 23.2.4 (Pomponius).

34 Quintilian, *Institutio Oratoria* 6. Preface 4–13. Quintilian uses the Latin word *orbitas*, which means generally "loss," but is frequently used specifically to mean "loss of a child" or "childlessness." In the "Turia" inscription, the husband comments that "Turia" was in anguish that her husband was childless: *dolens orbitate mea*.

35 De Pretis (2003) p. 137.

36 Cicero, *Epistulae ad Atticum* 5.1.3–4.

37 Dio 56.3.3.

38 Raepsaet-Charlier (1987) p. 511, #631.

39 Boatwright (1991) p. 515 suggests that Plotina may have been born about 58 CE.

40 Dio (Epitome) 68.5.5.

41 On Pliny's publication of his speeches, see Chapter 2, note 163. He refers to the *Panegyricus* in Letter 3.18.

42 In *Panegyricus* 66.4, Pliny uses the memorable phrase (cited in Chapter 1, note 70) that Trajan ordered the senators to be free. Pliny's gratitude may be interpreted as a reflection of the passivity of the Senate after 100 years of imperial rule.

43 Roche (2002) p. 43.

44 Roche (2002) p. 51.

45 Boatwright (1991) p. 520 observes that, in contrast to the wives of earlier emperors, and particularly Livia and Agrippina the Younger, Plotina played a much less conspicuous public role. She was not perceived to have influence over Trajan or to exercise power. Nor did she spend lavishly on public works.

46 Cf. the praise of "Turia": *CIL* 6.41062, left hand column (Column 1), line 31.

47 On the definition of *obsequium*, see note 5. An epitaph lauds a wife as "very obedient to her husband," *marito obsequentissima*, as well as being (like Plotina) "a woman of highest moral integrity," *sanctissima femina*: *CIL* 8.23808. Juvenal 6.224, criticizes a wife who gave orders to her husband.

48 Fischler (1994) 127.

49 Fischler (1994) 116, defines "authority" as deriving from the holding of public office, in contrast to "influence" which is exercised through informal channels. Men could have both authority and influence, women only influence.

50 Consider Livia's intercession on behalf of Plancina, as noted in Chapter 1.

51 The emperor Claudius, for example, is recorded by Suetonius as having yielded control to his wives and his freedmen. He therefore acted, Suetonius claims, not as a ruler, but as a servant, dispensing honors, military commands, pardons, and punishments according to the wishes of either his wives or his freedmen: Suetonius, *Claudius* 29.1. Freedmen who held positions on the emperor's staff were, like wives, without constitutional office, but they were confidants of the emperor and therefore suspected of possessing undue influence.

52 Zeiner (2007) p. 166, on symbolic capital in Statius.

53 Consider note 51. Claudius is castigated for having yielded control to his wives and acting like a servant.

54 *CIL* 6.20116 = *ILS* 8430.

55 G. Williams (1958) pp. 16–29, posits that *morem gerere* was a ritual phrase used in Roman wedding ceremonies.

56 Dionysius of Halicarnassus, *Roman Antiquities* 2.25.4.

57 G. Williams (1958) pp. 20 and 29.

58 Plautus, *Menaechmi* 787–788.

59 Livy 34.3.1–4. The Oppian Law had been passed after the disastrous defeat of the Romans by Hannibal at Cannae in 216 BCE. Its intent was to restrict the purchase and display of luxury items. The law prohibited women from owning more than about an ounce of gold, wearing dyed clothing, or riding in carriages within one mile of Rome.

   Carlon (2009) p. 140, n. 4: "Although Cato notes the presence of women during the delivery of his speech, he consistently refers to them in the third person, while addressing the men directly in the second person." He thereby denies women a role as actors in the political drama. On Livy's account, see Boyd (1987) pp. 191 and 192, and Wyke (1994) pp. 139–140.

60 Valerius Maximus 9.1.3. Spending by women was a common complaint made by Roman men, as it is in any culture where women do not have the opportunity to earn their own spending money. See Johnston (1980) pp. 143–159.

61 Tacitus, *Annals* 3.34.

62 Treggiari (1991) pp. 16–36; Evans Grubbs (2002) pp. 21–23. Note that *in manum* means "into (the) control," while *in manu* means "in (the) control."

63 *Digest* 23.3.9.3 (Ulpian).

64 Sherwin-White (1966) p. 153.

65 *CIL* 5.3496 = *ILS* 8457; *CIL* 6.10812 = *ILS* 8387; *CIL* 6.7581 = *ILS* 7804.

66 See note 54.

67 *CIL* 6.41062, left hand column (Column 1), line 28.

68 Plutarch, *Aemilius Paulus* 5.2.3, and *Conjugalia Praecepta* 22 (= *Moralia* 141 A, B).

69 Tacitus, *Agricola* 6.1.

70 Carlon (2009) pp. 141–142, believes that Pliny was familiar with the *Oeconomicus* of Xenophon, a late fifth early/fourth century Greek writer. In this work, Xenophon advises a husband on instructing his 15-year-old wife in the management of the household.

71 Pliny also praises the frugality of several acquaintances: *Letters* 1.22.4 (Titius Aristo), 5.19.9 (Zosimus), and 6.8.5 (Atilius Crescens).

72 Sallust, *Catiline* 25.3. In contrast, Pliny's contemporary, the poet Statius, wrote of his friend's wife, Priscilla, that she would have sacrificed her life for her honor: *Silvae* 5.1.63.

73 Sallust, *Catiline* 24.3.

74 Statius, *Silvae* 5.1.117–26.

75 Pliny, *Panegyricus* 83.7.

76 Recall that Amymone (mentioned earlier in the chapter text) was praised as thrifty (*CIL* 6.11602 = *ILS* 8402). See also *CIL* 6.26192, 8.11294, and 8.9520 = *ILS* 8398, 8444, and 8445.

77 See *Panegyricus* 1.3 and 20.2, where Trajan's *castitas* is said to be natural and inborn. Pliny also uses the word in reference to Titius Aristo (*Letter* 1.22.7) and Arrianus Maturus (*Letter* 3.2.2).

78 In *Letter* 7.19.4, however, when Pliny describes Fannia as possessing *castitas*, he probably means general moral purity.

79 Martial 1.13.

80 The word *caritas* was also used by Tacitus in reference to the marriage of his in-laws. See note 69.

81 Recitation: Roman men of Pliny's class invited friends to their homes to hear them recite speeches (or poetry) they had composed. A recitation was considered a form of entertainment for upper-class Roman men. In *Letter* 3.18, Pliny reports that he had assembled an audience to hear his revised (and enlarged) version of the *Panegyricus*. The recitation continued for three days! One purpose of a recitation was to invite constructive comments before a written version of the speech (or poetry) was published. See *Letters* 1.13, 2.19, 3.10, 4.5, 5.3, 5.12, 7.17, 8.12, and 8.21.

82 On Pliny's poetry, see *Letters* 4.14, 4.18, 5.3, 7.4, 7.9, 8.21, 9.25, and 9.34.

83 Pliny's contemporary, the poet Statius, uses the word *concordia* in reference to the marriage of a friend: *Silvae* 5.1.44.

84 Statius, *Silvae* 3.5.28–36. And Statius' stepdaughter set his poems to music: *Silvae* 3.5.63–65.

85 Statius, *Silvae* 5.1.66–70.

86 Hemelrijk (1999) p. 260, n. 7.

87 The precise age of Fundanus' daughter is addressed in Chapter 6.

88 Even in Rome, it was not usual for women to acquire fluency in Greek. Martial 10.68, and Juvenal 6.185–99, ridicule women who speak Greek as pretentious.

89 Ovid, *Ars Amatoria* 2.273–86. About Roman women writing poetry, see Hemelrijk (1999) pp. 146–153. In the Roman world, women were excluded as participants in recitations, which were the initial stage of publication. (On recitations, see note 81.) To go public with one's work was desirable for a man, but quite contrary to the conventions of feminine modesty. Even attendance at a recitation in one's own home might elicit criticism. Calpurnia modestly concealed herself behind a curtain when Pliny was reciting. In the epitaph of Murdia, mentioned in note 7, her son reflected that "it is difficult for a woman to win praise in new areas of endeavor because their lives are stimulated by less diversity of opportunities."

90 Chapter 1, note 33. Seneca, *Consolatio ad Marciam* 1.1, refers to the weakness of the female mind.

91 Sallust, *Catiline* 25.2–5.

92 On dancing girls from Gades (modern Cadiz), see Pliny, *Letter* 1.15.3 and Martial 3.63.5 and 5.78.27.

93 Boyd (1987) pp. 197–201.

94 Propertius, 1.2.27–30; 2.1.9–10; 2.3.17–21; 2.24c.21; 2.26b.25–26; 2.33b.38. On several occasions, he refers to her as a *docta puella*, "a learned girlfriend": 1.7.11, 2.11.6, 2.13.11.

95 Hemelrijk (1999) p. 79.

96 Plutarch, *Pompey* 55.1 and 2. Pompey was Cornelia's second husband. The difference in their ages was so great that some people believed that Cornelia would have been a better match for Pompey's son.

97 Plutarch, *Tiberius Gracchus* 1.5; Cicero, *Brutus* 211; Quintilian, *Institutio Oratoria* 1.1.6; Tacitus, *Dialogus* 28.

98 Juvenal 6.434–56. See note 88 on Juvenal's and Martial's views on women fluent in Greek. On invective against women in Roman satire, see Richlin (1984).

99 Martial 2.90.9–10.

100 On Musonius Rufus, see Chapter 2, note 144.

101 Musonius Rufus III and IV (Lutz (1947) pp. 38–49).

102 Plutarch, *Conjugalia Praecepta* 48 (= *Moralia* 145B–146A). Plutarch also states that he approved of instruction in geometry for women because it made them ashamed to be dancers.

103 Carlon (2009) p. 138.

104 Hemelrijk (1999) p. 34.

105 Seneca the Younger (Lucius Annaeus Seneca) was the philosopher and statesman whose suicide in 65 CE is discussed in Chapter 1. His father was Marcus Seneca Annaeus (Seneca the Elder) who published several books on rhetoric.

106 Seneca, *Consolatio ad Helviam* 17.3–4.
107 A letter written in Latin by Plotina is preserved at *CIL* 3.12283 = *ILS* 7784. Also preserved and published at *CIL* 3.12283 is a letter in Greek which Plotina addressed to Epicureans in Athens.
108 Rawson (1991) p. 20.
109 Foucault (1986) pp. 160–161.
110 De Pretis (2003) p. 142; also p. 137.
111 I have taken the word which Pliny uses, *libelli*, to mean his literary compositions, which is the meaning in *Letter* 4.19.2 where Pliny announces that Calpurnia reads his *libelli*. However, De Pretis (2003) p. 140, takes *libelli* in Letter 6.7 to mean the letters which Pliny has written to Calpurnia.
112 Foucault (1986) p. 79.
113 Calpurnia seems to have gone to an estate in Campania owned by her grandfather, and to have been joined there later by Pliny (*Letter* 6.30.2).
114 On the *exclusus amator* theme, see Copley (1956). Also De Verger (1998) p. 115.
115 Hemelrijk (1999) p. 81: "Pliny's letters demonstrate the eventual 'domestication' of the ideal of the *docta puella* by its incorporation into married life. ... Thus, the sophisticated and exciting *puella docta* of love poetry had turned into the well-educated, devoted wife." See Guillemin (1929) pp. 138–141, on Pliny's incorporation of the theme of conjugal love into Latin literature. See also Gunderson (1997).
116 Cicero, *Epistulae ad Familiares* 14.4.6.
117 Ovid, *Tristia* 3.4.59.
118 Statius, *Silvae* 3.5.21–28. Zeiner (2007) pp. 165–181.
119 See Hershkowitz, (1995) pp. 168–181.
120 See Chapter 2, note 187.
121 Pliny ends *Letter* 6.26.3 with a wish that Fuscus will, as soon as possible, make Servianus a grandfather.
122 Sherwin-White (1966) p. 732, suggests that a Caecilia recorded in an inscription may be a deceased sister of Pliny. (See note 30.) Nowhere, however, does Pliny mention having (had) a sister.
123 Treggiari (1991) pp. 256–257, cautions readers that Pliny may have edited out, before publication, expressions of grief.
124 Riddle (1992).
125 However, see Chapter 1, note 25.
126 Soranus, *Gynecology* 3.26.
127 Suetonius Tranquillus had no children (*Letter* 10.94). Corellius (*Letter* 1.12) and Titius Aristo (*Letter* 1.22) each had one daughter but no sons. Minicius Fundanus (*Letter* 5.16) had no sons and lost one of his two daughters.
128 Foucault (1986) especially pp. 78–80 and 150–164.
129 Musonius Rufus XIII A, XIII B and XIV (Lutz 1947, pp. 88–97). On Musonius Rufus, see Chapter 2, note 144.
130 Musonius Rufus XIII A (Lutz 1947, pp. 88–89).
131 Plutarch, *Conjugalia Praecepta* 11, 14, 22 (= *Moralia* 139D, 139F–140A, 141A and B).
132 It was Plutarch who preserved the story (cited earlier in the chapter text) of the man who divorced his wife because she irritated him like a pinching shoe.
133 On the identity of this Maximus, see Sherwin-White (1966) p. 401, who conjectures that Pliny's addressee was a man younger than he.
134 On the commissioning of a public building to honor the memory of a deceased family member, see *Letter* 5.11 where Pliny commends Calpurnia's grandfather for endowing a colonnade dedicated to his deceased son (Calpurnia's father).
135 Compare Pliny's shrewd comments in *Letter* 5.11 to his grandfather-in-law who seems, like Maximus, to have been reluctant to spend money on a memorial for a deceased family member.

136 We might compare the situation of Minicius Acilianus and Junia of *Letter* 1.14.

137 At the end of the letter, however, Pliny does mention needing to spend some time listening to the complaints of his tenant farmers. His several villas, to which he retired for respites from the hectic life of Rome, were also income-producing properties, whose agricultural land was farmed by tenants or share-croppers. Pliny's responsibilities as a landlord are discussed earlier in the text. In *Letter* 9.40, Pliny describes his activities when he visits his villa at Laurentum in the winter (a villa which was much closer to Rome – about 20 miles – than that in Etruria).

138 Bruttius Praesens later returned to the dutiful life of a senator, serving twice as consul and as governor of several provinces. See Sherwin-White (1966) p. 404, on his career.

139 Raepsaet-Charlier (1987) p. 408, #478 and p. 671, #871.

140 Bruttius Praesens had at least one son, also named Bruttius, whose mother may be either wife (though Raepsaet-Charlier declares Laberia to have been the mother). Bruttius, the son, then had a daughter, named Bruttia, who was married in 178 CE to Commodus, son of Marcus Aurelius. (Raepsaet-Charlier 1987, p. 149, #149; Marcus Aurelius was emperor 161–80 CE; Commodus was emperor 180–92 CE.) Several years into the marriage, Bruttia was accused of adultery, sent into exile on Capri, and then assassinated.

141 Sherwin-White (1966) p. 350 and Raepsaet-Charlier (1987) p. 129, #116.

142 Pliny suggests that the invitee preferred a dinner invitation with someone who offered more risqué entertainment: dancing girls from Gades; see note 92.

143 We learn in *Letter* 1.5.8–10 that Regulus asked Spurinna to intervene with Pliny on his behalf in 97 CE, when Pliny was considering how to avenge Helvidius II. See Syme (1991b) on the identity of Vestricius Spurinna.

144 Pliny used the same phrase in *Letter* 8.5 in reference to the wife of Macrinus (in the chapter text).

145 Raepsaet-Charlier (1987) p. 266, #298; Sherwin-White (1966) p. 155. Another native of Baetica was Herennius Senecio, one of "the Seven" (Chapter 2).

146 For other appearances of the terms in Pliny, see *Letters* 3.3.4 and 4.15.6, 9, 10, and 13.

147 For example, the name of the man mentioned in the previous paragraph, Acilianus, was apparently derived from his mother's family. See Chapter 2, note 191.

148 Consider the deaths of the Helvidiae (*Letter* 4.21), Junius Avitus (*Letter* 8.23), and the son of Regulus (*Letter* 4.2).

149 On the dates of Spurinna's military service and absence from Rome, see Sherwin-White (1966) pp. 154–156.

150 In all, only ten of the 247 letters in Books 1 to 9 were addressed to women (including Cottia as a co-recipient with her husband). And there were only seven different addressees, since two of the women (Calpurnia and her aunt) received more than one letter. Most of the female addressees may have been relatives of Pliny.

151 On recitations as an initial stage of publication, see note 81.

152 On the date and scope of Pliny's appointment, see Sherwin-White (1966) pp. 80–82. His commission was as *legatus Augusti pro praetore consulari potestate*, "propraetorian legate of the emperor with consular power."

153 On the situation in Bithynia: Levick (1979), and Chapter 7, note 72.

154 Pliny discusses these trials in *Letters* 4.9 (Julius Bassus) and 5.20 (Varenus Rufus). The definition of extortion is discussed later in this chapter.

155 The poet Horace's rather leisurely land journey to Brundisium, described in *Satire* 1.5, occupied about two weeks. In *Pro Plancio* 96, Cicero reports that he had decided to travel overland rather than by sea to Brundisium because a huge storm had made a maritime journey impossible.

156 *Letter* 1.4, written about 97 CE, is addressed to Pompeia Celerina, the mother of Pliny's previous wife. She is discussed in Chapter 5.

157 Elder Pliny, *Natural History* 19.1.3–4. Casson (1974); André and Baslez (1993).

158 For Cicero's journey, see the *Epistulae ad Atticum* 5.9, 5.10. 5.11, 5.12, 5.13. Cicero was not in a hurry to reach his province. He was unhappy about being sent away

from Italy at such a politically volatile time. Pliny and Calpurnia probably made the journey to Asia Minor in less time.

159 The adverse winds were the Etesians, mentioned by Cicero, *Epistulae ad Atticum* 6.8. They blow from the north for 40 days from about July 20.

160 Sherwin-White (1966), p. 581.

161 Scholars have generally believed that the letters to and from Trajan in Book 10 were gathered and published by an unknown person after the death of Pliny. Noreña (2007) pp. 239–277, however, contends that it was Pliny who selected and arranged the letters for publication and that he intended *Letters* 10.120 and 121 to be the final letters in the book. He argues that these letters depict Pliny's relationship with Trajan as so warm that Pliny felt confident enough to break the rule requiring prior imperial approval for private use of the imperial courier system (*cursus publicus*). According to Noreña it was important to Pliny's self-portrait that he be seen as having developed a good relationship with a good emperor, to counterbalance criticism of his success under the bad emperor, Domitian.

162 On Dasumia Polla: Raepsaet-Charlier (1987) p. 272, #308. On the hypothesis that the wife of Domitius Tullus was Dasumia Polla, see Syme (1985b), p. 54 (= RP 5, p. 535). Dasumia Polla may have been the daughter or (according to Syme) sister of Lucius Dasumius Hadrianus, a Spanish born senator who was suffect consul in 93 CE, the year that Pliny was praetor. If this assumption is correct, she was a distant cousin of the emperor Hadrian.

163 The surviving text of the will is available at *CIL* 6.10229, *FIRA* 3.48, Eck (1978), and Champlin (1986). On speculations about the identity of the testator and his wife, see Garcia (1982); Syme (1985b); Tate (2005); Konrad (1994).

164 On public interest in opening of wills, see Champlin (1991) pp. 5–28.

165 On *captatores*, see Chapter 2, note 52.

166 Champlin (1991) p. 123: "Usufruct and annuity share the important characteristic that each provides for the welfare of the widow without permanently reducing the patrimony."

167 Syme (1985b), p. 54 (= RP 5, p. 535).

168 Contrast, the stepmother of *Letter* 6.33, discussed in Chapter 4.

169 Syme (1985b), p. 54 (= RP 5, p. 535); (1984a) pp. 35 and 36 (= RP 4, 300 and 301). However, Birley (1987) p. 220, conjectures that Severus was the third husband of Domitia Lucilla (Domitius Tullus' adopted daughter). Sherwin-White (1966) p. 469, proposes that the daughter married Severus – or his son. There is more discussion of the marriage of Catilius Severus in Chapter 6.

170 However, in 120 CE, he incurred the displeasure of the emperor Hadrian and was removed in disgrace from the office of consul. Nonetheless, his family continued to be successful in public life, and his step great-grandson (Syme 1985b) or step grandson (Birley 1987) was Marcus Aurelius, emperor 161–80. See Birley (1987) p. 54.

171 The long list of additional beneficiaries includes several people who are mentioned in Pliny's published correspondence – that is, Junius Avitus, Minicius Justus, Sosius Senecio, and Fabius Rusticus. Much of the will is missing. It is possible that Pliny, too, was named as a beneficiary in it.

172 Syme (1949) p. 15. Raepsaet-Charlier (1987) p. 356, # 418.

173 On Corellius' mentorship of Pliny: *Letters* 4.17, 5.1.5, 7.11.3, 9.13.6.

174 Griffin (2007) 461–462: Pliny describes Corellius' deliberation upon suicide in terms of Stoic theory. Also: André (1975) 237–238.

175 Pliny reports in *Letter* 3.7.2 that Silius Italicus (an epic poet) committed suicide by starvation at the age of 75 because of an incurable tumor.

176 As noted in Chapter 1, Nero may have avoided this indictment in the case of Seneca's suicide by having soldiers prevent Paulina's suicide.

177 See note 14 of this chapter.

178 *Letters* 1.8.11 and 2.7.5.

179 Raepsaet-Charlier (1987) p. 684, #897.

180 Raepsaet-Charlier (1987) p. 126, #111.

181 Minicius Fundanus was the father of the girl who died at the age of 13 and on the brink of marriage (earlier in the text). She is discussed in Chapter 6. Pliny's *Letter* 5.16 reports her death.

182 The duties of a military tribune are discussed later in this chapter. On Pliny's posting as a military tribune, see note 256. Junius Avitus' commander, Lucius Julius Ursus Servianus, was married to the sister of Hadrian (emperor 117–138) and was a friend of Pliny. It was Servianus who recommended Pliny to Trajan for the "three-children privilege" (*Letter* 10.2). Pliny addressed two letters to Lucius Julius Ursus Servianus, 3.17 and 6.26, and mentioned him in *Letter* 7.6.8. In *Letter* 6.26, Pliny congratulates Servianus on arranging the marriage of his daughter to Fuscus Salinator. His daughter, discussed later, is mentioned in "The So-called Will of 'Dasumius'."

183 "A few years later": Sherwin-White (1966) p. 476, comments that an interval of eight or nine years between a military tribunate and a quaestorship was common, and cites Pliny's own career as an example. However, Avitus seems to have attained the rank of quaestor within about five years. On the office of quaestor, see Chapter 2, note 41.

184 On the term *adulescens*, see earlier in the text, and Chapter 4, note 88.

185 See note 14.

186 Recall that women could receive bequests and inheritances, but these were overseen by their *paterfamilias* or, if he were deceased, their *tutor* (guardian).

187 See note 171.

188 This was probably not Julius Ursus Servianus' first marriage. Domitia Paulina was about 30 years younger than he. On Domitia Paulina: Raepsaet-Charlier (1987), p. 35, #12. Plotina's support for Hadrian is mentioned earlier in this chapter.

189 The ultimate fates of the family of Julius Ursus Servianus were not happy. Servianus and his grandson (Julia's son) were accused of conspiring against Hadrian and condemned to death in 136 CE. They committed suicide. (*Scriptores Historiae Augustae: Hadrian* 15.8, 23.2 and 3).

190 Although our sources imply that Plotina maintained a "low profile" and did not intrude upon her husband Trajan's decisions, she was nonetheless perceived as having influence, and therefore people sought to cultivate a relationship with her.

191 This letter and the family of Ummidius Quadratus are discussed more extensively in Chapter 5.

192 Other *Letters*: 1.5, 1.20.14, 2.11.22, 2.20.2, 4.7, 6.2.1. See Chapter 2, note 133.

193 Champlin (1991) p. 99. On Regulus' career as a *delator*, see Tacitus, *Histories* 4.42.

194 For example, in *Letter* 1.5.15. See also Champlin (1991) p. 99–100 on the reliability of Pliny as a witness.

195 Hoffer (1999) pp. 55–91 (a chapter subtitled "Regulus, the Bad Senator"); Regulus is "a parody of the wise senior senator" (p. 55).

196 *CIL* 15.7421. Sherwin-White (1966) p. 266. Raepsaet-Charlier (1987) p. 162, #167.

197 Sherwin-White (1966) p. 278.

198 Regulus and his son are mentioned in Martial 6.38.

199 By contrast, he describes Arria's son in *Letter* 3.16.3 as a boy of "uncommon beauty and modesty." Also, in *Letter* 4.7, Pliny chides Regulus for composing and reciting publicly a biography of the boy, but Pliny prides himself in *Letter* 3.10 on composing and reciting a biography of Cottia and Vestricius Spurinna's son, Cottius (whose death is discussed earlier).

200 Saller (1994) pp. 114–132.

201 On the process of emancipation, see Gardner (1998) pp. 6–15.

202 Although Dixon (1988) p. 57, comments that Pliny's telling of the story suggests that the emancipation of a son was not a normal practice, she adds that Pliny's judgment need not be assumed to be objective.

203 On cognates: Chapter 1, note 29.

204 Gardner (1998) pp. 209–267, discusses the gradual changes made to Roman laws of succession to reflect the high value that people placed on the bonds between mothers and their children, and on non-agnate relatives. See also Dixon (1988) pp. 41–70.

205 *CIL* 6.1527, 41062, left-hand column (Column I), lines 37–39.

206 *CIL* 6.1527, 41062, right-hand column (Column II), lines 1–4.

207 Hoffer (1999) p. 57, suggests that Regulus' fawning behavior towards his liberated son was like that of a legacy hunter, a *captator* (which Regulus was: *Letter* 2.20), and that Regulus may have welcomed his son's death (despite his display of excessive mourning).

208 Tacitus, *Histories* 4.42.

209 "examining the entrails": The Romans, like many other ancient cultures, believed that the will of the gods could be discovered by the examination of the entrails of animals that had been sacrificed to them. Healthy internal organs were a sign that the gods were well-disposed. Any abnormality in the appearance or position of the internal organs was an unfavorable sign.

210 At *Letter* 2.20.11, Pliny remarks that Regulus "accepts inheritances and legacies as if he deserved them." Regulus' despicable behavior provides a striking contrast to Pliny's honorable behavior (as he describes it) in connection with receiving legacies and inheritances. See *Letters* 2.16, 4.10, 5.1, and 5.7, and the discussion in Chapter 4.

211 Raepsaet-Charlier (1987) p. 616, #788.

212 Raepsaet-Charlier (1987) p. 617, #789. *L'Année épigraphique* 1981, 825.

213 *Consul ordinarius*: During the imperial period, the term of office for a consul was reduced from one year to a few months, thereby enabling several men, rather than just two, to hold the office in one year. A man selected to hold the office at the beginning of the year was called the *consul ordinarius*. A man who held the office in later months was called a *consul suffectus* (suffect consul); see Chapter 1, note 6. Pliny was a suffect consul in 100 CE. This system allowed more men of senatorial rank to achieve the rank of consul. However, the position of *consul ordinarius* was more prestigious than that of *consul suffectus*. In official records, the names of the two *consules ordinarii* were given as the "name" of each year.

214 Tacitus, *Annals* 14.29.

215 *L' Année épigraphique* 1953, 251. It is not certain that the Verania of this and the previous inscription are the same person.

216 Tacitus, *Annals* 3.10–19.

217 The name of the father of Verania's husband was Marcus Licinius Crassus Frugi. The *nomen* of the father, Licinius, indicates that her husband had been born into the Licinius family, but later adopted into a branch of the Calpurnius family. His parents had perhaps arranged the adoption because they had four sons and therefore a "surplus." On the reasons for adoption, see Chapter 1. The addition of the name (*cognomen*) of Licinianus to his adoptive name was done to commemorate that his birth family was Licinius. The formation of adoptive names is examined by Solomies (1992) and Lindsay (2009).

On the First Triumvirate, see Chapter 7, note 19.

218 Seneca, *Apocolocyntosis* 11.2–5; Dio (Epitome) 60.29.6; Tacitus, *Histories* 1.48.

219 Tacitus, *Histories* 1.48 and 4.42.

220 Tacitus, *Histories* 4.42 and 43. It was at this same Senate meeting that Fannia's husband, Helvidius I, denounced the *delator*, Eprius Marcellus, causing dissension among the senators. See Chapter 2.

221 Tacitus, *Histories* 1.21, 38, 48.

222 Tacitus, *Histories* 1.15 and 29.

223 Tacitus, *Histories* 1.48.

224 Pliny, *Letter* 2.20.2; Tacitus, *Histories* 1.14–21; Plutarch, *Galba* 23; Suetonius, *Galba* 17. Lindsay (2009) pp. 203–206, discusses the process of adoption used by Galba. Syme (1982a) discusses the supporters of Galba.

225 Tacitus, *Histories* 1. 34–44; Plutarch, *Galba* 27.

226 Tacitus, *Histories* 4.42.

227 Tacitus, *Histories* 1.47; Plutarch, *Galba* 28. This brother was executed in 70 CE.

228 Plutarch, *Galba* 28.

229 *CIL* 6.31723 = *ILS* 240.

230 Champlin (1991) pp. 75–81, comments on witnesses to the signing of a will. Sherwin-White (1966) remarks, p. 204, on the importance of the seals which the witnesses applied to the will at the time that the testator signed it. Upon the opening of the will (after the death of the testator), the witnesses would be called upon to testify to the authenticity of the seals.

231 The Elder Pliny wrote an encyclopedic, multi-volume work titled *Naturalis Historia* (*Natural History*). The Younger Pliny provides a list of his uncle's written works in *Letter* 3.5.

232 Sherwin-White (1966) p. 373. However, Birley (2000) p. 82 disagrees. On the use of the ending-*ianus* to denote an adoption (Pomponius – Pomponianus, Licinius – Licinianus), see note 217.

233 Raepsaet-Charlier (1987) p. 535, #665.

234 *CIL* 2.3866.

235 See *Letters* 2.13 and 10.4, and discussion in Chapter 4.

236 The Centumviral Court was the chancery court of ancient Rome. We are not certain about its entire jurisdiction, but one area of its concern was cases involving wills and inheritance. On Pliny's participation in the court, see *Letters* 2.14, 4.24, 5.1, and 6.33, and discussion of *Letters* 5.1 and 6.33 in Chapter 4. The activities of this court are discussed in Chapter 4. See Chapter 4, note 185.

237 Carlon (2009) p. 39.

238 Sherwin-White (1966) p. 97.

239 *CIL* 6.12404. Syme (1968 a) p. 146 (= RP 2, p. 712).

240 Sherwin-White (1966) p. 97.

241 Ulpian, *Rules* 5.2. Treggiari (1991) p. 54 defines *affectio maritalis* as "the continuing will to regard the partner as *coniunx*" ("spouse"; literally: "joined together").

242 Gardner (1986) pp. 47–50.

243 Treggiari (1991) pp. 37–80.

244 *Digest* 23.2.4 (Pomponius).

245 *Digest* 23.2.2 (Paulus).

246 *Digest* 23.217.2 (Gaius). Evans Grubbs (2002) pp. 136–141.

247 Ulpian, *Rules* 5.2.

248 On the terms "irregular unions" and "quasi-marital unions," see Dixon (1992) p. 90; Gardner (1998) p. 254.

249 On the complexities of the Lex Minicia and mixed marriages, see Cherry (1990) pp. 244–266. Also Treggiari (1991, pp. 45–49) and Weaver (1986).

250 Gaius, *Institutes* 1.77 and 78.

251 Shelton (1987).

252 See also Chapter 2, note 144.

253 Musonius Rufus III and IV (Lutz 1947, pp. 38–49).

254 Musonius Rufus XIII A (Lutz 1947, pp. 88–89). Dillon (2004).

255 Tacitus, *Annals* 15.71; Dio (Epitome) 62.27; Philostratus, *Vita Apollonii*, 7.16.

256 Later in this chapter is more information about military tribunes. Pliny mentions his tribuneship in Syria also in *Letters* 1.10.2, 7.16.2, 7.31.2, 8.14.7, and 10.87. His duties, as he reveals in *Letter* 7.31.2, were to audit the financial accounts of the military units. He discovered a great deal of greed and neglect. He was probably not much older than 20 years at the time of his tribuneship. Griffin (2007) 454: "Pliny is keen to emphasize here that his own interest in philosophy was already manifest in his youth."

257 Sherwin-White (1966) p. 244, asserts that Pliny uses two names, the first a Roman *nomen*, for non-Romans who had acquired Roman citizenship, for example, Claudius Aristion (*Letter* 6.31.3) and Fonteius Magnus (*Letter* 5.20.4). "Greeks with single names

would seem to be non-citizens": Euphrates (*Letter* 1.10), Isaeus (*Letter* 2.3), and Polyaenus, (*Letter* 7.6.6).

258 For discussion of *Letter* 1.10, see Hoffer (1999) pp. 119–140.

259 Sherwin-White (1966) p. 108.

260 Philostratus, *Vita Apollonii* 8.7.11.

261 Sherwin-White (1966) p. 109.

262 Hoffer (1999) p. 130. Griffin (2007) 454–457, comments that Pliny portrays both Euphrates and Artemidorus as *exempla* of the virtues they preach.

263 Euphrates committed suicide in 119 CE by drinking hemlock. He was very old and ill. Dio (Epitome) 69.8.3.

264 On Casta, see Raepsaet-Charlier (1987) p. 188, #198.

265 Fear (1996); Haley (2003). Baetica is mentioned several times in Pliny's published correspondence. In *Letter* 7.33, for example, Pliny describes for Tacitus a hearing in 93 CE for which the Senate appointed Pliny to act as counsel for the Baetici in their indictment of the governor, Baebius Massa, on charges of extortion. Pliny's co-counsel was Herennius Senecio, who had been born in Baetica and served as a quaestor there. See also *Letters* 6.29.8 and 7.16.3.

266 Pliny laments Martial's death in *Letter* 3.21.

267 Tacitus, *Annals* 3.33–34. Also Martial 2.56.

268 Tacitus, *Annals* 4.19–20.

269 Children were usually allowed to retain possession of at least part of the estate of a condemned parent. See *Digest* 48.20.7.pref. (Paulus) and Tacitus, *Annals* 13.43. Also Chapter 1, note 50.

270 *Digest* 1.16.4.2 (Ulpian).

271 See Marshall (1990) p. 347, and Robinson (1995) pp. 81 and 82, on the controversy about when wives became liable.

272 On the Chronology of the extortion trials, see Sherwin-White (1966) pp. 56–62.

273 Seneca the Younger accompanied his maternal aunt and uncle to his uncle's posting in Egypt. On the exemplary conduct there of his aunt, see Chapter 1.

274 On Caecilia, see Raepsaet-Charlier (1987) p. 154, #154, and the discussion in Chapter 6.

275 During the imperial period, the minimum age for holding the office of praetor was 30 years, lowered from 40 in the republican period.

276 On the Lex Acilia and extortion trials, see Bauman (2000) pp. 51–66, and Brunt (1990) pp. 53–95.

277 In *Letter* 4.9, Pliny describes his defense of Julius Bassus who was charged with extortion as governor of Bithynia because he had accepted things from provincials (*Letter* 4.9.6). Pliny comments that the accusers called his acquisitions "theft" and "robbery," but Bassus called them "gifts." Nonetheless, as Pliny admits, the law forbade the acceptance even of gifts from provincials.

278 On the definition of "equestrian," see Chapter 2, note 144, and Chapter 4, note 75.

279 Whether or not the man was guilty, these punishments – corporal punishment, condemnation to the mines, and execution – were not the legally appropriate punishments for a Roman citizen of high-standing. However, see Sherwin-White (1966) pp. 164–166.

280 *Digest* 12.5.3 (Paulus). Also Sherwin-White (1966) p. 168. In *Letter* 2.11.19, Pliny states that money from bribes taken by Marius Priscus went into *aerarium Saturni*.
Pliny assumed an appointment as one of the prefects of the *aerarium Saturni* in 98 CE, replacing Bittius Proculus (husband of his former mother-in-law, *Letter* 9.13.13) and Publicius Certus (whom Pliny attempted to prosecute for the death of Helvidius II, *Letter* 9.13). Pliny remained prefect until selected for the suffect consulship in the autumn of 100 CE.

281 See Sherwin-White (1966) pp. 161–162, on the trial of Marius Priscus, who was charged with extortion with *saevitia* during his term as proconsul of Africa.

282 The occupation of Pliny's time with prefecture duties is discussed earlier in the text, in relation to the date of his marriage to Calpurnia. In *Letter* 3.4.2, Pliny reports that he

had just taken a brief leave of absence from his prefecture duties to travel to Tifernum to attend the laying of the foundation of a temple he had funded. *Letter* 10.8.4 contains his request to the emperor Trajan for permission for this leave. The temple is mentioned again in *Letter* 4.1, written several years later, in which Pliny announces to his grandfather-in-law that he and Calpurnia will be traveling to Tifernum and then on to Comum to visit him and Calpurnia's aunt.

283 In *Letter* 7.33, Pliny discusses the trial of Baebius Massa, at which he and Herennius Senecio were co-prosecutors. See note 265.

284 The Baetici believed that, by serving as their advocate in their case against Baebius Massa in 93 CE, Pliny had agreed to serve henceforth as their patron – that is, as someone who was bound to protect their interests. See Nichols (1980) pp. 370–378. The Romans had developed an elaborate patronage system. In its origins, it was an agreement by which a powerful, wealthy individual consented to provide legal or business assistance to more humble individuals in return for their political support. As the Roman elite expanded their interests throughout Italy and overseas, they took on the roles of patrons of entire communities, who might call on them not only for legal representation in Rome, but also for help in protecting their interests in the Senate or before the Emperor. The role of a patron usually also involved making gifts to the community of public buildings or entertainments. For Pliny's activities as a patron of his hometown, see earlier in this chapter. See also Wallace-Hadrill, (1989) pp. 63–87.

285 In *Letter* 2.11.12, Pliny speaks of the apprehension he felt when he stood before the Senate to prosecute Marius Priscus, a man of consular rank. (Nonetheless, he managed to speak for almost five hours, *Letter* 2.11.14.)

286 Sherwin-White (1966) p. 233, citing Cicero, *Verrine Orations* 1.56, comments that Verres extorted ten times more money (40 million sesterces), from a much smaller and poorer province (Sicily). On sesterces and their purchasing power, see Chapter 4, note 29.

287 On the practice of allowing the property of condemned people to pass to their children, see note 269.

288 Carlon (2009) p. 195.

289 Quintilian, *Institutio Oratoria* 7.3.10; *Codex Justinianus* 9.9.22. Treggiari (1991) pp. 262–319. Robinson (1995) pp. 58–68. Harries (2007) pp. 95–105.

290 Paulus, *Sententiae* 2.26.11 and 16.

291 *Digest* 48.5.6.1 (Papinianus) and 50.16.101 pr (Modestinus). On *stuprum*, Robinson (1995) pp. 59–60.

292 The use of concubines for sexual gratification is discussed in Chapter 7.

293 *Digest* 48.5.6.1 (Papinianus).

294 An infant did not become a legitimate member of an agnate *familia* until s/he had been formally accepted by the *paterfamilias*. If there were any doubt about the identity of an infant's father, the *paterfamilias* could refuse acceptance. The infant would then be "exposed" – that is, placed outside the family home, perhaps in an alley, garbage dump, or uninhabited area, and left to die of exposure.

295 Treggiari (1991) pp. 264–275. Also, Robinson (1995) p. 58.

296 Robinson (1995) pp. 58–59. *Digest* 48.5 is the section of the *Digest* which collects juristic interpretation of the Julian laws. See also Edwards (1993), especially pp. 34–62.

297 Augustus, *Res Gestae* 8.5.

298 Severy (2003) p. 56.

299 Harries (2007) pp. 96 and 89.

300 *Digest* 48.5.20 (21) (Papinianus) and 23 (Ulpian); Paulus, *Sententiae* 2.26.1. Robinson (1995) pp. 60–61.

301 *Digest* 48.5.24 (25). pr (Macer); Paulus, *Sententiae* 2.26.4. Robinson (1995) p. 61.

302 However, a husband who killed his wife after catching her with another man was to be punished more leniently because he committed the act while justifiably upset. Paulus, *Sententiae* 2.26.5; *Digest* 48.5.38.8 (*Papinianus*).

303 *Digest* 48.5.24 (25).1 (Macer); Paulus, *Sententiae* 2.26.6.

304 *Digest* 48.5.2.8 (Ulpian), 48.5.14 (15).2 (Scaevola).

305 *Digest* 48.5.4.1 (Ulpian); *Codex Justinianus* 9.9.6.

306 Digest 48.5.2.2 (Ulpian); *Codex Justinianus* 9.9.2; Paulus, *Sententiae* 2.26.8.

307 Paulus, *Sententiae* 2.26.14.

308 Horace, *Odes* 4.5.21–24.

309 Ovid's exile is discussed in Chapter 2. Of course, he expected his wife to remain loyal to him and to work tirelessly to have his sentence rescinded.

310 Tacitus, *Annals* 1.53.1, 3.24; Suetonius, *Augustus* 65, and *Tiberius* 11.4; 50.1.

311 Tacitus, *Annals* 3.24.5, 4.71.6; Suetonius, *Augustus* 65.

312 Suetonius, *Tiberius* 35.1 and 2; Tacitus, *Annals* 2.85.1; *Digest* 48.5.10.2 (Papinianus). In *Annals* 2.50.4, Tacitus reports that Tiberius rejected imposing on Appuleia Varilla the harsh penalties of the Julian law on adultery and urged that she be left to relatives to punish in accordance with ancestral precedent.

313 Tacitus, *Annals* 2.85.2–4. For a discussion of the trial, see Shotter (1966).

314 Treggiari (1991) Appendix 2, pp. 509–510, lists some of the adultery prosecutions under the Julio-Claudians.

315 Tacitus, *Annals* 6.47.2–48.6.

316 Pannonia: a Roman province bounded on the north and east by the Danube River. It included areas of what are now modern Hungary and Austria.

317 Tacitus, *Histories* 1.48.8; Dio 59.18.4; Plutarch, *Galba* 12.1 and 2.

318 Tacitus, *Histories* 1.2.

319 Garnsey (1970) p. 24.

320 Tacitus, *Annals* 6.40. Raepsaet-Charlier (1987) p. 51, #30.

321 At *Annals* 3.25, Tacitus reports that the enactment of Augustus' legislation encouraged the rise of informers who spied on households and reported violations. According to Tacitus, the activities of these informers ruined many families.

322 *Digest* 48.5.27.6 (Ulpian); *Codex Justinianus* 9.9.3. The mandatory torture of slaves while being questioned for evidence is discussed in Chapter 7.

323 *Digest* 48.5.27.15 (Ulpian). If an accused person was ultimately judged to be innocent, but his slave(s) had died or been permanently injured under torture, he was eligible for compensation (for destruction of his property).

324 Tacitus, *Annals* 3.23.

325 Raepsaet-Charlier (1987) p. 48, #28.

326 Tacitus, *Annals* 3.22 and 23; Suetonius, *Tiberius* 49.1. Quirinius is described by both Tacitus and Suetonius as rich and childless.

327 On the conviction for astrology of Vibia in 52 CE, see Chapter 1, note 79.

328 See Woodman and Martin (1996) p. 213, for the scholarly controversy about the date of the divorce. Townsend (1962) pp. 484–493.

329 Possibly the *Ludi Romani* which were held September 4–19. The "Games" included chariot races and theatrical performances which were financed with state funds for the enjoyment of the public.

330 Pompey: Gnaeus Pompeius Magnus had been Julius Caesar's colleague in the First Triumvirate. (On the First Triumvirate, see Chapter 7, note 19.) He was renowned for his successes as a military leader. He commissioned the construction of Rome's first permanent theater, which opened in 55 BCE and was known as the Theater of Pompey. Earlier in this chapter is mention of Pompey's fifth wife, Cornelia, who was knowledgeable in literature, music, geometry, and philosophy, and had "a nature that was free from that unpleasantness and meddlesomeness which such learning inflicts on young women." The husband of Verania Gemina (mentioned earlier: *Letter* 2.20) was also a descendant of Pompey.

331 Tacitus, *Annals* 3.23, reports that, although Lepida was banished, her property was not confiscated because she had a son by her second husband. His statement reminds us first, that emperors (here, Tiberius) sometimes showed compassion for the children of wealthy criminals by not confiscating the parent's property, and second, that there

was an assumption that mothers would bequeath property to their children even though their children were not their agnates.

332 Sherwin-White (1966) pp. 391–392. However, Crook (1955) p. 59, argues for one *consilium* whose composition changed. See also Devreker (1977).

Pliny may have been traveling to the council meeting, scheduled at Trajan's villa at Centum Cellae, when he stopped at his mother-in-law's villa at Alsium, mentioned in *Letter* 6.10. His mother-in-law is discussed in Chapter 5. Centum Cellae (modern Civitàvecchia) was about 50 miles northwest of Rome.

333 See note 256.

334 *Codex Justinianus* 9.9.2 and 9.

335 *Digest* 48.5.13 (14).5 (Ulpian).

4 Mothers, nurses, and stepmothers

1 Harlow and Laurence (2002) pp. 6–11.

2 Golden (1988) pp. 152–163.

3 Plutarch, *Consolatio ad uxorem* 2 and 5 (= *Moralia* 608 C and 609 D).

4 Cicero, *Tusculan Disputations* 1.39.93.

5 Seneca, *Letters* 99.1 and 2.

6 However, Golden (1988) p. 158, disputes this explanation. On the practice of exposure, see Chapter 3, note 294.

7 The English word "nurse" is cognate with the Latin *nutrire* through old French.

8 See Bradley (1986) pp. 211–213.

9 Pliny, *Letter* 4.21.

10 Juvenal 6.592–94.

11 Plutarch, *Cato the Elder*, 20.2 and 3. In a funerary inscription which a husband dedicated to his wife, who had died at the age of 24, he proudly records for posterity that she had fed her children with the milk of her own breasts: *CIL* 6.19128 = *ILS* 8451.

12 Tacitus, *Dialogus* 28 and 29.

13 Tacitus, *Germania* 20.

14 See Introduction, note 13.

15 Cicero, *Brutus* 211. The widowed Cornelia's fame as a *univira* is mentioned in Chapter 2.

16 Tacitus, *Dialogus* 28. See also Quintilian, *Institutio Oratoria* 1.1.6 on the eloquence which the Gracchi learned from their mother.

17 Aulus Gellius 12.1.5–23.

18 Plutarch's daughter invited her friends and her toys to breastfeed from her nurse, a small example perhaps of the many humiliations which slaves endured: *Consolatio ad uxorem* 2 (= *Moralia* 608 D). Plutarch, however, supplies the anecdote to demonstrate the kindness of the little girl. On the death of the daughter, see earlier in this chapter.

19 The child of a slave was born a slave and belonged to the owner of her/his mother. A mother might be bought or sold separately from her children, and they might be bought or sold separately from her.

20 Quintilian, *Institutio Oratoria* 1.1.4 and 5.

21 Soranus, *Gynecology* 2.19.

22 Galen, *Hygiene* (*De Sanitate Tuenda*) 1.8.

23 *Theodosian Code* 9.24.1.1

24 Suetonius, *Nero* 42. In section 50, Suetonius records that, after his death, the ashes of the friendless Nero were dutifully laid to rest by two nurses and his mistress. On the loyalty of Domitian's nurse, see Chapter 6, note 170.

25 Bradley (1986) pp. 202–213, provides examples of such inscriptions.

26 Line 32 (and 47) of "The So-called Will of 'Dasumius'" (*CIL* 6.10229); see Chapter 3, note 163.

27 In *Letter* 8.16, Pliny tells his addressee that he generously allows his slaves to acquire possessions and even to bequeath them, but that this privilege is valid only within the household. See note 165.

28 Propertius 4.7.73–74.

29 A *sestertius* ("sesterce") was an ancient Roman coin. Because of the very significant differences in ancient and modern economies, it is futile to try to determine the value of a sesterce in comparison with modern coinage or prices. From records found at Pompeii (a city buried by the eruption of Mount Vesuvius in 79 CE), we know that one sesterce would purchase four pounds of bread (a daily ration for two adults in an era when wheat was the mainstay of the average diet) or two liters of ordinary table wine. The price of a tunic (ordinary attire for working men) was 15 sesterces, and the price of a donkey was 500 sesterces. At Pompeii, the price for one slave is recorded as 2500 sesterces. However, Columella, who wrote a technical manual about agriculture in the early first century CE, recommends paying between 6000 and 8000 sesterces for a slave to work in a vineyard. We know that a rank and file soldier in the first century CE earned 900 sesterces per annum. Toward the end of the century, the emperor Domitian increased the military pay to 1200 sesterces per annum. Most people lived at subsistence level, and therefore few could afford to purchase real estate. Pliny, however, was very wealthy. In *Letter* 3.19, he asks a friend for advice on the purchase of an estate, probably in Etruria and adjoining the property he inherited from his uncle. The selling price of 3,000,000 sesterces was a bargain because the original selling price had been 5,000,000 (*Letter* 3.19.7). We do not know if Pliny purchased the property. In *Letter* 4.1 he announces to his grandfather-in-law that he is planning to visit his estates in Etruria (and carry out his duties as a town patron). (He describes one of these estates in great detail in *Letter* 5.6, and in *Letter* 9.36 he reports briefly on some of his and his wife's activities there.) In *Letter* 10.8.5, he requests permission from the emperor Trajan to make an inspection visit to his properties in Etruria which he reports brought in an income of more than 400,000 sesterces. And, of course, Pliny also owned large estates in the Comum area that he had inherited from his father and his mother, as well as a splendid villa on the coastline south of Rome (*Letter* 2.17).

30 On the basis of a passage from Columella, *De Re Rustica* 3.3.8, about land prices, Sherwin-White (1966) p. 358, estimates that the size of the property which Pliny gave his nurse was 40 to 50 acres. According to Columella's calculations, if the property were that size and devoted to viticulture, at least seven men would be required to work it.

31 On usufruct, see Chapter 3, note 166.

32 Gaius, *Institutes* 1.194. Gardner (1986) p. 194.

33 On attempts by ex-slaves to reunite their families after manumission, see Bradley (1984) pp. 77–80.

34 Dixon (1988) provides an excellent exploration of the topic.

35 Seneca, *De Providentia* 2.5.

36 A pedagogue (the word is formed from two ancient Greek words that mean "leading a child") was a male slave who looked after his owner's children. When a child was old enough to attend school, the pedagogue escorted him to and from his lessons, as well as to and from the baths and social functions. As was true of a nurse, it would be difficult for a pedagogue to discipline a child who was of a much higher social status.

37 Seneca, *De Ira* 2.21.1 and 6.

38 Seneca, *Consolatio ad Helviam* 15.1.

39 On the relationship of Marcus Aurelius to the family of Domitius Tullus of *Letter* 8.18, see Chapter 3, note 170; also Chapter 6, and Genealogy Chart 6.

40 Marcus Aurelius, *Meditations* 1.3.

41 Novatilla was the daughter of Seneca's elder brother, Novatus. Miriam Griffin (1976) p. 58–59.

42 Seneca the Younger, *Consolatio ad Helviam* 18.8.

43 In *Letter* 2.18, Pliny describes his search for a teacher for another family. In *Letter* 4.13, he describes his plan to establish a rhetorical school in his hometown of Comum so that the boys there do not need to go elsewhere for their continuing education. As noted in Chapter 3, few girls would have the opportunity to study with a rhetor.

44 As noted in Chapter 3, note 77, *castitas*, when used in reference to men, can denote an all-encompassing moral purity. Here, however, Pliny may be implying particularly that the school of Julius Genitor is free of sexual impropriety.

45 Julius Genitor was the man to whom Pliny addressed *Letter* 3.11, his account of his heroic support of "the Seven" in 93 CE. He also receives *Letters* 7.30 and 9.17 (where Pliny chides him for being a bit too rigid).

46 Tacitus, *Agricola* 4.2.

47 In the passage from Tacitus just cited, he uses the phrase *in sinu*, which I have translated as "at her side." The phrase could mean "at her breast" and refer to breastfeeding, but it seems here to have the wider meaning of "at her side," since Tacitus mentions that Agricola was *in sinu* of his mother, Julia Procilla, as an adolescent. The phrase, *in sinu*, is also used in the passage from Seneca (note 35) where it means "on their laps." The base meaning of the Latin noun *sinus* is "fold" or "hollow." By extension, it can mean "bosom" or "lap," and then "care" or "protection."

48 *Letters of Fronto*, Van den Hout (ed.: Teubner 1988) #62; Haines (ed.: Loeb 1962) vol. 1, p. 182.

49 Marcus Aurelius, *Meditations* 6.12.

50 Publilius Syrus, *Sententiae* 600 (p. 74 in Otto Friedrich).

51 *Letters of Fronto*, Van den Hout (ed.: Teubner 1988) #237; Haines (ed.: Loeb 1962) vol. 2, p. 228.

52 On recitations, see Chapter 3, note 81.

53 Sherwin-White (1966) p. 348: "In the earlier Principate the surviving Republican nobles played an undistinguished part in affairs, and the work of the empire was done by men like Pliny."

54 *auditorium*: the room where the recitation was held. The Latin verb for "to hear" is *audire*.

55 Rawson (1991) p. 20. See also Chapter 3.

56 Hemelrijk (1999) p.45.

57 In *Letter* 9.36.4, Pliny reports that, at their Tuscan villa, a book was read aloud to him and Calpurnia during dinner. After dinner, they were entertained by scenes from a comedy or by a lyre-player.

58 On the possible identity of the father, see Sherwin-White (1966) p. 349. He may be linked to the once numerous, but, by Pliny's time, nearly extinct family from which so many conspirators or political victims were drawn.

59 Fuscus Salinator was the recipient of the letter mentioned in note 57, describing Pliny's activities at his Tuscan villa.

60 The Elder Pliny provides autobiographical information in his voluminous encyclopedia, *Natural History*. A brief biography appears in Suetonius' *Lives of Famous Men*. For discussion about the career of the Elder Pliny, see Sherwin-White (1966) pp. 219–221; Syme (1969).

61 *CIL* 5, Supplementa Italica, #745. On this inscription, see Sherwin-White (1966) pp. 70 and 732.

62 Her father's family name would have been Plinius. Her mother's name may have been Marcella – that is, from the Marcellus family: *CIL* 5.3442.

63 Of his many writings, only the encyclopedia, *Natural History*, is extant. During Nero's reign, the Elder Pliny chose to write on the politically safe topics of grammar and rhetoric, or so the Younger Pliny tells us in *Letter* 3.5.5. See Chapter 2, note 13.

64 *CIL* 5.5262, 5.5263, 5.5267, 5.5279.

65 *CIL* 5, Supplementa Italica, #745.

66 An orphaned boy was assigned a *tutor* until he reached the age of puberty. Ulpian, *Rules* 11. 1 and 27.

67 Pliny wanted to spare boys of his community the need to leave the area for rhetorical training. On Pliny's establishment of a rhetoric school in Comum, see *Letter* 4.13.

68 In *Letter* 7.11.5, Pliny mentions the estates that he had inherited from his mother and father.

69 Syme (1985c) p. 196 (= RP 2, p. 644), declares that Pliny's adoption was testamentary.

70 In the inscriptions from his hometown of Comum (see note 64), he is listed as Gaius Plinius Caecilius Secundus, son of Lucius. The "Caecilius" preserved a record of his agnate birth family.

71 On the reference in *Letter* 4.1 to property and patronage in Etruria, near the town of Tifernum, see Chapter 3, note 29. On Pliny as a patron, see Nichols (1980).

72 Dixon (1988) p. 171, who considers *Letter* 6.20 "one of the most intimate portraits of a mother and son," believes that Plinia took responsibility for her son's actions and safety and made important decisions for him, even in such dire straits.

73 Lilja (1978) catalogues about ten references in the letters, three of them to women (*Letters* 5.16.9, 6.20.12, and 7.24.1). Most of the references are quite non-specific and do not allow us to form much of a mental image of the person: "a handsome appearance," " a ruddy complexion." The one exception is the description of the philosopher Euphrates given in *Letter* 1.10.6: "tall, with long hair, and a white beard." On Euphrates' marriage and appearance, see Chapter 3. In *Panegyricus* 4.7, Pliny describes Trajan as tall, strong, and dignified in appearance. His hair was prematurely old (grey? thin?), but said by Pliny to enhance his majesty.

74 On the relative value of 300,000 sesterces, see note 29. Romatius' net worth, before Pliny's gift, was 100,000 sesterces (which was also incidentally the purchase value of the property which Pliny gave to his nurse). This amount put Romatius in the upper bracket of Comum residents and qualified him for a position on the Comum town council. Socially, his family had apparently moved in the same circles as Pliny's family. That Pliny could easily afford to give Romatius 300,000 sesterces, his nurse a 100,000 sesterces property, and Calvina (*Letter* 2.4) 100,000 sesterces toward her dowry is an indication of his enormous personal wealth (although in *Letter* 2.4 he alleges that his resources are modest and that the income from his little farms – yes, he uses the diminutive – is small or uncertain). From *CIL* 5.5262, we learn that Pliny donated 500,000 sesterces in assistance to boys and girls in the town of Comum and 100,000 for upkeep of the library for whose construction he had paid. In *Letter* 1.8, he mentions that he gave a speech at the dedication of a library which he funded in Comum and that he planned to publish the speech. (Modesty was not a virtue among ancient Roman elite men.) In the same letter, he raises the topic of his philanthropy toward needy children, a topic mentioned again in *Letter* 7.18. In *Letter* 5.7.3, he announces that he gave 1,600,000 sesterces to the local community.

75 *Equites*, translated into English as "Equestrians" or "Knights" (although their historic connection to the Roman cavalry had lost its significance by the imperial period), were members of very affluent families whose wealth was derived from investments in real estate and trade and from a variety of business and banking enterprises. The minimum property requirement for admission to the equestrian order was 400,000 sesterces. (For the senatorial order, the minimum property requirement was 1,000,000 sesterces.) In the early imperial period, members of the equestrian order were eligible for several high-level military and administrative positions. See Sherwin-White (1966) p. 130, and note 101.

76 Pliny mentions problems with unproductive land and bad harvests also in *Letters* 4.6, 6.3, 8.15, 9.16, 9.20, 9.37, and 10.8. These letters remind us that much of the income for the wealthy depended on the cultivation of the many tracts of agricultural land that they owned.

77 The grandfather and *paterfamilias* of Pliny's wife was apparently concerned about the financial welfare of his granddaughter and of the great-grandchildren whom he expected (*Letter* 8.10.2) and who would inherit Pliny's property.

78 On patrons, see Chapter 3, note 284, and Saller (1989), Wallace-Hadrill (1989) and Braund (1989).

79 Cicero, *Epistulae ad Atticum* 1.5.8.

80 *Letters of Fronto*, Van den Hout (ed.: Teubner 1988) #62; Haines (ed.: Loeb 1962) vol. 1, p. 182.

81 Cicero, *De Amicitia* 1.

82 On the elder Pliny's military career, see Sherwin-White (1966) pp. 219–221.

83 Suetonius, *Vespasian* 21, records that Vespasian rose before dawn, read letters and official reports, and then admitted to his presence friends who offered their greetings.

84 Carlon (2009) p. 69.

85 See *PIR²* C 1294

86 *CIL* 16.28 = *ILS* 1995.

87 *Letters* 1.12, 3.3.1, 4.17, 5.1.5, 7.11.3, 7.31.4, 9.13.6.

88 Pliny uses the word *adulescentulus*, a diminutive of the word *adulescens*. *Adulescentulus* suggests a very young man. The term *adulescens* (used of Minicius Acilianus in *Letter* 1.14.10) could designate a man up to the age of about 40. For other appearances of the terms in Pliny, see *Letters* 2.7.5, 3.3.4; 4.15.6, 9, 10; and 13. On the early stages of Pliny's political career, see Syme (1991c).

89 If the supposition that Corellius had angered Domitian is correct, this emperor would be Domitian's successor, Nerva. Corellius died within a year or two of Nerva's becoming emperor.

90 *CIL* 16.28 = *ILS* 1995, and *CIL* 14.4276.

Carlon (2009) p. 72, examines the issue of Corellius Rufus' reputation among his senatorial colleagues and concludes that "it may be safely assumed that Corellius was well regarded."

91 In his conversation with Nerva (as it is recorded by Pliny), Corellius Rufus referred to his protégé not (as we might expect) by his *nomen*, Plinius, but as Secundus (one of Pliny's *cognomina*). Compare Arria's use of the *cognomen* Paetus in reference to her husband Caecina Paetus.

92 Pliny appears as a more forceful avenger in *Letter* 9.13, published perhaps about ten years after the publication of *Letter* 1.5.

93 Syme (1949), pp. 14 and 15; (1958), p.326, n. 5: the name Hispo was very rare.

94 On the preservation of family names through women, see Chapter 2, notes 57 and 191.

95 Carlon (2009) p. 76. She assumes (as I do not; see Chapter 3) that Pliny's marriage to Calpurnia predated the publication of any of his letters. We do not know whether *Letter* 3.3, addressed to Corellia Hispulla (about a teacher for her son), was written before or after the marriage. However, its publication (as opposed to its composition) probably post-dated the marriage, in which case Corellia Hispulla may have then been related to Pliny by his marriage to Calpurnia.

The one non-relative addressee, Cottia of *Letter* 3.10, receives the letter jointly with her husband.

96 Elder Pliny, *Natural History* 17.26.122. On the rarity of the name, see Syme, *Tacitus* (1958) p. 86, note 4. On the family of Corellius Rufus, see Zucker (1963).

97 Ateste (modern Este) was located about 22 miles southwest of Patavium (modern Padua). Thrasea Paetus was a native of Patavium (Tacitus, *Annals* 16.21; Dio, Epitome, 62.26.4), as was the maternal grandmother of Minicius Acilianus (*Letter* 1.14.6).

98 Laus Pompeia (modern Lodi) was located about 20 miles southeast of Mediolanum (modern Milan).

99 A Camp Prefect (*praefectus castrorum*) was often a man of equestrian rank (see note 75) who had made the military his career. He therefore came to his appointment as a senior officer with considerable experience, as opposed to the young men who were appointed to short terms as military tribunes, and then went on to senatorial careers. On Pliny's service as a military tribune, see Chapter 3, note 256. On his recommendation of a six-month military tribuneship for Varisidius Nepos (*Letter* 4.4), see later in this chapter.

100 Tacitus, *Histories* 3.7.

101 In the imperial period, members of the equestrian class could aspire to a public career which combined military and administrative posts. They served, for example, as military officers, working their way up to the rank of prefect (as did Corellia's husband, Minicius Justus). Several administrative posts in the provinces were reserved for equestrians, in particular the governorship of Egypt, which was considered the pinnacle of an equestrian career.

102 Pliny uses the verb *diligere* ("to be very fond of") to convey his affection for Corellia. He uses this same verb of his feelings toward Corellia Hispulla (*Letter* 3.3.1) and toward Fannia and Arria (*Letter* 7.19.10).

103 On "The So-called Will of 'Dasumius'," see Chapter 3, note 163.

104 On Junius Avitus, see *Letter* 8.23, and later in this chapter.

105 See Champlin (1991) pp. 21–28, on the motives of testators.

106 *consul ordinarius*: see Chapter 3, note 213. On the identification of Corellia's son as Lucius Minicius Rufus, see Carlon (2009) p. 75. However, Sherwin-White (1966) p. 415 and Birley (2000) p. 73 do not make this association.

107 The dating of Pliny's praetorship is controversial; see Sherwin-White (1966) pp. 763–771.

108 Dio 54.2.3.

109 Sherwin-White (1966) p. 414.

110 See also *Letter* 6.12 for the grandfather-in-law's bluntness in criticism of Pliny. For the desire for great-grandchildren, see *Letter* 8.10.

111 The properties would not have been owned jointly by his parents. Presumably each had inherited property from his/her own family, the Caecilii and the Plinii.

112 Carlon (2009) pp. 90 and 91, provides an excellent analysis of the rhetoric of this letter.

113 Carlon (2009) pp. 92–93, comments that it is rare for Pliny to begin a letter with the emphatic *tu*. "By opening these letters with *tu*, Pliny offers pointed counterinstructions to previous correspondence with his addressees."

114 Carlon (2009) p. 94: "Pliny uses her words to overturn her entreaty to him."

115 200,000 sesterces was not an insignificant amount; see note 29.

116 Griffin (2003) pp. 103–105, asserts that, in his letters, Pliny offers himself as an example of someone successfully practicing a code of ideal social behavior, a code that closely resembles that expounded by the younger Seneca in his *De Beneficiis*. See also Guillemin (1929), p. 8 and Dixon (1993)

117 PIR² N 55 has Corellia Hispulla married to Neratius Marcellus, agreeing with Syme. See note 120.

118 On the rarity of the *nomen*, see note 96.

119 On *consul ordinarius*, see Chapter 3, note 213.

120 Raepsaet-Charlier, (1987) pp. 238; Carlon (2009) pp. 73–75. Syme (1957), p. 492 (= RP 1, p. 350), maintains that Corellia's husband was Neratius Marcellus (not Priscus). On a possible connection by marriage of Anteia, wife of Helvidius II, and Corellia Hispulla, see Raepsaet-Charlier (1987) pp. 86 and 87, #68 and 69.

121 Also a matter of scholarly dispute is the identity of the father(s) of the Neratius brothers; see Raepsaet-Charlier (1987) p. 238.
Syme (1957) p. 491 (= RP 1, p. 350): Priscus was adopted by his uncle L. Neratius Priscus, suffect consul 87.

122 *CIL* 9.2456 = *ILS* 1032 or *AE* 1990, 217.

123 Carlon (2009) p. 74.

124 However, Sherwin-White (1966) rejects the identification with Neratius Priscus in his introductions to each of these letters.

125 On military tribunes, see note 99. Rather than accepting the appointment as military tribune, Suetonius asked that it be transferred to a kinsman (*propinquus*). From the tone of Pliny's letter, it seems that he was annoyed by the request. In *Letter* 4.4, Pliny requests of his addressee that he grant a six-month military tribuneship to Varisidius Nepos.

126 Pannonia: see Chapter 3, note 316.

127 On Pliny's term as prefect of the treasury of Saturn, see Chapter 3, note 282.

128 *Scriptores Historiae Augustae: Hadrian* 18.1. For Pliny's service on an emperor's council, see the story of Gallitta in Chapter 3.

129 *Scriptores Historiae Augustae: Hadrian* 4.8. On Plotina's efforts to make Hadrian the successor, see Chapter 3.

130 Schools in the ancient Roman world were privately funded, usually by the parents of the students. On Pliny's endowment of a rhetorical school, see *Letter* 4.13, and note 43.

131 On death of Arulenus Rusticus, and fate of his family, see Chapter 2.

132 On Pliny's use of the verb *diligere* to convey affection, see note 102.

133 On the meanings of *adulescens*, see note 88.

134 See note 73.

135 On the concern about the sexual vulnerability of boys to their teachers, see C. Williams (2010) pp. 78–84; Langlands (2006) p. 269.

136 Julius Genitor: see note 45.

137 Carlon (2009) p. 81.

138 Gaius Caecilius Strabo had been selected to be a suffect consul beginning in September of 105 CE.

139 In *Letter* 4.11.6 (which is discussed in Chapter 7), another female defendant, Cornelia the Vestal Virgin, is also absent from, and therefore unheard at her trial.

140 Carlon (2009) p. 88.

141 Consider Pliny's comment in *Letter* 3.4.7. He was willing to take on the prosecution of Caecilius Classicus for the Baetici because Classicus had died prior to the beginning of the trial. Pliny could therefore gain the gratitude of the Baetici without the risk of incurring the hatred of a fellow senator.

142 In *Letter* 9.13.6, Pliny refers to Corellius as the wisest man of his period.

143 Carlon (2009) p. 87. Nonetheless, in *Letter* 9.13.6, when Pliny admits to omitting a consultation with Corellius Rufus, he seems determined to impress upon his readers that he was bolder than his mentor.

144 On the use of Secundus as a name, rather than Plinius, see note 91.
   Cornutus was Gaius Julius Cornutus Tertullus; see Chapter 3, note 22.

145 Sosius Senecio was one of the beneficiaries listed in "The So-called Will of 'Dasumius'." See Chapter 3, note 171, on other of Pliny's friends who were beneficiaries.

146 See note 99.

147 The word *contubernalis* means literally "a person with whom one shares a tent," a reference deriving from army camps. By extension, it means a person with whom one has a very close friendship based on the sharing of many experiences. Perhaps it can be translated as "mate" or "chum." In *Letter* 1.19.1, Pliny refers to the addressee, Romatius Firmus (to whom he gave 300,000 sesterces), as "my fellow student and my *contubernalis* from an early age." He uses the word again of Voconius Romanus in *Letters* 2.13.5 and 10.4.1. In *Letter* 5.14.9, Pliny uses the related word *contubernium*: *contubernio nostro*, "our close companionship."

148 On Cornutus Tertullus, see note 144 in this chapter, and Chapter 3, note 22.

149 Pliny attributes two of these virtues, integrity and dignity, also to the much older Corellius Rufus in *Letter* 4.17.4; see earlier in the chapter text. The third virtue, influence (*auctoritas*), is certainly one which is more usually attributed to a man with greater experience. We might suppose that Pliny, first, wants to comfort the parents by exaggerating the virtues of their son, and, second, wants to answer critics who protested the approval of an honorific statue.

150 Sherwin-White (1966) p. 355, speculates that the surviving son/brother was Julius Naso of *Letter* 6.6, whose brother, Pliny reports there, was snatched away by a premature death. If this speculation is correct, we learn from *Letter* 6.6 that the husband/father was also dead.

151 There is additional discussion of Junius Avitus and his young wife in Chapter 3.

152　On the meaning of *orbitas*, see Chapter 3, note 34.

153　The laws dealing with such offenses were the *Lex Cornelia de falsis*, and the *Lex Cornelia de sicariis et veneficis*, passed about 81 BCE.

154　Several charges of deliberate poisoning are reported in Chapter 1, with regard, for example, to the untimely death of Germanicus.

155　Champlin (1991) p. 84. Pliny mentions two other charges of forgery. In *Letter* 6.31 (in which he also records the investigation into the adultery of Gallitta; see Chapter 3), he reports that the imperial council which Trajan had assembled at his villa heard a case about a falsified will. The correspondence of Pliny and Trajan in *Letters* 10.58 to 60 includes reference to a charge of forgery made by a woman, Furia Prima (see Chapter 7).
In *Panegyricus* 43.1, Pliny praises Trajan for not supporting forged, falsified, and unjust documents.

156　*Digest* 48.2.1 (Pomponius). Recall that "Turia" initiated the prosecution of the murderers of her parents; see Chapter 2, note 97.

157　*Digest* 48.2.12.2 (Venuleius Saturninus); Suetonius, *Titus* 8.5. On the anomalies of this case, see Sherwin-White (1966) pp. 409–410.

158　On Julius Ursus Servianus, see Chapter 3, notes 182, 188, and 189.

159　*Digest* 48.2.7.2 (Ulpianus).

160　See Chapter 3, note 196.

161　The family is mentioned in Martial 6.38. The son was not quite three years old at the time of the poem, and the poet prayed that his mother and father would, in the future, hear him pleading cases in court (that is, have a successful career). Neither mother nor son lived long enough to fulfill Martial's prayer.

162　Tacitus, *Histories* 4.42.

163　*Digest* 26.5.21.1 (Modestinus): A father who has emancipated his son cannot be appointed as his guardian.

164　Gardner (1998) pp. 107 and 108.

165　There are at least 14 letters in the collection in which Pliny mentions wills and/or inheritances: *Letters* 2.16, 2.20. 3.6, 4.10, 5.1, 5.5, 5.7, 6.22, 6.31, 6.33, 7.20, 7.24, 8.16, and 8.18. In several of these letters, he reveals that he was one of the beneficiaries of the will. (One of the benefits of having three children, or of being granted the "three-children privilege," was that it allowed one to receive more inheritances and legacies.) In *Letter* 1.9.2, moreover, he lists the witnessing of a will as a typical activity for an elite man on an average day in Rome. Roman law required that seven men – no women – gather to witness, sign, and seal a will which had been drawn up; see Chapter 3, note 230. When the author of the will died, the witnesses attested to the validity of the will. See Champlin (1991) pp. 75 and 76. In *Letter* 2.20.10, discussed in Chapter 3, we learn that Regulus was present for the signing of the will of Aurelia.
　　In *Letter* 8.16.1, Pliny informs his addressee with pride that he allows his slaves to make a "sort of" will (*quasi testamenta*). Since slaves were themselves "property," they could not legally possess property, and therefore their "wills" were not legally binding. However, Pliny permitted his slaves to draw up documents in which they indicated to whom they wished to bequeath items which they considered "theirs." However, they could not leave items to anyone outside of Pliny's household. Therefore, Pliny, as the *paterfamilias* of the slaves in his household, ultimately retained control of the items. Nonetheless, his gesture was more generous than that of many other slave owners.

166　Champlin (1991) pp. 5–28.

167　In *Letter* 7.20.6, Pliny comments to the addressee, the historian Tacitus: "You must have noticed how often we receive legacies of the same amount." Pliny was pleased that testators, in their wills, seemed to have judged him to be the equal of Tacitus.

168　Regulus' father's creditors had apparently claimed most of his estate; see note 162.

169　At the time of his death, Fannius was writing a book about the fates of people put to death or banished by Nero. It is unknown whether he was related to Fannia; see Chapter 2.

170 For similar statements, see *Letters* 4.10.2 and 5.7.2.

171 Carlon (2009) p. 129 comments on "the baldness with which (Pliny) expresses his delight in the advantages he gains behind the scenes because of his reputation for and exercise of integrity."

172 Arulenus Rusticus and his wife Verulana Gratilla: two of "the Seven" mentioned in Chapter 2.

173 Raepsaet-Charlier (1987) p. 516, #638 asserts that she was a "sister." Sherwin-White (1966) p. 312, states that she may be a "daughter." Carlon (2009) pp. 112–113, observes that this man and woman have the same name, Pomponius Gallus, but comments that "it was not unusual in the first century CE to give a female child names deriving from both her mother's and father's families, (*and*) there is no certainty that Pomponia Galla is the sister or daughter of a Pomponius Gallus rather than the child of some couple whose names were Pomponius and Galla." We might compare the name Corellia Hispulla.

174 Champlin (1991) pp. 15, 107–108; Nicholas (1962) pp. 260–264. Section 5.2 of the *Digest* is devoted to discussions of complaints about disinheritance.

175 On the *Lex Falcidia*: *Digest* 35.2.1 (Paulus). Nicholas (1962) p. 266. If there were several heirs, each received one-quarter of the net inheritance (after payment of debts and expenses). If a man had several children or several agnates, he might designate just one of them as heir and arrange for legacies for the others.

176 On marriage and *manus*, see Chapter 3.

177 See Chapter 2, note 87. While in exile, Cicero was concerned that Terentia might sell property she owned, rather than retaining it and eventually passing it on to their son.

178 *CIL* 6.10230 = *ILS* 8394. On Murdia, see also Chapter 3, note 7.

179 Valerius Maximus 7.8.2

180 *Digest* 5.2.5 (Marcellus). See Lewis (2007) pp.125–38. Gardner (1998) pp. 209–267, discusses the gradual changes made to Roman laws of succession to reflect the high value that people placed on the bonds between mothers and their children, and on non-agnate relatives.

In the Valerius Maximus passage cited in the previous note, he declares that the daughter who had not been nominated as a heir to her mother's estate chose not to challenge the will, which was further evidence of her sterling character and the injustice of her mother's action.

181 On the several meanings of *praeiudicium*, see Quintilian, *Institutio Oratoria* 5.1.2.

182 A *querela*, or "complaint," might be made by children, parents, or siblings. Pliny provides another anecdote about an allegedly unduteous will in *Letter* 6.33.

183 *Lex Cincia de donis et muneribus* was passed in 204 BCE. *Fragmenta Vaticana* 298–309 (Paulus). Sherwin-White (1966) pp. 312–313.
Zimmermann (1996) pp. 482–484.

184 Julius Frontinus served as governor of Britain about 76–78 CE and was also the author of books on aqueducts and military strategy. Pliny reports in *Letter* 4.8.3 that Julius Frontinus had recommended him to one of the colleges of priests. See also *Letter* 9.19.1.

185 The jurisdiction of the Centumviral Court included cases involving wills and inheritances. The court originally consisted of 100 jurymen (*centum* = "hundred," *viri* = "men"), but by the imperial period its numbers had been increased to 180. Sherwin-White (1966) p. 181, comments that "the Centumviral (*Court*) ranked at this time as the principal court of civil law for an advocate seeking to make a name." Pliny had much experience both as an advocate before and as a juryman on this court. In fact, in *Letter* 6.12.2, he calls the Centumviral Court "my arena." In *Letter* 2.14.1, he writes that he is stressed at the Centumviral Court by cases which bring more work than pleasure. In *Letter* 4.16.2 and 3, he reports that his speech in the court lasted for seven hours! See also *Letters* 4.24.1, 6.33.3, and 9.23.1. In *Letters* 1.5.4 and 5, he reports that he had appeared before the Centumviral Court on behalf of Arrionilla (see Chapter 3), but he does not indicate whether the case involved a will.

186 Suetonius, *Domitian* 8.1, reports that Domitian, in his efforts to reform the legal system, sometimes annulled decisions made by the Centumviral Court if he thought that the jurors had been swayed by bribery or bias. Pliny, however, has put a sinister angle on Domitian's actions.
Gardner (1986) p. 186 suggests that Asudius Curianus in some way blackmailed the men named as heirs.

187 Gardner (1998) p. 233.

188 His full name may have been Gaius Licinius Macrinus (or Marinus) Voconius Romanus. See *PIR²* L 210. He was born about 65 CE and was therefore about the same age as Pliny.

189 Two inscriptions from Roman Spain seem to refer to his family: *CIL* 2.3865 and 3866.

190 In both these letters, Pliny refers to Voconius Romanus as his *contubernalis*. On the meaning of *contubernalis*, see note 147.

191 *CIL* 2.3866. In *Letter* 9.28.2, Pliny comments that Voconius Romanus, to whom the letter is addressed, had referred to him a man named Popilius Artemisius. The name suggests that the man was a freedman (former slave) of the Popilius family – that is, the family of Voconius Romanus' wife. Freedpersons, upon emancipation, assumed the *nomen* (family name) of their former owner. Thus Artemisius became known as Popilius Artemisius. (As slaves, they had had no family or family name of their own, but belonged as property to their owner's family.)

192 Syme (1960) pp. 365–366 (= RP 2, pp. 480–482).

193 The title of his office was *flamen*, which is usually translated as "priest." The office-holder was not, however, expected to devote his life to religious duties. His term of service lasted only a year or two, during which time he would be responsible for ensuring that ceremonies and buildings dedicated to the continued well-being of the emperor were maintained.

194 We cannot determine whether Pliny applied to Nerva (emperor 96–98 CE) or his successor, Trajan, for the "three-children privilege" (for which see Chapter 1, note 25, and Chapter 3, note 14). Pliny himself obtained the privilege from Trajan in 98 CE, at the request of Julius Servianus (*Letter* 10.2). In *Letter* 10.94, Pliny asks Trajan to grant the privilege to his friend Suetonius.

195 On Plotina, see Chapter 3, especially note 190.

196 See note 189.

197 On the adoption of adults, see Chapter 1 and the story of the presumed son of Arria the Elder.

198 On sesterces, see note 29.

199 In *Letter* 1.19, Pliny wrote to Romatius Firmus, whose father was a friend of Pliny's mother and uncle, to offer him 300,000 sesterces towards the 400,000 sesterces necessary to qualify for admission into the equestrian order. See note 74.

200 On *mancipatio* – that is, the fictitious sale of agricultural land within Italy (or of slaves) to legalize the conveyance of property and transfer of ownership – see Nicholas (1962) p. 63; Schulz (1951) pp. 344–348. The ceremony required the presence of five witnesses, all of them Roman citizens.

201 P. Watson (1995); Gray-Fow (1988).

202 Vergil, *Georgics* 2.128–29: "whenever cruel stepmothers have poisoned the cups and mixed noxious plants and baleful spells." Ovid, *Metamorphoses* 1.147: "ruthless stepmothers mixed ghastly poisons." See Watson (1995) pp. 102–128.

203 Seneca the Elder, *Controversiae* 9.5 and 9.6. In *Controversiae* 4.5 he furnishes an exercise involving a stepson who, though a doctor, refused to treat his ill stepmother. His father disinherited him. Quintilian, *Institutio Oratoria* 2.10.5, remarks that school boys were asked to prepare declamations on topics that were not true to life, including the topic of cruel stepmothers. See P. Watson (1995) pp. 92–102.

204 Ovid, *Heroides* 12.187 and 188.

205 Propertius 4.11.86–90. On Cornelia and her pride in being a *univira*, see Chapter 1.

206 Seneca, *Consolatio Ad Helviam* 2.4.
207 Marcus Aurelius, *Meditations* 6.12.
208 Plutarch, *Antony* 87; *Dio* 51.15.5.
209 Fischler (1994) p. 118, comments that Octavia "exemplified the behavior of the Roman Matron, in contrast to the decadent, archetypally Eastern image of Cleopatra."
210 *Digest* 5.2.4 (Gaius).
211 *Codex Justinianus* 3.28.22 pr.
212 On the Centumviral Court, see note 185.
213 Compare *Letter* 3.13, also addressed to Voconius Romanus, which was a cover letter for a copy of a speech (now known as the *Panegyricus*; see Chapter 3) which Pliny delivered when he was suffect consul in 100 CE. There are numerous letters in the collected correspondence about the sending of literary works to friends, often with an invitation to the friend to offer a critique. See, for example, *Letters* 1.2, 1.8, 7.12, 7.20, 8.3, 8.13, 8.15, 8.19, 9.4, 9.18, 9.20, and 9.35.
214 Compare *Letters* 5.1.1, 6.15.1, and 6.25.1. See Sherwin-White (1966) p. 399.
215 *PIR*² A 1366. Attius Suburanus had served as adjutant to Julius Ursus Servianus (the other special judge named in *Letter* 7.6) during his prefectures of the grain supply and of Egypt between 81 and 84 CE. On the career of Sextus Attius Suburanus, see Syme (1980) 64–66.
216 For several examples of Regulus' activities as a legacy chaser, see Chapter 3.
217 The Centumviral Court met in the Basilica Julia in the Forum. See *Letter* 5.9.1. In the ancient Roman world, a "basilica" was a law court building (courthouse), not a religious structure.
218 Sherwin-White (1966) p. 399 and 400. Syme (1968a) pp. 138 and 139, 150 (= RP 2, pp. 700 and 701, 722. *PIR*² A 1366, 1370
219 Raepsaet-Charlier (1987) p. 134, #126, refers to Attia as the sister of the prefect/consul Suburanus. In a footnote, however, she adds that she does not exclude the possibility that Attia Viriola was his niece or cousin. Carlon (2009) writes on p. 113 that it is most likely that Attia was Suburanus' sister, and that their father had disinherited the two together. However, on p. 134, she writes that the Suburanus named in Letter 6.33 is, at best, a nephew or cousin of Attia Viriola.

5 Grandmothers, aunts, and mothers-in-law

1 Quintilian, *Institutio Oratoria* 6. Preface 4–13.
2 M. Cornelius Fronto, *De Nepote Amisso* 2.1, Haines (ed.: Loeb 1962) volume 2, p. 222.
3 Seneca the Younger, *Consolatio ad Helviam* 2.5.
4 On *captatores*, see Chapter 2, note 52.
5 *CIL* 6.18086.
6 Seneca, *Consolatio ad Helviam* 2.4.
7 On Novatilla, see Chapter 4, notes 41 and 42.
8 Quintilian, *Institutio Oratoria* 6. Preface 8.
9 *CIL* 6.1478.
10 Dixon (1988) p. 217.
11 Aulus Gellius 12.1.
12 Raepsaet-Charlier (1987) p. 649, #829.
13 Chapter 4, note 73.
14 Pliny uses the superlative adjective *robustissimus* in *Letter* 1.12.11: "Corellius Rufus completed his 67th year, which age is sufficiently long even for the 'most sturdy' people."
15 *PIR*¹ V 600. Also *CIL* 2.172 and 10.5182.
16 Syme (1968b), pp. 73–79 (= RP 2, pp. 660–665).
   However, there may have been only one son – that is, Gaius Ummidius Quadratus and Gaius Ummidius Sallustius may have been the same person.

17 On names after adoption, Chapter 3, notes 217 and 232.

18 Lusitania: the ancient Roman province corresponding approximately to modern Portugal.

19 It would be interesting to know if Ummidius Durmius Quadratus was in Illyricum in 42 CE. That was the year that Arria the Elder and her husband, Caecina Paetus, were in Illyricum and supported the attempted rebellion of Scribonianus. See Chapter 1.

20 Tacitus, *Annals* 12.48; 13.8 and 9; 14.26.

21 The site of the ancient town is now occupied by the Benedictine monastery of Monte Cassino.

22 Varro, *De Re Rustica* 3.3.9.

23 Horace, *Satires* 1.1.95–100.

24 For example, *CIL* 10.5182 = *ILS* 972 provides information about the career of Gaius Ummidius Durmius Quadratus.

25 *CIL* 10.5183 = *ILS* 5628.

26 On the generosity of Pliny's family members to their communities, see Chapter 3, notes 30 and 282. From *CIL* 5.5262, we learn that Pliny donated 500,000 sesterces in assistance to boys and girls in the town of Comum and 100,000 for upkeep of the library for whose construction he had paid. In *Letter* 1.8, he mentions that he gave a speech at the dedication of a library which he founded in Comum.

27 *CIL* 15.7567.

28 *AE* 1946, 174. See also Fora (1992).

29 *Notizie degli Scavi di Antichità* 1929, pp. 29–30.

30 Raepsaet-Charlier (1987) p. 649, #830.

31 Syme (1968b), p. 77 (= RP 2, p. 664).

32 The maternal grandmother of Minicius Acilianus, of *Letter* 1.14.6, was from Patavium.

33 Silius Italicus and Ummidia Quadratilla were about the same age. In *Letter* 3.7, Pliny reports his death in 103 CE. He starved himself to death in his villa at Naples because he had an incurable tumor. He was 75 years old when he died. The scholar Asconius Labeo is mentioned by Tacitus in *Annals* 13.10.1.

34 Syme (1968b), pp. 82–84 (= RP 2, pp. 669–671; (1979) p. 289 (= RP vol. 3, pp. 1159–1160).

35 93 CE was also the year of the deaths of three of "the Seven." On the violence of that period, see Suetonius, *Domitian* 10, and Dio (Epitome) 67.11.6.

36 *PIR*¹ S 397

37 Syme (1968b), p. 83 (= RP 2, p. 670).

38 He is also the addressee of *Letters* 6.29 and 9.13, and is mentioned in *Letter* 6.11.1.

39 *CIL* 3.7539. Syme (1968b), pp. 88–90 (= RP 2, pp. 675–677); (1979a), pp. 290–291 (= RP 3, pp.1161–1162). Lower Moesia corresponded approximately to the areas of modern Bulgaria and Romania along the Danube.

40 Birley (2000) p. 89, suggests that Sertorius Severus (Pliny's co-heir) may be the father or uncle of Ummidius Quadratus. See Syme (1979a), p. 292 (= RP 3, p. 1163); (1982b) p. 407 (= RP 5, p. 170); (1985c) p. 197 (= RP 5, p. 646).

41 *CIL* 6.32374.

42 Syme (1968b), p. 91 (= RP 2, p. 678).

43 Gaius Cassius Longinus was a famous scholar of jurisprudence. He was suffect consul in 30 CE and governor of Syria from 49 to 51. He was exiled by Nero in 65, but returned to Rome in 69.

44 Note that Pliny, when expressing his affection, uses the *cognomen* Quadratus (not the *nomen* Ummidius). He reports, in *Letters* 4.17.8 and 9, that Corellius Rufus similarly referred to him as Secundus (rather than Plinius), and, in *Letter* 3.16.6, that Arria E addressed her husband as Paetus.

45 In *Letter* 6.26, written about the same time as *Letter* 7.24, we learn that Fuscus Salinator was betrothed to the daughter of Julius Servianus. See Chapter 3, notes 182 and 183, and Chapter 4, note 59.

46 We might compare the younger Seneca's comment about his mother, Helvia, that she had converted her stepmother into a "mother" by her own exceptional obedience and *pietas* (*Consolatio Ad Helviam* 2.4).

47 "in the home": Latin *in contubernio* (*Letter* 7.24.3). Pliny uses the word *contubernium* also to describe the living arrangement of Corellia Hispulla and her son (*Letter* 3.3.3) and of Calpurnia Hispulla and her niece, Calpurnia (Pliny's wife: *Letter* 4.19.6). Although the word means in origin "sharing a tent (physical space)," as in the military, it came to mean also "sharing experiences," "sharing life." In the context of these letters of Pliny, *contubernium* imparts an image of a close family unit. See Chapter 4, note 147, on the related term, *contubernalis*.

48 Beacham (1999) pp. 141–146; Jory (1981) pp. 147–161.

49 Juvenal 6.60–81. Curiously Juvenal writes that a woman named Hispulla found pleasure in a tragic actor (*Satire* 6.74 and 75). We are not able to connect this Hispulla with any of the three Hispullas in Pliny: Hispulla, the wife of Corellius Rufus, Corellia Hispulla, his daughter, or Calpurnia Hispulla, Pliny's aunt-in-law

50 Galen, *De Praecognitione* (On Prognosis) 6.2–10 (631–633).

51 Dio 57.21.3. Slater (1994) pp. 122–128; Sick (1999) pp. 331–334.

52 *Digest* 23.2.42.1 (Modestinus) and 23.2.44. preface and 1 (Paulus).

53 Suetonius, *Domitian* 3.

54 Tacitus, *Annals* 1.77.

55 Tacitus, *Annals* 4.14; Suetonius, *Tiberius* 37.2.

56 Dio 59.2.5.

57 Suetonius, *Domitian* 7.1.

58 Pliny, *Panegyricus* 46.1–5: also 54.1–2.

59 Dio (Epitome) 68.10.2.

60 See *Letters* 1.15.2, 3.1.9, 9.17.3, and 9.36.4.

61 Guillemin (1929) p. 36, comments that Ummidia Quadratilla's involvement with pantomimists went beyond the bounds of decency. She is perhaps insinuating that the elite grandmother had sexual liaisons with her pantomimists, but there is no evidence for this.

62 Of course, the boar hunt which Pliny describes in *Letter* 1.6 did not require much exertion on his part.

63 Farney (2007) pp. 225–228.

64 Tacitus, *Annals* 3.55. Cf. *Annals* 16.5: People who came to Rome from elsewhere in Italy retained the traditional moral rigor and therefore did not enjoy the coarse public entertainments of Nero's reign.

65 Dio 56.3.3.

66 Sick (1999).

67 *CIL* 4.3891. *CIL* 4.2155 seems to mention a fan club: Actiani Anicetiani. Sick (1999) cites numerous other inscriptional records of the single name either Actius or Ancietus; these may be different people. See also Franklin (1987).

68 *CIL* 10.1946 = *ILS* 5183.

69 See Chapter 4, note 191.

70 *AE* 1985, 189.

71 In *Letter* 7.11.4, Pliny mentions entertainments that were produced during his praetorship.

72 Plutarch, *Cato the Elder* 21.7.

73 Elder Pliny, *Natural History* 7.39 (128).

74 *Digest* 38, Title 1, is devoted to this topic.

75 Sick (1999) p. 331. For Trimalchio, see Petronius, *Satyricon* 53.2; also Chapter 3, note 12.

76 Sick (1999) pp. 342 and 343.

77 Syme (1968b), p. 99 (= RP 2, p. 686); (1979), p. 308 (= RP 3, p. 1177).

78 On the marriage: *Scriptores Historiae Augustae: Marcus Aurelius*, 1.3 and 2.6, and *Didius Julianus* 1.3.

On Domitia Lucilla Maior: Raepsaet-Charlier (1987) p. 289, #328. On Domitia Lucilla Minor, Raepsaet-Charlier (1987) p. 290, #329.

79 *Scriptores Historiae Augustae: Hadrian* 15.7.
80 On the marriage of Pedanius Fuscus and Julius Servianus's daughter, see *Letter* 6.26 and Chapter 3.
81 *Contubernium*: see note 47.
82 Raepsaet-Charlier (1987) p. 507, #626; Syme (1968a) p. 144 (= RP 2, p. 709). On Lusitania, see note 18.
83 Raepsaet-Charlier (1987) p. 508, #627. *CIL* 11.1735.
84 Suetonius is addressed also in *Letters* 3.8, 5.10, and 9.34. He is mentioned in *Letters* 1.24 and 10.94 and 95.
85 In this letter, the Centumviral Court is called the Four Courts; the Centumviral Court was divided into four panels of judges. See Chapter 4, note 185.
86 On the terms *adulescens* and *adulescentulus*, see Chapter 4, note 88.
87 Sherwin-White (1966) p. 128, believes that the mother-in-law of *Letter* 1.18 is not Pompeia Celerina, but rather the mother of Pliny's first wife.
88 Aulus Gellius 12.1.
89 Pliny's sumptuous villa at Tifernum (also known as Tifernum Tiberinum) is described in loving detail in *Letter* 5.6. Another of his villas, at Laurentum, on the coast south-west of Rome, is described in *Letter* 2.17.
90 Cicero, *Pro Sestio* 3 (6).
91 See *Letters* 3.19.7, 5.19, 8.1, and 8.16, but also 1.21, and 3.14 where Pliny expresses no sympathy for slaves who attacked a very cruel master.
92 Sherwin-White (1966) p. 257. The estate which Pliny gave to his nurse was about 50 acres (*Letter* 6.3). See Chapter 4, note 30.
93 The duties of heirs are discussed in Chapter 4, in the section on Pomponia Galla. See also Chapter 6, note 110.
94 *Adfinis* is the word which Pliny uses in *Letter* 7.19.1 to define the relationship between Fannia and the Vestal Virgin, Junia. In *Letter* 2.4.2, he uses the word *adfinitas* to describe his relationship to a woman named Calvina (see Chapter 6).

6 Daughters and sisters

1 Corbier (2001) p. 54, maintains that the significant gesture was not the lifting up of the neonatal, but the giving of instructions to feed it.
2 Elder Seneca, *Controversiae* 10.4.21 enumerates causes of death of exposed infants. See Harris (1994) and Corbier (2001). The very foundation myth of Rome incorporates a story of exposure. The new-born Romulus and Remus were exposed by their evil great-uncle. However, rather than being killed and eaten by a wolf, they were rescued and fed by a wolf. Perhaps some people who exposed their infants hoped that their infants would enjoy a similar miraculous fate.
3 On strangulation and drowning of infants: Philo, *On Special Laws* 3.110–19; also Seneca the Younger, *De Ira* 1.15.2.
4 Sherwin-White (1966) pp. 650–655.
5 Cicero, *De Legibus* 3.8.19; Seneca the Younger, *De Ira* 1.15.2.
6 Plutarch, *De amore prolis* ("About Love for One's Offspring") 5 (= *Moralia* 497 E).
7 Golden (1988) p. 159, comments that "exposure of newborns could coexist with, and even be caused by, care for other children."
8 Musonius Rufus XV (Lutz (1947) pp. 96–101). On Musonius Rufus, see Chapter 2, note 144.
9 J. M. Riddle (1992).
10 Writing about the ancient Greek world, Golden (1981) p. 321 contends that, in classical Athens, 10% or more of female infants were exposed. He cites a fragment of the

Greek comic poet, Poseidippos: "Everyone, even if he happens to be a beggar, raises a son, but even if he is rich exposes a daughter."

11 Dionysius of Halicarnassus, *Roman Antiquities* 2.15.2.

12 Harris (1994) p. 5.

13 However, as noted earlier, in the imperial period there developed a tendency among elite families to give children the name of their mother's family as well as their father's.

14 However, the release of family estate was not necessarily permanent. In the case of a divorce, a woman's birth family would ask her former husband to return a substantial part of the dowry. If a man died intestate, his estate was divided in equal shares among his sons and daughters. However, most men, at least of the property-owning class, made wills, and frequently they left a larger amount of their estates to their sons than their daughters. The amount spent on a daughter's dowry might be considered her part of the estate. In addition, the sons might be designated as heirs (with the attendant responsibilities of heirship; see Chapter 5, note 93), while a daughter might receive only a bequest.

15 *Oxyrhynchus Papyri* 744 = *Select Papyri* 105.

16 Ovid, *Metamorphoses* 9.669–79.

17 Apuleius, *Metamorphoses* 10.23

18 Pliny, *Letters* 2.7.5 and 4.15.3 (in which Pliny relates that Asinius Rufus "fulfilled the obligation of the best of citizens because he was very willing to make use of the fertility of his wife, in an era in which the rewards of childlessness make even one child seem to many to be burdensome").

19 *Alimenta*: the Latin verb *alere* means "to nourish." Garnsey (1968); Duncan-Jones (1964) pp. 123–146, and (1974), pp. 291–310.

20 See also Dio (Epitome) 68.5.4.

21 Trajan and his successors promoted an image of the emperor, who held the title of *Pater Patriae* ("Father of the Fatherland"), as the *paterfamilias* of the state, a benevolent father whose primary concern was the welfare of his subjects, his "children." Pliny, *Panegyricus* 21.4: "You live with your citizens as a father with his children." On the use of coins and art work to publicize and celebrate this ideology, see Rawson (2001).

22 *CIL* 5.5262; *Letters* 1.8.10–11, and 7.18.2.

23 *CIL* 8.1641 = *ILS* 6818.

24 *Scriptores Historiae Augustae: Antoninus Pius* 8.1. Marcus Aurelius did the same upon death of his wife: *Scriptores Historiae Augustae: Marcus Aurelius* 26.6.

25 Garnsey (1991) pp. 49–51, warns against the pervasive assumption that all pre-modern societies shared callous attitudes toward children.

26 Hallett (1984) pp. 62–149.

27 *CIL* 4.294.

28 Plutarch, *Consolatio ad uxorem* 2 (= *Moralia* 608 C).

29 *CIL* 12.7113.

30 *CIL* 6.19159 = *ILS* 8005. See also *CIL* 6.8517 = *ILS* 1660.

31 *CIL* 3.2875.

32 *Fragmenta Vaticana* (Ulpian) 321 (= *Fontes Iuris Romani Antejustiniani* 2.536): Mourning for children over ten years of age should last a year (the same allowance as for parents). Mourning for children less than ten, but more than three years, should be limited to one month for every year lived. For children under three years, there should be no formal mourning, but only discreet mourning. For children under a year, there should be neither formal nor discreet mourning.

33 Cicero, *In Verrem* 2.1.112.

34 Treggiari (2007) p. 14, uses the terms "forename" for *praenomen*, and "clan name" for *nomen gentile*.

35 For example, *Epistulae ad Atticum* 1.5.8.

36 For example, *Epistulae ad Atticum* 5.19.2; also 7.2.4.

37 Treggiari (2007) p. 27, discusses the debate about the year of Tullia's birth. Scholars put her birth variously between 79 and 75 BCE.

38 Cicero, *Epistulae ad Atticum* 1.3.3.
39 Seneca the Younger, *Letter* 94.15.
40 On Piso, see Treggiari, (2007) p. 42.
41 Cicero, *Brutus* 272 (which was written in 46 BCE).
42 Cicero, *Epistulae ad Atticum* 1.18.
43 Treggiari (2007) pp. 52 and 53.
44 Cicero, *Epistulae ad Fratrem* 1.3.3.
45 Cicero, *Epistulae ad Familiares* 4.6.2.
46 Cicero, *Epistulae ad Atticum* 12.14 and 15. Also *Epistulae ad Familiares* 4.6. And Plutarch, *Cicero* 41.
47 *Letters* 1.9, 4.15, 6.6, and perhaps 7.12.
48 Sherwin-White (1966) p. 291. Syme (1991d).
49 Plutarch, *De Tranquillitate Animi* 1 (= *Moralia* 464 E).
50 Plutarch, *De Cohibenda Ira* ("On the Control of Anger") 2 (= *Moralia* 453 D).
51 On Musonius Rufus, see Chapter 2, note 144.
52 The word is used of Fundanus also in *Letter* 4.15.9, where it surely means "wise," not specifically "philosopher." See Griffin (2007) 477 on the definition.
53 The father of Asinius Bassus was Asinius Rufus (for whom see note 18).
54 Sherwin-White (1966) p. 355, speculates that Julius Naso of *Letter* 6.6 is the brother of Julius Avitus whose death on a sea voyage is reported in *Letter* 5.21; see Chapter 4. On Pliny's career and the disadvantages of running for office without a father, see Chapter 4.
55 Syme (1991d) pp. 608 and 609.
56 Plutarch, *De Cohibenda Ira* 6 (= *Moralia* 455 F).
57 *CIL* 6.16631 = *ILS* 1030.
58 *CIL* 6.16632.
59 Cf. *Letter* 1.14, where Pliny does not disclose the name of Arulenus Rusticus' daughter, for whom he is recommending a husband; see Chapter 2. Perhaps it was considered a breach of etiquette to disclose the name of a girl who was not yet married.
60 The numbers appear, of course, in Roman numerals: annos XII, menses XI, dies VII. It is interesting – but not uncommon – that the family kept such close track of the extent of her life. This recording of the life span down to the day may suggest that girls who were accepted into the family were cherished. Compare the inscription to Hateria Superba earlier in the chapter text.
61 Bodel (1995). He observes that the notion of "completing" a stage of life occurs frequently in Latin epitaphs.
62 Similarly *Letter* 7.19, which reports Fannia's illness, begins with "It grieves me – Fannia's ill health." Again Pliny brings to the forefront his own sense of bereavement.
63 Carlon (2009) p. 150.
64 Pliny expresses personal distress in other letters about deaths of people he knew. In 8.23.1, for example, reporting the death of the young man, Junius Avitus (who left behind a young bride, a new-born daughter, and an aging mother), he announces: "Grief has banished, driven off, and snatched away all work projects, concerns, and leisure activities." In this case, however, Pliny knew well the deceased, who was a protégé. It is unlikely that he knew the 13-year-old daughter of Fundanus well.
65 Cicero, *Epistulae ad Atticum* 1.12.4.
66 Cicero, *Epistulae ad Atticum* 5.19.2. However, the word *amabilis* is not restricted in Latin authors to characterizing women. It is used, for example, of Cicero's son in *Epistulae ad Familiares* 12.16.1.
67 Plutarch, *Consolatio ad uxorem* 2 (= *Moralia* 608 D).
68 Also described as possessing *gravitas* and *prudentia* was Publius Acilius, the uncle of the prospective bridegroom, Minicius Acilianus (*Letter* 1.14.6). Junius Mauricus, uncle of the prospective bride, was described in *Letter* 1.5.16 as being serious (*gravis*) and wise (*prudens*).

69 The phrase, a wife of singular example, is used also in *Letter* 3.1.5 in reference to Cottia. On Cottia and on Macrinus' wife, see Chapter 3.

70 Hoffer (1999) p. 184, discusses "the trope of the union of contrasting ages," and states in note 18 that Pliny uses the full version of the trope for Fundanus' daughter who "united elder, matron, and maiden." Cf. *Letter* 6.26.1, in which Fuscus Salinator (recently betrothed to the daughter of Julius Servianus) is described as possessing the virtues of a boy, a young man, and an old man.

71 Pedagogue: see Chapter 4, note 36.

72 The word "resolve" (*constantia*) is used also of Fannia in *Letter* 7.19.4, but in the context of her loyalty to her husband. On Pliny's attribution of virtues admired by Stoics, see André (1975) pp. 237–238.

73 Corellius Rufus faced his physical ailment with strength of mind (*Letter* 1.12.5). Titius Aristo bore his illness with patience (*Letter* 1.22.7).

74 Quintilian, *Institutio Oratoria*, 6. Preface.11

75 Hemelrijk (1999) p. 72.

76 The Latin word, *novissima*, can mean either "last/final" or "latest/most recent."

77 Hence Bodel's argument (see note 61) that, in writing that Minicia had not completed her fourteenth year, Pliny was informing his reader not of her exact age, but of the fact that she had not yet entered adulthood. In Roman law, a girl was judged to have entered puberty once she had completed 12 years: *Codex Justiniani* 5.60.3. However, readiness for marriage and child-bearing seems to have been considered 13 or 14 years.

78 Carlon (2009) p. 149, compares the styles of *Letters* 5.16 and 8.23. Both letters were addressed to the otherwise unknown Aefulanus Marcellinus.

79 Plutarch, *Consolatio ad uxorem* 9 (= *Moralia* 611C).

80 *CIL* 9.1817.

81 *CIL* 3.2875.

82 Since Pliny overheard the conversation, perhaps he had gone to Fundanus' home to console him during the nine days of home seclusion following the daughter's death; see Chapter 2, note 169, on Pliny's seclusion after his second wife's death. On the appropriate length of the mourning period for children, see note 32.

83 Pliny is referring to the advice of the Stoics and other philosophies to bear the death of a loved one calmly and to grieve with emotional restraint. Consider the harsh approach of the Stoic, Seneca the Younger, in *Letter* 99, about the immoderate grief of a friend who had lost a son. However, Griffin (2007) p. 464 points out that Seneca was primarily disturbed that the friend was deliberately prolonging his grief. Plutarch, in his consolation to his wife (*Consolatio ad uxorem*), recommends restraint.

84 On Pliny's recommendation of tolerance and indulgence of other's weaknesses, see *Letter* 8.22.3, where he cites Thrasea Paetus as saying: "He who hates faults, hates mankind." See Chapter 2, note 18.

85 Cicero, *Epistulae ad Fratrem* 1.3.3.

86 *Ostentatio doloris*: This same phrase appears in *Letter* 99.16 of Seneca the Younger, in which he counsels a friend against immoderate grief.

87 On the importance of grandchildren, see *Letters* 1.14.2, 6.26.3, and 8.10.1.

88 On the education of women, see Chapter 3.

89 Quintilian, *Institutio Oratoria*, 6. Preface. 11.

90 In Letter 1.14.3, Pliny refers to both himself and Minicius Acilianus with the word *iuvenis*; they were then both in their mid-30s.

91 On dowries, see Gardner (1986) pp. 97–116, Saller (1994) pp. 204–224, Treggiari (1991) pp. 323–364.

92 *In manu*: see Chapter 3, note 62.

93 In earlier periods of Roman history, when most wives were *in manu*, the dowry may have been considered a daughter's share of her birth family's property – that is, her patrimony. However, it was settled on her before the death of her natal *paterfamilias*. Once she wed, she moved formally into the agnate family of her husband, becoming

the daughter of her husband's *paterfamilias* or, if he were dead, the "daughter" of her husband. She would not expect a further inheritance from her natal *paterfamilias*.

94 There is some scholarly debate about whether the income from the dowry was intended only to cover expenditures on the wife (Saller 1994, p. 210), or to contribute to general expenses of running the household and maintaining children (Gardner 1986, p. 97).

95 Dixon (1986) p. 105.

96 Polybius 31.27.5.

97 Cicero *Epistulae ad Atticum* 11.2.2, 11.23.3, 11.25.3 and *Epistulae ad Familiares* 14.13.

98 Dixon (1986) pp. 102–111; Treggiari (1991) pp. 347 and 353.

99 Plutarch, *Cicero* 8.3.

100 Treggiari (1991) p. 345. Also Saller (1994) pp. 214–215.

101 Tacitus, *Annals* 2.86. On the Vestal Virgins, see Chapter 7.

102 Plautus, *Aulularia* 534–535.

103 Juvenal 6.136–140.

104 Cicero, *Pro Scauro* 8.

105 Treggiari (1991) p. 347, citing Elder, Pliny, *Natural History* 16.60.141.

106 *CIL* 6.1527, left hand column (Column I), line 46.

107 *CIL* 14.2298 = *ILS* 1949.

108 Cicero, *De Officiis* 2.55.

109 Her father's identity is unknown. Syme (1985a), p. 351 (= RP 5, p. 468 and n. 155), speculates that his name was Junius (*nomen*) Calvinus (*cognomen*). If this were correct, Calvina's full name would be Junia Calvina.

110 As noted in Chapter 4, in the section on Pomponia Galla, an heir, in contrast to a recipient of a bequest, was responsible for settling the estate of the deceased, which included the payment of debts, and for maintaining the family shrine.

111 Gaius, *Institutes* 2. 158–73; Ulpian, *Rules* 22.27 and 28.

112 Carlon (2009) p. 124, note 32.

113 Quintilian, *Institutio Oratoria* 6, Preface. Quintilian had been Pliny's teacher: *Letters* 2.14.9 and 6.6.3

114 Quintilian, *Institutio Oratoria* 3.1.21; Martial 5.56.6.

115 *CIL* 6.9785 = *ILS* 7779.

116 In *Letter* 6.25.3, probably written about the same time as *Letter* 6.32, Pliny relates that he had given a man, just appointed centurion, 40,000 sesterces to outfit himself appropriately.

117 In *Letter* 6.3.2, Pliny describes his gift of a farm, once valued at 100,000 sesterces, to his nurse as *munusculum* (the diminutive of *munus*, "gift").

118 Treggiari (1991), p. 342 (gift to the bride); Saller (1994), p. 212, note 26 (dowry).

119 Domitius Afer is mentioned by Pliny in *Letter* 2.14.10 as a teacher of the well-known rhetorician Quintilian, who was, in turn, one of Pliny's instructors.

120 In *Letter* 5.5.2, Pliny recounts that Gaius Fannius (mentioned in Chapter 2 as perhaps related to Fannia) died before he had changed his will. Thus he omitted some people whom he liked very much, and included some toward whom he was, at the time of his death, ill-disposed.

121 Martial 1.36 and 5.28.3.

122 Sherwin-White (1966) p. 470. Also de Zulueta (1935) pp. 19–32.

123 Pliny does not provide her name, but she appears as Domitia Lucilla, daughter of Gnaeus, in *CIL* 15.1010 = *ILS* 8652, and as Domitia in "The So-called Will of 'Dasumius'," which is now widely regarded as the Will of Gnaeus Domitius Tullus. See Chapter 3.

124 *CIL* 15.1010, 1046, 1048, 1050 = *ILS* 8652 and 8653; *CIL* 15.171 = *ILS* 8654; *CIL* 15.277 = *ILS* 8655. The Domitius family had been in the brick and pottery business for several generations, supplying materials for the construction of buildings in Rome and elsewhere. Bricks with their stamp have been discovered, for example, at the Colosseum, Market of Trajan, and Pantheon: *CIL* 15.979–83. One of the factories

has been discovered at Mugnano in Teverina, about 50 miles north of Rome: *CIL* 11.3042. See Gasperoni (2003) and Setälä (1977), pp. 34–37 and 107–109.

125   *Scriptores Historiae Augustae: Marcus Aurelius* 1.3. See Syme (1984b), p. 187, on this marriage.

126   Van den Hout (1999) p. 216, on the birth date of Domitia Lucilla Y.

127   Syme (1968b) p. 95 (= RP 2, p. 682 and 683), and (1979) pp. 299 and 305 (= RP 3, pp. 1168 and 1174). Birley (1987) pp. 33 and 245 and genealogy chart, p. 237. See also Chapter 3, note 169.

128   Birley (1987) p. 31.

129   *Scriptores Historiae Augustae: Marcus Aurelius* 1.4 and 9.

130   Marcus Aurelius, *Meditations* 1.3.

131   Fronto's loss of five children is noted in Chapter 5.

132   Hemelrijk (1999) pp. 199–200, and p. 269, n.64.

133   The efforts of the mother of Voconius Romanus to have him admitted to the Senate are discussed in Chapter 4.

134   *Digest* 5.2.4 (Gaius).

135   *Codex Justinianus* 3.28.22 pr.

136   Fannia and Helvidius II serve as an example of a good relationship between a stepmother and stepson.

137   We may recall Seneca's statement, cited in Chapter 4, that "even a good stepmother is a great burden" and his recollection that his mother, Helvia, had had a good relationship with her stepmother because she had displayed exceptional obedience. The credit belonged to the daughter. But Seneca is biased.

138   Voconius Romanus was the addressee of the *Letter* 6.33, about Attia Viriola and the stepmother who tried to deprive her of her inheritance. Perhaps Pliny intended the reader to see a contrast between Voconius Romanus' experience with a benevolent stepfather and Attia Viriola's experiences with a stepmother.

139   The issue of the number of Pliny's wives is addressed in Chapter 3.

140   Raepsaet-Charlier (1987) p. 670, #869. *CIL* 11.1735.

141   See *Letter* 7.19.8, discussed in Chapter 2.

142   Catilius Severus was the maternal *proavus* of Marcus Aurelius; see earlier in the chapter text.

143   His wife is discussed in Chapter 3.

144   De Blois (2001) maintains that Pliny emphasizes friendship in his letters in order not only to highlight his own good character, but also to publicize that Trajan was fostering an era of co-operation and harmony.

145   Sherwin-White (1966) p.716. Both *equestris* and *equitata* can mean "of cavalry."
      In keeping with the Roman custom of assigning auxiliary military units to posts far removed from the provinces in which they were recruited, the *cohors prima Hispanorum* was recruited in Spain, but stationed in Britain, and the *cohors prima Brittonum* was recruited in Britain, but stationed in Pannonia (for which, see Chapter 3, note 316).

146   Holder (1980) pp. 86–88.

147   A centurion was the commanding officer of the smallest unit of the Roman army, a "century" (roughly 100 men). Gallitta, who is mentioned in Chapter 3, was accused of adultery with a centurion.

148   Phang (2001) pp. 13–21, 53–58.

149   Wolff (1974) p. 509.

150   On marriages between citizens and non-citizens, see Chapter 3.

151   For example, she is identified as "Julia" in *CIL* 6.941. Ancient literary sources about Julia are: Suetonius, *Titus* 4.2 and 5.2, and *Domitian* 17.3 and 22; Philostratus, *The Life of Apollonius* 7.7; Dio Cassius (Epitome) 67.3; Juvenal 2. 29–33; Martial 9.1.7. The epigraphical sources are listed in Raepsaet-Charlier (1987) p. 323, #371. A good discussion of the sources is available in Vinson (1989) pp. 431–450, and Jones (1992) pp. 38–46.

152 Suetonius, *Titus* 5.2, records that Titus captured Jerusalem on the anniversary of his daughter's birthday. The month of the capture has been determined to have been September.

153 Suetonius, *Titus* 4.2. Raepsaet-Charlier (1987) p. 324, and Jones (1984) p. 19, and (1992), p. 38, argue for the first wife as mother. See also Castritius (1969) pp. 492–494.

154 Marcia Furnilla was the niece of (Quintus Marcius) Barea Soranus, a man of consular rank and possibly a Stoic sympathizer, who was tried and executed for treason at the same time as Thrasea Paetus (Chapter 2): Tacitus, *Annals* 16.30–32, *Histories* 4.7; Dio (Epitome) 62.26.

155 Philostratus, *The Life of Apollonius* 7.7, states that Titus had more than one daughter.

156 Suetonius, *Domitian* 17.3, provides the name of the nurse.

157 Suetonius, *Domitian* 3.1, records the birth of a son. His death is implied in Martial 4.3.

158 Tacitus, *Annals* 12.7.2; Suetonius, *Claudius* 26.3. Such a decree was apparently passed, but applied only to nieces who were the daughters of brothers. It remained illegal to marry the daughter of a sister: Gaius, *Institutes* 1.62.

159 Suetonius, *Domitian* 22. Levick (2002) offers a creative biography of Domitia and an interpretation of events during her life.

160 Philostratus, *The Life of Apollonius* 7.7, provides name Titus Sabinus. Raepsaet-Charlier (1987) Stemma XII, speculates that Arrecina Clementia, sister of Arrecina Tertulla, was mother of Sabinus.

161 The honorific title for Julia is recorded in *CIL* 6.2059. The title "Augusta" was first bestowed on Livia by her husband Augustus as part of his will.

162 Suetonius, *Domitian* 10.4.

163 See Jones (1984) p. 19, on the sources for dating Flavia Julia's death between 87 and 90 CE. Vinson (1989) p. 436, speculates that the year was 89.
Sources for her deification include *CIL* 3.13524 and Martial 9.1.7. Deification: a deceased emperor or deceased member of his family could be nominated by the Senate to be elevated to the stature of a deity and henceforth to receive public divine honors.

164 See Chapter 5, note 53.

165 Philostratus, *The Life of Apollonius* 7.7; Suetonius, *Domitian* 22; Juvenal 2.29–33; Dio (Epitome) 67.3.

166 Vinson (1989) pp. 431–450; Jones (1992) pp. 33–40.

167 Juvenal 2. 29–31.

168 Jones (1992) p. 39; Martial 6.3.

169 Suetonius, *Domitian* 10.4. In this same passage, Suetonius relates that Domitian ordered the execution of Flavia Julia's husband.
On the death of Helvdius II in 93 CE, along with Arulenus Rusticus and Herennius Senecio, see Chapter 2.

170 Suetonius, *Domitian* 17.3. It is noteworthy that the nurse owned property. Perhaps she had been given it by Domitian, even as Pliny gave his nurse a farm (*Letter* 6.3). On the loyalty of nurses, compare the story related in Chapter 4, note 24 that, when Nero received the devastating news of Galba's revolt in 68 CE, his nurse was at his side, trying to console him when he had been abandoned by his "friends." After his death, two of his nurses and his mistress dutifully laid his ashes to rest: Suetonius, *Nero* 42 and 50.

171 Hallett (1984) pp. 150–210.

172 Plautus, *Aulularia* 120–128.

173 Musonius Rusus, XV (Lutz 1947, pp. 100–101). On Musonius Rufus, see Chapter 2, note 144. In the Greek text, the word *adelphoi* is used, which may mean "brothers" or "siblings" (that is, both brothers and sisters).

174 Festus, *De Significatione Verborum*, on *amita* (Lindsay 2009, p. 13).

175 Festus claimed that the word *matertera* meant "another mother (*mater*)" (Lindsay 2009, p. 121), while the word *amita* was derived from the verb *amare*, "to love" (Lindsay 2009, p. 13).

176 *CIL* 5, Supplementa Italica, #745. Sherwin-White (1966) p. 732.

177 On Plotina, see Chapter 3.
178 Her husband was Gaius Salonius Matidius Patruinus. The couple had a daughter, named Salonia Matidia.
179 Both Trajan's wife, Pompeia Plotina, and sister, Ulpia Marciana, were granted the honorific title Augusta. See note 161 on Flavia Julia.

7 Women outside the family

1 See Chapter 1 on Augustus' identification of himself as *Pater Patriae*, "Father of the Fatherland." On Trajan's promotion of himself as *paterfamilias* of the state, see Chapter 6, note 21.
2 The Latin word *aedes* means "building," rather than specifically "temple." Aulus Gellius 14.7.7, cites Varro as stating that the *aedes Vestae*, "building of Vesta," had not been consecrated as a temple. It is, however, commonly referred to in English as the Temple of Vesta.
3 Ovid, *Fasti* 6.291–98. The temple was, however, the repository of the Palladium, a statue of the goddess Pallas which was believed to have been brought to Italy by Aeneas when he sailed from Troy: Dionysius of Halicarnassus 1.69.2 and 2.66. 5 and 6; Plutarch, *Camillus* 20.5.
4 Ancient sources for the Vestal Virgins include Plutarch, *Numa* 9–11; Dionysius of Halicarnassus 2.67–69; Aulus Gellius 1.12.
   Modern scholarship includes: Guizzi (1968); Gardner (1986) pp. 22–26; Hallett (1984) pp. 83–89; Beard (1980) and (1995); Parker (2004); Staples (1998); Wildfang (2006); Cornell (1981); Takács (2008).
5 In ancient Rome, there existed a group or "college" (*collegium*) of priests. The Latin word for "priest" is *pontifex*. Hence the *Collegium Pontificum*. The head of this College, and of the other religious groups, including the Vestal Virgins, was the *Pontifex Maximus*, the "Highest (or: Greatest) Priest." In the republican period, the Pontifex Maximus was a political figure who was elected by a popular assembly to a lifelong term. Julius Caesar, for example, became Pontifex Maximus in 63 BCE, and subsequently also was elected consul for 59 BCE and led his army into Gaul in 58 BCE. From the time of Augustus on, the emperor received the appointment as Pontifex Maximus. (The title Pontifex Maximus is used today by the Pope.)
6 Dio 55.22.5.
7 Tacitus, *Annals* 2.86.
8 On the size of dowries, see Chapter 6.
9 Gardner (1986) pp. 5–22.
10 In a marriage in which the wife had not entered into the *manus* of her husband (and this was the case for most marriages in Pliny's time), she remained in the *potestas* of her own *paterfamilias*.
11 On the emancipation of Regulus' son, see Chapter 3.
12 Cicero, *Pro Fonteio* 21.46–47. The speech was delivered about 69 BCE. Only parts of it are extant. We do not know if Fonteius was acquitted or convicted.
13 Note that, although their formal ties with their *familia* were severed, Vestal Virgins retained their family names – that is, Fonteia, and, in Pliny's *Letter* 4.11, Cornelia.
14 Staples (1998), p. 143: "It was the Roman state that was a Vestal's sole heir at law." She argues that, as a Vestal Virgin was no longer a member of a particular family, she became a representative of the state – that is, the whole "family" of citizens.
15 Dio 56.10.2. On the Julian legislation and the "three-children privilege," see Chapter 1.
16 Livy 1.20.3.
17 Tacitus, *Annals* 4.16. In his will, Tiberius left legacies to Vestal Virgins: Suetonius, *Tiberius* 76.
18 Plutarch, *Crassus* 1.2.

19 The two other members of the First Triumvirate were Gaius Julius Caesar (assassinated in 44 BCE) and Gnaeus Pompeius Magnus (Pompey). On Pompey, see Chapter 3, note 330.

20 Gardner (1986) pp. 25–26, on the legal status and possible marriage of retired Vestal Virgins.

21 Plutarch, *Numa* 10.2; Dionysius of Halicarnassus 2. 67. 2.

22 However, Wildfang (2006), p. 98, contends that Cicero and his political allies were helped by his wife Terentia's half-sister, the Vestal Virgin, Fabia. See note 45.

23 *CIL* 6.2131. On auxiliary units, see Chapter 6. On similar patronage by Pliny, see *Letters* 1.19 (advancement to equestrian rank), and 3.8 and 4.4 (military tribune).

24 Aulus Gellius, 1.12.14 and 19. The word *amata*, formed from the Latin verb *amare*, "to love," means "beloved." Gellius proposes that the word "Amata" was the name of the first Vestal Virgin. Wildfang (2006), pp. 40 and 41, discusses several other suggested explanations, but accepts that of Gellius, commenting that the formulaic use of the name emphasizes the continuity of the institution.

According to Gellius' report, the Vestal Virgins acted "on behalf of the Roman people." Schultz (2006) pp. 127 and 128, enumerates the duties of the Vestal Virgins and comments that their duties in the public realm were paralleled in private homes by women's roles within household religions.

25 Wildfang (2006), pp. 16–18, sees this role of the Vestal Virgins as their being the protectors of Rome's symbolic grain storehouse.

26 Suetonius, *Julius Caesar* 83.1; Plutarch, *Antony* 58.3; Tacitus, *Annals* 1.8.1.

27 Peace treaties: Appian, *Civil Wars* 5.73; Dio 48.37.1.

28 Tacitus, *Histories* 1.43; Plutarch, *Galba* 27.

29 On the special seating at the gladiatorial games, see Cicero, *Pro Murena* 73.

30 Dio 47.19.4 reports that the Second Triumvirate allowed the Vestal Virgins to have the use of one lictor each because one of them had been insulted when she was returning from a dinner in the evening. However, Plutarch, *Numa*, 1.10.3, attributes to Numa the use of lictors by Vestal Virgins. [The three members of the Second Triumvirate were Gaius Octavianus (who later became known as Augustus), Marcus Aemilius Lepidus (to whom "Turia" unsuccessfully appealed on behalf of her husband: see Chapter 2), and Marcus Antonius, or Mark Antony, (who was married to Octavian's sister, Octavia; see Chapter 4.)]

31 On the Vestal Virgin's lictor as a symbol of power, see Staples (1998) p. 145.

32 On the meaning of *incestum*, see the discussion of Flavia Julia in Chapter 6.

33 Livy 4.44.11. Also: Livy 8.15.7. On the special hairstyle of the Vestal Virgins, see Wildfang (2006), pp. 11–13.

34 Parker (2004) p. 568. Also Staples (1998) pp. 129–130.

35 Schultz (2006) p.141.

36 Livy 2.42.11 (gives the Vestal's name as Oppia); Dionysius of Halicarnassus 8.89.4 and 5 (gives her name as Opimia). Parker (2004) pp. 593–595, provides a list of all the accusations and punishments of the Vestal Virgins over time.

37 Dionysius of Halicarnassus 9.40.3 and 4.

38 Livy 22.57. 2–6; Plutarch, *Fabius*, 18.3.

39 Livy, *Periochae* 63. Plutarch, *Roman Questions* 83. Dio 26.87 and 88.

40 Parker (2004) p. 585.

41 Dionysius of Halicarnassus 2.67.5. If a Vestal Virgin had accidentally allowed the fire to go out, she was punished with a whipping, not death. Dionysius of Halicarnassus 2.67.3.

42 Staples (1998) p. 135.

43 Plutarch, *Numa* 10. 4–7; Dionysius of Halicarnassus 2. 67. 3 and 4.

44 The Greeks and Gauls, however, were buried in Forum Boarium (between the Capitoline and the Tiber River), not at the Colline Gate.

45 Asconius on Cicero, *In toga candida*, 91.19–23. See Cadoux (2005) pp. 162–179. Fabia seems to have continued in her position as a Vestal Virgin after her acquittal. As

mentioned in Chapter 2, in 58 BCE, Terentia took refuge with the Vestal Virgins when Cicero was in exile: *Epistulae ad Familiares* 14.2.2.

46 Suetonius, *Domitian* 8, provides an extensive list of the various actions Domitian took to reduce immorality. Also Statius, *Silvae* 1.1.36.

47 Tacitus, *Histories* 1.2.

48 Sherwin-White (1966) p. 283 on the dates of 83 or 84. Suetonius, *Domitian* 8.3. On "free choice of death," see Chapter 1. Philostratus, *Life of Apollonius* 7.6 reports only that Domitian put to death three Vestal Virgins who had broken their vows.

49 Dio (Epitome) 67.3.3 and 4.

50 The Greek word which Dio uses means "to breathe out," "expire." The priest may have fainted, or perhaps have died.

51 Juvenal, a contemporary of Pliny and Suetonius, makes reference in *Satire* 4.8–10 to a priestess who was punished for *incestum* by being buried alive. He is presumably referring to Cornelia. He names her lover as Crispinus, whose name does not appear in Suetonius or Pliny. Stewart (1994) argues convincingly that in Satire 4, which is ostensibly the story of the presentation to Domitian of a very large fish, Juvenal alludes continually to the trial of Cornelia and thereby mocks Domitian's religious pretensions.

52 Traub (1955).

53 Cornelius Minicianus also received *Letter* 3.9, the account of the extortion trial of Caecilius Classicus and his family; see Chapter 3.

54 On deification, see Chapter 6, note 163.

55 Sherwin-White (1966) p. 283. Traub (1955), p. 213, conjectures that the letter was published about 15 years after the incident.

56 Tacitus, *Annals* 15.22. Raepsaet-Charlier (1987) p. 245, #274 and 275; Pigon (1999).

57 Juvenal 4.144–49, suggests that Domitian regularly summoned councils at his villa. On the references to *incestum* in *Satire* 4, see note 51.

58 Vinson (1989) pp. 431–450, discusses the charges that Domitian did not punish the adultery of his wife. More specifically, he divorced her, as was required by the Julian laws, but then remarried her: Suetonius, *Domitian* 3.1. And yet he removed a Roman equestrian from a list of judges because, after divorcing his wife for adultery, he then remarried her: Suetonius, *Domitian* 8.3. On Domitian's wife's alleged adultery with the actor, Paris, see Suetonius, *Domitian* 3.

59 Vinson (1989) p. 449: "Domitian became the posthumous victim of a smear campaign directed by Trajan and his circle. No aspect of the Domitianic era was overlooked in the attempt to glorify the new regime by condemning the old."

60 On Pliny's use of quotations from Arria and Fannia, see Chapters 1 and 2.

61 Plutarch, *Numa* 10.4–7.

62 Vinson (1989) p. 434.

63 On equestrian rank, see Chapter 4, note 75.

64 See note 51.

65 Pliny, *Letter* 3.11; also *Letters* 1.5.3, 7.19.5, and 7.33.4.

66 The confiscation of the property of people convicted of capital offences is discussed in earlier chapters.

67 Carlon (2009) p. 196: "Pliny arguably creates a work of historical fiction, making innocent and noble a woman firmly condemned by all other sources."

68 On Pliny's assignment in Bithynia-Pontus, see Chapter 3.

69 I Peter 1.1 (New Testament) attests to the spread of Christianity into the Bithynia-Pontus regions. Lucian, *Alexander* 25: "He proclaimed that Pontus was overrun with atheists and Christians."

70 Minicius Felix, *Octavius* 8.4; 9.2, 4–7; 10.2.5; 12.5.

71 On the suppression of Bacchic rites in 186 BCE: Livy 39. 8, 9, 14, 17, 18.

72 Johnson (1988) 417–422.

73 For example, Dio Chrysostom, *Orations* 39 and 43. (Dio Chrysostom is also known, and is referred to by Pliny in *Letters* 10.81 and 82, as Cocceianus Dio; see Chapter 4.)

74 *hetaeriae*: a Greek word. Bithynia-Pontus was in the Greek-speaking area of the Roman Empire.

75 Dio Chrysostom, *Orations* 45. 7 and 8.

76 Consider Gallitta of *Letter* 6.31.4, whose adultery is discussed in Chapter 3. Also Acts 22.25–27: "And as they bound him with thongs, Paul said unto the centurion that stood by, Is it lawful for you to scourge a man that is a Roman, and uncondemned? When the centurion heard that, he went and told the chief captain, saying, Take heed what thou doest: for this man is a Roman. Then the chief captain came, and said unto him, Tell me, art thou a Roman? He said, Yea." Also Acts 16.37; 25.9–12. Paulus, *Sententiae* 5.26.1; Digest 48.6.7 (Ulpian).

77 1 Timothy 3.8–13.

78 Harrill (2006).

79 Harrill (2006) pp. 115–123. The Lares were familiar figures in Roman religion, serving as Guardians of Individual Families (*Lares Familiares*) and Guardians of Neighborhoods or Communities (*Lares Compitales*). Harrill examines Augustus' innovation of uniting all residents of the Roman Empire in the public worship of the Guardian Deities of *his* family (*Lares Augusti*). On Augustus' assumption of the role of *pater patriae*, "father of the fatherland" and his construction of a model of the state as a family writ large and its residents as his children, see Chapters 1 and 3.

80 Harrill (2006) p. 114.

81 DuBois (1991) focuses on the torture of slaves in the Greek legal system which, like the Roman system, assumed that a slave "will lie unless compelled by physical force to speak truly and that when compelled he will speak truly" (p. 68).

82 Tacitus, *Annals* 3.14.

83 Hadrian issued a ruling that, if a slave-owner was murdered in his house, only those slaves who had been near enough to have been aware of the murder should be interrogated under torture: *Scriptores Historiae Augustae: Hadrian* 18.11. However, see note 95 on Hadrian's less sympathetic ruling about punishing slaves.

84 Cicero, *Pro Cluentio* 63. 176 and 177.

85 Cicero, *Pro Milone* 21.57–22.58.

86 Suetonius, *Nero* 16.2, commenting on Nero's punishment of Christians, writes that they were a class of men adhering to a new and nefarious superstition: *superstitio malefica*. At no point in *Letter* 10.96 does Pliny suggest that the Christians in his province were nefarious.

87 Bradley (1984 and 1994); Joshel and Murnaghan (1998); McKeown (2007a); Andreau and Descat (2011).

88 The addressee of *Letter* 3.19 is Gaius Calvisius Rufus, the man whose nephew Pliny recommends for a six-month military tribunate in *Letter* 4.4; see Chapters 4 and 6.

89 Fitzgerald (2000) provides a study of how the ubiquitous presence of slaves in Roman society affected the thoughts and behavior of free persons and produced "attendant ironies of domination" (p. 13). Also Hoffer (1999), p. 47.

90 See the calculations of K. Williams (2006) p. 410, n. 6.

91 Seneca, *Letter* 47.5.

92 Seneca, *Letter* 4.8.

93 The text of the *senatus consultum Silanianum* of 10 CE, dealing with the murder of slave owners, has not survived. However, it was commented on extensively by later jurists – see *Digest* 29.5 – and therefore we have a good idea about its contents. It apparently required the torture and execution of all slaves in a household where a slave was suspected of having murdered the owner. It was probably not a new judicial decision, but rather a codification of a traditional practice. For discussion, see A. Watson (1987) pp. 134–138.

94 Rosivach (2007) p. 224.

95 *Digest* 29.5.1.28 (Ulpian).

96 Tacitus, *Annals*, 14.42–45.
97 On the cost of slaves see Chapter 4, note 29; also Chapter 5, about the costs and training of pantomimists.
98 Gamauf (2007) pp. 148–149.
99 Nothing more is known about Larcius Macedo. He is the only certain instance of a senator having had a father who was a slave. It would be interesting to know how he acquired the enormous amount of money, as well as the political connections, to gain public office. Sherwin-White (1966) p. 247, notes that his son was a consul under Hadrian.
100 McKeown (2007b).
101 McGinn (1991) and Rawson (1974).
102 On *conubium*, the legal capacity to enter into a valid marriage with one another, see Chapter 3. On prohibitions, see Treggiari (1991) pp. 44 and 61–66.
103 Of the asymmetry of concubinage, Treggiari (1991) p. 52, observes that there is no word to describe the male partner of a *concubina*.
104 Suetonius, *Domitian* 22.1.
105 Tacitus, *Histories* 1.72.
106 K. Williams (2006) p. 413.
107 Treggiari (1969), Mouritsen (2011), especially pp. 120–205. (On the meaning of *manus* with reference to wives, see Chapter 3, note 62.)
108 Some owners manumitted slaves to prevent them from being tortured to provide incriminating evidence against their owner. When threatened with the confiscation of his property, Cicero considered manumitting his slaves in order to deprive the state of the income from their sale. (See Chapter 2.) A less generous reason for manumission might be to rid the household of a sick or old slave.
109 *CIL* 3.14206.21 = *ILS* 7479. This young man, Vitalis, was born in the home of his owner and worked in his shop. He was manumitted and adopted by his owner. He died at the age of 16. We do not know if his mother was manumitted when he was.
110 One example of an affectionate relationship between a freedman and his former owner has been mentioned in Chapter 6. *CIL* 14.2298 = *ILS* 1949: Marcus Aurelius Cotta Maximus ordered his freedman, Zosimus, to raise – that is, not expose – the children born to him, and provided for their maintenance. He also provided dowries for Zosimus' daughters and obtained for Zosimus' son the rank of military tribune.
111 *Digest* 38.1.35 (Paulus); *Digest* 38.1.46 (Valens).
112 In *Letter* 7.16.2, Pliny recalls that Calestrius Tiro had been selected for the office of tribune earlier than him because he had a child. See Chapter 3, note 14.
113 *Digest* 29.5.1.22 (Ulpian).
114 Tacitus, *Annals* 13.32.1.
115 In *Letter* 4.4, Pliny requested of Sosius Senecio that he grant a military tribuneship to the son of the sister of Calvisius Rufus. See Chapter 4. Pliny describes Calvisius Rufus as his *contubernalis* (for which term, see Chapter 4, note 147, and Chapter 5, note 47).
116 Carlon (2009) pp. 128–129.
117 Sherwin-White (1966) pp. 567 and 568. Ulpian, *Rules* 1.17.
118 Ulpian, *Rules* 3.2.
119 In the manuscripts, the word Antonia was omitted before the name Hedia. There is little doubt, however, that she, like her fellow slave, Harmeris, assumed the name of her patroness once she was manumitted.
120 Sherwin-White (1966) p. 641, discusses special privileges granted to philosophers, teachers, and doctors by the Flavian emperors.
121 We learn in *Letter* 10.81 that Flavius Archippus had petitioned Pliny, when he was governor of Bithynia-Pontus, to investigate Dio Chrysostom's financial accounts and

his placing of a statue of the emperor in the same building in which the bodies of his wife and son had been buried. (See earlier in this chapter.)

122 See *Letter* 7.6.8–13, which is discussed in Chapter 4. Here a mother whose son had died had brought charges of forging or falsifying his will and of poisoning against his freedmen.

123 Sherwin-White (1966) p. 643.

Bibliography

André, Jean-Marie (1975) "Pensée et Philosophie dans les *Lettres* de Pline le Jeune", *Revue des Etudes Latines* 53: 225–247.

André, Jean-Marie and Marie-Françoise Baslez (1993) *Voyager dans l'Antiquité*, Paris: Fayard.

Andreau, Jean and Raymond Descat (2011) *The Slave in Greece and Rome*, tr. Marion Leopold, Madison: University of Wisconsin Press.

Archer, Léonie, Susan Fischler, and Maria Wyke (eds) (1994) *Women in Ancient Societies: an illusion of the night*, New York: Routledge.

Ash, Rhiannon (2003) " 'Aliud est enim epistulam, aliud historiam … scribere' (Epistles 6.16.22): Pliny the Historian?", *Arethusa* 36: 211–225.

Aubrion, Étienne (1990) "La 'Correspondance' de Pline le Jeune: Problèmes et orientations actuelles de la recherche", *Aufstieg und Niedergang der römischen Welt* II 33.1: 304–374.

Barrett, Anthony (1996) *Agrippina: sex, power, and politics in the early Empire*, New Haven: Yale University Press.

——(2005) "Aulus Caecina Severus and the military woman", *Historia* 54: 301–314.

Bauman, Richard (1974) *Impietas in Principem: a study of treason against the Roman emperor*, Munich: Beck.

——(2000) *Human Rights in Ancient Rome*, London; New York: Routledge.

Beacham, Richard (1999) *Spectacle Entertainments of Early Imperial Rome*, New Haven; London: Yale University Press.

Beard, Mary (1980) "The Sexual Status of Vestal Virgins", *Journal of Roman Studies* 70: 12–27.

——(1995) "Re-reading (Vestal) Virginity", in Richard Hawley and Barbara Levick (eds), *Women in Antiquity: New Assessments*, London; New York: Routledge: 166–177.

Bell Jr., Albert (2002) *All Roads Lead to Murder: a case from the notebooks of Pliny the Younger*, Boone, NC: High Country Publishers.

Birley, Anthony (1987) *Marcus Aurelius: a biography* (2nd edition), New Haven: Yale University Press.

——(2000) *Onomasticon to the Younger Pliny*, Munich; Leipzig: K. G. Saur.

Boatwright, Mary (1991) "The Imperial Women of the Early Second Century A.D.", *American Journal of Philology* 112: 513–540.

Bodel, John (1995) "Minicia Marcella: taken before her time", *American Journal of Philology* 116: 453–460.

Boyd, Barbara Weiden (1987) "*Virtus Effeminata* and Sallust's Sempronia", *Transactions of the American Philological Association* 117: 183–201.

Bradley, Keith (1984) *Slaves and Masters in the Roman Empire: a study in social control*, Bruxelles: Latomus.

——(1986) "Wet-nursing at Rome: a study in social relations", in Beryl Rawson (ed.) *The Family in Ancient Rome: New Perspectives*, London; Sydney: Croom Helm: 201–229.

——(1994) *Slavery and Society at Rome*, Cambridge: Cambridge University Press.

Braginton, Mary (1944) "Exile under the Roman Emperors", *Classical Journal* 39: 391–407.

Braund, David (1989) "Function and Dysfunction: personal patronage in Roman imperialism", in Andrew Wallace-Hadrill (ed.) *Patronage in Ancient Society*, London; New York: Routledge: 137–152.

Braund, Susanna (2002) *Latin Literature*, London; New York: Routledge.

Brunt, P. A. (1990) *Roman Imperial Themes*, Oxford: Clarendon Press; New York: Oxford University Press.

Bütler, Hans-Peter (1967) *Die geistige Welt des jüngeren Plinius. Studien zur Thematik seiner Briefe*, Heidelberg: Carl Winter Universitätsverlag.

Cadoux, T. J. (2005) "Catiline and the Vestal Virgins", *Historia* 54: 162–179.

Cairns, John and Paul du Plessis (eds) (2007) *Beyond Dogmatics: law and society in the Roman world*, Edinburgh: Edinburgh University Press.

Cantarella, Eva (1987) *Pandora's Daughters: the role and status of women in Greek and Roman antiquity*, tr. Maureen Fant, Baltimore: Johns Hopkins University Press.

Carlon, Jacqueline (2009) *Pliny's Women: constructing virtue and creating identity in the Roman world*, Cambridge; New York: Cambridge University Press.

Casson, Lionel (1974) *Travel in the Ancient World*, Baltimore: Johns Hopkins University Press.

Castritius, Helmut (1969) "Zu den Frauen der Flavier", *Historia* 18: 492–502.

Champlin, Edward (1986) "Miscellanea testamentaria", *Zeitschrift für Papyrologie und Epigraphik:* 62: 247–255.

——(1991) *Final Judgments: duty and emotion in Roman wills*, Berkeley: University of California Press.

——(2001) "Pliny's Other Country", in Michael Peachin (ed.) *Aspects of Friendship in the Greco-Roman World, Journal of Roman Archaeology* 43 (supplementary series): 121–128.

Cherry, David (1990) "The Minician Law: marriage and the Roman citizenship", *Phoenix* 44: 244–266.

Chilver, G. E. F. (1979) *A Historical Commentary on Tacitus' Histories I and II*, Oxford: Clarendon Press.

Claassen, Jo-Marie (1999) *Displaced Persons: the literature of exile from Cicero to Boethius*, Madison: University of Wisconsin Press.

Copley, Frank O. (1956) *Exclusus Amator: a study in Latin love poetry*, Madison: American Philological Association.

Corbier, Mireille (1991) "Constructing Kinship in Rome: marriage and divorce, filiation and adoption", in David Kertzer and Richard Saller (eds) *The Family in Italy from Antiquity to the Present*, New Haven: Yale University Press: 127–144.

——(2001) "Child Exposure and Abandonment", in Suzanne Dixon (ed.) *Childhood, Class, and Kin in the Roman World*, London; New York: Routledge: 52–73.

Cornell, T. J. (1981) "Some observations on the 'crimen incesti'", in J. Scheid (ed.) *Le Délit religieux dans la Cité antique*, Rome: Ecole Française de Rome: 27–37.

Crook, J. A. (1955) *Consilium Principis: imperial councils and counsellors from Augustus to Diocletian*, Cambridge: Cambridge University Press.

Damon, Cynthia, and Sarolta Takács (eds) (1999) *The Senatus consultum de Cn. Pisone patre. Text, Translation, Discussion, American Journal of Philology* 120 (special issue): 1–186.

De Blois, Lukas (2001) "The Political Significance of Friendship in the *Letters* of Pliny the Younger", in Michael Peachin (ed.) *Aspects of Friendship in the Greco-Roman World, Journal of Roman Archaeology* 43 (supplementary series): 129–134.

De Pretis, Anna (2003) " 'Insincerity,' 'Facts,' and 'Epistolarity': approaches to Pliny's *Epistles* to Calpurnia", *Arethusa* 36: 127–146.

De Verger, Antonio Ramirez (1998) "Erotic Language in Pliny, *Ep.* VII 5", *Glotta* 74: 114–116.

De Zulueta, Francis (1935) "The New Fragments of Gaius', *Journal of Roman Studies*" 25: 19–32.

Devreker, John (1977) "La continuité dans le Consilium Principis sous les Flaviens", *Ancient Society* 8: 223–243.

Dillon, John (2004) *Musonius Rufus and Education in the Good Life*, Dallas: University Press of America.

Dixon, Suzanne (1986) "Family Finances: Terentia and Tullia", in Beryl Rawson (ed.) *The Family in Ancient Rome: new perspectives*, London: Croom Helm: 93–120.

——(1988) *The Roman Mother*, Norman, OK: University of Oklahoma Press.

——(1992) *The Roman Family*, Baltimore: Johns Hopkins University Press.

——(1993) "The Meaning of Gift and Debt in the Roman Elite", *Echos du Monde Classique* 37 (n.s. 12): 451–464.

——(ed.) (2001a) *Childhood, Class and Kin in the Roman World*, London; New York: Routledge.

——(2001b) *Reading Roman Women: sources, genres, and real life*, London: Duckworth.

——(2007) *Cornelia, Mother of the Gracchi*, London; New York: Routledge.

DuBois, Page (1991) *Torture and Truth*, London; New York: Routledge.

Duncan-Jones, Richard (1964) "The Purpose and Organization of the *Alimenta*", *Papers of the British School at Rome* 32: 123–146.

——(1974) *The Economy of the Roman Empire: Quantative Studies*, Cambridge: Cambridge University Press.

Eck, Werner (1978) "Zum neuen Fragment des sogenannten Testamentum Dasumii", *Zeitschrift für Papyrologie und Epigraphik* 30: 277–295.

Edwards, Catherine (1993) *The Politics of Immorality in Ancient Rome*, Cambridge; New York: Cambridge University Press.

——(2007) *Death in Ancient Rome*, New Haven; London: Yale University Press.

Evans Grubbs, Judith (2002) *Women and Law in the Roman Empire: a sourcebook on marriage, divorce and widowhood*, London; New York: Routledge.

Farney, Gary (2007) *Ethnic Identity and Aristocratic Competition in Republican Rome*, Cambridge; New York: Cambridge University Press.

Fear, A. T. (1996) *Rome and Baetica. Urbanization in Southern Spain, C. 50 BC – AD 150*, Oxford: Clarendon Press.

Fischler, Susan (1994) "Social Stereotypes and Historical Analysis: the case of the imperial women at Rome", in Léonie Archer, Susan Fischler, and Maria Wyke (eds) *Women in Ancient Societies: an illusion of the night*, New York: Routledge: 115–133.

Fitzgerald, William (2000) *Slavery and the Roman Literary Imagination*, Cambridge: Cambridge University Press.

Fora, Maurizio (1992) "Ummidia Quadratilla ed il Restauro del Teatro di Cassino", *Zeitschrift für Papyrologie und Epigraphik* 94: 269–273.

Foubert, Lien (2011) "The Impact of Women's Travels on Military Imagery in the Julio-Claudian Period", in Olivier Hekster and Ted Kaizer (eds) *Frontiers in the Roman World*, Leiden and Boston: Brill: 349–362.

Foucault, Michel (1986) *The Care of the Self*, tr. Robert Hurley, New York: Pantheon Books.

Franklin, James (1987) "Pantomimists at Pompeii: Actius Anicetus and his troupe", *American Journal of Philology* 108: 95–107.

Gallivan, Paul (1981) "The Fasti for A. D. 70–96", *Classical Quarterly* 31: 186–220.

Gamauf, Richard (2007) "'Cum aliter nulla domus tuta esse possit ... ': Fear of Slaves and Roman Law", in Anastasia Serghidou (ed.) *Fear of Slaves – Fear of Enslavement in the Ancient Mediterranean*, Crete: Presses universitaires de Franche-Comté: 145–164.

Gamberini, Federico (1983) *Stylistic Theory and Practice in the Younger Pliny*, Hildesheim; New York: Olms.

Garcia, Carmen Castillo (1982) "El famoso testamento del Cordobes 'Dasumio'", *Actas del I Congreso Andaluz de Estudios Clásicos*: 159–163.

Gardner, Jane (1986) *Women in Roman Law and Society*, London: Croom Helm.

——(1998) *Family and Familia in Roman Law and Life*, Oxford: Clarendon Press.

Garnsey, Peter (1968) "Trajan's Alimenta: Some Problems', *Historia* 17: 367–381.

——(1970) *Social Status and Legal Privilege in the Roman Empire*, Oxford: Clarendon Press.

——(1991) "Child-rearing in Ancient Italy", in David Kertzer and Richard Saller (eds) *The Family in Italy from Antiquity to the Present*, New Haven: Yale University Press: 48–65.

Gasperoni, Tiziano (2003) *Le Fornaci dei Domitii*, Viterbo: Università degli studi della Tuscia.

Gibson, Roy (2003) "Pliny and the Art of (in)Offensive Self-Praise", *Arethusa* 36: 235–254.

Ginsburg, Judith (1993) "*In maiores certamina*: past and present in the *Annals*", in T. J. Luce and A. J. Woodman (eds) *Tacitus and the Tacitean Tradition*, Princeton: Princeton University Press: 88–96.

Golden, Mark (1981) "Demography and the Exposure of Girls at Athens", *Phoenix* 35: 316–331.

——(1988) "Did the ancients care when their children died?", *Greece and Rome* 35: 152–63.

Gowing, Alain (1992) "Lepidus, the Proscriptions and the *Laudatio Turiae*", *Historia* 41: 283–296.

Gray-Fow, Michael (1988) "The Wicked Stepmother in Roman Literature and History: an evaluation", *Latomus* 47: 741–757.

Grete, Sabine (2003) "Marriage and Exile: Cicero's letters to Terentia", *Helios* 30: 127–146.

Griffin, Miriam (1976) *Seneca: A Philosopher in Politics*, Oxford: Clarendon Press.

——(1984) *Nero: the end of a dynasty*, London: Batsford.

——(1986) "Philosophy, Cato, and Roman Suicide", *Greece and Rome* 33: 64–77, 192–202.

——(2003) "*De Beneficiis* and Roman Society", *Journal of Roman Studies* 93: 92–113.

——(2007) "The Younger Pliny's Debt to Moral Philosophy", *Harvard Studies in Classical Philology* 103: 451–481.

Grisé, Yolande (1982) *Le suicide dans la Rome antique*, Paris: Les Belles Lettres.

Guillemin, Anne Marie (1929) *Pline et le vie littéraire de son temps*, Paris: Les Belles Lettres.

Guizzi, Francesco (1968) *Aspetti Giuridici del Sacerdozio Romano: Il Sacerdozio di Vesta*, Napoli: Jovene.

Gunderson, Erik (1997) "Catullus, Pliny, and Love-Letters", *Transactions of the American Philological Association* 127: 201–231.

Hahn, Johannes, and Paul Leunissen (1990) "Statistical Method and Inheritance of the Consulate under the Early Roman Empire", *Phoenix* 44: 60–81.

Haley, Evan (2003) *Baetica Felix: people and prosperity in Southern Spain from Caesar to Septimius Severus*, Austin: University of Texas Press.

Hallett, Judith (1984) *Fathers and Daughters in Roman Society: women and the elite family*, Princeton: Princeton University Press.

——(1990) "Perspectives on Roman Women", in Ronald Mellor (ed.) *From Augustus to Nero: The First Dynasty of Imperial Rome*, East Lansing: Michigan State University Press: 132–144.

Harlow, Mary and Ray Laurence (2002) *Growing Up and Growing Old in Ancient Rome: a life course approach*, London; New York: Routledge.

Harries, Jill (2007) *Law and Crime in the Roman World*, Cambridge; New York: Cambridge University Press.

Harrill, James Albert (2006) "Servile Functionaries or Priestly Leaders? Roman Domestic Religion, Narrative Intertextuality, and Pliny's Reference to Slave Christian *Ministrae*

(Ep. 10,96,8)", *Zeitschrift für die neutestamentliche Wissenschaft und die Kunde der älteren Kirche* 97: 111–130.

Harris, W. V. (1994) "Child-exposure in the Roman Empire", *Journal of Roman Studies* 84: 1–22.

Hawley, Richard and Barbara Levick (eds) (1995) *Women in Antiquity: New Assessments*, London; New York: Routledge.

Hemelrijk, Emily (1999) *Matrona Docta: educated women in the Roman Elite from Cornelia to Julia Domna*, London; New York: Routledge.

——(2004) "Masculinity and Femininity in the *Laudatio Turiae*", *Classical Quarterly* 54: 185–197.

Henderson, John (2002) *Pliny's Statue: the letters, self-portraiture and classical art*, Exeter: University of Exeter Press.

——(2003) "Portrait of the Artist as a Figure of Style: P.L.I.N.Y.'s Letters", *Arethusa* 36: 115–125.

Hershkowitz, Debra (1995) "Pliny the Poet", *Greece and Rome* 42: 168–181.

Hill, Timothy (2004) *Ambitiosa Mors: suicide and the self in Roman thought and literature*, London; New York: Routledge.

Hoffer, Stanley (1999) *The Anxieties of Pliny the Younger*, Atlanta: Scholar's Press.

Holder, Paul (1980) *Studies in the Auxilia of the Roman Army from Augustus to Trajan*, Oxford: British Archaeological Reports Series 70.

Hopkins, Keith (1983) *Death and Renewal: sociological studies in Roman history*, vol. 2, Cambridge: Cambridge University Press.

Horsfall, Nicholas (1983) "Some Problems in the 'Laudatio Turiae'", *Bulletin of the Institute of Classical Studies* 30: 85–98.

Hutchinson, G. O. (1998) *Cicero's Correspondence: a literary study*, Oxford: Clarendon Press.

Johnson, Gary (1988) "*De conspiratione delatorum*: Pliny and the Christians revisited", *Latomus*, 47: 417–422.

Johnston, Patricia (1980) "*Poenulus* 1.2 and Roman Women", *Transactions of the American Philological Association* 110: 143–159.

Jones, Brian W. (1984) *The Emperor Titus*, London: Croom Helm.

——(1992) *The Emperor Domitian*, London; New York: Routledge.

Jory, E. J. (1981) "The Literary Evidence for the Beginnings of Imperial Pantomime", *Bulletin of the Institute of Classical Studies* 28: 147–161.

Joshel, Sandra (1992) "The Body Female and the Body Politic: Livy's Lucretia and Verginia", in Amy Richlin (ed.) *Pornography and Representation in Greece and Rome*, New York: Oxford University Press: 112–130.

Joshel, Sandra and Sheila Murnaghan (eds) (1998) *Women and Slaves in Greco-Roman Culture: differential equations*, London; New York: Routledge.

Kelly, Gordon (2006) *A History of Exile in the Roman Republic*, Cambridge: Cambridge University Press.

Kertzer, David and Richard Saller (eds) (1991) *The Family in Italy from Antiquity to the Present*. New Haven: Yale University Press.

Kleiner, Diana (1978) "The Great Friezes of the Ara Pacis Augustae", *Mélanges de l'Ecole française de Rome, Antiquité* 90: 753–785.

Konrad, Christof (1994) " 'Domitius Calvisius' in Plutarch", *Zeitschrift für Papyrologie und Epigraphik* 103: 139–146.

Langlands, Rebecca (2006) *Sexual Morality in Ancient Rome*, Cambridge: Cambridge University Press.

Lattimore, Richmond (1942) *Themes in Greek and Latin Epitaphs*, Urbana: University of Illinois Press.

Leach, Eleanor Winsor (1990) "The Politics of Self-Presentation: Pliny's *Letters* and Roman portrait sculpture", *Classical Antiquity* 9: 14–39.

Levick, Barbara (1979) "Pliny in Bithynia – and What Followed", *Greece and Rome* 26: 119–131.

——(2002) "Corbulo's Daughter", *Greece and Rome* 49: 199–211.

Lewis, A. D. E. (2007) "The Dutiful Legatee: Pliny, Letters V.1", in John Cairns and Paul du Plessis (eds) *Beyond Dogmatics: law and society in the Roman world*, Edinburgh: Edinburgh University Press: 125–138.

L'Hoir, Francesca Santoro (1994) "Tacitus and Women's Usurpation of Power", *Classical World* 88: 5–25.

——(2006) *Tragedy, Rhetoric, and the Historiography of Tacitus' Annales*, Ann Arbor: University of Michigan Press.

Lightman, M. and W. Zeisel (1977) "Univira: an example of continuity and change in Roman society", *Church History* 46: 19–32.

Lilja, Saara (1978) "Descriptions of Human Appearance in Pliny's Letters", *Arctos* 12: 55–62.

Lindsay, Hugh (2009) *Adoption in the Roman World*, Cambridge: Cambridge University Press.

Lovén, Lena Larsson (1998) "LANAM FECIT: woolworking and female virtue", in Lena Larsson Lovén and Agneta Strömberg (eds) *Aspects of Women in Antiquity*, Jonsered: Aströms Forlag: 85–95.

Lovén, Lena Larsson and Agneta Strömberg (eds) (1998) *Aspects of Women in Antiquity*, Jonsered: Aströms Forlag.

Lutz, Cora (1947) *Musonius Rufus. "The Roman Socrates"*, *Yale Classical Studies*: 10: 3–147.

McGinn, Thomas (1991) "Concubinage and the *Lex Julia* on Adultery", *Transactions of the American Philological Association* 121: 335–375.

——(2008) *Widows and Patriarchy: ancient and modern*, London: Duckworth.

McKeown, Niall (2007a) *The Invention of Ancient Slavery?*, London: Duckworth.

——(2007b) "The Sound of John Henderson Laughing: Pliny 3.14 and Roman slaveowners' fear of their slaves", in Anastasia Serghidou (ed.) *Fear of Slaves – Fear of Enslavement in the Ancient Mediterranean*, Crete: Presses universitaires de Franche-Comté: 265–279.

McNeill, Randall (2001) *Horace: image, identity, and audience*, Baltimore: Johns Hopkins University Press.

Malitz, Jürgen (1985) "Helvidius Priscus und Vespasian. Zur Geschichte der 'stoischen' Senatsopposition", *Hermes* 113: 231–246.

Marshall, Anthony (1975a) "Tacitus and the Governor's Lady: a note on Annals iii. 33–34", *Greece and Rome* 22 (1975) 11–18.

——(1975b) "Roman Women and the Provinces", *Ancient Society* 6: 109–127.

——(1989) "Ladies at Law: the role of women in the Roman civil courts", *Studies in Latin Literature and Roman History* 5 (*Collection Latomus*): 35–54.

——(1990) "Women on Trial before the Roman Senate", *Echos du Monde Classique* 34: 333–366.

Mayer, Roland (1991) "Roman Historical Exempla", in B. L. Hijmans and Pierre Grimal (eds) *Sénèque et la prose latine*, Genève: Fondation Hardt: 141–170.

——(2003) "Pliny and *Gloria Dicendi*", *Arethusa* 36: 227–234.

Morello, Ruth (2003) "Pliny and the Art of Saying Nothing", *Arethusa* 36: 187–209.

Morello, Ruth and Roy Gibson (2003) "Introduction", *Arethusa* 36: 109–113.

Mouritsen, Henrik (2011) *The Freedman in the Roman World*, Cambridge: Cambridge University Press.

Nicholas, Barry (1962) *An Introduction to Roman Law*, Oxford: Clarendon Press.

Nichols, John (1980) "Pliny and the Patronage of Communities", *Hermes* 108: 365–385.

Noreña, Carlos (2007) "The Social Economy of Pliny's Correspondence with Trajan", *American Journal of Philology* 128: 239–277.

Notizie degli Scavi di Antichità (1929), Rome: Accademia Nazionale dei Lincei.

Parker, Holt (1998) "Loyal Slaves and Loyal Wives: the crisis of the outsider-within and Roman *exemplum* literature", in Sandra Joshel and Sheila Murnaghan (eds) *Women and Slaves in Greco-Roman Culture: differential equations*, London; New York: Routledge: 152–173.

——(2004) "Why Were The Vestals Virgins? Or The Chastity of Women and the Safety of the Roman State", *American Journal of Philology* 125: 563–601.

Peachin, Michael (ed.) (2001) *Aspects of Friendship in the Greco-Roman World*, *Journal of Roman Archaeology* 43 (supplementary series).

Phang, Sara Elise (2001) *The Marriage of Roman Soldiers (13 B.C – A.D. 235): Law and Family in the Imperial Army*, Leiden; Boston; Koln: Brill.

Pigon, Jakub (1992) "Helvidius Priscus, Eprius Marcellus, and *Iudicium Senatus*: observations on Tacitus, *Histories* 4.7–8", *Classical Quarterly* 42: 235–246.

——(1999) "The Identity of the Chief Vestal Cornelia", *Mnemosyne* 52: 206–213.

Plass, Paul (1995) *The Game of Death in Ancient Rome: arena sport and political suicide*, Madison: University of Wisconsin Press.

Potter, D. S., and Cynthia Damon (1999) "The 'Senatus Consultum de Cn. Pisone Patre': Text, Translation, Discussion", *American Journal of Philology* 120: 1–186.

Radice, Betty (tr.) (1963) *The Letters of the Younger Pliny*, Harmondsworth; New York: Penguin.

Radicke, Jan (1997) "Die Selbstdarstellung des Plinius in seinen Briefen", *Hermes* 125: 447–469.

Raepsaet-Charlier, Marie-Thérèse (1982) "Épouses et familles de magistrats dans les provinces romaines aux deux premiers siècles de l'Empire", *Historia* 31: 56–69.

——(1987) *Prosopographie des femmes de l'ordre senatorial (Ier-IIe siècles)*, Louvain: Peeters.

Rawson, Beryl (1974) "Roman Concubinage and Other *De Facto* Marriages", *Transactions of the American Philological Association* 104: 279–305.

——(ed.) (1986) *The Family in Ancient Rome: new perspectives*, London; Sydney: Croom Helm.

——(ed.) (1991) *Marriage, Divorce, and Children in Ancient Rome*, Oxford: Clarendon Press.

——(1991) "Adult-Child Relationships in Roman Society", in Beryl Rawson (ed.) *Marriage, Divorce, and Children in Ancient Rome*, Oxford: Clarendon Press: 1–30.

——(2001) "Children as cultural symbols: imperial ideology in the second century", in Suzanne Dixon (ed.) *Childhood, Class and Kin in the Roman World*, London; New York: Routledge: 21–42.

Riccobono, Salvatore (ed.) (1945) *Acta Divi Augusti*, Roma: Regia Accademia italica.

Richlin, Amy (1984) "Invective Against Women in Roman Satire", *Arethusa* 17: 67–80.

——(ed.) (1992) *Pornography and Representation in Greece and Rome*, New York: Oxford University Press.

Riddle, John (1992) *Contraception and Abortion from the Ancient World to the Renaissance*, Cambridge, MA: Harvard University Press.

Riggsby, Andrew (1995) "Pliny on Cicero and Oratory: self-fashioning in the public eye", *American Journal of Philology* 116: 123–135.

——(1998) "Self and Community in the Younger Pliny", *Arethusa* 31: 75–97.

Robinson, O. F. (1995) *The Criminal Law of Ancient Rome*, Baltimore: Johns Hopkins University Press.

Roche, Paul (2002) "The Public Image of Trajan's Family", *Classical Philology* 97: 41–60.

Rogers, R. S. (1935) *Criminal Trials and Criminal Legislation under Tiberius*, Middletown: American Philological Association.

——(1960) "A Group of Domitianic Treason-Trials", *Classical Philology* 55: 19–23.

Rosenmeyer, Thomas (1989) *Senecan Drama and Stoic Cosmology*, Berkeley; Los Angeles: University of California Press.

Rosivach, Vincent (2007) "Murdered Masters", *New England Classical Journal* 34: 217–224.

Rudich, Vasily (1993) *Political Dissidence under Nero: the price of dissimulation*, London; New York: Routledge.

Saller, Richard (1989) "Patronage and Friendship in Early Imperial Rome: drawing the distinction", in Andrew Wallace-Hadrill (ed.) *Patronage in Ancient Society*, London; New York: Routledge: 49–62.

——(1994) *Patriarchy, Property and Death in the Roman Family*, Cambridge: Cambridge University Press.

Schultz, Celia (2006) *Women's Religious Activity in the Roman Republic*, Chapel Hill: University of North Carolina Press.

Schulz, Fritz (1951) *Classical Roman Law*, Oxford: Clarendon Press.

Serghidou, Anastasia (ed.) (2007) *Fear of Slaves – Fear of Enslavement in the Ancient Mediterranean*, Crete: Presses universitaires de Franche-Comté.

Setälä, Päivi (1977) *Private Domini in Roman Brick Stamps of the Empire*, Helsinki: Suomalainen tiedakatemia.

Severy, Beth (2003) *Augustus and the Family at the Birth of the Roman Empire*, New York: Routledge.

Shelton, Jo-Ann (1987) "Pliny's Letter 3.11: Rhetoric and Autobiography", *Classica et Mediaevalia* 38: 121–139.

——(1990) "Pliny the Younger and the Ideal Wife", *Classica et Mediaevalia* 41: 163–186.

——(1995) "Paradigm and Persuasion in Seneca's *Ad Marciam*", *Classica et Mediaevalia* 46: 157–188.

Sherwin-White, A. N. (1966) *The Letters of Pliny: a historical and social commentary*, Oxford: Clarendon Press.

Shotter, D. C. A. (1966) "Tiberius' Part in the Trial of Aemilia Lepida", *Historia* 15: 312–317.

Sick, David (1999) "Ummidia Quadratilla: cagey businesswoman or lazy pantomime watcher?", *Classical Antiquity* 18: 330–348.

Slater, William (1994) "Pantomime Riots", *Classical Antiquity* 13: 120–144.

Solomies, Olli (1992) *Adoptive and Polyonymous Nomenclature in the Roman Empire*, Helsinki: Societas Scientiarum Fennica.

Southern, Pat (1997) *Domitian: tragic tyrant*, London; New York: Routledge.

Staples, Ariadne (1998) *From Good Goddess to Vestal Virgins: sex and category in Roman religion*, London; New York: Routledge.

Stewart, Roberta (1994) "Domitian and Roman Religion: Juvenal, *Satires* Two and Four", *Transactions of the American Philological Association* 124: 309–332.

Syme, Sir Ronald (1949) "Personal Names in Annals I–VI", *Journal of Roman Studies* 39: 6–18.

——(1957) "The Jurist Neratius Priscus", *Hermes* 85: 480–493 (= *Roman Papers*, volume 1: 339–352).

——(1958) *Tacitus*, Oxford: Clarendon Press.

——(1960) "Pliny's Less Successful Friends", *Historia* 9: 362–379 (= *Roman Papers*, volume 2: 477–495).

——(1968a) "People in Pliny", *Journal of Roman Studies* 58: 135–151 (= *Roman Papers*, volume 2: 694–723).

——(1968b) "The Ummidii", *Historia* 17: 72–105 (= *Roman Papers*, volume 2: 659–693).

——(1969) "Pliny the Procurator", *Harvard Studies in Classical Philology* 73: 201–236 (= *Roman Papers*, volume 2: 742–773).

——(1979a) "Ummidius Quadratus, *capax imperii*", *Harvard Studies in Classical Philology* 83: 287–310 (= *Roman Papers*, volume 3: 1158–1178).

——(1979b) *Roman Papers*, volumes 1, 2, and 3, Ernst Badian (ed.), Oxford: Oxford University Press.

——(1980) "Guard Prefects of Trajan and Hadrian", *Journal of Roman Studies* 70: 64–80 (= *Roman Papers*, volume 3: 1276–1302).

——(1982a) "Partisans of Galba", *Historia* 31: 460–483 (= *Roman Papers*, volume 4: 115–139).

——(1982b) "Clues to Testamentary Adoption", in Silvio Panciera (ed.) *Epigrafia e ordine senatorio*, Rome: Edizioni di storia e letteratura: 397–410 (= *Roman Papers*, volume 5: 159–173).

——(1983) "Domitian: the last years", *Chiron* 13: 121–146 (= *Roman Papers*, volume 4: 252–277).

——(1984a) "Hadrian and the Senate", *Athenaeum* 62: 31–60 (= *Roman Papers*, volume 4: 295–324).

——(1984b) "P. Calvisius Ruso. One Person or Two?", *Zeitschrift für Papyrologie und Epigraphik* 56: 173–192 (= *Roman Papers*, volume 4: 397–417).

——(1985a) "Correspondents of Pliny". *Historia* 34: 324–359 (= *Roman Papers*, volume 5: 440–477).

——(1985b) "The Testamentum Dasumii: some novelties", *Chiron* 15: 41–63 (= *Roman Papers*, volume 5: 521–545).

——(1985c) "The Paternity of Polyonymous Consuls", *Zeitschrift für Papyrologie und Epigraphik* 61: 191–198 (= *Roman Papers*, volume 5: 639–647).

——(1988) *Roman Papers*, volumes 4 and 5, Anthony Birley (ed.), Oxford: Oxford University Press.

——(1991a) *Roman Papers*, volumes 6 and 7, Anthony Birley (ed.), Oxford: Oxford University Press.

——(1991b) "Vestricius Spurinna", in *Roman Papers*, volume 7: 541–550.

——(1991c) "Pliny's Early Career", in *Roman Papers*, volume 7: 551–567.

——(1991d) "Minicius Fundanus from Ticinum", in *Roman Papers*, volume 7: 603–619.

Takács, Sarolta (2008) *Vestal Virgins, Sibyls, and Matrons: Women in Roman Religion*, Austin: University of Texas Press.

Tate, Joshua (2005) "New Thoughts on the 'Will of Dasumii'", *Zeitschrift der Savigny-Stiftung für Rechtsgeschichte* 122: 166–171.

Townsend, G. B. (1962) "The Trial of Aemilia Lepida in AD 20", *Latomus* 21: 484–493.

Toynbee, J. M. C. (1971) *Death and Burial in the Roman World*, Ithaca, N.Y.: Cornell University Press.

Traub, Henry (1955) "Pliny's Treatment of History in Epistolary Form", *Transactions of the American Philological Association* 86: 213–232.

Treggiari, Susan (1969) *Roman Freedmen During the Late Republic*, Oxford: Clarendon Press.

——(1991) *Roman Marriage: Iusti Coniuges from the time of Cicero to the time of Ulpian*, Oxford: Clarendon Press.

——(2007) *Terentia, Tullia and Publilia: the women of Cicero's family*, London; New York: Routledge.

Van den Hout, Michael Petrus (1999) *A Commentary on the Letters of M. Cornelius Fronto*, Leiden: Brill.

Van Hooff, Anton (1990) *From Autothanasia to Suicide: self-killing in classical antiquity*, London; New York: Routledge.

Vinson, Martha (1989) "Domitia Longina, Julia Titi, and the Literary Tradition", *Historia* 38: 431–450.

Wallace-Hadrill, Andrew (ed.) (1989) *Patronage in Ancient Society*, London; New York: Routledge.

——(1989) "Patronage in Roman Society: from republic to empire", in Andrew Wallace-Hadrill (ed.) *Patronage in Ancient Society*, London; New York: Routledge: 63–87.

Walsh, P. G. (2006) *Pliny the Younger: complete letters*, Oxford; New York: Oxford University Press.

Watson, Alan (1987) *Roman Slave Law*, Baltimore: Johns Hopkins Press.

Watson, Patricia (1995) *Ancient Stepmothers: myth, misogyny, and reality*, Mnemosyne Supplementum 143, Leiden: Brill.

Weaver, P. R. C. (1986) "The Status of Children in Mixed Marriages", in Beryl Rawson (ed.) *The Family in Ancient Rome: new perspectives*, Ithaca, N.Y.: Cornell University Press: 145–169.

Wildfang, Robin Lorsch (2006) *Rome's Vestal Virgins*, London; New York: Routledge.

Williams, Craig Arthur (2010) *Roman Homosexuality*, 2nd edition, Oxford; New York: Oxford University Press.

Williams, G. W. (1958) "Some Aspects of Roman Marriage Ceremonies and Ideals", *Journal of Roman Studies* 48: 16–29.

Williams, Kathryn (2006) "Pliny and the Murder of Larcius Macedo", *Classical Journal* 101: 409–424.

Wirszubski, Chaim (1950) *Libertas as a Political Ideal at Rome During the Late Republic and Early Principate*, Cambridge: Cambridge University Press.

Wistrand, Erik (1979) "The Stoic Opposition to the Principate", *Studi Classice* 18: 93–101.

Wolff, Hartmut (1974) "Zu den Bürgerrechtsverleihungen an Kinder von Auxiliaren und Legionaren", *Chiron* 4: 479–510.

Woodman, A. J. and R. H. Martin (eds) (1996) *The Annals of Tacitus. Book 3*, Cambridge: Cambridge University Press.

Wyke, Maria, (1994) "Women in the Mirror: the rhetoric of adornment in the Roman world", in Léonie Archer, Susan Fischler, and Maria Wyke (eds) *Women in Ancient Societies: an illusion of the night*, New York: Routledge: 134–151.

Zeiner, Noelle (2007) "Perfecting the Ideal: molding Roman women in Statius' *Silvae*", *Arethusa* 40: 165–181.

Zimmermann, Reinhard (1996) *The Law of Obligations: Roman foundations of the civilian tradition*, Oxford: New York: Oxford University Press.

Zucker, Friedrick (1963) "Der jüngere Plinius und die Familie des Konsulars Q. Corellius Rufus", *Das Altertum* 9: 37–43.

Index of Pliny's letters

Index of ancient names

Index of subjects